A Special Issue of
Memory

Short-term and Working Memory

Edited by

Susan E. Gathercole
University of Durham, UK

Psychology Press
Taylor & Francis Group
New York London

First published 2001 by Psychology Press Ltd

This edition published 2012 by Psychology Press

Psychology Press
Taylor & Francis Group
711 Third Avenue,
New York, NY 10017

Psychology Press
Taylor & Francis Group
27 Church Road, Hove
East Sussex BN3 2FA

First issued in paperback 2015

Psychology Press is an imprint of the Taylor & Francis Group, an informa business

British Library Cataloguing in Publication Data
A catalogue record for this book is available from the British Library

ISBN 978-1-138-87786-3 (pbk)
ISBN 978-1-84169-918-9 (hbk)

ISSN 0965-8211

Cover design by Jim Wilkie
Typeset in the UK by DP Photosetting, Aylesbury, UK.

Contents*

---

*This book is also a special issue of the journal *Memory*, and forms issues 4, 5, & 6 of Volume 9 (2001). The page numbers are taken from the journal and so begin with p. 209.

MEMORY, 2001, *9* (4/5/6), 209–221

When the central executive lets us down: Schemas, attention, and load in a generative working memory task

P.J. Barnard and S.K. Scott
MRC Cognition and Brain Sciences Unit, Cambridge, UK

J. May
University of Sheffield, UK

Participants were asked to generate a single sequence of numbers in between two bounds. By varying the requested sequence length and way in which the question is posed, this paradigm enables assessment of the contributions to central executive functioning of schema, focus of attention, and load. With sequences of three or four numbers, a quarter of the sample failed fully to comply with the instructions. They generated an incorrect number of numbers or went outside the specified bounds. With sequences of six numbers, more than half of the sample infringed one or more of the constraints. Participants consistently generated sequences with particular generic properties. The overall frequency and patterns of infringements suggest that a substantial proportion of participants focused their conceptual attention on sequence content and often neglected the problem of how the length and boundary constraints were going to be evaluated either before or during response delivery.

Most research within the working memory (WM) framework has concentrated on the role of the two slave systems, the phonological loop (Baddeley, 1986) and the visuo-spatial sketchpad (Logie, 1995). From its inception (Baddeley & Hitch, 1974), much of the utility of the working memory model was linked to the presence of a central executive component that controlled and co-ordinated the two slave systems. The executive component originally enabled the WM framework to account for the variability in memory capacity observed across tasks, as well as across presentation and response modalities. It was hypothesised to have its own storage and processing capacities, additional to those of the slave systems, but was deliberately left underspecified. Despite its figurative representation as a single "box", it was not intended to be a single theoretical component. It was simply proposed as a pool of general-purpose resources that could either fulfil control functions or provide supplementary storage. In a subsequent theoretical development the storage function was dropped and Baddeley (1986) incorporated the Supervisory Attention System of Norman and Shallice (1986) into the WM model. This development acted as a preliminary fractionation of executive resources and led to a pragmatic approach to specifying executive functions. These included not only the role of controlling and co-ordinating the slave systems but also the capabilities to direct or switch attention, and the capability to activate representations in long-term memory (Baddeley, 1996; Baddeley & Logie, 1999). Most recently, Baddeley (2000) has added an additional component to the working memory model: an episodic buffer that provides interfacing storage in between executive resources and episodic long-term memory.

The initial fractionation of executive resources enabled the WM model to extend its interpretation of empirical phenomena to domains such as dual task performance, the generation of random

Requests for reprints should be sent to P.J. Barnard, MRC Cognition and Brain Sciences Unit, 15 Chaucer Road, Cambridge, CB2 2EF, UK. Email: philip.barnard@mrc-cbu.cam.ac.uk

http://www.tandf.co.uk/journals/pp/09658211.html DOI:10.1080/09658210143000191

sequences, ageing, and attention switching as well as individual differences in working memory capacity (Baddeley, 1996). Because of all of the intricate relationships that can hold between the activation of long-term memory structures, the control of attention, and the co-ordination of the different slave systems, our understanding of executive functions is unlikely to proceed with any great rapidity. One of the major impediments to progress is the lack of paradigms that provide opportunities for empirical investigation of the different facets of executive functioning, especially the activation of schemas or action plans from long-term memory, the active evaluation of performance against task demands during schema execution, and switching between schemas.

Number-processing tasks have featured prominently in studies of both executive function and dysfunction in the general working memory literature. Random number generation is traditionally seen as involving a high degree of executive load (e.g., see Baddeley, Emslie, Kolodny, & Duncan, 1998). Mental arithmetic has also been widely used to explore how storage within the phonological loop is co-ordinated with more computational aspects of central executive functions (Hitch, 1978; Logie & Duff, 1996). The executive function of activating and using numeric representations in long-term memory can also be severely disrupted in patients with frontal lobe damage, which Baddeley and Wilson (1988) considered more appropriately labelled as dysexecutive syndrome. On the cognitive estimates task, such patients typically give estimates of numeric attributes, such as the height of a building, that are well outside the range given by a normal sample (Shallice & Evans, 1978).

In an attempt to specify both the representations and processes involved in an executive task requiring access to schemas, Scott, Barnard, and May (2001) adopted a number-generation paradigm in which the task instructions were varied systematically. Over 1300 people were asked to generate a single large number in between two widely spaced bounds. The actual questions asked were phrased in slightly different ways, such as "Can you please give me a number in between one million and ten million?", "Can you please give me a 7 figure number, that is a number between one million and ten million?", or "Can you please give me a number between one million and nine million, nine hundred and ninety-nine thousand, nine hundred and ninety-nine?". While the task remained essentially unaltered, the variations of phrasing placed differing degrees of emphasis on either the "randomness" of the number, its structure, or the boundaries of the selection range.

Although participants generated a huge variety of specific numbers, Scott et al. found that the numbers conformed in their internal thematic structure to a small number of different generic schemas. To codify the numbers, they used a variant of systemic grammar (Halliday, 1970). Each number was decomposed into two components, its psychological subject and its psychological predicate. The psychological subject was the first component of the verbal response that, in the case of spoken English numbers, indicates overall magnitude. The psychological predicate was the elaboration, if any was given, in the thousands, hundreds, and units ranges. In the case of a number such as "One million five hundred and forty two thousand three hundred and twenty-five", one million is the subject, and the remainder is the predicate.

In these schemas the subject and predicate components were "marked" by generic features such as magnitude, parity, and complexity. Some combinations of features occurred with high frequency, whereas other combinations rarely occurred. The distribution of schemas underlying the responses was strongly influenced by the specific question asked. When range boundaries were mentioned in unmarked form (e.g., one to ten million), the predominant response was to produce a round number of millions, with a low, odd psychological subject and no elaborated predicate. In contrast, when the question posed mentioned the number of digits in the number, participants more often produced a complex numeric predicate, with the subject most often being formed by re-using the lower boundary or by taking the lowest available number of odd parity. When the question marked the upper boundary in complex form, the numbers generated tended to have a minimally elaborated predicate, such as "a million and one".

Scott et al. were working within a theoretical framework that regards executive functions as fulfilled by processing exchanges between two levels of meaning (Barnard, 1999). One level, that of propositional representation, encodes meaning in terms of referentially specific semantic properties and relationships. The other level, that of implicational representation, is a more abstract form of meaning based on generically encoded schema. Scott et al. interpreted their data as evidence that the propositional content of the question was used to activate different distributions of number schemas encoded at an implicational level of meaning. Exchanges between schematic and propositional meaning were linked, not only to the generation of the response itself but also to the way in which the responses were evaluated against the task demands prior to or during output. This account has similarities with the hypothesis that people generate and edit responses to be implicitly "appropriate" in such number-generation tasks (Kubovy, 1977; Kubovy & Psotka, 1976).

In the Scott et al. study, there was an unexpectedly high overall error rate. Across 11 different conditions, responses were outside the bounds specified in the question on between 4% and 24% of occasions. On average 1 in 8 participants produced responses outside the range, with far more going below the specified range than above it. These errors were not random, but conformed to the same kind of schemas as the correct responses. They would have been correct according to participants' generically represented "implicational" understanding of the task instructions, although not according to the instructions' detailed propositional content. Scott et al. argued that the occurrence of errors in this one-trial task indicated limitations in "normal" executive functioning. They concluded that a substantial proportion of responses were generated by participants activating a generic schema to produce a referentially specific number, and then outputting the number without evaluating its content against all the explicit conditions in the propositional representation of the original request. The errors were thus associated with a failure of executive function linked directly to the processing of meaning.

In other contexts, people's attention to meaning is highly selective. When asked the question "How many animals of each kind did Moses take into the ark?" respondents frequently answer "Two", apparently not evaluating their knowledge that the agent of the action was Noah rather than Moses (Erickson & Mattson, 1981). The effect is not obtained when the question mentions "Nixon". The Moses illusion works because both Moses and Noah fit the same generic schema of "significant-male-figure-in-old-testament-with-two-syllable-name" whereas Nixon does not. This kind of question focuses the attention of executive processing on a particular attribute, in this case also a number, while evaluation of different attribute is attenuated, in this case referential identity. Scott et al. argued that the different questions posed to elicit a large number brought a subset of numeric attributes into relatively sharp semantic focus, while other attributes of the number were subjected to attenuated evaluation.

The evidence from the number-generation task, coupled with that from language understanding, suggests a simple hypothesis concerning the limitations on executive functioning and how they may relate to representations activated from long-term memory. If the task-relevant representations are multi-attribute, then central executive processes may be able to attend to only a subset of the constituents of these representations at any one time. Limitations of this sort are most likely to be apparent in one-off tasks like single number generation or the Moses illusion. In novel situations, any limited capacity of the central executive is most likely to be exposed for examination. In more conventional experiments participants are typically given some practice and then asked to perform the task many times. They thus have plenty of opportunities to develop and hone special-purpose representations for the executive control of performance, perhaps involving deliberative and temporally extended evaluations, to help minimise the effects of executive limitations.

A relatively simple extension of one-off number-generation tasks (Kubovy, 1977; Scott et al., 2001) can be used to examine the relationship between executive demands and error under circumstances where storage requirements, and hence use of slave system resources, are minimal. Rather like continuous random number generation, participants can be asked to generate a single sequence of numbers of some specified sequence length, where all the numbers need to lie between two bounds. The basic task makes real demands on central executive functions. They include a requirement to construct a schema for organising the response, such as an ascending or descending sequence, the generation of the particular numbers in the sequence, and demands to evaluate the responses for conformity with the length and boundary constraints.

This paradigm allows the contributions of schema, the focus of executive attention, and load to be assessed. A question of the form "Can you please give me a sequence of any three numbers in the range 100 up to 500?" implies an ascending schema, whereas "Can you please give me a sequence of any three numbers in the range 500 down to 100?" implies a descending schema. In these two examples the bounds are expressed as round numbers of hundreds. By specifying only the subject component in the two numbers, the request effectively marks the overall magnitude range. However, if the bounds are specified in a way that includes some additional precision in the numeric predicate (e.g., "...499 down to 101"), then the overall range is only minimally adjusted, but the detailed identity of the boundaries is explicitly marked. This should focus the attention of executive processes on the actual identity of the bounds. Load can then be manipulated by increasing the length of the sequence of numbers.

Given a window of some 400 numbers and a request to generate a sequence of just 3 numbers, most people should be able to complete the task without error. In perceptual tasks it is well known that people can "subitise" up to four entities with no increase in reaction time (Mandler & Shebo, 1982). In a generation task, they may be able to utilise a representation held in a peripheral slave system to accomplish something analogous to subitisation for short sequence lengths. However, as sequence length rises beyond three or four complex numbers, the ability of executive processes for both the boundaries and the number of numbers being output should be compromised. There should be a general increase in infringements of the task constraints as sequence length rises. There should also be more detailed consequences of an increase in demands if the capability of executive resources for the concurrent evaluation of multiple attributes is restricted. For example, there should be a trade-off between infringements of the length constraint and the boundary constraints. Where the initial request is phrased with a complex numeric bound, boundary errors should be reduced, but at a likely cost of infringing the length constraint.

Increasing the length of the sequence to be generated is not the only way that demands on executive processes are likely to vary in this task context. The processing load on executive resources can vary implicitly as a function of the particular number schemas adopted to control sequence generation. Across the sequence of numbers they generate, participants are free to vary one or more attributes of number. They can optionally vary the number of hundreds (the numeric subject), the numbers in the tens and units ranges (the numeric predicate), or both. They can also maintain direction (ascending or descending) or change direction. Again, if executive resources are devoted to manipulating several different features of numbers across the sequence, then participants should be more likely to infringe boundaries or length constraints than if fewer features of number are being manipulated: errors should be more frequent when participants select complex number schemas for their response sequences.

Other than assuming that participants will tend to follow the direction implied by the question phrasing, we are aware of no evidence that would enable us to predict the precise distribution of strategies that will be adopted. Given the evidence of Scott et al., it is quite likely that specifying boundaries as a round number of hundreds will invoke a different distribution of strategies than when they are specified with detail in the numeric predicate. As explicit and implicit load on executive processes rises there should be more infringements of constraints. However, the exact relationship between implicit and explicit load and any interactions with question phrasing can only be expected to emerge when the distribution of strategies is known.

METHOD

Participants were each individually asked to generate a single sequence of numbers, according to two objective constraints: *range* and *length*. The sequences were to be generated within two bounds specified in the question, and the length of the required sequence was varied from three to six numbers. For each sequence length the question was posed in one of four different ways by varying two components of the instructions: *direction* and *complexity*. The first component varied the implied direction of the sequence by manipulating the presentation order of the bounds ("up to" or "down to"). The second component varied the implied complexity of individual numbers by manipulating the "subject–predicate" composition of the bounds: In the "simple" conditions both upper and lower bounds were round hundreds; in the "complex" conditions the bounds marked additional detail in the numeric predicate.

To ensure a consistent frame of parity within each question, the parity of the bounds and predicate (where specified) was matched with the sequence length, so that sequences of odd length (three and five numbers) were in the ranges 100–500 or 101–499, and sequences of even length (four and six numbers) were in the ranges 200–600 or 202–598. The actual selection ranges thus varied slightly, allowing between 401 and 397 candidate numbers. The combinations of bounds, implied direction and sequence lengths are summarised in Table 1.

Participants

A total of 384 people participated in the experiment. Half of the participants in each condition were recruited in scientific research units. These included scientific staff, support staff, and graduate students. The other half of the participants in each condition were recruited in a general university setting. No personal details were recorded.

Procedure

Participants were approached in several research units and three universities. An experimenter first asked if they would be prepared to take part in a study of how people think about concepts and ideas. They were then told that the experimenter would ask them a question involving numbers and that they should respond as quickly as possible by speaking their answer clearly into a hand-held tape-recorder. For simple bounds and implied ascending sequences, the question was then posed in the following form:

> *Could you please give me a sequence of any three numbers within the range one hundred up to five hundred?*

An example of the equivalent question for descending sequences with complex bounds was:

> *Could you please give me a sequence of any six numbers within the range five hundred and ninety-eight down to two hundred and two?*

The first of these examples is the wording for top left-hand cell of Table 1, while the second example is the wording for the bottom right-hand cell of that table. The other variants can be established by substituting the other sequence lengths and upper and lower numeric bounds into these sentence frames. Participants were approached in public areas or their offices and anyone who might have overheard another carry out the task was not asked to participate. Data were collected by three experimenters. Each rotated through a list of the 16 questions as successive participants were recruited.

RESULTS

The individual sequences were analysed both in terms of their compliance with the experimental instructions (constraint infringements) and according to the type of sequence generated. Constraint infringements occurred when participants generated two many or too few numbers or when they included numbers that were either above or below the specified boundaries. Type of sequence was codified according to the direction of the sequence that was generated, and whether or not a consistent psychological subject was used within the sequence.

Analysis of constraint infringements

Of the 384 participants, 143 (37%) failed to comply fully with the constraints mentioned in the question. There were 172 specific infringements including 29 cases where participants generated both the wrong number of numbers and went outside the range given in the question. When they did go outside the range, it was not uncommon for most or all of the sequence to be outside the range. Multiple instances in the same sequence were counted as a single infringement of

TABLE 1
The 16 conditions for the generation of number sequences

Length	*Odd context* 3	*Even context* 4	*Odd context* 5	*Even context* 6
Up simple	100–500	200–600	100–500	200–600
Up complex	101–499	202–598	101–499	202–598
Down simple	500–100	600–200	500–100	600–200
Down complex	499–101	598–202	499–101	598–202

24 participants were used in each cell (N = 384).

one constraint. The wrong number of numbers could only be too many or two few. However, it was possible for participants to give one number in a sequence that was below the range and another in the same sequence that was above the range. This only occurred in two cases and the first instance only was counted. In one case this resolved to above and in the other case to below.

Table 2 shows the number of sequences that failed fully to comply with the experimental instructions. The number of responses involving at least one infringement increased with the length of sequence requested, $\chi^2(3) = 24.5$, $p < .0001$. Responses involving multiple infringements also rose with sequence length, $\chi^2(3) = 7.87$, $p < .05$. Although there were fewest infringements in the "up simple" conditions, the total number of responses involving one or more infringements did not differ systematically across the four question types, $\chi^2(3) = 6.27$, $p > .05$.

Table 3 presents a more detailed breakdown of the specific infringements of sequence length and upper and lower bounds. Participants were just as likely to generate too many numbers with the two shorter sequence lengths as they were with the two longer sequence lengths. There was a significant contingency between length infringement category (too many/too few/none) and sequence length, $\chi^2(6) = 48.0$, $p < .0001$. For sequence lengths 3, 4, and 5 relatively few participants generated sequences that were too short. There is a very marked discontinuity at sequence length 6, where there is a dramatic rise in the number of participants who generated too few numbers. Of the 96 participants, 30 simply stopped when they had generated five numbers, and two stopped even earlier.

Participants were far more likely to err by including one or more numbers below the lower bound than by including one or more numbers above the upper bound. Again, there was a significant contingency between range errors and sequence length, $\chi^2(6) = 17.5$, $p < .01$. They were more than twice as likely to go too low in the longer sequences than in the shorter ones.

Increasing the sequence length clearly has a detrimental effect on the ability of participants to generate a sequence of the required length, and to keep within the specified range. Overall, the question type did not influence the number of errors. However, when the type of errors made is broken down a relationship with question type does become apparent. Table 4 shows the frequencies of specific infringements as a function of the question posed. Although the table suggests that participants were more likely to perseverate

TABLE 2
The number of sequences containing at least one infringement of a constraint (range or sequence length)

Length	*Odd context* 3	*Even context* 4	*Odd context* 5	*Even context* 6	*total*
Up simple	3	4	7	12	26
Up complex	6	5	14	12	37
Down simple	9	6	12	15	42
Down complex	6	11	7	14	38
Any infringements	24	26	40	53	143
Infringements as %	25%	27%	42%	55%	37%
Multiple infringements	3	7	6	13	29

TABLE 3
Infringements of the length and range constraints tabulated in relation to the length of sequence requested

	Length infringements			*Range infringements*		
Length	*Too many*	*Too few*	*None*	*Too high*	*Too low*	*None*
3	14	4	78	0	9	87
4	15	8	73	4	6	86
5	16	6	74	3	21	72
6	13	32	51	5	16	75
Total	58	50	276	12	52	320

TABLE 4
Infringements of the length and range constraints tabulated in relation to the phrasing of the initial question

	Length infringements			*Range infringements*		
Question	*Too many*	*Too few*	*None*	*Too high*	*Too low*	*None*
Up simple	11	12	73	0	9	87
Up complex	18	11	67	2	10	84
Down simple	12	14	70	3	24	69
Down complex	17	13	66	7	9	80
Total	58	50	276	12	52	320

and produce more numbers than required when the bounds were specified in complex form (35) rather than simple form (23), there was no contingency between length infringements and question type, $\chi^2(6) = 3.39$, $p > .7$. However, the frequency with which they produced numbers that were out of the specified range was contingent upon the question posed, $\chi^2(6) = 23.5$, $p < .001$.

Errors below the lower bound were concentrated in the "down simple" condition. Closer inspection of these errors showed that there were two patterns. Of the 52 sequences where the lower boundary was infringed, 30 involved the very first number that was generated being below the lower bound. In many of these cases all or most of the numbers generated subsequently in the sequence were out of bounds. These instances were quite evenly distributed across the four variants of the question posed (up simple: 7; up complex: 9; down simple: 9; down complex: 5). The increase in this type of error following the down simple question is largely accounted for by errors that occurred later in the sequence (up simple: 2; up complex: 1; down simple: 15; down complex: 4). Of these errors, 17 occur at sequence lengths 5 and 6. Taken in conjunction with the length errors, the evidence for a direct trade-off between length and bound infringements is mixed. With an implied descending sequence, there are fewer "too low" errors but more "too many" errors in the complex than in the simple condition. In the case of an implied ascending sequence, there is no real indication of a systematic trade-off.

The variation in infringements of the constraints at the longer sequence lengths has two distinct components. The first is a dramatic rise in the number of sequences with too few numbers at sequence length 6. The second is an increase in the number of occasions when participants generate a number below the lower boundary having started off within the specified range. The rise in these infringements occurred when the bounds were specified in simple form, when the implied direction for the sequence was down, and were most frequent at sequence lengths 5 and 6. The occurrence of "low" infringements later in the sequence could be linked either to the re-use of a bound, to a switch in the use of strategies, or both.

Analysis of sequence type

As noted in the introduction, participants have considerable strategic freedom. They can generate sequences that systematically ascend, descend, or change direction. They can use a restricted range of numbers on much of the range specified. They can use a constant or variable increase or decrease. The increase or decrease can be small or large, and so on. There is also an obvious strategy to keep within the constraints. Anyone who counts up in intervals of 1, 10, or 100 can simply stop at the point where the number varied corresponds to the number of numbers to be generated (e.g., 101, 102, 103...; 110, 120, 130...; 100, 200, 300...). Across the full set of 394 responses, a wide range of detailed strategies were used. However, as with Scott et al. (2001), there were a number of dominant strategies, which can be taken to reflect the underlying schemas called into play, and whose use depended on the way in which the question was posed.

Table 5 shows the frequency with which five types of sequences were generated, and the number of responses with one or more infringements. Those sequences where all numbers were in ascending (up) or descending (down) order were distinguished from those where there was a change in direction (direction varied). The latter category included changes in direction in midstream and those on the last item of the sequence where it seemed likely that participants were

TABLE 5
The numbers of sequences conforming to five patterns, with the number of sequences involving at least one infringement in parentheses

	Up same subject	*Down same subject*	*Up different subject*	*Down different subject*	*Direction varied*	*U/c*	*Total*
Up simple	17 (4)	0 (–)	57 (13)	0 (–)	21 (8)	1 (1)	96 (26)
Up complex	34 (11)	2 (0)	30 (10)	0 (–)	28 (14)	2 (2)	96 (37)
Down simple	2 (1)	8 (3)	17 (10)	36 (12)	33 (16)	0 (–)	96 (42)
Down complex	14 (4)	8 (0)	16 (9)	19 (7)	35 (14)	4 (4)	96 (38)
Total	67 (20)	18 (3)	120 (42)	55 (19)	117 (52)	7 (7)	384 (143)
% infringements	29.9%	16.7%	35.0%	34.5%	44%	–	37%

changing direction to avoid the risk of infringing a boundary constraint.

Following Scott et al., the ascending and descending strategies were further distinguished on the basis of the "subject–predicate" distinction. The subject here is the "number of hundreds", while the predicate is the numeric detail in the tens and units range. Those sequences with the "same subject" have an invariant number of hundreds, the variation coming from increasing or decreasing the number in the predicate ($n = 85$). Those sequences with a different subject are those where the numbers generated referenced ranges of two or more hundreds ($n = 175$). When counting up in round hundreds, the subject would have the feature incrementing while the predicate would have an invariant feature. Sequences with the same subject and systematic ascent or descent in the predicate component have the lowest rates of infringement. Ascending and descending sequences characteristically involving changes to both subject and predicate give intermediate levels of error, while those involving changes in the subject, changes in the predicate, and changes in direction are associated with the highest error rates.

When the subject was varied in either an ascending or descending sequence, the vast majority of participants also varied the interval and/or number used to specify the elements of the predicate. Of the 175 ascending and descending sequences with different subjects, 142 also varied predicate elements and used different intervals. Of the 117 sequences showing varied direction, only 2 involved use of the same subject throughout, none used the same predicate, and only 1 used the same interval between numbers. Seven responses were unclassifiable because they involved no variation. They were all errors. Six were instances where participants responded with a single number rather than a sequence and one involved the repetition of the digit "1" for the required sequence length. Repetition, although not explicitly ruled out by the instructions, was extremely rare, occurring in only two other sequences.

The way in which the question was posed clearly influenced the distribution of strategies adopted in a systematic way. When the question was phrased with simple boundaries and implied an ascending sequence, the dominant strategy was to produce an ascending sequence varying both subject and predicate elements across the sequence. When the implied sequence was "up" and also had the range specified in more complex form, participants made far greater use of the strategy of restricting the range of the sequence, varying only the predicate attached to a single hundred. Where an ascending sequence was implied, only two participants adopted a strategy of systematic descent. With questions phrased to imply a descending sequence with simple bounds, the most frequent strategy was to produce responses where the numbers generated descended, again with variation in both subject and predicate. However, in this condition a considerable fraction of the participants adopt an ascending strategy, again varying the subject over the sequence. When the implied descent questions were phrased with complex bounds, there was no increase in the use of the "down same subject" strategy. The switch was to an "up same subject" strategy. Although there was something of an increase in the generation of sequences with direction varied as the "unusualness" of the question posed increased from "up simple" to "down complex", this variation did not approach significance, $\chi^2(3) = 5.74$, $p > .1$.

Table 6 shows the specific infringements as a function of the type of sequence actually generated. Infringements of the lower bound are now

TABLE 6
The different forms of infringement tabulated by type of sequence generated

	Same subject	*Different subject*	*Direction varied*	*Unclassified*	*Total*
N of sequences	85	175	117	7	384
Too Many	14	22	22	0	58
Too Few	7	22	15	6	50
% length errors	25%	25%	32%		
Too High	0	5	6	1	12
Too low on 1st no.	6	11	12	1	30
Too low later	0	10	12	0	22
% bound errors	7%	15%	26%		

subdivided into those that occur on the very first number generated and those that occur later in the sequence. In those sequences where the same subject is used infringements of the length constraint occur on 25% of sequences, and a range infringement on 7% of sequences. When the subject (and most often the predicate too) varies, infringements of the length constraint are also at 25% but the percentage of sequences in which the range is infringed rise to 15%. If subject, predicate, and direction are all varied in the same sequence, then the percentage of sequences with length infringements rises to 32% and the percentage of range infringements to 26%. Although it appears that the likelihood of going out of range increases quite systematically with the number of attributes that are varied as the sequence evolves, use of the same subject strategy inherently reduces the risk of committing this sort of infringement. These data are nonetheless suggestive that varying direction carries some additional risk of infringing either the length or the range constraints.

One effect of posing a question with complex bounds was to increase the proportion of participants who generated sequences with a restricted range (repeatedly using the same subject) and to reduce the proportion of participants varying both subject and predicate components. The analysis of errors within each type of sequence indicates that the effect of this shift would be broadly cost-neutral for length errors, as both types of sequences are associated with the same likelihood of a length infringement. The different distribution of strategies would also have had only a marginal effect on boundary errors in the down simple and down complex conditions. The most error-prone form of sequence, where the direction is varied, is generated with comparable frequency in both of the conditions. The main difference in the distribution of strategies in these two conditions is that 12 more participants used the same subject strategy in the complex condition. Assuming a simple relationship between error and type of sequence in simple and complex sequences, the 8% difference in error rate between the two strategies would have saved the complex condition no more than a single "low bound" error. In the down complex condition there were 35 sequences in which the subject varied and 35 in which the direction was varied. In both cases only two "late low" errors occurred (6%). In the down simple condition there were 33 sequences in which the subject varied and there were 7 (21%) late low errors. There were 53 sequences in which the direction was varied and 8 (15%) late low errors. The greater occurrence of low errors in the down simple condition compared to the down complex condition seems to be related to the extent to which the bounds were actually evaluated during sequence output rather than the shift in the type of sequence actually generated.

DISCUSSION

Faced with the simple, once-off task of generating a sequence of three numbers in between two bounds, around one in four participants failed fully to comply with the request. When the requested sequence length rose to six, more than half of our participants infringed one or more of the constraints. In one way or another, the central executive let them down.

Our general hypothesis was that central executive processes would be able to attend to only a subset of task-relevant attributes at any one time. It was argued that infringements of constraints would increase with the processing load imposed by sequence length, and that specifying the range in a complex form should reduce boundary errors at the expense of length errors. It was also conjectured that participants might place themselves at increased risk of infringing constraints by manipulating many rather than few attributes of number over the sequences they actually generated. The results provide some support for each of the more specific hypotheses, but only in qualified form. Infringement of length and range constraints is not a simple function of increased explicit loading, nor is there a straightforward trade-off of the two types of constraint in all conditions. Neither of the two ways of infringing the length constraint rises systematically with length. Range infringements do depend on how they were originally expressed in the question posed, but only when the implied sequence was that of descent.

It is possible that some of the participants simply didn't hear the question in all its detail. However, the effects of failing to hear part of the question should be just as apparent at the short sequence lengths as at the longer ones. It is also possible that they encoded the question perfectly well but that its representation degraded in some way while the responses were being generated. As phonological and articulatory processes are obviously occupied for more time with each increase in sequence length, more errors would be expected at the longer lengths. Such an account does not readily accommodate the pattern of range infringements. Errors above the upper boundary were infrequent at all sequence lengths, while 30 of the 52 errors below the lower boundary involved the very first number generated.

The overall frequency of infringements, and the distributions of particular infringements, suggests that a substantial proportion of participants may have focused their conceptual attention on formulating sequence content. As with the application of the concept of goal neglect to dual task performance (Duncan, 1995), while attending to sequence content, our participants may simply have disregarded, or overlooked, the problem of how the length and boundary constraints were going to be evaluated either before or during response delivery. Indeed, the frequencies of infringements actually observed are quite likely to have underestimated the true extent of this problem. Having neglected to craft an adequate executive control structure, many of the participants may well have conformed to the constraints more by good fortune than by intent. When asked to generate six numbers, 30 participants stopped short when they had generated five numbers. Many of those asked to generate five numbers may also simply have stopped at the same point without knowing exactly how many numbers they had generated. Peripheral mechanisms, such as the phonological loop of the WM memory model or its equivalent in other theories, may then have had a part to play in shaping the precise patterning of observed errors. At the point at which participants realised they were at risk of infringing a constraint, and in a context where compound, polysyllabic numbers are being generated, a limited-capacity phonological trace of recent output would preclude effective counting of the number of numbers that had actually been output.

It is equally possible that executive representations for staying within the boundary constraints may have been not much more effective in the shorter sequences than the longer ones. Range errors may have been less frequent at the shorter lengths because they were generating fewer numbers with strategies that inherently kept their responses within bounds. Had participants been given multiple trials, then it seems highly likely that they would have developed specific strategies to help them keep within both length and boundary constraints at the longer sequence lengths as well. Once exposed to the "Moses" illusion (Erickson & Mattson, 1981), people are unlikely to be caught out again. Hence, the once-off nature of the experimental procedure and the implicit demand to produce an immediate, novel response does seem to provide conditions under which natural properties of the intersections between control structures and schema content are likely to emerge.

In the Scott et al. (2001) study of the generation of individual large numbers in between two bounds, participants were far less likely to infringe the upper boundary than the lower one, an effect replicated here in sequences of numbers. In that study the lower bound was commonly used to anchor output. It formed the psychological subject of participants' output when the generation schema led to detail being incorporated in the numeric predicate, but not when the generation schema led to a simpler form specifying only a round number of millions. Asymmetric use of upper and lower bounds may reflect how numeric schemas tend to be organised in long-term memory. According to Benford's Law, lower numbers occur more frequently in our environment (Benford, 1938). In addition smaller numbers appear to be more richly represented, and this worsens in a logarithmic manner with magnitude (Poulton, 1979). Asymmetry also exists in how bounds are "marked" in normal linguistic expression. It is well known from studies of language (e.g., Clark & Clark, 1977) that the unmarked form for natural dimensions is asymmetric with respect to magnitude. We normally ask "How tall/rich/many?" rather than "How short/poor/few?". The latter forms are used only under specific circumstances, when it is presupposed that the answer lies in the lower range of the magnitude dimension. When the direction implied by the question was down, participants were more likely to infringe the lower bound when it had been expressed in simple unmarked form as a round number of hundreds than when detail was marked in the form of a more complex numeric predicate. The presence of complexity was clearly salient in this context, in that it led to clear adjustments in generation strategies. It may also have had the effect of focusing executive attention on the precise identity of the lower bound.

The overall pattern of infringements may thus be best understood as arising in circumstances where a subset of task demands are neglected, and where executive priority is assigned to translating the content of different generation schemas into overt response sequences. Some three-quarters of the participants clearly interpreted the question as a request to generate, not just a sequence of so many numbers, but a sequence that covered a substantial proportion of the specified range. Coverage of the range requires participants to vary the number of hundreds. In addition, a substantial proportion of participants also invoke schemas for sequence generation that involve varying numeric detail. They manipulate both subject and predicate components over numbers. In many cases, either intentionally or because they are approaching a bound, they additionally vary direction. In those conditions where the implied direction was ascent, two thirds of participants in both the simple and complex bound conditions opened their sequence by repeating the number of hundreds specified in the lower bound. They overwhelmingly ascended. High levels of re-using the lower bound, and an ascending sequence, naturally protect most participants from going too low once they have started off within bounds. Only two participants subsequently infringed the upper bound and only three the lower bound. Sixteen participants (10%) started their sequences below the bound when the implied direction was ascent. When the implied direction was down and the questions was phrased with simple bounds, very few participants simply re-used the upper bound. Under these circumstances 10% of participants again infringed the lower boundary from the very first item in their response sequence and a further 16% infringed this boundary after having started out within range. This suggests that the preference for using the lower bound as the psychological subject of a sequence occurs not only when it comes first, but because it is generally easier to anchor sequence content to lower numbers. Consistent with the view that participants' attention was focused on sequence content, one effect of specifying the boundaries in complex form was increased use of the strategy of ascent using the same psychological subject. This restricts the range of output and implicitly reduces the likelihood of infringing an upper bound.

At least in the context of this one-off task, the number-generation question is not simply understood in terms of its literal "propositional" meaning. The influence of schema and inference, be it implicit or explicit, is pervasive. As with the Scott et al. (2001) study, the number schemas preferentially adopted have consistent abstract properties. In general, people tend to follow the directionality implied in the question, they tend to cover much of the range in preference to restricted range, and they tend to generate complex numbers in preference to simple ones. A deceptively simple question appears to allow executive processes to focus their attention on developing a number schema and on governing generation of the next number, rather than on the problem of how the length and boundary constraints are going to be evaluated either before or during response delivery. Such control by default is inherently error-prone, although quite capable of producing a correct result when an appropriate strategy has been adopted, and the sequence actually produced does not conflict with task-imposed constraints. When an inappropriate strategy has been adopted, the simultaneous requirements to limit both sequence length and magnitude while paying attention to other implied features, such as sequence organisation or changing a complex numeric predicate, appear to exceed the capacity of the executive processes and errors slip through unnoticed.

In a recent comparison of some 10 theoretical models of working memory, Miyake and Shah (1999) described a number of common themes. They noted that both long-term knowledge and executive control were generally regarded as playing an integral role in the determination of working memory performance. They also noted that the limits of working memory capacity are now very widely viewed as multiply determined and that in some models such limits are viewed as an emergent property of the cognitive system (e.g., Barnard, 1999; O'Reilly, Braver, & Cohen, 1999; Schneider, 1999; Young & Lewis, 1999). The overall pattern of results in our number-generation task supports this general orientation. The majority of errors do occur under conditions where the load on executive processes is high. They occur most frequently when more rather than fewer numbers are being generated and they are concentrated in circumstances where participants are manipulating many attributes of sequence content. However, beyond this simple association of circumstance, concepts such as load or capacity appear to be of limited value for understanding the empirical variation in error patterns, and hence for developing more specific theories of executive functioning. The overall effect of load is composed of a set of quite distinct underlying influences. These influences are more readily understood by considering how knowledge in long-term memory is initially accessed, and then subsequently used in the dynamic control and co-ordination of ongoing cognition. Potential mechanisms can obviously be specified in alternative frameworks, such as Baddeley's new proposal (2000) for incorporating an "episodic buffer" in between the central executive and long-term memory, or Scott et al.'s (2001) theory based on exchanges between different levels of meaning. The further development of empirical paradigms that focus on the role of domain-specific schemas in novel tasks offers one route by which alternative theories can been developed and contrasted. Such a schema-based route may ultimately prove more productive for our understanding of central executive functioning than continued reliance on studying the effects of global manipulations of load.

REFERENCES

Baddeley, A.D. (1986). *Working memory*. Oxford: Oxford University Press.

Baddeley, A.D. (1996). Exploring the central executive. *Quarterly Journal of Experimental Psychology*, *49A*, 5–28.

Baddeley, A.D. (2000). The episodic buffer: A new component of working memory? *Trends in Cognitive Science*, *4*, 417–423.

Baddeley, A.D., Emslie, H., Kolodny, J., & Duncan, J. (1998). Random generation and the executive control of working memory. *Quarterly Journal of Experimental Psychology*, *51*A, 819–852.

Baddeley, A.D., & Hitch, G.J. (1974). Working memory. In G.A. Bower (Ed.), *Recent advances in learning and motivation* (Vol. 8, pp. 47–89). New York: Academic Press.

Baddeley, A.D., & Logie, R.H. (1999). Working memory, the multi-component model. In A. Miyake & P. Shah (Eds.), *Models of working memory: Mechanisms of active maintenance and executive control* (pp. 28–61). Cambridge: Cambridge University Press.

Baddeley, A.D., & Wilson, B. (1988). Frontal amnesia and the dysexecutive syndrome. *Brain and Cognition*, *7*, 212–230.

Barnard, P.J. (1999). Interacting cognitive subsystems: Modelling working memory phenomena within a multi-processor architecture. In A. Miyake & P. Shah (Eds.), *Models of working memory: Mechanisms of active maintenance and executive control* (pp. 298–339). Cambridge: Cambridge University Press.

Benford, F. (1938). The law of anomalous numbers. *Proceedings of the American Philosophical Society*, *78*, 551–572.

Clark, H.H., & Clark, E.V. (1977). *Psychology and language: An introduction to psycholinguistics*. New York: Harcourt, Brace Jovanovich, Inc.

Duncan, J. (1995). Attention, intelligence and the frontal lobes. In M.S. Gazzaniga (Ed.), *The cognitive neurosciences* (pp. 721–733). Boston, MA: MIT Press.

Erickson, T.D., & Mattson, M.E. (1981). From words to meaning: A semantic illusion. *Journal of Verbal Learning and Verbal Behavior*, *20*, 540–551.

Halliday, M.A.K. (1970). Language structure and language function. In J. Lyons, (Ed.), *New horizons in linguistics* (pp. 140–165). Harmondsworth, UK: Penguin Books.

Hitch, G.J. (1978). The role of short-term working memory in mental arithmetic. *Cognitive Psychology*, *10*, 302–323.

Kubovy, M. (1977). Response availability and the apparent spontaneity of numerical choices. *Journal of Experimental Psychology: Human Perception and Performance*, *3*, 359–364.

Kubovy, M., & Psotka, J. (1976). The predominance of seven and the apparent spontaneity of numerical choices. *Journal of Experimental Psychology: Human Perception and Performance*, *2*, 291–294.

Logie, R.H. (1995). *Visuo-spatial working memory*. Hove, UK: Lawrence Erlbaum Associates Ltd.

Logie, R.H., & Duff, S.C. (1996). *Processing and storage in working memory: Multiple component?* Poster presented at the annual meeting of the Psychonomic Society, Chicago IL.

Mandler, G., & Shebo, B-J. (1982). Subitizing: An analysis of its component processes. *Journal of Experimental Psychology: General*, *111*, 1–22.

Miyake, A., & Shah, P. (Eds.) (1999). *Models of working memory: Mechanisms of active maintenance and executive control*. Cambridge: Cambridge University Press.

Norman, D.A., & Shallice, T. (1986). Attention to

action: Willed and automatic control of behaviour. In R.J. Davidson, G.E. Schwarts, & D. Shaprio (Eds.), *Consciousness and self regulation, Advances in research and theory* (Vol. 4, pp. 1–18). New York: Plenum Press.

O'Reilly, R.C., Braver, T.S., & Cohen, J.D. (1999). A biologically based computational model of working memory. In A. Miyake & P. Shah (Eds.), *Models of working memory: Mechanisms of active maintenance and executive control* (pp. 375–411). Cambridge: Cambridge University Press.

Poulton, E.C. (1979). Models for biases in judging sensory magnitude. *Psychological Bulletin*, *86*, 777–803.

Schneider, W. (1999). Working memory in a multilevel hybrid connectionist control architecture In A. Miyake & P. Shah (Eds.), *Models of working memory: Mechanisms of active maintenance and executive control* (pp. 341–374). Cambridge: Cambridge University Press.

Scott, S.K., Barnard, P.J., & May, J. (2001). Specifying executive representations and processes in number generation tasks. *Quarterly Journal of Experimental Psychology*, *54A*, 641–664.

Shallice, T., & Evans, M.E. (1978). The involvement of the frontal lobes in cognitive estimation. *Cortex*, *4*, 294–303.

Young, R.M., & Lewis, R.L. (1999). The SOAR cognitive architecture and human working memory. In A. Miyake & P. Shah (Eds.), *Models of working memory: Mechanisms of active maintenance and executive control* (pp. 224–256). Cambridge: Cambridge University Press.

MEMORY, 2001, 9 (4/5/6), 223–231

Patterns of errors in short-term forgetting in AD and ageing

Maria Victoria Sebastian
Universidad Complutense, Madrid, Spain

Julio Menor
Universidad de Oviedo, Spain

Rosa Elosua
Universidad Nacional de Educación a Distancia, Madrid, Spain

This study examined whether the low performance of 40 AD patients in the Brown-Peterson task could be explained by a pattern of errors that differed from 55 elderly controls. Our quantitative results showed that AD patients had a lower performance level in the three retention intervals than controls but a significant interaction between group and interval was not found, indicating that the rate of forgetfulness was similar in the two groups. In our qualitative analysis, errors were categorised as confusions, perseverations, omissions, and order alterations. Contrary to other studies (Dannenbaum, Parkinson, & Inman, 1988; Kopelman, 1985) where an AD forgetfulness tendency of omissions was observed, our data showed an excess of perseveration (even more than five repetitions), indicating problems in the central executive. This could be interpreted in terms of problems in updating the contents of working memory.

The ailment Alzheimer's disease (AD) is a degenerative disorder at the cortical level which causes multiple cognitive deficits, the most important of which is the progressive loss of memory. This memory loss is manifested, according to the traditional classification, in both short-term and long-term memory tasks. Among the most frequently used short-term memory tasks are verbal memory span tasks and the Brown-Peterson task (Brown, 1958; Peterson & Peterson, 1959). In the former, some investigators have found significant differences between AD patients and normal elderly (Becker, 1988; Belleville, Peretz, & Malenfant, 1996; Cherry, Buckwalter, & Henderson, 1996; Collette, Van der Linden, Bechet, & Salmon, 1999; Kaszniak, Garron, & Fox, 1979; Kopelman, 1985; Morris, 1984, 1986, 1987; Orsini, Trojano, Chiachio, & Grossi, 1988) whereas others (Botwinick, Storandt, & Berg, 1986; Corkin, 1982; Lines et al., 1991; Martín, Brouwers, Cox, & Fedio, 1985; Weingartner et al., 1983) have not found such differences.

As regards the Brown-Peterson task, it has been used to determine whether the rate of forgetting is similar to that of the control group or, on the contrary, the AD patients forget more quickly. Previous results (for example, Sullivan, Corkin, & Growden, 1986) would seem to indicate that the loss of information was, indeed, quicker in the patient group. Nevertheless, subsequent studies (Dannenbaum et al., 1988; Kopelman, 1985, 1991) that were able to equate

Requests for reprints should be sent to Maria Victoria Sebastian, Universidad Complutense, Department of Basic Psychology I, Somosaguas, 28223, Madrid. Spain. Email: *mvsebastian@psi.ucm.es*

This work was supported by the Dirección General de Investigación Científica y Técnica of Spanish Ministry of Education and Culture (grant number DGICYT PB94-1573). We would like to thank Michael Kopelman and Robin Morris for their helpful comments on an earlier draft and James Hollander for his help with the English version.

http://www.tandf.co.uk/journals/pp/09658211.html DOI:10.1080/09658210143000038

the initial level of acquisition demonstrated that although AD patients clearly performed less well than the controls, they did not forget more quickly: that is, the forgetting curves were parallel for the two groups with verbal and non-verbal material.

The two tasks were used in the context of the working memory model of Baddeley (1986, 1997). This model is a multi-component system that contains both storage and processing functions, with two slave subsystems: the phonological loop and the visual-spatial sketch pad, responsible for retaining speech-based and visuo-spatial information respectively, and an attention component called the central executive, which controls and co-ordinates the activity of the slave systems as well as the available processing resources.

The working memory model (Baddeley, 1986) has been used to explain short-term memory deficit both in normal ageing (Anderson & Craik, 2000; Craik, 1977, 1994; Light, 1991; Morris, Craik, & Gick, 1990) and in Alzheimer patients (see the review by Kopelman, 1994; Vallar & Papagno, 1995) and to determine which component or components might be affected in either case. In the first case, the elderly have a poorer performance when, for example, they are asked to carry out two tasks (dual task procedure), indicating that the central executive is performing less adequately in the elderly than in the younger group. In studies of Alzheimer, Morris (1986) has suggested that the low performance rates attained by AD patients in the Brown-Peterson task is due to a dysfunction of the central executive, which would otherwise allow the subject to review the items while doing the distracting task. Morris manipulated the complexity of the task and found that the more difficult it was, the lower was the performance of AD patients in serial recall of the items. More recent studies (Belleville et al., 1996; Collette et al., 1999) have also examined the phonological loop and central executive functioning in this disease and have found a deficit in both components.

In addition to quantitative analyses of performance in the Brown-Peterson task, qualitative assessments of participants' performance in this task are possible. Such errors might aid in determining which of the cognitive mechanisms may have a deficit. Nevertheless, few studies (Dannenbaum et al., 1988; Kopelman, 1985) have followed this route. For example, Kopelman compared performance in the Brown-Peterson task in three groups of participants: AD patients, Korsakoffs patients, and controls. He used a series of three one-syllable words, and the distractor task consisted of counting backwards by twos or threes for 2, 5, 10, and 20 seconds. Errors were classified into omissions, intrusions (intra- and extra-list items), and confusions. Kopelman found that omissions predominated in the AD group whereas intrusions did so in the Korsakoff group. In the control group, distribution of errors was more homogeneous. In the other study conducted by Dannenbaum et al. (1988), there was also a predominance of omissions.

The primary aim of this study is to analyse the pattern of errors committed in the Brown-Peterson task by an AD patient group in order to determine whether it differed from the control group and whether such a difference has any functional significance; that is, whether this pattern enables a determination of which mechanisms suffer from a deficit in this illness. The Brown-Peterson task employed differs slightly from the original. First, the series of letters were presented visually and were made up of two items instead of the usual three in order to avoid overloading the memory of the subject. Second, participants were asked to read the letters aloud in order to check articulation and encoding. Third, the distractor task entailed counting forwards one by one, as a pilot study showed that AD patients encountered great difficulties in counting backwards.

As previously reported (Kopelman, 1985), the errors in this task are first those of omission, indicating that the information has not been encoded. Second, confusions might reflect the manner in which the subject is storing or retrieving the material. As presentation is visual in our procedure, and participants are asked to read the items aloud, it was expected that they make a visual and phonological representation of them. These confusions could thus be of two main types: visual or phonological. If the confusions are visual, it may indicate that the participants have not phonologically recoded the material, presumably because the phonological loop is not performing properly, and they rely mainly on visual features. If the confusions are phonological, it would suggest that the participants have stored the material phonologically but might be having problems in recirculating the information between the phonological store and the phonological output buffer, as proposed by Vallar and Papagno (1995), so the trace may lose quality or be degraded in its phonological features because similar traces could not be distinguished ("the phonological similarity effect", reported by Conrad & Hull, 1964; Baddeley, 1966); or patients may engage in confusions when they are asked to give the response (phonological buffer output).

Moreover, errors may be of a different nature, reflecting the deficient functioning of another component of working memory. Thus, the presence of prolonged perseverance errors or the repetition of the response given in the immediately preceding test may signal the subject's difficulty in renewing or updating the contents of working memory. Therefore, the objective of this study is to determine whether the poor performance of AD patients in the Brown-Peterson task might be accompanied by a pattern of errors that is qualitatively different from that of the control group; or whether the errors are of the same type but only in large numbers.

METHOD

Participants

A total of 95 participants carried out the experiment: 40 Alzheimer (AD) patients, with a mean age of 73.17 ($SD = 4.68$), 13 males and 27 females, with 10.6 years of education ($SD = 2.48$), and with MMSE of 20.30 ($SD = 2.14$) from three outpatient clinics, diagnosed in accordance with NINCDS/ADRDA standards (McKhann et al., 1984) with a digit span of 4.20 ($SD = .65$); and 55 elderly control participants from three different outpatient centres with a mean age of 73.00 ($SD = .82$), 22 males and 33 females, with 10.9 years of education ($SD = 1.05$); and with a MMSE of 27.77, ($SD = 1.70$) and a digit span of 4.64 ($SD = .82$). All participants were able to read and write correctly.

Material

The material consisted of 21 items. Each item comprised two upper-case consonants, the letters combined randomly with the constraint that they were not repeated in the following item. Selection of consonants was random, but the order of presentation was constant. The items were each presented typed in upper-case letters in the centre of white 10 × 15 cm cards, which were spiral bound.

Procedure

The task was administered individually to all participants. The participant sat in front of the researcher, who placed the notebook of cards so that the person could read them easily. A practice item was administered previously to ensure that the participant understood the task correctly. The participants were informed that they would see a series of cards with two letters and that they would have to read them aloud and look at them attentively because they would later have to remember them in the same order in which they had seen them.

There were three experimental conditions: a retention interval of 7, 14, and 21 seconds. Once the participant had read the item, the researcher turned the card and said a number, which was of two digits in every case, cueing the subject to begin counting forwards one by one beginning from that number. When the time had elapsed, according the retention level, the participant was asked to recall the letters that had just been presented. The entire task was tape recorded for subsequent transcription and analysis.

RESULTS

First of all, data were analysed on digit span in direct order of the two subject groups, and significant differences were found between the groups $F(1, 93) = 7.72$, $MSE = 4.41$, $p < .0006$. The AD group (4.20) had a lower span than the control (C) (4.64).

The results of the Brown-Peterson task were analysed in two different ways. First, the proportion of accurate recall was examined, and second, the different types of errors were analysed. Both forms were analysed in terms of subject groups (AD and C).

Analysis of accurate recall

An accurate recall was considered to be the serial recall of two letters according to how the participant had read them, regardless of the original items. The score obtained by each participant is the mean of recall of all items. In the case of 0 or 1 values, they were transformed, following the suggestion of Bartlett (1947, cited by Kirk, 1982, p. 83).

With these data (transformed by arc sine in degrees), an initial analysis of variance was made with two factors: Group and Retention Interval (7, 14, and 21 s). The analysis of variance showed that the main factors, Group $F(1,93) = 137.83$, $MSE = 124.18$, $p < .0001$, and Interval $F(2,186) = 4.54$, $MSE = .71$, $p < .012$ were significant, but not the interaction $F(2,186) = 1.68$, $MSE = .26$ $p = .189$. In Table 1, it can be seen that the AD group (.32) have a considerably inferior memory to the C group (.85). Pairwise comparisons with the Bonferroni adjustment showed that both groups recalled more letters in the 7 s (.62, $p < .013$) interval than in the 21 s interval but no significant differences were found in the other two intervals (interval 14 = .59 and interval 21 = .55, $p = .154$).

Analyses of errors

Errors committed by the participants were grouped into the following exclusive categories: *confusions*, *perseverations*, *omissions*, and *order alterations*. In each category, proportions (based on the number of errors) were computed and transformed by arc sine in degrees in order to compare the groups. In the case of 0 or 1 values, Bartlett's suggestion was again followed (1947, cited by Kirk, 1982, p. 83). First, confusions of one or two letters were analysed. *Confusion of one letter* was when the participant said a letter other than those presented. This confusion could be *visual* (when the letter recalled visually resembled the one presented; e.g., the item "ZB" presented, "ZB" read, "ZH" recalled); *phonological* (when the letter was similar phonetically, according to the classification in traditional Spanish grammar, i.e., sonority, point, and form of articulation; e.g., the item "ZB" presented, "ZB" read, "ZV" recalled); *both criteria* (when the letter was similar both visually and phonologically; e.g., the item "ZB" presented, "ZB" read, "ZP" recalled); or *others* (when the letter answered was neither visually nor phonologically similar to the one presented). This last category would be similar to "intrusions" used by other authors (Dannenbaum et al., 1988; Kopelman, 1985). *Confusion of two letters* was a response of two letters that were different from those presented.

TABLE 1
Mean proportions (and standard deviations) of correct recall in relation to groups and retention intervals

Group	*Retention Interval* 7	14	21	*Mean*
AD	.37 (.30)	.32 (.30)	.27 (.30)	.32
C	.86 (.14)	.86 (.20)	.82 (.22)	.85
Mean	.62	.59	.55	

Comparing the confusions between one and two letters (from total confusions) by groups [Group $F(1,93) = 27.80$, $MSE = 15.55$, $p < .0001$; type of confusion $F(1,93) = 124.44$, $MSE = 100.27$, $p < .0001$; and interaction, $F(1,93) = 4.49$, $MSE = 3.62$, $p < .037$], it was found (Table 2) that both the interaction and the principal factors were significant. Interaction indicated that the difference between AD (.84) and C (.50) was greater in those of one letter, $F(1,93) = 15.40$, $MSE = 17.09$, $p < .0002$, than in those of two letters, AD = .15, C = .07; $F(1,93) = 8.15$, $MSE = 2.08$, $p < .0053$.

To examine one-letter confusions with more specificity, a variance analysis was conducted according to the four error types (visual, phonological, both, and others) and groups, and it was found (Table 2) that only the principal factors, Group $F(1,93) = 36.34$, $MSE = 10.38$, $p < .0001$, and type of confusions $F(3, 279) = 27.59$, $MSE = 17.13$, $p < .0001$ were significant, but not the interaction $F(3, 279) = 2.33$, $MSE = 1.45$, $p = .074$. AD (.25) committed more confusions than C (.14). Pairwise comparisons indicated that phonological confusions (.44, all $ps < .0001$) were more frequent than visual ones (.12), any combinations thereof (.11) or those in the subcategory "other confusions" (.13), which are called "intrusions" by other authors.

Introducting the retention interval as a factor, the data showed the same pattern of errors as the previous one in confusions of one letter; it would not appear that this factor has any influence either as a principal factor or in interaction with the other factors. However, in the case of confusion of two letters, the only significant effect was interval as a main factor $F(2,186) = 6.98$, $MSE = .4.13$, $p < .001$. Pairwise comparisons of the three intervals indicated that these confusions were significantly more frequent (all $ps < .018$) in the 21 second interval (.13) than the other two (7 s = .09; 14 s = .11).

Second, perseverations were analysed according to whether they were of *one letter* or of *two letters*. Perseveration is understood as repetition by the participant of the response given in the immediately preceding test. In turn, these were subdivided according the number of times they were repeated consecutively, resulting in six

TABLE 2
Mean proportions (and standard deviations) of the different types of confusions of one letter and two letters by group

Group	One letter Visual	Phonological	Both	Others	Two letters
AD	.16 (.21)	.56 (.31)	.14 (.24)	.15 (.19)	.15 (.16)
C	.08 (.22)	.31 (.40)	.07 (.16)	.11 (.25)	.07 (.19)
Mean	.12	.44	.11	.13	.11

different ones. *Perseveration of one letter* was the repetition by the participant of a letter that was the same as in the previous response. Such repetition could occur once (perseveration of a letter one consecutive time), twice (perseveration of a letter two consecutive times) three times (perseveration of a letter three consecutive times), four times (perseveration of a letter four consecutive times), five times (perseveration of a letter five consecutive times) or more than five (perseveration of a letter more than five consecutive times).

In like manner, *perseveration of two letters* consisted of the repetition of two letters that were the same as in the previous response. As in the case of perseveration of one letter, this perseveration could occur once (perseveration of two letters one consecutive time), twice (perseveration of two letters two consecutive times), three times (perseveration of two letters three consecutive times), four times (perseveration of two letters four consecutive times), five times (perseveration of two letters five consecutive times), or more than five (perseveration of two letters more than five consecutive times).

Comparing the perseverations of one (Table 3) and two letters (Table 4) from total perseverations by group, Group $F(1,93)=11.54$, $MSE=7.83$, $p<.001$; type of perseverations $F(1,93)=75.51$, $MSE = 69.70$, $p<.0001$; and interaction, $F(1,93)=.09$, $MSE=.09$, $p=.760$, both groups had a larger number of errors of one (.60) than of two letters (.13), and the AD group (.46) made more perseverations than group C (.30).

As can be seen in Table 3, group C committed practically no perseveration of one letter more than twice. Thus, the first two levels were taken into account according to group, and an analysis of variance conducted. This showed that both the interaction $F(1,93)=4.23$, $MSE=3.72$, $p<.04$, and the principal factors Group $F(1,93)=4.04$, $MSE=2.81$, $p<.04$; perseveration $F(1,93)=72.54$, $MSE=63.78$, $p<.0001$ were significant. Interaction indicated the difference between AD (.19) and C (.03) was only significant in the case of perseveration of one letter twice. The groups (AD = .54; C = .56) committed a similar number of perseverations where they occurred once.

Continuing with these two levels of perseverations and adding the factor of retention interval, the only new result that was significant was the interaction between perseveration and interval $F(2,186) = 5.50$, $MSE = 4.08$, $p < .005$. Neither interval as a principal factor, $F(2,186)=1.88$, $MSE=1.46$, $p=.156$, nor the group × interval interaction, $F(2, 186) = .20$, $MSE = .16$, $p = .818$, nor triple interaction, $F(2,186)=2.65$, $MSE=1.96$, $p=.073$, was significant. Subsequent analysis showed that only those that occurred once (.24) were significantly more numerous than those occurring twice (.10). Pairwise comparisons showed that only the perseverations that occurred once in 7 second intervals (.32) were more frequent than in the 14 (.19, $p<.02$) and 21 second (.20, $p<.05$) intervals, and no differences were found between the last two.

Pairwise comparisons were made for the AD group, and it was found that the once-repeated

TABLE 3
Mean proportions (and standard deviations) of the different types of perseverations of one letter by group

Group	Once	Twice	Three times	Four times	Five times	Five times +
AD	.54 (.33)	.19 (.24)	.08 (.12)	.06 (.16)	.03 (.05)	.06 (.11)
C	.56 (.47)	.03 (.06)	.01 (.03)	.01 (.00)	.01 (.00)	.01 (.00)
Mean	.55	.11	.05	.04	.02	.04

TABLE 4
Mean proportions (and standard deviations) of the different types of perseverations of two letters by group

Group	*Once*	*Twice*	*Three times*	*Four times*	*Five times*	*Five times +*
AD	.48 (.43)	.09 (.15)	.03 (.06)	.03 (.05)	.02 (.02)	.02 (.05)
C	.15 (.34)	.02 (.04)	.01 (.00)	.01 (.00)	.01 (.00)	.01 (.00)
Mean	.32	.06	.02	.02	.02	.02

perseverations were most frequent (.54, all $ps < .002$), amounting to significantly more than the rest, and that twice-repeated perseverations (.19, $p < .001$) had a higher score than those of five (.03) or more than five (.06). However, in group C there were significant differences, $F(1, 54) = 66.74$, $MSE = 58.37, p < .0001$, only between the first (.56) and the second type (.03), as scores were practically null at other levels.

As regards the two-letter perseverations in Table 4, as there so few scores in group C, there was an analysis of variance only for the first level (repeated once). The results indicated a significant difference between the groups, $F(1, 93) = 17.97$, $MSE = 20.37$, $p < .0001$. The AD group committed a significantly larger number of perseverations repeated once (.48) than group C (.15).

Introducing retention interval as a factor, the data showed the same pattern of errors as previously; it would not appear that this factor has any influence either as a principal factor or in interaction with the other factors.

In group AD, patients followed the same result pattern as in the one-letter perseverations in relation to number of times occurred.

Third, omissions of one or two letters were measured (Table 5). *Omission of a letter* implied that the subject did not reproduce the first or second letter presented, while *omission of two letters* indicated a blank response by the subject.

To analyse omissions (of one and two letters) by group (Table 5), an analysis of variance was performed. It showed that the principal factor, Group $F(1, 93) = 30.92$, $MSE = 18.88$, $p < .0001$, was significant but the second factor, omission $F(1, 93) = 2.11$, $MSE = 1.73, p = .15$ and interaction were not, $F(1, 93) = .18$, $MSE = .15$, $p = .673$. The AD group (.29) committed more omissions than group C (.07).

When introducing retention interval as a factor, data showed that this interval as a principal factor, $F(2, 186) = 7.50$, $MSE = 2.00$, $p < .001$, was significant, though no significant interactions were found in the other factors [omission × interval, $F(2, 186) = 1.55$, $MSE = .48$, $p = .214$; group × interval, $F(2, 186) = 1.50$, $MSE = .40$, $p = .226$; triple interaction, $F(2, 186) = .22$, $MSE = .07$, $p = .804$]. Pairwise comparisons were made and showed that omissions in the interval 21 s (.12, all $ps < .026$) were more frequent than in the rest (.06 in interval 14 s, and .07 in interval 7 s, respectively).

The fourth error, alterations in the order of one or two letters, was then evaluated. *One letter order alteration* meant that the subject accurately recalled one of the two letters presented but in a different order, whereas a *two letter order alteration* was an accurate recall of both letters, though in a different order.

To analyse order alterations (of one and two letters) by group (Table 6), an analysis of variance was performed. It showed that both the principal factors, Group $F(1, 93) = 15.87$, $MSE = 12.68$, $p < .0001$ and order alterations $F(1, 93) = 38.12$, $MSE = 38.35$, $p < .0001$ in addition to interaction were significant, $F(1, 93) = 20.47$, $MSE = 20.59$, $p < .0001$. This indicated that the difference between AD (.69) and C (.26) was greater in

TABLE 5
Mean proportions (and standard deviations) of the different types of omission of one and two letters by group

Group	*Omission of one letter*	*Omission of two letters*
AD	.26 (.39)	.32 (.42)
C	.02 (.07)	.11 (.29)
Mean	.14	.22

TABLE 6
Mean proportions (and standard deviations) of different order alterations (one and two letters) by group

Group	*One letter order alteration*	*Two letter order alteration*
AD	.69 (.39)	.11 (.19)
C	.26 (.40)	.17 (.32)
Mean	.48	.14

alterations of one letter, $F(1,93) = 27.26$, $MSE = 32.80$, $p < .00001$, than in those of two letters; AD = .11 and C = .17, respectively, $F(1,93) = .79$, $MSE = .48$, $p = .38$.

When introducing retention interval as a factor, the data showed that neither as a principal factor, $F(2, 186) = .54$, $MSE = .33$, $p = .581$, nor in interactions [alteration × interval, $F(2, 186) = 1.96$, $MSE = 1.36$, $p = .144$; group × interval, $F(2, 186) = 1.65$, $MSE = 1.01$, $p = .195$; triple interaction, $F(2,186) = 1.16$, $MSE = .81$, $p = .314$] was it significant.

Finally, a two-way analysis of variance was carried out to determine which of the previously mentioned error types (confusions, perseverations, omissions, and order alterations) was most frequent by group. The data indicated that only the principal factors Group $F(1, 93) = 14.85$, $MSE = 3.18$, $p < .0001$, and error type $F(3,279) = 23.54$, $MSE = 11.85$, $p < .0001$, were significant but not interaction, $F(3,279) = .57$, $MSE = .29$, $p = .636$. AD (.26) committed more errors than C (.21). Both groups committed a larger number of perseverations (.37) and confusions (.30) although there was no difference between them; both types of errors were more frequent than the other two (omissions = .09, $p < .0001$; order alterations = .15, $p < .0001$). These last two were not significantly different ($p = .062$).

DISCUSSION

In this study, a quantitative and qualitative analysis was made of the performance of patients with probable AD and control participants in the traditional Brown-Peterson task. From a quantitative point of view, the AD patients performed worse than the controls in the three retention intervals analysed. However, no interaction between group and interval was found, indicating that the rate of forgetting in the three intervals considered (7, 14, and 21 seconds) was similar in the two participant groups. But this is not to rule out a quicker rate of forgetfulness in the Alzheimer group, because in the first interval tested (7 seconds), significant differences were found between the Alzheimer group and the control group.

The qualitative analysis was based on the proportions of errors by the participant groups in the task. Errors were categorised as confusions, perseverations, omissions, and order alterations. The AD group committed a larger number of confusions than the control group, and phonological ones were more frequent than the other three types, though no interaction between group and type of confusion was found. In perseveration errors, the AD group perseverated up to more than five consecutive times, whereas the controls generally perseverated once. This pattern of results was also found in two-letter perseverations. Omission errors were more frequent in AD patients than in controls, but two-letter omissions were not more frequent than one-letter ones, and no interaction between group and type of omission was found. Finally, in order alterations, the AD group had more errors than the controls only in those of one letter and not those of two letters.

As regards the quantitative analysis of data from the Brown-Peterson task, the lack of interaction between group and interval corroborated the results of previous authors (for example, Belleville et al., 1996; Dannenbaum et al., 1988; Kopelman, 1985). Nevertheless, as noted earlier, the AD group showed a poorer performance than group C in the first interval of 7 seconds. As the groups were not equal in performance, a possible problem of encoding cannot be excluded. One alternative explanation, as suggested by Morris (1986), is based on a dysfunction of the central executive, which makes holding of material and initiating the distractor task more difficult for AD patients, causing rapid forgetting in the first few seconds.

Moreover, in our study the series of items comprised two letters and not three, in order to avoid the "floor effect" in AD patients, as several studies (for example, Belleville et al., 1996; Cherry et al., 1996; Collette et al., 1999; Dannenbaum et al., 1988; Kopelman, 1985; Morris, 1984) have shown that these patients' verbal memory span is significantly lower than in controls. In addition, our AD patients had a span of 4.20 digits, which was considerably lower than that of the controls. Thus, the use of series of two letters ensured to a greater degree that the short-term memory of the participant would not be overloaded. Noteworthy is the low digit span of the controls, for while it is higher than the AD patients, it is lower than that obtained in English-language studies. A tentative explanation would be the number of syllables making up the digits in Spanish compared to English (Naveh-Benjamin & Ayres, 1986). In Spanish, all the digits except 2 ("*dos*") and 3 ("*tres*") are composed of two syllables (for example, 4 is "*cua-tro*" and 5 "*cin-co*") whereas in English it is the opposite: there are more digits composed of one syllable than of two. Given the known role of subvocal rehearsal in memory span, and the fact that this span is mediated by the number of syllables that can be uttered in 2 seconds, digit series composed of two syllables will be more poorly recalled than those of one syllable (the "word-length effect" reported by Baddeley, Thomson, & Buchanan, 1975). A similar explanation has been put forth by Ellis and Hennelly (1980) in comparing the digit spans of English and Welsh children.

The aim of analysing errors was to determine whether these errors might provide any information on the Brown-Peterson task. In contrast to the results of Kopelman (1985) and Dannenbaum et al. (1988) which found a predominance of omissions, our study found mostly confusions and perseverations. Error patterns might reflect task difficulty; thus, remembering two letters with a distraction consisting of counting forwards by ones is easier than remembering three words and counting backwards by twos (Kopelman, 1985). However, this remains to be demonstrated empirically.

The high rates of perseverations in a single series (even more than five times) would seem to suggest a clear inability by the patient to renew or update the contents of working memory; that is, it is as if a patient had become fixated on a particular item. The ability to constantly renew the contents of working memory is considered a control mechanism, and it would be the function of the central executive to indicate, therefore, that there is a deficit in these patients.

In addition to this type of error, the AD patients had a larger number of confusions than the control group, while both groups showed a high proportion of phonological confusions. It must be borne in mind that the letters were presented visually, though the participants were asked to read them aloud as they were presented, and before beginning the distractor task. The participants were thus aided in making both a visual and phonological encoding of the letters. However, the errors committed were above all of a phonological nature, which would seem to indicate the predominance of phonological coding over visual coding. This might result in a greater reliance on an intact phonological store, thereby increasing the probability of this type of error when participants are asked to give the response, presumably because both groups may have problems in recirculating the information between the phonological store and the phonological output buffer (Vallar & Papagno, 1995).

The greater prevalence of omissions in AD patients may be a reflection, as suggested by Kopelman (1985), of an encoding or storage deficit, as the distractor task employed (counting forwards one by one) alters patient performance in series as short as two letters.

Finally, errors of altered order usually occur when the series used coincides with or exceed the memory span of AD patients. In our study, however, the series presented was below the span of AD patients. Furthermore, the larger number of order alterations produced by AD patients occurred only in those of one letter and not in two. It should be noted that these alterations consist of accurate recall of one of the letters but in a different order than the presentation, implying that recall of the other item is yet another error, but this is usually a perseveration from the previous series or a confusion. As such, order alterations are closely related to the presence of another type of error (perseverations, for example), making them difficult to interpret.

In sum, our data, taken as a whole, would suggest that the performance deficit shown by AD patients in the Brown-Peterson task is primarily due to a difficulty in renewing or updating the contents of working memory.

REFERENCES

Anderson, N.D. & Craik, F.I.M. (2000). Memory in the aging brain. In E. Tulving, & F.I.M. Craik (Eds.), *The Oxford handbook of memory*. Oxford: Oxford University Press.

Baddeley, A. (1966). Short-term memory for word sequences as a function of acoustic, semantic and formal similarity. *Journal of Experimental Psychology, 18*, 362–365.

Baddeley, A. (1986). *Working memory*. Oxford: Oxford University Press.

Baddeley, A. (1997). *Human memory. Theory and practice*. Hove, UK: Psychology Press.

Baddeley, A.D., Thomson, N., & Buchanan, M. (1975). Word length and the structure of short-term memory. *Journal of Verbal Learning and Verbal Behavior, 14*, 575–589.

Becker, J.T. (1988). Working memory and secondary memory deficits in Alzheimer's disease. *Journal of Clinical and Experimental Neuropsychology, 6*, 739–753.

Belleville, S., Peretz, I., & Malefant, D. (1996). Examination of the working memory components in normal aging and in dementia of the Alzheimer type. *Neuropsychologia, 3*, 195–207.

Botwinick, J., Storandt, M., & Berg, L. (1986). A longitudinal, behavioral study of senile dementia of the Alzheimer type. *Archives of Neurology, 43*, 1124–1127.

Brown, J. (1958). Some tests of the decay theory of immediate memory. *The Quarterly Journal of Experimental Psychology*, *10*, 12–21.

Cherry, B.J., Buckwalter, J.G., & Henderson, V.W. (1996). Memory span procedures in Alzheimer's disease. *Neuropsychology*, *2*, 286–293.

Collette, F., van der Linden, M., Bechet, S., & Salmon, E. (1999). Phonological loop and central executive functioning in Alzheimer's disease. *Neuropsychologia*, *37*, 905–918.

Conrad, R., & Hull, A.J. (1964). Information, acoustic confusion and memory span. *British Journal of Psychology*, *55*, 429–432.

Corkin, S. (1982). Some relationships between global amnesias and the memory impairments in Alzheimer's disease. In S. Corkin, K.L. Davies, & J.H. Growdon (Eds.), *Alzheimer's disease: A report of progress in research Vol. 19*. New York: Raven Press.

Craik, F.I.M. (1977). Age differences in human memory. In J.E. Birren & K.W. Schaie (Eds.), *Handbook of the psychology of aging*. New York: Van Nostrand-Reinhold.

Craik, F.I.M. (1994). Memory changes in normal aging. *Current Directions in Psychological Science*, *3*, 155–158.

Dannenbaum, S.E., Parkinson, S.R., & Inman, V.W. (1988). Short-term forgetting: Comparisons between patients with dementia of the Alzheimer type, depressed and normal elderly. *Cognitive Neuropsychology*, *5*, 213–233.

Ellis, N.C., & Hennelly, R.A. (1980). A bilingual word-length effect: Implications for intelligence testing and the relative ease of mental calculation in Welsh and English. *British Journal of Psychology*, *71*, 43–51.

Kaszniak, A.W., Garron, D.C., & Fox, J. (1979). Differential aspects of ages and cerebral atrophy upon span of immediate recall and paired associates learning in older patients with suspected dementia. *Cortex*, *15*, 285–295.

Kirk, R.E. (1982). *Experimental design* (2nd edn). Monterey, CA: Brooks/Cole.

Kopelman, M.D. (1985). Rates of forgetting in Alzheimer type dementia and Korsakoff's syndrome. *Neuropsychology*, *23*, 623–638.

Kopelman, M.D. (1991). Non-verbal, short-term forgetting in the alcoholic Korsakoff syndrome and Alzheimer-type dementia. *Neuropsychologia*, *8*, 737–747.

Kopelman, M.D. (1994). Working memory in the amnesic syndrome and degenerative dementia. *Neuropsychology*, *8*, 555–562.

Light, L.L. (1991). Memory and aging: four hypotheses in search of data. *Annual Review of Psychology*, *42*, 333–376.

Lines, C.R., Dawson, C., Preston, G.C., Reich, S., Foster, C., & Traub, M. (1991). Memory and attention in patients with senile dementia of the Alzheimer type and in normal elderly subjects. *Journal of Clinical and Experimental Neuropsychology*, *13*, 691–702.

Martin, A., Brouwers, P., Cox, C., & Fedio, P. (1985). On the nature of the verbal memory deficit in Alzheimer's disease. *Brain and Language*, *25*, 323–341.

McKhann, G., Drachman, D., Folstein, M., Katzman, R., Price, D., & Stadlan, E.M. (1984). Clinical diagnosis of Alzheimer's disease: Report of the NINCDS-ADRDA Work Group under the auspices of Department of Health and Human Services Task Force on Alzheimer's disease. *Neurology*, *34*, 939–944.

Morris, R.G. (1984). Dementia and the functioning of the articulatory loop system. *Cognitive Neuropsychology*, *1*, 143–157.

Morris, R.G. (1986). Short-term forgetting in senile dementia of the Alzheimer's type. *Cognitive Neuropsychology*, *3*, 77–97.

Morris, R.G. (1987). Articulatory rehearsal in Alzheimer-type dementia. *Brain and Language*, *30*, 351–362.

Morris, R.G., Craik, F.I.M., & Gick, M.L. (1990). Age differences in working memory task: The role of secondary memory and the central executive system. *Quarterly Journal of Experimental Psychology*, *42*A, 67–86.

Naveh-Benjamin, M., & Ayres, T.J. (1986). Digit span, reading rate, and linguistic relativity. *The Quarterly Journal of Experimental Psychology*, *38*A, 739–751.

Orsini, A., Trojano, L., Chiacchio, L., & Grossi, D. (1988). Immediate memory spans in dementia. *Perceptual Motor Skills*, *67*, 267–272.

Peterson, L.R., & Peterson, M.J. (1959). Short-term retention of individual verbal items. *Journal of Experimental Psychology*, *58*, 193–198.

Sullivan, E.V., Corkin, S., & Growden, J.H. (1986). Verbal and nonverbal short-term memory in patients with Alzheimer's disease and in healthy elderly subjects. *Developmental Neuropsychology*, *2*, 387–400.

Vallar, G., & Papagno, C. (1995). Neuropsychological impairments of short-term memory. In A.D. Baddeley, B.A. Wilson, & F.N. Watts (Eds.), *Handbook of memory disorders*. Chichester, UK: Wiley.

Weingartner, H.J., Grafman, J., Boutelle, W., Kaye, W., & Martin, P. (1983). Forms of cognitive failure. *Science*, *221*, 380–382.

MEMORY, 2001, *9* (4/5/6), 233–247

How does the severity of a learning disability affect working memory performance?

Lucy A. Henry
Institute of Psychiatry, Kings College London, UK

Working memory performance was examined in children aged 11–12 years who had borderline, mild, and moderate learning disabilities. Comparisons with children of average abilities were used to determine whether those with more severe learning disabilities had greater impairments in working memory. Seven measures of working memory span were used to assess temporary phonological short-term storage (digit span, word span), temporary visuo-spatial short-term storage (pattern span, spatial span), and temporary short-term storage with additional processing, or central executive, demands (listening span, odd one out span, reverse digit span). Children with mild and moderate learning disabilities were impaired on all measures of working memory compared to children of average abilities. Children with borderline learning disabilities were just as good as children with average abilities on visuo-spatial and complex span tasks, but showed an impairment on phonological span tasks. Children with moderate learning disabilities were indistinguishable from children with mild learning disabilities on simple span tasks, but were significantly poorer than the mild group on the more demanding complex span tasks. For the group as a whole, working memory was strongly related to mental age.

The working memory model (Baddeley, 1986; Baddeley & Hitch, 1974) provides a very useful framework for looking at temporary storage and processing of information and has been applied to children without learning disabilities very successfully (see Gathercole, 1998; Henry & Millar, 1993 for reviews). Working memory is divided into a central executive or attentional control system plus two "slave" storage systems for the temporary retention of information. One storage system, the phenological loop, is for phonological material and the other, the visuo-spatial sketch pad is for visual and spatial information. These two subsystems are limited in capacity to a few items and decay is very rapid. Items can be maintained in each system for short periods of time by using modality-specific rehearsal mechanisms. Evidence for rehearsal derives from studies showing that engaging in concurrent visual or spatial activity disrupts short-term visuo-spatial storage (Brooks, 1967, Byrne, 1974) and engaging in concurrent speech (e.g., "the, the, the...") disrupts phonological short-term storage (Baddeley, Lewis, & Vallar, 1984; Murray, 1968).

Recent work has begun to explore working memory in children with learning disabilities (e.g., Hulme & Mackenzie, 1992; Hulme & Roodenrys, 1995; Jarrold & Baddeley, 1997; Jarrold, Baddeley, & Hewes, 1999; 2000; Russell, Jarrold, & Henry, 1996; Varnhagen, Das, & Varnhagen, 1987; Vicari, Carlesimo, & Caltagirone, 1995). However, much of this research has concentrated on a minority of children with learning disabilities—those with an identifiable syndrome or disorder (e.g., William's syndrome, Down's syndrome, autism). This paper is concerned with the

Requests for reprints should be sent to Lucy A. Henry, Department of Psychology, Institute of Psychiatry, De Crespigny Park, Denmark Hill, London SE5 8AF, UK. Email: *L.Henry@iop.kcl.ac.uk*

This research was funded by the Wellcome Trust, grant number 042860. I would like to thank the children and teachers from the following schools who kindly took part in this project: Garratt Park School, Southfields Community College, Lilian Baylis School, and Highshore School.

http://www.tandf.co.uk/journals/pp/09658211.html DOI:10.1080/09658210042000085

larger numbers of children with learning disabilities who do not suffer from an identified syndrome. These children may be simply the lower end of the normal distribution of ability, they may have suffered some form of brain damage before or after birth due to obstetric complications, or they may have suffered from a disease during childhood (e.g., meningitis). Often there will be no clear explanation for the learning disability. The focus of this study was the effect of *severity* of learning disability (LD) on working memory performance in each of the three systems.

Several previous studies have examined aspects of working memory in children with learning disabilities. Most have used one or two memory span measures and included one group of children with learning disabilities (e.g., mild, moderate, or severe LD) together with a comparison group of typically developing children matched for mental age. For example, Hulme and Mackenzie (1992) looked at children with moderate to severe learning disabilities (IQ levels between 20 and 50), finding lower digit and word spans compared to children matched for mental age. Memory span scores also increased at a much slower rate over five years for the children with learning disabilities compared to the mental age matched children. Similar studies have replicated these deficits in auditory digit span (Marcell & Weeks, 1988; Marinosson, 1974) and word span (Russell et al., 1996), and found additional deficits in visual sequential memory (Marinosson, 1974) and complex span (Russell et al., 1996). However, there are also a number of studies that have not found such deficits in forwards or backwards digit span (Brown, 1974; Jarrold & Baddeley, 1997; Vicari et al., 1995), word span (Jarrold et al., 2000) or forwards and backwards Corsi (spatial) span (Jarrold & Baddeley, 1997; Vicari et al., 1995).

This conflicting picture of the working memory performance in children with learning disabilities remains because none of the studies used a wide range of working memory measures, to enable conclusions to be drawn about working memory performance as a whole in children with learning disabilities. In fact, between-experiments comparisons in this area are particularly difficult to make because the studies described used children with different levels of learning disability (ranging from borderline to severe) and different assessment tools to estimate general ability. Most common was a receptive vocabulary measure to estimate IQ (e.g., Jarrold & Baddeley, 1997; Jarrold et al., 2000; Marinosson, 1974; Russell et al., 1996), but test results from school records (e.g., Brown, 1974) and the Leiter Performance Intelligence Scales (Vicari et al., 1995) were also used.

One recent study has used a much wider battery of memory span tasks within the same study. Gathercole and Pickering (in press) found differences between children with and without special educational needs on a variety of working memory measures including phonological short-term memory tasks involving nonwords, visuo-spatial tasks involving recalling the position and order of a sequence of black squares and recalling routes through mazes, and central executive measures (reverse digit span and listening span). However, we do not know from this study exactly what levels of learning disability the children had.

Therefore, no one study has included a full range of working memory measures, a range of children with differing levels of learning disabilities, and a consistent method of assessing general ability. This type of comprehensive design is crucial in order to examine the role of severity of learning disability in working memory performance. The current study looked at groups of children with clearly defined and varying degrees of learning disability on a wide range of working memory span tasks that tapped each component of the working memory system. In order to present a distinct picture of how each group performed, every learning disability subgroup was compared to the same comparison group (namely typically developing children of the same chronological age). In this way, the role of severity of learning disability could be examined rather than the separate (but important) issue of whether working memory skills keep pace with mental age.

Of additional theoretical interest was the extent to which the measures of working memory were related to general ability. Hulme and Makenzie (1992) noted the longstanding evidence of a moderate correlation between measures of digit span and IQ. The present study will allow comparisons of the relationships between general ability and measures of each component of working memory separately, plus a consideration of the overall relationship between general ability and working memory. Correlations cannot, of course, address the issue of whether working memory impairments may be a cause or a consequence of learning disabilities. However, comparing relationships between general ability and working memory performance in each of the three components of working memory can at least give some idea of whether *particular* working memory skills are compromised in those with learning disabilities or whether *all* working memory skills are compromised.

Knowing the strengths and limitations of children with varying degrees of learning disabilities should allow teaching methods to be more specifically tailored for different ability groups. We would also gain a clearer insight into just how much information in different modalities children with varying degrees of learning disability can deal with at one time. Again, this could directly influence teaching methods, for example, with respect to the type and length of instructions given for learning tasks—whether presented by the teacher or via computer-assisted learning tasks. Many classroom-based activities rely heavily on verbal instructions such that any deficits in phonological short-term memory may have disproportionate effects on learning basic skills such as reading, writing, and mental arithmetic that rely on using phonological short-term storage as a "mental workspace".

Another reason for examining working memory performance in children with mixed aetiology learning disabilities is to provide data on comparison groups for research on working memory in children with specific disorders or genetic syndromes associated with intellectual disability (e.g., Down's syndrome, William's syndrome, autism). This phenotypic research (e.g., Dykens, 2000) is becoming increasingly valuable in identifying and remediating different disorders, but it is vital that we understand how the comparison groups perform on working memory tasks so that differences in performance among subgroups of children with learning disabilities can be properly evaluated.

Therefore, working memory spans on a range of tasks were examined in samples of 11- to 12-year-old children with varying degrees of learning disabilities. These included children with borderline (IQ between 70 and 79), mild (IQ between 55 and 69), and moderate (IQ between 40 and 54) learning disabilities. Children with severe learning disabilities were not included, as at a chronological age of 11–12 years, those with severe learning disabilities were unable to manage the central executive loaded span tasks. The comparison group was a chronological age matched group with average abilities (i.e., IQ of 80 or higher). The other alternative would have been to use separate mental age matched comparison groups for each of the learning disability subgroups. However, it was felt that it would be more instructive in this initial study to establish what types of impairments were present in each of our groups with respect to chronological age. This allows for the possibility that the less severely impaired children, particularly those with borderline learning disabilities, may not actually have memory deficits in some or all of the span tasks.

Working memory tasks were selected to cover all three working memory systems, the phonological loop, the visuo-spatial sketch pad, and the central executive. Typically, the capacity of the phonological loop is assessed using materials that can be stored phonologically, usually words, nonsense words, or digits. Memory span, the longest list that can be repeated in order, was used here for all of the working memory tasks to facilitate comparisons between tasks. The phonological memory span tasks were digit span and word span. Temporary visual and spatial storage, the domain of the visuo-spatial sketch pad, were assessed using memory span for nonsense pictures (nonsense pictures were used to reduce the likelihood of them being labelled and remembered as words) and memory span for spatial positions.

Simple rote retention of visuo-spatial or phonological materials can be contrasted with span tasks that require some form of processing together with recall of the results of that processing (e.g., Daneman & Carpenter, 1980). The processing requirement calls for central executive resources on top of the rote retention. Span tasks of this nature can be referred to as "complex" span tasks or central executive loaded span tasks. One complex span task requiring phonological processing and storage (listening span—derived from Leather & Henry, 1994) was included as well as one requiring visual and spatial processing and storage (odd one out span—derived from Hitch & McAuley, 1991). Listening span requires the child to state whether a sentence is true of false, and then retain the last word of that sentence while subsequent sentences are presented and processed. Odd one out span requires the child to choose one of three nonsense pictures that is different from the other two and retain its spatial position while subsequent odd one out decisions are made. A third central executive loaded span task was reverse digit span. This task requires that a list of numbers be retained and reversed before recall, calling upon central executive resources to manipulate the information (e.g., Lehto, 1996). Overall, the current battery of working memory tasks was similar to that used by Gathercole and Pickering (in press) except that the focus here was purely on span measures to facilitate comparisons between the different working memory components.

The following predictions were made. First, that children with learning disabilities would obtain generally poorer memory span scores than the average ability control group. This prediction was based on previous work showing that memory performance in general is impaired in children with learning disabilities compared to typically developing children (e.g., review by Borkowski, Peck, & Damberg, 1991), although it must be noted that the working memory related studies using mental age matched comparison groups were less consistent (see earlier).

With respect to the severity of the learning disability, it was predicted that memory span performance would show progressive decreases as the severity of the learning disability increased. In other words, a general picture would emerge whereby average-ability children would obtain slightly higher scores than children with borderline learning disabilities, children with borderline learning disabilities would obtain higher scores than children with mild learning disabilities, and children with mild learning disabilities would obtain higher scores than children with moderate learning disabilities—i.e., mental age (general ability level) would be strongly related to working memory performance. Note however, that there is no guiding literature to suggest whether these relationships might be equally strong for each working memory task. Theoretical accounts of short-term memory deficits in those with learning disabilities have often focused on rehearsal deficits in verbal short-term recall tasks (e.g., Ellis, 1970) so one might predict greater deficits on phonological memory.

A further question of interest was whether differences between groups would emerge for all of the span tasks. It was speculated that more marked differences between groups might be found for the complex span tasks (listening span, odd one out span, and reverse digit span) than the simple span tasks (digit span, word span, pattern span, spatial span). This is because complex span tasks require more planning and organisation and it might be expected that children with learning disabilities may find such tasks particularly difficult. There is some evidence that children with learning disabilities are impaired on executive tasks such as the Tower of Hanoi (Borys, Spitz, & Dorans, 1982) and complex memory span tasks (Russell et al., 1996). However, unlike the evidence for specific central executive impairments in children with autism (e.g., review by Pennington & Ozonoff, 1996), there is no direct evidence for such deficits in children with general learning disabilities. Therefore, the predictions were only speculative.

METHOD

Participants

Participants were 78 children aged between 11 and 12 years. Of these, 25 were of average intellectual ability as assessed by the British Ability Scales II (Elliott, 1996) (mean General Conceptual Ability 104.5, range 84–123); 10 were of borderline intellectual ability (mean GCA 75.3, range 70–79); 21 had mild learning disabilities (mean GCA 60.5, range 55–68); and 22 had moderate learning disabilities (mean GCA 45.8, range 40–52. The ability bands corresponded to those in the Diagnostic and Statistical Manual of Mental Disorders, Fourth Edition (DSM-IV).

The average-ability children came from two mainstream inner-city schools in South London. Some of the children with learning disabilities came from the same two mainstream schools (n = 9) and the remainder came from two special schools for children with learning disabilities also in South London. The sample contained more boys (n = 52) than girls (n = 26) as this reflected the composition of the classes in the special schools. It was not possible to match exactly for gender in each of our subgroups. All children were tested individually in their schools. Table 1 gives full details of the sample.

For two children with moderate LD, there were missing data for some span tasks: digit span, pattern span, and reverse digits for one child; and listening span and odd one out span for another. In the former case, the child did not want to participate in the final session, in the latter case, the child did not want to attempt the two complex span tasks (this probably means he was unable to manage them). There were also missing data for two children in the average-ability control group: pattern span, spatial span, and odd man out span for both of them. This was because one child was excluded from school and another moved away during the testing period.

Ethical approval for the study was obtained from the institution at which it was carried out and full written consent was obtained from parents prior to participation.

TABLE 1
Participants

Group	Age	Mental Age	GCA	Number
CA control	11 yr 11 m (4 m)	13 yr 0 m (15 m)	104.5 (9.3)	25 (10)
Borderline LD	12 yr 0 m (5 m)	9 yr 4 m (7 m)	75.3 (3.3)	10 (8)
Mild LD	11 yr 11 m (5 m)	7 yr 9 m (6 m)	60.5 (3.9)	21 (18)
Moderate LD	11 yr 11 m (7 m)	6 yr 4 m (7 m)	45.8 (4.0)	22 (16)

Characteristics of the four ability groups: CA (chronological age matched controls with average abilities), borderline learning disabilities (LD), mild LD and moderate LD. Numbers of boys are given in brackets in the "Number" column, standard deviations are given in brackets in the other columns. GCA = General Conceptual Ability (BAS II).

Procedure and materials

Children were given seven memory span tests over two sessions as part of a larger study on eyewitness memory. They were also given four subtests of the British Ability Scales II (BAS II—Elliott, 1996), namely Word Definitions and Verbal Similarities (comprising the verbal reasoning scale) and Matrices and Quantitative Reasoning (comprising the non-verbal reasoning scale). General Conceptual Ability (GCA) was pro-rated from these two core scales (we did not administer the third core scale, Spatial Reasoning).

For all the groups of children with learning disabilities, four of the memory span tests were administered in the same session as the BAS II: word span, spatial span, listening span, and odd one out span (in that order). Three further span tests were given as part of the Test of Learning and Memory (TOMAL—Reynolds & Bigler, 1994) in another session: digit span, pattern span, and reverse digits. Overall, two span tasks assessed phonological short-term memory (digit span and word span), two assessed visuo-spatial short-term memory (spatial span and pattern span), and three assessed "complex" memory span involving central executive resources (listening span, odd one out span, and reverse digit span). Within the complex memory span tasks, two were verbal tasks (listening span, reverse digits) and one was a visuo-spatial task (odd one out span). The order of testing was slightly different for the average ability control group because of greater constraints imposed by lesson times. These children received the tasks in the same order as the children with learning disabilities, except that pattern span, spatial span, and odd man out span were administered separately in a final extra session. Each span task is described separately next.

Word span. The child was required to recall a series of one-syllable words in order orally. The words were presented by the experimenter at a rate of one per second and were drawn from a pool of eight high-frequency words (cake, sheep, frog, bus, clown, kite, drum, boot). Children were presented with lists of increasing length beginning with a list length of two words. There were three trials at each list length. As long as the participant passed two trials at any particular list length, they went on to the next list length. Memory span was the longest list at which two correct responses were given, plus one half-point credit if one list out of three was correctly recalled at the next (longer) list length.

Spatial span. This was based on Corsi span. The child was presented with an A4-sized array of nine black-and-white drawings of cubes on a white background. The cubes were drawn in perspective with one side shaded and were randomly arranged on the background. The experimenter pointed to a series of cubes and the child was asked to point to the same cubes in the same order immediately afterwards. List lengths began at two for all children and progressed up to eight. There were two trials at each list length. In order to proceed to the next list length, one out of the two trials at least had to be reported accurately. Spatial span was scored as the longest list length correctly recalled at least once. Testing ceased if the participant failed to recall a list length on either of the two trials.

Listening span. This task was based on one used by Leather and Henry (1994). Participants heard short sentences that could either be true or false (e.g. "children go to school" or "grass grows in the house"). Sentences were presented in groups of one to four and the child was asked to listen to each sentence, say whether it was true or false, and then recall the last word from each of the sentences. All children began by hearing just one sentence, saying whether it was true or false, and then recalling the last word. Once the child had passed three trials with one sentence (i.e., a list length of one), two sentences were presented and the child attempted to recall two sentence-final words. Three trials were administered at each list length. Testing continued to longer list lengths (i.e., lists of three and then four sentences), provided the participant recalled the sentence-final words correctly on at least two of the trials. Listening span was the longest list length at which two trials were passed, plus an extra half-point credit if one list at the next list length was correctly recalled. Sentence-final words could be recalled in any order on this task. The full span task is given in the Appendix.

Odd one out span. This task was loosely based on one used by Hitch and McAuley (1991) and involved remembering the spatial locations of nonsense pictures over trials. First, children were shown an A4 sheet with two elongated rectangular blank boxes drawn on it, one above the other. Each box was divided into three sections from left to right (see Figure 1). The child was then presented with a card containing three similar-looking figures in a row from left to right. The card was the same size as the blank boxes on the A4 sheet and was placed just above the top blank box. It was pointed out that each figure corresponded to one section in the blank box. Figures were black-on-white line drawings of various shapes and symbols. On each card, two of the figures were identical, with the third differing slightly from the other two (see Figure 2 for two examples). The child was asked to point to the figure that was different from the others—i.e. the odd one out. The Experimenter then placed her finger on the section in the blank box corresponding to the position of the odd one out and said "The odd one out goes here, in this space—try to remember where it goes because I am taking the card away." The card was removed and a second card with three figures on it was placed just above the second, lower blank box. Again, the child was asked to point to the odd one out and the Experimenter demonstrated that the new odd one out belonged in the corresponding section of the lower blank box. The card was removed and the child was asked to try to recall the positions of the upper and lower odd one out pictures by pointing to the appropriate sections on the A4 sheet.

Figure 1. Response card at list length 2 showing two rectangular blank boxes, divided into three sections for the odd one out span task.

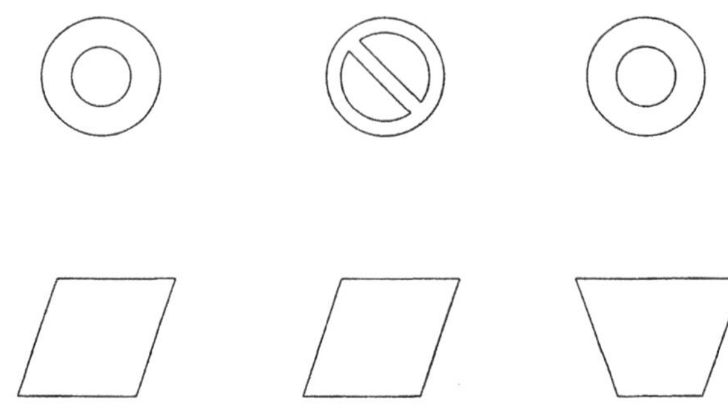

Figure 2. Examples of figures used in the odd one out span task.

This first trial was to demonstrate the task and two further practice trials using list lengths of two items were administered. However, there was one change to the procedure in subsequent trials. The blank boxes were covered up during presentation of the cards with figures on them. This was to prevent children using their fingers to mark the spatial positions of the odd ones out. Provided the child passed the two practice trials, the next list length was administered (three cards). A new A4 sheet with three blank boxes (upper, middle, and lower) was presented and the child was told that this time three cards would be presented. List lengths increased to five cards, with new A4-sized response cards containing four and then five rectangular blank boxes, and testing continued provided the child obtained at least two out of three trials correct at any particular list length. Odd one out span was the longest list length at which two trials were passed, plus an extra half-point credit if one trial at the next, higher, list length was correct.

The other three span tasks were taken from the Test of Learning and Memory (TOMAL—Reynolds & Bigler, 1994).

Digit span. The Experimenter presented lists of digits verbally at a rate of one per second. Recall was oral and the child had to recall items in order. The test began with a list length of two items and continued with successively longer lists, always with two trials for each list length. Testing ceased when both lists at a particular list length were incorrect. Span was the longest list length correctly recalled.

Pattern span. This task is called visual sequential memory in the TOMAL. Lists of nonsense pictures were presented to the child. Pictures were presented in an array from left to right and were black-on-white line drawings. After viewing each array for 5 seconds, a second array was presented in which the nonsense drawings were presented in a different order. The child was asked to point to the nonsense pictures in the order in which they appeared on the first array. Testing began with two lists of two nonsense pictures. Successively longer lists were presented, always with two trials at each list length, and testing ceased when both lists at a particular list length were incorrect. Span score was the longest list length correctly recalled.

Reverse digit span. This was identical to the digit span test, except that recall was in reverse order. One practice trial was administered to check that the child understood the instructions. Span was the longest list length correctly recalled and testing ceased when both lists at a particular list length were incorrect.

RESULTS

Reliability and validity of the span measures

Each span task consisted of two or three presentations (i.e., trials) at each list length. In order to assess the reliability of each measure, span scores were calculated from each set of first presentations (i.e., all trial 1's scores), each set of second presentations (all trial 2's), and each set of third presentations (all trial 3's) where three trials were always administered (listening span and odd one out span). Together with the total span score, calculated as described in the previous section, there were three or four estimations of span for each task that could be used to estimate reliability (this method is similar to that used by Engle, Tuholski, Laughlin, & Conway, 1999). The correlations between the span estimations for total span as well as the first, second, and third (where available) trial estimations were calculated and the average of these correlations provides a measure of task reliability. The means of the correlations for each span task were as follows: digit span .78 (range .69 to .82); word span .76 (range .60 to .84); pattern span .71 (range .66 to .79); spatial span .84 (range .71 to .92); listening span .76 (range .63 to .89); odd one out span .80 (range .66 to .90); and reverse digit span .78 (range .65 to .92). All of the span measures, therefore, were reasonably reliable. Even the lowest correlations between alternative span measures (i.e. the lowest in the range) were still moderately reliable.

A different issue concerns the construct validity of our span tasks. It was expected that many of the span tasks, having been used in previous research for some time, would be good measures of the three working memory components, namely phonological short-term storage, visuo-spatial short-term storage, and central executive-loaded short-term storage. However, the odd one out span task was new (although closely based on one used by Hitch & McAuley, 1991) and there is very little research of this kind using samples of children with learning disabilities. Therefore, it was desirable to present some evidence concerning the construct validity of the span tasks.

Correlations between the span tasks are given in Table 2. One-tailed tests were used because relationships between span measures were expected, and a level of significance of greater than 1% was required given the relatively large number of correlations carried out. Every span measure was significantly related to every other span measure (the size of the correlations ranged from .38 to .67 and all were highly significant). Mental age was strongly related to every span measure (range .62 to .73) suggesting that it was a mediating factor in the relationships between the span measures. Therefore, the correlations were repeated, partialling out the effects of mental age. Table 2 gives these data in italics. Here, only three correlations were significant at beyond the 1% level: those between digit span and word span, $r(74) = .41$, $p < .001$; spatial span and pattern span, $r(72) = .31$, $p < .01$; and odd one out span and listening span, $r(72) = .29$, $p < .01$. These results

TABLE 2
Correlations

	Word	*Pattern*	*Spatial*	*Listening*	*Odd one out*	*Reverse*	*MA*
Digit span	.65**	.48**	.44**	.51**	.54**	.54**	.65**
	.41**	*.11*	*−.02*	*.07*	*.15*	*.21*	
Word span		.38**	.38**	.52**	.51**	.48**	.62**
		−.04	*−.09*	*.11*	*.13*	*.13*	
Pattern span			.62**	.57**	.53**	.34**	.64**
			.31*	*.18*	*.14*	*−.14*	
Spatial span				.64**	.62**	.46**	.70**
				.27	*.26*	*.00*	
Listening span					.66**	.59**	.74**
					.29*	*.22*	
Odd one out span						.48**	.70**
						.04	
Reverse digits							.65**

Correlations between the memory span measures and mental age. Correlations between the span measures with mental age controlled are given in italics.
** $p < .001$.
* $p < .01$

provide good evidence for the construct validity of the span tasks indicating that, even controlling for mental age, the measures chosen to assess phonological, visuo-spatial, and central executive loaded working memory span respectively were significantly related to each other and not to span tasks in different domains. The exception to this was reverse digit span which was weakly (and non-significantly) related to both listening span and digit span. Given its weak and non-domain-specific relationships with the other span measures, reverse digit span was analysed separately. Note that previous authors have found evidence for a visuo-spatial component in reverse span for visually presented letters or words (Engle et al., 1999; Li & Lewandowsky, 1995). There was no evidence for a visuo-spatial component in the current auditory reverse digit span task, probably because auditory presentation does not encourage visuo-spatial processing.

Severity of learning disability and working memory

The next analysis examined the extent to which working memory performance was affected by the severity of the learning disability. Span scores were combined within each domain, namely digit span with word span, pattern span with spatial span, and listening span with odd one out span, to provide measures of phonological, visuo-spatial and complex working memory span respectively. Table 3 gives these data, together with the individual span scores for each span task. In order to compare the scores between domains, *z*-scores for each measure were used in this analysis. A multivariate analysis of variance (group[4] × span task [3]) revealed a very strong effect of group, $F(3,70) = 57.98$, $p < .001$. However, there was no effect of working memory task, nor any interaction between task and group.

However, specific predictions with regard to the effects of severity of learning disability on working memory performance within each working memory component had been made, namely that more marked differences between LD groups should be obtained for complex memory span measures as opposed to simple memory span measures. Therefore, three further analyses examined the effects of severity of learning disability on span scores in each working memory component separately. One-way analyses of variance was used with post hoc Scheffe test (significance values of better than .05 required) to examine group differences in detail. Although these tests were necessarily post hoc, we were concerned that the overall analysis might mask more subtle differences between groups on the working memory span tasks.

There were highly significant differences between groups on all three composite span measures: $F(3,73) = 21.45$, $p < .001$; $F(3,71) = 29.2$, $p < .001$; and $F(3,71) = 40.44$, $p < .001$ for phono-

TABLE 3
Mean and combined scores

Span Measure	*CA Control*	*Borderline LD*	*Mild LD*	*Moderate LD*
Digit	5.6 (.9)	4.9 (.9)	4.3 (.8)	4.0 (.8)
Word	4.8 (.7)	4.1 (.7)	3.8 (.5)	3.5 (.7)
Phonological	10.4 (1.4)	9.0 (1.4)	8.1 (1)	7.5 (1.4)
Pattern	4.9 (1)	4.8 (1)	3.7 (.7)	3.2 (.6)
Spatial	6.1 (1)	5.6 (.8)	4.4 (1.1)	3.9 (1.1)
Visuo-spatial	11.0 (1.6)	10.4 (1.7)	8.1 (1.5)	7.1 (1.3)
Listening	3.3 (.4)	2.7 (1)	2.3 (.8)	1.5 (.6)
Odd one out	4.5 (.7)	4.0 (1.1)	3.0 (.8)	2.5 (.8)
Complex	7.8 (1)	6.7 (1.6)	5.3 (1.3)	4.0 (1.1)
Reverse digit	4.4 (1)	3.4 (.7)	3.2 (.7)	2.9 (.7)

Mean memory span scores and combined working memory scores (see text) for children with average abilities (CA control group) borderline learning disabilities (LD), mild LD, and moderate LD. Standard deviations are given in brackets.

logical, visuo-spatial, and complex memory span tasks respectively—just repeating the result of the previous analysis. Post hoc Scheffe tests were used to examine the differences between ability groups. For *phonological* memory span, the CA group obtained significantly higher scores than the borderline LD ($p < .05$), the mild LD ($p < .001$), and the moderate LD ($p < .001$) groups. The borderline LD group obtained significantly higher scores than the moderate LD group ($p < .05$). All other comparisons were non-significant. Therefore, all of the LD groups showed an impairment in phonological memory span compared to their CA counterparts. There were fewer differences among the LD subgroups—only the borderline LD group was significantly better than the moderate LD group.

For *visuo-spatial* memory span, the CA and borderline groups did not differ from each other and the mild and moderate groups did not differ from each other. However, there were significant differences between the CA/borderline and mild/moderate groups ($ps < .001$) with the former obtaining much higher visuo-spatial memory span scores. No other comparisons were significant. These results showed a clear split between the CA and borderline groups and the mild/moderate LD groups. The CA/borderline groups were significantly better on visuo-spatial span tasks than the mild/moderate LD groups.

For *complex* memory span, the CA group obtained significantly higher scores than the mild LD group ($p < .001$) and the moderate LD group ($p < .001$). The borderline LD group obtained significantly higher scores than the mild LD group ($p < .03$) and the moderate LD group ($p < .001$). Finally, the mild LD group obtained significantly higher scores than the moderate LD group ($p < .02$). Therefore, all comparisons between the groups were significant, except that between CA and borderline LD. These results indicated that there were clear and marked differences between all of the LD groups on complex memory span—far more so than on the measures of simple memory span. There was also clear evidence of increased impairment depending on severity of LD, such that with every increase in LD from borderline to mild to moderate, there was a significant and marked decrease in performance. Those with borderline LD were not impaired on the complex span tasks compared with the average-ability CA group. However, there was some evidence of a ceiling effect on odd one out span for the CA group, so it might be that with a more demanding task differences may emerge between the CA group and those with borderline learning disabilities.

As mentioned earlier, reverse digit span was analysed separately because it did not relate strongly to the other measures of complex memory span and, therefore, could not be regarded as an unambiguous measure of central executive loaded memory span. A one-way analysis of variance with post hoc Sheffe tests (significance values of better than 5% required) showed a significant effect of learning disability group, $F(3, 76) = 17.21$, $p < .001$. The CA group obtained higher scores than all the other groups, borderline ($p < .05$), mild ($p < .001$), and moderate ($p < .001$) which did not differ. Therefore, having any degree of learning disability reduced performance on this task compared to typically developing children, but the severity of the LD made no difference.

The final analysis examined the extent to which the three combined span measures (phonological, visuo-spatial, and complex span) could explain variations in mental age. The correlations between all span measures and mental age were very high, as described earlier, but it was of interest to see whether these relationships were reflecting some common portion of variance, or whether span measures for the different components of working memory accounted for separate portions of the variance in mental age. Six fixed-order hierarchical multiple regressions were carried out using phonological span, visuo-spatial span, and complex span scores to predict mental age. Each predictor variable was entered in every possible order to see whether it accounted for shared or unique portions of the variance. Table 4 gives these regressions in brief. All three working memory measures accounted for significant portions of the variance regardless of which order they were entered. In total, an impressive 74% of the variance was accounted for. Therefore, in this very heterogeneous sample, working memory was closely linked to mental age. In addition, the three components of working memory all contributed separately to the variance in mental age. The considerable shared variance suggests that there are common mechanisms involved in span tasks generally as well as domain-specific skills.

DISCUSSION

In this study, children with borderline, mild, and moderate learning disabilities were compared to age-matched typically-developing children on a range of working memory span tasks. The aim was to assess whether the severity of the learning disability was closely related to working memory performance in all three components of working memory, namely the phonological loop, the visuo-spatial sketch pad, and the central executive (Baddeley, 1986). The tasks assessed temporary phonological storage (digit span and word span), temporary visuo-spatial storage (pattern span and spatial span), and central executive-loaded temporary storage (listening span and odd one out span). A seventh task, initially intended to measure central executive loaded storage (reverse digit span) was not closely related to any of the other measures, so was analysed separately.

The overall analysis produced a clear and emphatic picture of working memory performance in children with learning disabilities. Across the board, working memory was markedly lower in children with mild and moderate learning disabilities and somewhat lower in children with borderline learning disabilities (this group is discussed in detail later on). Relationships between working memory and mental age were uniformly high in all of the seven memory span tasks (correlations ranged from .62 to .73—all highly significant). Therefore, over the whole sample, all three components of working memory were strongly related to general ability. This supports the view that all working memory skills are related

TABLE 4
Regression analyses

Predictors	*R Square*	*R Square change*	F *Value*	*Significance*
Phonmem	.49	.49	68.65 (d.f. 1,72)	$p < .001$
Vismem	.69	.20	46.60 (d.f. 1,71)	$p < .001$
Complex	.74	.05	14.17 (d.f. 1,70)	$p < .001$

Summary of six fixed order hierarchical multiple regression analyses with the dependent variable mental age and the predictor variables phonological memory (Phonmem), visuo-spatial memory (Vismem) and complex memory (Complex).

R Square change values for the other five possible orders of entry were as follows—all R Square change statistics were highly significant ($p < .001$):
Phonmem (.49), Complex (.20), Vismem (.055)
Vismem (.56), Phonmem (.13), Complex (.05)
Vismem (.56), Complex (.13), Phonmem (.06)
Complex (.61), Phonmem (.075), Vismem (.055)
Complex (.61), Vismem (.07), Phonmem (.06)

to measures of general ability (although this leaves open the possibility that particular aspects of working memory could be related to particular skills such as vocabulary knowledge or mathematical ability). Regression analyses indicated that as much as 74% of the variance in mental age could be accounted for by the three composite working memory measures. All accounted for both unique and shared portions of the variance, suggesting that phonological, visuo-spatial, and complex memory span abilities tapped into separate *and* shared aspects of general ability as indexed by mental age. It is important to emphasise that the current sample of 11–12-year-olds covered a huge range of ability (IQ from 40 to 123) so that it is not surprising to have found such strong relationships. It is not clear whether relationships between mental age and working memory would be as strong in more homogeneous samples.

Although no overall interaction was found between learning disability group and memory span task, specific predictions had been made that larger effects of learning disability subgroup should be found for the complex memory span measure as opposed to the two simple memory span measures (phonological memory and visuo-spatial memory). Therefore, more sensitive tests for group differences were used to examine this.

These analyses showed that all the groups of children with learning disabilities obtained significantly lower scores for *phonological* memory span than the CA control group. There was only limited evidence that more severe learning disabilities led to *greater* phonological working memory impairments. Children with borderline learning disabilities obtained significantly higher phonological span scores than children with moderate learning disabilities, but no other comparisons between groups with learning disabilities were significant. These results must be taken in the context of there being no overall task by group interaction, but hint at a general deficit in phonological working memory for all children with learning disabilities, regardless of severity.

Interestingly, this pattern was found for reverse digit span as well. This task was initially included as a measure of central executive loaded memory span, but the pattern of intercorrelations between tasks indicated that it was only weakly and non-significantly related to digit span and listening span. This meant that it spanned phonological short-term memory and complex memory—but was not definitely related to either task. It would seem that reverse digit span requires some combination of phonological memory and attentional resources to recite the sequence backwards. However, given its weak correlations with these skills it clearly taps something else as well. It would be tempting to dismiss reverse digit span on theoretical grounds as not clearly reflecting any one component of working memory, except that it very effectively differentiated between those with and without learning disabilities. Having any degree of learning disability, whether borderline, mild, or moderate, led to reduced performance, but performance was no worse with a greater severity of learning disability. This is a particularly striking result because it dovetails with a recent study by Gathercole and Pickering (in press). They found that of all of their working memory tasks (phonological short term memory, visuo-spatial short-term memory, and central executive tasks), reverse digit span was the one task that consistently differentiated between children with and without special educational needs at ages 7 and 8 years. Therefore, although the status of reverse digit span as a central executive loaded span task is in question, it does appear to be extremely effective in discriminating between children with and without learning disabilities and as such warrants further research. It is worth pointing out that deficits in verbal rehearsal (e.g., Ellis, 1970) could potentially explain poor phonological memory and poor reverse digit span, and this issue merits further research.

For the *visuo-spatial* memory span measure, children with borderline learning disabilities were indistinguishable from their average-ability peers. They were also significantly better than children with mild and moderate learning disabilities, who were themselves indistinguishable. Therefore, children with borderline learning disabilities did *not* have a visuo-spatial working memory deficit compared to typically developing children of the same age. By contrast, children with mild and moderate learning disabilities showed clear impairments on the visuo-spatial span tasks as they had done on the phonological span tasks.

For the *central executive* loaded span measure (i.e., listening span and odd one out span—or "complex" memory span), there were clear and significant differences between every group except the CA and borderline groups. Children with borderline LD were not impaired on complex memory span tasks (although their raw scores were somewhat lower and there was some evidence of a ceiling effect for odd one out span in the CA group—further research may well indicate that there is a slight impairment in complex memory with more demanding tasks for the CA group). However, as the learning disability increased from borderline to mild to moderate, each group obtained significantly lower scores. It had been predicted that complex span might be the task where children with learning disabilities were particularly hampered, as it required both storage and concurrent processing. Indeed, the greatest differences between groups were obtained on complex span and it was the only measure to successfully distinguish between mild and moderate LD subgroups.

As children with mild and moderate learning disabilities were significantly poorer than the CA group on all of the span measures, it can be concluded that they showed a consistent and general working memory impairment relative to age-matched typically-developing children. However, it must be noted that although the purpose of this research was not to examine individual differences, children in all groups did show wide variations in patterns of strength and weakness across the working memory span tasks. Therefore, there were islands of ability for many of the children on particular span tasks. For example, one girl with moderate learning disabilities nevertheless showed completely average digit and word span scores for her age (she was an interesting case—teachers had assumed she was far more able than she was, probably because she was able to retain and act upon verbal instructions using her very good phonological short-term memory).

What are the implications of the performance of the children with borderline learning disabilities? These children showed evidence of a phonological memory impairment and an impairment in reverse digit span, but not a visuo-spatial impairment or an impairment in the combined complex memory span measure (although see earlier comments on potential ceiling effects obscuring impairments here). It may be that one feature of a borderline learning disability is a form of relative phonological short-term memory weakness (possibly related to lack of verbal rehearsal) that is tapped by forward and reverse simple span performance. Even children with relatively good visual and spatial working memory may have difficulties with much classroom-based learning because of the pivotal role of temporary phonological short-term storage in tasks such as reading, spelling, arithmetic, and vocabulary acquisition.

To take one example, there is a substantial body of evidence suggesting a relationship between vocabulary acquisition and phonological memory ability (e.g., Gathercole & Baddeley, 1989, 1990; Gathercole, Willis, Emslie, & Baddeley, 1992; Michas & Henry, 1994). Although all children with learning disabilities might be expected to show vocabulary deficits, those with borderline learning disabilities are in the position of having a comparative advantage on visuo-spatial working memory. However, this advantage does not appear to impact on vocabulary development because phonological short-term storage is required to maintain and learn new vocabulary items. Whether visuo-spatial methods (e.g. presenting pictures or moving scenes together with printed and spoken words) could be used to improve vocabulary has yet to be examined. Computer-based packages providing visual cues were, in fact, already being used in one of the mainstream schools that took part in this study to enhance reading and spelling in their children with learning disabilities. However, several factors mean that this issue warrants further research. The current sample of children with borderline learning disabilities was relatively small and there was no overall interaction between memory task and LD group to offer more substantial support for the notion that the borderline group showed a differential impairment in phonological short-term memory.

The absolute working memory capacity of children with learning disabilities for different types of materials can be deduced from Table 3. Mean simple spans for phonological material, even for the moderate LD group who had the lowest scores, were 4 digits and 3.5 words. This suggests that if verbal instructions contain no more than three units of information (i.e. three meaning-carrying words) they should be appropriate for 11–12-year-old children with borderline through to moderate learning disabilities. This contrasts with children of average ability who may manage about five units of information. Similarly, children with mild and moderate learning disabilities were able to recall at least three items in tests of simple visual and spatial recall. Again, instructions or information presented visually or spatially should be manageable even for children with moderate learning disabilities provided only three units of meaningful information are presented at once.

When we look at the complex memory tasks (listening span and odd one out span), it is apparent that all of the children obtained much lower spans. Clearly, remembering information while carrying out a processing task was more difficult, regardless of ability. However, looking at listening span, arguably the most relevant task for typical classroom learning—the child hears an instruction and must keep that in mind while listening to something else or beginning the activity—the average-ability children could still obtain a mean score of over 3 items. This contrasts with the moderate LD group's score of only 1.5 items and implies that children with moderate learning disabilities can maintain comfortably only one item of information while carrying out a processing task. This may be a considerable handicap in a classroom setting. The moderate LD group was the poorest on this task even compared to the other LD subgroups. Their corresponding score on the visuo-spatial complex task was higher at 2.5 items, which hints that teaching methods may better exploit concurrent processing and storage capacity of children with moderate learning disabilities if visual and spatial means of instruction are used instead of verbal ones.

In summary, it was found that the severity of a child's learning disability had implications for working memory performance. All of the groups of children with learning disabilities showed an impairment in *phonological* short-term storage and reverse digit span compared to typically-developing children of the same age. By contrast, only children with mild and moderate learning disabilities showed impairments on *visuo-spatial* short-term storage and the other measures of *central executive* loaded working memory span. The tasks that distinguished most starkly between learning disability subgroups were the measures of central executive loaded memory span (excluding reverse digit span). Here, clear differences were obtained between all subgroups except the borderline and CA groups. The good performance of children with borderline LD on visuo-spatial tasks, the phonological memory difficulties of all of the children with learning disabilities, and the numerically higher visuo-spatial as opposed to phonological complex span scores in all groups point towards the potentially greater effectiveness of teaching methods utilising visual and spatial working memory in children with learning disabilities. Finally, all the measures of working memory were strongly related to mental age in this very heterogeneous sample. Phonological short-term memory, visuo-spatial short-term memory, and central executive loaded working memory all accounted for both unique and shared portions of the variance in mental age, together explaining 74% of the total variance. Therefore, working memory was strongly linked to general ability, although further research will be required to elucidate the exact nature and direction of this relationship.

REFERENCES

Baddeley, A.D. (1986). *Working memory*. Oxford: Oxford University Press.

Baddeley, A.D., & Hitch, G.J. (1974). Working memory. In G. Bower (Ed.), *The psychology of learning and motivation*, Vol. 8, pp. 47–89. New York: Academic Press.

Baddeley, A.D., Lewis, V.J., & Vallar, G. (1984). Exploring the articulatory loop. *Quarterly Journal of Experimental Psychology*, *36*, 233–252.

Borkowski, J.G., Peck, V.A., & Damberg, P.R. (1991). Attention, memory and cognition. In J.L. Matson & J.A. Mulick (Eds.), *Handbook of mental retardation* (2nd Edn.), pp. 479–497. New York: Pergamon.

Borys, S.V., Spitz, H.H., & Dorans, B.A. (1982). Tower of Hanoi performance of retarded young adults and nonretarded children as a function of solution length and goal state. *Journal of Experimental Child Psychology*, *33*, 87–110.

Brooks, L.R. (1967). The suppression of visualization by reading. *Quarterly Journal of Experimental Psychology*, *19*, 289–299.

Brown, R.M. (1974). Effects of recall order, cue placement, and retention interval on short-term memory of normal and retarded children. *Perceptual and Motor Skills*, *39*, 167–178.

Byrne, B. (1974). Item concreteness vs. spatial organisation as predictors of visual imagery. *Memory and Cognition*, *2*, 53–59.

Daneman, M., & Carpenter, P.A. (1980). Individual differences in working memory and reading. *Journal of Verbal Learning and Verbal Behavior*, *19*, 450–466.

Dykens, E.M. (2000). Psychopathology in children with intellectual disability. *Journal of Child Psychology and Psychiatry*, *41*, 407–417.

Elliott, C.D. (1996). *British Ability Scales Second Edition (BAS II)*. Windsor, UK: NFER-Nelson.

Ellis, N.R. (1970). Memory processes in retardates and normals. In N.R. Ellis (Ed.), *International review of research in mental retardation*, Vol. 4. New York: Academic Press.

Engle, R.W., Tuholski, S.W., Laughlin, J.E., & Conway, A.R.A. (1999). Working memory, short-term memory, and general fluid intelligence: A latent variable approach. *Journal of Experimental Psychology: General*, *128*, 309–331.

Gathercole, S.E. (1998). The development of memory. *Journal of Child Psychology and Psychiatry*, *39*, 3–27.

Gathercole, S.E., & Baddeley, A.D. (1989). Evaluation of the role of phonological STM in the development of vocabulary in children: A longitudinal study. *Journal of Memory and Language*, *28*, 200–215.

Gathercole, S.E., & Baddeley, A.D. (1990). The role of phonological memory in vocabulary acquisition: A study of young children learning new words. *British Journal of Psychology*, *81*, 439–454.

Gathercole, S.E., & Pickering, S.J. (in press). Working memory deficits in children with special educational needs. *British Journal of Special Education*.

Gathercole, S.E., Willis, C.S., Emslie, H., & Baddeley, A.D. (1992). Phonological memory and vocabulary development during the early school years: A longitudinal study. *Developmental Psychology*, *5*, 887–898.

Henry, L.A., & Millar, S. (1993). Why does memory span increase with age? A review of the evidence for two current hypotheses. *European Journal of Cognitive Psychology*, *5*, 241–287.

Hitch, G.J., & McAuley, E. (1991). Working memory in children with specific arithmetic learning difficulties. *British Journal of Psychology*, *82*, 375–386.

Hulme, C., & Mackenzie, S. (1992). *Working memory and severe learning difficulties*. Hove, UK: Lawrence Erlbaum Associates Ltd.

Hulme, C., & Roodenrys, S. (1995). Verbal working memory development and its disorders. *Journal of Child Psychology and Psychiatry*, *36*, 373–398.

Jarrold, C., & Baddeley, A.D. (1997). Short-term memory for verbal and visuo-spatial information in Down's syndrome. *Cognitive Neuropsychiatry*, *2*, 101–122.

Jarrold, C., Baddeley, A.D., & Hewes, A.K. (1999). Dissociating working memory: Evidence from Down's and Williams Syndrome. *Neuropsychologia*, *37*, 637–651.

Jarrold, C., Baddeley, A.D., & Hewes, A.K. (2000). Verbal short-term memory deficits in Down Syndrome: A consequence of problems in rehearsal? *Journal of Child Psychology and Psychiatry*, *40*, 233–244.

Leather, C.V., & Henry, L.A. (1994). Working memory span and phonological awareness tasks as predictors of early reading ability. *Journal of Experimental Child Psychology*, *58*, 88–111.

Lehto, J. (1996). Are executive function tests dependent on working memory capacity? *The Quarterly Journal of Experimental Psychology*, *49*A, 29–50.

Li, S.-C., & Lewandowsky, S. (1995). Forward and backward recall: Different retrieval processes. *Journal of Experimental Psychology: Learning, Memory and Cognition*, *21*, 837–847.

Marcell, M.M., & Weeks, S.L. (1988). Short-term memory difficulties and Down's syndrome. *Journal of Mental Deficiency Research*, *32*, 153–162.

Marinosson, G.L. (1974). Performance profiles of matched normal, educationally subnormal and severely subnormal children on the revised ITPA. *Journal of Child Psychology and Psychiatry*, *15*, 139–148.

Michas, I., & Henry, L.A. (1994). The link between phonological memory and vocabulary acquisition. *British Journal of Developmental Psychology*, *12*, 147–163.

Murray, D.J. (1968). Articulation and acoustic confusability in short-term memory. *Journal of Experimental Psychology*, *78*, 679–684.

Pennington, B.F., & Ozonoff, S. (1996). Executive functions and developmental psychopathology. *Journal of Child Psychology and Psychiatry*, *37*, 51–87.

Reynolds, C.R., & Bigler, E. (1994). *Test of Memory and Learning*. Austin, Texas: Pro-Ed.

Russell, J., Jarrold, C., & Henry, L. (1996). Working memory in children with autism and with moderate learning difficulties. *Journal of Child Psychology and Psychiatry*, *37*, 673–686.

Varnhagen, C.K., Das, J.P., & Varnhagen, S. (1987). Auditory and visual memory span: Cognitive processing by TMR individuals with Down Syndrome or other etiologies. *American Journal of Mental Deficiency*, *91*, 398–405.

Vicari, S., Carlesimo, A., & Caltagirone, C. (1995). Short-term memory in persons with intellectual disabilities and Down's syndrome. *Journal of Intellectual Disability Research*, *39*, 532–537.

APPENDIX: LISTENING SPAN TASK

Sentence	Response	Recall
Children go to SCHOOL	T	SCHOOL
People are covered in FUR	F	FUR
Grass grows in the HOUSE	F	HOUSE
Trees are covered in LEAVES	T	
People live in a NEST	F	LEAVES, NEST
I drink with a FORK	F	
Worms live in the GROUND	T	FORK, GROUND
There are swings at the PARK	T	
My toes are on my HAND	F	PARK, HAND
I wash my face with MILK	F	
At school I sit on CHAIRS	T	
Snakes and spiders can BITE	T	MILK, CHAIRS, BITE
Babies sleep in a COT	T	
I wear lipstick on my NOSE	F	
The sun comes out at NIGHT	F	COT, NOSE, NIGHT
I can brush my HAIR	T	
Giraffes have a long NECK	T	
The colour of water is RED	F	HAIR, NECK, RED
I write with a PEN	T	
Dogs fly in the SKY	F	
I talk with my EYES	F	
I eat from a PLATE	T	PEN, SKY, EYES, PLATE
In winter it is HOT	F	
The sky is GREEN	F	
Fish live in the SEA	T	
At school I learn to READ	T	HOT, GREEN, SEA, READ
I swim in the SAND	F	
Cars drive on the ROAD	T	
Oranges are BLUE	F	
Food goes in my MOUTH	T	SAND, ROAD, BLUE, MOUTH

MEMORY, 2001, 9 (4/5/6), 249–259

Contribution of lexico-semantic processes to verbal short-term memory tasks: A PET activation study

F. Collette and S. Majerus
University of Liège, Belgium

M. Van der Linden
University of Liège, Belgium, and University of Geneva, Switzerland

P. Dabe, C. Degueldre, G. Delfiore, A. Luxen, and E. Salmon
University of Liège, Belgium

Recent studies have demonstrated the intervention of long-term memory processes in verbal STM tasks and several cognitive models have been proposed to explain these effects. A PET study was performed in order to determine whether supplementary cerebral areas are involved when subjects have to execute short-term memory tasks for items having representations in long-term memory (in comparison to items without such representations: words vs non-words). Results indicate that verbal STM for words specifically involves the left middle temporal gyrus (BA 21) and temporo-parietal junction (BA 39). These areas can be associated with lexical and semantic processes. These results are in agreement with cognitive models that postulate the simultaneous influence of lexical and semantic long-term representations on verbal STM processes and/or a lexico-semantic buffer.

The cerebral areas involved in the maintenance of a small amount of verbal information in memory during a brief period of time have been investigated in many positron emission tomography (PET) and functional magnetic resonance imaging (fMRI) activation experiments. These studies showed that a network of primarily left-sided brain regions was activated during the realisation of these tasks (Awh et al., 1996; Becker et al., 1994; Paulesu, Frith, & Frackowiack, 1993; Salmon et al., 1996). These regions include the left supramarginal gyrus and Broca's area, as well as the supplementary motor area, premotor cortex, anterior cingulate, insula, thalamus, cerebellum and para-hippocampal gyrus.

The multi-component model of verbal short-term memory (STM) proposed by Baddeley and Hitch (Baddeley, 1986; Baddeley & Hitch, 1974) was frequently used to interpret these results. This model comprises a modality-free controlling central executive that is aided by a number of subsidiary slave systems ensuring temporary maintenance of different kinds of information. Among these slave systems, the phonological loop has been the most thoroughly explored. This system is specialised for processing verbal material and is composed of two subsystems: a passive phonological input store and an articulatory rehearsal process. Numerous functional imagery studies have investigated the neural basis of the different subcomponents of the phonological loop.

Requests for reprints should be sent to F. Collette, Service de Neuropsychologie, Boulevard du Rectorat 3 (B33), 4000 Liège (Sart-Tilman), Belgium. Email: f.collette@ulg.ac.be

This work was supported by the Belgian National Fund for Scientific Research (FNRS), the "Fondation Médicale Reine Elisabeth", and the InterUniversity Pole of Attraction Program P4/22, Belgian State, Prime Minister's Office, Federal Office for Scientific, Technical and Cultural Affairs. F. Collette is a Post-doctoral Researcher and S. Majerus is a Research Fellow at the FNRS. This work was presented as a poster at the Fifth International Conference on Functional Mapping of the Human Brain (Dusseldörf, June 1999).

http://www.tandf.co.uk/journals/pp/09658211.html DOI:10.1080/09658210143000056

In a first study, Paulesu et al. (1993) showed that activation of the supramarginal gyrus was related to the phonological store of the phonological loop, whereas activation in Broca's area was associated with the rehearsal component. These results have been confirmed by subsequent studies (e.g., Salmon et al., 1996; Schumacher et al., 1996). In a recent review paper, consisting of a finer-grained analysis of published experiments about the phonological loop, Becker, MacAndrew, and Fiez (1999) emphasised the existence of two possible foci of the phonological store within the parietal cortex: Under some experimental conditions, storage mechanisms appear in the region of the inferior supramarginal gyrus (Becker et al., 1994; Paulesu et al., 1993; Salmon et al., 1996) whereas in other studies the locus of the phonological system appears much more superior within the parietal lobe at the border of BA 37, BA 39 and BA 40/7 (Awh et al., 1996; Smith, Jonides, & Koeppe, 1996).

Furthermore, studies show that verbal STM tasks are influenced by representations stored in verbal long-term memory. Indeed, verbal STM span performance is larger for words than for non-words (Hulme, Roodenrys, & Mercer, 1995; Schweickert, 1993), for high-frequency and high-imageability words than for low-frequency and low-imageability items (Bourassa & Besner, 1994; Walker & Hulme, 1999; Watkins & Watkins, 1977), and also for words belonging to the same semantic category than for words from different semantic categories (Poirier & Saint-Aubin, 1995). These data indicate that lexical and semantic information contributes to verbal STM span. In the same vein, developmental studies have shown that non-word repetition, a measure of verbal STM, is better for more wordlike non-words (Gathercole, Willis, Emslie, & Baddeley, 1991). This wordlikeness effect suggests that immediate memory for non-words is supported by some knowledge of the phonological structure of words in a given language. Thus the influence of representations stored in long-term memory on verbal STM functioning seems to be quite a robust effect in cognitive and developmental psychological studies.

Although the neural network underlying the phonological loop processes is relatively well established at present, no functional imagery study has been specifically designed to investigate the influence of long-term memory representations on verbal STM. Indeed, some of these studies used verbal items (e.g., letters, words . . .) both in control and experimental tasks, whereas the remaining studies used verbal items in the experimental condition (e.g., letters) and non-verbal items in the control condition (e.g., meaningless objects). In the first case, both types of items had pre-existing long-term representations and in the second, the experimental and control tasks differed about other cognitive characteristics than the existence of pre-existing phonological or lexical long-term representations. Interestingly, Crosson et al. (1999) demonstrated that different brain regions were activated in a verbal STM task, depending on the kind of information that had to be processed. Indeed, when the short-term memory task required the retention of semantic information, left middle temporal and posterior-inferior temporal regions, inferior frontal cortex, posterior thalamus, Broca's area, and pre-SMA were activated, whereas the left extrastriate cortex and Broca's area were activated when orthographic information had to be retained. Finally, increases of cerebral activity were found in the inferior temporal-occipital junction, prefrontal cortex, pre-SMA, cerebellum, and midbrain regions when phonological information had to be maintained in verbal short-term memory. However, in the study of Crosson et al. (1999), the stimuli used in the phonological, semantic, and orthographic STM tasks were words and thus all had pre-existing representations in long-term memory. Therefore, it is not possible to determine whether there is additional brain activation for the short-term storage of stimuli that have or that do not have pre-existing representations in long-term memory.

Consequently, the aim of the present study was to evaluate whether there is differential brain activation for verbal STM of items that have or do not have representations in long-term memory, in this case familiar words versus non-words. If long-term memory does support verbal STM, as predicted by empirical studies, then there should be activation of additional brain regions for the short-term retention of lists of words as compared to lists of non-words.

MATERIAL AND METHODS

Subjects

A total of 12 European right-handed volunteers (5 males and 7 females), aged from 18 to 30 years gave written informed consent to take part in this study, which was approved by the University of Liège Ethics Committee. None had any past medical history or used any medication.

Positron emission tomography scanning

PET data were acquired on a Siemens CTI 951 R 16/31 scanner in 3D mode. The subject's head was stabilised by a thermoplastic facemask secured to the head holder (Truscan imaging, MA), and a venous catheter was secured in a left antebrachial vein. First, a 20-min transmission scan was acquired for attenuation correction using three rotating sources of 68Ge. Then, regional cerebral blood flow, taken as a marker of local neuronal activity (Jueptner & Weiller, 1995), was estimated during 12 emission scans. Each scan consisted of two frames: a 30-second background frame and a 90-second acquisition frame. The slow intravenous water ($H_2{}^{15}O$) infusion began 10 seconds before the second frame. Six mCi (222 MBq) were injected for each scan, in 5 cc saline, over a period of 20 seconds. The infusion was totally automated in order not to disturb the subject during the scanning period. Data were reconstructed using a Hanning filter (cutoff frequency: 0.5 cycle/pixel) and corrected for attenuation and background activity. The cognitive tasks were randomly distributed between subjects, with the exception that a cognitive task was not administered twice in succession.

Cognitive tasks

Subjects performed four different verbal repetition tasks. The tasks administered consisted of an auditory presentation of item lists that subjects had to recall aloud in serial order immediately after their presentation. Two types of items were used: words and non-words. Moreover, for each type of items, two list lengths were administered: recall of lists of one or three items. A factorial design was thus obtained that allowed exploration of the variables "memory load" (1 vs 3 items) and "pre-existing representations in long-term memory" (words vs non-words), as well as the influence of pre-existing representations in long-term memory on verbal STM functioning.

Details of the different tasks are as follows:

1. One non-word condition: auditory presentation of series of one non-word that the subject had to recall immediately.
2. One word condition: auditory presentation of series of one word that the subject had to recall immediately.
3. Three non-words condition: auditory presentation of series of three non-words that the subject had to recall immediately in serial order.
4. Three words condition: auditory presentation of series of three words that the subject had to recall immediately in serial order.

A pool of 349 bisyllabic non-words was drawn up by combining French phonotactically legal syllables. From these non-words, 234 were selected in a pre-experimental phase as having a low wordlikeness with French words (for a description of the procedure, see Gathercole et al., 1991). The words used in this study were selected from the database Brulex (Content, Mousty, & Radeau, 1990) with the following criteria: the items were bisyllabic nouns of high or medium frequency and the consonant–vowel structure of each word was closely matched to that of a non-word.

From these items three lists of one word, three words, one non-word, and three non-words were selected and were recorded on a computer. No item was repeated from one list to another. For each task, items were presented with an interval of 1 second and the response time allocated was 2 (one-item lists) or 5 (three-item lists) seconds. The three lists of each condition were randomly presented, with the restriction that two lists in the same condition were not successively presented. Subjects' responses were recorded on a tape microphone. The recall score was termed as the number of items correctly recalled in serial order. Subjects were trained on each cognitive task before the PET session. Before each acquisition, the instructions were repeated. In order to have similar requirements in auditory processes and motor response, each task consisted of 39 items (13 series of 3 items for the three items repetition conditions, or 39 series of 1 item for the one item repetition conditions). Because of the duration of the scanning period, specific analysis of the changes of regional cerebral metabolism during encoding, storage, and retrieval were not possible.

Data analysis

Data were analysed using statistical parametric mapping (SPM99; Welcome Department of Cognitive Neurology, Institute of Neurology, London, UK) implemented in MATLAB. For each subject, all scans were realigned together, then normalised to a standard PET template using the same transformations (Frackowiak et al., 1997). Finally, PET images were smoothed using a Gaussian kernel of 16 mm full width at half maximum to accommodate inter-subject differences in gyral and functional anatomy and to suppress high-frequency noise in the images. Such transformations of the data allow for voxel by voxel averaging of data across subjects and for direct cross-reference to the anatomical features in the standard stereotactic atlas (Talairach & Tournoux, 1988).

Differences in global activity within and between subjects were removed by analysis of covariance on a voxel by voxel basis with global count as covariate and regional activity across subjects for each task as treatment (Friston et al., 1990). The across-task comparisons were first performed by averaging between paired measurements (fixed effect model). For each voxel in stereotactic space, the analysis of covariance (ANCOVA) generated a condition-specific adjusted mean rCBF value (normalised to 50 ml/100 ml/min) and an associated adjusted error variance. The ANCOVA allowed the comparison of the means across conditions on a voxel by voxel basis using the t statistic. The resulting sets of t values constituted statistical parametric maps [SPM(t)] (Friston, Frith, Liddle, & Frackowiak, 1991). The SPM(t) were transformed to the unit normal distribution [SPM(Z)]. We used a SPM thresholded at $p < .001$ (voxel level), with further correction for multiple comparisons ($p < .05$). SPM was thresholded to $p < .001$ (uncorrected for multiple comparisons), when looking for activation in a region predicted from previous studies.

RESULTS

Cognitive performance

Results indicate significant differences between the four conditions: the recall score in the one and three words conditions did not differ (one word: 38.87 $\pm$ 0.24; three words: 38.72 $\pm$ 0.33) and performances were superior to the performance in the one non-word condition (37.74 + 0.77), while more errors were found during the recall of three non-words, 29.27 $\pm$ 0.33; χ^2 *ANOVA* (8, 3) = 34, $p < .0001$.[1]

[1] As the number of errors (omissions, inversions, and intrusions) differed in the four cognitive conditions, data analysis was also performed by using the individual performance as covariable in order to control for a possible influence of task difficulty. These analyses demonstrated similar results to those described hereafter.

Imaging data

Conjunction analysis: Memory load. In order to determine the cerebral areas involved in both verbal short-term memory tasks, a conjunction analysis was performed in which the changes in cerebral activity common to the comparison of three to one items (both for words and non-words) were assessed. This analysis showed increases of activity in the left medial frontal area (BA 8), in the anterior cingulate gyrus, in the left thalamus, and left insula. Supplementary foci of activation (non-corrected for multiple comparisons) were also found in Broca's area, in the anterior cingulate (BA 24/32) as well as in the cerebellum bilaterally (Table 1 and Figure 1).

Conjunction analysis: type of items. The cerebral areas specifically involved in the processing of words (with no regard to the memory load) are right-sided and include the superior temporal gyrus (BA 22) and the middle frontal gyrus (BA 9) (Table 2 and Figure 1).

Conversely, the cerebral area most involved in the processing of non-words is the right cerebellum. Supplementary activation foci (non-corrected for multiple comparisons, see Table 3 and Figure 1) were found in the left cerebellum and the left superior temporal gyrus (BA 22).

TABLE 1
Conjunction analysis for the memory load

Brain area	*Stereotactic coordinates* *x*	*y*	*x*	*Z-score*
p-value < .001, with further comparison for multiple comparisons				
Medial frontal gyrus (BA 8)	2	28	40	5.76
Anterior cingulate gyrus (BA 32)	4	28	32	4.95
L thalamus	−2	−4	0	4.77
L insula	−24	20	−6	4.80
p-value < .001, not corrected for multiple comparisons				
L inferior frontal gyrus (BA 44)	−46	52	2	3.13
	−58	16	8	3.13
R and L cerebellum	10	−78	−22	4.31
	60	−58	−26	4.07
	−46	−68	−26	3.97
	−34	−64	−34	3.75
	−44	−74	−32	3.63

Coordinates and Z-scores for voxels in which there was significant activation foci when repetition of three items was compared to the repetition of one item. L = left hemisphere; R = right hemisphere. x, y, z (in mm) refer to coordinates in the Talairach space (Talairach & Tournoux, 1988).

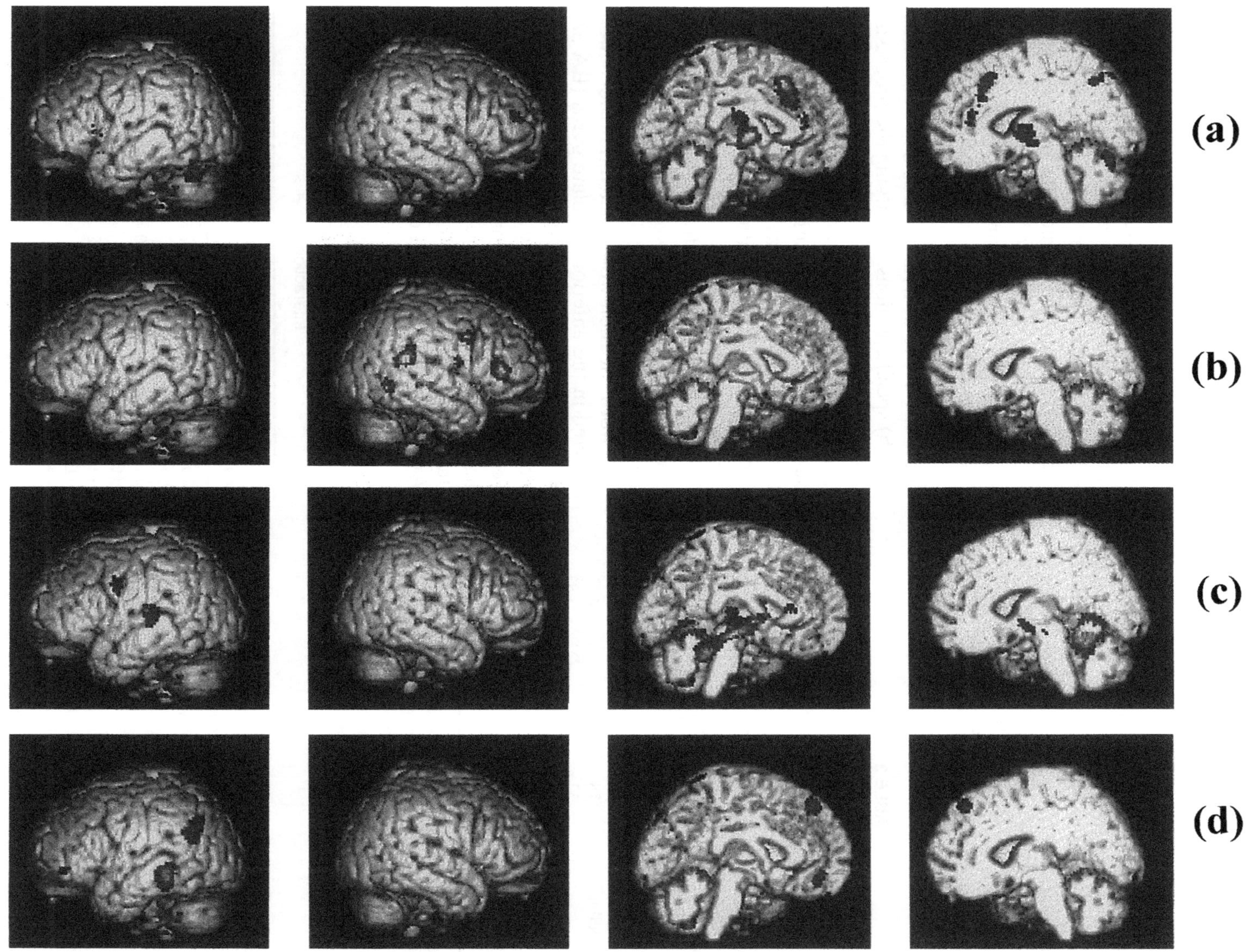

Figure 1. Brain activation (corrected for multiple comparisons) observed (a) when the memory load for three items was compared to the memory load for one item; (b) in the processing of words in comparison to non-words; (c) in the processing of non-words in comparison to words; (d) in the interaction analysis between memory load and type of items. Coordinates of all significant regions are given respectively in Tables 1, 2, 3, and 4. Brain areas are rendered on a standard brain conforming to stereotactic space.

TABLE 2
Conjunction analysis for the item type: words–non-words

Brain area	Stereotactic coordinates x	y	x	Z-score
p-value <.001, with further corrections for multiple comparisons				
R superior temporal gyrus (BA 22)	64	−42	18	5.05
	70	−36	18	4.70
R middle frontal gyrus (BA 9)	50	14	30	5.00

Coordinates and Z-scores for voxels in which there was significant activation foci when the processing of words was compared to the processing of non-words. L = left hemisphere; R = right hemisphere. *x*, *y*, *z* (in mm) refer to coordinates in the Talairach space (Talairach & Tournoux, 1988).

TABLE 3
Conjunction analysis for the item type: non-words–words

Brain area	Stereotactic coordinates x	y	x	Z-score
p-value <.001, with further corrections for multiple comparisons				
R cerebellum	4	−58	−6	5.25
	22	−60	−24	5.10
p-value <.001, not corrected for multiple comparisons				
R and L cerebellum	18	−56	−16	4.61
	52	−78	−22	3.83
	−10	−40	−22	4.43
	−12	−52	−20	3.63
L superior temporal gyrus (BA 22)	−70	−26	4	4.22

Coordinates and Z-scores for voxels in which there was significant activation or deactivation foci when the processing of non-words was compared to the processing of words. L = left hemisphere; R = right hemisphere. *x*, *y*, *z* (in mm) refer to coordinates in the Talairach space (Talairach & Tournoux, 1988).

Interaction analysis. Our factorial design allows us to study the effect that one variable has on the expression of the other variable. In this study, the two variables were memory load (one or three items) and the representations in long-term memory (present or absent). The interaction between these factors identifies areas where the functioning of verbal STM varies depending on the presence or absence of pre-existing representations in long-term memory. In the present case, the influence of pre-existing representations in long-term memory on the functioning of verbal STM was assessed (see Price, Moore, & Friston, 1997). Results showed increased rCBF specific to the storage of words in short-term memory in the left middle temporal gyrus (BA 21) and left temporo-parietal junction (BA 39) (see Table 4 and Figure 1).

DISCUSSION

The aim of the present study was to determine whether similar cerebral areas are involved in verbal short-term memory for words and non-words, with only the former having pre-existing representations in long-term memory. We first performed two conjunction analyses in order to determine (a) cerebral areas involved in the functioning of the phonological loop and common to the two types of items (words and non-words) and (b) specific regions underlying the processing of words versus non-words, whereby the items have or have not to be stored in verbal STM. Next, the cerebral areas specific to the short-term storage of information having pre-existing long-term memory representations were isolated by interaction analysis.

When the cerebral activity in the conditions requiring recall of three words or non-words was contrasted with that found during the repetition of one word or non-word, activation foci were detected in the anterior cingulate gyrus (BA 32), medial frontal gyrus (BA 8), left insula, thalamus, and cerebellum bilaterally as well as in Broca's area (BA 44). This network of brain areas was classically devoted in previous studies to the functional anatomy of the phonological loop (Awh et al., 1996; Paulesu et al., 1993; Salmon et

TABLE 4
Interaction analysis

Brain area	Stereotactic coordinates x	y	x	Z-score
p-value <.001, with further corrections for multiple comparisons				
L middle temporal gyrus (BA 21)	−60	−38	−14	5.05
L temporo-parietal gyrus (BA 39)	−52	−62	18	5.00

Coordinates and Z-scores for voxels in which there was significant activation foci with an interaction analysis between the variables "memory load" and "representations in long-term memory". L = left hemisphere; R = right hemisphere. *x*, *y*, *z* (in mm) refer to coordinates in the Talairach space (Talairach & Tournoux, 1988).

al., 1996). More precisely, Paulesu et al. (1993) related the activity in Broca's area to the articulatory rehearsal system. However, no foci of activation were found in the supramarginal gyrus, a region that has been related to phonological short-term storage of information (Paulesu et al., 1993; Salmon et al., 1996). Recently Rypma et al. (1999) did not observe any activity in that region when verbal STM for three letters was compared to verbal STM for one letter, whereas such activity was found in the comparison of memory for six letters and for one letter. The authors interpreted these results by the existence of minimal differences in the storage requirements between three-letter and one-letter memory loads which yield similar levels of activation in the parietal cortex. Such an explanation is consistent with our results, as we have compared memory loads for three items and one item.

The cerebral areas involved in the processing of words (without regard to the memory load) are the right superior temporal gyrus (BA 22) and right middle frontal gyrus (BA 9). These results show that the processing of words, in comparison to non-words, implicates additional cerebral areas in the right hemisphere, but none in the left-sided language-processing brain regions. Many PET studies for single word processing have shown activation of bilateral temporal areas (e.g., Mummery, Ashburner, Scott, & Wise, 1999; Petersen et al., 1989; Price et al., 1996). The fact that the right-sided increases of activity remain significant in the contrast of word versus non-word suggests that only words activate language-processing areas in the right hemisphere. This is also compatible with the recent hypothesis of Pulvermüller (1999) who suggests, on the basis of electrophysiological data, that content words (nouns) in particular, as used in this study, are represented bilaterally in the brain. On the other hand, the absence of significant activation of the left temporal areas in the word versus non-word contrast is probably caused by the fact that both words and non-words activate those areas. This is compatible with a recent study by Paulesu et al. (2000) who showed that non-word reading yielded even greater activation of left hemisphere areas than word reading, probably reflecting different item processing in the left and right brain region.

Surprisingly, increase of activity during the processing of words in comparison to non-words was also found in the right middle frontal gyrus (BA 9). A major distinction between words and non-words is that the former have associated semantic representations. Studies exploring the semantic representations of words showed increases of activity in prefrontal, temporal, anterior cingulate, and cerebellar regions (for a review, see Cabeza & Nyberg, 2000). However, prefrontal activity during semantic memory tasks has almost always been found in the left hemisphere but not in the right (e.g., Démonet et al., 1992; Shaywitz et al., 1995; Thompson-Schills, D'Esposito, Aguirre, & Farah, 1997; Warburton et al., 1996). We have to note that previous studies exploring the neural substrates of semantic representations used a very different methodology from that of the present study and did not require subjects to encode and retrieve lists of items. Consequently, we could suggest that the right prefrontal activation is related to the retrieval and/or monitoring of semantic information previously presented to the subject. For example, Buckner et al. (1995) demonstrated selective activation in a right prefrontal area (close to the area found in the present study) when subjects were presented with the beginning of words and asked to recall words previously studied beginning with these letters, in comparison to a task in which subjects had to produce any word beginning with these letters.

It must be emphasised that one specific cerebral area intervening in the processing of non-words in comparison to words is the left superior temporal gyrus (BA 22). That area was classically involved in verbal tasks requiring the use of phonological representations associated to language processes (Démonet et al., 1992, 1994; Paulesu et al., 1993, 1996; Petersen et al., 1989; Sergent, Zuck, Levesque, & McDonald, 1992). Such an increase of activity in the present study indicates that the repetition of non-words was based on a phonological network similar to that intervening in word processing. These data do not appear surprising, as the non-words were drawn up on the basis of French syllables and their structure was similar to that of words in the language. Specific foci of activation were also found in the cerebellum when subjects had to store and repeat non-words, which could be related to the necessity of considerable articulatory motor programming in the processing of these items (e.g., Paulesu et al., 1993).

Taken as a whole, these conjunction analyses demonstrated that our results were mostly in agreement with previous studies that explored the functional network of verbal STM or the cerebral areas involved in the processing of phonological and semantic information. Thus, this experimental design does appear relevant to exploring whether supplementary cerebral areas are involved in verbal STM for items having pre-existing long-term representations.

The interaction analysis demonstrated that the left middle temporal (BA 21) gyrus and temporo-parietal (BA 39) junction are specifically involved during a STM task requiring the short-term maintenance of verbal items having pre-existing long-term representations. In previous studies exploring the neural substrate of language processing, these regions have been mostly associated with lexical and semantic language representations (e.g., Binder et al., 1997; Démonet et al., 1992, 1994; Howard et al., 1992; Mummery, Patterson, Hodges, & Wise, 1996; Vandenberghe et al., 1996). With reference to these studies, the increase of activity in the left temporo-parietal junction in our study is in agreement with an implication of semantic processes in short-term memory for words (Demonet et al., 1992; Mummery et al., 1996; Vandenberghe et al., 1996). Data are less clear-cut concerning the left middle temporal gyrus. Indeed, for some authors, that region would support a spoken-word lexicon (e.g., Howard et al., 1992) or phonological processes (Mazoyer et al., 1993; Zatorre, Evans, Meyer, & Gjedde, 1992) while others studies have shown that this region is also involved in semantic processes (Demonet et al., 1992). Overall, it appears that the regions that are additionally activated for the storage of words versus non-words in our study are regions mostly associated with lexical and semantic, rather than purely phonological processing. However, it is not yet possible to characterise these regions clearly with regard to their implication in auditory lexical processing (the sound-based word form) and in semantic processing (the meaning associated with the word form) (for a review concerning the intervention of these regions in cognitive processes, see Price, Indefrey, & van Turenhout, 1999). An alternative explanation for the additional brain activation for the storage of words versus non-words is that these regions could reflect the intervention of a lexico-semantic buffer. Indeed, Crosson et al. (1999) recently observed activation of the left middle temporal gyrus, close to the activation focus of our study, in a verbal STM task that required short-term retention of semantic information (in comparison to the retention of phonological and orthographic representations). A similar activation was noted by Vandenberghe et al. (1996) during semantic judgments about words, a condition that also probably requires the intervention of temporary semantic storage. However, in the studies of Crosson et al. and Vandenberghe et al. it cannot be ruled out that the activation of the left middle temporal gyrus in the semantic working memory condition reflects the intervention of lexical and semantic language representations that support performance in the semantic working memory condition rather than a semantic buffer *per se*. In fact, activation of the posterior ventral temporal gyrus has also been reported in studies where the demands on a semantic buffer were minimal or non-existent, as in simple object naming tasks (A. Martin, Wiggs, Ungerleider, & Haxby, 1996).

The results of this study can be summarised in the following way. First, the short-term memory tasks using both words and non-words involved increase of activity in Broca's area. This region was associated with the rehearsal of verbal information in the phonological loop of working memory (Baddeley, 1986). Moreover, the processing of words (but not non-words) in short-term memory involved an increase of activity in cerebral areas involved in the storage (and/or processing) of semantic and lexical long-term knowledge or in a lexico-semantic buffer. These findings can be used to discuss the relevance of different verbal short-term memory models. So far, we can reasonably make the assumption that these data are consistent with the existence of both a verbal STM system and long-term memory stores. But they also indicate that these systems closely interact, especially for the short-term retention of words. This is partially compatible with Baddeley's revised model of the phonological loop (Baddeley, Gathercole, & Papagno, 1998), at least with regard to the intervention of lexical long-term representations. Indeed, their revised model postulates a close interactive relationship between the phonological store and a phonological lexicon. However, the model should be extended in order to account also for the support of semantic knowledge in verbal short-term storage tasks (see Logie, 1996, for an implication of semantic representations in verbal STM tasks). In this context, our data are also consistent with the interactive model of language and short-term memory processing of R.C. Martin, Lesch, and Bartha (1999), which has the advantage of including a semantic level of processing. R.C. Martin and colleagues propose that the phonological, lexical, and semantic long-term representations involved in language perception and production are closely associated to phonological and lexico-semantic buffers. The maintenance of activation in the buffers for verbal short-term memory tasks depends on the correct feedback from the long-term language representations. In our study, the activation of areas involved in lexical and semantic processing for the storage of words versus non-words supports this theoretical proposal. Interestingly, this model also postulates specific buffers for the temporary storage of phonological and lexical-semantic information. This is consistent with the alternative interpretation that we have given to the activation of the posterior middle temporal lobe in our study as well as with the study by Crosson et al. (1999). Further studies are clearly needed to determine whether activation of the posterior left middle temporal gyrus in STM tasks only reflects the intervention of lexical and semantic long-term representations or if this region also constitutes the neurobiological basis for a semantic buffer.

In conclusion, the results of the present study demonstrate that there exists a support of lexico-semantic processing during STM tasks, and that this influence comprises the intervention of a phonological lexicon and semantic long-term representations or, alternatively, of a lexico-semantic buffer. These data allowed us to discuss the relevance of verbal STM models and demonstrate that the models that are the most in agreement with our data are those that postulate the simultaneous influence of lexical and semantic long-term representations on information-specific STM processes (e.g., R.C. Martin et al., 1999). No activity in cerebral areas specifically devoted to phonological processes was found during the STM task for words. This is probably related to the fact that the items (words and non-words) used in the different tasks had a similar phonotactic structure and were consequently based on a similar phonological network. Thus, using STM tasks in which the wordlikeness of the non-words is systematically varied could emphasise the intervention of phonological representations specific to words and non-words in STM tasks. More generally, the present study demonstrated that neuroimaging data could be used to challenge cognitive theoretical formulations and, in the line with this study, to better specify the functional architecture of STM. For example, functional imagery techniques would be fruitful in resolving the questions of the relationships between STM and perception, or the temporal course of the different processes involved in the short-term storage of information.

REFERENCES

Awh, E., Jonides, J., Smith, E.E., Schumacher, E.H., Koeppe, R.A., & Katz, S. (1996). Dissociation of storage and rehearsal in verbal working memory: Evidence from positron emission tomography. *Psychological Science*, *7*, 25–31.

Baddeley, A.D. (1986). *Working memory*. Oxford: Clarendon Press.

Baddeley, A.D., Gathercole, S., & Papagno, C. (1998). The phonological loop as a language learning device. *Psychological Review*, *105*, 158–173.

Baddeley, A.D., & Hitch, G.J. (1974). Working memory. In G. Bower (Ed.), *Recent advances in learning and motivation* (Vol. 8, pp. 47–90). New York: Academic Press.

Becker, J.T., MacAndrew, D.K., & Fiez, J.A. (1999). A comment on the functional localization of the phonological storage subsystem of working memory. *Brain and Cognition*, *41*, 27–38.

Becker, J.T., Mintum, M.A., Diehl, D.J., Dobkin, J., Martidis, A., Madoff, D.C., & DeKosky, S.T. (1994). Functional neuroanatomy of verbal free recall: A replication study. *Human Brain Mapping*, *1*, 284–292.

Binder, J.R., Frost, J.A., Hammeke, T.A., Cox, T.W., Rao, S.M., & Prieto, T. (1997). Human brain language areas identified by functional magnetic resonance imaging. *Journal of Neuroscience*, *17*, 353–362.

Bourassa, D.C., & Besner, D. (1994). Beyond the articulatory loop: A semantic contribution to serial order recall of subspan lists. *Psychonomic Bulletin & Review*, *1*, 122–125.

Buckner, R.L., Petersen, S.E., Ojemann, J.G., Miezin, F.M., Squire, L.R., & Raichle, M.E. (1995). Functional anatomical studies of explicit and implicit memory retrieval tasks. *The Journal of Neurosciences*, *15*, 12–29.

Cabeza, R., & Nyberg, L. (2000). Imaging cognition II: An empirical review of 275 PET and fMRI studies. *Journal of Cognitive Neuroscience*, *12*, 1–47.

Content, A., Mousty, P., & Radeau, M. (1990). BRULEX. Une base de données lexicales informatisée pour le français ecrit et parlé. [BRULEX: A computerised lexical database for the French language]. *Année Psychologique*, *90*, 551–566.

Crosson, B., Rao, S.M., Woodley, S.J., Rosen, A.C., Bobholz, J.A., Mayer, A., Cunningham, J.M., Hammeke, T.A., Fuller, S.A., Binder, J.R., Cox, R.W., & Stein, E.A. (1999). Mapping of semantic, phonological, and orthographic verbal working memory in normal adults with functional magnetic resonance imaging. *Neuropsychology*, *13*, 171–187.

Démonet, J.-F., Chollet, F., Ramsay, S., Cardebat, D., Nespoulous, J.L., Wise, R., Rascol, A., & Frackowiak, R.S.J. (1992). The anatomy of phonological and semantic processing in normal subjects. *Brain*, *115*, 1753–1768

Démonet, J.-F., Price, C.J., Wise, R., & Frackowiack, R.S.J. (1994). Differential activation of right and left posterior cerebral regions by semantic and phonological tasks: A positron emission tomography study. *Neuroscience Letters*, *182*, 25–28..

Frackowiak, R., Friston, K., Frith, C., Dolan, R., & Mazziotta, J.C. (1997). *Human brain function*. London: Academic Press.

Friston, K.J., Frith, C.D., Liddle, P.F., Dolan, R.J., Lammertsma, A.A., & Frackowiak, R.S.J. (1990). The relationship between global and local changes in PET scans. *Journal of Cerebral Blood Flow and Metabolism*, *10*, 458–466.

Friston, K.J., Frith, C.D., Liddle, P.F., & Frackowiak, R.S.J. (1991). Comparing functional (PET) images: The assessment of significant changes. *Journal of Cerebral Blood Flow and Metabolism*, *11*, 690–699.

Gathercole, S.E., Willis, C., Emslie, H., & Baddeley, A.D. (1991). The influences of number of syllables and wordlikeness on children's repetition of nonwords. *Applied Psycholinguistics*, *12*, 349–367.

Howard, D., Patterson, K., Wise, R., Brown, W.D., Friston, K.J., Weiller, C., & Frackowiak, R.S.J. (1992). The cortical localization of the lexicons. *Brain*, *115*, 1769–1782.

Hulme, C., Roodenrys, S., & Mercer, R. (1995). The role of long-term memory mechanisms in memory span. *British Journal of Psychology*, *86*, 527–536.

Jueptner, M., & Weiller, C. (1995). Review: Does measurement of regional cerebral blood flow reflect synaptic activity? Implications for PET and fMRI. *NeuroImage*, *2*, 148–156.

Logie, R.H. (1996). The seven ages of working memory. In M. Richards, R.W. Engle, L. Hasher, R.H. Logie, E.R. Stoltzfus, & R.T. Zacks (Eds.), *Working memory and human cognition* (pp. 31–65). Oxford: Oxford University Press.

Martin, A., Wiggs, C.L., Ungerleider, L.G., & Haxby, J.V. (1996). Neural correlates of category-specific knowledge. *Nature*, *379*, 649–652.

Martin, R.C., Lesch, M.F., & Bartha, M.C. (1999). Independence of input and output phonology in word processing and short-term memory. *Journal of Memory and Language*, *41*, 3–29.

Mazoyer, B.M., Tzourio, N., Frak, V., Syrota, A. et al. (1993). The cortical representation of speech. *Journal of Cognitive Neuroscience*, *5*, 467–479.

Mummery, C.J., Ashburner, J., Scott, S.K., & Wise, R.J.S. (1999). Functional neuroimaging of speech perception in six normal and two aphasic subjects. *Journal of the Acoustical Society of America*, *106*, 449–457.

Mummery, C.J., Patterson, K., Hodges, J.R., & Wise, R.J.S. (1996). Generating "tiger" as an animal name or a word beginning with T: Differences in brain activation. *Proceedings of the Royal Society of London (B)*, *263*, 989–995.

Paulesu, E., Frith, C.D., & Frackowiak, R.S.J. (1993). The neural correlates of the verbal component of working memory. *Nature*, *362*, 342–345.

Paulesu, E., McCrory, E., Fazio, F., Menoncello, L., Brunswick, N., Cappa, S.F., Cotelli, M., Cossu, G., Corte, F., Lorusso, M., Pesenti, S., Gallagher, A., Perani, D., Price, C., Frith, C.D., & Frith, U. (2000). A cultural effect on brain function. *Nature Neuroscience*, *3*, 91–96.

Petersen, S.E., Fox, P.T., Posner, M.I., Mintum, M., & Raichle, M.E. (1989). Positron emission tomography studies of the processing of single words. *Journal of Cognitive Neuroscience*, *1*, 153–170.

Poirier, M., & Saint-Aubin, J. (1995). Memory for related and unrelated words: Further evidence on the influence of semantic factors in immediate serial recall. *The Quarterly Journal of Experimental Psychology*, *48*A, 384–404.

Price, C.J., Indefrey, P., & van Turenhout, M. (1999). The neural architecture underlying the processing of written and spoken word forms. In C.M. Brown & P. Haggort (Eds.), *The neurocognition of language* (pp. 211–240). Oxford: Oxford University Press.

Price, C.J., Moore, C.J., & Friston, K.J. (1997). Substractions, conjunctions and interactions in experimental design of activation studies. *Human Brain Mapping*, *5*, 264–272.

Price, C.J., Wise, R.J.S., Warburton, E.A., Moore, C.J., Howard, D., Patterson, K., Frackowiak, R.S.J., & Friston, K.J. (1996). Hearing and saying. The functional neuro-anatomy of auditory word processing. *Brain*, *119*, 919–931.

Pulvermüller, F. (1999). Words in the brain's language. *Behavioral and Brain Sciences*, *22*, 253–336.

Rypma, B., Prabhakaran, V., Desmond, J.E., Glover, G.H., & Gabrieli, J.D.E. (1999). Load dependent roles of frontal brain regions in the maintenance of working memory. *Neuroimage*, *9*, 216–226.

Salmon, E., Van der Linden, M., Collette, F., Delfiore, G., Maquet, P., Degueldre, C., Luxen, A., & Franck, G. (1996). Regional brain activity during working memory tasks. *Brain*, *119*, 1617–1625.

Schumacher, E.H., Lauber, E., Awh, E., Jonides, J., Smith, E.E., & Koeppe, R.A. (1996). PET evidence for an amodal verbal working memory system. *Neuroimage*, *3*, 79–88.

Schweickert, R. (1993). A multinomial processing tree model for degradation and redintegration in immediate recall. *Memory and Cognition*, *21*, 168–175.

Sergent, J., Zuck, E., Levesque, M., & MacDonald, B. (1992). Positron emission tomography study of letter and object processing: Empirical findings and methodological considerations. *Cerebral Cortex*, *2*, 68–80.

Shaywitz, B.A., Shaywitz, S.E., Pugh, K.R., Constable, R.T., Skudlarski, P., Fulbright, R.K., Bronen, R.A., Fletcher, J.A., Shankweller, D.P., Katz, L., & Gore, J.C. (1995). Sex differences in the functional organization of the brain for language. *Nature*, *373*, 607–609.

Smith, E.E., Jonides, J., & Koeppe, R.A. (1996). Dissociating verbal and spatial working memory using PET. *Cerebral Cortex*, *6*, 11–20.

Talairach, J., & Tournoux, P. (1988). *Co-planar stereotaxic atlas of the human brain: 3-dimensional proportional system: An approach to cerebral imaging.* Stuttgart: Thieme.

Thompson-Schill, S.L., D'Esposito, M., Aguirre, G.K., & Farah, M.J. (1997). Role of left inferior prefrontal cortex in retrieval of semantic knowledge: A reevaluation. *Proceedings of the National Academic of Sciences, USA*, *94*, 14792–14797.

Vandenbergh, R., Price, C.J., Wise, R.J.S., Josephs, O., & Frackowiak, R.S.J. (1996). Functional anatomy of a common semantic system for words and pictures. *Nature*, *383*, 254–256.

Walker, I., & Hulme, C. (1999). Concrete words are easier to recall than abstract words: Evidence for a semantic contribution to short-term serial recall. *Journal of Experimental Psychology: Learning, Memory, and Cognition*, *25*, 1256–1271.

Warburton, E., Wise, R.J.S., Price, C.J., Weiller, C., Hadar, U., Ramsay, S., & Frackowiak, R.S.J. (1996). Noun and verb retrieval by normal subjects. Studies with PET. *Brain*, *119*, 159–179.

Watkins, O.C., & Watkins, M.J. (1977). Serial recall and the modality effect: Effects of word frequency. *Journal of Experimental Psychology: Human Learning and Memory*, *3*, 712–718.

Zatorre, R.J., Evans, A.C., Meyer, E., & Gjedde, A. (1992). Lateralization of phonetic and pitch discrimination in speech processing. *Science*, *256*, 846–849.

MEMORY, 2001, 9 (4/5/6), 261–280

Short-term retention of lexical-semantic representations: Implications for speech production

Randi C. Martin and Monica L. Freedman
Rice University, Texas, USA

Patients with semantic STM deficits have difficulty comprehending sentences that require the retention of several lexical-semantic representations prior to their integration into higher-level propositions (Martin, 1995; Martin & Romani, 1994). In Experiment 1, patients with a semantic retention deficit had difficulty with the same type of constructions in speech production, namely noun phrases with one or two prenominal adjectives. Their performance improved when they could produce the nouns and adjectives in sentence form, which placed smaller demands on lexical-semantic retention. In Experiment 2 these patients were better able to produce syntactically complex sentences than the prenominal adjective phrases having an equal number of content words, indicating that the findings in Experiment 1 could not be attributed to syntactic complexity. These patients produced more pauses in the sentence constructions in Experiments 1 and 2, suggesting that the timing of such productions is abnormal. In contrast, patient EA, with a phonological retention deficit, performed better than the patients with a semantic retention deficit on the AN phrases despite having a smaller STM span. She showed no significant benefit of producing sentence compared to phrase constructions, and also made fewer and shorter pauses than the other patients. These findings support the multiple capacities view of verbal working memory and suggest that the same semantic retention capacity used in language comprehension is used in speech production.

INTRODUCTION

In contrast to numerous studies on the role of working memory in sentence comprehension, only a few have examined its role in sentence production. Current models of production imply, however, that working memory is involved. These models assume that lexical, syntactic, and phonological representations for several words are maintained simultaneously at different stages in the production process and, moreover, that the representations at one level remain available while representations at the next are constructed. The question to be addressed in this study is the relation between the short-term memory capacities tapped by standard memory span tasks and the working memory capacities involved in language production. This issue was investigated by examining brain-damaged patients who have very reduced short-term memory spans. The patients differed in the nature of their short-term memory deficits. One of the patients has a short-term memory deficit primarily for the retention of phonological information, whereas two others have a deficit primarily in the retention of lexical-semantic information. Consequently, it was possible to investigate whether these different deficits had different consequences for production that related to capacity demands involved in planning at the semantic or phonological levels.

Speech production models and working memory demands

There is general agreement concerning the stages of planning and levels of representation that are involved in sentence production (Bock & Levelt,

Requests for reprints should be sent to Randi C. Martin, Department of Psychology, Rice University, P.O. Box 1892, Houston, TX 77251, USA. Email: rmartin@rice.edu

This research was supported by NIH grant DC 00218 to Randi C. Martin at Rice University. The authors would like to thank Mike Katz, Ann-Marie Lobo, and Frank Tamborello for assistance in patient testing and data analysis.

http://www.tandf.co.uk/journals/pp/09658211.html DOI:10.1080/09658210143000173

1994; Dell, 1986). At the highest level, the message to be expressed is represented in a nonverbal format. The message is used to select lexical representations and a syntactic structure to express the relations among the lexical representations. It should be noted that the lexical representations at this level are presumed to be representations of semantic and syntactic information (i.e., "lemmas"; Kempen & Huijbers, 1983) rather than phonological representations. Some recent speech production models have implied that lemmas contain purely syntactic representations (Bock & Levelt, 1994; Levelt, Roelofs, & Meyer, 1999). However, lemmas are portrayed in graphical depictions of these models as being essentially empty nodes that link conceptual representations to syntactic information. In this paper we will use "lemma" to refer to this type of representation that provides a means of connecting conceptual and syntactic specifications of words. Further downstream in the planning process, the phonological representations for the words are retrieved. In these models, information may flow from one level to the next before a complete representation of the entire utterance is constructed at the prior level. For example, phonological encoding of the first noun phrase may proceed while construction of the syntactic representation of the second noun phrase is in progress.

The scope of planning, in terms of the proportion of the message being planned, appears to vary depending on the level at which the planning is taking place. At the message level, the entire thought may be represented. However, at subsequent levels, smaller portions may be planned. Data from naturally occurring speech errors and from experimental studies suggest that the scope of planning is greater at the level of lemma selection than at the phonological level (Garrett, 1980; Meyer, 1996; Smith & Wheeldon, 1999). For instance, whole word exchange errors (e.g., "I left the cigar in my briefcase" → "I left the briefcase in my cigar") tend to occur across a larger number of intervening words than do sound exchange errors (e.g., "strictly speaking" → "spictly streaking") (Garrett, 1980). Also, in a picture description paradigm with spoken word distractors, Meyer (1996) found that onset latencies for a phrase such as "the boat and the car" were delayed by the presentation of a word semantically related to either the first or second noun. Facilitation in onset latencies was observed for words phonologically related to the first noun but there was no phonological effect for words related to the second noun. Given this evidence of a greater scope of planning at the semantic level, it is possible that there are greater capacity demands at the level involved in maintaining lemma representations.

Components of verbal short-term memory and their relation to sentence planning

Recent evidence suggests that a number of different types of representations are involved in the maintenance of words during standard memory span tasks. A large body of research implicates a role for phonological representations, and many models of short-term memory have focused on the retention of phonological codes (Baddeley, 1986; Schweickert, Guentert, & Hersberger, 1990). However, other studies involving normal subjects and brain-damaged patients indicate that semantic representations are involved as well. For example, studies of normal subjects have shown that span is greater for words than nonwords (Crowder, 1978; Hulme, Maugham, & Brown, 1991; Schweickert, 1993), greater for words from the same category than for words from different categories (Poirier & St. Aubin, 1995), and greater for high than low imageability words (Bourassa & Besner, 1994). Also, span for foreign words increases when subjects learn the meanings of the foreign words (Hulme et al., 1991). Neuropsychological evidence comes from the work of Patterson and colleagues and of N. Martin and Saffran. Patterson, Graham, and Hodges (1994) and Knott, Patterson, and Hodges (1997) demonstrated that patients with dementia that affects semantic representations show a larger word span for known words than for unknown words (that is, words for which they no longer know the meaning). Saffran and N. Martin (1990; Martin & Saffran, 1992, 1997) analysed the word-processing and short-term memory deficits of patients with phonological vs semantic processing deficits and found distinctive short-term memory patterns with regard to recency and primary effects in serial recall and the effects of imageability and frequency at early vs late serial positions. That is, patients with phonological processing deficits tend to show greater primacy than recency effects and greater effects of imageability at late serial positions, whereas patients with semantic processing deficits tend to show greater recency than primacy effects and large effects of imageability at early list positions. Thus, there is evidence from both normal subjects and brain-damaged patients supporting the involvement of multiple linguistic codes in verbal short-term memory.

Neuropsychological data have also indicated that the phonological and semantic retention capacities may be selectively affected by brain damage, independently of damage to phonological and semantic processing abilities. Martin, Shelton, and Yaffee (1994) reported two patients who both had very reduced spans, but who showed different effects of phonological and semantic variables on span. Both patients showed normal or near normal levels of single word processing in both comprehension and production tasks. Patient EA demonstrated reduced phonological effects, but preserved semantic effects on memory span. For example, she showed no phonological similarity effect in the visual modality and no word length effect in either auditory or visual modalities, and showed better performance with visual than auditory presentation (the reverse of the normal pattern). However, she showed a large advantage for words over nonwords, suggesting that the semantic information in the words aided her performance. Two short-term memory probe tasks were administered, a rhyme probe task that tapped phonological retention and a category probe task that tapped semantic retention. EA performed slightly better on the category probe than the rhyme probe task, whereas normal subjects showed a substantial advantage on the rhyme probe task. In contrast to EA, patient AB showed normal phonological effects in span tasks but no advantage for words over nonwords. AB performed worse than EA on the category probe task, but better than EA on the rhyme probe task. Thus across the two patients there was a double dissociation between deficits in semantic vs phonological retention. This dissociation has recently been replicated in a study of two children who had sustained severe closed head injury (Hanten & Martin, 2000).

In addition to the distinction between semantic and phonological retention capacities, there is evidence that a further distinction needs to be made between the capacities involved in the retention of input and output phonological codes (Allport, 1984; Romani, 1992; Shallice & Butterworth, 1977; but see N. Martin & Saffran, 1992). Evidence for a selective impairment of a phonological output buffer is provided by patients who show poor performance on list recall tasks that require phonological output, but good performance on recognition tasks tapping input retention, such as digit matching span tasks or probe tasks (Allport, 1984; Romani, 1992; Shallice, Rumiati & Zadini, 2000). The opposite dissociation of an impaired phonological input buffer but preserved output buffer is demonstrated by patients who have very reduced spans and poor performance on input tasks like those just mentioned, but who produce speech that is within normal range in terms of sentence length, grammatical complexity, and rate of pausing and hesitations (R. Martin et al., 1994; Shallice & Butterworth, 1977). Under the assumption that an output phonological buffer is needed to plan speech production, the good language production for these patients suggests that the output buffer is preserved despite the severe restriction in the input buffer.

Patient MS (Martin, Lesch, & Bartha, 1999) provides another source of evidence for the separation of input and output buffers. We have hypothesised that MS has difficulty, not with the output buffer *per se*, but rather with activating output phonological representations from lexical-semantic representations. His picture naming is severely impaired, but when he is unable to produce a picture name, he typically produces a long description of the object, indicating preserved semantic knowledge. This patient has unimpaired speech perception but has difficulty specifically in retrieving output phonological representations. He performed normally on nonword list recall, suggesting that both his input and output buffers are preserved and that he can translate directly between input and output phonological representations. On short-term memory tasks involving only input phonological representations for words (such as rhyme probe or order probe tasks), he performs at a normal level. However, when required to reproduce a list of words, his performance was impaired, particularly for low-frequency, low-imageability words. He would sometimes provide semantic descriptions of the words in the list. His performance suggests that the connections used for activating output phonological representations from lexical-semantic representations are damaged, which has a greater impact on his production of low- than high-frequency words in both naming and list recall. Thus, he does not show the boost in performance for words compared to nonwords that is shown by normal subjects because normal subjects receive activation both from direct translation from the input phonological representations and from activation flowing from lexical-semantic representations.

Based on the findings of semantic and phonological contributions to memory span, we have developed a model of short-term memory in which there is a close connection between levels of representation in language processing and those involved in short-term memory. As shown in Figure 1 (Martin et al., 1999), language processing is supported by interactive activation of representations in the long-term knowledge store. During word recognition, acoustic information is mapped onto a phonological form, which then accesses a lexical form, which then activates a semantic representation. In word production, activation begins at the semantic level, which then activates a lexical representation, which then activates its phonological representation, which is used to guide articulation. The output from language processing is maintained in limited-capacity buffers specific to each level of representation.

The lexical knowledge network represented on the left-hand side of Figure 1 is similar to that proposed by Dell and colleagues in their model of word production (Dell, 1986; Dell & O'Seaghdha, 1992; Dell et al., 1997). In Dell's (1986) model of sentence production, the different levels of representation in the lexical network are tied to slots in syntactic, morphological, and phonological planning frames. It seems plausible to assume that the phonological buffer that we have hypothesised is identical to the phonological planning frame in Dell's model. The relation between the lexical-semantic buffer in Figure 1 and Dell's planning frames could take different forms. One possibility is that the lexical-semantic buffer is used to hold semantic and syntactic specifications of several words simultaneously and then these representations are linked to a separate syntactic frame. A second possibility is that the lexical-semantic buffer is equivalent to the syntactic planning

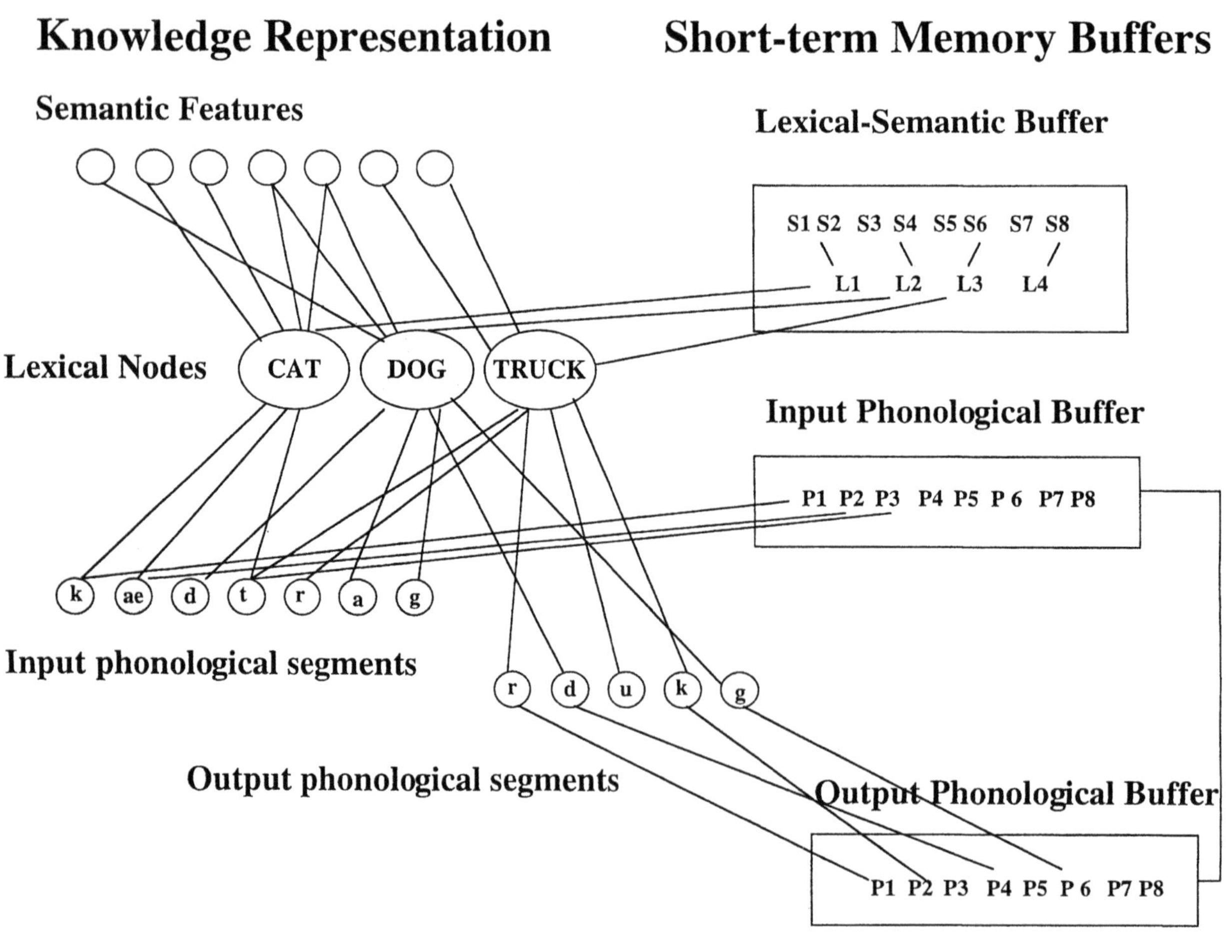

Figure 1. Model of language processing and short-term memory (based on Martin et al., 1999).

frame. If so, then to account for the patients' short-term memory deficits, one would have to assume that a syntactic frame was involved in serial list recall. As Barnard (1985) suggested, one might assume that the syntactic frame for a word list was quite simple and similar to that involved in representation of a compound noun phrase (e.g., "Jeeps, cars and buses..."). In either case, we would assume that links between the lexical-semantic buffer or syntactic frame to the representations in the knowledge store would serve to keep these representations active, and damage to the buffer or to the links should have negative consequences for production. We prefer the former hypothesis that there is a separate lexical-semantic retention buffer that feeds into a syntactic frame, rather than equating the lexical-semantic buffer with the frame. It seems easier to account for the patients' span deficits in terms of overly active decay or increased interference among lexical-semantic representations. If the buffer were equated with the syntactic frame, one would have to assume some deficit in the capacity of the syntactic frame itself or possibly in the links between the frame and the knowledge store. The results from Experiment 2 provide some data on this issue.

Relation between capacities involved in language production and language comprehension

As discussed earlier, evidence suggests that there are separate buffers involved in retaining input phonological forms and output phonological forms. This separation raises the question of whether there are separate lexical-semantic retention capacities involved in comprehension and production. Kempen and Hoenkamp (1987) suggested that the same syntactic procedures are involved in production and comprehension and recent empirical evidence supports this view (Branigan et al., 1995). However, as indicated earlier, it is possible that the lexical-semantic retention buffer is separate from the syntactic frame, and thus other evidence would be needed to address whether this buffer is shared in comprehension and production. In a number of previous studies, we have demonstrated that patients with a semantic STM deficit have difficulty with sentences with a high semantic load (Martin & Feher, 1990; Martin & Romani, 1994; Martin et al., 1994). More specifically, Martin and Romani (1994) and Martin (1995) demonstrated that patients who show semantic retention deficits on memory span tasks perform poorly on sentence comprehension when they have to maintain several lexical-semantic representations prior to their integration into higher-level propositional representations. These studies employed an auditory sentence anomaly judgement task, manipulating the number of adjectives before or after a noun or the number of nouns before or after a verb. For example, the "before" condition with adjectives used anomalous sentences such as "The rusty, old, red swimsuit..." or "The rusty swimsuit...". The "after" condition used anomalous sentences of the form "The swimsuit was old, red, and rusty..." or "The swimsuit was rusty...". Matching sensible sentences were also presented (for example, "The rusty pail..."). A similar manipulation was used for sentences that varied the number of nouns that came before or after a verb. For example, a "before" sentence with three nouns was "The cloth, the vase and the mirror cracked..." and the matching "after" sentence was "The movers cracked the mirror, the vase and the cloth...". It was reasoned that the "before" conditions should make a larger demand on lexical-semantic retention because integration of lexical-semantic information was delayed. In the "after" conditions, integration was immediate. That is, the meaning of an adjective had to be maintained until it could be integrated with a noun, and the meaning of a noun had to be maintained until it could be integrated in terms of its thematic role with respect to the verb.

Martin and Romani (1994) and Martin (1995) showed that two patients (AB and ML) with semantic STM deficits performed very poorly in the "before" condition when two or three words had to be maintained prior to integration. They made a large number of errors and showed a very large effect of the number of nouns or adjectives that had to be maintained prior to integration. In fact, both performed near chance level with two or three adjectives or nouns in the "before" condition (about 37–40% errors for each patient in these conditions where 50% would be chance), compared with 10–15% errors with one preceding adjective or noun. In contrast, in the "after" condition, they made many fewer errors overall and showed little effect of the number of adjectives or nouns. In contrast, patient EA, with a phonological retention deficit, performed like normal subjects with slightly worse performance overall in the "before" condition. However, she did not show the interaction between the "before/after" manipulation and distance that was shown by the semantic retention deficit patients.

If the same lexical-semantic retention capacities are used in both comprehension and production, then patients with semantic retention deficits might have difficulty producing the same types of constructions that caused difficulty in comprehension (namely, noun phrases with several prenominal adjectives and subject noun phrases with more than one noun). Recent models of language production have assumed that planning proceeds incrementally (de Smedt, 1996; Kempen & Hoenkamp, 1987; LaPointe & Dell, 1989; Smith & Wheeldon, 1999). Whereas a message-level representation may be developed that spans an entire clause or more, planning at the syntactic level proceeds in a phrase-by-phrase fashion in terms of both development of grammatical structure and the attachment of lexical-semantic representations to this structure. If we assume that all the lexical-semantic representations in a phrase must be planned simultaneously prior to the initiation of phonological encoding of the phrase, then patients with a lexical-semantic retention deficit should have difficulty producing phrases containing several content words. A phonological retention deficit that is limited to an input buffer deficit would be predicted to have no effect on production, as only the output phonological buffer should be involved in planning phonological representations for speech production (Martin & Freedman, 2001; Martin et al., 1999; Shallice & Butterworth, 1977).

It might be argued that even though normal subjects might plan all of the lexical-semantic representations for a phrase simultaneously, there may be no necessity to do so. That is, if patients can keep the message to be expressed in mind, they might be able to retrieve the lexical-semantic representations for each word sequentially—provided that they can maintain the syntactic structure for the phrase in order for the words to be produced in the right order. However, it is possible that in order to produce speech fluently with normal intonational contours, several lexical-semantic representations must be planned and maintained in parallel while phonological encoding is carried out. In the present paper, we investigated what we have termed the "lexical head principle", that is, that speakers must plan the lexical-semantic representation for the head of the phrase and that for all of the content words prior to that head within the same phrase (Martin & Freedman, 2001). Thus, in an adjective-noun or adjective-adjective-noun phrase, where the head of the phrase is the noun, the noun plus all preceding adjectives must be planned at the lexical-semantic level prior to phonological encoding of the phrase. Patients who are unable to maintain all of these lexical-semantic representations simultaneously might either fail entirely at producing the phrase, or produce it in a piecemeal fashion with pauses intervening between each content word.

Some evidence from normal subjects is consistent with this lexical head principle. Schriefers (1993) examined the effects of visually presented distractor words on the production of adjective-noun phrases (in Dutch) describing coloured objects (e.g., "groen bed" → "green bed"). Distractor words semantically related to either the noun or the adjective delayed onset latencies relative to unrelated distractors, suggesting that subjects were planning both words at the semantic level prior to speech onset. However, this effect was obtained only for phrases without a determiner. For phrases with a determiner ("het groene bed" → "the green bed"), interference was obtained only for distractor words semantically related to the noun. This latter result might suggest that only the lexical head needs to be planned at the semantic level and not the preceding adjective. In Dutch, however, when both a determiner and adjective are present, only the determiner agrees in gender with the noun. When no determiner is present, the adjective agrees in gender. Thus, for the phrases with determiners, it is possible that determiner selection was slow relative to adjective selection, with the result that interfering effects of the semantically related adjective distractor were hidden by the relatively long time needed to select the correct determiner.

Other results that are somewhat relevant to the lexical head principle come from a recent study by Smith and Wheeldon (1999). They contrasted onset latencies to describe moving pictures with sentences of two types: (1) simple/complex: The ball moves above the faucet and the sock; (2) complex/simple: The ball and the faucet move above the sock. Even though the two sentence types were matched in length and content words, initiation times were longer for the complex/simple sentences than the simple/complex sentences. The results suggest that speakers were planning both nouns in the subject noun phrase at least at the semantic level in the complex/simple sentences prior to initiating articulation. However, the use of a compound noun phrase somewhat complicates the issue of what constitutes a phrase. The compound noun phrase consists of two noun phrases, each of which has its own head. Thus, if subjects were only planning the first noun phrase of the compound noun phrase, then no effect of complexity should have been obtained. The results suggest instead that subjects planned the entire subject noun phrase.

A preliminary study from our lab (Martin & Freedman, 2001; Martin & Romani, 1995) supported the contention that patients with a semantic retention deficit would have difficulty producing utterances that, according to the lexical head principle, would require the maintenance of two or more lexical-semantic representations. Patients were asked to describe pictures using simple adjective-noun (AN) and adjective-adjective-noun (AAN) phrases. Patient EA, with an input phonological retention deficit, was predicted to have no difficulty with this task. Patients ML and AB, who had lexical-semantic retention deficits and who had done poorly on comprehending sentences with several prenominal adjectives, were predicted to have difficulty, particularly with the AAN phrases. To elicit the phrases, pictures of three different objects (hair, leaf, and curtain) were constructed, which varied on three different dimensions (e.g., Hair—long vs short, blonde vs black, straight vs curly). The AN phrases were elicited by showing two pictures side by side, which were identical except for one relevant dimension (e.g., *long* straight black hair vs *short* straight black hair). The target picture was highlighted to indicate which picture should be described. Subjects were instructed to produce an AN phrase to describe the highlighted picture which would differentiate it from the other picture. The AAN phrases (e.g., "long curly hair") were elicited by showing three pictures. The target picture was highlighted, and the other pictures differed from the target on only one of the relevant dimensions (e.g., long curly hair [target] shown with long *straight* hair and *short* curly hair; see Figure 2).

As shown in Table 1, patient EA with a phonological STM deficit performed normally on both the one- and two-adjective conditions in the noun phrase production task. The two patients with semantic retention deficits were able to name the single nouns and adjectives perfectly, but performed very poorly on the AN and AAN combinations, well below the range of controls.

Figure 2. Stimuli for eliciting adjective noun phrases.

TABLE 1
Patient performance on preliminary noun phrase production task

	Adj.	*N.*	*Adj. N*	*AAN*
Controls	100	88	92	77
(n = 6)		(93)	(97)	(82)
Phonological STM				
EA	100	90	90	70
		(90)	(100)	(80)
Semantic STM				
AB	100	100	30	0
			(30)	(0)
ML	100	100	20	10
			(80)	(40)

Percent correct (numbers in parentheses are percent correct after self-correction).

These patients struggled to produce a phrase of the appropriate type, often producing pieces of it separately. For example, for the target "small leaf" AB responded "It's a leaf. It's small." In the case of ML, he often worked his way up to the appropriate phrase. For example, when trying to produce the target "small, rough leaf" ML responded "small . . . small . . . rough, rough leaf . . . small, rough leaf." These patients' difficulties in producing these simple phrases, together with their difficulty in understanding the sentences with two or three adjectives before a noun suggest that the same semantic retention buffer that is used in comprehension is used in production. Accordingly, their difficulty with AN and AAN phrases would stem from an inability to maintain multiple semantic representations in memory at one time, although they have no difficulty accessing them individually.

If this interpretation is correct, then these patients should be better able to produce the same content information if the task required a syntactic construction in which each phrase contained no content words preceding the lexical head. This issue was addressed in Experiment 1 where the patients' ability to produce phrases with prenominal adjectives was compared to their ability to produce sentences with an adjective phrase following a copula (e.g., "The leaf is small"). An alternative interpretation of ML and AB's difficulty with the AN phrases is that adding prenominal adjectives increases syntactic complexity, and these patients have difficulty with more complex syntactic constructions. Experiment 2 addressed this issue. The patients were asked to produce syntactically complex utterances which could be produced, according to lexical head principle, in a series of phrases each containing only one content word. If difficulty with the AN phrases derives from restricted capacity for maintaining lexical-semantic representations, then performance of patients with semantic retention deficits should improve rather than decrease on these sentences with greater grammatical complexity but lesser demands on semantic retention capacity.

PATIENT DESCRIPTIONS

Patient ML

ML is a 55-year-old man who suffered a left hemisphere CVA in 1990. CT scan indicated an infarction involving the left frontal and parietal operculum, with atrophy in the left temporal operculum and mild diffuse atrophy. He completed two years of college and had been employed as a draftsman. ML demonstrates good comprehension and single word processing. His speech is halting and characterised by reduced phrase length.

Patient GR

GR is a 54-year-old man who had received his bachelor's degree in English and History and was working at the Texas Employment Commission before suffering a stroke in 1989. CT scan revealed a large frontoparietal temporal wedge-shaped middle cerebral artery distribution stroke. GR exhibits good comprehension but reduced output. His speech is characterised by short utterances, which are grammatically correct, and by word-finding difficulty.

Patient EA

EA is a 66-year-old college-educated woman who is a homemaker and participates in a competitive synchronised swimming team. She suffered a left hemisphere stroke in 1975, involving the left temporal and parietal lobes, and including the primary auditory cortex, Wernicke's area, and the superior and inferior parietal lobules. She demonstrates good comprehension and fluent speech, with very occasional phonological paraphasias in multi-syllable words.

PATIENT SHORT-TERM MEMORY PERFORMANCE

All three patients have reduced STM spans. On the Philadelphia List Repetition task, which is part of the Philadelphia Comprehension Battery (Saffran, Schwartz, Linebarger, & Bochetto, 1989), patients are asked to repeat one-, two-, three- and four-word lists which are manipulated for frequency and imageability. Collapsing across all item types at each list length, each patient's span was calculated as the estimated list length at which he or she would achieve 50% correct. ML and GR had spans of 2.7 and 3.2 words, respectively. EA had the lowest span of 1.9. As mentioned earlier, the short-term memory patterns for EA and ML differed, with EA showing primarily a phonological retention deficit and ML a semantic retention deficit (Freedman & Martin, 2001; R. Martin & Lesch, 1996; R. Martin & Romani, 1995; R. Martin et al., 1994). GR also has more difficulty retaining semantic than phonological information (Martin & Freedman, 2001). Freedman and Martin tested all three patients (and two others) on a variety of tasks designed to require the retention of semantic or phonological information. Their scores on each of the tasks were converted to z-scores and added together to yield a composite phonological STM score and a composite semantic STM score. The semantic STM score included performance on four tasks: a category probe task, the difference between a three-choice and two-choice relatedness task, an attribute judgement task, and the difference between word vs nonword span, where better performance with words was assumed to reflect a benefit from retention of the words' semantic representations. The phonological STM score included performance on three tasks: a rhyme probe task, the difference between repetition of long (three- and four-syllable) and short (one- and two-syllable) nonwords, and the difference between phoneme discrimination between items presented one after the other and those having a 5-second filled delay between them. Of the five patients in the study, EA had the lowest composite phonological STM score (−4.14) and the highest composite semantic STM score (3.86). Both ML and GR showed the opposite pattern of higher phonological STM scores than semantic STM scores. ML scored −.23 on the phonological STM score vs −2.59 on the semantic STM score. Although ML may show some impairment of phonological retention, it is much better preserved than his semantic retention ability. GR scored .98 on the phonological STM score compared to .53 on the semantic retention score. Thus GR does not seem to be as impaired as ML on these retention tasks, but he shows the same pattern of better preserved phonological than semantic retention.

EXPERIMENT 1

In this experiment, subjects were asked to produce AN or AAN phrases as in the preliminary study. They were also asked to produce the same information as in the noun phrases using a sentence construction. If a speaker must only access the lexical-semantic representation for the head of the phrase and all words that precede it in the phrase before beginning phonological retrieval, then we might expect these patients to demonstrate better performance in the sentence format, as only one lexical-semantic representation must be maintained at a time. For example, rather than saying "green leaf" or "small green leaf", they might be better able to say "the leaf is green" or "the leaf is small and green". In "the leaf is green" there is only one noun in the subject noun phrase and only one adjective in the adjective phrase following the copula. In "The leaf is small and green" there are now two adjectives in the adjective phrase, so patients may still have some difficulty with that construction.

Method

Materials

Similar to the preliminary study, pictures of three objects (hair, book, and curtain) were used which each varied on three different dimensions. These pictures were presented on computer using the PsyScope program (Cohen, MacWhinney, Flatt, & Provost, 1993).

Design and procedure

The procedure was similar to that described in the preliminary study, but the patients completed two versions of the task, one in which they produced phrases to describe pictures and one in which they produced sentences to describe the pictures. They were tested in two sessions separated by at least 2 weeks. Both sessions were tape-recorded.

Phrase production task. Subjects first saw a labelled display on the computer screen, which familiarised them with the different pictures and dimensions to be described. Subjects then completed 18 trials naming only the nouns and 18 trials naming only the adjectives. The adjectives were elicited by showing two pictures side by side, which were identical except for one relevant dimension (e.g., *long* straight black hair vs *short* straight black hair). One picture was highlighted to indicate which adjective should be produced (e.g., "long"). The single noun and single adjective blocks were each repeated three times to ensure that subjects were well practised in producing the individual nouns and adjectives prior to attempting the phrases. Next the subjects completed one block of AN phrases (e.g., "long hair") and one block of AAN phrases (e.g., "long curly hair"). Before each test block of 18 trials, subjects were shown two examples and given six practice trials with feedback. The AN phrases were elicited using the same picture format as the adjective productions, but subjects were instructed to produce an AN phrase to describe the highlighted picture which would differentiate it from the other picture. The AAN phrases were elicited by showing three pictures. The target picture was highlighted, and the other pictures differed from the target on only one of the relevant dimensions (e.g., long curly hair [target] shown with long *straight* hair and *short* curly hair). For each test trial, a beep sounded simultaneously with the onset of the picture. The patients' responses were digitised and scored for accuracy. For each trial, the time from the beep to the onset of their response and any pauses (including silence, false starts, and fillers such as "uh...") were measured. Any delay over 1 second in length between consecutive words was counted as a pause.

Sentence production task. The procedure was exactly the same as for the phrase production task except that, rather than producing AN or AAN phrases in the test blocks, patients were instructed to produce descriptions of the pictures in the form of a sentence (e.g., "The hair is long" or "The hair is long and curly"). Again the responses were digitised and scored for accuracy, time to onset, and pausing.

Results

Table 2 presents the percentage of trials that were correct on the patient's first response and, in parentheses, the percentage of responses that were correct by the patient's final attempt, for both the phrase and sentence versions of the task. As in the preliminary study, patient EA's performance was substantially better than ML's in the initial correct response data for the phrase constructions (78% vs 50%, $\chi^2 = 6.02$, $p = .01$, when combining across the AN and AAN conditions). She also performed better than GR (78% vs 39%, $\chi^2 = 11.2$, $p = .001$). These results are striking given that EA has a smaller memory span than either ML or GR. All three of the patients showed a drop in performance between the one-adjective and two-adjective phrase conditions, although the drop was larger for ML and GR than for EA, particularly in the last correct data (56% and 44% decline for ML and GR, respectively, and 22% for

TABLE 2

Patient performance on noun phrase and sentence production in Experiment 1

Noun Phrases	*Adj*	*N*	*Adj N*	*AAN*
Controls	94 (97)	100 (100)	90 (95)	70 (81)
Phonological STM EA	83 (100)	94 (100)	89 (100)	67 (78)
Semantic STM ML	94 (100)	100 (100)	78 (100)	22 (44)
GR	67 (89)	94 (100)	50 (83)	28 (39)
Sentences	***Adj***	***N***	***N is A***	***N is A and A***
Controls	99 (99)	99 (99)	98 (98)	76 (84)
Phonological STM EA	100 (100)	100 (100)	83 (83)	89 (89)
Semantic STM ML	83 (83)	94 (100)	89 (100)	28 (34)
GR	78 (94)	94 (100)	83 (83)	44 (61)

Percent correct (numbers in parentheses are percent correct after self-correction).

EA).[1] It should be noted that the control subjects showed a mean decline of 15% across these conditions in all the preliminary study.

The major issue addressed in this experiment was whether the patients with a semantic retention deficit would show an improvement in performance in the sentence constructions compared to the phrase constructions. Table 3 lists the time to response onset, mean number of pauses, and mean pause length for the correct trials. Both ML and GR showed an improvement in performance in the sentence constructions, although ML's improvement was most evident in time to onset, whereas GR's was most evident in percent correct (shown in Table 2). ML's increase in percent correct (11% for the one-adjective and 6% for the two-adjective conditions) was not significant, $\chi^2 = .5$, $p = .48$, when combining his data across the one-adjective and two-adjective conditions. However, the time to onset data did show a significant decrease in the sentence constructions. For the one-adjective condition, he began his correct responses 8 seconds faster in the sentence than the phrase version, $t(28) = 2.73$, $p = .005$, and for the two-adjective condition, he was 12 seconds faster in the sentence version, $t(7) = 2.76$, $p = .01$. ML's long onset latencies were filled with silence, "uh", or isolated phonemes from the beginnings of words (e.g., "s-, s- uh ... straight hair"). Although he was faster to begin his sentence responses, ML produced more pauses within his responses for the sentence than the phrase versions. In the one-adjective condition, he made an average of 0.8 pauses in the sentence vs 0.2 pauses in the phrase versions, $t(28) = 2.9$, $p = .004$. In the two-adjective condition, he made 2.4 pauses in the sentence productions compared to 1.0 pauses in the phrase productions, $t(7) = 3.09$, $p = .009$.

TABLE 3
Patient response onset latencies (in seconds) and pausing in phrase and sentence production tasks in Experiment 1

	Phrases	*Sentences*
One Adjective		
Controls		
Time to onset	1.4	1.0
Mean # pauses	0.2	0.2
Mean pause length	1.1	1.1
Semantic STM Deficit		
ML		
Time to onset	10.0	2.0
Mean # pauses	0.2	0.8
Mean pause length	2.8	2.9
GR		
Time to onset	3.0	2.5
Mean # pauses	0.2	0.9
Mean pause length	3.6	2.2
Phonological STM Deficit		
EA		
Time on onset	1.3	0.8
Mean # pauses	0.0	0.1
Mean pause length	0.0	1.1
Two Adjectives		
Controls		
Time to onset	2.8	1.2
Mean # pauses	1.8	2.8
Mean pause length	1.8	1.5
Semantic STM Deficit		
ML		
Time to onset	14.6	2.6
Mean # pauses	1.0	2.4
Mean pause length	2.4	3.1
GR		
Time to onset	4.2	3.6
Mean # pauses	1.0	2.0
Mean pause length	1.7	2.4
Phonological STM Deficit		
EA		
Time to onset	1.4	1.0
Mean # pauses	0.3	0.6
Mean pause length	1.3	1.3

GR showed a large effect of phrase vs sentence construction on percent correct (improving 33% in the one-adjective condition and 16% in the two-adjective condition). Collapsed across the one- and two-adjective conditions, he was significantly more accurate in the sentence than in the phrase versions of the task, $\chi^2 = 4.5$, $p = .03$. GR showed

[1] ML performed substantially better on the AN phrases and somewhat better on AAN phrases in Experiment 1 than he did in the preliminary study, even though his production of the single adjectives and nouns was slightly better in the preliminary study. In the earlier study, he self-corrected to the appropriate response on 60% of the trials in the AN condition and 30% of the trials in the AAN condition. In Experiment 1, he self-corrected to the correct response on 22% of the trials in both conditions. His accuracy on final responses was similar across the two experiments. A possible explanation of the differing results is that ML delayed his onset of the adjective-noun phrases in Experiment 1 more so than in the preliminary study in order that he could self-correct his utterance internally before beginning speaking. In the preliminary study, he may have begun speaking quickly and then self-corrected overtly to the correct utterance. However, we do not have latency data from the preliminary study to test this hypothesis.

only relatively small effects in response onset. For the one-adjective condition, GR was 0.5 seconds faster in the sentence than the phrase constructions, $t(21) = .83, p = .21$, and for the two-adjective condition, he was 0.6 seconds faster producing the sentence construction, $t(11) = .50$, $p = .31$. Like ML, GR also showed an increase in the mean number of pauses within the response for the sentence compared to the phrase productions, increasing from 0.2 to 0.9 pauses in the one-adjective condition, $t(21) = 2.6, p = .008$ and from 1.0 to 2.0 in the two-adjective condition, $t(11) = 2.06, p = .03$).

EA showed a 6% decline in performance from the phrase to the sentence constructions for the one-adjective condition, but an improvement of 22% for the two-adjective condition. The difference between the phrase and sentence constructions was non-significant for the combined data (78% vs 86% correct, $\chi^2 = .84$, $p = .36$). EA showed a small advantage in onset times in the sentence constructions that was similar to that of GR. However, the differences were highly significant for EA, due to her much lower variance in onset latencies. For the one-adjective condition, she was 0.5 seconds faster for the sentence than the phrase version, $t(20) = 4.9$, $p < .001$. For the two-adjective condition, she was 0.4 seconds faster, $t(26) = 3.9$, $p < .001$. Although both EA and ML showed a significant effect of construction type on onset latency, the effect was clearly much larger for ML. A two (patient) × two (condition) ANOVA on the combined data from the one- and two-adjective conditions confirmed that there was a significant interaction between patient and condition, $F(1,94) = 17.9$, $p < .001$. Furthermore, EA demonstrated many fewer pauses in all construction types, and a smaller increase in number of pauses between the phrase and sentence constructions. For the one-adjective condition, she increased from 0.0 pauses in the phrase constructions to 0.1 pauses in the sentence constructions, $t(29) = 1.03$, $p = .15$. In the two-adjective condition, she increased from 0.3 to 0.6 pauses, $t(26) = 1.46$, $p = .08$, which was only marginally significant.

The types of errors for the patients' final attempts are presented in Table 4. The errors on final responses fell into four types. Most of the errors consisted of producing a grammatically appropriate phrase or sentence, but using one incorrect adjective (e.g., producing "short blonde hair" instead of "short curly hair"). The errors listed under "incorrect adjective" were always correct for describing the picture, but were not the appropriate ones for distinguishing the target picture from the comparison picture(s). On the two-adjective trials (averaging across phrase and sentence constructions), EA produced incorrect adjectives on 17% of the trials, whereas ML did this on 42% and GR on 61% of the trials. Thus, it appears that ML and GR had a great deal of difficulty suppressing the irrelevant information in the pictures for the two-adjective condition, although EA also had some difficulty. "Opposite adjective" refers to producing a phrase with an adjective opposite to the target adjective (e.g., "short hair" for the target "long hair"). "Omit adjective" refers to producing a phrase but leaving out one of the target adjectives (e.g., "blonde hair" for the target "long blonde hair"). GR was the only patient to commit these two error types. Finally, EA used incorrect verb agreement on two sentence trials (e.g., "The curtain are red").

Discussion

We had predicted that ML and GR would be better able to produce the sentence form than the phrases, whereas this manipulation should have little effect for EA. These predictions were borne out for the most part. GR, but not ML or EA, showed significantly greater accuracy in the sentence constructions. ML showed substantially faster onset latencies for correct initial responses in the sentence than in the phrase constructions. Although EA also showed significantly faster onset latencies in the sentence constructions, the effect for ML was about 20 times as large. (ML was 8.0–12.0 seconds faster in the sentence than the phrase condition, whereas EA was 0.4–0.5 seconds faster).[2] This difference between GR and ML, in that GR shows a large benefit of construction type in his accuracy while ML shows most of the benefit in his time to

[2] It is likely that control subjects would also show longer onset latencies for the phrases than the sentences. As discussed in the introduction, Smith and Wheeldon (1999) found that subjects were faster to initiate single-clause sentences beginning with a simple phrase than matched single-clause sentences beginning with a complex phrase. The difference in onset for the different sentence types was on the order of 78 ms and onset latencies were around 1 second for their young normal subjects. Although there are many differences between their experiment and ours, EA's onset latencies and her difference between the sentence and phrase constructions may fall close to the range of older (age-matched) control subjects. ML's mean onset latencies and differences between phrase and sentence latencies are certain to fall far outside this range.

TABLE 4
Percent correct and percent error types in phrase and sentence productions in Experiment 1

			Errors Types in Final Response:			
Error Types	*First Correct*	*Last Correct*	*Incorrect Adjective*	*Opposite Adjective*	*Omit Adjective*	*Verb Agreement*
Controls						
One adjective						
Phrase	90	95	5	0	0	0
Sentence	98	98	2	0	0	0
Two adjectives						
Phrase	70	81	19	0	0	0
Sentence	76	84	16	0	0	0
ML						
One adjective						
Phrase	78	100	0	0	0	0
Sentence	89	100	0	0	0	0
Two adjectives						
Phrase	22	44	56	0	0	0
Sentence	28	34	67	0	0	0
GR						
One adjective						
Phrase	50	83	17	0	0	0
Sentence	83	89	6	6	0	0
Two adjectives						
Phrase	28	39	56	0	6	0
Sentence	44	61	28	11	0	0
EA						
One adjective						
Phrase	89	100	0	0	0	0
Sentence	83	83	6	0	0	11
Two adjectives						
Phrase	67	78	22	0	0	0
Sentence	89	89	11	0	0	0

onset, may reflect different strategies or degrees of deficit for the two patients.

The better performance of EA than ML and GR on these production tasks is consistent with the hypothesis that the semantic-retention capacity that has been affected in ML and GR is involved in planning for speech production, presumably at the lexical-semantic level. Their substantially better performance in the sentence than the phrase construction is consistent with the lexical head principle, that is, the hypothesis that all content words in a phrase up to and including the head of the phrase must be planned at the lexical-semantic level prior to initiating phonological retrieval. ML and GR apparently have great difficulty in maintaining more than one lexical-semantic representation simultaneously. Given that the sentence forms contained only one noun in the initial noun phrase, a simple copula as the verb, and one or two adjectives in the adjective phrases, they were better able to produce these forms. However, while their accuracy or time to onset improved, they showed greater pausing in the sentence forms. This greater pausing suggests that they produced the sentence in a piecemeal fashion, producing one phrase (and one content word) at a time and then moving on to the next.

EA, with a phonological retention deficit, was less affected by the amount of lexical-semantic information to be maintained in a phrase, and showed less pausing and shorter pauses during her sentence productions. These results suggest one of two possibilities with regard to the role of phonological retention capacity. The first is that the phonological capacity that is affected for patient EA is a capacity involved in the retention of input phonological forms. The output phonological capacity that is involved in planning speech production has been unaffected for this patient. The second is that phonological planning does not occur across a very long span in terms of number of words, perhaps covering only one or two words. This minimal storage demand may be within EA's reduced capacity. We favour the former possibility, given other evidence of a separation between input and output capacities (Martin et al., 1999; Romani, 1992). However, the second cannot be ruled out on the basis of the data presented here.

Although the results from Experiment 1 indicated better performance in the sentence constructions for the patients with a semantic retention deficit, their errors included a large proportion of incorrect adjectives in both the phrase and sentence constructions, particularly for the two-adjective condition. Patient EA also showed some errors of this type. This suggests that having the comparison pictures presented alongside the target picture created interference for the patients, particularly for the patients with a semantic retention deficit. If these patients' difficulty in production is specifically with retaining lexical-semantic representations, then they should have difficulty producing the AN phrases even when a single picture is presented. Pictures could be selected with dimensions that are salient enough to evoke a target response without having comparison pictures. Work along these lines is currently in progress.

EXPERIMENT 2: PRODUCTION OF SYNTACTICALLY COMPLEX SENTENCES

Experiment 2 addressed the issue of whether ML's and GR's difficulty with prenominal adjective phrases might be attributed to difficulties with syntactically complex constructions. That is, it might be argued that producing an AAN phrase involves more complex syntactic planning than producing an AN phrase, which in turn involves more complex planning than producing a single noun or adjective. In this experiment, patients were asked to produce grammatically complex sentences in which the amount of semantic information in each phrase was limited. The syntactic constructions that were used were one-clause active and passive sentences (e.g., "The rabbit chased the monkey" or "The monkey was chased by the rabbit") and cleft-subject sentences having either an active or passive form in the relative clause (e.g., "That's the rabbit that chased the monkey" or "That's the monkey that was chased by the rabbit"). The surface structure of the sentences is shown next, according to the government and binding theory of syntactic structure (Chomsky, 1981; Radford, 1988) with traces (e_i) indicated for the cleft sentences:

(1) The rabbit chased the monkey.
$[[[\text{the}]_{det}\ [\text{rabbit}]_{N}]_{NP}\ [[[\text{chased}]_{V}\ [[\text{the}]_{det}\ [\text{monkey}]_{N}\ ]_{NP}\ ]_{VP}\ ]_{I''}]_{S}$

(2) The monkey was chased by the rabbit.
$[[[\text{the}]_{det}\ [\text{monkey}]_{N}]_{NP}\ [[\text{was}]_{I}\ [\text{chased}]_{V}\ [[\text{by}]_{prep}\ [[\text{the}]_{det}\ [\text{rabbit}]_{N}\ ]_{NP}\ ]_{pp}\ ]_{VP}\ ]_{`I'}\ ]_{S}$

(3) That's the rabbit_i that e_i chased the monkey.
$[[[\text{that}]_{N}]_{NP}\ [[[\text{is}]_{V}\ [[[\text{the}]_{det}\ [\text{rabbit}]_{N}]_{NP}\ [[\text{that}]_{comp}\ [[[[\text{chased}]_{V}\ [[\text{the}]_{det}\ [\text{monkey}]_{N}\ ]_{NP'}]_{VP}\ ]_{I'}\ ]_{ip}\ ]_{CP'}]_{NP}\ ]_{VP}\ ]_{IP}\ ]_{S}$

(4) That's the monkey_i that e_i was chased by the rabbit.
$[[[\text{that}]_{N}]_{NP}\ [[[\text{is}]_{V}\ [[[\text{the}]_{det}\ [\text{monkey}]_{N}]_{NP}\ [[\text{that}]_{comp}\ [[[\text{was}]_{comp}\ [[[\text{was}]_{aux}\ [[\text{chased}]_{V}\ [[\text{by}]_{prep}\ [[\text{the}]_{det}\ [\text{rabbit}]_{N}\ ]_{NP}\ ]_{PP}\ ]_{PP}\ ]_{VP}\ ]_{I'}\ ]_{ip}\ ]_{CP'}\ ]_{NP}\ ]_{VP}\ ]_{IP}\ ]_{S}$

All of these sentence types allow for production in a phrase-by-phrase fashion in which each phrase (NP, VP, PP) has at most one content word up to the lexical head (i.e., the noun, the verb, or preposition). Even though the verb phrase in all of these examples contains two content words (e.g., "chased the monkey"), the verb (e.g., "chased") is the head of the phrase. According to the lexical head principle, only the verb and words preceding it in the same phrase have to be represented in a semantic form prior to phonological encoding. As no content words precede the verb in the same phrase, only the verb would have to be planned.

In this experiment, actions carried out with stuffed animals were used rather than pictures in order to elicit the target productions. The experimental procedure was similar to one developed by Hamburger and Crain (1984) to elicit complex constructions from children. We used this procedure because it was easier to portray different verbs (e.g., "chased", "tickled") with this method than with static pictures.

Method

Materials

Eight different stuffed animals were used to act out scenes to be described by the patient.

Design and procedure

Before producing the sentences, subjects were familiarised with the animal names (bear, dog, alligator, fish, monkey, rabbit, frog, and elephant) and the actions (chase, kick, push, and tickle) that would be used. The experimenter first named each animal and demonstrated each action for the patient. Then the patient named each animal and each action three times.

In the first part of the experiment, subjects produced three sets of sentences: blocked active, blocked passive, and mixed active and passive. To ensure that the patients understood the constructions they were supposed to produce, they received seven practice trials with feedback before each blocked set, and eight practice trials before the mixed set. There were 16 test trials in each of the blocked sets, and 24 test trials in the mixed set. The active and passive blocks always preceded the mixed block. The experimenter acted out a brief scene with the animals and then pointed to one of the animals to elicit either an active or a passive sentence. The subject was asked to describe what occurred, beginning the sentence with the animal pointed to by the experimenter.

For the cleft sentences, the same type of scene was acted out, but there were two animals of one kind and one animal of another kind present. One of the animals of the pair acted on or was acted upon by the other animal. The experimenter pointed to that animal, and the patients were instructed to describe what had occurred, beginning each sentence with "That's the..." in order to invoke a relative clause construction. (For example, if there were two frogs and one bear, and one of the frogs kicked the bear, the experimenter would point to that frog, and the target response would be "That's the frog that kicked the bear"). Again, subjects received practice trials with feedback before each block, and the subject relative clause block and the object relative clause block preceded the mixed block. Alternative cleft productions that were appropriate for the picture (e.g., "It was the frog that kicked the bear") were counted as correct.

The entire session was tape-recorded and the patients' responses were digitised. Their responses were scored for accuracy and were timed to measure the number and length of pauses within their responses as in Experiment 1. It was not possible to measure time to onset of their responses because the scenes were acted out and subjects could begin planning and initiating their response during the scene. There was no audible signal to begin timing for each trial.

GR did not complete the mixed cleft sentence condition because he refused to do any more tests with the stuffed animals used to elicit these constructions.[3]

Results

Both the AAN phrases from Experiment 1 and these more grammatically complex sentence constructions in Experiment 2 required production of three content words. Table 5 compares the results for these tasks. The table includes results both for initial correct responses (first correct) and those that the subject produced eventually after making self-corrections (last correct). Both ML and GR performed much better on the syntactically more complex sentences in the active-passive and cleft sentences than they did on the AAN phrases, both for first correct and last correct responses. Comparing their "last correct" scores, ML performed significantly worse on the AAN phrases (44%) than on the mixed one-clause sentences (92%), $\chi^2 = 11.24$, $p < .001$ and the mixed cleft sentences (96%), $\chi^2 = 14.05$, $p < .001$. GR also performed significantly worse on the AAN phrases (39%) than on the mixed one-clause sentences (71%), $\chi^2 = 4.23$, $p = .04$. As noted earlier, he refused to perform the mixed cleft sentence condition. However, it is apparent that he did quite well on the blocked active and passive cleft sentences in comparison to the AAN phrases. Patient EA showed no significant difference in performance between the AAN phrases (78%), the mixed one-clause sentences (92%) and the mixed cleft sentences (79%), $p > .05$ for all comparisons.

Table 6 reports the number of pauses and pause lengths for these sentence types for first correct responses. As in the sentence constructions in Experiment 1, patients ML and GR had more pauses, and their pauses (particularly ML's) were longer than EA's in all conditions. Collapsing across all correct responses in all six sentence conditions, ML made significantly more pauses than EA, $t(166) = 5.54$, $p < .0005$, and his pauses were also significantly longer than hers, $t(141) = 3.22$, $p = .002$. Comparing the five sentence condition blocks that GR completed, GR also made significantly more pauses than EA, $t(131) = 3.86$, $p < .0005$, and his pauses were significantly longer than EA's, $t(100) = 3.26$, $p = .002$.

Although ML's and GR's performance on these sentence constructions was better than their

[3] It is not clear why he refused to complete this condition. Perhaps he found the use of the stuffed animals demeaning.

TABLE 5
Percent correct on tasks requiring production of three content words

	Phrases	*One-clause sentences*			*Cleft sentences*		
	AAN	*Active*	*Passive*	*Mixed*	*Active*	*Passive*	*Mixed*
ML							
First correct	22	75	94	67	88	88	54
Last correct	44	81	100	92	88	100	96
GR							
First correct	28	81	81	58	100	81	—
Last correct	39	87	81	71	100	94	—
EA							
First correct	67	88	94	92	88	81	79
Last correct	78	94	94	92	88	81	79

TABLE 6
Number of pauses and mean pause length (in seconds) for Experiment 2

	Active	*Passive*	*Mixed*	*Subject Relative*	*Object Relative*	*Mixed*
ML						
Mean # pauses	1.1	1.3	1.1	1.3	0.9	1.8
Mean pause length	3.1	3.5	2.5	2.2	2.6	2.3
GR						
Mean # pauses	1.2	0.5	1.4	1.0	1.0	—
Mean pause length	2.1	1.9	2.9	2.4	2.0	—
EA						
Mean # pauses	0.5	1.1	0.4	0.0	0.5	0.5
Mean pause length	1.7	1.6	1.7	0.0	1.3	1.5

performance on the AAN phrases, they both did show some breakdown on the mixed conditions, particularly in terms of first correct responses. Table 7 repeats the first correct and last correct percentages and provides a breakdown of errors for final utterances (i.e., for sentences that were never produced correctly). These errors were categorised into four types. "Wrong verb" refers to trials in which the subject used a different verb from the one acted out in the scene (e.g., "The dog chased the fish" instead of "The dog tickled the fish"). "Verb form" refers to trials in which the patient produced a grammatically incorrect form of the verb (e.g., "The rabbit tickle the dog"). This was the primary error type for ML and GR. "Sentence form" errors were those in which the target was a complex (cleft) sentence form but the patient produced a simple form (e.g., "The dog chased the fish" instead of "That's the dog that chased the fish"). Only EA produced this type of error. Finally, "Active/Passive" errors include those responses in which the patient produced a sentence using the wrong voice.

Although few of ML and GR's errors on final utterances were the wrong voice, they produced many such errors in their initial attempts in the mixed conditions. Interestingly, these initial voice errors were always passive responses to active targets, rather than active responses to passive targets (see Table 8). The inappropriate passive constructions usually occurred after a passive sentence had been elicited in the previous trial. For these incorrect passive responses, the patients (especially ML) sometimes realised the form was incorrect and self-corrected to the correct form. For example, for the target "That's the rabbit that chased the dog", ML responded "It was the uh, rabbit that was chased the dog. It was the rabbit that chased the dog". (As in this example, some of these initial utterances were incomplete passive forms.) Patient EA did not produce a voice error on any of the trials.

TABLE 7
Percent correct and percent error types on final utterances in Experiment 2

			Errors Types in Final Response:			
Error Types	*First Correct*	*Last Correct*	*Wrong Verb*	*Verb Form*	*Sentence Form*	*Active/ Passive*
ML						
Actives (n = 16)	75	81	0	19	0	0
Passives (n = 16)	94	100	0	0	0	0
Mixed (n = 24)	67	92	0	4	0	4
Subject Relative (n = 8)	88	88	0	12	0	0
Object Relative (n = 16)	88	100	0	0	0	0
Mixed (n = 24)	54	96	0	0	0	4
GR						
Actives (n = 16)	81	87	0	13	0	0
Passives (n = 16)	81	81	0	19	0	0
Mixed (n = 24)	58	71	13	8	0	8
Subject Relative (n = 8)	100	100	0	0	0	0
Object Relative (n = 16)	81	94	6	0	0	0
Mixed (n = 24)	—	—	—	—	—	—
EA						
Actives (n = 16)	94	94	0	6	0	0
Passives (n = 16)	94	94	6	0	0	0
Mixed (n = 24)	92	92	8	0	0	0
Subject Relative (n = 8)	88	88	0	0	12	0
Object Relative (n = 16)	81	81	13	0	6	0
Mixed (n = 24)	79	79	4	0	17	0

TABLE 8
Number of active/passive voice errors on initial utterances in Experiment 2

				Passive responses	
	Total # errors	*# Active responses to passive targets*	*# Passive responses to active targets*	*# Preceded by passive targets*	*# Self-corrected*
ML					
Mixed Act/Pass	8	0	3	2	2
Mixed Sub/Obj Rel.	11	0	5	4	4
GR					
Mixed Act/Pass	10	0	4	3	1
EA					
Mixed Act/Pass	2	0	0	0	0
Mixed Sub/Obj Rel.	5	0	0	0	0

Discussion

Both ML and GR showed better performance with the sentences from Experiment 2 than with the phrases from Experiment 1, even though the phrases had the same number of content words and were much simpler grammatically. In contrast, EA did not show an effect of the amount of lexical-semantic content that must be planned. Although she performed much better than ML and GR on the phrase production task, she performed comparably or slightly worse than they did on the sentence productions. As in the sentence conditions in Experiment 1, ML and GR produced more frequent and longer pauses than EA in Experiment 2, in line with the idea that they are unable to plan all of the lexical-semantic representations simultaneously, and thus must pause frequently to plan the subsequent phrase.

Although ML and GR showed a good ability to produce the complex sentences in Experiment 2, their performance did drop from the blocked to the mixed conditions, at least in terms of first correct responses. (Their final responses in the mixed condition were highly accurate.) As discussed in the results section, a large proportion of their initial errors in the mixed condition were the inappropriate production of a passive form for an active target. This finding is surprising given that active forms are much more frequent in naturally occurring speech and one might have predicted the production of actives for passives rather than the reverse. Most of these passive response errors (75%) occurred following the correct production of a passive form on the immediately preceding trial, thus indicating a tendency to perseverate on a passive form. Studies with normal subjects have demonstrated a syntactic priming effect—that is, use of a given syntactic construction in one utterance primes the production of that same syntactic form on the next utterance (Bock, 1986). However, the amount of priming appears to be equivalent for active and passive primes (Bock, 1986; Bock, Loebell, & Morey, 1992). It would seem that it is something about the difficulty of the passive form for these aphasic patients that leads to its persistence. It is unclear, however, why a difficult passive form should show more persistence than an active form, which should be generally more available.

In the introduction we discussed the possibility that the lextical-semantic retention buffer might be equivalent to the syntactic planning frame hypothesised by Dell (1986). The results from Experiment 2 argue against this possibility. That is, in order for patients to produce, for example, the cleft sentences, which contain an embedded clause, we would assume that they must maintain something like the syntactic tree structure in the sentence types shown in examples (3)–(4). Even though we are assuming that syntactic planning is incremental rather than carried out simultaneously for an entire clause, the syntactic choices that are made for each fragment that is planned must be retained in order to ensure that the structure of subsequent fragments can be integrated with the structure of the earlier fragments to construct a syntactically coherent sentence (de Smedt, 1996; Kempen & Hoenkamp, 1987). Thus, there is a need for a capacity for retaining the syntactic structure generated so far so that subsequent fragments may be integrated with this structure. The patients' success at producing the complex structures would suggest that their capacity restrictions are not at the level of maintaining complex syntactic frames. Their difficulty seems instead to be in maintaining the lexical-semantic representations that would be attached to such frames. Thus, these results support the hypothesis that the lexical-semantic retention buffer is separate from the syntactic planning frame, and serves to hold simultaneously several representations that will be attached to the syntactic frame.

GENERAL DISCUSSION

As discussed in the introduction, patients with a semantic retention deficit have difficulties comprehending sentences containing noun phrases with several adjectives preceding a noun, but do better when the adjectives follow the noun (Martin, 1995; Martin & Romani, 1994). In Experiment 1, patients with a semantic retention deficit had difficulty with the same prenominal adjective constructions in speech production. Although they could name single nouns and adjectives accurately, their performance declined substantially when they had to produce AN or AAN phrases. However, their performance improved in Experiment 1 when they could produce the nouns and adjectives in a sentence form with the adjectives following the noun. We have argued that the sentence form placed fewer demands on semantic retention because of the lexical head principle—that is, the number of content words up to and including the head of the phrase was smaller in the sentence condition. Experiment 2 demonstrated that these patients' difficulty with the prenominal adjective phrases could not be attributed to syntactic complexity of the phrases, as they were better able to produce syntactically complex sentences including sentences with a passive form in a relative clause than they could prenominal adjective phrases with an equal number of content words. The findings from both experiments support the contention that the same lexical-semantic retention capacity is involved in comprehension and production.

To provide a comparison with the patients with a semantic retention deficit, patient EA, with a phonological retention deficit, was also included in these experiments. Despite her smaller memory span, she performed better than the patients with a semantic retention dificit did on the AN phrases. She showed no significant improvement in the sentence forms in terms of accuracy, and showed a decrease in onset latencies that was much smaller than that observed for one of the semantic retention deficit patients (ML). Also, her performance in Experiment 2 did not show the significant improvement between the AAN phrase and the complex syntactic constructions that was demonstrated by the other patients. Thus, the contrast between EA and the other two patients supports the separation between semantic and phonological retention capacities, and indicates that the semantic retention capacity is crucial to planning phrases with several content words preceding the head of the phrase. The results also suggest that the input phonological capacity that is disrupted for patient EA is not crucial for speech output.

These data support a model of production in which semantic and syntactic planning proceed in a phrase-by-phrase fashion with phonological production awaiting retrieval of the semantic representation of the head of a phrase. The consequences of a deficit in semantic retention capacity can be minimal for utterances that can be produced in a series of phrases with each containing only one content word. However, the increased number and length of pauses by the patients with semantic retention deficits demonstrates that the timing of production of such utterances is abnormal. This increased pausing occurred primarily in the sentence constructions in both Experiments 1 and 2, in which the subjects could produce their responses in a phrase-by-phrase fashion. These findings suggest that while the phrase is a minimal planning unit, normal subjects may typically be planning more than an individual phrase at a lexical-semantic level in order that production may proceed in a smooth fashion.

At a more general level, the results presented here are consistent with the multiple components view of verbal working memory that we have advocated in the past (Martin et al., 1999; Martin & Romani, 1994; Romani & Martin, 1999). That is, these results support the distinction between separable capacities for semantic and phonological retention, and within phonological retention, separate capacities for input and output phonological forms. Overall, our view is that the phonological and semantic capacities uncovered in verbal span tasks are closely linked to the representations and processes involved in the perception and production of language, and exist in order to support these processes.

REFERENCES

Allport, D.A. (1984). Auditory verbal short-term memory and conduction aphasia. In H. Bouma & D.G. Bouwhuis (Eds.), *Attention and performance X: Control and language processes* (pp.351–364). Hove, UK: Lawrence Erlbaum Associates Ltd.

Baddeley, A. (1986). *Working memory*. Oxford: Clarendon Press/Oxford University Press.

Barnard, P. (1985). Interacting cognitive subsystems: A psycholinguistic approach to short-term memory. In A. Ellis (Ed.), *Progress in the psychology of language* (pp.197–258). Hove, UK: Lawrence Erlbaum Associates Ltd.

Bock, K. (1986). Syntactic persistence in language production. *Cognitive Psychology*, *18*, 355–387.

Bock, K., & Levelt, W. (1994) Language production: Grammatical encoding. In M.A. Gernsbacher (Ed.), *Handbook of psycholinguistics* (pp.945–984). San Diego, CA: Academic Press.

Bock, K., Loebell, H., & Morey, R. (1992). From conceptual roles to structural relations: Bridging the syntactic cleft. *Psychological Review*, *99*, 150–170.

Bourassa, D.C., & Besner, D. (1994). Beyond the articulatory loop: A semantic contribution to serial order recall of subspan lists. *Psychonomic Bulletin and Review*, *1*, 122–125.

Branigan, H., Pickering, M., Liversedge, S., Stewart, A., & Urbach, T. (1995). Syntactic priming: Investigating the mental representation of language. *Journal of Psycholinguistic Research*, *24*, 489–506.

Chomsky, N. (1981). *Lectures on government and binding*. Dordrecht: Foris.

Cohen, J.D., MacWhinney, B., Flatt, M., & Provost, J. (1993). PsyScope: A new graphic interactive environment for designing psychology experiments. *Behavioral Research Methods, Instruments and Computers*, *25*(2), 257–271.

Crowder, R.G. (1978). Memory for phonologically uniform lists. *Journal of Verbal Learning and Verbal Behavior*, *17*(1), 73–89.

Dell, G.S. (1986). A spreading-activation theory of retrieval in sentence production. *Psychological Review*, *93*(3), 283–321.

Dell, G.S., & O'Seaghdha, P.G. (1992). Stages of lexical access in language production. *Cognition*, *42*, 287–314.

Dell, G.S., Shwartz, M.F., Martin, N., Saffran, E.M., & Gagnon, D.A. (1997). Lexical access in aphasic and nonaphasic speakers. *Psychological Review*, *104*(4), 801–838.

de Smedt, K. (1996). Computational models of incremental grammatical encoding. In T. Dijkstra & K. de Smedt (Eds.), *Computational psycholinguistics: AI and connectionist models of human language processing* (pp.279–307). London: Taylor & Francis.

Freedman, M., & Martin, R.C. (2001). Dissociable components of short-term memory and their relation to long-term learning. *Cognitive Neuropsychology*, *18*, 193–226.

Garrett, M. (1980). Levels of processing in sentence production. In B. Butterworth (Ed.), *Language production, Vol. 1: Speech & talk* (pp.177–220). London: Academic Press.

Hamburger, H., & Crain, S. (1984). Acquisition of cognitive compiling. *Cognition, 17*(2), 85–136.

Hanten, G., & Martin, R.C. (2000). Contributions of phonological and semantic short-term memory to sentence processing: Evidence from two cases of closed head injury in children. *Journal of Memory and Language, 43*, 335–361.

Hulme, C., Maughan, S., & Brown, G. (1991). Memory for familiar and unfamiliar words: Evidence for a long-term memory contribution to short-term span. *Journal of Memory and Language, 30*, 685–701.

Kempen, G., & Hoenkamp, E. (1987). An incremental procedural grammar for sentence formulation. *Cognitive Science, 11*, 201–258.

Kempen, G., & Huijbers, P. (1983). The lexicalization process in sentence production and naming: Indirect election of words. *Cognition, 14*, 185–209.

Knott, R., Patterson, K., & Hodges, J. (1997). Lexical and semantic binding effects in short-term memory: Evidence from semantic dementia. *Cognitive Neuropsychology, 14*, 1165–1216.

LaPointe, S.G., & Dell, G. (1989). A synthesis of some recent work in sentence production. In G.N. Carlson & M.K. Tanenhaus (Eds.), *Linguistic structure in language processing* (pp.107–156). Boston, MA: Kluwer Academic Publishers.

Levelt, W., Roelofs, A., & Meyer, A. (1999). A theory of lexical access in speech production. *Behavioral & Brain Sciences, 22*, 1–75.

Martin, N., & Saffran, E.M. (1992). A computational account of deep dyslexia: Evidence from a single case study. *Brain and Language, 43*, 240–274.

Martin, N., & Saffran, E.M. (1997). Language and auditory-verbal short-term memory impairments: Evidence for common underlying processes. *Cognitive Neuropsychology, 14*(5), 641–682.

Martin, R. (1995). *A multiple capacities view of working memory in language*. Symposium presentation, Psychonomic Society meeting, Los Angeles.

Martin, R., & Freedman, M. (2001). Verbal working memory: The ins and outs of phonological and lexical-semantic retention. In H.L. Roediger, J.S. Nairne, I. Neath, & A.M. Suprenant (Eds.), *The nature of remembering: Essays in honor of Robert G. Crowder* (pp.331–349). Washington, DC: American Psychological Association Press.

Martin, R.C., & Feher, E. (1990). The consequences of reduced memory span for the comprehension of semantic versus syntactic information. *Brain and Language, 38*, 1–20.

Martin, R.C., & Lesch, M.F. (1996). Associations and dissociations between language impairment and list recall: Implications for models of STM. In S.E. Gathercole (Ed.), *Models of short-term memory* (pp.149–178). Hove, UK: Psychology Press.

Martin, R.C., Lesch, M.F., & Bartha, M.C. (1999). Independence of input and output phonology in word processing and short-term memory. *Journal of Memory and Language, 40*, 1–27.

Martin, R.C., & Romani, C. (1994). Verbal working memory and sentence comprehension: A multiple-components view. *Neuropsychology, 8*(4), 506–523.

Martin, R.C., & Romani, C. (1995). Remembering stories but not words. In R. Campbell & M. Conway (Eds.), *Broken memories* (pp.267–284). Cambridge, UK: Blackwell.

Martin, R.C., Shelton, J., & Yaffee, L.S. (1994). Language processing and working memory: Neuropsychological evidence for separate phonological and semantic capacities. *Journal of Memory and Language, 33*, 83–111.

Meyer, A.S. (1996). Lexical access in phrase and sentence production: Results from picture–word interference experiments. *Journal of Memory and Language, 35*, 477–496.

Patterson, K., Graham, N., & Hodges, J.R. (1994). The impact of semantic memory loss on phonological representations. *Journal of Cognitive Neuroscience, 6*, 57–69.

Poirier, M., & St. Aubin, J. (1995). Memory for related and unrelated words: Further evidence on the influence of semantic factors in immediate serial recall. *Quarterly Journal of Experimental Psychology, 48*(A), 384–404.

Radford, A. (1988). *Transformational grammar: A first course*. New York: Cambridge University Press.

Romani, C. (1992). Are there distinct input and output buffers? Evidence from an aphasic patient with an impaired output buffer. *Language & Cognitive Processes, 7*(2), 131–162.

Romani, C., & Martin, R. (1999). A deficit in the short-term retention of lexical-semantic information: Forgetting words but remembering a story. *Journal of Experimental Psychology: General, 128*(1), 56–77.

Saffran, E.M., & Martin, N. (1990). Neuropsychological evidence for lexical involvement in short-term memory. In G. Vallar & T. Shallice (Eds.), *Neuropsychological impairments of short-term memory* (pp.428–447). London: Cambridge University Press.

Saffran, E.M., Schwartz, M.F., Linebarger, M., & Bochetto, P. (1989). *The Philadelphia Comprehension Battery* [unpublished].

Schriefers, H. (1993). Syntactic processes in the production of noun phrases. *Journal of Experimental Psychology: Learning, Memory and Cognition, 19*, 841–850.

Schweickert, R. (1993). Degradation and redintegration in immediate recall: A multinomial processing tree model. *Memory and Cognition, 21*, 168–175.

Schweickert, R., Guentert, L., & Hersberger, L. (1990). Phonological similarity, pronunciation rate, and memory span. *Psychological Science, 1*(1), 74–77.

Shallice, T., & Butterworth, B. (1977). Short-term memory impairment and spontaneous speech. *Neuropsychologia, 15*, 729–735.

Shallice, T., Rumiati, R.I., & Zadini, A. (2000). The selective impairment of the phonological output buffer. *Cognitive Neuropsychology, 17*, 517–546.

Smith, M., & Wheeldon, L. (1999). High level processing scope in spoken sentence production. *Cognition, 73*, 205–246.

MEMORY, 2001, *9* (4/5/6), 281–299

A re-evaluation of the phonological similarity effect in adults' short-term memory of words and nonwords

Arild Lian, Paul J. Karlsen, and Bendik Winsvold
University of Oslo, Norway

The phonological similarity effect (PSE) was studied in two tasks of serial recall, in one task of serial recognition and one item identification task. PSE occurred only in the former three tasks involving memory of order when study items were words and nonwords with an associative connectedness to long-term memory. Nonwords that, according to a reaction time assessment of associative value, were less well connected to long-term memory mechanisms, were not sensitive to phonological similarity. These results are discussed in relation to contemporary models of short-term memory that explain the PSE as a result of confusions of items that are similarly encoded in a phonological layer. This layer is identified as a higher-level phonological space that is accessed by words and nonwords of high associative value and not by nonwords of low associative value.

In immediate serial recall tasks, lists of verbal items that are phonologically similar are typically recalled less well than lists of phonologically distinct items. This means that the list *mad, cap, cat* is usually more difficult to remember than the list *cow, bar, pen*. This has been called the phonological similarity effect (PSE). It was first reported by Conrad and Hull (1964) and has since been extensively explored in the literature of verbal short-term memory (Baddeley, 1966; Conrad, 1964; Estes, 1973; Longoni, Richardson, & Aiello, 1993; Murray, 1968; Salame & Baddeley, 1986; Wickelgren, 1965). Nairne (1990) brands PSE as a benchmark fact of that literature; Gathercole (1997) identifies it as one of five key empirical findings that any plausible model of short-term memory must explain; Page and Norris (1998) state the explanation of PSE as an essential test of such models.

The initial problem of our study applies to the generality of PSE. In most earlier works on short-term memory, items to be remembered were familiar words, digits, or single letters. For literate adults these materials generally form well-known sound patterns with specific representations at lexical and semantic levels in long-term memory. How is the memory of unfamiliar speech sound patterns affected by manipulation of the phonological similarity of the material to be remembered? In the present work we raise the problem of whether PSE applies to both words and nonwords with differing associative values. This is a new concept based on an independent and open-ended reaction time test introduced in our study. This initial test makes it possible to distinguish between the associative values of individual words and nonwords by measuring how fast subjects come up with associations to each of these utterances. The pretest makes up an effective tool in defining our stimulus material and is thoroughly discussed later.

The PSE was studied in two tasks of serial recall, in one task of serial recognition, and one item identification task. Brown (1997) distinguishes between the memory for individual items and the memory for serial order of these items. He

Requests for reprints should be sent to Arild Lian, Institute of Psychology, Box 1094, Blindern, N-0317 Oslo, Norway. Email: arild.lian@psykologi.uio.no

The authors gratefully acknowledge the assistance of Marte Mengshoel Linnae and Per Magne Nilsen for running the experiments and for examining the speech sound files. This work was supported in part by a grant from the Norwegian Research Council to the first author.

http://www.tandf.co.uk/journals/pp/09658211.html DOI:10.1080/09658210143000074

claims that any recall task makes demands on both sorts of memory. Some studies indicate that PSE is mainly associated with confusion of serial order, or transpositions among the phonologically similar items in the list (Conrad, 1965; Drewnowski, 1980; Ellis, 1980; Healy, 1974; Murdock & vom Saal, 1967; Wickelgren, 1965). Item errors—like omissions, repetitions, missed repetitions, and intrusions—do not increase to the same extent. How is the memory of unfamiliar speech sounds affected in tasks that focus especially on memory of order and memory of items respectively, compared to the memory of words and familiar speech sounds in the same tasks? We look into that in the serial recognition task and the item identification task in Experiment 2.

The classical explanation of PSE involves an interference interpretation and has been adopted by all models that explicitly deal with PSE. At what specific level or layer of representation do the assumed interferences or confusions between phonologically similar items occur? If PSE is grounded on a confusion of phonologically similar items causing transition errors during serial recall, it might be claimed that it should apply equally well to words and nonwords, regardless of their associative value, as the phonological level of representation may be assumed to be the same for any verbal material auditorily encoded. Based on the interference interpretation, it might even be claimed that PSE should be stronger for nonwords than for words. As unfamiliar nonwords may depend to a lesser extent than words on semantic or lexical long-term representations, it is reasonable to think that the encoding of unfamiliar nonwords is more dependent on acoustic or phonological features than the encoding of familiar words. The fact that the activation of these features may also be less stable for nonwords than for words, should make them especially vulnerable to random decay and following confusion.

Any robust differences in the way familiar and unfamiliar speech sound patterns are affected by phonological similarity, then, may give us valuable information about how verbal material is dealt with in short-term memory. Some phonological representation level is assumed to be active for any verbal material, independent of the semantic meaningfulness, or association value, of the material to be remembered. PSE may be assumed to be a result of confusion of items at that level. As a result of our study, however, it seems necessary to distinguish between different levels or layers of phonological representation. The classical PSE seems to be a result of confusion in a late, lexical layer that is highly activated or accessed by the more familiar speech sounds. Confusions at this level may involve clusters of phonological segments already represented in long-term memory and that are associated with meaningful material.

MODELS AND BACKGROUND DATA

How has PSE been dealt with so far in the literature? In her 1997 article, Gathercole surveys four major contemporary models of short-term memory and finds that none of them sufficiently explains PSE. The models are the phonological loop (Baddeley, 1986), the network model of the phonological loop (Burgess & Hitch, 1992), the trace decay model (Brown & Hulme, 1995), and the interactive model (Gathercole & Martin, 1996). The former two seem to be the only ones to have addressed the problem directly. As Brown and Hulme acknowledge, their 1995 model is unable to accommodate the PSE, as it does not "represent" the phonological structure of a memory item in any way other than the amount of time it occupies, and as the interactive model is not explicit on the issue of how the serial order of activated phonological elements is represented, it too provides no explanation for the disruptive effects of phonological similarity between memory items.

Baddeley's phonological loop comprises two components, the phonological short-term store and the subvocal rehearsal process. The phonological store represents the material in a phonological code that decays with time. A process of articulatory-like rehearsal serves to refresh the decaying representations in the phonological store and so to maintain the memory items. According to the phonological loop model, the source of PSE in immediate serial recall is the phonological store. It is argued that memory items that share a similar phonological structure will become more rapidly indiscriminable from one another due to decay than items with non-overlapping phonological structures (Baddeley, 1986). In the network model of the phonological loop, the similarity effect is due to the operation of the feedback weights running from the output phoneme layer to the input phoneme layer, as these weights implement the phonological store in the model (Burgess & Hitch, 1992, 1999).

As information in the phonological store

decays, it needs to be reconstructed through rehearsal. The reconstruction is assumed to depend on some other information that has not been subject to the same speed of decay. This information is presumably lexical long-term memory representations that were somewhat activated by the original presentation of the memory list.

According to some researchers, a controlled rehearsal process is not necessary for the reconstruction of decayed information. Instead, a redintegration process has been postulated, akin to pattern completion in speech perception (Brown & Hulme, 1995; Schweickert, 1993). This process was said to depend on lexical long-term representations in the phonological form of words, a representation that is supposed to be generally lacking for nonwords (Hulme, Newton, Cowan, Stuart, & Brown, 1999). This redintegration process, then, accounts for the lexicality and the word familiarity effect. As some nonwords may activate long-term representations, the redintegration process may also account for the wordlikeness effect. If phonological information in short-term memory generally decays with the same speed, and the phonological redintegration process is not activated, there should be no PSE, and very low recall span.

Another model of interest here is Nairne's (1990) feature model of immediate memory. This model involves another disadvantage interpretation of phonologically similar items, in the sense that long-term representations of items that share one or more vowels are assumed to contain many overlapping features. If features or lower-level segments of an item in short-term memory have been overwritten or forgotten, a matching process similar to redintegration occurs. Again, an item is likely to be confused with other items in a list if they have confusable long-term representations. If there were hardly any long-term lexical representations activated by certain lists of nonwords, there should be a clear lexicality effect when compared to words, and there should be nothing to confuse; that is, no PSE for nonwords compared to words, or an interaction effect between lexicality and phonological similarity.

Schweickert (1993) postulates two parallel redintegration processes: one that attempts to form a word, and another that attempts to form a phoneme string. According to Schweickert, the two processes are autonomous and can be selectively influenced by lexicality and phonological similarity. Schweickert predicts that there should be no interaction between phonological similarity and lexicality: he sees that as a necessary implication of the two mechanisms being autonomous. An experiment by Besner and Davelaar (1982) is taken to be in agreement with this prediction. In our view, however, it is not necessary to postulate two parallel redintegration processes to account for the PSE, the lexicality effect, and the lack of an interaction between the two found in Besner and Davelaar's experiment.

Besner and Davelaar (1982) demonstrated that the phonemically similar lists were less accurately recalled than lists of phonemically distinct items, irrespective of the wordlikeness of the visually presented materials. This finding disagreed with the results of a pilot experiment with 18 subjects run in our laboratory. The pilot experiment involved a serial recall task almost identical to that reported in our Experiments 1A and 1B, except that the earlier stimulus material was not assessed for associative values. We found, in agreement with both Besner and Davelaar (1982) and Hulme et al. (1999), that memory span is substantially longer for words than nonwords. However, our results also showed a significant interaction effect between lexicality and phonological similarity, indicating in our case that the phonological similarity factor affected words but not nonwords. The reason why the results of our pilot experiment differed from those of Besner and Davelaar's (1982) experiment may be that we made use of auditory representation. That would indicate a modality effect. Also, the vowels in Besner and Davelaar's items seem to be of longer duration than ours, indicating a possible vowel duration effect. The difference observed between the two experiments could also be the result of Besner and Davelaar's less wordlike nonwords being insufficiently unwordlike.

Hulme (1984) and Hulme and Tordoff (1989) found an interesting interaction between the size of PSE and age for immediate serial recall of words. The growth of memory span with age was attributed to the increasing number of distinct words being recalled; the number of similar words recalled showed very little growth with age. When speech rate was controlled for, the effect of age was no longer significant. A new interpretation of this result in line with our study would be that the increase in speech rate and PSE are both associated with growth of vocabulary and the development of the lexical phonological layer.

More recently, Gathercole, Pickering, Hall, and Peaker (2001) have compared degrees of sensitivity to phonological similarity for words and nonwords in two experiments on serial recall and two experiments on serial recognition. All items were one-syllable consonant-vowel-consonants (CVCs) drawn from a pool of 150 words and 150 nonwords. The phonologically similar lists were made up of items that had different consonants but shared a vowel, and in the phonologically distinct list all vowels were different. These nonwords seem rather similar to the ones used in our experiments. Another point of convergence was the use of auditory presentation.

The two serial recall experiments (Experiment 3A with children and Experiment 4A with adult subjects) demonstrated a significant interaction effect between lexicality (words vs nonwords) and phonological similarity (phonologically similar vs distinct lists) showing that the sensitivity to phonological similarity is higher for words than for nonwords. Also, in the serial recognition experiments the difference in scores between similar and distinct lists was greater for words than nonwords, but the interaction between the two factors was not significant. Gathercole et al.'s (2001) data, then, indicate that PSE is higher for words than nonwords in serial recall but not in serial recognition tasks.

Nonwords that are wordlike and more likely to activate lexical long-term memory representations may be more sensitive to phonological similarity compared to nonwords that are less wordlike and more or less meaningless items for the participating subjects. It may be that these types of nonwords activate lexical layers to a greater extent than unwordlike nonwords, but also that they do not activate semantic layers to the same extent as words. Wordlike nonwords, then, may be especially vulnerable to phonological similarity. Therefore, Gathercole et al.'s (2001) demonstration of a significant interaction effect between lexicality and phonological similarity in two out of four experiments may depend on the selection of nonword items for the four experiments. In the present work we shall re-examine this issue by studying PSE for both words and nonwords in serial recall and serial recognition tasks while taking into consideration the associative values among the items.

THE PRETEST

The aim of the pretest is to separate items that have the lexical status of nonwords but are wordlike and likely to produce some long-term association when spoken to language-competent adult listeners, and nonword items that are less likely to call forth any long-term association by adults. To categorise items in respect to meaningfulness or associative value, a rating task could be used, in which case judgements of, say, wordlikeness are done without any time constraint. However, the encoding of items in serial recall and serial recognition experiments will take place under some time constraint. Items in the list cannot be studied for an unlimited time. They are presented successively at a certain time rate, with a short pause between each item, giving little time for associative processes and rehearsal. Also, they are usually presented only once. During the recall stage there may be less time constraints as subjects are usually told that they may recall items at their own pace. Before that stage, however, forgetting may already have occurred. Hence we prefer to assess the degree of associative value of items by way of a reaction time task. This involves the use of an independent pretest that to our knowledge has not formerly been used to assess verbal material in short-term memory tasks. We think, however, that this associative pretest may be a more sensitive measure of the status of items than subjective rating of familiarity and worldlikeness, and objective frequency rating based on the counting of occurrences in text sources, like newspapers. Subjects participating in this pretest will be instructed to express verbally as fast as possible an association to the presented item, and to press a key simultaneously with the verbal response. An itemwise tabulation of mean reaction times makes possible the selection of a group of items that are less likely to produce meaningful associations under time constraints, and a group of items that under similar conditions are more likely to be meaningfully encoded. The response latencies will not distinguish types or breadths of associations, but probabilities with which items will under time constraints activate some long-term memory representation. In this way we come up with items of low and high associative value, respectively.

More details about the selection of study items will be presented in the introductory section of Experiments 1A and 1B. Both experiments deal with serial recall of words and nonwords of high and low association value. However, Experiment 1B is a replication of 1A with a new set of stimuli that are generated according to the same procedure used in Experiment 1A. Experiment 2 deals with serial recognition of words and nonwords, and a new task designed to study the recognition of items independent of order. The two tasks, serial recognition and item identification, make equal demands on the response system.

EXPERIMENT 1A

Gathercole (1995) showed that repetition accuracy in nonword repetition tests depended on the rated wordlikeness of the nonwords. A phonological sound pattern constitutes a nonword in the sense that there is no lexical entry or *lexeme* (Lyons, 1981) corresponding to the item. Some nonwords may activate long-term representations in the capacity of their wordlikeness, but generally great variation prevails among nonwords as to their associative connectedness to long-term semantic knowledge. Also, words may differ with respect to the probability or speed of activation of some long-term memory representation. In the following we shall refer to this property as associative value of study items.

The main objective of this experiment is to study immediate serial recall of words and nonwords as a function of the associative value of the study items. Second, we also want to study serial recall of words and nonwords for two rates of presentation. In the fast condition items will be presented with a shorter inter-item interval than in the slow condition. Baddeley and Lewis (1984), who demonstrated a relative independence of span and presentation rate, argued that trace decay in the slow presentation condition is generally compensated for by a rehearsal process between presented items. They also argued, however, that meaningful materials will benefit more from a slow presentation rate, as more time permits an activation of supporting associations. Brown and Hulme's (1995) multicomponent model, which predicts item length effects without a rehearsal mechanism, argues for a trace decay system that is relatively insensitive to presentation rate for both words and nonwords.

At first, however, we shall present a pretest that was run to assess the associative value of candidate words and nonwords and to select the pool of items to be used in the present experiment. The aim of this study is to create eight categories of lists corresponding to the factorial combinations of Lexicality (2) by Associative value (2) by Phonological similarity (2). The levels of the former two factors will include different items, but we intend to make use of the same items to form phonologically similar and distinct lists. However, a full overlap of items in these categories cannot be warranted, as the distinct group will include more vowels than those selected for the similar group (e.g. *a* and *e*). The categories of lists will be created in such a way that the number of repetitions in each condition will be the same across subjects. As memory span has been shown to be greater for words than nonwords, more words than nonwords will be needed.

Reaction time assessment of the associative value of study items

The word and nonword stimuli were selected from a pool of 112 one-syllable words and 79 one-syllable nonwords. The words were high-frequency words in the Norwegian language characterised by an approximately equal length of pronunciation. They all included one vowel between a consonant or consonant cluster in the beginning and the end of the word (i.e. *Blest, Rull*). The words were divided into two groups. In the first group of 56 words the eight vowels in the Norwegian alphabet (excluding *æ*) were about equally represented. Hence, these words formed a group of phonologically distinct items. In the second group 28 words included the vowel *a*, and 28 included the vowel *e*., and thus each of these halves formed a group of phonologically similar items. The nonwords constituted only consonant-vowel-consonant (CVC) combinations, and they were always pronounced with a short vowel; 39 of them included all vowels used in the words about equally often. This half formed the group of phonologically distinct items. As to the rest of the nonwords, 20 included the vowel *a* and 20 the vowel *e*, i.e., two groups of phonologically similar nonwords.

Every word and nonword item was read aloud in a female voice to a computer that recorded and digitised the items. All items in a randomised and intermixed list of words and nonwords were played back to a subject, who was told to press the space bar on a computer once he/she could come up with an associated word or statement to the item presented, or a word that he/she thought the item sounded like. Simultaneously with the key press, the subject was required to say aloud his/her associated word/statement. It was emphasised that a mere sound-pattern reproduction of the auditory stimulus would not be accepted. Otherwise, a liberal practice with respect to the acceptance of associative responses was followed. Key press reaction times (RT) were recorded as indices of associative value of the presented items. A total of 24 undergraduate students served as subjects in the pretest.

In an itemwise tabulation of the data, the mean and standard deviation of RTs to phonologically distinct words were 2179 ms and 388 ms respectively, and for the phonologically similar words the mean and standard deviation were, with the *a* vowel, 2321 ms and 371 ms, and with the *e* vowel, 2204 ms and 377 ms, respectively. The means of the three word groups did not differ significantly from each other. The mean and standard deviation of RTs for distinct nonwords were 2846 ms and 421 ms, while mean and standard deviation for phonologically similar nonwords with the *a* vowel were 2625 ms and 264 ms, and with the *e* vowel, 2796 ms and 472 ms, respectively. The means of the three groups of nonwords did not differ significantly from each other, whereas the mean (2216 ms) of all three groups of words differed significantly from the mean (2778 ms) of all three groups of nonwords ($t = 9.70$, $df = 189$, $p < .001$).

In the itemwise tabulation of RTs we defined the mean RT as an inverse measure of Associative value, i.e., items with low mean RTs were considered high on associative value and vice versa for items with high mean RTs. The mean/SD ratio was taken as a measure of agreement across subjects on the item. The median RT in each of the word and nonword groups was used to distinguish items of low and high associative value in the group, and thus we created eight groups of items altogether. From each of the eight item groups we selected a few items to be used in the memory span experiment. We took care to include items of high agreement ratios and to keep overlapping RTs between groups of different associative value at a minimum. In this way we decided to use 12 items in the low associative value group and 12 items in the high associative value group for the phonologically distinct words. Likewise, from the phonologically similar words we selected 8 items with the *a* vowel and 8 items with the *e* vowel in each of the low and high associative groups. (The similar group was made larger due to the representation of two vowels.) The number of items selected for the phonologically similar nonwords was 12 (6 with an *a* vowel and 6 with an *e* vowel) in each of the two meaningfulness groups, and for each of the two groups of phonologically distinct nonwords we selected 10 items. (We selected more word than nonword items because word spans are expected to be higher than nonword spans.)

Distinct and similar word items within each of the low and high associative value groups did not differ significantly from each other with respect to mean RT, nor did distinct and similar nonword items. Thus, for instance, for words of low associative value, the three categories (similar with *a* vowel, similar with *e* vowel and distinct) did not differ significantly from each other. However, items in low associative value groups always differed significantly from the corresponding word or nonword items in the high associative value groups.

Table 1 shows the statistical descriptives of the RT data and mean presentation time of the eight groups of items used in the experiment. The phonologically similar words and phonologically similar nonwords each contained one half of *a*-vowel items and one half of *e*-vowel items. As pointed out, the difference in the set size for words

TABLE 1
Statistical descriptives of words and nonwords used in Experiment 1A

	Words				*Nonwords*			
	Similar		*Distinct*		*Similar*		*Distinct*	
	Low	*High*	*Low*	*High*	*Low*	*High*	*Low*	*High*
Number	16	16	12	12	12	12	10	10
Mean	2372	1902	2394	1782	3493	2625	3436	2607
Agreement	2.47	3.08	2.65	3.58	1.70	2.16	1.68	2.19
Minimum	2143	1587	2147	1587	2759	2439	3014	2374
Maximum	2601	2245	2680	1971	5277	2874	3900	2897
Pres. time	859	799	855	788	707	732	727	678

Mean, minimum, and maximum refer to reaction time in milliseconds. Pres. time = presentation time in milliseconds. Similar, distinct = phonological similarity. High, low = associative value.

and nonwords is due to an expected difference of span between the two groups' items.

To summarise, the complete set of items selected for the present experiment can be categorised as words and nonwords that give rise to the factor of Lexicality with two levels. However, Lexicality is not fully independent from the factor of Associative value. The selected words have all higher RTs compared to nonwords. On the other hand, words and nonwords may differ in a way that is not revealed by the present RT data, and this possibility warrants the use of Associative value and Lexicality as separate factors, each with two levels. Although the two may be reduced to one factor of Meaningfulness with four levels, data analysis will primarily be undertaken to test the effect of both factors separately. As previously mentioned, we shall use the term Associative value for Meaningfulness, which we think will be more consistent with the present operationalisation of the term.

Method

Subjects. A total of 32 undergraduate students, 26 females and 14 males, from the University of Oslo served as paid subjects in the experiment. All were native speakers of Norwegian in the age range 20–30 years. The subjects signed an informed consent.

Design. The experiment was run according to a repeated measures design with the factors of Presentation rate (2) × Lexicality (2) × Phonological similarity (2) × Associative value (2).

Materials and procedure. The word and nonword groups shown in Table 1 were used to construct lists for the serial recall tasks. In the phonologically similar conditions we alternated between lists sharing the *a* vowel and lists sharing the *e* vowel, and due to the representation of two vowels these categories have two more items compared to the distinct categories in Table 1. However, phonologically distinct lists were created by using some items from the similar group within the same level of Lexicality and Associative value, i.e., a procedure that eliminated differences of set size between groups of phonologically similar and distinct categories, and which warranted a partial overlap of items in the two conditions. Before testing, subjects were asked to listen to all words and nonwords to be used in the experiment. They were told to repeat each of the words and each of the nonwords to check their audibility, and to ascertain the subject's ability to articulate each item correctly. All subjects who signed up for the experiment and who took part in the test for audibility of items fulfilled all serial recall tasks.

Word and nonword lists of varying lengths were generated randomly without replacement from each of the eight pools of items (Table 1). For each of the word conditions there were generated four lists of three items, and six lists of each of the succeeding list lengths, to a maximum list length of eight words. Correspondingly, for nonwords four lists of two items, and six lists of each of the list lengths from three to six items were generated. For practical reasons, no lists of the same length within the same category started with identical items.

In the experiment the presentation of lists was blocked with respect to the eight groups. However, the presentation of phonologically similar lists was made possible by randomly alternating between *a* vowel and *e* vowel lists. Span measurements started by presenting subjects with two lists, randomly selected from the set of four, at the lowest sequence length, and with four lists, randomly selected at each of the other list lengths. Testing was discontinued when subjects made errors at all four lists of a certain length. Subjects were credited with a score corresponding to the list length tested when they recalled all lists at that length and a score of .25 for each subsequent list recalled correctly.

The subjects were told to recall the presented list of items by saying each item aloud in the same order, and they were told to say "pass" for an item they could not remember. A response was scored as correct only when all the sounds/speech segments of the item were properly articulated, i.e., a conservative scoring regime was maintained throughout the experiment.

The experiment was run in two sessions, once for each of two rates of presentation. In one session items were presented with an interval of 300 ms between the offset of one item and the onset of another (the fast condition) and in the other session items were presented with an interval of 1000 ms between items (the slow condition). The order of the two sessions was balanced across subjects, and the break between sessions was a minimum of 1 hour, but varied from 1–4 hours for most subjects. The subjects were told they would hear a list of words or nonwords, that these categories of items were not mixed in a list, and that all items were selected from the series of words and nonwords presented to check for their audibility before testing. They were then told to listen carefully to be able to repeat them back in the same order with a clear and well articulated voice.

The entire testing session was audiotaped and replayed later to moderate the online scoring.

Results and discussion

No significant main effect of Presentation rate on memory span was observed. Nor did Presentation rate interact significantly with any of the other independent variables. We shall therefore present mean span measures by collapsing scores for the fast and slow presentation rates. Figure 1 shows mean span measure and 95% confidence interval for each of the eight experimental conditions. Standard error of means varied between .07 and .11 for the different conditions. A significant main effect of Lexicality, $F(1, 31) = 221.35$, $MSE = .51$, $p < .001$, supports Hulme, Roodenrys, Brown, and Mercer's (1995) finding that memory span for words is substantially better than memory span for nonwords. There is also a main effect of Phonological similarity, $F(1, 31) = 159.74$, $MSE = .19$, $p < .001$, which conforms to a number of other reports (Baddeley, 1966; Conrad, 1964; Longoni et al., 1993), and there is a main effect of Associative value, $F(1, 31) = 69.82$, $MSE = .21$, $p < .001$, which is a new finding.

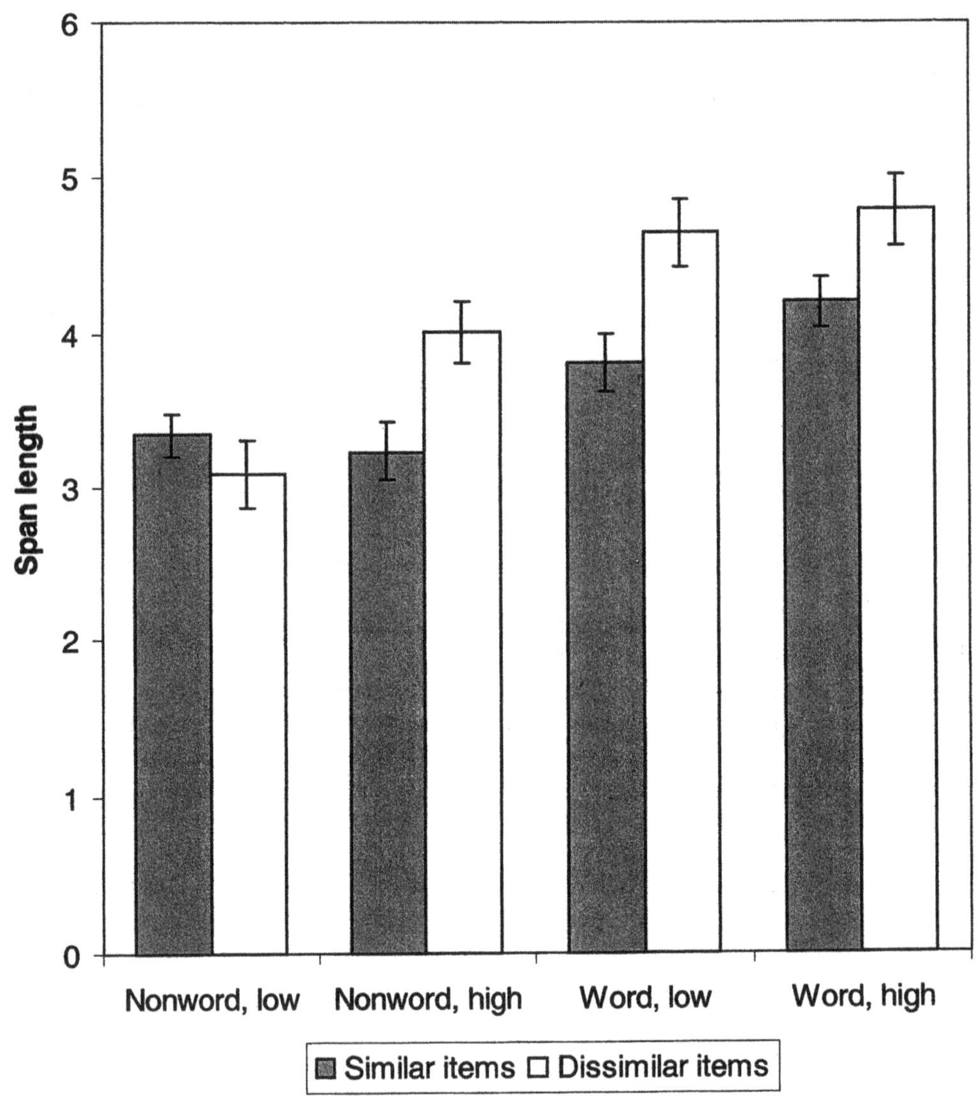

Figure 1. Mean short-term memory span and 95% confidence interval for each of the eight experimental conditions for phonologically similar and distinct words and nonwords with low and high associative value in Experiment 1A.

Figure 1 also shows that Phonological similarity affects the word and nonword span differently as documented by a significant interaction between Phonological similarity and Lexicality, $F\ (1, 31) = 19.73$, $MSE = .34$, $p < .001$. PSE is clearly present in the recall of nonwords with high associative value, but on the contrary the recall of nonwords with low associative value benefited from phonological similarity of the presented items. This finding is reflected by the significant interaction between Phonological similarity and Associative value, $F\ (1, 31) = 21.32$, $MSE = .23$, $p < .001$. Also, the three-way interaction between Lexicality, Phonological similarity, and Associative value was significant, $F\ (1, 31) = 52.33$, $MSE = .25$, $p < .001$, meaning that sensitivity to phonological similarity is affected by the associative value of nonwords, not words.

The recall data of the nonwords with low associative value shows a reversed effect of Phonological similarity. Thus mean span for phonologically similar nonwords is 3.35 and for distinct nonwords in this category 3.09, i.e., a difference that is significant on a *t*-test of paired samples ($t = 3.40$, $df = 31$, $p = .002$). The reversed effect of Phonological similarity by low associative nonwords is surprising. We cannot come up with a consistent explanation of this finding, unless it can be shown that phonologically similar lists of nonwords but not words contain less information than phonologically distinct lists in presemantic processing. In any case, when associative value is taken into account, we can conclude that words and nonwords are processed differently in short-term memory.

Effect of repeating items across sessions. Because no effect of Presentation rate has been demonstrated, our data do not contradict Brown and Hulme's (1995) model. The two presentation rates were tested in separate sessions, and therefore we are in a position to test the effect of repetition of items. In the experiment some proactive interference may be expected due to the fact that the items that are presented across trials are drawn from an extremely restricted set. Cross-trial confusions are more likely to occur when items are repeated, and such confusions may serve to increase PSE. As our subjects were tested twice, once for each of the two presentation rates, we should find more cross-trial confusions in the second session. Table 2 shows PSE in the four item categories in the first and second session of the experiment. The effect size did not differ significantly between sessions for any of the item categories. Yet it should be emphasised that PSE changes in opposite directions for words and nonwords with high associative value on the one side and nonwords with low associative value on the other. In the last session, PSE becomes more negative for nonwords with low associative value and more positive for the other item categories.

TABLE 2
Effects of phonological similarity, Experiment 1A

Item category	Associative value	Effect of phonological similarity: First session	Second session
Nonwords	Low	−.13	−.38
Nonwords	High	.76	.78
Words	Low	.80	.88
Words	High	.56	.62

Effects of phonological similarity (span of phonologically distinct–span of phonologically similar items) for each of four item categories in the first and second sessions of Experiment 1A.

Summary of results. The main finding in Experiment 1A has to do with PSE that occurs by words and nonwords with high associative value and not by nonwords of low associative value. In fact, the immediate serial recall of novel and meaningless nonwords shows a reversed PSE, in the sense that nonwords that are phonologically similar have a slight recall advantage compared to nonwords that are phonologically distinct. This shows that verbal items that have long-term memory representations, either as words or nonwords with high associative value, are processed differently from nonwords without such representations. Furthermore, our main finding undermines the generality of PSE, and hence it is worthwhile to explore the critical conditions that constrain the operation of a phonological similarity factor. At first, however, we shall present a replication of the present experiment with other nonword items categorised with respect to associative value.

EXPERIMENT 1B

The validity of our findings for nonwords in Experiment 1A will be tested with an independent set of stimuli that is generated by the same assessment procedure. In the first experiment phonologically similar lists were created by selecting items that shared a vowel, either *a* or *e*. This time we shall enhance the phonological similarity of items in a list by selecting CVC syllables that share a vowel and a final consonant sound. Thus *tev kev pev* will constitute a phonologically similar list, whereas items in phonologically distinct lists have different vowel and final consonant sounds, for example, *kev dob tiv*. If PSE is due to a failure of discrimination in encoding, we have provided more optimal conditions for demonstration of this effect by adding a rhyme component to the phonologically similar lists.

Two inclusion criteria were used for the selection of CVC syllables. (1) They should have no single form occurrences in *The Oslo corpus of tagged Norwegian texts* (2000), which includes a database of 18.5 million words. (2) They should not be included in the pool of nonwords used in Experiment 1A. To follow these criteria as closely as possible, we decided to use the consonants *b, d, g, k, p, r, t* as the first consonant in the syllable. These consonants were then combined with the following vowels: *a, e, i, o, u, ø, å*. To reduce the likelihood of creating single syllables that had single form occurrences in *The Oslo corpus* we decided to use *b* and *v* as the final consonants. From the 7 × 7 × 2 CVC combinations we excluded 9 that also constituted familiar words in the Norwegian language when spoken with a short vowel. As all CVC were spoken with a short vowel, we checked each of them for occurrences in *The Oslo corpus* by writing them with a double *v* or *b, i.e. tevv, revv, pabb, gabb*. (When checked with only one final consonant we found more occurrences of these syllables due to the assumption of a long vowel pronunciation.) Of the remaining 89 CVC syllables 87 had zero occurrences in *The Oslo corpus* when items with a double consonant ending were checked, this spelling being closer to actual pronunciation of the CVC syllables. Of the remaining two items, *kub*, had four occurrences, and *dub* had one occurrence, which are extremely low frequencies. Interestingly, they both became nonwords of high associative value.

The 89 CVC combinations were all different from the one-syllable nonwords used in Experiment 1A except for three items, *keb, dav, kib*. To make possible the creation of phonologically similar lists of five and six items these were included in the pool of candidate items.

Reaction time assessment of the associative value of study items

The 89 nonwords were spoken by a male voice, audiotaped, and digitised for presentation by a computer. A total of 20 students from the University of Oslo (12 females and 8 males with a mean age of 24 years) participated in a reaction time study designed to assess the degree of associative value for each item in the pool. Reaction times for a spoken word or phrase as an association to the auditory presentation of items were tabulated itemwise; items above the median reaction time were considered as nonwords of low associative value, and those below the median as nonwords of high associative value. By excluding six items from above and six items from below the median that had the lowest agreement scores, we defined two sets of 38 nonwords to be used in the experiment. Mean reaction time of the 38 nonwords from above the median was 4762 ms, and hence these formed the items with low associative value. Mean reaction time of the 38 nonwords from below the median was 2880 ms, and hence, these formed the items with high associative value.

Method

Subjects. A total of 22 other students from the University of Oslo, 12 females and 10 males, served as participants in the study. Mean age was 26 years, range 19–31 years. All were native speakers of Norwegian, and none of them had any known hearing or language disability.

Design. The experiment was run according to a simple 2 by 2 design for repeated measures, i.e. nonword span as a function of Phonological similarity (2) by Associative value (2).

Materials and procedure. The 38 nonwords of low associative value were organised into lists of phonologically similar nonwords with the lengths of two, three, four, five, and six items. Four lists were created for each of these list lengths. The same nonwords were then rearranged into lists of phonologically distinct nonwords, four lists at each of the five list lengths. Similarly, the 38 nonwords of high associative value were organised into the same number of phonologically similar and distinct lists at each of the five list lengths. Thereby we created four conditions that were presented blocked to the subject. However the four types of lists, phonologically similar items of low and high associative value and phonologically distinct items with low and high associative value, were presented in a random order for each subject. The subjects were told that lists of nonwords, which might be more or less meaningless, were to be presented for immediate serial recall. Testing started with the shortest lists, four lists at each list length, and testing was discontinued when the subject made errors on each of the four lists of a given length. Memory span was measured according to the maximum length at which the subject recalled all lists correctly, and above this level we added a score of .25 for each list correctly recalled. The same strict scoring practice as in Experiment 1A was maintained.

Results and discussion

Figure 2 shows the mean scores together with 95% confidence intervals for the four conditions. Standard error of mean varied between .08 and .12 for the four conditions. As in Experiment 1A, nonwords of low associative value show a negative PSE, but the similar—distinct difference does not reach significance ($t = 2.01$, $df = 21$, $p = .057$). This discrepancy between tests of significance for low associative nonwords in the two experiments may be due partly to fewer subjects in Experiment 1B, partly to a difference of effect size in the two experiments. The mean span difference between similar and distinct items may be expressed in terms of a z score for the whole set of low asso-

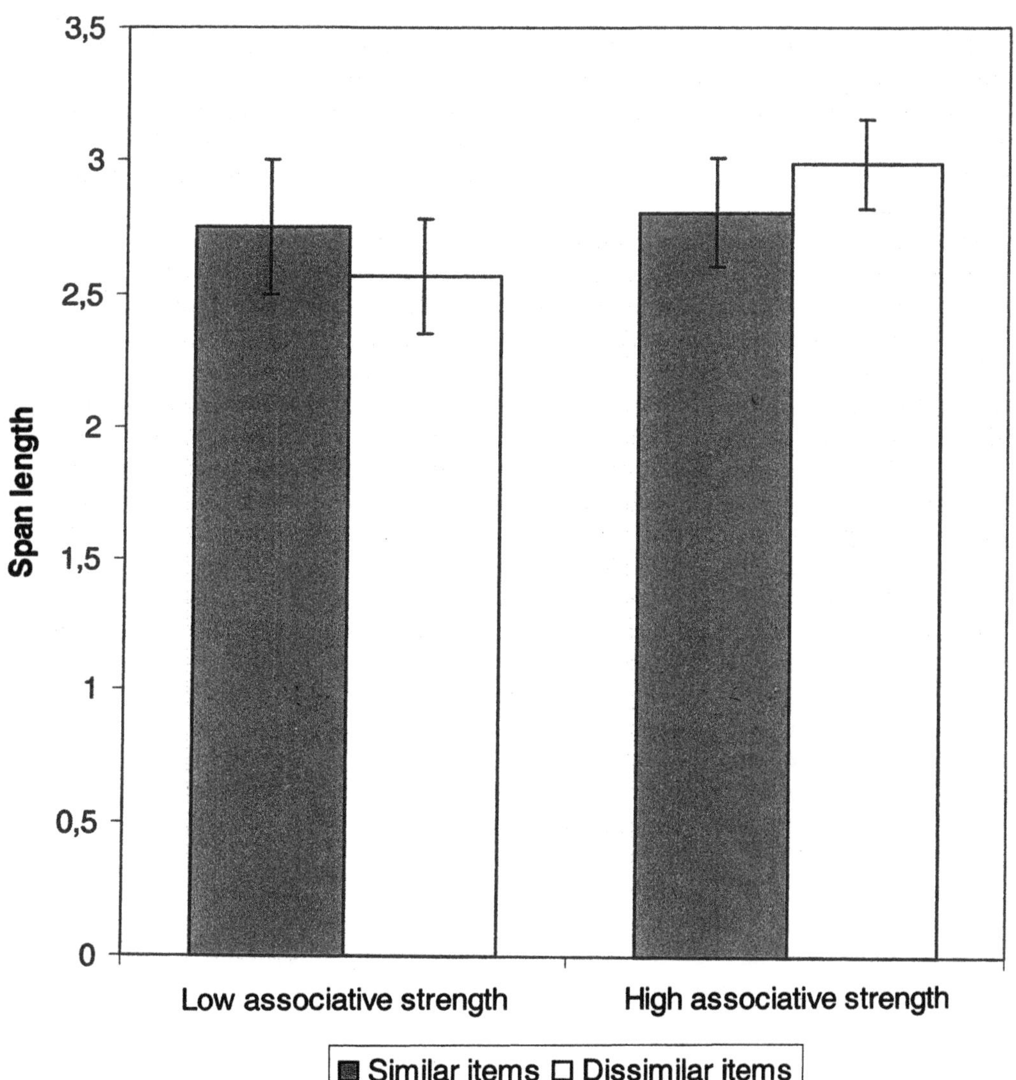

Figure 2. Mean short-term memory span and 95% confidence interval for phonologically similar (rhyming) and phonologically distinct nonwords with low and high associative value in Experiment 1B.

ciative nonwords. In Experiment 1A this difference yields a z of 6.44, and in Experiment 1B this difference yields a z of 5.06, showing that the effect size is somewhat stronger in the former experiment. Phonologically distinct nonwords of high associative value are significantly better recalled than phonologically similar nonwords of high associative value ($t = 2.52$, $df = 20$, $p = .02$), i.e., an effect that agrees with the one found in Experiment 1A.

As the effects of Phonological similarity are opposite for nonwords at the two levels of Associative value, no main effect of this variable is demonstrated in the ANOVA for repeated measures. A main effect of Associative value, $F(1, 20) = 7.97$, $MSE = .17$, $p = .011$ validates the procedure used to categorise the study items with respect to their connectedness to long-term memory representations. Nonwords of high associative value are more like words in a serial recall task, and although the level of performance is very low in the present experiment, the main effect of Associative value is comparable to the lexicality effect reported by Hulme et al. (1995) and Gathercole et al. (2001).

Finally, the variance analysis demonstrates a significant effect of interaction between Phonological similarity and Associative value, $F(1, 20) = 25.21$, $MSE = .03$, $p < .001$. This effect supports our findings in Experiment 1A and shows that serial recall sensitivity to phonological similarity for nonwords depends on the ease with which these items can activate long-term memory representations by the subjects. In the present experiment a rhyme component increased the similarity between items in similar lists, and no PSE is found for the low associative nonwords. However, the rhyme component means that the final consonant of nonwords was either *v* or *b*, and thereby we reduced the overall phonological variance in the pool and made the test a very difficult one.

The serial recall task in Experiments 1A and 1B depended on the retention of both items and order. Our experiments cannot tell which of these components, the memory of items or the memory of order, is associated with PSE for words and nonwords with high associative value. However, there is a considerable empirical literature (Conrad, 1965; Drewnowski, 1980; Ellis, 1980; Healy, 1974; Murdock & vom Saal, 1967; Wickelgren, 1965) that supports the claim that PSE turns up in tasks that require memory of order. Burgess and Hitch (1992, 1999) and Page and Norris (1998) have reviewed the literature on computational models of short-term memory designed to simulate the relationship between memory of order and PSE.

In view of the extended empirical literature in the field (Conrad, 1965; Drewnowski, 1980; Ellis, 1980; Healy, 1974; Murdock & vom Saal, 1967; Wickelgren, 1965) we assume that PSEs of words and nonwords of high associative value in serial recall depend on the processing of order rather than items. If this assumption is correct, performance on a free recall task should be insensitive to the phonological similarity of items. We therefore ran a pilot experiment of free recall of words, i.e. words that in Experiment 1A turned out to be sensitive to this factor. A set of 16 one-syllable words, 8 phonologically similar (sharing the *e* vowel), and 8 phonologically distinct words was selected for the experiment, and random sequences of the similar and distinct items were auditorily presented to subjects with the instruction to recall, in any order, as many of them as possible. Also, the 40 participating subjects were randomly assigned one of two groups. The subjects of group A were tested without any previous exposure to the test items, whereas the subjects of group B listened to all items spoken by a female voice with an inter-item pause of 1 second. This pretest presentation of the study items was made twice, each time in a randomised order.

The results showed a slight PSE in group A but not in group B. The effect in group A was nonsignificant. This shows that memory performance is unaffected by the phonological similarity factor, independent of any pre-exposure to the study items. Yet we need more evidence to show (1) that PSEs are restricted to tasks requiring order and do not occur in tasks that make a similar demand on the response system but require memory of items independent of order. Furthermore, we want to demonstrate (2) that the relationship between PSE and memory of order only applies to words and nonwords with high associative value and not to meaningless nonwords of low associative value. These will be the objectives of the next experiment.

EXPERIMENT 2

To study whether the association between phonological memory and vocabulary knowledge depends on speech output constraints or some prior encoding or storage component Gathercole et al. (1999) introduced the serial nonword recognition task. Two lists of nonwords are auditorily presented to the subject. The lists contain the same items, but are either identical (e.g. "sev, rof, dab" ... "sev, rof, dab") or different with respect to order (e.g. "sev, rof, dab" ... "sev, dab, rof"). The two lists of a trial may be composed of words or nonwords, in either case the subject is given a two-choice recognition task. Moreover, the lists may be composed of phonologically similar or distinct items. The main point to be stressed is that the lists to be compared are either identical or different with respect to order, but they always contain the same words/nonwords.

The serial recognition paradigm makes minimal demands on speech output abilities, and therefore it has been adopted in studies of short-term memory in individuals with language and speech pathologies (Campbell & Butterworth, 1985; Martin & Breedin, 1992; Shallice & Warrington, 1977). Also, serial recognition performance is strongly correlated with vocabulary knowledge and capacity for immediate serial recall (Gathercole & Pickering, 1999; Gathercole, et al., 1999).

The serial word/nonword recognition task, which requires the retention of order, must be contrasted with another task that requires the retention of specific items. This time the subject will be presented with two lists of items which always differ in order, but are composed either of identical items (e.g. "teb, lef, ker" ... "lef, ker, teb") or items that are identical except for one (e.g. "teb, lef, ker" ... "lef, sev, teb"). We shall refer to this task as the item identification task: The subject is given a two-choice recognition task according to which he/she decides whether the two auditorily presented lists contained exactly the same items or if they were identical except for one item. Also in this task the items in a list may be either phonologically similar or distinct. In the negative trials where the lists do not contain exactly the same items, the one new item may be phonologically similar (contain the same vowel) or distinct compared to the one that is replaced. In this way, the item identification task will include three kinds of trials: (1) Trials with phonologically similar items in the two sequences, as in the examples just given. The new item in negative trials always includes the same vowel as the other items in the list. (2) Trials with phonologically distinct items in the two lists, and here too negative trials include a new item with the same vowel as the one in the replaced item (e.g. "koff, rav, sik" ... "koff, sik, tad"). (3) Trials with phonologically distinct items in the two lists; negative trials include a new item with a vowel that differs from the one in the replaced item (e.g. "bev, sor, fab" ... "sor, bev, fud"). In brief we shall refer to the three types of trials as (1) "similar", (2) "distinct, same vowel", and (3) "distinct, different vowel".

Contemporary models of short-term memory (Baddeley, 1986; Burgess & Hitch, 1992; Nairne, 1990) which relate PSE to the confusability of phonologically similar items will predict lower scores on the "similar" trials in the item identification task compared to the "distinct, same vowel" and the "distinct, different vowel" trials. It may also be argued that confusability of items may interfere with the retention of order, and thus according to the contemporary models a PSE may also be predicted in the serial recognition task. On the other hand, if the present view that this effect is associated with the retention of order and not the retention of items is correct, we will predict a PSE in the serial recognition task and no such effect in the item identification task.

Besides the problem of an interpretation of the PSE, we shall also deal with the problem of whether words and nonwords are processed differently by the phonological loop. Although there are capacity differences for the processing of the two types of items, there may be no qualitative differences in the short-term memory of words and nonwords. In the latter case, any predictions with respect to PSE will apply equally to words and nonwords. On the other hand, if there are qualitative differences it is likely that conditions that favour PSE by one type of items do not do so for the other type of items. The results of the two preceding experiments indicate that this effect occurs for words having a long-term memory representation and not at all for nonwords that do not have a similar representation.

Method

Subjects. A total of 31 students of psychology, 17 females and 14 males, from the University of Oslo served as subjects in the experiment. All were native speakers of Norwegian and none of them had any documented hearing or language disabilities.

Materials and procedure. The 22 nonwords (12 phonologically similar and 10 distinct) with low associative value and the 28 words (16 phonologically similar and 12 distinct) with high associative value were used as test items in the present experiment. Several schemes of test lists were prepared for each of the two tasks, the serial recognition task and the item identification task. For example, eight pairs of lists with phonologically similar words were presented at each of five list lengths, beginning with four words in a list and ending with eight. The eight pairs of lists at each list length included four identical and four different list pairs. As the computer selected at random six pairs for presentation at each list length, the number of identical and different pairs did not always match within a block but was distributed 50–50 across conditions and subjects. For nonword sequences pairs were first presented at list length three and ending with list length seven. In addition to the Task factor (serial recognition and item identification) the experiment included the factor of Lexicality (words and nonwords) and the Phonological similarity factor (similar and distinct items in the serial recognition task, similar and two types of distinct pairs in the item identification task). As in the examples described earlier, we presented six pairs of lists at each of five list lengths for each of the eight plus two factorial combinations.

Although list pairs in all conditions were presented in ascending series, we could not find a reliable criterion of span that was applicable to all subjects. To obtain a span measure for each subject we would have had to extend testing above the maximum list lengths. Instead we decided to measure the subjects' performances in the range of list lengths presented. At the lowest list length, i.e., three and four for nonwords and words respectively, errors were rare, and at the highest list lengths most subjects scored close to chance. With only six lists presented at each list length, and with a two-choice recognition task, an element of chance must be taken into consideration. We shall therefore record the total number of correct responses over the range of list lengths for each of the factorial combinations included in the experiment. Yet it is important to demonstrate a main effect of List length, which is therefore included as a factor in the design. However, in ANOVA this factor is given four levels corresponding to the four list lengths shared by the word and nonword items.

All subjects served in both the serial recognition task and the item identification task. The experiment was therefore run according to a design for repeated measures with the factors of Task (2) × Lexicality (2) × Phonological similarity (2) × List length (4). In defining the Phonological similarity factor with two levels we shall run the analysis twice, first by using the distinct condition in the item identification task with the same vowel in the replaced item in negative trials, and second with a different vowel in the replaced item.

Results and discussion

To compare serial recognition and item identification scores for words and nonwords, we have summed the scores over the four list lengths shared by the two categories of items. Maximum score when the number of correct responses is summed over these lengths is 24. Mean summed score (M) and standard deviation (SD) are listed in Table 3 for each of four conditions in the serial recognition task and for each of six conditions in the item identification task.

Conditions where both lists consist of phonologically similar items are listed as "similar" and should be compared to conditions where both lists consist of phonologically distinct items, listed as "distinct". The PSE with higher mean scores for "distinct" occurs in the serial recognition task for words ("similar" = 17.25 vs "distinct" = 19.77) and in the item identification task for words when "similar" is compared to "distinct" with different vowel replacement in the negative trials ("similar" = 17.96 vs "distinct" = 18.68). Only the former difference turns out to be significant on a t-test for paired samples ($t = 3.04$, $df = 30$, $p = .005$).

TABLE 3
Mean scores, Experiment 2

	Words		*Nonwords*	
	M	*SD*	*M*	*SD*
Serial recognition				
Similar	17.25	2.59	17.71	2.37
Distinct	19.77	2.01	17.65	2.98
Item identification				
Similar	17.97	2.50	16.42	3.01
Distinct				
• negative: same vowel	17.29	2.55	16.13	2.60
• negative: different vowel	18.68	2.91	15.87	2.84

Mean scores summed over the four list lengths shared by words and nonwords in the four conditions of the serial recognition task and the six conditions of the item identification task. M = mean. SD = standard deviation.

The latter difference is far from significant ($t = .79$, $df = 30$, $p = .439$).

The comparison of means shows that PSE occurs only in the serial recognition task that requires the retention of order independent of items. Moreover, this effect is demonstrated for words and not nonwords, and in this respect the data agree with the results of Experiment 1A. Notice that the immediate serial recall task in Experiments 1A and 1B and the serial recognition task in Experiment 2 both require the retention of order.

Figure 3 shows the mean scores by List length in the two tasks, including list lengths 3 and 8 that are not shared by the two categories of items. Graphs are plotted separately for phonologically similar and distinct nonwords (a and b) and words (c and d). Results from the item identification task

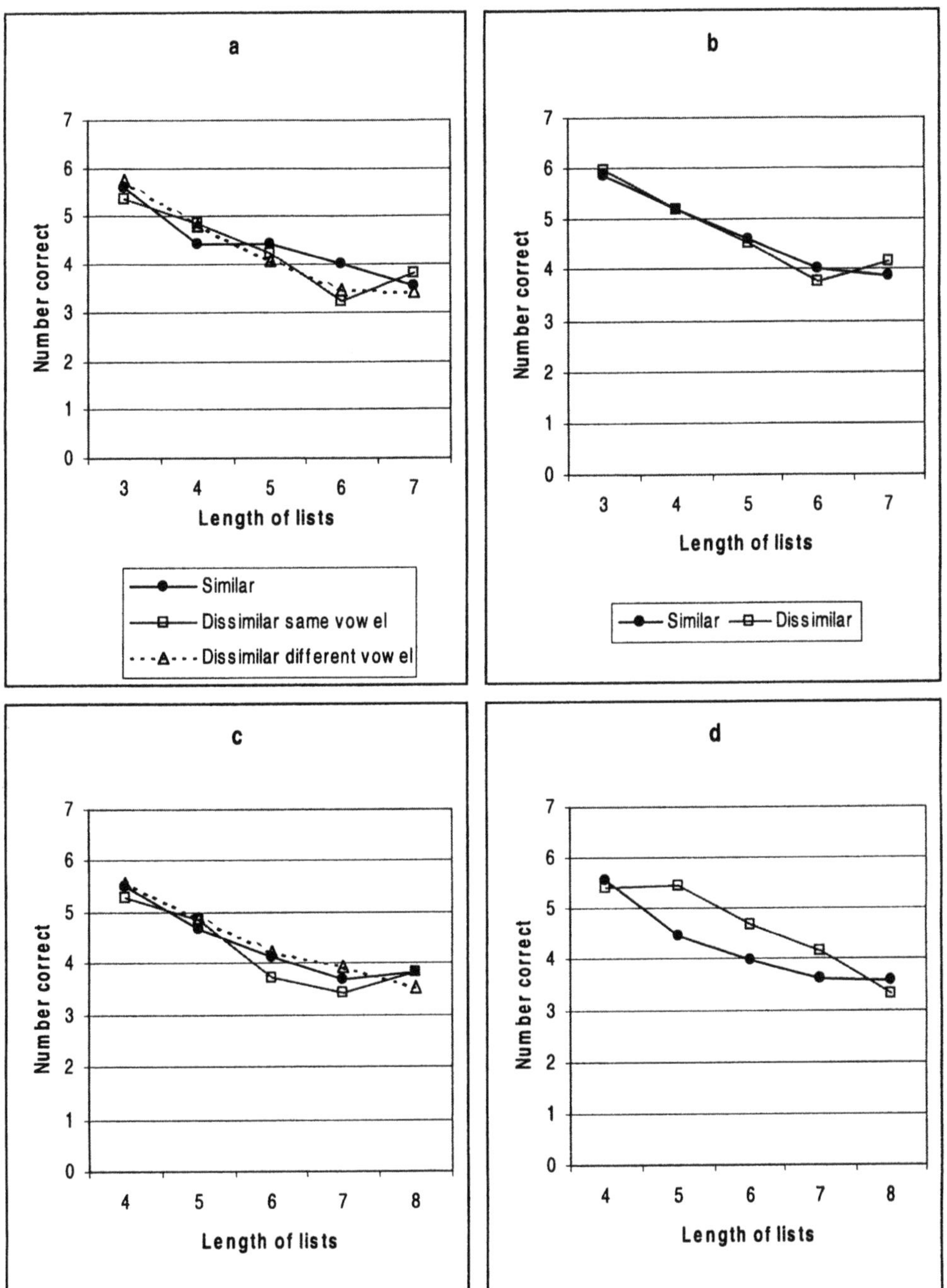

Figure 3. Mean number of lists with similar and distinct vowels correctly recognised in the item identification task (a and c) and the serial recognition task (b and d) for nonwords (a and b) and words (c and d) at each of five list lengths in Experiment 2.

with the two types of study items are shown in (a) and (c), and the results from the serial recognition task are shown in (b) and (d). The analysis of variance, however, is based on the summed scores across the four list lengths shared by the two categories of items. We shall start by disregarding the "distinct, different vowel" condition in the item identification task. We then find a strong main effect of List length, $F(3, 90) = 68.09$, $MSE = 1.54$, $p < .001$, which shows the increasing difficulty of both tasks with increasing list length. Note that there is a main effect of Task, $F(1, 30) = 14.95$, $MSE = 1.60$, $p = .001$, which shows that the item identification task (mean score across conditions: 33.05) has been more difficult than the serial recognition task (mean score across conditions: 36.19). Finally, we find a main effect of Lexicality, $F(1, 30) = 31.67$, $MSE = .70$, $p < .001$, which shows that scores are higher for words (mean score across tasks and conditions: 18.07) than nonwords (mean score across tasks and conditions: 16.98).

There is no main effect of Phonological similarity. On the other hand, we find a significant interaction between Task and Phonological similarity, $F(1, 30) = 6.11$, $MSE = 1.46$, $p = .019$, which shows that PSE only occurs in the serial recognition task. This finding supports our hypothesis that the effect is related to the processing of information about order of items and not to the retention of separate items. In comparing Figure 3 b and d we also find that PSE in recognition of order is limited to words. The order of nonwords is recognised equally well regardless of whether the lists constitute series of phonologically similar or distinct items. Thus, we find a significant three-way interaction effect between Task, Phonological similarity, and Lexicality, $F(1, 30) = 5.71$, $MSE = 5.71$, $p = .023$.

A second ANOVA for repeated measures was undertaken when the "distinct" condition in the item identification task was changed from same vowel replacement to different vowel replacement. This means that the second list in negative trials included an item with a vowel that did not appear in the items of the first list. This may have created a pop-out effect, and the probability of the detection of change will be high. The three main effects (i.e. effects of List, Task, and Lexicality) remain significant in the second analysis, and this time the analysis also demonstrates a main effect of Phonological similarity, $F(1, 30) = 4.24$, $MSE = 1.13$, $p = .048$, which means that memory performance is better for lists of phonologically distinct items. However, Table 3 shows that this difference is mostly due to the similar–distinct difference for words in the serial recognition task. But phonologically distinct lists of words are also scored higher than phonologically similar lists in the item identification task. Subjects easily noticed the new item with a different vowel in word but not nonword lists. This shows that the absence of a significant two-way interaction effect between Task and Phonological similarity, $F(1, 30) = 3.29$, $MSE = 1.07$, $p = .08$, is due to sensitivity to vowel replacement in the word list rather than an effect of phonological similarity in the similar conditions.

The last ANOVA also demonstrates a significant Lexicality by Phonological similarity interaction, $F(1, 30) = 11.00$, $MSE = 1.05$, $p = .002$, which shows that PSE is restricted to words. In any case, the summed scores for "similar" and "distinct" conditions do not differ significantly in the item identification task, which means that no PSE has been demonstrated in this test. Moreover, we find no evidence for this effect when the presented items consist of nonwords, neither in the serial recognition task nor in the item identification task.

GENERAL DISCUSSION

The effect of phonological similarity (PSE) on short-term memory for words and nonwords has been tested in two tasks of serial recall, in one task of serial recognition, and one item identification task. This effect has been replicated in a vast number of experiments; thus Nairne and Kelley (1999) characterised the effect as the benchmark finding in short-term memory literature. Despite its assumed robustness, we have only demonstrated PSE in tests of serial recall and serial recognition of order. No significant PSE is demonstrated in an item identification task, and the results of a pilot experiment on free recall of words indicate that the effect is absent when items do not have to be recalled in the correct order. These data support the claim made in the empirical literature, that PSEs are generally restricted to tasks that require the retention of order (Conrad, 1965; Drewnowski, 1980; Ellis 1980; Healy, 1974; Murdock & vom Saal, 1967; Wickelgren, 1965).

Researchers in the field of short-term memory have generally proposed some form of interference interpretation of PSE (Baddeley, 1968;

Brown, Hulme & Preece, 2000; Burgess & Hitch, 1992, 1999; Houghton, 1990; Nairne, 1990; Page & Norris, 1998; Schweickert, Guentert, & Hersberger, 1990). This interpretation involves a disadvantage for the retrieval of phonologically similar items, and applies equally to the short-term memory of words and nonwords. The literature includes reports that indicate that this is in fact the case. Thus Besner and Davelaar (1982) have demonstrated that phonological similarity affects the retention of verbal items regardless of the wordlikeness of these items, and Papagno and Vallar (1992) found that the phonological similarity factor affects the learning of novel words more than familiar words. The definition and selection of nonwords may have influenced these results. This is why we made a reaction-time-based assessment of the associative value of items to be used in our experiments. Moreover, we found that the serial recall of nonwords, which according to this assessment had high associative value, was affected by the phonological similarity of items in the list. However, the span measures with items having low associative value were not equally affected by the phonological similarity factor. On the contrary, lists of phonologically similar items of this category were more likely to be recalled than lists of phonologically distinct items in a serial recall task. Furthermore, we have shown that PSE in recognition of order applies to words but not nonwords having a low associative value.

The finding that PSE occurs with words and nonwords of high associative value, and not with nonwords of low associative value, shows that the effect depends on the activation of long-term memory mechanisms. However, we also found that nonwords of high associative value are more prone to phonological similarity in serial recall than words of high associative value. However, the difference in PSE between the high associative nonwords and the two groups of words is non-significant, indicating that semantic processes do very little to reduce PSE, as predicted by Schweickert (1993). However, the difference between PSE for nonwords of high associative value and the negative phonological similarity effect seen for nonwords of low associative value is significant, indicating that the disappearance of PSE for nonwords of low associative value is not due to a floor effect.

In our opinion these results reflect that PSE occurs in a fundamental lexical-phonological layer. This layer may also be identified as the higher phonological space, in contrast to the lower-level phonological network found in the interactive model proposed by Gathercole and Martin (1996). Both words and nonwords of high associative value easily access this fundamental layer, where stable, lexical clusters and their similar neighbours are activated. These activations cannot be overruled by their respective connections to unrelated and less confusable semantic representations. If, however, the activation of these clusters decays, or is already low or non-existent, there should be less to confuse, and PSE should be reduced. This will happen for words when there is a delay between presentation and recall (Nairne & Kelley, 1999). It will not happen for some nonwords which do not rely on stable, semantic representations and are not sensitive to phonological similarity in the first case. Also, if item representations in the lexical phonological layer are activated to a very small extent simply because they are not accessed, then PSE too will be very small or absent, as we see for nonwords of low associative value. Indeed, at this level we see a negative phonological similarity effect. This may be due to the unusually low level of representation relied upon for these items. At a lower and pre-lexical phonological layer, phoneme or syllable segments may be represented and activated in new, unstable clusters. Hartley and Houghton (1996) would predict PSE also at this level, based on the activation of syllable templates of related phonemes. As each remembered item consists of several phonemes, there will be a very heavy memory load when that level of representation must be relied upon. Perhaps a list of phonemically similar items simply implies a lower memory load than a list of phonemically distinct items at this level of representation.

It seems unlikely that the opposite effects of phonological similarity for nonwords of high and low associative value are due to different types of controlled strategy. The two classes of nonwords are highly similar, the subjects do not know what class of nonwords they will be hearing next, and there are clear time restrictions imposed by the steady presentation rate. This indicates that a systematic adoption of different strategies for the two classes of nonwords will be extremely difficult.

During the redintegration process (Brown & Hulme, 1995) or the similar matching process (Nairne, 1990), clusters of segments at the lower-level phonological layer are reconstructed by the activated long-term units of the higher-level phonological layer. If there are few long-term lexical-phonological units activated, memory span will decrease, and there will be less PSE.

A somewhat different interpretation of our findings in Experiments 1A and 1B is related to the redintegration process (Brown & Hulme, 1995) or the similar matching process (Nairne, 1990) described briefly in our introduction. Instead of focusing on different layers of item representations, one may look at the connections between the different representational layers. In this case PSE is due to inhibition of certain connections between different layers rather than interference between activated items at a certain layer. The excitation of a certain connection between a lexical-phonological layer and a semantic layer due to the presentation of a familiar verbal item may lead to the inhibition of connections from related neighbours of that item at the lexical-phonological layer to their respective and unrelated semantic representations. When neighbours at the lexical-phonological layer are presented together, that will lead to the same connections being both excited and inhibited. The net excitation will thereby be lower for each item than for items that are not lexical-phonological neighbours. Such a system would be tuned for variance in verbal material. In this case phonologically distinct sounds have an advantage compared to phonologically similar sounds when semantic connections are activated. Such a system would also secure great precision in the semantic processing.

REFERENCES

Baddeley, A.D. (1966). The influence of acoustic and semantic similarity on long-term memory for word sequences. *Quarterly Journal of Experimental Psychology, 18*, 302–309.

Baddeley, A.D. (1968). How does acoustic similarity influence short-term memory? *Quarterly Journal of Experimental Psychology, 20*, 249–263.

Baddeley, A.D. (1986). *Working memory*. Oxford: Oxford University Press.

Baddeley, A.D., & Lewis, V.J. (1984). When does rapid presentation enhance digit span? *Bulletin of the Psychonomic Society, 22*, 403–405.

Besner, D., & Davelaar, E. (1982). Basic processes in reading: Two phonological codes. *Canadian Journal of Psychology, 36*, 701–711.

Brown, G.D.A. (1997). Formal models of memory for serial order: A review. In M.A. Conway (Ed.), *Cognitive models of memory* (pp. 47–77). Cambridge, MA: MIT Press.

Brown, G.D.A., & Hulme, C. (1995). Modelling item length effects in memory span: No rehearsal needed? *Journal of Memory and Language, 34*, 594–621.

Brown, G.D.A., Hulme, C., & Preece, T. (2000). Oscillator-based memory for serial order. *Psychological Review, 107*, 127–181.

Burgess, N., & Hitch, G.J. (1992). Toward a network model of the articulatory loop. *Journal of Memory and Language, 31*, 429–460.

Burgess, N., & Hitch, G.J. (1999). Memory for serial order: A network model of the phonological loop and its timing. *Psychological Review, 106*, 551–581.

Campbell, R., & Butterworth, B. (1985). Phonological dyslexia and dysgraphia in highly literate subjects: A developmental case with associated deficits of phonemic processing and awareness. *Quarterly Journal of Experimental Psychology, 37*A, 435–476.

Conrad, R. (1964). Acoustic confusions in immediate memory. *British Journal of Psychology, 55*, 75–84.

Conrad, R. (1965). Order error in immediate recall of sequences. *Journal of Verbal Learning, 4*, 161–169.

Conrad, R., & Hull, A.J. (1964). Information, acoustic confusion and memory span. *British Journal of Psychology, 55*, 429–432.

Drewnowski, A. (1980). Attributes and priorities in short-term recall: A new model of memory span. *Journal of Experimental Psychology: General, 109*, 208–250.

Ellis, A.W. (1980). Errors in speech and short-term memory: The effects of phonemic similarity and syllable position. *Journal of Verbal Learning and Verbal Behavior, 19*, 624–634.

Estes, W.K. (1973). Phonemic coding and rehearsal in short-term memory for letter strings. *Journal of Verbal Learning & Verbal Behavior, 12*, 360–372.

Gathercole, S.E. (1995). Is nonword repetition a test of phonological memory or long-term knowledge? It all depends on the nonwords. *Memory & Cognition, 23*, 83–84.

Gathercole, S.E. (1997). Models of verbal short-term memory. In M.A. Conway (Ed.), *Cognitive models of memory* (pp. 13–45). Cambridge, MA: MIT Press.

Gathercole, S.E., & Martin, A. (1996). Interactive processes in phonological memory. In S.E. Gathercole (Ed.), *Models of short-term memory*. Hove, UK: Lawrence Erlbaum Associates Ltd.

Gathercole, S.E., & Pickering, S.J. (1999). Estimating the capacity of phonological short-term memory. *International Journal of Psychology, 34*, 378–382.

Gathercole, S.E., Pickering, S.J., Hall, M., & Peaker, S.M. (2001). Dissociable lexical and phonological influences on serial recognition and serial recall. *The Quarterly Journal of Experimental Psychology, 54A*, 1–30.

Gathercole, S.E., Service, E., Hitch, G.J., Adams, A-M., & Martin A.J. (1999). Phonological short-term memory and vocabulary development. Further evidence on the nature of the relationship. *Applied Cognitive Psychology, 13*, 65–77.

Hartley, T., & Houghton, G. (1996). A linguistically-constrained model of short-term memory for nonwords. *Journal of Memory and Language, 35*, 1–31.

Healy, A.F. (1974). Separating item from order information in short-term memory. *Journal of Verbal Learning and Verbal Behavior, 13*, 644–655.

Houghton, G. (1990). The problem of serial order: A neural network memory of sequence learning and recall. In R. Dale, C. Mellish, & M. Zock (Eds.), *Current research in natural language generation*. Hove, UK: Lawrence Erlbaum Associates Ltd.

Hulme, C. (1984). Developmental differences in the effects of acoustic similarity on memory span. *Developmental Psychology*, *20*, 650–652.

Hulme, C., Newton, P., Cowan, N., Stuart, G., & Brown, G. (1999). Think before you speak: Pauses, memory search, and trace redintegration processes in verbal memory span. *Journal of Experimental Psychology: Learning, Memory and Cognition*, *25*, 447–463.

Hulme, C., Roodenrys, S., Brown, G.D.A., & Mercer, R. (1995). The role of long-term memory mechanisms in memory span. *British Journal of Psychology*, *86*, 527–536.

Hulme, C., & Tordoff, V. (1989). Working memory development: The effects of speech rate, word length, and acoustic similarity on serial recall. *Journal of Experimental Child Psychology*, *47*, 72–87.

Longoni, A.M., Richardson, J.T.E., & Aiello, A. (1993). Articulatory rehearsal and phonological storage in working memory. *Memory & Cognition*, *21*, 11–22.

Lyons, J. (1981). *Semantics, Vol. 1*. London: Cambridge University Press.

Martin, R.C., & Breedin, S.D. (1992). Dissociations between speech perception and phonological short-term memory deficits. *Cognitive Neuropsychology*, *9*, 509–534.

Murdock, B.B., & vom Saal, W. (1967). Transpositions in short-term memory. *Journal of Experimental Psychology*, *74*, 137–143.

Murray, D.J. (1968). Articulation and acoustic confusability in short-term memory. *Journal of Experimental Psychology*, *78*, 679–684.

Nairne, J.S. (1990). A feature model of immediate memory. *Memory & Cognition*, *18*, 251–269.

Nairne, J.S., & Kelley, M.R. (1999). Reversing the phonological similarity effect. *Memory & Cognition*, *27*, 45–53.

Page, M.P.A., & Norris, D. (1998). The primacy model: A new model of immediate serial recall. *Psychological Review*, *105*, 761–781.

Papagno, C., & Vallar, G. (1992). Phonological short-term memory and the learning of novel words: The effect of phonological similarity and item length. *The Quarterly Journal of Experimental Psychology*, *44*A, 47–67.

Salame, P., & Baddeley, A.D. (1986). Phonological factors in STM: Similarity and the unattended speech effect. *Bulletin of the Psychonomic Society*, *24*, 263–265.

Schweickert, R. (1993). A multinominal processing tree model for degradation and redintegration in immediate recall. *Memory & Cognition*, *23*, 168–175.

Schweickert, R., Guentert, L., & Hersberger, L. (1990). Phonological similarity, pronunciation rate, and memory span. *Psychological Science*, *1*, 74–77.

Shallice, T., & Warrington, E.K. (1977). Auditory-verbal short-term memory impairment and conduction aphasia. *Brain and Language*, *4*, 479–491.

The Oslo corpus of tagged Norwegian texts. (Last updated June 2000). http://www.tekstlab.uio.no/norsk/bokmaal/english.html

Wickelgren, W.C. (1965). Short-term memory for phonemically similar lists. *American Journal of Psychology*, *78*, 567–574.

MEMORY, 2001, 9 (4/5/6), 301–311

Modelling serial position curves with temporal distinctiveness

Jeffrey N. Rouder
University of Missouri-Columbia, USA

Pablo Gomez
Northwestern University, USA

We offer a critique of the temporal distinctiveness model of serial position effects (Nairne, Neath, Serra, & Byun, 1997). The temporal distinctiveness model combines a precise definition of stimulus distinctiveness with a memory perturbation process. The critique is empirically motivated—we show that with a more complete analysis, the temporal distinctiveness model does not adequately account for Nairne et al.'s experimental data. To better account for the data, we independently modified two components of Nairne et al.'s model: the mathematical form of the definition of temporal distinctiveness and the mathematical form of the mapping from distinctiveness to free-recall probabilities. Both of these modifications provided for better fits. Yet both Nairne et al.'s definition and our modified definition are fairly arbitrary. We show that a significant challenge to this approach is to find theoretically motivated constraints of the temporal distinctiveness model while providing for adequate fits to data.

When participants are asked to free-recall a list of previously studied items, they tend to produce more items from the beginning and end of the list than from the middle of the list. These findings, respectively termed primacy and recency, have traditionally been cited in support of Atkinson and Shiffrin's (1968) two-store memory model (see, for example, Rundus, 1971). The gist of the argument is that end-of-list items are recalled more frequently than middle-of-list items because the recall of end-of-list items is from both the short-term store and the long-term store, whereas recall of the middle-of-list items is from only the long-term store. Beginning-of-list items are better recalled than middle-of-list items because at the beginning of the list there is a smaller mnemonic burden and hence better transfer from the short-term store to the long-term store. Several alternative explanations of primacy and recency (e.g., Craik & Lockhart's, 1972, levels of processing framework, or Baddeley & Hitch's, 1977, working memory framework) are closely related to the two-store model in that explanations of primacy and recency are based on the assumption that different mnemonic processes operate at different serial positions. For example, in the levels of processing framework, recency effects occur because shallow traces are available for end-of-list items only. Neuropsychological research yields additional support for the notion that recency and primacy are supported by separate stores and/or separate processes for auditory stimuli. Patients with damage to anterior perisylvian region exhibit preserved recency but diminished primacy. But patients with damage to parts of the inferior parietal lobule exhibit the opposite result: pre-

Requests for reprints should be sent to Jeffrey N. Rouder, 210 McAlester Hall, Department of Psychology, Columbia, MO, USA, 65211.

This research was supported by National Science Foundation Grant BCS-9917561 to J. Rouder and National Institute of Mental Health Grants HD MH44640, National Institute for Deafness and other Communications Disorders Grant R01-DC01240, and National Science Foundation Grant SBR-9221940 to R. Ratcliff and G. McKoon. We are grateful to Ian Neath for providing detailed information on the temporal distinctiveness model.

http://www.tandf.co.uk/journals/pp/09658211.html DOI:10.1080/09658210042000102

served primacy but diminished recency (Gordon, 1983). These results are consistent with the idea that primacy and recency may be mediated by different brain structures.

Nairne, Neath and their colleagues (Nairne et al., 1997; Neath, 1993) propose an alternative account of primacy and recency effects based on a single mnemonic process operating on a single store. The account is based on the observation that items at the beginning and end of the list are different from items in the middle of the list. Items at both ends of the list are presented near unique temporal events (namely, the beginning and end of the list). These items, therefore, are more *temporally distinct* than middle-of-list items. Participants encode the temporal position of an item as part of the general context and use the temporal distinctiveness of these beginning- and end-of-list items to aid in free-recall. The idea that distinctiveness is an important determinant in free-recall comes from interference theories of memory (e.g., Einstein, McDaniel, & Lackey, 1989; Postman & Stark, 1969). Interference from competing items explains omission errors in free-recall. Distinctive items are relatively immune to interference and are less likely to be omitted.

To account for variability in performance, Nairne, Neath, and colleagues assume that there is flux or change in memory through time (e.g., Estes, 1997). The record of an item's temporal position may change randomly after encoding. For example, at recall, the participant may mistakenly remember the first item as being in the second position. In this case, the temporal distinctiveness of the first item would be lessened. Beginning-of-list items are more likely to have their temporal positions confused (they need to be retained longer) than end-of-list items, and hence the temporal distinctiveness of beginning-of-list items is less than that of the end-of-list items. This explains why recency effects are larger than primacy effects for immediate free-recall tasks.

Temporal distinctiveness is not a new theoretical construct; it can be traced back to Murdock (1960). What is new is that Nairne et al. (1997, henceforth referred to as NNSB) have incorporated temporal distinctiveness in a rigorous and parsimonious formal model which accounts for primacy and recency effects under a number of experimental conditions. Because the model offers an elegant explanation of primacy and recency effects without postulating multiple mnemonic stores or processes, it merits further evaluation. In this paper, we demonstrate that the NNSB model-fitting endeavour is flawed and fails to capture several aspects of NNSB's own experimental data. We present two different ways of refining the NNSB model so that it does indeed provide a better fit to the data. In the process of refining the model, we demonstrate that some of the original NNSB assumptions, as well as our refinements, are arbitrary and lack theoretical backing. The unfortunate state of affairs is that the goodness-of-fit of the NNSB model is largely dependent on the particular forms of these atheoretical assumptions. Therefore, fitting the NNSB data with the NNSB model does not provide a satisfactory test of the core components of the temporal distinctiveness framework. Our conclusion is that temporal distinctiveness is not yet sufficiently developed to provide a satisfactory alternative to the modal two-store model.

THE TEMPORAL DISTINCTIVENESS DIFFUSION MODEL

It is easiest to understand the NNSB model within the context of a specific experimental paradigm. NNSB performed a number of free-recall experiments in which participants studied lists of letters and digits. Letters served as targets for a subsequent free-recall test while digits served as distractors. Participants were not required to commit the distractors to memory. There were always six target letters, but the number of distractor digits varied from condition to condition in two ways. First, the number of distractor digits between target letters was manipulated from two to twelve digits. Second, the number of distractor digits following the last target was also manipulated from two to twelve digits. NNSB did not manipulate these factors in a factorial manner; instead they chose nine different pairings. The conditions can be represented as ordered pairs in which the first argument denotes the number of distractors between targets, and the second argument denotes the number of distractors after the last target. The nine conditions were (2,2), (2,4), (2,8), (2,16), (2,24), (4,2), (8,2), (16,2), (24,2). The first five conditions are used to explore the effects of increasing the number of distractors after the presentation of targets, while the last four conditions are used to explore the effects of increasing the number of distractors between targets.

It is standard to plot the probability of an item being recalled as a function of its serial position during study. Such plots are referred to as serial position curves. A rising left tail indicates primacy effects whereas a rising right tail indicates recency effects. In NNSB Experiment 1, each list contained six targets, and hence there were six points for each serial position curve. Figure 1 shows these empirical serial position curves. Each of the nine panels corresponds to a different condition, and the small circles are correct recall proportions.

It is helpful to have confidence intervals around the free-recall proportions in evaluating formal models. Unfortunately, NNSB did not provide this information. Instead, we have "guesstimated" .95% confidence intervals in a manner described in the Appendix. These "guesstimates" are graphed as error bars in the figure. As discussed in the Appendix, the "guesstimates" are most likely larger than the true confidence intervals. By overestimating the confidence intervals, we are more confident that if several predictions are outside their respective confidence intervals, then the model is misspecified.

The NNSB model is predicated on three assumptions: first, that the temporal position of each item is stored; second, that the stored value of temporal position randomly changes in time; and third, that free-recall probabilities are based on the distinctiveness of these randomly-changed temporal positions. To implement the first assumption we assume that the participant accurately stores the temporal position of the item at the time of study. For example, when the fifth

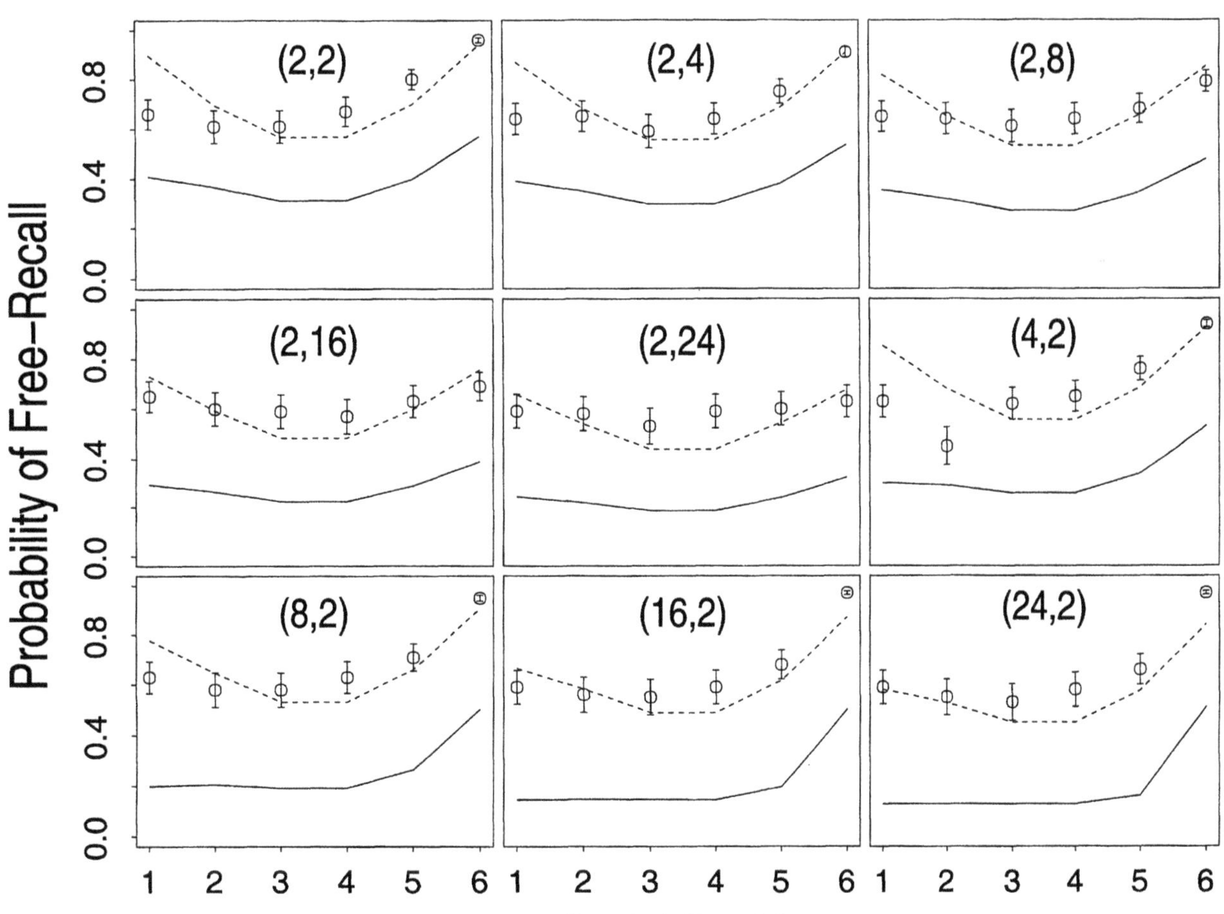

Figure 1. Serial position curves from NNSB's Experiment 1. The small circles are the data. The solid lines that grossly underestimate the data are from the temporal distinctiveness model evaluated with the parameters NNSB used to fit recency slopes. The dotted lines are fits from the temporal distinctiveness model with optimised parameters.

target is studied, the temporal position value of 5 is stored.[1]

The second assumption is that the temporal position of items can change. This is implemented by assuming that the temporal position of items undergoes a perturbation process or random walk (e.g., Estes, 1997). Suppose the stored temporal position of an item is x. A short time later, the stored temporal position may change to $x + 1$ with probability $\theta/2$, where θ is a free parameter. The stored temporal position may also change to $x - 1$ also with probability of $\theta/2$. Alternatively, the position may not change with probability $1 - \theta$. There are exceptions to those probabilities which occur when the temporal position is at the beginning of the list ($x = 1$) or at the end of the list ($x = 6$ for the NNSB experiments). In these cases, the temporal position remains unchanged with probability $1 - \theta/2$ or it can move one position towards the middle of the list with probability $\theta/2$. This change process is known as a random walk with reflecting boundaries (e.g., Feller, 1965). The number of changes in temporal position is directly related to the time between the study of an item and the start of recall. Therefore, end-of-list items undergo fewer changes on average than beginning-of-list items.

The most intriguing assumption is the third one, in which these perturbed temporal positions are used to calculate free-recall probabilities. The temporal distinctiveness of each item, denoted D_i, is the sum of distances between the item's temporal position and each of the other items' temporal positions.

$$D_i = \sum_{j=1}^{6} |x_i - x_j| \qquad (1)$$

where x_i denotes the temporal position of the ith target at the time of recall. The last step is to specify a function that relates distinctiveness (D_i) to free-recall probabilities. NNSB did not want the success of their model to hinge on tertiary assumptions like the form of the relationship between distinctiveness and free-recall probability. Their solution was to use simplicity as a guide, and they chose to scale distinctiveness linearly. The probability of free-recalling the ith target (denoted P_i) is D_i/k, where k is the scaling parameter.

In its minimalist form, the NNSB model has only three free parameters: the probability of a change (θ), the number of opportunities that a temporal position change may occur per unit time, and the scaling factor (k). In their implementation, NNSB used a fourth free parameter. They assumed that the number of change-opportunities per unit time in the retention interval was different from that during presentation of target items. This assumption is plausible as there may be different mnemonic loads while maintaining information in the retention interval than while storing new information in the study period. It is reasonable in this framework to expect the rate of temporal positions change to vary with mnemonic load.

In their paper NNSB did not fit the model to the serial position curves. Instead, they derived a quantity from their data called the *recency slope* (see Glenberg, Bradley, Kraus, & Renzaglia, 1983). The recency slope is the slope of the best fitting line through the correct free-recall proportions of the three most recent items (or the three right-most points in Figure 1). Although fitting the recency slopes is impressive, these fits do not imply that the model actually fits the serial position curves. The solid lines in Figure 1 show the model's predictions for the nine serial position curves for the parameters used by NNSB. These fits to the serial position curves are poor and grossly underestimate the correct free-recall proportions. To quantify the fit, we used a root-mean-squared (RMS) error statistic. The root-mean-squared error is the average discrepancy between the predicted probability of correct free-recall and the proportion of correct free-recall. When the parameters reported by NNSB are used to predict serial position curves the RMS error is .38, which is unsettling. It is evident from inspection that the predicted recency slopes fit the empirical recency slopes (this was the main empirical support NNSB provided for the model), but the gross underestimation of the serial position curves obviates this close fit.

[1] There are a few ambiguities in the NNSB article about whether distractors are items that receive temporal position assignments. In describing and illustrating the model, NNSB assigned temporal positions to both targets and distractors (see NNSB, p. 157). Hence the temporal position of the fifth target would be one more than the total number of preceding targets and distractors in the list. But, in fitting the temporal distinctiveness model to data, NNSB did not assign serial positions to distractors (Neath, personal communication). Therefore, as stated earlier, the fifth target was assigned temporal position 5. There is no a priori reason to prefer either approach. We follow the latter NNSB approach of assigning temporal position only to targets because this version of the model is sufficiently tractable that the parameters can be optimised to fit data.

The NNSB choice of parameters to evaluate their model was motivated by fitting the recency slopes. To find parameters that best fit the entire serial position curves, we used the SIMPLEX routine[2] (Nelder & Mead, 1965). The predictions from the best-fitting parameters are shown in Figure 1 as dotted lines. Although there is a capital improvement over the NNSB fit, the model still does a relatively poor job of accounting for the data (the root-mean-squared error was .099). Both NNSB's original parameters and the optimised parameters are shown in the first two rows of Table 1. These rows appear under the sub-heading "Murdock-NNSB Distinctiveness".

The bottom line is that the NNSB model fails to provide a satisfactory fit to the serial position curves. Even when the parameters are optimised, there are still large and systematic misses. The preceeding analysis shows how researchers may be led astray if they focus on derived statistics in the data at the expense of more fundamental ones. In the remainder of the paper, we attempt a few revisions of the NNSB model.

FROM DISTINCTIVENESS TO FREE-RECALL

Are there any models that keep the core assumptions of the framework and that adequately fit the data? The core assumptions are: (a) temporal position is encoded, (b) temporal position perturbs, and (c) the distinctiveness of the perturbed positions is predictive of free-recall performance. To answer this question, we generalised the tertiary assumption about the form of the function that relates distinctiveness to free-recall while leaving intact the core assumptions. In the NNSB model, distinctiveness is scaled by a constant (k), e.g., $P_i = D_i/k$. This function relating distinctiveness to recall probability can be generalised to an affine form, e.g., $P_i = k_0 + D_i/k$. The model with this function relating probability to distinctiveness was fit (see the dotted lines in Figure 2), and the resulting root-mean-squared error was 0.044. The best fitting parameters for this model are presented in Table 1 in the row labelled *Affine scaled*. The model fits much better with the affine scaling function than with the original linear one.

Establishing that there exists some scaling of distinctiveness to free-recall probability that, when coupled with the core assumptions, provides for a good fit of the data is a critical first step. If we were unable to provide such an existence demonstration, we could have rejected the core of the framework. But this existence result is only a first step. There is a serious problem in leaving the functional form unconstrained in theory. If researchers are unconstrained and find the best functional form to fit the data, one is never sure that the core components can be rejected. For any given set of data, there may exist some function form of the scaling from distinctiveness to free-recall probability that, when coupled with the core assumptions, will provide an adequate fit. Fitting

TABLE 1
Parameters and fits for NNSB models

	θ	*Change-opportunities per second* In-between targets	*Recency*	*Scale* k	k_0	*Threshold*	γ	*RMS error*
Murdock-NNSB Distinctiveness								
Original parameters	.05	17	7	22	—	—	—	.3761
Optimised parameters	.027	3	7	15.18	—	—	—	.0984
Affine scaled	.056	56	12	23.30	.492	—	—	.0438
Response process	.059	11	5	—	—	8.66	—	.0878
Flexible Distinctiveness								
Scaled	.149	5	3	5.49	—	—	.85	.0428
Response process	.223	5	3	—	—	9.107	1.56	.0691

[2] The NNSB model is ill-suited to optimisation in SIMPLEX because two of the parameters, the number of change-opportunities per unit time in the recency interval and the interval between targets, are integer valued. We used the following approach to mitigate this problem. First, a grid was set up over a large range of numbers for the change-opportunity parameters. For each point on the grid, we estimated the other two parameters with SIMPLEX and calculated the RMS error. The point on the grid with the lowest RMS then served as the best values for the two change-opportunity parameters.

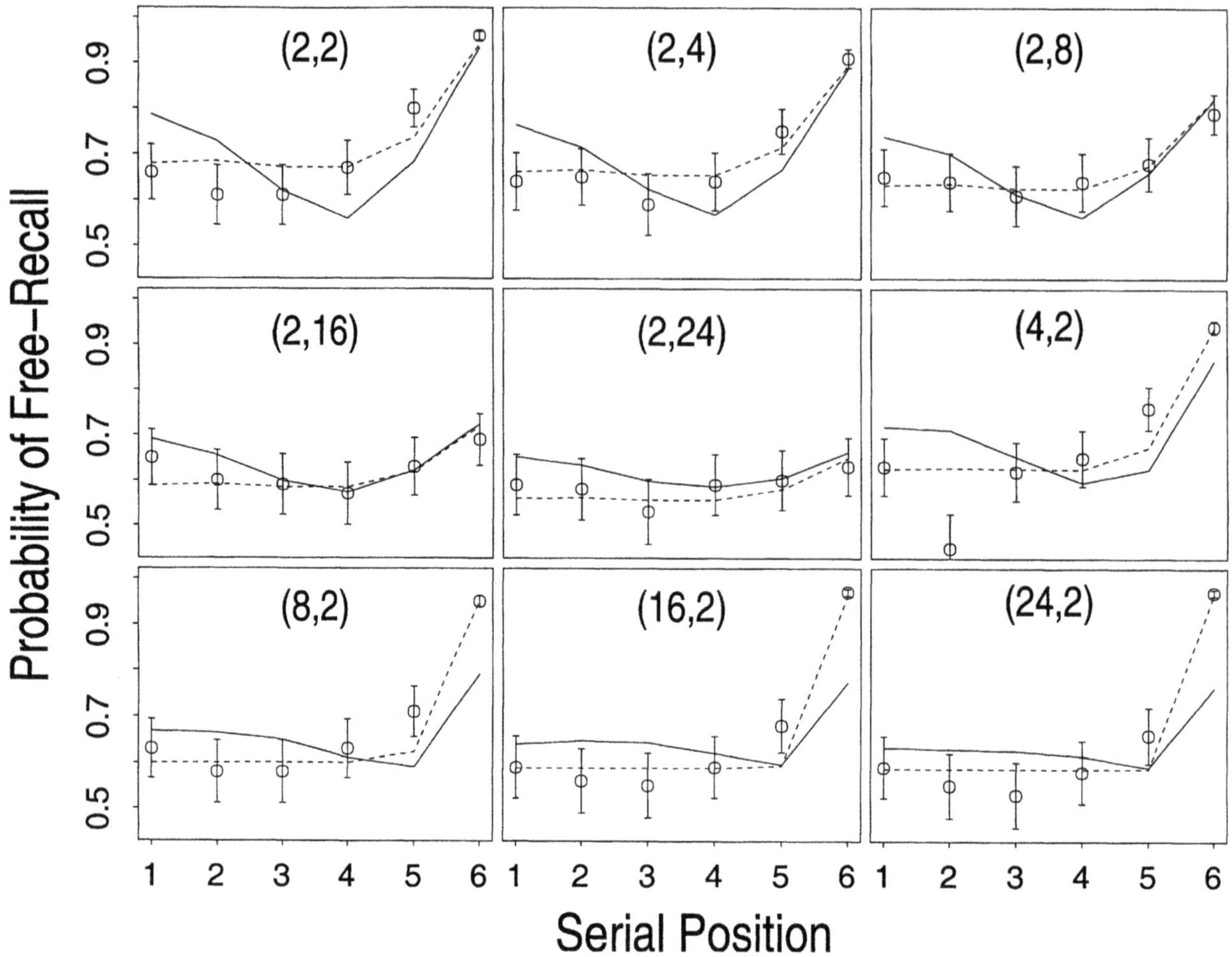

Figure 2. Fits of the affine scaled NNSB model (dotted lines) and the NNSB model with a theoretically grounded response process (solid lines).

the model with an unconstrained functional form may be more an exercise in curve fitting than a test of psychological theory.

Both the original linear scaling function and our affine scaling function are arbitrary in nature. There is no reason to prefer one over the other. The next step in testing the core assumptions is to postulate a theoretically grounded response process for relating distinctiveness to free-recall probabilities. We implemented a threshold approach. If, on a given trial, the distinctiveness of an item was greater than a threshold, it was sufficiently distinct to be immune to interference from other items and was recalled. Conversely, if the temporal distinctiveness was below the threshold, then the participant failed to recall that item due to interference. The mechanics of this response process are very similar to the Theory of Signal Detection and are used in other memory models such as SAM (Gillund & Shiffrin, 1984), TODAM (Murdock, 1982, 1983), and Atkinson and Juola's (1973, 1974) two-process model. It would be a strong demonstration if, when coupled to a theoretically grounded response process, the core assumptions of the temporal distinctiveness framework can account for the data.

To understand how this response process operates, it is necessary to examine how NNSB calculated distinctiveness values. At the time of test, an item has undergone a number of temporal position perturbations. In fact, because the perturbations are random, the temporal position of an item at test is represented by a discrete probability distribution with mass at several temporal positions. NNSB used the mean temporal position to calculate average distinctiveness. This approach of computing an average distinctiveness forces the researcher to specify a function to relate average distinctiveness to free-recall response probability. Of course, the choice of the form of the function is arbitrary. But, as has been shown, the form of this function greatly influences the fit of the model.

The major advantage to the threshold-based alternative is that there is no need to specify a functional form to relate average distinctiveness to response probability. To calculate free-recall probabilities, one must calculate the whole distribution of distinctiveness from the whole distribution of temporal positions. Free-recall probabilities correspond to the probability mass of distinctiveness that is greater than a criterion. Monte Carlo simulation was used to calculate the distribution of temporal positions. Based on this simulated distribution, the probability mass of distinctiveness was calculated as well as the proportion that exceeded the criterion. This approach is far more principled than the NNSB approach because the trial-by-trial variability in the perturbation process drives the variability in the distinctiveness distribution and, consequently, the proportion of that distribution over threshold.

We used SIMPLEX in conjunction with Monte Carlo simulations to find the best-fitting parameters. The results are shown as solid lines in Figure 2, and the best-fitting parameters are shown in Table 1 in the row labelled *Response process*. The fit is not much better than the original NNSB model with optimised parameters. The conclusion is that when coupled with a theoretically grounded method of mapping distinctiveness to response probability, the core assumptions provide at best a rough fit to the data. Certainly, there are systematic deviations, and we do not find the fit sufficient.

FROM SERIAL POSITION TO TEMPORAL DISTINCTIVENESS

In this section, we search for a means of revising one of the core assumptions. Up to this point, the functional form of temporal distinctiveness was considered part of the core assumptions. Temporal distinctiveness in the NNSB and Murdock formulations is the sum of position differences (see Equation 1). The intuition captured in this formulation is that (a) the beginning and end of the list are more distinct than the middle, and (b) distinctiveness is symmetric, favouring the beginning and end equally. One advantage of this formulation is its simplicity—it requires no parameters. The drawback is that the function is rather rigid. The approach pursued here is to find a temporal distinctiveness function that preserves the symmetry and bowed shape of the sums-of-differences function, but is more flexible. One such function, henceforth termed the *flexible distinctiveness function*, is:

$$D_i = \left[\frac{x}{n+1}\left(1 - \frac{x}{n+1}\right)\right]^{-\gamma} \quad \gamma \geq 0. \tag{2}$$

In the flexible distinctiveness function, x is the temporal position of an item at recall and n is the list length. Both the Murdock-NNSB temporal distinctiveness function and the new flexible distinctiveness function are shown in Figure 3. The reason for the $(n + 1)$ term in the denominators in Equation 2 is to preserve symmetry. The exponent of the power function (γ) acts as a tuning parameter. Large values correspond to a sharp tuning in which both beginning- and end-of-list items are much more distinct than middle-of-list items. Small values correspond to a shallow tuning in which beginning- and end-of-list items are only somewhat more distinct than middle-of-list items.

It is important to recognise a lack of theoretical grounding in flexible distinctiveness. A key concept in the Murdock-NNSB distinctiveness is that distinctiveness of an item is a function of the temporal position of the item as well as the temporal positions of all other items in the list. Brown, Neath, and Chater (1998) termed the Murdock-NNSB distinctiveness as *global* because of this property. They critiqued[3] global properties in distinctiveness formulations and recommend a *local* distinctiveness in which the distinctiveness is a function of the item's temporal position and its nearest neighbours.

The flexible distinctiveness formulation is neither global nor local; the distinctiveness of an item depends solely on its temporal position without regard to the positions of other items. The best way of viewing flexible distinctiveness is as a form that may mimic other formulations of local or

[3] Brown et al. (1998) presented participants with serial lists in which the time between items was varied within the list. There was a large temporal gap between the middle item and all of the others. The Murdock-NNSB distinctiveness predicts greater primacy and recency in this paradigm than in the one in which the time between items is constant. In Brown et al.'s experiments, there was an increase for correct recall for the middle item at the expense of the primacy and recency. Brown et al. concluded that distinctiveness was local in nature, and because the isolate in the middle of the list had no near neighbours, it was distinct. But, for the paradigm presented here, there are no differential predictions between global and local temporal distinctiveness. Both global and local distinctiveness predict symmetric u-shaped functions.

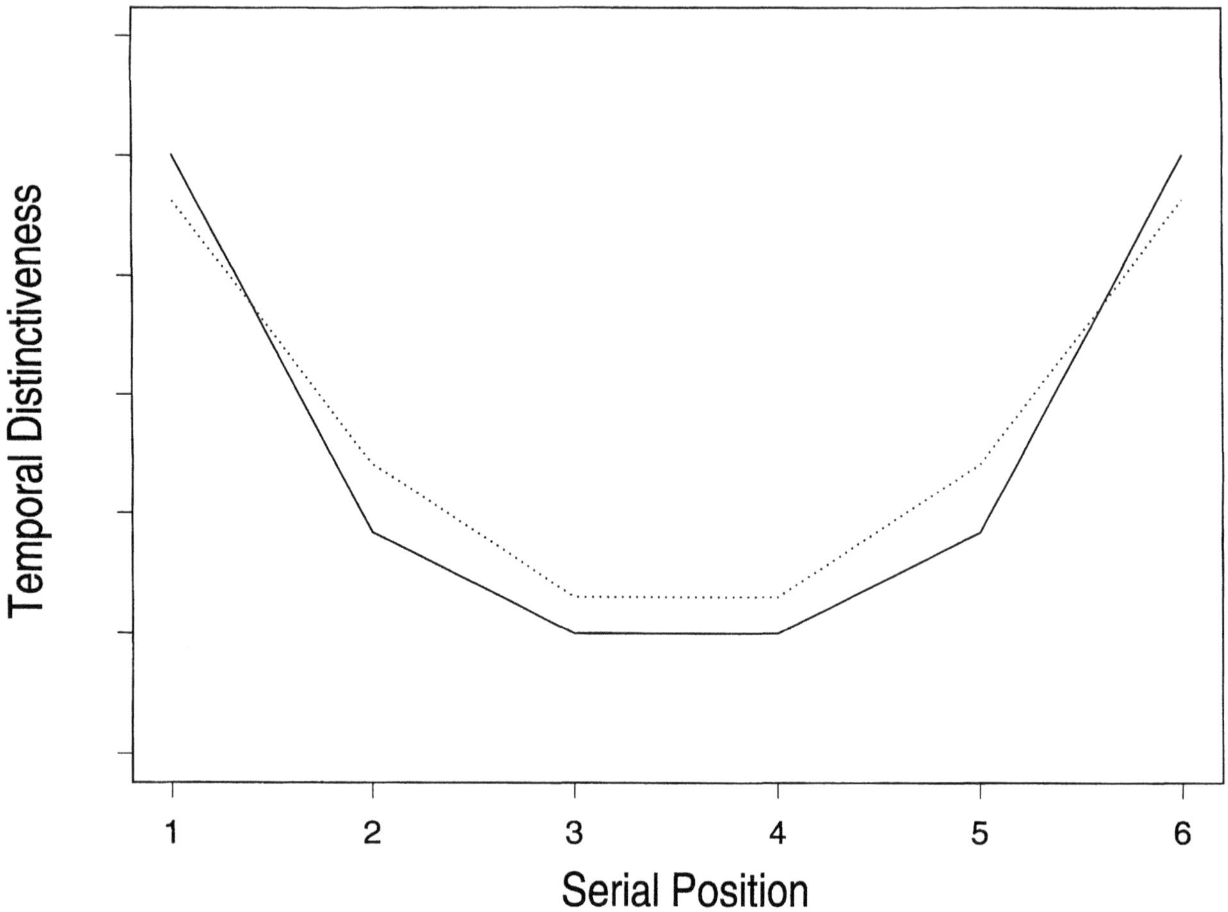

Figure 3. Temporal distinctiveness functions. The solid line corresponds to flexible distinctiveness (Equation 2) evaluated with γ = .85, and the dotted line corresponds to the Murdock-NNSB temporal distinctiveness function (Equation 1).

global temporal distinctiveness for this task. Flexible distinctiveness is designed to mimic u-shaped, symmetrical distinctiveness functions. Therefore, if a model with flexible distinctiveness does not account for the data, we can be fairly confident that this failure is not due to a mis-specification of the u-shaped temporal distinctiveness function. Instead, a failure represents a deeper failure of the core assumptions of the perturbation-distinctiveness approach.

The first step is to provide an "existence" demonstration. We show that there exists a functional form from distinctiveness to free-recall probabilities that, when coupled with the core assumptions and flexible distinctiveness, can fit the data. We used a linear function to relate distinctiveness to free-recall probabilities. The resulting model has five parameters, θ, the two change opportunities per unit time parameters, k (the multiplicative scaling parameter), and γ (the tuning parameter). As shown by the dotted lines in Figure 4, this model provides a relatively satisfactory account of the NNSB serial position curves (rms = .043). The best fitting parameters are shown in Table 1 under the sub-heading *Flexible distinctiveness* in the row labelled *Scaled.*

As mentioned before, these fits are necessary, but not sufficient. The good fit may be a function of the arbitrary relationship between distinctiveness and free-recall. As a final test, we coupled flexible temporal distinctiveness with the more theoretically motivated response process discussed earlier. The best-fitting parameters are shown in Table 1 (in the row labelled *Response process*), and the predictions from these parameters are shown as solid lines in Figure 4. Although this fit is better than the corresponding fit with Murdock-NNSB distinctiveness (this is not surprising as there is an additional parameter), the fit still misses some points (rms = .070).

This last model fit (represented by the solid lines) is the fairest test of the temporal distinctiveness framework. We have generalised temporal distinctiveness while still requiring the u-

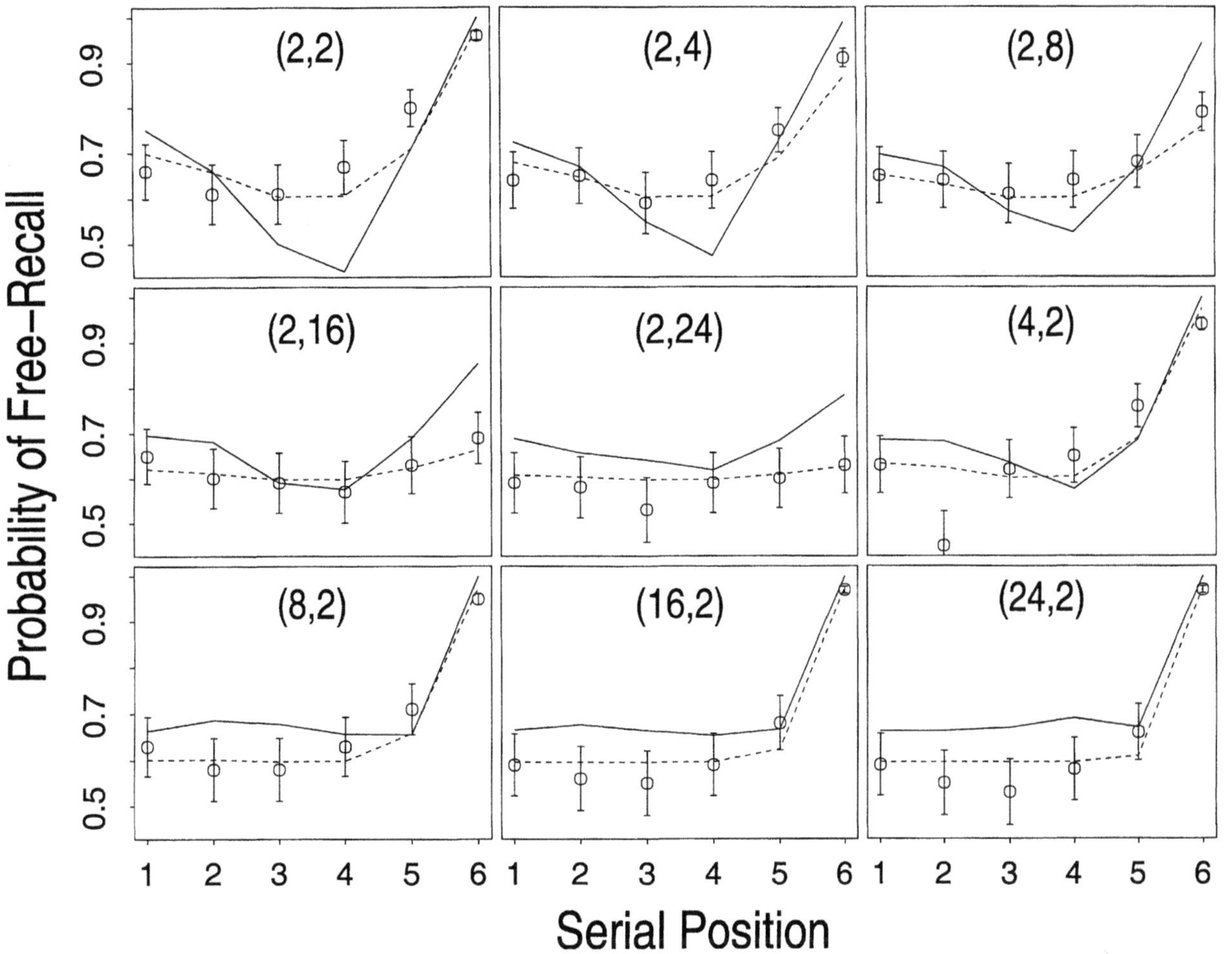

Figure 4. Fits to models with flexible distinctiveness (Equation 2). The dotted lines are for the flexible distinctiveness model with the original NNSB scaling. The solid lines are for the flexible distinctiveness model with the theoretically motivated response process.

shaped and symmetry properties. We have have implemented a theoretically grounded response process such that the fit is not a function of the flexibility of tertiary assumptions. With only a "guesstimate" of the variability in the data, evaluative statements must be made cautiously. On one hand, this is a good fit for a field with a history of accounting for only summary trends in data. On the other hand, the systematic nature of the misses leaves us unsatisfied. In the end, we suspect that those inclined to favour the model may view our fits as somewhat supportive of the temporal distinctiveness framework. Those less inclined to favour the framework may be less convinced that the fits are acceptable.

SUMMARY

The conclusion of the preceding analyses are threefold. First, the NNSB temporal distinctiveness model fails to account for serial position curves. Second, there are ways of modifying the NNSB temporal distinctiveness model that yield much better fits. We were able to generalise the scaling from distinctiveness to free-recall performance. Although this generalisation fits better, it is quite arbitrary and points to perhaps the most important issue—the fit of the model depends on tertiary and arbitrary assumptions. When we coupled the core assumptions of the temporal distinctiveness framework to a more theoretically grounded response process, we were unable to provide satisfactory fits. Third, the same basic pattern of results holds when the form of temporal distinctiveness is generalised. That is, the core framework provided satisfactory fits with arbitrary assumptions but failed when coupled with a theoretically grounded response process. In sum, temporal distinctiveness models may have the potential of providing a single process account of serial position effects that is elegant and parsimonious. Yet, as shown here, they have not been shown to fit benchmark data without recourse to arbitrary, and probably all-too-flexible, assumptions.

REFERENCES

Atkinson, R.C., & Juola, J.F. (1973). Factors influencing the speed and accuracy of word recognition. In S. Kornblum (Ed.), *Attention and Performance IV* (pp. 583–612). New York: Academic Press.

Atkinson, R.C., & Juola, J.F. (1974). Search and decision processes in recognition memory. In D.H. Krantz, R.C. Atkinson, R.D. Luce, & P. Suppes (Eds.), *Contemporary development in mathematical psychology (Vol 1)* (pp. 242–293). San Francisco: Freeman.

Atkinson, R.C., & Shiffrin, R.N. (1968). Human memory: A proposed system system and its control processes. In K.W. Spence & J.T. Spence (Eds.), *The psychology of learning and motivation: Advances in research and theory. Vol. 2* (pp. 89–195). New York: Academic Press.

Baddeley, A.D., & Hitch, G.J. (1977). Recency revisited. In S. Dornic (Ed.), *Attention and Performance 6*, (pp. 647–667). Hillsdale, NJ: Lawrence Earlbaum Associates Inc.

Brown, G.D.A., Neath, I., & Chater, N. (1998). *Scale-independent memory and perception.* Paper presented at the 39th Annual Meeting of the Psychonomic Society. Dallas, TX.

Craik, F.I.M., & Lockhart, R.S. (1972). Levels of processing: A framework for memory research. *Journal of Experimental Psychology: General, 104*, 671–684.

Einstein, G.O., McDaniel, M.A., & Lackey, S. (1989). Bizarre imagery, interference, and distinctiveness. *Journal of Experimental Psychology: Learning, Memory, & Cognition, 15*, 137–146.

Feller, W. (1968). *Introduction to probability theory and its applications* (Vol. 1, 3rd ed.). New York: Wiley.

Estes, W. (1997). Processes of memory loss, recovery, and distortion. *Psychological Review, 104*, 148–169.

Gillund, G., & Shiffrin, R. (1984). A retrieval model for both recognition and recall. *Psychological Review, 91*, 97–123.

Glenberg, A.M., Bradley, M.M., Kraus, T.A., & Renzaglia, G.J. (1983). Studies of the long-term recency effect: Support for a contextually guided retrieval hypothesis. *Journal of Experimental Psychology: Learning, Memory, & Cognition, 9*, 231–255.

Gordon, W. (1983). Memory disorders in aphasia: I. Auditory immediate recall. *Neuropsychologia, 21*, 325–339.

Johnson, N.L., Kotz, S., & Balakrishnan, N. (1994). *Continuous Univariate Distributions. Volume 2 (Second ed.).* Chichester, UK: Wiley.

Murdock, B.B. (1960). The distinctiveness of stimuli. *Psychological Review, 67*, 16–31.

Murdock, B.B. (1982). A theory for the storage and retrieval of item and associative information. *Psychological Review, 89*, 609–626.

Murdock, B.B. (1983). A distributed memory model for serial-order information. *Psychological Review, 90*, 316–338.

Nairne, J.S., Neath, I., Serra, M., & Byun, E. (1997). Positional distinctiveness and the ratio rule in free recall. *Journal of Memory and Language, 37*, 155–166.

Neath, I. (1993). Distinctiveness and serial position effects in recognition. *Memory and Cognition, 21*, 689–698.

Nelder, J.A., & Mead, R. (1965). A simplex method for function minimization. *Computer Journal, 7*, 308–313.

Postman, L., & Stark, K. (1969). Role of response availibility in transfer and interference. *Journal of Experimental Psychology, 79*, 168–177.

Rundus, D. (1971). Analysis of rehearsal processes in free recall. *Journal of Experimental Psychology, 89*, 63–77.

APPENDIX

NNSB published only mean correct free-recall proportions for their Experiment 1. We provide a reasonable "guesstimate" of confidence intervals. Our approach is to assume that each participant's recall proportion is a sample from a beta distribution (Johnson, Kotz, & Balakrishnan, 1994). The beta distribution is a functional form that can describe densities with high variability on the [0, 1] interval. The beta is described by two parameters α and β. We set $\beta = 1.2$ for all conditions and serial presentation positions. We then adjusted α such that the expectation of the beta density equalled the observed response proportion. For example, the value of the response proportion for the first serial position in the condition (2, 2) is .66. By choosing $\alpha = 2.33$, the resulting beta density has an expected value of .66, matching the observed response proportion. Figure 5 shows such a density and, as can be seen, it is quite variable. In fact, it is far more variable than the differences in individual participants. The variance of this density is used to compute confidence intervals. Because the variance of the beta is an overestimation of variability across participants, the confidence intervals are inflated. This, in turn, makes it harder to reject ill-fitting models. If a model can be rejected by an ill fit, then the rejection is made with more confidence than would be if the confidence intervals were estimated without such bias.

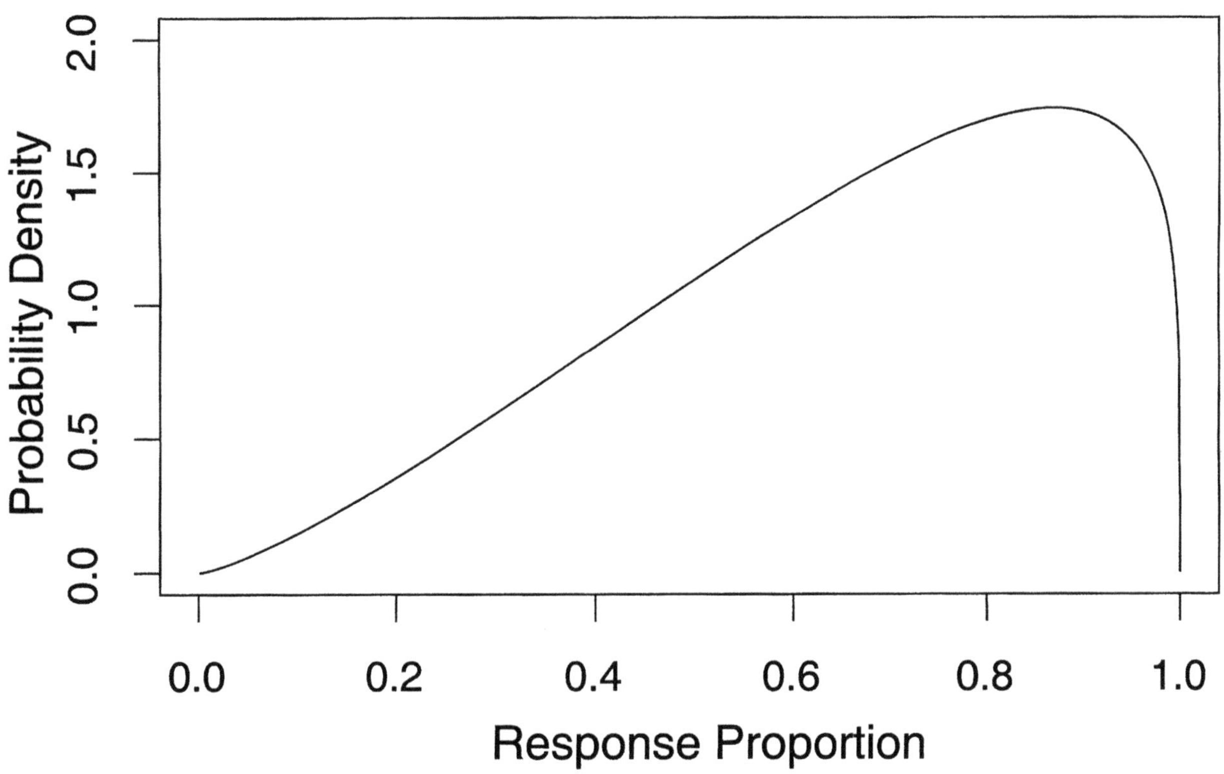

Figure 5. A beta-density model of variability across individuals in free-recall proportions. The figure shows the density for a mean response proportion of .66.

MEMORY, 2001, 9 (4/5/6), 313–322

The phonological loop and memory for rhythms: An individual differences approach

Satoru Saito

Osaka University of Education, Japan

The purpose of the current study was to examine the relationship between short-term memory for rhythm and the phonological loop in working memory. Results showed that digit span scores significantly correlated with the scores on the rhythmic memory task, and that the correlation between the two scores remained significant even after the common variance with reading speed was partialled out. Partial correlation and regression analyses indicated that the relation between memory for rhythm and digit span scores is mediated by the third component in the phonological loop, the component that is responsible for regulation of timing mechanisms in immediate memory tasks.

The role of working memory in everyday cognition has been examined intensively throughout the last three decades. In particular, the function of the phonological working memory in language-related activities, such as reading (Baddeley, Eldridge, & Lewis, 1981), counting (Logie & Baddeley, 1987), and language learning (Baddeley, Gathercole, & Papagno, 1998; Gathercole & Baddeley, 1993), has been adequately explained by the concept of the phonological loop (originally called the articulatory loop, Baddeley, 1986; Baddeley & Hitch, 1974) in Baddeley's working memory model (1990).

It is generally accepted that the phonological loop is a system for retaining phonemic information and comprises a phonological store and an articulatory control process (Baddeley, 1990). Materials presented auditorily have direct access to the phonological store, which can hold speech-based information for about 2 seconds. On the other hand, visual materials only have access to the store through the articulatory control process, which serves to allow visually presented materials to be phonologically coded by an articulatory mechanism. This process can also maintain materials within the phonological store by subvocal repetition.

A number of studies have shown the role of phonemic representations in the phonological loop. For example, it is well known that phonemically similar sequences of letters or words lead to poorer immediate serial recall than dissimilar ones (Baddeley, 1966; Conrad & Hull, 1964). In contrast to the phonemic features, other aspects of phonology, such as prosody, have not received much attention in working memory research. Some studies, however, have dealt with individual elements of prosody, e.g., stress judgements of written words (Burani, Vallar, & Bottini, 1991; Campbell, Rosen, Solis-Macias, & White, 1991), memory for pitch (Keller, Cowan, & Saults, 1995; Pechmann & Mohr, 1992), and memory for duration (Wearden, 1993; Wearden & Ferrara, 1993; Wearden & Culpin, unpublished data quoted

Requests for reprints should be sent to Satoru Saito, Department of Psychology, Osaka University of Education, 4-698-1 Asahigaoka, Kashiwara City, Osaka 582-8582, Japan. E-mail: saito@cc.osaka-kyoiku.ac.jp

Satoru Saito is a Visiting Fellow at the Department of Experimental Psychology, University of Bristol, UK.

This research was supported by a Grant-in-Aid for Scientific Research from the Ministry of Education, Science, Sports and Culture in Japan (#11710063).

Parts of the data in this article were reported at the 18th Annual Conference of the Japanese Psychonomic Society (1999). I am grateful to Erina Saeki and Maki Taniguchi for their assistance in collecting and scoring data in this study.

http://www.tandf.co.uk/journals/pp/09658211.html DOI:10.1080/09658210143000164

by Wearden, 1993). Most, but not all, of these studies have suggested that an articulatory component, probably the articulatory control process, serves to carry out the tasks concerned. These results suggest that the phonological loop might be a system for maintaining prosody of language.

Another line of evidence for this assertion comes from studies of language acquisition. It is known that there is a specific association between the phonological loop and language development (Baddeley et al., 1998; Gathercole & Baddeley, 1993). Research in language acquisition has suggested that the prosodic aspects of language are among the important linguistic features acquired by infants, showing, for example, that the prosodic features of adult speech to infants are more informative than those in speech to other adults (Fernald, 1989) and that younger infants can imitate the pitch of sounds that they have heard (Kessen, Levine, & Wendrich, 1979). Moreover, Masataka (1992) demonstrated that when the sound characteristics of maternal speech to infants were exaggerated, the type of fundamental frequency contour of the 3- to 4-month-old infant's response could be predicted from the type of the mother's preceding utterance. Masataka (1993) also demonstrated that repetition behaviour of prosodic features of maternal speech by infants affects later development of language ability. What is important about this research is that the repetition behaviour by infants is based on their immediate memory ability, and such ability should be supported by some kind of memory system. If we regard the phonological loop as a language acquisition device (Baddeley et al., 1998), it is a promising candidate for this supporting system. From this point of view, it seems reasonable to assume that the phonological loop is a short-term retention system not only for phonemic features of speech, but also for prosody, which involves accent, intonation, and rhythm of language.

A series of experimental studies has also shown the relation between the phonological loop and the prosodic feature of language. Saito (1994) suggested that the articulatory control process of the phonological loop involved some form of speech motor programming or planning (see also Baddeley & Wilson, 1985; Martin, Blossom-Stach, Yaffee, & Wetzel, 1995; Shallice & Vallar, 1990; Waters, Rochon, & Caplan, 1992), and that speech motor programming deals with rhythmic aspects of speech. Saito (1994) investigated the phonological loop by using a method of complex rhythmic finger tapping. The result showed that a concurrent rhythmic tapping task caused the phonological similarity effect for visual letter material to disappear; in other words, tapping out a rhythm distracted the activity of the phonological loop. He suggested that this speech motor programming, which deals with rhythmic information of speech, aids a control system for rhythmic activities in performing the complex rhythmic tapping. When the speech motor programming is used for rhythmic tapping, it cannot control the phonological loop for serial recall of letter materials.

This study addresses the issue of memory for rhythm, one of the prosodic features of language and an issue that has previously been neglected in the field of working memory. Although some researchers have investigated the reproduction of rhythms (e.g., Glenberg & Jona, 1991; Glenberg et al., 1989; Martin, 1972; Povel, 1981), no studies have examined rhythms in the framework of working memory. Recently, however, Saito and Ishio (1998) tested whether phonemic and rhythmical information was coded and maintained in a common system (the phonological loop). They reported an experiment in which participants undertook a task that required them to remember temporal sequences of rhythms. The results showed that the reproduction of rhythms was dramatically reduced by an articulatory suppression, and that the deterioration of the rhythm memory was larger than that effected by a concurrent spatial task, which does not diminish the activity of the phonological loop directly. They concluded that an articulatory component of the phonological loop apparently plays an important role in how memory for rhythms performs the task.

The purpose of the present article is to explore the relationship between the phonological loop and rhythmic memory performance through an individual difference approach. Participants are tested using a series of tasks, which include the following: (a) reproduction of the temporal rhythm sequence; (b) digit span task, which is a reliable measure of the phonological loop functioning; (c) articulation and reading speed, an ordinal task for measuring the ability of the articulatory control process. Two points are examined in this study. First, the correlation between two measures, (a) and (b), is verified. If retention of rhythmic information is supported by the phonological loop, scores on the rhythm memory task should correlate with scores on the memory span task for verbal materials. Second, the origin of the correlation between the two measures is sought. As mentioned before, some researchers have suggested that an articulatory component might serve to carry out phonological or sound tasks, even when the tasks do not involve phonemic processing (Pechmann & Mohr, 1992; Wearden, 1993; Wearden & Ferrara, 1993). In particular, Saito and Ishio (1998) suggested that the articulatory control process in the phonological loop plays an important role in maintaining temporal patterns of rhythms. The correlation between memory span and rhythmic memory performance may be mediated by the articulatory component in working memory. If the correlation between the two measures originates in the functioning of the articulatory control process, then the coefficient of the correlation should approach *zero* after the common variance with the articulation or reading speed is partialled out, because the speech rate is thought to be a good measure of the functioning of the articulatory control process (Chincotta & Underwood, 1996, 1997). On the other hand, if the correlation is mediated by other components, then the partial correlation should remain significant even after the common variance with reading speed is controlled.

METHOD

Participants

A total of 57 undergraduates and graduates from Osaka University of Education served as volunteers for this experiment. Their ages ranged from 19–24, with a mean of 19.6 years. All of them were non-musicians.

Materials and procedure

All participants engaged in a rhythm memory task, an auditory digit span task, an articulation speed task, a reading speed task, and a mental rotation task. In addition to these five tasks, 36 of the 57 participants performed a visual digit span task.

Rhythm memory. Presentation of stimuli was controlled by a personal computer (NEC; PC-9801RX). The stimulus set of rhythmic patterns was identical to that used in Saito and Ishio (1998), except that the tone duration and the interval within the rhythmic patterns were longer than those used in their research. The stimulus set consisted of 24 rhythmic patterns with six practice trials. Each rhythm pattern was composed of two parts: a tone part (●) and a silent part (—). A "●" represents a 56 ms tone duration followed by a 224 ms silent interval. A "—" represents a 280 ms silent interval. Consequently, "●" has a 280 ms SOA (stimulus onset asynchrony), "●—●" has a 560 ms SOA, and "●——●" has a 840 ms SOA. Figure 1 shows the stimuli for the test trials.

A total of 24 test rhythm patterns were presented in random order. In each trial, the participants heard a rhythm pattern. The participants' task was to reproduce the pattern by tapping a key of the computer with the index finger of their writing hand. Following a visual signal on the computer display, a rhythm pattern was presented

No.	
1	●–●–●–●
2	●●●–●–●
3	●–●●●–●
4	●–●–●●●
5	●–●●––●
6	●–●––●●
7	●––●●–●
8	●●––●–●
9	●●●––●●
10	●●●●––●
11	●–●●–●●
12	●––●●●●
13	●●●–●–●–●
14	●–●●●–●–●
15	●–●–●●●–●
16	●–●–●–●●●
17	●––●●–●–●
18	●–●––●●–●
19	●–●–●––●●
20	●●––●–●–●
21	●●●●●–●–●
22	●–●●●●●–●
23	●–●–●●●●●
24	●●●–●–●●●

Figure 1. Temporal structure of the rhythmic patterns used as to-be-remembered items in the present study. "●" represents a 56 ms tone duration followed by a 224 msec silent interval, and "—" represents a 280 ms silent interval.

from the personal computer. A 5-second unfilled delay followed the termination of the last tone. The end of the delay was indicated by a signal, which also informed the participants of the start of the recall period. The signal was a question mark on the computer display. Participants moved their writing hand to the keyboard of the computer from the side of the desk. By tapping a key (the XFER key) that produced the same tone used in the rhythm stimuli, participants reproduced the pattern of rhythm that had just been presented. The tapping intervals were recorded by the personal computer. When the participants finished their response, they pushed the "Q" key to indicate the end of their response to a rhythm.

Auditory digit span. To determine memory span, each participant took part in a standard digit span task. Random-digit strings were presented auditorily at the rate of one digit per second, via stereo dynamic headphones from a recording of a male voice stored digitally on a Macintosh computer. The end of a string was indicated by a question mark on the computer display and an auditory beep, which signalled the start of the recall period, when the participant had to repeat the digit sequence in the same order. The test commenced with two five-digit lists; the length of the lists was increased by one item each time until the participant made errors on both lists at a given length. If participants failed to recall one or two five-digit list(s), they were given two four-digit lists. Identical items appearing contiguously and ascending and descending sequences were avoided. Span was calculated as the greatest list length at which the participant was able to recall all lists correctly, plus half a point for each subsequent list recalled correctly.

Visual digit span. Random-digit strings were presented visually on a display (Macintosh computer) at the rate of one digit per second. The end of a string was indicated by a question mark on the display and an auditory beep which signalled the start of the recall period. The participant then had to answer the digit sequence in the same order orally. As for the auditory span task, the test commenced with two five-digit lists. The span calculation method was identical to that used in the auditory span task.

Articulation speed. Participants counted five times from one to ten in Japanese. They did this as quickly as they could, and were timed by stopwatch. This digit-articulation time was measured three times; one for practice and two for test trials. The mean times in seconds of the two test trials were used as the articulation speed scores.

Reading speed. Following Chincotta and Underwood (1996, 1997), a list of 200 random digits varying from zero to nine was constructed for measurement of reading speed. Consecutive repetition of digits and ascending and descending sequences of more than two digits were avoided. The list was printed in 20 rows each containing 10 numbers. Participants were asked to read the list accurately and as quickly as possible, pronouncing each digit individually and audibly. Time taken was measured by a stopwatch.

Mental rotation. To test non-verbal, visuospatial ability, a paper-and-pencil mental rotation task was administered. Each trial in this test consisted of five drawings of a two-dimensional picture; one was a target and the other four were alternatives; of those, three were different pictures from the target and one was the same picture as the target, rotated in different orientations. Participants were asked to select, from the four alternatives, the same drawing of the target picture. They were given 2 minutes to solve 18 trials. The number of correct trials was the score for this test for each participant.

RESULTS

Results are reported in two stages. The first section examines performance on the rhythm memory task. The second section further tests the phonological loop hypothesis by examining the patterns of correlations among different measures.

Rhythm memory

Tapping intervals as a response to a rhythm were recorded by the personal computer. When the rhythm consisted of n tones, the response to this rhythm had $n-1$ intervals (e.g., the rhythm that consisted of six tones had five intervals). If a response to a rhythmic pattern had one or more response intervals that were regarded as an error, the response was treated as an error trial. Two criteria were used for determining whether an interval was correct or not. That is, there are two types of the reference intervals for scoring data.

Reference interval for relative criterion. When a response preserved the relative structure of a rhythmic pattern, in spite of a breakdown in absolute time, it was regarded as a correct trial for the relative criterion. Each reference interval was calculated from total time of the all intervals for a rhythm. For example, the first interval of rhythm No. 4, which consists of four intervals (●●●—●—●), has a duration of one-sixth the total time of the four intervals. That is, the reference of this interval on the relative criterion is equal to the total response time divided by six. If the response interval differed from that reference by 15% or more, it was counted as an error. Mean and observed ranges of the correct responses for this criterion are presented in Table 1.

Reference interval for absolute criterion. The absolute criterion was based on a reference to the actual note that was presented. On this criterion, if a response interval differed from the presented one by 15% or more, it was counted as an error. The absolute criterion required punctual responses. Mean and observed ranges of the correct responses for this criterion are also presented in Table 1.

Correlation analyses

One of the main goals of this study was to examine the correlation between memory span, which is a measure of phonological loop functioning, and rhythm memory performance. As expected from the hypothesis, the auditory memory span correlated significantly with the scores on rhythm memory task, in both the absolute criterion, $r(55) = .43$, $p < .01$, and the relative criterion, $r(55) = .39$, $p < .01$. Furthermore, the visual memory span score also correlated with the rhythm memory score in both the absolute criterion, $r(34) = .48$, $p < .01$, and the relative criterion, $r(34) = .50$, $p < .01$. This positive correlation implies that an individual with high span produced a high number of correct responses on the rhythm memory task. A summary of descriptive statistics for the measures used in this study is presented in Table 1. Table 2 shows the entire correlation matrix of this experiment.

As predicted, the memory spans also correlated significantly with a measure of the reading speed for the auditory span, $r(55) = -.41$, $p < .01$, and for the visual span, $r(34) = -.33$, $p < .05$. The correlations replicate several previous studies, indicating that the span performance is supported by some kind of articulatory mechanism. However, the articulation speed correlated only marginally with the auditory span, $r(55) = -.22$, $p < .1$, and did not correlate with the visual span, $r(34) = -.11$. For this reason, only reading speed scores are used as a measure of speech rate in the following analyses.[1]

To summarise observations from Table 2, the memory spans significantly correlated with

TABLE 1
Summary of descriptive statistics for the measures used

			Observed score range	
Measure	*M*	*SD*	*Minimum*	*Maximum*
Memory for rhythms (relative)	18.65	3.27	9.00	24.00
Memory for rhythms (absolute)	17.05	4.22	6.00	24.00
Auditory memory span	6.90	1.29	4.00	10.50
Visual memory span (n = 36)	7.35	1.61	4.50	10.50
Articulation speed	8.13	1.34	5.72	11.24
Reading speed	55.31	8.83	37.81	83.45
Mental rotation	10.81	2.30	5.00	16.00

n = 57.

[1] There is a possible reason why correlation between memory span and the articulation speed scores did not reach statistical significance. Generally, the articulation rate has been measured by timing the several repetitions of a word-set (e.g., word-triplet, Baddeley, Thomson, & Buchanan, 1975; word-pair; Caplan, Rochon, & Waters, 1992). On the other hand, the rates of articulation in the present study were measured by using single words. The repetitions of a word-set would need somewhat complex speech motor programming, that is, the complex operation of phonological representations for the utterance. Then, the articulation rate in the previous studies could be a measure of the articulatory "control" process. In contrast, single-word repetitions seem to be performed automatically, particularly with a high-familiarity word as was used in the current study, and seem to be simply a measure of the speed of speech "muscle" operation. For this reason, the articulation measures in this study would not be expected to reflect the functioning of the speech motor programming and of the articulatory control process. However, the reading rate in this study was measured by the same procedure as the previous ones (Chincotta & Underwood, 1996, 1997), and correlated with the span scores successfully. This measure would include at least two components; (1) translation of visual materials to phonological codes, (2) speech motor programming for random sequence of digits. As both of them are thought to be functions of the articulatory control process in the phonological loop, it is not surprising that the reading rate measure is a good predictor of the memory span scores.

TABLE 2
Correlation matrix

	1	*2*	*3*	*4*	*5*	*6*	*7*
1. Memory for rhythms (relative)	–	.72**	.39**	.50**	.04	.02	.19
2. Memory for rhythms (absolute)		–	.43**	.48**	−.05	−.05	.03
3. Auditory memory span			–	.78**	−.22+	−.41**	.08
4. Visual memory span (n = 36)				–	−.11	−.33*	.32*
5. Articulation speed					–	.41**	−.01
6. Reading speed						–	.25+
7. Mental rotation							–

n = 57.
+$p < .10$. *$p < .05$. **$p < .01$.

rhythmic memory task and reading speed. Reading speed and articulation speed also correlated with each other, but the correct responses in the rhythm memory task did not show significant correlation with either of these two measures. The mental rotation task score correlated significantly with visual span score and marginally with reading speed, indicating the involvement of visual-spatial processing in these tasks.

A series of partial correlation analyses was used to examine the relationship among three measures: digit span, rhythm memory, and reading speed. These analyses will clarify the cause of a significant correlation between the scores on the rhythm memory task and memory span. If the correlation between the two scores comes from the same mechanisms that cause a correlation between memory span and reading speed, the degree of the correlation coefficient between the rhythm reproduction score and memory span should disappear after the common variance with the reading speed is partialled out. This is not the case: the partial correlation between auditory span and rhythm memory was significant both for absolute criterion, $r(54) = .44$, $p < .001$, and for relative criterion, $r(54) = .43$, $p < .001$, even after the common variance with reading speed was partialled out. In addition, the correlation between auditory memory span and reading speed also remained significant both after the absolute scores on rhythm memory task were controlled, $r(54) = -.42$, $p < .001$, and after the relative scores were partialled out, $r(54) = -.45$, $p < .001$. The pattern of the partial correlation between visual memory span and rhythm memory and between visual memory span and reading speed was identical to the one reported earlier for auditory span—respectively, $r(33) = .52$, $p < .002$, $r(33) = .56$, $p < .001$, $r(33) = -.39$, $p < .01$, and $r(33) = -.43$, $p < .01$. In addition, all these patterns are reproduced even when mental rotation scores were also controlled. These patterns suggest that the correct response score obtained from the rhythm reproduction task is uniquely associated with memory span scores. We can predict memory span significantly from reading speed and rhythmic memory performance on relative criteria, e.g., for the auditory span, $R = .59$, $F(2, 54) = 14.243$, $p < .001$.

As can be seen in Table 2, visual memory span showed stronger correlation with rhythm memory score, $r(34) = .50$, than did the auditory span, $r(55) = .39$ for all participants; $r(34) = .38$ for the corresponding participants. To examine the relation between visual span and rhythm memory, a hierarchical regression analysis was conducted using visual memory span score as a dependent variable and auditory memory span score, reading speed, mental rotation, and score on rhythm memory task as predictors. Table 3 shows the correlation between visual memory span score and four other measures from 36 participants,

TABLE 3
Visual memory span

Measure	*Correlation coefficient*	*Simple regression (% variance)*	*Hierarchical regression (% variance)*
Auditory memory span	.78	61**	61**
Reading speed	−.33	11*	0
Mental rotation	.32	10*	5*
Memory for rhythms (relative)	.50	25**	5*
Total	.84	71**	—

Correlation between visual memory span score and four other measures with percentage of variance accounted for by each based on simple and hierarchical regression (n = 36).
*$p < .05$. **$p < .01$.

TABLE 4
Auditory memory span

Measure	*Correlation coefficient*	*Simple regression (% variance)*	*Hierarchical regression (% variance)*
Visual memory span	.78	61**	61**
Reading speed	−.35	12*	1
Mental rotation	.15	2	0
Memory for rhythms (relative)	.38	14**	0
Total	.79	62**	—

Correlation between auditory memory span score and four other measures with percentage of variance accounted for by each based on simple and hierarchical regression (n = 36).
*p < .05. **p < .01.

together with percentage of variance accounted for by each based on simple and hierarchical regression. All simple regressions were statistically significant. The greater amount of variance in the visual memory span score was accounted for by auditory span, 61%. Reading speed score, mental rotation, and rhythm memory score were significant, accounting for 11%, 10%, and 25% of the variance in the visual memory span score respectively. Although reading speed did not account for any variance beyond that of the auditory span score, mental rotation score still accounted for 5% of the variance after the variances accounted for by auditory span and reading speed were partialled out from the visual span score. Furthermore, the rhythm memory score still accounted for 5% of the variance after the variances accounted for by auditory span, reading speed, and mental rotation score were partialled out. On the other hand, reading speed, mental rotation, and rhythm memory score did not account for any variance after those accounted for by visual span were partialled out from the auditory span score (see Table 4).

DISCUSSION

The present results indicate a close relationship between the phonological loop and short-term memory for rhythms. Partial correlation and regression analyses, however, did not support the hypothesis that the correlation between memory span and rhythmic memory originates in the articulatory control process in the phonological loop. In fact, the correlation coefficient remained unchanged even after the common variance with reading speed was partialled out, supporting the alternative explanation that the correlation is mediated by other components.

Three possibilities have to be discussed here. (1) An acoustic or auditory memory, distinct from components within the phonological loop, may contribute to the correlation between the two measures. (2) As mentioned in the introduction, there seem to be two components in the phonological loop—the articulatory control process and the phonological store. The latter may support the reproduction of rhythms. (3) A third component in the phonological loop may contribute to the correlation. Burgess and Hitch (1992, 1999) have recently proposed a new component in the phonological loop, a component apparently responsible for regulation of timing mechanisms in immediate memory tasks (see Hitch, Burgess, Towse, & Culpin, 1996). Contribution of other factors (e.g., attentional control) to the correlation between memory span and scores on memory for rhythms would be outside the range of possibility, because the correlation was still significant after reading speed and non-verbal mental rotation scores were partialled out. These three points are discussed in the order listed.

Because digits in both the auditory memory span task and tones in the rhythmic memory task were presented auditorily, there is a possibility that the correlation between auditory span and scores on the rhythm reproduction task might be mediated by an acoustic or auditory memory. In order to eliminate any contribution of acoustic or auditory memory to the correlation, a visual digit span task was included in this experiment. If the correlation between memory span scores and scores on memory for rhythms is mediated by the acoustic or auditory memory, visual digit span scores should not correlate with rhythm memory scores. However, the results showed a significant correlation between them, suggesting that acoustic or auditory memory mechanisms do not mediate the correlation. These results are unsurprising: the procedures forced participants to use a modality-free phonological coding. In the current procedures, a 5-second unfilled delay preceded the recall period in the rhythm memory task, and the participants were expected to rehearse the presented rhythms repeatedly. In order to maintain the rhythmic information, they had to reactivate the information. The activated representation would not be acoustic or auditory in nature, but instead would be an internally generated, and therefore possibly phonological, representation.

The correlation and regression analyses indicated that the mechanisms that cause a correlation between memory span and reading speed do not mediate the correlation between memory span and rhythm memory. As reading speed is thought to be a good measure of articulatory control functioning (Baddeley et al., 1975; Chincotta & Underwood, 1996, 1997), the factor behind the correlation between memory span and reading speed would be the articulatory control process in the phonological loop. The prevailing model of the phonological loop consists of two components (e.g., Baddeley, 1986), of which the phonological store remains.

The phonological store may partially support memory for rhythms. There are, however, some difficulties in accepting the hypothesis that the correlation between memory span and rhythm memory is mediated only by the phonological store. First, it is not clear from this hypothesis why visual span showed a stronger association with rhythm memory than did auditory span score. In general, auditory presentation of to-be-remembered items has an advantage over visual presentation in accessing the phonological store. For example, the phonological similarity effects with auditorily presented materials withstand an articulatory suppression, whereas those with visual materials do not (Baddeley, Lewis, & Vallar, 1984). Second, along this line, the phonological store hypothesis cannot explain the fact that the rhythm memory score still accounted for some variance after the variances accounted for by auditory span, reading speed, and mental rotation score were controlled. Third, the phonological store hypothesis contradicts the fact that the reproduction of rhythms was dramatically reduced by the concurrent articulation task (Saito & Ishio, 1998). Although this result does not rule out the possibility of involvement by the phonological store, it does indicate that another component that is abolished by concurrent articulation contributes to performance of the memory task for rhythms. What component contributes to both digit span and memory for rhythms, affected by articulatory suppression but independent from reading speed? Such a system might be the third component in the phonological loop proposed by Burgess and Hitch (1992) and Hitch et al. (1996), and recently extended by Burgess and Hitch (1999).

Previous investigations of immediate serial recall have shown a beneficial effect of temporal grouping (e.g., Frankish, 1985, 1989; Hitch et al., 1996). For instance, pause grouping of nine-digit lists into threes is effective for improving recall. In a later study, Hitch et al. (1996) found that articulatory suppression removed the pause grouping effect for visual lists, but not for auditory lists. They consequently assumed the involvement of the phonological loop in temporal grouping, and proposed a third component in the loop, responsible for controlling timing mechanisms in the immediate memory tasks.

Hitch et al. (1996) suggested that articulatory suppression requires speech production at a regular rate and it might be controlled by the same timing mechanism as the memory task. For this reason, the temporal grouping effects for visual materials disappeared under the articulatory suppression. They have also noticed the possibility that presentation through the auditory modality has an inherently temporal nature. In other words, the auditory presentation of verbal materials seems to induce relatively automatic activation of temporal information, whereas visual presentation needs stronger involvement of the timing production mechanisms to use temporal information for memory, because visual presentation of verbal materials gives list items less clear temporal distinctiveness than auditory presentation (see Glenberg & Swanson, 1986). This might explain why articulatory suppression did not affect temporal grouping with auditory presentation, but did with visual presentation.

Grouping by inserting pauses in a list seems to be an addition of rhythmic information onto the list; such information positively affects the immediate memory performance. A hypothesis here is that the same timing mechanisms that support the immediate memory would contribute to the retention of a temporal structure of rhythms. This hypothesis has three major advantages that overcome the flaws of the earlier two hypotheses. First, it assumes that the visual memory span task requires more involvement of the timing production mechanisms than does the auditory span task, and consequently predicts the fact that visual span associated more strongly with rhythm memory than did auditory span score. Second, as this mechanism might be independent from articulation itself (i.e., independent from the speed of the speech motor programming action), the rhythm reproduction score should be irrelevant to the correlation between memory span score and reading speed. Third, articulatory suppression needs a production of speech sounds at a constant rate and is thought to be regulated by the timing mechanisms used for memory tasks. Consequently, memory for rhythms would compete with articulatory suppression for the timing system, and should be abolished by the suppression.

Furthermore, this hypothesis is also supported by conclusions from time estimation literature. Recently, Fortin and Masse (1999) showed that short-term memory processing of letter order information interfered with time production, in which participants are required to accumulate the amount of temporal information corresponding to the target interval. They suggested that the accumulation of temporal information would be controlled by processing in short-term memory or working memory without the use of pure storage capacity (Fortin & Breton, 1995; Fortin & Masse, 1999). This assumption is consistent with the results from the current study, indicating that the correlation between memory span and memory for rhythms would be mediated by the timing control mechanisms.

In conclusion, a close link between memory span and memory for rhythms has been verified from the current results with musically untrained participants. In contrast to the initial assumption, it was found that such a relationship is independent of the articulatory control process in the phonological loop. A promising hypothesis that can account for the present results and the previous findings in a coherent way is to postulate a third component within the phonological loop (Hitch et al., 1996) which is responsible for the timing control in immediate memory tasks. Although this hypothesis may need to be refined, emphasising the importance of the timing mechanisms in working memory provides new insights and should contribute to progress in this field.

REFERENCES

Baddeley, A.D. (1966). Short-term memory for word sequences as a function of acoustic, semantic and formal similarity. *Quarterly Journal of Experimental Psychology*, *18*, 362–365.

Baddeley, A.D. (1986). *Working memory*. New York: Oxford University Press.

Baddeley, A.D. (1990). *Human memory: Theory and practice*. Hove, UK: Lawrence Erlbaum Associates Ltd.

Baddeley, A.D., Eldridge, M., & Lewis, V. (1981). The role of subvocalisation in reading. *Quarterly Journal of Experimental Psychology*, *33*A, 439–454.

Baddeley, A.D., Gathercole, S.E., & Papagno, C. (1998). The phonological loop as a language learning device. *Psychological Review*, *105*, 158–173.

Baddeley, A.D., & Hitch, G.J. (1974). Working memory. In G. Bower (Ed.), *Psychology of learning and motivation, Vol.VIII* (pp. 47–90). New York: Academic press.

Baddeley, A.D., Lewis, V., & Vallar, G. (1984). Exploring the articulatory loop. *Quarterly Journal of Experimental Psychology*, *36*A, 233–252.

Baddeley, A.D., Thomson, N., & Buchanan, M. (1975). Word length and the structure of short-term memory. *Journal of Verbal Learning and Verbal Behavior*, *14*, 575–589.

Baddeley, A.D., & Wilson, B.A. (1985). Phonological coding and short-term memory in patients without speech. *Journal of Memory and Language*, *24*, 490–502.

Burani, C., Vallar, G., & Bottini, G. (1991). Articulatory coding and phonological judgments on written words and pictures: The role of the phonological output buffer. *European Journal of Cognitive Psychology*, *3*, 379–398.

Burgess, N., & Hitch, G.J. (1992). Towards a network model of the articulatory loop. *Journal of Memory and Language*, *31*, 429–460.

Burgess, N., & Hitch, G.J. (1999). Memory for serial order: A network model of the phonological loop and its timing. *Psychological Review*, *106*, 551–581.

Campbell, R., Rosen, S., Solis-Macias, V., & White, T. (1991). Stress in silent reading: Effects of concurrent articulation on the detection of syllabic stress patterns in written words in English speakers. *Language and Cognitive Processes*, *6*, 29–47.

Caplan, D., Rochon, E., & Waters, G.S. (1992). Articulatory and phonological determinants of word length effects in span tasks. *Quarterly Journal of Experimental Psychology*, *45*A, 177–192.

Chincotta, D., & Underwood, G. (1996). Mother tongue, language of schooling and bilingual digit span. *British Journal of Psychology*, *87*, 193–208.

Chincotta, D., & Underwood, G. (1997). Bilingual memory span advantage for Arabic numerals over digit words. *British Journal of Psychology*, *88*, 295–310.

Conrad, R., & Hull, A.J. (1964). Information, acoustic confusion and memory span. *British Journal of Psychology*, *55*, 429–432.

Fernald, A. (1989). Intonation and communicative intent in mothers' speech to infants: Is the melody the message? *Child Development*, *60*, 1497–1510.

Fortin, C., & Breton, R. (1995). Temporal interval production and processing in working memory. *Perception & Psychophysics*, *57*, 203–215.

Fortin, C., & Masse, N. (1999). Order information in short-term memory and time estimation. *Memory & Cognition*, *27*, 54–62.

Frankish, C. (1985). Modality-specific grouping effects in short-term memory. *Journal of Memory and Language*, *24*, 200–209.

Frankish, C. (1989). Perceptual organization and PAS. *Journal of Experimental Psychology: Human Learning & Memory*, *15*, 469–479.

Gathercole, S.E., & Baddeley, A.D. (1993). *Working memory and language*. Hove, UK: Lawrence Erlbaum Associates Ltd.

Glenberg, A.M., & Jona, M. (1991). Temporal coding in rhythm tasks revealed by modality effects. *Memory & Cognition, 19*, 514–522.

Glenberg, A.M., Mann, S., Altman, L., Forman, T., & Procise, S. (1989). Modality effects in the coding and reproduction of rhythms. *Memory & Cognition, 17*, 373–383.

Glenberg, A.M., & Swanson, N.C. (1986). A temporal distinctiveness theory of recency and modality effects. *Journal of Experimental Psychology: Learning, Memory, and Cognition, 12*, 3–15.

Hitch, G.J., Burgess, N., Towse, J.N., & Culpin, V. (1996). Temporal grouping effects in immediate recall: A working memory analysis. *Quarterly Journal of Experimental Psychology, 49*A, 116–139.

Keller, T.A., Cowan, N., & Saults, J.S. (1995). Can auditory memory for tone pitch be rehearsed? *Journal of Experimental Psychology: Learning, Memory, and Cognition, 21*, 635–645.

Kessen, W., Levine, J., & Wendrich, K.A. (1979). The imitation of pitch in infants. *Infant Behavior and Development, 2*, 93–99.

Logie, R.H., & Baddeley, A.D. (1987). Cognitive processes in counting. *Journal of Experimental Psychology: Learning, Memory, and Cognition, 13*, 310–326.

Martin, J.G. (1972). Rhythmic (hierarchical) versus serial structure in speech and other behavior. *Psychological Review, 79*, 487–509.

Martin, R.C., Blossom-Stach, C., Yaffee, L., & Wetzel, F. (1995). Consequences of a central motor programming deficit for rehearsal and reading comprehension. *Quarterly Journal of Experimental Psychology, 48*A, 536–572.

Masataka, N. (1992). Pitch characteristics of Japanese maternal speech to infants. *Journal of Child Language, 191*, 213–223.

Masataka, N. (1993). Effects of contingent and non-contingent maternal stimulation on the vocal behaviour of three- to four-month-old Japanese infants. *Journal of Child Language, 20*, 303–312.

Pechmann, T., & Mohr, G. (1992). Interference in memory for tonal pitch: Implications for a working-memory model. *Memory & Cognition, 20*, 314–320.

Povel, D. (1981). Internal representation of simple temporal patterns. *Journal of Experimental Psychology: Human Perception and Performance, 7*, 3–18.

Saito, S. (1994). What effect can rhythmic finger tapping have on the phonological similarity effect? *Memory & Cognition, 22*, 181–187.

Saito, S., & Ishio, A. (1998). Rhythmic information in working memory: Effects of concurrent articulation on reproduction of rhythms. *Japanese Psychological Research, 40*, 10–18.

Shallice, T., & Vallar, G. (1990). The impairment of auditory-verbal short-term storage. In G. Vallar & T. Shallice (Eds.), *Neuropsychological impairment of short-term memory* (pp. 11–53). New York: Cambridge University Press.

Waters, G.S., Rochon, E., & Caplan, D. (1992). The role of high-level speech planning in rehearsal: Evidence from patients with apraxia of speech. *Journal of Memory and Language, 31*, 54–73.

Wearden, J.H. (1993). Decisions and memories in human timing. *Psychologia Belgica, 3*, 241–253.

Wearden, J.H., & Ferrara, A. (1993). Subjective shortening in humans' memory for stimulus duration. *Quarterly Journal of Experimental Psychology, 46*B, 163–186.

MEMORY, 2001, *9* (4/5/6), 323–331

The impact of broadband noise on serial memory: Changes in band-pass frequency increase disruption

Sébastien Tremblay, William J. Macken, and Dylan M. Jones
Cardiff University, UK

Irrelevant sound consisting of bursts of broadband noise, in which centre frequency changes with each burst, markedly impaired short-term memory for order. In contrast, a sequence of irrelevant sound in which the same band-pass noise burst was repeated did not produce significant disruption. Serial recall for both visual-verbal (Experiment 1) and visual-spatial items (Experiment 2) was sensitive to the increased disruption produced by changing irrelevant noise. The results provide evidence that sounds that are largely aperiodic can produce marked disruption of serial recall in a similar manner to periodic sounds (e.g., speech, musical streams, and tones), and thus show a changing-state effect.

By its mere presence background sound may be detrimental to cognitive performance. Interest in this effect is long-standing (e.g., Broadbent, 1958), but early studies were largely confined to the impact of noise on cognitive performance with the major variable of interest being the level of noise. In a classic study, Colle and Welsh (1976) found that background speech disrupted serial recall of visually presented items, despite the fact that participants were instructed to ignore the speech. In contrast to the robust and marked detrimental effect of irrelevant speech on serial recall, continuous noise sometimes produces modest effects (e.g., Salamé & Baddeley, 1982; LeCompte, 1994), but many studies fail to produce any such disruption (e.g., Jones, Miles, & Page, 1990; Salamé & Baddeley, 1987). The current study examines the role of noise in relation to the disruption of serial memory by irrelevant sound.

Subsequent work has shown that not only is narrative speech more disruptive than continuous white noise (e.g., Colle & Welsh, 1976), but, for instance, repeating a single token (e.g., J, J, J, J) results in substantially less disruption of serial recall than presenting a sequence of different tokens (e.g., C, H, J, U). The so-called changing-state effect refers to the phenomenon that an auditory signal exhibiting appreciable change between its components causes a marked deficit in recall performance as opposed to steady signals (e.g., Jones, Madden, & Miles, 1992; LeCompte, 1995). Likewise, tones varying in frequency or timbre produce a much greater irrelevant sound effect than a repeated tone (e.g., Jones & Macken, 1993; Neath, Surprenant, & LeCompte, 1998) and instrumental music with many sharp changes is more disruptive than music with slow changes (e.g., Klatte, Kilcher, & Hellbrück, 1995). According to the empirically based concept of changing-state, little or no disruption will occur if the background stream consists of a repeated or continuous sound, but a stream containing change, will disrupt serial recall appreciably.

Whether the irrelevant sound is meaningful (e.g., Jones et al., 1990), or similar to the to-be-remembered items (e.g., Jones & Macken, 1995;

Requests for reprints should be sent to Dylan Jones, School of Psychology, Cardiff University, PO Box 901, Cardiff CF1 3YG, UK. Email: JonesDM@cardiff.ac.uk

Sébastien Tremblay is now at Laval University, Québec, Canada.

Special thanks are due to Dr John Culling for his help in editing the noise stimuli. We would also like to thank Robert Hughes for critical reading of an earlier draft. This work was supported in the form of a project grant to Dylan M. Jones from the Defence Evaluation & Research Agency (Farnborough, Hants), Centre for Human Sciences.

http://www.tandf.co.uk/journals/pp/09658211.html DOI:10.1080/09658210143000010

LeCompte & Shaibe, 1997) plays a minor role in the irrelevant sound effect. What seems to be critical is whether the irrelevant sound is changing or steady. The applicability of the changing-state assumption has been verified with a range of speech and nonspeech stimuli. There is a large body of evidence to suggest that speech and nonspeech are functionally similar in relation to disruption of serial recall, (see Jones & Tremblay, 2000, for a discussion). A compelling demonstration is the finding that the same physical stimulus (sinewave speech), whether perceived as speech or nonspeech sound, disrupts serial recall to the same degree (Tremblay, Nicholls, Alford, & Jones, 2000). The latter contrast was performed by manipulating the speech-likeness perceivability of the same sinewave speech stimuli through pre-exposure to the sound and instructions given to the participants. Sinewave speech is an ambiguous stimulus consisting of a number of sinusoids that replicate natural speech utterances (see, e.g., Remez & Rubin, 1990). The group of participants who had been trained to perceive the sinewave stimuli as speech were not more susceptible to disruption by those sounds than the untrained group of participants who reported the same sinewave stimuli to sound like "electronic music" or "computer bleeps".

The main objective of the current work is to test the possibility that the changing-state phenomenon applies not only to speech and nonspeech but also to noise. The results of the current series have a bearing on the literature reporting a range of inconsistent effects of noise on short-term memory. Although many studies have investigated the issue of noise interference, the findings are rather equivocal and it is not yet possible to state with a certain degree of confidence what type of noise and what kind of tasks will result in significant disruption of performance.

Early work on the impact of noise (pink or white noise) on performance centred on the effects of the level of intensity. Such sounds are referred to generally as aperiodic, in that they have no clear cycle of repetition and hence have no clear tonal quality. One key objective of this work was to establish the threshold of intensity at which loud noise impaired mental performance. For example, performance on vigilance tasks may either be facilitated (Poulton, 1977) or reduced (Broadbent, 1979) by continuous white noise. Broadbent (1979) stated that detrimental effects on vigilance depend mainly on the noise being over 95 dB(A). Additionally, other tasks such as mental arithmetic (e.g., Woodhead, 1964) were affected by intermittent white noise, but only if the bursts arrived during the execution of the response or the intake of information, respectively. This early literature seems to suggest that in order to be disruptive noise needs to be very loud and its presentation restricted to certain parts of the task.

In most of the studies on the effects of noise on short-term memory, the to-be-remembered (TBR) items were presented auditorily and the noise used a means of masking (e.g., Rabbitt, 1968). In the case of visually presented verbal items, the noise was very loud and the effects modest (see, e.g., Salamé & Baddeley, 1982, Experiment 3), or, again, timing between TBR items and bursts of pink noise was very important (Salamé & Wittersheim, 1978). In some other studies the presence of continuous noise actually improved recall performance, though marginally, compared to a quiet background (e.g., Hockey & Hamilton, 1970; see also Davies & Jones, 1975). In contrast to effects of noise, speech and nonspeech sounds such as tones or music have consistently been shown to impair markedly serial recall. Irrelevant sound played at levels as low as 40 dB(A) was shown to disrupt serial recall substantially (e.g. Colle, 1980; see also Tremblay & Jones, 1999), a level far below the threshold of 95 dB(A) necessary for white noise to impair visual vigilance. However to our knowledge, in most if not all studies, the impact of noise has been tested using either continuous noise or intermittent noise with the same burst presented repeatedly. By contrast, the changing-state effect has been demonstrated with many types of periodic sounds such as speech and tones, but is yet to be tested with aperiodic sounds such as noise.

Like the effect of loud aperiodic sound, the degree of interference by irrelevant periodic sound depends on the characteristics of the prevailing cognitive task. Serial recall in particular has been shown to be susceptible to disruption, especially to the increased effect caused by changing-state sound (see Beaman & Jones, 1998). The extent to which seriation (the process of placing items into order) is involved in a memory task seems to be related to the degree of disruption caused by irrelevant sound. For example, the effect of irrelevant sound on free recall is relatively small (Richardson, 1984; Salamé & Baddeley, 1990) unless participants are encouraged to use a serial rehearsal strategy (Beaman & Jones,

1998; LeCompte, 1994). Other tasks with a burden on memory other than strict serial recall, such as the missing-item task (LeCompte, 1994; Beaman & Jones, 1997), mental arithmetic (Buchner, Steffens, Irmen, & Wender, 1998) and memory for prose (Banbury & Berry, 1998) are relatively sensitive to the deleterious effect of irrelevant sound, though to a lesser degree (see, e.g., Jones & Macken, 1993). However these tasks seem to also rely on rote rehearsal (see Beaman & Jones, 1997, for a discussion). Some other tasks with neither memory nor a seriation component—sentence acceptability tests (Boyle & Coltheart, 1996) and a range of perceptual tasks (e.g., Baddeley & Salamé, 1986; Burani, Vallar, & Bottini, 1991)—proved to be immune to disruption by irrelevant sound.

It is reasonable, on the basis of precedent, to claim that tasks requiring memory for order are more sensitive to disruption by varying irrelevant sound. The key question addressed by the present series is whether the disruptive effect observed at low levels with periodic sounds can be observed with aperiodic sounds. In order to achieve this, the noise meets the key criterion of changing in composition by using bursts of band-pass noise that change in centre frequency. If the changing-state phenomenon extends to aperiodic sounds, bursts of broadband noise should disrupt serial recall substantially only when the auditory sequence is made up of bursts from different bands, not when the same band is repeated.

EXPERIMENT 1

In the first experiment we contrast the effects of noise bursts on immediate serial recall for visually presented verbal items. The main contrast is between two different types of sequences: one type consisting of repeated presentations of the same burst of noise, and the second type made up of noise bursts at different band-pass frequencies.

Method

Participants. A total of 20 participants, male and female students, volunteered to take part in the study. All reported normal hearing and normal (or corrected-to-normal) vision.

Materials. Seven item lists of to-be-remembered items were constructed using random orders of the consonants *f*, *k*, *l*, *m*, *q*, *r*, and *y*. The letters were presented in lower-case 48-point Geneva font and were black on a light grey background on the screen of a *Macintosh LC* computer using *HyperCard* software. The rate of presentation was at one letter per second (on for 0.8 s, off for 0.2 s). A *Consilium Industrie* (*Model PN11*) generator produced white noise (with equal energy over the audio frequency range) that was then filtered at one of a range of centre frequencies, at 250, 500, 1000, 2000, and 4000 Hz. The bandwidth of the filters measured at points that were 10 dB down from the peak of the pass band were 150, 300, 600, 1200, and 2400 Hz, respectively (see Moore, 1996). Thus, the ratio of centre-frequency to bandwidth was $Q_{10} = 1.66$, which indicates that the band-pass noises had a low degree of tonality, and sounded noisy rather than tonal (see, for example, Rosen & Howell, 1991, for a general account of the characteristics of filters). A pilot study confirmed that the bands were of approximately equal loudness.

Using these filters, two sets of noise sequences were created: In one, the steady-state condition, bursts of noise at the same centre frequency were repeated (randomly chosen with the constraint of being equally represented through the experiment); in the other, the changing-state condition, bursts from each of the five centre frequencies were assembled in a random order. In neither case could the sounds be mistaken for speech. Each burst of noise lasted 300 ms and was separated from the next burst by a gap of silence lasting 200 ms. Sound was played back to the participant through headphones at approximately 65 dB(A) as measured by a sound-level meter from an artificial ear (*Brüel & Kjaer, Naerum*).

Design and procedure. Participants initiated each trial via a HyperCard button on the screen of the computer using a mouse. After the seven consonants had been presented, participants were prompted to recall the list by writing it in its order of presentation. Three auditory conditions were presented during the presentation and rehearsal phases of the task—changing-state, steady-state, and quiet—varying in a random fashion from trial to trial, but with the constraint that there were no two successive trials of the same condition. In each case recall took place in silence. There were 60 trials in all, 20 for each auditory condition. Each band-pass noise centre frequency was represented equally (that is four times) over the 20 trials in the steady-state condition. Before the experiment proper, participants were given five practice trials in quiet; the experimental session lasted 35–40 minutes.

Results and discussion

Participants' responses were scored by a strict serial order criterion: Each item had to be in the correct position in order for the response to be scored correct. Probability of serial recall error (pooled over serial positions) in relation to auditory condition is reported in Table 1. Data were subjected to a 3 (auditory condition) × 7 (serial position) repeated-measures analysis of variance. The effect of conditions was significant, $F(2,38) = 9.38$, $MSE = 7.26$, $p < .001$, as was the effect of serial position, $F(6,114) = 21.57$, $MSE = 7.89, p < .0001$, but there was no interaction between serial position and conditions, $F(12,220) = MSE = 2.24$, $p > .05$. Typical serial position curves with primacy and recency recall advantages were obtained, and the effect of noise was similar for all positions as supported by the absence of significant interaction between serial position and condition (see Figure 1).

Planned comparisons between the three components of the main effect showed that changing-state noise was significantly more disruptive than quiet, $F(1,38) = 14.72$, $p < .0005$, but the effect of steady-state noise was not significantly different

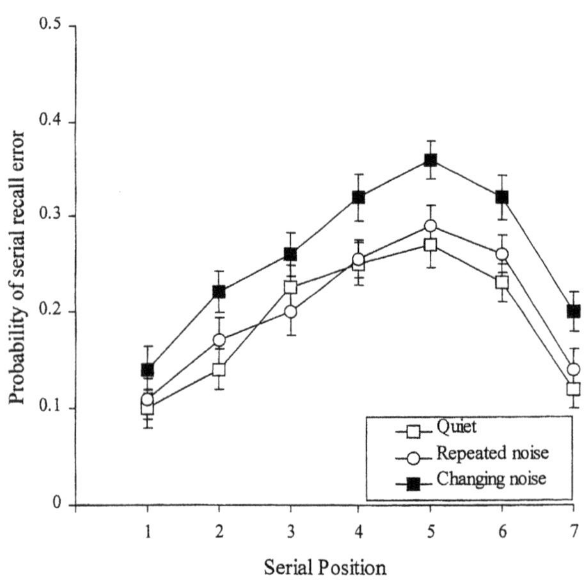

Figure 1. Results from Experiment 1: Probability of serial recall error in relation to serial position for the three auditory conditions (quiet control, repeated noise, and changing noise). Error bars represent the standard errors.

TABLE 1
Results from Experiments 1 and 2

Conditions	*Verbal*	*Spatial*
Quiet control	.19	.43
Repeated noise	.20	.41
Changing noise	.26	.54

Probability of serial recall error, averaged over serial positions, in relation to quiet control, repeated noise, and changing noise. Serial recall for both visual-verbal and visual-spatial items is impaired by changing noise.

from quiet, $F(1,38) = 0.31$, $p > .05$. Changing-state was also significantly more disruptive than steady-state noise, $F(1,38) = 13.39$, $p < .001$.

The results of Experiment 1 are unequivocal: There are clear-cut effects of changing-state noise. In other experiments studying the disruption of serial recall in which noise was used (e.g., Salamé & Baddeley, 1989), the sound was continuous rather than occurring in discrete bursts of changing centre frequency. The results of Experiment 1 show that when discontinuous and unchanging noise is used, the effect on serial recall is rather modest (see Salamé & Wittersheim, 1978). The results are also novel in showing a changing-state effect with noise, an effect until now confined to periodic stimuli such as tones and speech.

EXPERIMENT 2

In Experiment 2 we tested whether serial recall for non-verbal, visual-spatial items is also sensitive to the increased disruption produced by changing irrelevant noise, using a short-term memory task that requires serial recall for the order in which a sequence of dots was presented within a two-dimensional matrix. Given that the to-be-remembered dots are re-presented at recall, retrieval of order rather than item information is predominant (see Jones, Farrand, Stuart, & Morris, 1995). There is ample evidence to show that such a task produces typical serial position curves with marked primacy and recency recall advantages (see, e.g., Farrand & Jones, 1996), and is sensitive to the suffix effect (Parmentier, Tremblay, & Jones, 2001). Generally, this visual-spatial serial recall task may be regarded as a good analogue of the classical verbal serial recall task.

Method

Participants. A total of 18 Cardiff University undergraduates took part in this experiment in exchange for course credits. All of them reported normal vision or corrected-to-normal vision.

Materials. A visual-spatial version of the immediate serial recall task was employed. The task was similar to that used in Jones et al. (1995). A sequence of seven black dots 1 cm in diameter was presented randomly, one dot at a time, within a 600 × 600 pixel matrix. The matrix took up a 16.5 cm × 16.5 cm white area on the computer screen (*PC compatible machine*). For each trial, the coordinates for positioning the dots were randomly generated in software (*Visual Basic 5.0*), but constrained by the rule that if any randomly generated dots were to appear closer than 60 pixels (2 cm) in either axis of the matrix, another set of coordinates was generated. Only the dots, not the matrix, were visible on the display. On each trial, a sequence of seven dots was displayed at a rate of one dot every second (700 ms on, 300 ms off). After the presentation of the seventh dot, all dots were simultaneously re-presented in the spatial locations in which they had been presented originally. Participants responded by using the mouse to locate and click on the dots in the order they were presented initially. To indicate when a dot had been selected by the participant, the colour of the dot changed from black to green and remained so until the whole response sequence had been produced.

The irrelevant noise sequences were the same as those for Experiment 1. The sound was played through headphones at approximately 65 dB(A).

Design. Three conditions were tested: a quiet control and two noise conditions, one with repeated and the other with changing noise. There were 15 trials in each condition. The presentation of the conditions was randomised with the restriction that there could be a maximum of three successive trials of the same condition.

Procedure. Participants were seated approximately 50 cm from the computer screen on which the visual-spatial task was displayed. Written instructions encouraged participants to respond as quickly and as accurately as possible, and stated that once an item had been selected it would not be possible to alter it. There were 3 practice trials followed by 30 experimental trials. The presentation of trials was self-paced; participants mouse-clicked on a button on the screen to initiate a trial. Immediately following the presentation of the last to-be-remembered item (seventh) the whole set of dots was re-presented simultaneously, which prompted participants to begin retrieval. Participants were tested individually and the experiment took 25–30 minutes.

Results and discussion

As in Experiment 1, a strict serial recall criterion was used to score the data. The probability of serial recall error for visual-spatial items in relation to auditory condition is presented in Table 1. A repeated-measure ANOVA was carried out on the data with serial position (7 levels) and conditions (3 levels). The main effects of both condition, $F(1,17) = 22.04$, $MSE = 7.08$, $p < .001$ and serial position, $F(6,102) = 21.10$, $MSE = 3.49$, $p < .001$, were significant. However, the interaction between condition and serial position was not significant, $F(6,102) = 0.72$, $MSE = 1.69$, $p = .73$. The pattern of interaction was similar to the one found in Experiment 1 (see Figure 2).

Planned contrasts revealed that the difference between quiet control and the repeated-noise

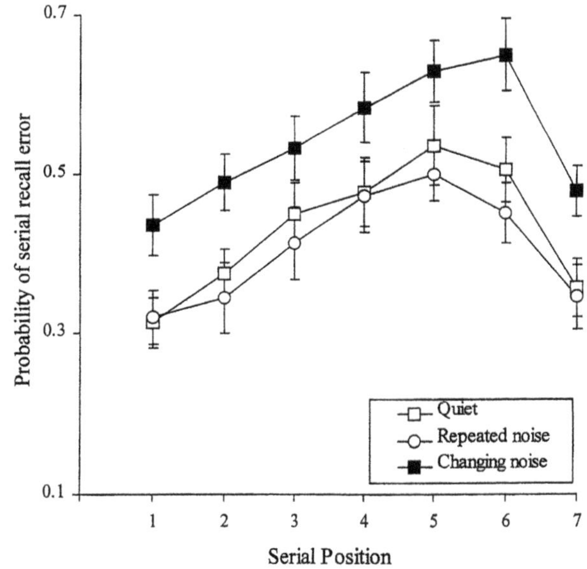

Figure 2. Results from Experiment 2: Probability of serial recall error in relation to serial position for the three auditory conditions (quiet control, repeated noise, and changing noise). Error bars represent the standard errors.

condition was not significant, $F(1, 17) = 1.61$, $p = .21$, and that serial performance under changing noise was significantly worse than that under repeated noise, $F(1, 17) = 39.31$, $p < .0001$.

The results of Experiment 2 replicate those obtained in Experiment 1 and extend the demonstration of a changing-state noise effect to serial recall for visual-spatial items. It seems reasonable to claim that the disruptive effect of irrelevant sound is not restricted to irrelevant speech or other periodic sounds such as tones, and does not only affect retrieval of verbal stimuli. Visual inspection of the recall probabilities reported in Table 1 reveals that recall of verbal items is greater than that of spatial items. This difference in performance may arise as a result of the fact that the categorical or semantic representations associated with the verbal items may assist recall (see Jones et al., 1995).

GENERAL DISCUSSION

The current experimental series extends the changing-state effect to broadband noise. The increased disruption by irrelevant noise bursts varying in band-pass frequency impaired serial recall of visual-verbal as well as serial recall of visual-spatial items. Whether the irrelevant sound is periodic such as speech and tones, or aperiodic such as noise, it has the potential to disrupt serial recall markedly.

The present results challenge the notion of a memory system whose contents are confined to speech or periodic sounds. In order to account for the large detrimental effect of irrelevant speech on serial recall in contrast to the absence or little effect of noise, Salamé and Baddeley (1982) suggested that a phonological filter allowed only speech sounds, or sounds similar to speech, to have access to short-term memory. The material allowed in a phonological store would then contaminate the visual TBR items transferred into the same store via rehearsal. However, subsequent work has shown that nonspeech sounds such as tones and pitch glides also produce similar disruption of recall (e.g., Jones & Macken, 1993). It has been suggested that the effect of tones and the absence of any substantial effect of noise can be reconciled by supposing that a filter could allow passage of tonal stimuli, leaving only non-periodic sounds, such as noise, to be excluded (Salamé & Baddeley, 1989). The notion of a filter has difficulty explaining why changing-state stimuli, periodic and aperiodic, have a much stronger disruptive effect than repeated stimuli.

The phonological store account of the irrelevant sound effect comes with the assumption that phonological similarity between the irrelevant material and the TBR items is related to the degree of disruption of serial recall. The feature model (Nairne, 1990; Neath, 2000) that has some success in explaining a number of irrelevant speech effects and other short-term memory effects is also based on the assumption that similarity is a determinant factor (see Jones & Tremblay, 2000, for a discussion). However, in the present experiments, no content is shared between the irrelevant noise and either the visual-verbal or the visual-spatial to-be-remembered items. The findings lend some additional support to the view that interference by irrelevant sound is not due to the similarity of the sound to the material held in memory (see Jones & Macken, 1995, for discussion). Neath (2000; see also Neath et al., 1998) states that the feature model specifically fails to embody an account for the irrelevant nonspeech effects.

One intuitively appealing and parsimonious account of the irrelevant sound, which may apply to any types of auditory stimuli, is based on the concept of orienting response (see Sokolov, 1963). It is suggested that irrelevant sound gives rise to some kind of orienting response, and that when a sound is repeated the orienting response (and hence the distraction from the serial recall task) is diminished (Cowan, 1995). However, this approach has the difficulty of explaining why generally no reduction of response to irrelevant sound (and hence no diminution of the detrimental effect), whether repeated or changing, is observable within or between experimental sessions (Hellbrück, Kuwano, & Namba, 1996; Jones, Macken, & Mosdell, 1997; see also Tremblay & Jones, 1998, for a related demonstration). A further difficulty is a logical one. If the irrelevant sound effect was due wholly to the recruitment of attention from the task, it seems problematic that the nature of the task determines in part the degree of disruption (e.g., Beaman & Jones, 1997; Salamé & Baddeley, 1990).

An alternative view is that any changing-state sound will produce disruption of serial recall (e.g., Jones et al., 1992; Jones & Macken, 1993). According to the theoretical framework that originated from the changing-state phenomenon, interference by irrelevant sound is not the product of attentional capture or similarity of content in the irrelevant and TBR material, but seems to result from a clash between similar *processes*. That is, the disruption is assumed to arise when two sources of information require similar processing modes. Specifically interference arises because there are two concurrent processes of seriation within the irrelevant sound effect (see Jones et al., 1999). One process is the automatic and pre-attentive organisation of the sound in its appropriate serial order. Generally, it has been assumed that the greater the quantity of changing information within the sound sequence, the stronger the cues to seriation (and so the greater the disruption). However, there is some evidence to suggest that the degree of disruption is not predicted solely by a consideration of the degree of change, but that the effects of change can be modulated by the rules of auditory organisation generally known as "streaming" (Bregman, 1990). Thus changing-state, the construct that predicts the degree of disruption, maps onto physical changes through auditory streaming: Physical change will predict disruption only within a single-stream percept. If more than one stream is formed then the degree of change within the streams will be the determinant factor. The effect of degree of change can be understood only in relation to the organisation of sounds into streams and to the ensuing consequences of change within such streams. The second process is deliberate and reflects the seriation of the TBR items. In the present study, serial recall was the common requirement to both verbal and spatial memory tasks, and both were sensitive to disruption by irrelevant changing noise. Serial recall has been shown to be particularly susceptible to disruption (see, e.g., Beaman & Jones, 1998). Therefore, it is assumed that the obligatory ordering of irrelevant sound interferes with the deliberate seriation of the TBR material.

Although no effect of repeated noise bursts was found in the present study and others (e.g., Jones et al., 1990; Salamé & Baddeley, 1989), there are some studies in which small but significant effects (either beneficial or detrimental) are found (e.g., Hockey & Hamilton, 1970; LeCompte, 1994). Poulton (1978; see also Broadbent, 1977) offered a composite theory of human performance in noise that identifies four key determinants of noise interference: (1) masking of auditory cues or inner speech; (2) distraction, much in the sense of Sokolov's (1963) concept of orienting response; (3) noise-induced changes in behavioural arousal; and (4) positive and negative transfer from noise to quiet. In the case of changing-state irrelevant sound, the effect is consistently one of disruption, strong rather than modest, and seems to influence particularly maintenance of order information (see Beaman & Jones, 1998). The by now considerable body of research on irrelevant sound suggests that Poulton's (1978) framework has little explanatory value, at least for sounds of low intensity.

First, let us discuss the masking hypothesis in detail. In the 1970s, irrelevant speech was thought to interfere with memory by masking "inner speech" (Poulton, 1977) or some other form of auditory recoding of visually presented items (Colle, 1980; Colle & Welsh, 1976). The idea of masking implies that the similarity between the irrelevant sound and the TBR stimuli is an important factor, but it is not.

Another view related to masking is that the impact of irrelevant sounds in processing visual information is located at perception, when stimuli are registered (Broadbent, 1983). A key prediction of perceptual masking is that conflict, in terms of timing, between relevant and irrelevant information should affect the degree of disruption. This issue has been tested by manipulating the timing of exposure to irrelevant material during the course of a serial recall trial. The clearest demonstration against this prediction is that serial recall is markedly impaired even when irrelevant speech is presented after the presentation of the to-be-remembered items (Miles, Jones, & Madden, 1991). Hence, in this condition, the visual stimuli must have been perceived accurately before any irrelevant sound was presented (see LeCompte, 1994, for a replication).

The finding that the irrelevant sound effect does not diminish over time and has a greater impact on memory for order (see earlier discussion of the habituation account) rules out the applicability of the second and third factors of the composite theory. Distraction or habituation to attentional capture plays little or no role in the irrelevant sound effect. Likewise, that the irrelevant sound effect is enduring is problematic to that arousal factor, which states that the impact of noise is transient. Also, as opposed to continuous or repeated noise effects on performance, disruption by irrelevant sounds such as speech and tones is as great at low intensity, 40 dB(A), as it is at much higher intensity, up to 95 dB(A). This finding rules out the view that the irrelevant sound effect may be related to the participant's level of arousal (see Colle, 1980; see also Ellermeier & Hellbrück, 1998; Tremblay & Jones, 1999).

The concept of interference by similarity of process offers a single construct that can account for both the characteristics of the task and those of the irrelevant sound that modulate the degree of disruption. With regard to the effects of noise on cognitive performance, according to the process-oriented approach, tasks requiring memory for order in the presence of changing-state sound will result in substantial interference.

REFERENCES

Baddeley, A.D., & Salamé, P. (1986). The unattended speech effect: Perception or memory. *Journal of Experimental Psychology: Learning, Memory and Cognition*, *12*, 525–529.

Banbury, S., & Berry, D.C. (1998). The disruption of speech and office-related tasks by speech and office noise. *British Journal of Psychology*, *89*, 499–517.

Beaman, C.P., & Jones, D.M. (1997). The role of serial order in the irrelevant speech effect: Tests of the changing state hypothesis. *Journal of Experimental Psychology: Learning, Memory and Cognition*, *23*, 459–471.

Beaman, C.P., & Jones, D.M. (1998). Irrelevant sound disrupts order information in free as in serial recall. *Quarterly Journal of Experimental Psychology: Human Experimental Psychology*, *51*A, 615–636.

Boyle, R., & Coltheart, V. (1996). Effects of irrelevant sounds on phonological coding in reading comprehension and short-term memory. *Quarterly Journal of Experimental Psychology: Human Experimental Psychology*, *49*A, 398–416.

Bregman, A.S. (1990). *Auditory scene analysis: The perceptual organization of sound*. Cambridge, MA: MIT Press.

Broadbent, D.E. (1958). *Perception and communication*. Oxford: Pergamon.

Broadbent, D.E. (1977). Precautions in experiments on noise. *British Journal of Psychology*, *68*, 427–429.

Broadbent, D.E. (1979). Human performance and noise. In C.M. Harris (Ed.), *Handbook of noise control* (pp. 17.1–17.20). New York: McGraw Hill.

Broadbent, D.E. (1983). *Recent advances in understanding performance in noise*. Paper presented at Noise as a Public Health Problem; Proceedings of the Fourth International Congress, Milan.

Buchner, A., Steffens, M.C., Irmen, L., & Wender, K.F. (1998). Irrelevant auditory material affects counting. *Journal of Experimental Psychology: Learning, Memory, & Cognition*, *24*, 48–67.

Burani, C., Vallar, G., & Bottini, G. (1991). Ariculatory coding and phonological judgements on written words and pictures: The role of the phonological output buffer. *European Journal of Cognitive Psychology*, *3*, 379–398.

Colle, H.A. (1980). Auditory encoding in visual short-term recall: Effects of noise intensity and spatial location. *Journal of Verbal Learning and Verbal Behavior*, *19*, 722–735.

Colle, H.A., & Welsh, A. (1976). Acoustic masking in primary memory. *Journal of Verbal Learning and Verbal Behavior*, *15*, 17–31.

Cowan, N. (1995). *Attention and memory: An integrated framework*. Oxford: Oxford University Press.

Davies, D.R., & Jones, D.M. (1975). The effects of noise and incentives upon attention in short-term memory. *British Journal of Psychology*, *66*, 61–68.

Ellermeier, W., & Hellbrück, J. (1998). Is level irrelevant in 'irrelevant speech'? Effects of loudness, signal-to-noise ratio, and binaural masking. *Journal of Experimental Psychology: Human Perception & Performance*, *24*, 1406–1414.

Farrand, P., & Jones, D.M. (1996). Direction of report in spatial and verbal serial short-term memory. *Quarterly Journal of Experimental Psychology: Human Experimental Psychology*, *49*A, 140–158.

Hellbrück, J., Kuwano, S., & Namba, S. (1996). Irrelevant background speech and human performance: Is there long-term habituation? *Journal of the Acoustical Society of Japan*, *17*, 239–247.

Hockey, R., & Hamilton, P. (1970). Arousal and information selection in short-term memory. *Nature*, *226*, 866–867.

Jones, D.M., Alford, D., Bridges, A., Tremblay, S., & Macken, W.J. (1999). Organizational factors in selective attention: The interplay of acoustic distinctiveness and auditory streaming in the irrelevant sound effect. *Journal of Experimental Psychology: Learning, Memory and Cognition*, *25*, 464–473.

Jones, D.M., Farrand, P., Stuart, G., & Morris, N. (1995). Functional equivalence of verbal and spatial information in serial short-term memory. *Journal of Experimental Psychology: Learning, Memory and Cognition*, *21*, 1008–1018.

Jones, D.M., & Macken, W.J. (1993). Irrelevant tones produce an irrelevantl speech effect: Implications for phonological coding in working memory. *Journal of Experimental Psychology: Learning, Memory and Cognition*, *19*, 369–381.

Jones, D.M., & Macken, W.J. (1995). Phonological similarity in the irrelevant speech effect: Within- or between-stream similarity? *Journal of Experimental Psychology: Learning, Memory and Cognition*, *21*, 103–115.

Jones, D.M., Macken, W.J., & Mosdell, N. (1997). The role of habituation in the disruption of recall performance by irrelevant sound. *British Journal of Psychology*, *88*, 549–564.

Jones, D.M., Madden, C., & Miles, C. (1992). Privileged access by irrelevant speech to short-term memory: The role of changing state. *Quarterly Journal of Experimental Psychology: Human Experimental Psychology*, *44*A, 645–669.

Jones, D.M., Miles, C., & Page, J. (1990). Disruption of proof-reading by irrelevant speech: Effects of attention, arousal or memory? *Applied Cognitive Psychology*, *4*, 89–108.

Jones, D.M., & Tremblay, S. (2000). Interference in memory by process or content? A reply to Neath (2000). *Psychonomic Bulletin & Review*, *7*, 550–558.

Klatte, M., Kilcher, H., & Hellbrück, J. (1995). Wirkungen der zeitlichen Struktur von hintergrundscall auf das Arbeitsgedachtnis und ihre theoretischen und praktischen Implikationen [The effects of temporal structure of background noise on working memory: theories and applications]. *Zeitschnift für Experimentelle Psychologie*, *42*, 517–544.

LeCompte, D.C. (1994). Extending the irrelevant speech effect beyond serial recall. *Journal of Experimental Psychology: Learning, Memory and Cognition*, *20*, 1396–1408.

LeCompte, D.C. (1995). An irrelevant speech effect with repeated and continuous background speech. *Psychonomic Bulletin and Review*, *2*, 391–397.

LeCompte, D.C., & Shaibe, D.M. (1997). On the irrelevance of phonological similarity to the irrelevant speech effect. *Quarterly Journal of Experimental Psychology: Human Experimental Psychology*, *50A*, 100–118.

Miles, C., Jones, D.M., & Madden, C.A. (1991). Locus of the irrelevant speech effect in short-term memory. *Journal of Experimental Psychology: Learning, Memory and Cognition*, *17*, 578–584.

Moore, B.C.J. (1996). *Introduction to the psychology of hearing*. London: Academic Press.

Nairne, J.S. (1990). A feature model of immediate memory. *Memory & Cognition*, *18*, 251–269.

Neath, I., Suprenant, A.M., & LeCompte, D.C. (1998). Irrelevant speech eliminates the word length effect. *Memory & Cognition*, 26, 343–354.

Neath, I. (2000). Modeling the effects of irrelevant speech on memory. *Psychonomic Bulletin & Review*, *7*, 403–423.

Parmentier, F.P., Tremblay, S., & Jones, D.M. (2001). Recency and sufix effects in serial memory for visual spatial items. *Manuscript submitted for publication*.

Poulton, E.C. (1977). Continuous intense noise masks auditory feedback and inner speech. *Psychological Bulletin*, *84*, 977–1001.

Poulton, E.C. (1978). A new look at the effects of noise upon performance. *British Journal of Psychology*, *69*, 435–437.

Rabbit, P. (1968). Channel-capacity, intelligibility and immediate memory. *Quarterly Journal of Experimental Psychology: Human Experimental Psychology*, *20*, 241–248.

Remez, R.E., & Rubin, P.E. (1990). On the perception of speech from time-varying acoustic information: Contributions of amplitude variations. *Perception & Psychophysics*, *48*, 313–325.

Richardson, J.T. (1984). Developing the theory of working memory. *Memory and Cognition*, *12*, 71–83.

Rosen, S., & Howell, P. (1991). *Signals and systems for speech and hearing*. London: Academic Press.

Salamé, P., & Baddeley, A.D. (1982). Disruption of short-term memory by unattended speech: Implications for the structure of working memory. *Journal of Verbal Learning and Verbal Behavior*, *21*, 150–164.

Salamé, P., & Baddeley, A.D. (1987). Noise, unattended speech and short-term memory. *Ergonomics*, *30*, 1185–1194.

Salamé, P., & Baddeley, A.D. (1989). Effects of background music on phonological short-term memory. *Quarterly Journal of Experimental Psychology: Human Experimental Psychology*, *41*, 107–122.

Salamé, P., & Baddeley, A.D. (1990). The effects of irrelevant speech on immediate free recall. *Bulletin of the Psychonomic Society*, *28*, 540–542.

Salamé, P., & Witterseim, G. (1978). Selective noise disturbance of the information input stage in short-term memory. *Quarterly Journal of Experimental Psychology: Human Experimental Psychology*, *30*, 693–704.

Sokolov, E.N. (1963). *Perception and the conditioned reflex*. London: Pergamon Press.

Tremblay, S., & Jones, D.M. (1998). The role of habituation in the irrelevant sound effect: Evidence from the effects of token set size and rate of transition. *Journal of Experimental Psychology: Learning, Memory and Cognition*, *24*, 659–671.

Tremblay, S., & Jones, D.M. (1999). Change of intensity fails to produce an irrelevant sound effect: Implications for the representation of unattended sound. *Journal of Experimental Psychology: Human Perception and Performance*, *25*, 1005–1015.

Tremblay, S., Nicholls, A., Alford, D., & Jones, D.M. (2000). Irrelevant sound effect: Does speech play a special role? *Journal of Experimental Psychology: Learning, Memory, and Cognition*, *26*, 1750–1754.

Woodhead, M.M. (1964). The effect of bursts of noise on an arithmetic task. *American Journal of Psychology*, *77*, 627–633.

MEMORY, 2001, *9* (4/5/6), 333–348

Word length and phonological similarity effects in simple, complex, and delayed serial recall tasks: Implications for working memory

Gerald Tehan, Liam Hendry, and David Kocinski

University of Southern Queensland, Australia

Some current models of working memory argue that a passive short-term store is not involved in more dynamic working memory tasks. Other models argue that standard short-term memory and working memory tasks rely on common storage facilities. We examine these issues by exploring two signature effects of passive short-term storage in simple span, complex span, and Brown-Peterson tasks. The finding that all three tasks show word length and phonological similarity effects suggests that common processes or storage mechanisms are involved in all tasks. The implications for models of working memory are discussed.

In the mid 1970s Baddeley and Hitch (1974) proposed a model of working memory that incorporated three structures: a central executive, a phonological loop, and a visuo-spatial sketchpad. The three structures had very different characteristics and performed different functions. In the earliest formulation of the model the central executive was depicted as a limited-capacity workspace whose resources could be flexibly allocated to processing or storage[1]. The other two components were seen as limited-capacity slave systems that could be used for temporary storage without impacting on the functioning of the central executive. The visuo-spatial sketchpad could store small amounts of visual/spatial material and the phonological loop could maintain small amounts of verbal material in serial order for brief periods of time.

In recent times there has been debate as to the need to specify either separate slave systems for each modality (Farrand & Jones, 1996; Jones, Farrand, Stuart, & Morris, 1995; Shah & Miyake, 1996; Swanson, 1996) or to maintain a separation between the central executive and slave systems (Adams, Bourke, & Willis, 1999; LaPointe & Engle, 1990; Lehto, 1996). As a result, alternative models of working memory have emerged that do not involve the same set of assumptions.

In the current research we seek to test two general classes of working memory models in which active working memory interacts or does not interact with passive, verbal short-term storage. The first class of model assumes that a short-term memory buffer does not support working memory performance (Baddeley, 1986; Brainerd & Kingma, 1985; Swanson, 1996). We focus on Baddeley's model as a representative of this class. The second class takes the opposite view and argues that short-term storage does support

[1] Baddeley's original view of the central executive has changed in his subsequent writings and he no longer particularly holds to the description of the central executive as a flexible workplace that can be used for both storage and processing. However this conception is still popular in terms of other models of working memory and is a commonly used description of Baddeley's work (Daneman & Carpenter, 1980; LaPointe & Engle, 1990; Miyake & Shah, 1999). Thus, although the current article continually refers to "Baddeley's" model and the central executive, the term is used more as a descriptor of what other people commonly attribute to the model than as an accurate reflection of Baddeley's current views concerning the properties of the central executive.

Requests for reprints should be sent to Gerry Tehan, Department of Psychology, University of Southern Queensland, Toowoomba, QLD, Australia 4350. Email: tehan@usq.edu.au

http://www.tandf.co.uk/journals/pp/09658211.html DOI:10.1080/09658210042000049

working memory performance (Cowan, 1999; Engle, 1996; Engle, Kane, & Tuholski, 1999). We focus on Cowan's (1999) embedded process model as an instance of the second class of models, primarily because it explicitly incorporates a role for long-term memory (LTM) which Baddeley's model does not.

Immediate serial recall has been the task of choice for exploring the effects of the phonological loop. Performance on this task has resulted in a number of signature effects, two of which form the basis of the current research. The first is the word length effect; the finding that lists containing words of short spoken duration are better recalled than lists containing words of long spoken duration (Baddeley, Thompson, & Buchanan, 1975). The word length effect is attributed to the fact that items in the phonological store decay within approximately 2 seconds if rehearsal is prevented. As rehearsal is the necessary process for maintaining item availability and rehearsal happens in real time, the word length effect results from the fact that more short words can be rehearsed in a given period of time than long words. The second feature of interest is the phonological similarity effect; the finding that lists that contain similar-sounding words are not as well remembered as lists that contain dissimilar-sounding words (Baddeley, 1966). The phonological similarity effect is based on the assumption that items in the phonological store are registered in terms of their phonological features. Discrimination among traces is seen to be more difficult if the traces are very similar to one another than if they are easily distinguishable. For current purposes, the key factor is that both the word length effect and the phonological similarity effect are due to the operation of the phonological loop. No role for the central executive or LTM is proposed for either of these effects. Consequently, from this perspective, phonological similarity and word length effects should be limited to tasks that access the phonological loop. There is no reason to suppose that these effects would be present in tasks that access the other components of memory, provided that rehearsal is effectively prevented in these tasks.

Cowan's model consists of three components: an automatic attention orienting system, a central executive, and a memory store. For present purposes the latter two are the most important. The central executive is seen as a pool of effortful processes that can be used to control attention. The memory component consists of three hierarchically embedded components. At the base of all performance is LTM, which is assumed to be both unlimited in capacity and to have some base level of activation. In any short-term retention task, some of the LTM representations become activated. Central executive resources can be used to determine which items are attended to and, consequently, such items become highly activated in the focus of attention. The focus of attention is seen to be capacity limited to approximately four items. Items that have passed from the focus of attention but remain above baseline levels of activation are said to be in active memory and are readily accessible at retrieval. According to Cowan, active memory is the main database for the focus of attention to draw upon. However, the utility of active memory is limited in that an item's activation is assumed to rapidly decay to resting levels unless it is brought back into the focus of attention. In linking these notions to prior research Cowan identifies the combined storage of focus of attention and active memory with traditional notions of a short-term store.

The dynamics of Cowan's model are readily demonstrated with respect to the word length effect in immediate serial recall. Cowan et al. (1992) found that forgetting of the late items in a list was most pronounced when the items in the early positions were long words. They assumed that as early items were being recalled, later items were being forgotten. That is, while the long items were being recalled, the representations of the late items were undergoing more decay in active memory than when the short ittems were being recalled first. The longer it took to recall the initial items the harder it became to retrieve the late items. Thus the word length effect results from differential amounts of decay in active memory and decay starts once the items are no longer in the focus of attention.

Given Cowan's assumptions, word length effects should be evident in any task that involves active memory. Take for example complex span tasks in which simultaneous storage and processing are requirec. In the operations span procedure that Turner and Engle (1989) developed, participants are presented with a series of simple maths problems and word pairs (e.g., $7 \times 2 - 3 = 12$ BOMB). Subjects have to read the maths problem aloud, then say if the provided answer is correct or not and then read the word aloud. Following a series of these pairs (starting with two pairs and increasing in length thereafter) subjects are required to recall the words that had been paired with the maths problem. From Cowan's perspective, at certain times during learning, the maths problems are going to be the focus of attention. While this is happening the representations of the words that have been studied are likely to be undergoing decay in active memory. At recall, accessing the words in active memory is attempted. Provided the words remain active above baseline levels and can be retrieved, then the same factors that produce the word length effect on simple span tasks should influence performance on the complex span task. LaPointe and Engle (1990) provide relevant data. They examined word length effects under a range of different conditions in simple and complex span tasks. Generally they found identical patterns of effects across the two types of taks. Most importantly, word length effects were observed in the complex span taks, as Cowan's model might predict.

The interesting question involves what will happen on a delayed test in which items have decayed from active memory. For example, in the Brown-Peterson task (Brown, 1958; Peterson & Peterson, 1959) where the presentation of a small number of items is followed by a distractor task, no traces in active memory should be available to support performance if a sufficiently long retention interval is used. Participants would then have to access LTM in order to be able to recall the list items. There is nothing in Cowan's model that predicts word length effects in LTM. Cowan, Wood, and Borne (1994) provide relevant data. They had their participants study six item lists for backward serial recall. In one condition short and long words were presented under standard short-term memory conditions. That is, the words were presented individually at a fairly rapid rate and recall was tested immediately after the final item in the list. In the second condition, a continuous distractor task was employed. That is, each of the six words was preceded and followed by 15 seconds of distractor activity. Cowan et al. (1994) found the standard word length effect under immediate presentation rates, but not under the continuous distractor conditions; if anything long words were better remembered than short words. Cowan et al. argued that the word length effect in the immediate presentation condition reflected differential amounts of decay during recall. The absence of the word length effect on the continuous distractor task was explained by arguing that the distractor activity was of a sufficient duration to ensure that neither the short nor the long items remained active in memory.

The complex span and continuous distractor tasks have features in common in that in both tasks the to-be-remembered word is accompanied by some distractor activity. As far as the embedded process model is concerned, the key difference between these tasks appears to be the duration of the distractor activity. If the duration is relatively short as in the complex span tasks, items in memory can remain above baseline levels of activation. When the distractor activity is longer, then item strength returns to baseline levels. Thus, the central feature of the embedded processes model for current purposes is the rate of decay of items in active memory. Unfortunately, while Cowan is quite specific about the capacity of the focus of attention, decay rates in active memory are not specified, so precise predictions are hard to make.

In sum, the Cowan model assumes that a short-term store supports recall in any task that involves an immediate test or very short short retention intervals. Thus, the pattern of performance on simple span and complex span tasks should be similar if active memory is involved in both tasks. Any discontinuity in performance should only emerge when extended retention intervals are used, as is the case with the Brown-Peterson task. For Baddeley's model, the discontinuity is between simple span and the other memory tests, provided that rehearsal is effectively prevented on those tasks. Complex span tasks are not thought to rely on the same structures as simple span (Daneman & Carpenter, 1980; Towse, Hitch, & Hutton, 1998) although the LaPointe and Engle's results (1990) would cast some doubt on this conclusion. Vallar and Baddeley (1982) explicitly tested the notion that the phonological loop supported recall in the Brown-Peterson task. They found no evidence to support such a conclusion.

EXPERIMENT 1A AND B

In the first experiment we examined word length effects in three tasks, all of which required the serial recall of four-word lists. The simple version of the task involved the recall of the four words immediately after presentation. In the complex version of the task we adapted the Turner and Engle (1989) operation span task by presenting four WORD-maths problems on each trial. In the Brown-Peterson task we presented the four words and then had subjects engage in 12 seconds of distractor activity.

In sum, both the Baddeley and Cowan models predict the standard word length effect on an immediate test. The two models diverge on what to expect on the complex span task. If the task is not supported by the phonological loop and rehearsal is prevented, the Baddeley model predicts an attenuation of effect. The Cowan model predicts that the effect will still be present if the items remain at above baseline levels of activation. Given the LaPointe and Engle (1990) results, we expected to find word length effects on the task. Both models predict that word length effects should not be present on a delayed test.

Method

Participants. A total of 40 undergraduate students from the University of Southern Queensland volunteered to participate in the experiment, in return for course credit or tickets in a cash prize draw. All participants were tested individually in sessions averaging 30 minutes' duration: 20 students participated in Part A of the Experiment and a different 20 participated in Part B.

Materials. The long and short words used in the experiment were those utilised by Baddeley et al. (1975). The short word pool consisted of *sum hate harm wit bond yield worst twice*. The long words were *association opportunity representative organisation considerable immediately university individual*. The word pool was supplemented by a pool of 128 simple maths problems of the type used by LaPointe and Engle (1990). These consisted of either a simple product or dividend, followed by either a simple addition or subtraction, then an answer which was either true or false (e.g., $7 \times 2 - 3 = 12$). The false answers differed from the true answer by one or two and there were equal numbers of true and false problems.

Participants studied 48 trials in which they were requested to remember four words. For 24 of the trials the four words on each trial were randomly sampled from the pool of short words and for the other 24 trials the words on each trial were randomly sampled from the long pool. Eight each of the short and long lists were randomly allocated to the immediate recall condition (e.g., *hate harm wit bond*), eight each were randomly allocated to the operation span task, and eight each were allocated to the delayed racall task. To create each trial on the delayed task, four maths problems were randomly selected from the pool and placed after the four words (e.g., *twice sum yeild worst 8/4 + 1 = 6 3 × 2 − 1 = 5 10/2 − 3 = 4 4 × 2 + 7 = 14*). To create each operations span trial, four maths problems were randomly selected from the pool and these were interleaved with the four words such that each word was placed before its associated maths problem words (e.g., *bond 8/4 + 1 = 6 sum 2 × 2 − 1 = 6 wit 10/2 − 3 = 2 twice 4 × 2 + 7 = 15*). The order of the 48 trials was then randomised. This procedure was conducted for each subject such that 20 different sets of trials were generated.

Procedure. Participants were told that on each trial they would be presented with four words and that their primary task was to be able to remember the four words in order. They were also told that on some trials there were a number of simple maths problems and that their task was to decide as quickly as possible if each maths problem was true or false.

The immediate serial recall lists contained word stimuli presented at a rate of one word per second. Subjects were instructed to read each word aloud as it appeared on the screen. A row of question marks appeared after the fourth word as a cue to commence recall. On the delayed lists the words were again presented at a rate of one word per second and subjects read each word aloud. The four words were immediately followed by four maths problems presented at a rate of one problem every 3 seconds. Subjects were instructed not to read the problem aloud; instead they were to simply make a decision and say "yes" or "no". A row of question marks again cued the end of the list. On the operations span trials, a word and maths problem appeared simultaneously on the screen. The instructions indicated that the word was to be first read aloud and then the maths problem was to be read silently and then solved with a "yes" or "no" decision. The four word-problem pairs were presented at a rate of one pair every 4 seconds and the recall cue appeared at the end of the list. One each type of trial serial recall was requested and participants were instructed to say "something" if they could not recall a particular word, in order to preserve the serial order of the remaining recalled words.

After conducting Part A of the experiment using the procedure just described, we were somewhat concerned about the low level of performance on the delayed and operations span trials. To see if floor effects influenced our results, we reduced the difficulty of the processing component of the maths problems in Part B of the experiment. In Part B, instead of solving the maths problems all subjects had to do was to read the digits of the maths problems aloud. So for the problem *4 × 2 + 7 = 15* subjects would respond by saying "four two seven fifteen". Thus on the delayed test, subjects read the four words aloud and then shadowed four maths problems. In the operations span task, they first read the word aloud then read the digits of each problem aloud.

Results

Scoring. While serial recall was required on all trials, it is possible to score the output in different ways. The most common way is to score an item as correct only if it is recalled in its appropriate serial position. Other researchers have argued that serial recall involves a two-part discrimination process. One has to discriminate items on the present trial from items on earlier trials. Then the correct position of an item within a list has to be determined. These two discrimination tasks can be measured by socring the data in alternative ways. First, it is possible to score items by ignoring the output position. Thus a list item is scored as correct if it appears somewhere in the recall protocol, irrespective of what position it was recalled in. This form of item scoring has been used most widely in scoring the complex span tasks (LaPointe & Engle, 1990). Second, the ability to discriminate serial positions within a list can be determined by scoring the number of order errors made, corrected for item recall (Poirier & Saint-Aubin, 1995). Here the number of order errors made is calculated as a proportion of the total number of items recalled. We provide analyses of all three types of scores. In each case an alpha level of .05 has been used to determine statistical reliability. Furthermore, F statistics are reported for both parts of the experiment, the first being obtained for Part A and the second for Part B.

Mathematics problems. On average subjects solved the maths problems at an 86% level of accuracy on the delayed and operations span trials. Most importantly, accuracy did not differ as a function of the type of task or word length, $Fs < 1$.

Correct in position. Performance on the correct in position is summarised in the upper panels of Figure 1. It is clear that across all tasks short words were better recalled than long words. A 3 × 2 repeated measures ANOVA confirmed these results. In both parts of the experiment short words were better recalled than long words, $F(1, 19) = 47.48$, $MSe = 21.50$ and $F(1, 19) = 83.51$, $MSe = 16.36$ for Part A and Part B respectively. There were task differences in both parts of the experiment, $F(2, 19) = 85.58$, $MSe = 33.76$ and $F(2, 19) = 132.50$, $MSe = 12.72$. In both parts of the experiment immediate recall was better than operation span, $F(1, 19) = 112.33$, $MSe = 460.80$ and $F(1, 19) = 197.00$, $MSe = 17.09$, and recall in the operation span task was better than delayed recall in Part B of the experiment, $F(1, 19) = 63.67$, $MSe = 11.49$, but not in Part A of the experiment, $F(1, 19) = 2.85$, $MSe = .05$. The interaction between word length and task approached significance in Part A, $F(2, 38) = 3.11$, $MSe = 24.88$, $p = .056$, but was not significant in Part B, $F(2, 38) = 1.84$, $MSe = 12.22$.

Item recall. Item recall, where list items were scored as correct irrespective of the order in which they were recalled, is summarised in the middle panels of Figure 1. Again across all tasks short words were better recalled than long words. A 3 × 2 repeated measures ANOVA confirmed these results. In both parts of the experiment short words were better recalled than long words, $F(1, 19) = 45.24$, $MSe = 8.35$ and $F(1, 19) = 93.91$, $MSe = 8.91$ for Part A and Part B respectively. There were task differences in both parts of the experiment, $F(2, 19) = 53.37$, $MSe = 22.54$ and $F(2, 19) = 75.08$, $MSe = 10.72$. In both parts of the experiment immediate recall was better than operation span, $F(1, 19) = 58.49$, $MSE = 38.60$ and $F(1, 19) = 91.17$, $MSE = 17.67$, and recall in the operation span task was better than delayed recall, $F(1, 19) = 15.45$, $MSe = 11.26$, and, $F(1, 19) = 56.26$, $MSe = 7.11$. The interaction between word length and task was not significant in either instance.

Order errors. The probability of making an order error conditionalised on item recall is summarised in the lower panels of Figure 1. Again across all tasks fewer order errors were made with short words than long words. A 3 × 2 repeated measures ANOVA confirmed these results. In both parts of the experiment there were more order errors for the long words than the short words, $F(1, 19) = 22.43$, $MSe = .023$ and $F(1, 19) = 24.16$, $MSe = .015$ for Part A and Part B respectively. There were task differences in both parts of the experiment, $F(2, 19) = 28.78$, $MSe = .042$ and $F(2, 19) = 39.27$, $MSe = .014$. There were fewer

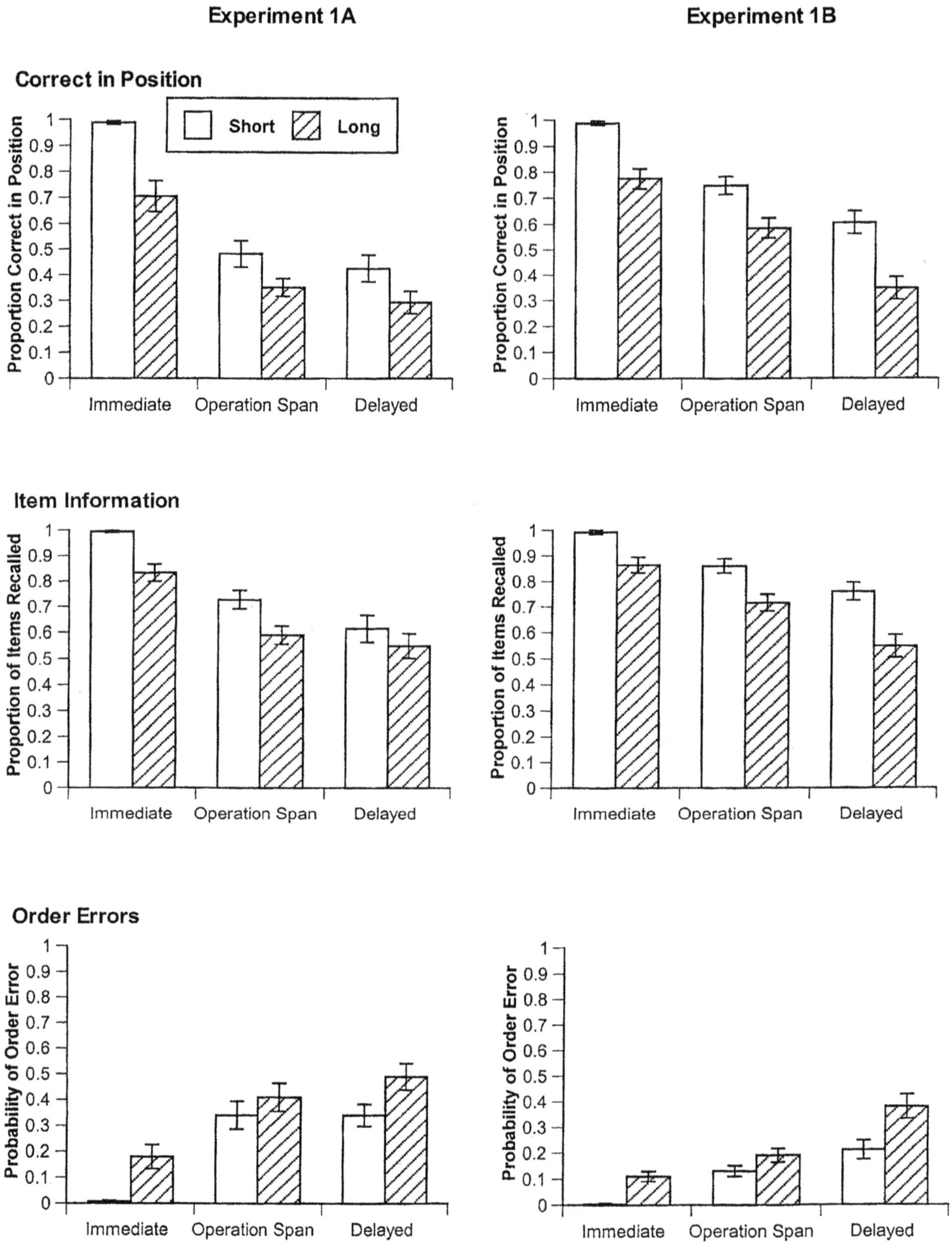

Figure 1. Word length effects in immediate, delayed, and operations span serial recall tasks. Error bars represent the standard error of the mean.

order errors on an immediate test than on the operations span, $F(1, 19) = 62.93$, $MSe = .032$ and $F(1, 19) = 61.62$, $MSe = .018$, and recall in the operation span task was better than delayed recall in Part B of the experiment, $F(1, 19) = 18.23$, $MSe = .019$, but not in Part A of the experiment, $F(1, 19) = .62$, $MSe = .046$. The interaction between word length and task was not significant in either case.

Discussion

The results are quite straightforward. Across all tasks and across all scoring procedures, short words were better recalled than long words. We thus replicate the standard word length effect in immediate serial recall and we also replicate LaPointe and Engle's (1990) finding that word length effects could be found in a complex span task. We extend these findings to show that word length effects can be observed in the Brown-Peterson task as well.

Finding word length effects on the complex span task is consistent with Cowan's model if it is assumed that items remain active in memory. This probably requires the further assumption that early list items need to be brought back into the focus of attention and thereby reactivated at some time during presentation. That is, the early list items need to be rehearsed. The finding of word length effects on the delayed test does not replicate the Cowan et al. (1994) results with the continuous distractor task. However, in both experiments a substantial period of distractor activity followed the final list items; 12 seconds in the current experiment and 15 seconds in the Cowan et al. experiment. It is unlikely that this 3-second difference is crucial. It is more likely that the effects could be attributable to different retrieval processes involved in forward and backward recall. The presence of a word length effect after a substantial period of distractor activity presents a challenge to the Cowan model.

The results also pose some problems for the Baddeley model. However, there are two possible ways in which the model could explain the data. The first is that the phonological loop is involved in all three tasks. We and others (Towse et al., 1998; Vallar & Baddeley, 1982) doubt this is correct but will return to this issue in the general discussion.

The second possibility is that the word length effect in immediate recall is due to the rehearsal function of the phonological loop, but that other factors are responsible for the word length effect on the remaining two tasks. It is clear that monosyllabic and polysyllabic words differ on multiple dimensions such as the number of phonemic units, complexity in output planning, prosody, concreteness, and linguistic origin to name but a few. For example, Caplan, Rochon, and Waters (1992) have argued that word length effects are the result of differences in the complexity of output plans for the different words. In their research they equated words on spoken duration (a correlate of rehearsal speed) but had differences in output complexity. If duration was the key variable then there should have been little difference in recall. Instead they found that recall depended on complexity and not on duration. Likewise, Service (1998) was able to manipulate duration and complexity separately using Finnish non-words. She too found that recall was a function of complexity rather than spoken duration. Given that complexity of output gestures are a long-term component of memory, it is possible that the word length effect in the operation span and delayed tasks reflects output complexity effects rather than rehearsal effects.

Of course, the Caplan et al. (1992) and the Service (1998) data could indicate that it is these long-term factors that are important in all three tasks. It is now commonly accepted that immediate serial recall involves redintegration processes that involve LTM phonological representations of words (Brown & Hulme, 1995; Tehan & Humphreys, 1998). It is likely that complexity may impact on the redintegration process. Finally, the case for the word length effect being due to rehearsal speed has been seriously weakened by a re-examination of the original Baddeley et al. (1975) procedures and results. Lovatt, Avons, and Masterson (2000) matched disyllabic words on a number of variables but maximised spoken duration differences between these words. In none of their experiments were they able to find word length effects. The only time they did so was when they conducted a direct replication of Baddeley et al. using their material. They concluded that the word length effects in the Baddeley et al. (1975) study are probably due to accidental differences in the list items.

The results of Experiment 1 are problematic for both models. However, the case for and against could be better made if a similar pattern of performance emerged with a second marker of immediate recall performance. In Experiment 2 we examine phonological similarity effects across the three tasks.

EXPERIMENT 2A AND B

Lists of similar-sounding words are harder to recall than lists of dissimilar-sounding words (Baddeley, 1966). The phonological similarity effect has been explained within the working memory model by assuming trace discrimination problems within the phonological store. From this perspective, the phonological similarity effect should be very transient, especially for visually presented items. That is, in the absence of rehearsal, traces should rapidly decay and the phonological similarity effect should be attenuated.

The Cowan (1999) model suggests that short-term memory can be supported by a range of codes, including phonological ones. Cowan adopts similar assumptions to Baddeley. First, discrimination among items with similar representations will be difficult. Second, once an item leaves the focus of attention the phonological codes decay rapidly in active memory. Thus, the Cowan model also predicts that phonological similarity effects will be present on an immediate test but not on a delayed test. However, if the results in Experiment 1 are any guide, the operations span task is supported by active memory and as such phonological similarity effects would be expected in that task.

As far as predictions on the delayed test go, the data are reasonably consistent with the predictions of both models when correct-in-position scoring is utilised (Fallon, Groves, & Tehan, 1999; Nairne & Kelley, 1999; Tehan & Humphreys, 1995). For instance, Tehan and Humphreys (1995, Experiment 1) had participants study four-word, visually presented, phonologically similar or dissimilar lists. These lists were tested immediately or after a 2-second distractor period filled with verbal shadowing. They found strong similarity effects on an immediate test and no effect on the delayed test. At face value this suggests that items are rapidly lost from a phonological loop or from active memory.

However, rapid decay of phonological codes is harder to justify when other measures of performance are utilised. That is, phonological similarity effects on a delayed test critically depend on the way in which phonological similarity is operationalised and the scoring measure used. Fallon et al. (1999) manipulated phonological similarity in two ways: the words on their similar lists either all rhymed with each other (e.g., *hat rat mat cat bat pat*) or had high levels of phonological overlap but did not come from the single rhyme category (e.g., *man cap mad can cat map cad mat*). When phonological similarity was operationalised in terms of high overlap but no categorisation, similar lists were always less well remembered than dissimilar lists on immediate and delayed tests using correct-in-position scoring. There were always more order errors in the similar lists and there was also an item advantage for the dissimilar lists. The pattern changed when similar lists contained rhyming items. With correct-in position scoring there was no difference between dissimilar and rhyming lists. However, rhyming items always produced a higher level of order errors than the dissimilar lists on both immediate and delayed tests. With item scoring, the rhyme category did not have any effect on an immediate test compared with the dissimilar items; but on a delayed test the rhyming items were better recalled than the dissimilar items. Thus, the absence of a phonological similarity effect on a delayed test using correct-in-position scoring did not come about by the decay of phonological codes, it was an artefact of superior item information for the rhyming lists being counterbalanced by increased order errors. A re-analysis of the Tehan and Humphreys (1995) data described earlier also indicated that the lack of a phonological similarity effect on a delayed test resulted from the trade-off between item and order scores.

In sum, both the Baddeley and Cowan models suggest that at retrieval when a word has to be recalled in its correct position, the presence of similar representations in memory increases the difficulty of an order discrimination process. The Fallon et al. results indicate that correct-in-position scoring may not be the best metric for observing phonological similarity effects, in that item enhancement for rhyming lists can mask order deficits and thereby give the impression that phonological traces have decayed to baseline levels. Their research argues that a better index for observing active phonological traces is the number of order errors. If phonological traces have truly decayed, then order errors should be equivalent for both similar and dissimilar lists. Consequently, a strong test of the Baddeley and Cowan models would involve the number of order errors across the three tasks. On an immediate test both models would predict that there would be more order errors for similar lists than dissimilar lists. On a delayed test, if the representations have decayed to baseline levels, order errors should be equivalent for similar and dissimilar lists. For the complex span task, the models would probably make differential predictions.

In the following experiment we examine phonological similarity effects in the three serial order tasks. We operationalise phonological similarity in the same way as Fallon et al. (1999). That is, participants study three types of list: phonologically dissimilar lists, phonologically similar lists in which there is high phonemic overlap among items but they do not rhyme with each other, and lists in which all items rhyme with each other. The Fallon et al. data indicated that phonological similarity effects were not equivalent for the two types of similar lists. We thought that if we could replicate this pattern of findings across tasks it would provide compelling evidence for the equivalence of the three tasks as is suggested by the results of Experiment 1.

Method

Participants. A total of 40 undergraduate students from the University of Southern Queensland volunteered to participate in the experiment, in return for course credit or tickets in a cash prize draw. All participants were tested individually in sessions averaging 30 minutes' duration: 20 students participated in Part A of the Experiment and the remaining 20 participated in Part B.

Materials. Four single-syllable instances were selected from each of 45 rhyme categories from the Univeristy of South Florida rhyme category norms (Walling, McEvoy, Oth, & Nelson, 1984), with relative category dominance controlled at between 5 and 14%. For each subject, 45 four-item lists were randomly assigned to three groups of 15 as the first step in creating the three types of lists. In the similar rhyming condition the four rhyming items within each category were simply randomised in order (e.g., *torn horn corn shorn*). For the 15 similar-non-rhyming trials, two instances were selected from two different rhyme categories (e.g., *coat ship goat skip*) and then ordered in such a way that the two rhyming items never appeared adjacent to one another. Compared to the dissimilar lists, this procedure increased the level of phonological similarity without the benefit of a single rhyme category. For the dissimilar condition, the 15 lists were pooled, and the resulting 60 words were randomly assigned to dissimilar four-item lists, with the restriction that no two rhyming words were in the same list (e.g., *wart buff rest hoot*). Five of each type of trial was then randomly assigned to immediate test, operations span test, or delayed test conditions. The latter two types of trials were constructed in the same way as for Experiment 1. The order of the 45 trials was randomised for each subject as well.

Procedure. The procedure was identical to that used in Experiment 1. Again we employed two different versions of processing the maths problems. In Part A of the experiment, the maths problems were solved and a 'yes"/"no" response was given. In Part B subjects simply read the digits within each problem aloud.

Results

Maths problems. The overall mean for correct verification of maths problems in Part A was 87.4%. A 2×3 repeated measures ANOVA revealed a significant main effect for similarity, $F(2, 38) = 3.47$, $MSe = 1.78$, but not for task type, $F(1, 19) < 1$, $MSe = 2.20$. The interaction was not significant, $F(2, 38) = 2.48$, $MSe = 1.61$. Orthogonal contrasts showed that more maths errors were made in the rhyming lists than in the dissimilar and similar lists, which did not differ. The difference between the mean score for rhyming (17.05) and the combined means of the dissimilar and similar conditions (17.69) was 0.64 of a maths problem.

Correct in position. The data for the correct in position measure are presented in the top panels of Figure 2. A 3×3 repeated measures ANOVA was conducted to analyse these data. There was a main effect for task type, $F(2, 38) = 169.22$, $MSe = 13.73$ for Part A and $F(2, 38) = 138.87$, $MSe = 11.09$ for Part B. More words were recalled from the immediate task than words from the delayed and operations span tasks in both parts of the experiment, $F(1, 19) = 169.22$, $MSe = 18.32$, and $F(1, 19) = 195.74$, $MSe = 11.80$. Operations span did not differ from delayed recall in Part A, but more words were recalled in the operations span test than on the delayed test in Part B, $F(1, 19) = 74.20$, $MSe = 10.38$. The main effect for phonolo-

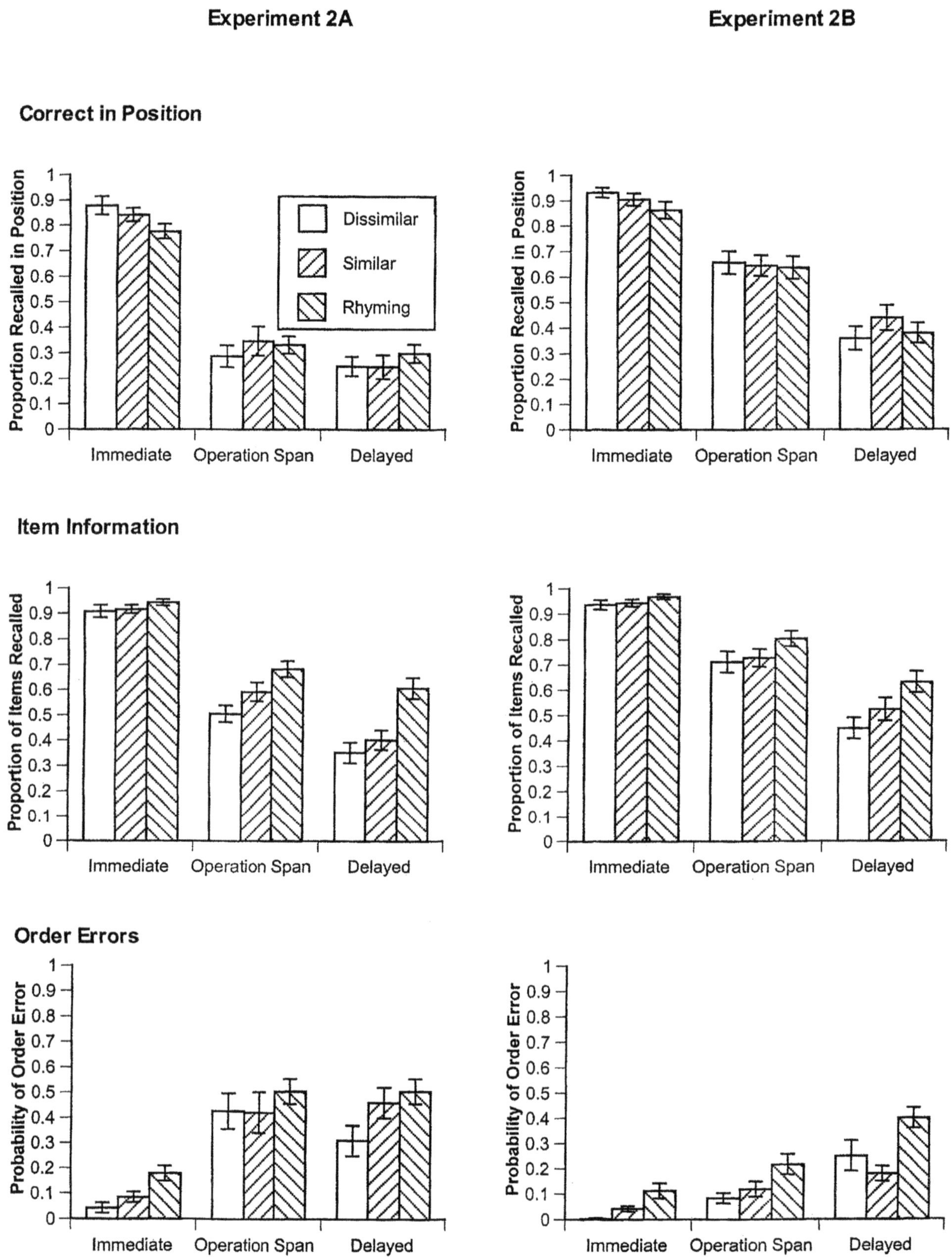

Figure 2. Phonological similarity effects in immediate, delayed, and operations span serial recall tasks. Error bars represent the standard error of the mean.

gical similarity was not significant, F (2, 38) < 1, MSe = 7.28, and F (2, 38) = 1.28, MSe = 6.46. A small significant interaction between task and phonological similarity was found in Part A, F (4, 76) = 3.55, MSe = 5.04, but not in Part B, F (4, 76) = 1.33, MSe = 6.17. In Table 1, we support these analyses of the phonological similarity effect by comparing performance first between the dissimilar and similar lists and second between dissimilar and rhyming lists. We use two indexes of the strength of the phonological similarity effects. The first is a measure of effect size where we report Cohen's d statistic. Traditionally, effect sizes around the .2 level have been seen as weak; around the .5 level as medium, and above the .8 level as strong. In Table 1, the effect size estimates above .40 have been emboldened. The second supporting measures have involved standard repeated measures Student's t-test. The t values are presented in brackets in Table 1 and those that reach the .05 level of significance have been starred. Those effect sizes between .40 and .45 approached statistical significance (p = .06).

Clearly, the difference in recall between dissimilar and similar lists was not all that strong in any of the tests; the only strong effect was with the operations span test in Part A of the Experiment. The difference between the dissimilar and rhyming lists was very strong on an immediate test but not on the operations span and delayed test.

Item recall. A significant main effect was also observed for task type using the item measure, F (2, 38) = 157.35, MSe = 8.79, and F (2, 38) = 95.62, MSe = 10.81. More words were recalled in the immediate condition than in the working memory task, F (1, 19) = 131.18, MSe = 9.86, and F (1, 19) = 113.25, MSe = 13.9, which in turn showed better recall than the delayed task, F (1, 19) = 190.80, MSe = 7.72, and F (1, 19) = 63.35, MSe = 7.64. There was also a main effect for phonological similarity, F (2, 38) = 36.64, MSe = 4.17, and F (2, 38) = 14.34, MSe = 4.51. The interaction of task type with phonemic information was significant, F (4, 76) = 8.70, MSe = 3.40, and F (4, 76) = 4.40, MSe = 2.68. It is clear that this interaction stems from the differing effects that rhyming lists had on the different tests. In Table 1 it is evident that the difference between dissimilar and similar trials was sporadic. There was no difference on an immediate test and no consistently strong effects on the other two types of test. However, the differences between dissimilar and rhyming lists were consistent. There was no effect of similarity on an immediate test, but a strong similarity advantage on the operations span and delayed test.

Order errors. Analyses of order errors again showed a significant main effect for task type, F (2, 38) = 29.52, MSe = 0.08, and F (2, 38) = 60.38, MSe = 0.01. Proportion of transposition errors in the immediate task was significantly lower than in the delayed and working memory tasks, F (1, 19) = 24.06, MSe = 0.04, and F (1, 19) = 88.36, MSe = 0.02, which did not differ in Part A. However in Part B there were fewer order errors in the operations task than in the delayed task, F (1, 19) = 20.93, MSe = 0.01. There was a significant main

TABLE 1
Experiment 2

	Correct in Position		*Item*		*Order*	
	Similar	*Rhyming*	*Similar*	*Rhyming*	*Similar*	*Rhyming*
Immediate A	.20	**.63**	.05	.28	.29	**1.07**
	(0.89)	**(2.83)***	(0.25)	(1.28)	(1.39)	**(4.79)***
Immediate B	.30	**.53**	.10	.37	**.62**	**.87**
	(1.37)	**(2.38)***	(0.45)	(1.68)	**(2.80)***	**(3.92)**
Operations A	**.53**	.34	**.98**	**1.57**	.03	.31
	(2.37)*	(1.55)	**(4.41)***	**(7.02)***	(0.15)	(1.55)
Operations B	.08	.14	.12	**.77**	.20	**.82**
	(0.37)	(0.65)	(0.54)	**(3.45)***	(0.92)	**(3.66)***
Delayed A	.01	.36	.26	**1.65**	**.50**	**.46**
	(0.05)	(1.62)	(1.18)	**(7.41)***	**(2.25)***	**(2.09)***
Delayed B	.34	.08	**.44**	**1.28**	.18	**.43**
	(1.55)	(0.40)	(1.98)	**(5.72)***	(0.82)	(1.96)

Cohen's d effect size estimates (and Student t statistic) of the phonological similarity effect as a function of memory task, scoring method, and type of phonological similarity.

Student t statistic based on 19 degrees of freedom. Starred statistics are significant at .05.

effect for phonological similarity, F (2, 38) = 6.43, MSe = 0.04, and F (2, 38) = 13.69, MSe = 0.02. The interaction of task type with phonological similarity for the order measure was not significant, F (4, 76) = 1.24, MSe = 0.03, and F (4, 76) = 1.47, MSe = 0.02. In looking at effect size data, it is clear that the differences between dissimilar and similar lists were again quite variable. However, recall of the rhyming lists was characterised by frequent misordering of the list words as reflected by the large effect size estimates under almost all conditions.

Discussion

The first point that needs to be made is that creating phonologically non-rhyming similar lists did not prove overly effective. There are indicators that in some conditions subjects are sensitive to the categorical nature of the two items. Furthermore, longer lists are probably required to maximise the effect of similarity without category. Effect size measures were generally quite weak for all of the measures and any effects that did emerge were not replicated across tasks or across Parts A and B of the experiment. Consequently, the rest of the discussion centres on the comparisons involving the dissimilar lists and the rhyming lists. Here the effects were more consistent across tasks and across the two parts of the experiment.

Using the correct-in-position scoring we replicate the standard phonological similarity effect on an immediate test; dissimilar lists were better recalled than the rhyming lists. We also replicate the Tehan and Humphreys (1995) and Fallon et al. (1999) results in showing that the phonological similarity effect is attenuated on a delayed test. Like Fallon et al., the attenuation of the effect on a delayed test is due to an item advantage in the rhyming lists being offset by an order decrement.

The new findings are that the differences between dissimilar and rhyming lists are equivalent for the operations span and delayed test conditions for all measures used. Furthermore, in all three tasks, more order errors are made in the rhyming lists than in the dissimilar lists. In fact the only difference between the three tasks on item and order scores is that there is an absence of an item advantage for the rhyming lists on the immediate test. The most likely explanation for this is that performance on the immediate test is on ceiling. The Fallon et al. (1999) research suggests that as list length increases and as performance comes off ceiling, then the item advantage for rhyming list emerges. Thus, although a concentration soley on the correct in position measure would indicate that the immediate recall task is different from the delayed and working memory tasks, an analysis of item and order effects suggests that all three tasks are affected by phonological similarity in the same way. In all tasks order errors are more prevalent in the rhyming lists, and as long as performance is off ceiling, item recall is better on the rhyming lists than on the dissimilar lists.

The results suggest that the three tasks are quite similar and the item/order analysis clearly indicates that performance on the operations span and delayed tests is being supported by phonological representations. The strong test of the Baddeley and Cowan models assumed that phonological representations would decay to baseline levels and that there would be equivalent order errors for similar and dissimilar lists. The evidence is that order errors are more frequent in rhyming lists in all three tasks. If one accepts the proposition that increased order errors for phonologically similar lists are due to activated representations in memory, then the conclusion can only be that all three tasks are supported by active phonological representations. That is, there is no evidence that representations of items have decayed to baseline levels in any of the tasks.

Although the presence of phonological representations on the delayed test is problematic for both models, they could explain the results by arguing that the phonological representations for auditory items decay at a slower rate than for visually presented items. Thus even after 12 seconds of distractor activity, the phonological representations of the list items could still be above threshold levels. This assumption might be plausible. With auditory presentation or when subjects read items aloud, as was the case in the current experiment, phonological codes are assumed to be stronger than those derived through visual presentation (Penney, 1989). Furthermore, there is empirical evidence showing that auditorially derived phonological codes can remain active for periods of at least 10–15 seconds under some circumstances (Longoni, Richardson, & Aiello, 1993; Tolan & Tehan, 1999). However, the circumstances in the Longoni et al. and the Tolan & Tehan experiments are quite different from those utilised here.

GENERAL DISCUSSION

The pattern of performance observed in the two experiments seriously questions the need to distinguish separate passive and active storage components in a working memory system. Two of the cornerstone indicators of the phonological loop, the word length and phonological similarity effects, are also evident in a task that has been assumed to measure central executive functioning and one that has been assumed to measure LTM. A parsimonious explanation for the results would argue that the same structures or the same processes are involved in each task.

From the Baddeley perspective, the data could be explained by arguing that the phonological loop underlies performance in the complex span and delayed recall tasks. In the introduction it was noted that Daneman and Carpenter (1980) clearly thought that the phonological loop was not involved in standard working memory tasks. Although LaPointe and Engle (1990) challenged the Daneman and Carpenter interpretation, they did not come to the conclusion that the phonological loop supported both simple and complex span tasks. Instead, they concluded that an undifferentiated pool of working memory resources supported both tasks. It is fair to say that currently, when complex span tasks are being used, the assumption is that they are measuring something other than the processes encapsulated by the concept of the phonological loop.

However, a role for the phonological loop could be argued if the key processes that underpin the loop are common to all tasks. Thus, if subjects are able to rehearse at some stage during the distractor task, word length and phonological similarity effects might emerge. Can we rule this possibility out? The answer is obviously no; participants *might* rehearse at various stages during the task. No researcher in this area can exercise complete control over the covert mental strategies that subjects adopt. Furthermore, covert rehearsal processes are notoriously difficult to measure and as Brown and Hulme (1995) note there are many aspects of rehearsal in short-term tasks that have yet to be resolved. Thus, it is impossible to say whether participants are or are not rehearsing. The tenable position is that activities like articulatory suppression, counting backwards in threes, shadowing digits, or doing maths problems, reduce the opportunity to rehearse or decrease the cumulative number of rehearsals, but are unlikely to prevent rehearsal totally. As such, inferences about the degree of rehearsal taking place can only be made on the basis of indirect behavioural indicators.

Although it is possible that participants might rehearse during our tasks, there is not a lot of evidence for substantial cumulative rehearsal. For a start, performance on the maths problems is good, but it is by no means on ceiling. Our impression was that subjects found this task quite demanding within the time allotted and did not have time available for rehearsals. These observations are supported by the fact that in Part A of both experiments, performance on the delayed task and the operations span task appears to be very close to floor, with subjects only being able to recall about one or two of the four items. The absolute level of performance does not seem to indicate that much rehearsal is going on, yet reliable word length and phonological similarity effects are observed.

Second, the difficulty of the distractor task changed with Part A and Part B. Shadowing digits is presumably easier than doing maths problems and would provide a better opportunity to rehearse. Performance on Part B was higher in terms of absolute levels of performance and is consistent with an increased opportunity to rehearse. However, even with an increased opportunity to rehearse, the pattern of effects did not change in any way. Word length and phonological similarity effects were present under both hard and easy distractor tasks.

The Cowan model fares little better than the phonological loop model. The results on the immediate test and on the operations span test are consistent with the notion that recall is supported time-limited active memory. However, the presence of a word length effect and phonological errors on the delayed test are hard to reconcile with the notion of rapidly decaying representations in active memory. The Cowan model could probably be salvaged if it were assumed the items could be periodically reactivated during the distractor tasks. Thus, once again, if subjects were able to rehearse during the distractor task, the items could be reactivated in active memory and standard memory effects would follow.

The foregoing discussion suggests that both the working memory and embedded processes models could be adapted to explain performance on all three tasks by assuming that participants rehearse/reactivate items during distractor periods. The problem is that while rehearsal/reactivation is a central feature of these models, the rehearsal/

reactivation process is unspecified. As Brown and Hulme (1993, p. 599) note, "...if rehearsal does exert an important causal influence on memory span, it is clearly necessary to know exactly when such rehearsal is taking place."

Given that no firm conclusions concerning the presence or absence of rehearsal in these tasks is possible, the only appeal left is to the writing of the various authors involved. Both Baddeley and Cowan have at one time suggested that neither the phonological loop nor active memory are involved in Brown-Peterson type tasks. Vallar and Baddeley (1982) explicitly tested the notion that the phonological loop was involved in the Brown-Peterson task by manipulating the distractor activity employed during the distractor task. They argued that if the phonological loop was involved, then using articulatory suppression as a distractor task should have a detrimental effect on recall in the same way that it does in immediate serial recall. They compared performance on the task where half the subjects counted backwards in threes during the retention interval and the other half repeated the word "the" continuously during the retention interval. They found that counting backwards in threes over a 15-second retention interval produced the standard Brown-Peterson forgetting curve. However, articulatory suppression produced no effect over shorter retention intervals (5 seconds) and only weak effects at the long retention intervals. On the basis that articulatory suppression had virtually no influence on recall, Vallar and Baddeley concluded that the phonological loop did not support performance on the Brown-Peterson task. Given the obvious difference in processing demands associated with the two types of distractor activity they suggested that the central executive supported performance on the task.

Cowan et al. (1994) argued for the need to maintain a distinction between short-term storage and long-term storage. Word length effects were found in backward recall on immediate test, but not on a continuous distractor task in which 15-second distractor periods were utilised. They argued that word length effects on an immediate test indicated that items were present in a short-term store (activated in active memory). The absence of effects on the continuous distractor task was taken as evidence that the items were recalled from a long-term store. That is, the memories for the list items had returned to baseline levels. In short, memories might maintain some residual activity on our operations span task where a 3-second distractor task was employed, but LTM should be accessed on the delayed task.

The role of active memory in complex span tasks has also been questioned. Towse et al. (1998) have also argued that the retention characteristics of complex span tasks seems to be too great to be supported by the phonological loop. Certainly other researchers (Brainerd & Kingma, 1985; Daneman & Carpenter, 1980; Swanson, 1996) argue that working memory tasks are not supported by a short-term store.

If neither the Baddeley nor Cowan model provides a complete account of the results of the two experiments, are there viable alternatives that can? Clearly the data strongly support the notion that very similar processes or structures underlie the three tasks. It may be that all three tasks reflect the use of similar codes but differ in the levels of temporal decay (Towse et al., 1998) or differences in temporal distinctiveness (Neath & Crowder, 1990). Furthermore, existing models of short-term memory that make no reference to active central executive resources can probably explain the results. Nairne's (1990) feature model already models word length (Neath & Nairne, 1995) and phonological similarity effects in immediate serial recall, and it also models performance on the Brown-Peterson task. It could easily be extended to handle the operations span data. As forgetting in the model is based on interference rather than temporal decay, similar patterns of performance would be expected across all tasks.

In sum, our results imply that similar processes and/or structures are involved in simple, complex, and delayed recall tasks. However, they do not specify what those processes and/or structures are. The current research was motivated by the need to distinguish between two classes of working memory models that assume both active and passive storage. One class assumes that a passive store is not involved in active working memory, the other class insists that it is. When it comes to performance on simple and complex span tasks, the data clearly indicate that both tasks are supported by a common storage system. However, our research also suggests that the same storage system is involved in delayed recall as well. Neither of the representative models provided a totally satisfactory answer for this finding. Finally, our starting proposition was that the phonological similarity and word length effects were signature effects of the operation of the phonological loop. The current data would suggest that these effects are more general and should be considered more as signature variables of performance over short retention intervals.

REFERENCES

Adams, A., Bourke, L., & Willis, C. (1999). Working memory and spoken language comprehension in young children. *International Journal of Psychology, 34*, 364–373.

Baddeley, A.D. (1966). Short-term memory for word sequences as a function of acoustic, semantic and formal similarity. *Quarterly Journal of Experimental Psychology, 18A*, 362–365.

Baddeley, A.D. (1986). *Working memory*. London: Oxford University Press.

Baddeley, A.D., & Hitch, G. (1974). Working memory. In K.W. Spence & J.T. Spence (Eds.), *The psychology of learning and motivation, vol 8* (pp. 67–89). New York: Academic Press.

Baddeley, A.D., Thomson, N., & Buchanan, M. (1975). Word length and the structure of short-term memory. *Journal of Verbal Learning and Verbal Behaviour, 14*, 575–589.

Brainerd, C.J., & Kingma, J. (1985). On the independence of short-term memory and working memory in cognitive development. *Cognitive Psychology, 17*, 210–247.

Brown, G.D.A., & Hulme, C. (1995). Modeling item length effects in memory span: No rehearsal needed? *Journal of Memory and Language, 34*, 594–621.

Brown, J.A. (1958). Some tests of the decay theory of immediate memory. *Quarterly Journal of Experimental Psychology, 10*, 12–21.

Caplan, D., Rochon, E., & Walters, G. (1992). Articulatory and phonological determinants of word length effects in span tasks. *Quarterly Journal of Experimental Psychology, 45A*, 177–192.

Cowan, N. (1999). An embedded-process model of working memory. In A. Miyake & P. Shah (Eds.), *Models of working memory: Mechanisms of active maintenance and executive control* (pp. 102–134). New York: Cambridge University Press.

Cowan, N., Day, L., Saults, J.S., Keller, T.A., Johnson, T., & Flores, L. (1992). The role of verbal output time in the effects of word length on immediate memory. *Journal of Memory and Language, 31*, 1–17.

Cowan, N., Wood, N.L., & Borne, D.N. (1994). Reconfirmation of the short-term storage concept. *Psychological Science, 5*, 103–106.

Daneman, M., & Carpenter, P.A. (1980). Individual differences in working memory and reading. *Journal of Verbal Learning and Verbal Behavior, 19*, 450–466.

Engle, R.W. (1996). Working memory and retrieval: An inhibition-resource approach. In J.T.E. Richardson, R. Engle, L. Hasher, R. Logie, E. Stolzfus, & R. Zacks (Eds.), *Working memory and cognition* (pp. 89–120). New York: Oxford University Press.

Engle, R.W., Kane, M.J., & Tuholski, S.W. (1999). Individual differences in working memory capacity and what they tell us about controlled attention, general fluid intelligence, and functions of the prefrontal cortex. In A. Miyake & P. Shah (Eds.), *Models of working memory: Mechanisms of active maintenance and executive control* (pp. 102–134). New York: Cambridge University Press.

Fallon, A.B., Groves, K., & Teyhan, G. (1999). Phonological similarity and trace degradation in the serial recall task: When CAT helps RAT, but not MAN. *International Journal of Psychology, 34*, 301–308.

Farrand, P., & Jones, D. (1996). Direction of report in spatial and verbal serial short term memory. *Quarterly Journal of Experimental Psychology, 49A*, 140–158.

Jones, D., Farrand, P., Stuart, G., & Morris, N. (1995). Functional equivalence of verbal and spatial information in serial short-term memory. *Journal of Experimental Psychology: Learning, Memory, and Cognition, 21*, 1008–1018.

LaPointe, L.B., & Engle, R.W. (1990). Simple and complex word spans as measures of working memory capacity. *Journal of Experimental Psychology: Learning, Memory, and Cognition, 16*, 1118–1133.

Lehto, J. (1996). Are executive function tests dependent on working memory capacity? *Quarterly Journal of Experimental Psychology, 49A*, 29–50.

Longoni, A.M., Richardson, J.T.E., & Aiello, A. (1993). Articulatory rehearsal and phonological storage in working memory. *Memory and Cognition, 21*, 11–22.

Lovatt, P., Avons, S.E., & Masterson, J. (2000). The word-length effect and disyllabic words. *Quarterly Journal of Experimental Psychology, 53A1*, 1–22.

Miyake, A., & Shah, P. (1999). *Models of working memory: Mechanisms of active maintenance and executive control*. New York: Cambridge University Press.

Nairne, J.S. (1990). A feature model of immediate memory. *Memory and Cognition, 18*, 251–269.

Nairne, J.S., & Kelly, M.R. (1999). Reversing the phonological similarity effect. *Memory andCognition, 27*, 45–53.

Neath, I., & Crowder, R.G. (1990). Schedules of presentation and temporal distinctiveness in human memory. *Journal of Experimental Psychology: Learning, Memory, and Cognition, 16*, 316–327.

Neath, I., & Nairne, J.S. (1995). Word-length effects in immediate memory: Overwriting trace decay theory. *Psychonomic Bulletin and Review, 2*, 429–441.

Penney, C.G. (1989). Modality effects and the structure of short-term verbalmemory. *Memory and Cognition, 17*, 398–422.

Peterson, L.R., & Peterson, M.J. (1959). Short-term retention of individual items. *Journal of Experimental Psychology, 58*, 193–198.

Poirier, M., & Saint-Aubin, J. (1995). Memory for related and unrelated words: Further evidence on the influence of semantic factors in immediate serial recall. *Quarterly Journal of Experimental Psychology, 48A*, 384–404.

Service, E. (1998). The effect of word length on immediate serial recall depends upon complexity, not articulatory duration. *Quarterly Journal of Experimental Psychology*, *51A*, 283–304.

Shah, P., & Miyake, A. (1996). The separability of working memory resources for spatial thinking and language processing: An individual differences approach. *Journal of Experimental Psychology: General*, *125*, 4–27.

Swanson, H.L. (1996). Individual differences in children's working memory. *Memory and Cognition*, *24*, 70–82.

Tehan, G., & Humphreys, M.S. (1995). Transient phonemic codes and immunity to proactive interference. *Memory and Cognition*, *23*, 181–191.

Tehan, G., & Humphreys, M.S. (1998). Creating proactive interference in immediate recall: Building a dog from a dart, a mop and a fig. *Memory and Cognition*, *26*, 477–489.

Tolan, G.A., & Tehan, G. (1999). Determinants of short-term forgetting: Decay, retroactive interference or proactive interference? *International Journal of Psychology*, *34*, 285–292.

Towse, J.N., Hitch, G.J., & Hutton, U. (1998). A reevaluation of working memory capacity in children. *Journal of Memory and Language*, *39*, 195–217.

Turner, M., & Engle, R.W. (1989). Is working memory capacity task dependent? *Journal of Memory and Language*, *28*, 127–154.

Vallar, G., & Baddeley, A.D. (1982). Short-term forgetting and the articulatory loop. *Quarterly Journal of Experimental Psychology*, *34A*, 61–77.

Walling, J.R., McEvoy, C.L., Oth, J.E., & Nelson, D.L. (1984). *The University of South Florida rhyme category norms*. Unpublished manuscript, University of South Florida.

MEMORY, 2001, 9 (4/5/6), 349–363

Phonological short-term memory contributions to sentence processing in young children

Catherine S. Willis
Liverpool Hope University College, UK

Susan E. Gathercole
University of Bristol, UK

Two experiments investigated the contribution of phonological short-term memory to the processing of spoken sentences by 4- and 5-year-old children. In Experiment 1, sentences contained either short or longer words, and varied in syntactic structure. Overall, repetition but not comprehension of the sentences was significantly influenced by word length. In Experiment 2, children selected on the basis of their high phonological short-term memory ability were founded to be superior at repeating sentences to children of lower phonological short-term memory ability, although the two groups did not differ in their comprehension accuracy for the same sentences. In both experiments, comprehension and repetition performance were differently influenced by particular sentence structures. It is proposed that sentence repetition in children is constrained by phonological memory capacity, and is therefore directly influenced by memory-related factors that include the length and number of words in sentences, and individual differences in memory skills.

Immediate repetition of spoken sentences is a paradigm that has been used extensively to investigate the processes involved in comprehending language. Evidence that the language-processing system is involved in sentence repetition is provided by findings that normal individuals have a capacity to repeat words in meaningful sentences that greatly exceeds conventional memory span assessments using sequences containing unrelated digits, letters, or words. For example, whereas the number of words recalled from a list during serial recall is typically five or six, Miller and Selfridge (1950) reported almost 100% accuracy in the recall of 20-word sentences. Another key finding is that when errors in recalling verbatim form of sentences do occur, the gist of the sentence is often preserved (e.g., Jarvella, 1971; Saffran & Martin, 1975).

Several theoretical accounts of this enhanced memory span for sentences over sequences of unrelated words have been advanced. Potter and Lombardi (Lombardi & Potter, 1992; Potter & Lombardi, 1990, 1998) proposed that the high level of accuracy of sentence repetition is achieved by regenerating the original form of the sentences from three sources: the conceptual representations of the meaning of the sentence that were constructed during initial sentence processing, activated lexical items, and syntactically primed sentence structures. These authors argue that immediate memory for sentences is largely conceptually based and reconstructive in nature, and

Requests for reprints should be sent to Dr Catherine Willis, Centre of Applied Psychology, Liverpool John Moores University, Henry Cotton Building, 15–21 Webster Street, Liverpool L3 2ET, UK. Email: C.Willis@livjm.ac.uk

This research was supported by an ESRC studentship (no. R00429234340) awarded to the first author, and forms part of her doctoral thesis at Lancaster University. The authors thank Graeme Stead and James Smith for the artwork in the comprehension picture book, and the staff and children of St. Mary's & St. Benedict;s R.C. Primary School, Bamber Bridge Methodist School, Walton-le-Dale C.P. School, and Clayton Brook C.P. School for their participation in the experiments.

http://www.tandf.co.uk/journals/pp/09658211.html DOI:10.1080/09658210143000155

does not call on the capacity-constrained phonological short-term storage system believed to underpin the recall of sequences of unrelated items (e.g., Baddeley, 1986; Baddeley, Thomson, & Buchanan, 1975).

McCarthy and Warrington (1987a,b) have also distinguished between the processes typically involved in list recall and sentence repetition. Their investigations of the immediate memory capacities of neuropsychological patients identified a double dissociation between list and sentence repetition. Two individuals with severe impairments of phonological memory showed deficient recall of unrelated stimulus items but good capacities for the immediate verbatim recall of meaningful sentences. In contrast, a patient with unimpaired memory span more accurately recalled word lists than sentences (McCarthy & Warrington, 1987a). On the basis of these findings, it was argued that phonological short-term memory supports list recall, whereas sentence repetition is underpinned by a dynamic memory system with access to lexical semantic information. This system shares some important features with the "episodic buffer" component recently added by Baddeley (2000) to the working memory model. The episodic buffer provides an amodal workspace in which information from other working memory subsystems and long-term memory (such as lexical and semantic knowledge) can be integrated, and could therefore readily accommodate the superior memory span for words presented within meaningful sentences rather than unrelated strings.

McCarthy and Warrington (1987b) do not rule out any contribution of phonological short-term memory to sentence repetition, and indeed present evidence of deficits in sentence repetition in short-term memory patients under certain highly constrained conditions, such as sentences containing syntactically complex constructions relating to order of occurrence (see also, Martin, 1990; Saffran & Martin, 1990; Vallar & Baddeley, 1984). In line with other theorists (e.g., Caramazza & Zurif, 1976; Saffran & Martin, 1975; Vallar & Baddeley, 1984), McCarthy and Warrington propose that although under most circumstances the language processor operates on-line without recourse to buffer storage, phonological memory representations may be consulted to enable backtracking and possibly re-analysis of spoken language under conditions where on-line comprehension is not possible. Such conditions include fast rates of presentation, and slow latencies of the analytic processes underlying language comprehension.

Martin and colleagues (Hanten & Martin, 2000; Martin, Lesch, & Bartha, 1999; Martin, Shelton, & Yaffee, 1994) propose that phonological memory makes a more direct contribution to sentence repetition, pointing to evidence that individuals with short-term memory deficits do show impairments of sentence repetition (Butterworth, Campbell, & Howard, 1986; Friedrich, Martin, & Kemper, 1985; Martin et al., 1994), and often produce gist rather than verbatim recall of sentences (Martin, 1993; Saffran & Martin, 1975). This group has advanced a multiple systems model of short-term memory in which phonological, lexical, and semantic knowledge representations are activated during processing, and pass on activation to more temporary phonological and semantic storage buffers. Supported by striking neuropsychological dissociations, Martin et al. (1999; see also, Hanten & Martin, 2000) propose that sentence repetition is supported by access to both phonological and semantic short-term stores, while sentence comprehension depends primarily on semantic short-term storage.

The majority of previous research on this topic has used individuals with histories of normal language development who acquired deficits in short-term memory following neuropsychological damage in adulthood. The purpose of the research reported in the present article was to investigate the extent to which phonological short-term storage contributes to sentence repetition in young children. One possibility is that children may depend on phonological short-term memory to support language processing to an even greater extent than adults. During the early years of life when the processes involved in syntactic and semantic analysis of sentence are still being acquired and the analytic processes that have been acquired operate relatively slowly, off-line analysis requiring phonological memory support may be more common. This conjecture fits well with McCarthy and Warrington's (1987b) proposal that phonological memory support is necessary under conditions of slow latencies of language-analytic processes, as a consequence of resulting delays in transcoding incoming language into the necessary central cognitive representations. Early language development may represent one such case of this condition being satisfied, and hence of significant phonological memory involvement in sentence repetition. It may also be the case that sentence processing is more directly constrained by phonological memory factors in children than in adults because children's memory capacity is smaller. Phonological memory capacity develops dramatically over the middle childhood years, with a two- to three-fold increase in memory span between about 4 and 11 years of age (see Gathercole, 1999, for review). The typical phonological memory capacities of two or three items at around 5 years of age may impose a much more severe constraint on memory support for sentence processing than adult capacities of six or seven items.

There have been a small number of studies exploring phonological memory involvement in sentence processing in children. Hanten and Martin (2000) recently reported findings from two 10-year old children with short-term memory impairments resulting from closed head injuries. One child with a clear profile of phonological memory deficits was severely impaired in repeating sentences, but showed normal detection of semantic anomalies in sentences. These findings are consistent with these authors' claims that phonological storage contributes to the repetition although not the comprehension of sentences, in children as well as adults.

This view also receives some support from findings of two studies comparing the sentence-processing abilities of 8-year old children selected on the basis of good and poor reading ability, but who were also distinguished in their immediate memory spans. Shankweiler, Smith, and Mann (1984) found that poor readers made significantly more errors in repeating some types of sentences (those containing reflexive pronouns) than good readers, although the two groups did not differ significantly in their ability to understand the same sentences when tested on a separate occasion using a forced-choice picture verification task. Mann, Shankweiler, and Smith (1984), however, reported findings that poor readers were impaired in following verbal instructions that contained relative clause structures, suggesting that the sentence-processing deficit in this population may extend beyond repetition to more central comprehension processes.

The present two experiments investigated phonological memory involvement in sentence processing in younger children, aged 4 and 5 years, whose language abilities were normal but still developing. In both experiments, the children heard spoken sentences, attempted to repeat the verbatim form of the sentences, and then demonstrated their comprehension by selecting the line drawing that corresponded to the meaning of the sentence. Including the comprehension test in this way provided an opportunity to evaluate the extent to which sentence repetition and comprehension were subject to the same constraints.

Phonological memory load in sentence processing was manipulated by varying word length in Experiment 1. The children were presented with spoken sentences that varied in number of syllables but not in number of words. The length of words in a memory sequence has a powerful effect on immediate recall of unrelated word lists, with superior recall consistently found for lists containing short rather than long words (Baddeley et al., 1975). Early accounts of the word-length effect located its influence in a time-dependent articulatory rehearsal process which allowed more opportunity for decay of long than short memory items (Baddeley et al., 1975; Baddeley, Lewis, & Vallar, 1984). More recently, it has been argued that the word-length effect may alternatively arise from differences in either the phonological structure of short and long words (Caplan & Waters, 1994; Caplan, Rochon, & Waters, 1992; Lovatt, Avons, & Masterson, 2000), or in their delays prior to output (Cowan et al., 1992; Dosher & Ma, 1998). For the present purposes, debates concerning the detailed origins of the word-length effect are not crucial; the important point is that the phenomenon is widely believed to originate in phonological short-term memory.

If phonological memory does contribute significantly to sentence repetition but not comprehension, as claimed by Martin and colleagues (e.g., Hanten & Martin, 2000), the accuracy of repetition but not comprehension should be poorer for the sentences containing the lengthier words. If, on the other hand, sentence processing proceeds independently of buffer storage (Potter & Lombardi, 1990, 1998), no influence of word length should be found on either measure.

Links between phonological memory function and sentence processing established in both adults and children to date have been found to be highly specific to sentence structures, and in particular to complex and lengthy constructions (e.g., Mann et al., 1984; McCarthy & Warrington, 1987a; Saffran & Martin, 1975). In order to explore the specificity of possible memory contributions to sentence processing in our experiments, a range of sentence structures were included. Six sentence types from the Test for Reception of Grammar (Bishop, 1982), found by Willis (1997) to show close links with phonological memory ability, were selected. The sentences contained either the prepositions *above* and *below*, the prepositions *in* and *on*, reversible constructions, relative clauses, X-but-not-Y constructions, or embedded structures. Incorporating a range of grammatical structures also provided the opportunity to investigate whether repetition and comprehension were equivalently influenced by syntactic form.

In summary, Experiment 1 was designed to investigate phonological memory contributions to sentence processing in 4- and 5-year-old children. The children attempted sentence repetition followed by a comprehension measure. Phonological memory load was manipulated by varying the length of words in the sentences, and the syntactic structure of the sentences was also varied.

EXPERIMENT 1

Method

Design. Repetition and comprehension accuracy were each tested as a function of two within-subject variables: sentence length (short and longer), and sentence type. There were four sentences in each experimental condition. For both the repetition and comprehension dependent variables, the number of sentences on which correct responses were made was scored.

Participants. A total of 30 reception class children with a mean age of 4 years 6 months (SD = 4.28 months) participated in the study. The children all attended a state primary school in an urban area near Preston, north-west England.

Materials. Six sentence types from the Test for Reception of Grammar (TROG; Bishop, 1982) were selected for use in this study. Sentences contained either (i) the prepositions *above* and *below* (mean length 6.0 words), (ii) the prepositions *in* and *on* (mean length 6.5 words), (iii) reversible sentences (e.g., *The fox is chased by the horse*, mean length 7.1 words), (iv) sentences containing a relative clause (e.g., *The book is on the box that is red*, mean length 8.5 words), (v) sentences of an X-but-not-Y construction (e.g., *The box but not the chair is red*, mean length 7.6 words), or (vi) embedded sentences (e.g., *The shoe the comb is on is blue*, mean length 8.0 words).

The stimuli are listed in the Appendix. Four short and four long sentences of each sentence type were constructed, matched individually for syntactic structure and verb. Word length within sentences was manipulated mainly by contrasting the number of syllables in the nouns: the nouns contained one syllable in the short sentences but either two or three syllables in the long sentences. Where possible, multi-syllable adjectives were included in the long sentences, and monosyllabic adjectives in the short sentences. The mean number of syllables in the short and long sentences, for each sentence type, was as follows: *in/on*, 6.50 (short), 9.75 (long); *above/below*, 7.00 (short), 10.00 (long); reversible actives, 7.00 (short), 9.00 (long); X-but-not-Y, 8.00 (short), 10.75 (long); embedded sentences, 8.50 (short), 12.75 (long); relative clauses, 9.00 (short), 12.75 (long). The sentences containing short and longer nouns were randomly sequenced, with sentences of each type being blocked at presentation as in the TROG test (Bishop, 1982). The materials therefore consisted of six blocks each containing eight sentences, half of which contained short and half of which contained longer words. The sentences were presented to each child in the same order.

A picture book was constructed to test children's comprehension of the sentences. A new page was used for each sentence. As in the TROG test (Bishop, 1982), four line drawings were constructed for each sentence, with one drawing corresponding to the precise sentence meaning, and three foils. Both lexical and syntactic foils were used. For example, for the sentence *The fox is chased by the horse*, the foils were drawings depicting the following sentences: *The cat is chased by the horse*, *The horse is chased by the fox*, and *The rabbit is chased by the fox*.

Procedure. Each child was tested individually in a quiet testing area, seated facing the text administrator. At the beginning of the testing session, the child was instructed to "listen carefully while I say a sentence, then say the sentence back to me. When you have done that I will show you some pictures and I want you to point to the one which shows what I said." Simple sentences from a block of TROG (e.g., *The boy is running*) were used as practice sentences. On each trial, the child was required to repeat each sentence and then to point to one of the four drawings on the page that he or she believed corresponded to the meaning of the sentence. The page was not displayed to the child until the repetition attempt had been made. The accuracy of repetition and comprehension responses were recorded on each trial at the time of testing.

Results

Repetition and comprehension accuracy for each participant was scored as a function of sentence length and sentence type. Mean scores and standard errors in each condition are shown in Table 1. Accuracy was greater for the sentences containing short than longer words in both the repetition and comprehension tasks, although the magnitude of the decrement with longer nouns was greatest for repetition.

The repetition and comprehension data were analysed separately, as they represent distinct dependent variables Two-way analyses of variance, with sentence length (two levels) and sentence type (six levels) as the within-subject factors, were performed on the repetition and comprehension scores. In the analysis of the repetition scores, there was a significant main effect of sentence length, $F(1, 29) = 10.000, p < .005$, reflecting the superior level of performance found with sentences containing short rather than longer nouns. The effect of sentence type was also highly significant, $F(5, 145) = 41.072, p < .001$. Pairwise comparisons by Tukey's HSD test of the different sentence structures established that both reversible sentences and sentences containing *in* and *on* were repeated with significantly greater accuracy than sentences containing X-but-not-Y structures, relative clauses, and embedded clauses ($p < .001$ in each case). Significantly greater accuracy was also found for sentences containing X-but-not-Y structures and *above/below* than relative clauses and embedded clauses ($p < .001$ in each case).

The interaction between sentence length and sentence type was also significant, $F(5, 145) = 2.34$, $p < .05$. Planned comparisons of the sentences containing short and longer words revealed significant differences for sentence types containing *in/on*, $F(1, 29) = 8.398, p < .01$, and X-but-not-Y structures, $F(1, 29) = 4.619, p < .05$. No other significant differences were found.

The corresponding analysis of variance performed on the comprehension scores revealed a highly significant main effect of sentence type, $F(5, 145) = 18.804, p < .001$. Tukey's HSD pairwise comparisons established superior performance for reversible sentences compared to sentences containing relative clauses ($p < .05$), and for sentences containing *above/below* and embedded clauses ($p < .001$, both cases). Sentences containing *in/on* were associated with higher performance than sentences containing X-but-not-Y structures, *above/below*, relative and embedded clauses ($p < .001$, in each case). Embedded sentences were also more poorly understood than either sentences containing X-but-not-Y structures or relative clauses ($p < .001$, both cases).

The main effect of sentence length was non-significant in this analysis, $F(1, 29) = 1.526, p > .05$, although the interaction between sentence length and sentence type was significant, $F(5, 145) = 3.324$, $p < .01$. Planned comparisons of the short and longer sentences for each sentence type revealed a significant advantage for the short over the longer embedded sentences, $F(1, 29) = 12.362$, $p < .005$.

To aid direct comparison of the strengths of association between each of the independent variables (sentence length and sentence type) and performance on the repetition and comprehension measures, partial η^2 was computed in each case. For sentence length, partial η^2 was .26 on the repetition task, and .05 on the comprehension

TABLE 1
Mean scores and standard errors as a function of task, word length, and sentence type

	Repetition				*Comprehension*			
	Short		*Longer*		*Short*		*Longer*	
Sentence type	*Mean*	*S.E.*	*Mean*	*S.E.*	*Mean*	*S.E.*	*Mean*	*S.E.*
In/on	3.50	0.20	3.07	0.18	3.20	0.17	2.90	0.15
Above/below	3.20	0.21	2.77	0.24	1.87	0.22	2.90	0.19
Reversible passive	2.93	0.27	3.13	0.23	2.57	0.22	2.90	0.19
X-but-not-Y	2.20	0.27	1.67	0.28	2.23	0.21	2.27	0.21
Embedded sentence	1.10	0.27	0.97	0.28	1.80	0.18	1.03	0.19
Relative clause	0.83	0.26	0.83	0.21	2.03	0.15	2.27	0.19

* $p < .05$
** $p < .01$

task. For sentence type, partial η^2 was .59 on the repetition measure, and .39 on the comprehension measure. Both independent variables therefore had greater influences on repetition than comprehension performance, probably due to greater task sensitivity. However, the association between sentence length was 5.1 times stronger for repetition than comprehension, whereas the association for sentence type was 1.5 times stronger in the former than the latter task. These comparisons suggest that the influence of sentence length is genuinely greater on sentence repetition than sentence comprehension, even after differences in overall task sensitivity have been taken into account.

A further issue of interest concerns the possible differential influences of sentence type on the two tasks, repetition and comprehension. Four of the sentence types led to comparable relative levels of performance across the two tasks: sentences containing *in/on*, reversible sentences, X-but-not-Y constructions, and embedded sentences. However, there were two notable differences across the tasks. First, sentences containing *above/below* were repeated with a relatively high degree of accuracy, but were comprehended poorly. Indeed, repetition scores were considerably higher than comprehension scores in absolute terms (80% versus 46%), despite the higher chance levels of correct responses in the forced-choice comprehension task (.25) than the repetition task (virtually zero). All other things being equal, superior levels of performance would therefore be expected on comprehension compared to repetition for all sentence types. Second, sentences containing relative clauses were associated with poorest levels of repetition performance of all six sentence types (21% accuracy), but intermediate comprehension scores (51% accuracy).

Differences between repetition and comprehension were explored in a series of one-way analyses of variance performed on repetition and comprehension scores for each sentence type, collapsed across sentence length. As the nature of these analyses was essentially exploratory, a Bonferroni correction was applied to yield a criterion significance level of .008 for each comparison. The outcomes of these analyses confirmed the earlier observations. For four of the sentence types (reversibles, *in/on*, X-but-not-Y, and embedded sentences), there were no significant differences in scores on the repetition and comprehension measures. For the sentences containing *above* and *below*, however, repetition scores significantly exceeded comprehension scores, $F(1, 29) = 27.23$, $p < .001$, despite the lower baseline guessing levels in repetition than comprehension. On sentences containing relative clauses, in contrast, accuracy was significantly greater for comprehension than repetition scores, $F(1, 29) = 34.09$, $p < .001$.

Discussion

Four- and five-year old children were significantly more accurate at repeating spoken sentences containing short rather than longer words. However, selection of pictures depicting the sentence meaning was not significantly influenced by sentence length. Sensitivity to length of the memory sequence is a ubiquitous finding in immediate recall of lists of unrelated words, and has been widely interpreted as reflecting the time-limited nature of the rehearsal process leading to slower rates of either rehearsal or output of long rather than short words (e.g., Baddeley et al., 1975; Cowan et al., 1992). The disruptive effect of increasing word length on accuracy of sentence repetition is therefore consistent with the proposal that representations of the verbatim form of sentences in phonological short-term memory are used to support their immediate recall (Hanten & Martin, 2000; Martin et al., 1999). In contrast, these findings provide no support for Potter and Lombardi's (1998) contention that sentence repetition is mediated by access to conceptual, lexical, and syntactic representations of sentences but not to phonological short-term memory.

The sentence-length effect found in this experiment was relatively small in magnitude, and indeed a significant advantage to short lists was obtained only for three of the six sentence types (*in/on*, *above/below*, X-but-not-Y). Of the remaining three sentence types in which no difference was found, two (embedded sentences, and relative clauses) were associated with low levels of repetition accuracy which may have obscured any potential length effects. Although a more robust and substantial word-length effect would have provided stronger support for the view that phonological memory does support sentence repetition in young children, it is important to note that the difference between the number of syllables contained in the short and long sentences was itself only moderate in comparison with experiments contrasting word length in list recall. The long sentences contained on average 10.8 syllables as opposed to 7.8 syllables in the short sentences, an increase of 41% which is many times less than the 200–400% contrast typically made in serial recall experiments (e.g., Baddeley et al., 1975, 1984). The fact that the somewhat weak manipulation of word length in the present experiment yielded a significant effect at all is therefore notable.

In contrast, sentences containing lengthier words were not associated with increased errors in picture-selection comprehension measure overall. This pattern of phonological memory influence on the repetition but not comprehension of sentences replicates findings from studies of both neuropsychological patients (Martin et al., 1994) and children (Hanten & Martin, 2000; Shankweiler et al., 1984). However, a word-length effect was obtained for the comprehension of one sentence type (embedded sentences), and the absence of an effect for the remaining sentence types could conceivably reflect a relative insensitivity of this particular dependent variable to word length. Compared with the repetition task on which chance levels of correct responding approach zero, reduced sensitivity of scores would certainly be expected from a four-choice task with a chance baseline guessing rate of .25 which increases to .50 if lexical information is retained, as only one distractor included the lexical items present in most sentences. However, comparisons of the strengths of association of independent variables with performance on the repetition and comprehension tasks do provide some reassurance on this point. Although the comprehension scores were less strongly associated with both sentence type and word length than with repetition scores, the magnitude of the reduced sensitivity was three times greater for word length than sentence type.

Scores on both the repetition and comprehension tasks were highest for the reversible sentences and sentences containing *in/on* clauses, at intermediate levels for X-but-not-Y structures, and poor for sentences containing embedded clauses. Thus, there appears to be a large degree of commonality in the language-processing mechanisms supporting performance on the two tasks, despite the apparent differential sensitivities of the tasks to word length. Repetition and comprehension accuracy did, however, diverge for two of the sentence types. High repetition but relatively low comprehension scores were obtained on sentences containing *above* and *below*, whereas there were poor repetition scores but reasonably high comprehension scores for sentences containing relative clauses. These findings are particularly surprising as the repetition and comprehension tasks were not independent, with the child first attempting to repeat each sentence and then to select a picture corresponding to its meaning.

How can these findings be explained? The comprehension data are possibly best understood as reflecting the particular stage of syntactic competence reached by this 4- to 5-year-old age group: their understanding of structures containing embedded clauses and the spatial adverbs *above* and *below* appears to lag behind sentences containing reversible constructions and *in* and *on*.

Because sentences containing *above* and *below* are repeated more accurately than reversible sentences and those containing *in* and *on*, it appears that verbatim recall is either not as highly constrained by the maturity of syntactic processes as sentence comprehension, or is also sensitive to other factors, which masks this developmental difference. One possible explanation for these findings relates to the variation in the number of words in the different sentence types. Sentences containing *above* and *below* were relatively short, and contained a similar number of words to sentences containing *in* and *on*. Both sentence types were associated with comparably high levels of repetition accuracy, although their comprehension accuracy differed. In contrast, the sentences containing relative clauses, which were associated with much poorer repetition than comprehension performance, contained more words than did each of the five other sentence types. These findings can therefore be readily explained in terms of differences in the phonological memory burdens imposed by the sentence types, as the capacity of phonological short-term memory is known to be limited by the amount of phonological information (e.g., Baddeley et al., 1975; Caplan & Waters, 1994). According to this account, and all other things being equal, short sentences should be more effectively maintained in phonological memory and will therefore be better recalled than lengthier sequences, irrespective of whether the length variation relates to number of syllables (as in the short and longer sentences in Experiment 1) or number of words (see also, Baddeley, Vallar, & Wilson, 1987).

The contributions of phonological short-term memory to young children's repetition and comprehension of sentences were investigated further in Experiment 2, which employed a different memory manipulation. Children with relatively low and high scores on two measures of phonological memory—auditory digit span and nonword repetition—but matched on a measure of nonverbal reasoning ability were selected to participate in the experiment. As in Experiment 1, children were required to repeat a sentence and then to demonstrate their understanding by choosing an appropriate line drawing that depicted the sentence on each trial. In order to explore further the differential effects of sentence structure on repetition and comprehension performance, 16 different sentence structures taken from the TROG (Bishop, 1982) were employed in the experiment.

On the basis both of Shankweiler et al.'s (1984) comparison of sentence processing in older good and poor readers and Hanten and Martin's (2000) report of sentence processing in a child with an acquired phonological memory impairment, it was predicted that the children with relatively poor phonological memory function would show deficits in the repetition but not the comprehension of spoken sentences. This pattern of findings would lend substantial further support to the view that sentence repetition is significantly constrained by phonological memory (e.g., Martin et al., 1999; McCarthy & Warrington, 1987b). By contrasting a wide range of syntactic structures, the experiment also provided a further opportunity to explore the dissociations in the sensitivity of repetition and comprehension to sentence type established in Experiment 1.

EXPERIMENT 2

Method

Design. The sentence-processing performance of two groups of children, selected as having either relatively high or low phonological memory abilities, was compared on two tasks: sentence repetition and sentence comprehension. Sixteen different types of sentence structure were included in each task as a within-subject variable. Each child received four sentences of each type in blocked sequence taken from the TROG test (Bishop, 1982), in each task.

Participants. A total of 61 reception class children (mean age 5 years 2 months, SD = 3.65 months, range = 4 years, 8 months to 5 years, 8 months) attending state primary schools near Preston, an urban region of north-west England, participated in an initial screening phase. The children were tested individually on two measures of phonological STM and one nonverbal ability test. The two memory tests were the Children's Test of Nonword Repetition (Gathercole & Baddeley, 1996) and auditory digit span (Gathercole, 1995). The mean score on the nonword repetition test was 18.87 (SD = 5.85), and mean digit span was 3.75 (SD = .91). The standard score of each child's performance was calculated for each measure, and the two standard scores were averaged to yield a composite phonological memory score for each child.

Raven's Coloured Progressive Matrices test (1978) was given to each child to provide a measure of his or her nonverbal reasoning abilities. The mean score on this test was 14.2 (SD = 3.17). The screening data were used to identify 13 children with high short-term memory scores and 13 children with low short-term memory scores were selected to participate in Experiment 2. The groups were matched for nonverbal scores, and their profiles are shown in Table 2. The difference in the groups' composite memory scores was highly significant, $t(24) = 11.09$, $p < .001$. The groups also differed on their nonword repetition scores, $t(24) = 7.98$, $p < .001$, and digit span, $t(24) = 8.49$, $p < .001$. The mean chronological ages and nonverbal ability scores for each group did not differ significantly, $t(24) < 1$, in both cases.

Materials and procedure. Each child was tested individually. Their repetition and understanding of spoken sentences was tested using sentences from the Test for Reception of Grammar (TROG; Bishop, 1982). The first 12 TROG items are single words and were used to check knowledge of the vocabulary used in the test, but were not included in the analyses. The next four sentences (containing two elements combined, such as *the boy is running*) were used for practice. A further four sentences in each of sixteen sentence structures were then presented, these were: (i) negative sentences (e.g., *The boy is not running*, mean length 5.0 words); (ii) sentences combining three elements (e.g., *The boy is jumping over the box*, mean length 6.5 words); (iii) sentences containing plural personal pronouns (e.g., *They are sitting on the table*, mean length 5.75; (iv) reversible active sentences (e.g., *The girl is pushing the horse*, mean length 6.0 words; (v) sentences containing masculine/feminine personal pronouns (e.g., *She is sitting on the chair*, mean length 5.75); (vi) sentences containing a plural noun inflection

TABLE 2
Mean scores on screening measures for the two phonological memory groups and sample as a whole

	Group		
	High phonological memory	*Low phonological memory*	*Sample*
Chronological Age (mos)	62.85 (3.29)	62.00 (4.53)	62.22 (3.65)
Non-verbal ability	14.00 (2.08)	14.00 (2.27)	14.16 (3.17)
Nonword repetition	25.15 (3.05)	13.00 (4.56)	18.87 (5.85)
Digit span	4.77 (0.73)	2.85 (0.38)	3.75 (0.91)
Composite memory score	1.10 (0.48)	–1.00 (0.48)	0.00 (0.90)

Standard deviations shown in parentheses.

(e.g., *The cats look at the ball*, mean length 5.5 words); (vii) sentences involving a comparison (e.g., *The knife is longer than the pencil*, mean length 7.0 words); (viii) reversible passive sentences (e.g., *The girl is chased by the horse*, mean length 7.0 words); (ix) sentences containing the prepositions *in* and *on* (mean length 6.5 words); (x) sentences containing a postmodified subject (e.g., *The boy chasing the horse is fat*, mean length 7.0 words); (xi) sentences of an X-but-not-Y construction (e.g., *The box but not the chair is red*, mean length 7.5 words); (xii) sentences containing the prepositions *above* and *below* (mean length 6.0 words); (xiii) sentences of a not-only-X-but-also-Y construction (e.g., *not only the bird but also the flower is blue*, mean length 9.75 words); (xiv) sentences containing a relative clause (e.g., *The book is on the box that is red*, mean length 8.5 words); (xv) sentences containing a neither-X-nor-Y construction (e.g., *Neither the dog nor the ball is brown*, mean length 7.5 words); and (xvi) embedded sentences (e.g., *The shoe the comb is on is blue*, mean length 8.0 words).

The experimenter read aloud each sentence for the child to repeat immediately. After a repetition attempt had been made, the child was shown an array of four pictures on a page. One picture showed a correct depiction of the sentence, while the other three pictures included lexical and syntactic foils. The child was asked to point to the correct picture of the sentence. At the time of testing, repetition and comprehension responses

TABLE 3
Mean repetition and comprehension scores as a function of STM group and sentence type

	Repetition				*Comprehension*			
	Short		*Low*		*Short*		*Low*	
Sentence type	*Mean*	*S.E.*	*Mean*	*S.E.*	*Mean*	*S.E.*	*Mean*	*S.E.*
Negative	3.92	0.08	3.31	0.38	3.69	0.21	3.85	0.10
3 elements combined	4.00	0.00	3.38	0.27	4.00	0.00	3.69	0.17
Plural personal pronoun	3.85	0.10	3.38	0.33	3.46	0.18	2.92	0.29
Reversible active	3.85	0.10	3.62	0.31	3.77	0.12	3.69	0.17
Singular personal pronoun	3.77	0.12	3.54	0.31	3.15	0.27	2.77	0.26
Plural noun inflection	3.54	0.18	2.38	0.35	3.15	0.19	2.54	0.29
Comparative adjective	3.92	0.08	2.69	0.43	3.15	0.25	2.85	0.30
Reversible passive	3.92	0.08	2.92	0.33	2.69	0.35	2.38	0.33
In/on	3.92	0.08	3.23	0.38	3.46	0.18	2.85	0.32
Postmodified subject	3.38	0.27	2.15	0.27	2.85	0.36	2.00	0.34
X-but-not-Y	3.46	0.22	1.69	0.33	2.38	0.35	2.08	0.31
Above/below	3.54	0.22	2.85	0.27	2.31	0.35	1.46	0.29
Not-only-X-but-also-Y	0.69	0.38	0.00	0.00	1.23	0.32	1.62	0.35
Relative clause	2.00	0.45	0.31	0.21	2.23	0.36	1.54	0.31
Neither-X-nor-Y	0.92	0.33	0.00	0.00	1.54	0.37	0.69	0.21
Embedded sentence	2.38	0.43	0.15	0.10	0.77	0.20	0.77	0.20

were scored as correct or incorrect. The session was recorded to allow checking of scoring.

Results

Repetition and comprehension scores as a function of short-term memory group are shown in Table 3. Scores on both the repetition and comprehension measures were greater for the high than the low short-term memory group. The group difference was considerably greater, however, on the repetition than the comprehension task.

Table 3 summarises scores on the repetition and comprehension tasks as a function of memory group and sentence type. Separate two-way analyses of variance, with short-term memory group as the between-subjects factor and sentence type as the within-subject factor, were performed on the scores on the two tasks. All terms in the analysis of the repetition data were highly significant: group, $F(1, 24) = 58.451$, $p < .001$; sentence type, $F(15, 60) = 18.335$, $p < .001$, group by sentence type, $F(15, 36) = 3.216$, $p < .001$. The main effect of group reflects the superior repetition accuracy of the children in the high compared to the low short-term memory group. Tukey's HSD pairwise comparisons of sentence types established that the final four sentence types (not-only-X-but-also-Y, relative clauses, neither-X-nor-Y, and embedded sentences) were less accurately repeated than the first twelve sentence type shown in Table 3 ($p < .001$, in each case). Embedded sentences were also associated with lower performance than sentences containing not-only-X-but-also-Y structures ($p < .005$), and neither-X-nor-Y structures ($p < .05$). Sentences containing postmodified subjects and X-but-not-Y structures showed lower levels of repetition accuracy than sentences with the following features: negatives, three combined, plural personal pronouns, reversible constructions, singular personal pronouns, and *in/on* ($p < .05$ in each case). X-but-not-Y constructions were also repeated with significantly less accuracy than reversible sentences ($p < .05$).

The interaction term was explored in a series of planned comparisons, which established significant group effects for the following sentence types: three elements combined, $F(1, 24) = 5.333$, $p < .05$; plural noun inflection, $F(1, 24) = 8.544$, $p < .01$; comparative adjective, $F(1, 24) = 7.959$, $p < .01$; reversible, $F(1, 24) = 8.741$, $p < .01$ postmodified subject $F(1, 24) = 10.378$, $p < .005$; X-but-not-Y, $F(1, 24) = 20.346$, $p < .001$; relative clause $F(1, 24) = 11.524$, $p < .005$; neither-X-nor-Y, $F(1, 24) = 7.854$, $p < .01$; and embedded sentence, $F(1, 24) = 25.230$, $p < .001$.

The only significant term in the corresponding analysis of the comprehension scores was sentence type, $F(15, 360) = 28.919$, $p < .001$. The non-significant terms were: memory group, $F(1, 24) = 4.206$, $p > .05$, and group by sentence type, $F(15, 360) = 1.093$, $p > .05$. Tukey's HSD pairwise comparisons established a large number of significant differences across sentence type, of which only those that differ from the outcomes of the corresponding analysis of the repetition data are noted here. Higher scores were found for sentences containing three elements than for either singular personal pronouns ($p < .05$) or plural pronoun inflection ($p < .01$). Negative sentences were more accurately understood than sentences containing singular personal pronouns ($p < .05$). Scores were higher on reversible sentences than on sentences containing either negatives, three elements combined, or reversible active structures ($p < .001$ in each case). Sentences containing *above/below* were more poorly understood than the following structures: negatives, three elements combined, plural personal pronouns, reversible actives, singular personal pronouns, plural noun inflections, comparative adjectives, and *in/on* ($p < .005$ in each case). Poorer scores were obtained on embedded sentences than relative clauses ($p < .005$).

In order to compare more directly the strength of association between the two independent variables (memory group and sentence type) on repetition and comprehension, partial η^2 values were calculated in each case. For short-term memory group, partial $\eta^2 = .43$ on repetition and .15 on comprehension. For sentence type, partial $\eta^2 = .71$ on repetition and .55 on comprehension. The association between groups was therefore 2.90 times stronger on repetition than comprehension scores, whereas he sentence type effect was only 1.30 times stronger on repetition than comprehension. Thus, as in Experiment 1, the short-term memory variable (in this case, memory group) had a more marked effect on sentence repetition than comprehension.

In order to explore possible differential effects of sentence type on repetition and comprehension, a series of one-way analyses of variance were performed on each sentence type collapsed across short-term memory group, with task (repetition, comprehension) as the within-subject factor. A Bonferroni correction was applied to yield a criterion significance level of .003. There were no significant advantages to comprehension over repetition scores. However, a significant advantage to repetition over comprehension scores was found for sentences containing *above* and *below*, $F(1, 25) = 20.01, p < .001$. None of the remaining sentence types yielded significant task effects.

Discussion

Children with good phonological short-term memory skills were more accurate than children with poor memory skills at repeating spoken sentences, but did not differ significantly in their capacities to understand the sentences. This result is consistent with Shankweiler et al.'s (1984) findings that relative to children with good reading ability, children who were poor readers and obtained low scores on short-term verbal memory measures were impaired in the repetition but not the comprehension of spoken sentences. It also fits well with Hanten and Martin's (2000) report that an older child with an acquired phonological memory deficit was impaired at repeating sentences but showed normal sentence comprehension. Together, the findings provide substantial support for claims that in children, temporary representations of the phonological form of sentences play a greater role in attempts to repeat than to understand sentences (e.g., Martin et al., 1999), and run counter to the notion that the repetition of sentences is guided by access to conceptual, lexical, and syntactic representations rather than to phonological short-term memory (Potter & Lombardi, 1990).

A further important feature of the results of Experiment 2 concerns the selective effects of sentence structure on repetition and comprehension performance. As in Experiment 1, children were more accurate at repeating than understanding sentences containing the spatial adverbs *above* and *below*, despite the greater baseline guessing probability in the comprehension than the repetition tasks. We propose that such a repetition advantage will arise in conditions under which the sentences are relatively short and therefore impose a reduced minimal phonological memory load, but the children's syntactic analytic skills for those structures are not fully developed. Comprehension accuracy, which depends directly on the adequacy of the syntactic and semantic analytic process, is therefore relatively poor for such sentences. However, good levels of sentence repetition performance are achieved by direct access to phonological memory representations of the verbatim forms of the sentences.

GENERAL DISCUSSION

The findings of Experiments 1 and 2 converge in demonstrating a greater contribution of phonological short-term memory to young children's repetition than comprehension of spoken sentences. Repetition accuracy was more strongly affected by the length of words in the sentences than comprehension in Experiment 1, in line with a substantial research literature establishing poor short-term memory for stimuli of longer compared to short spoken durations (e.g., Baddeley et al., 1975). Furthermore, children selected as having high short-term memory skills were superior at repeating sentences compared to low memory children, but did not differ in their capacities to understand the same sentences in Experiment 2.

These results are entirely consistent with proposals made by Martin and associates (Hanten & Martin, 2000; Martin et al., 1999) that temporary phonological representations as well as conceptual representations are used to support the repetition of sentences, whereas sentence comprehension depends more directly on access to temporary semantic representations. The findings of Experiment 2 also extend reports of specific links between phonological memory ability and sentence repetition but not comprehension in children by Hanten and Martin (2000), and by Shankweiler et al. (1984).

Although increasing word length exerted a significant disruptive effect overall on sentence repetition but not comprehension, the effect of word length was significant for only three of the six sentence structures employed in Experiment 1. There are at least two possible reasons for this inconsistency. First, in two of the remaining sentence types (embedded sentences and relative clauses), repetition accuracy was generally poor, with only around 25% of repetition attempts correct on average. There may therefore have been a floor effect in the data which limited measurable effects of word length in these conditions. We suggest later that the children's low repetition accuracy for such sentences is itself a function of the significant role played by phonological memory in sentence repetition. Second, the word-length manipulation was not very powerful in this experiment, with the longer sentences containing on average only 41% more syllables than the short sentences. This contrasts with the standard-word length manipulations employed in serial recall experiments, in which long word lists contain 200–400% more syllables than short word lists (e.g., Baddeley et al., 1975, 1984). The relatively weak contrast in word length within sentences may therefore lie at the root of the failure to obtain word-length effects for all six sentence structures in Experiment 1.

The children participating in Experiment 2 were selected on the basis of obtaining relatively good or poor scores on two tests of phonological short-term memory—nonword repetition and auditory digit span—but comparable levels of nonverbal reasoning ability. The poor repetition accuracy of the low memory group has therefore been interpreted here as reflecting their reduced phonological memory capacities imposing a greater constraint on recall of the verbatim form of the sentences than for the high memory group. It is highly likely that the two groups differed in other respects, too. For example, we would expect that the low memory group would also have less extensive vocabulary knowledge than the high memory group, on the basis of the close associations established between phonological memory and vocabulary acquisition (see Baddeley, Gathercole, & Papagno, 1998, for review). There may also be differences in the speech-production abilities of the two groups (Adams & Gathercole, 1995, 1996). Other researchers have argued that individual differences in children's phonological short-term memory skills reflect more fundamental differences in phonological processing *per se* (e.g., Metsala, 1999).

As our assessment of the children's abilities in Experiment 2 was restricted to phonological memory tasks and nonverbal reasoning, we are not able to explore the extent to which differences between the memory groups in sentence repetition are also associated with variation in these other domains of ability. Although individual differences correlated with phonological memory raise an important interpretational issue for the group difference in repetition performance in Experiment 2, it is not clear how alternative accounts of that finding relating, for example, to differences in vocabulary knowledge or phonological processing would readily accommodate either the word-length effect found in sentence repetition in Experiment 1, or the contrasting sensitivity of repetition and comprehension performance to particular sentence types. The phonological memory account is more parsimonious, identifying a single mechanism underpinning the broad profile of findings from the two experiments.

Post hoc comparisons of the differential influences of type of sentence structure on the repetition and comprehension measures provided further evidence of a more direct association between phonological short-term memory and sentence repetition than comprehension in young children. There was a reasonable degree of correspondence in the accuracy of repetition and comprehension scores for the majority of sentence forms. However, the children were more accurate at repeating than comprehending sentences containing *above* and *below* in both Experiments 1 and 2, whereas in Experiment 1 there was a comprehension advantage for sentences containing relative clauses. We suggest that the crucial determinant of whether repetition and comprehension performances are evenly matched or show disparities in one or other direction in young children is the balance of loads imposed by particular sentences on the maturity of the syntactic and semantic processes and phonological short-term storage. The sentences showing the repetition advantage were relatively short in length, and so imposed a relatively minor burden on phonological storage capacity. The poor comprehension scores for these sentences suggest that children of this age are still in the process of acquiring the relevant syntactic and semantic analytic processes, resulting in errorful performance on the picture-pointing task. In older children and adults who have mastered these syntactic analyses, comprehension performance would presumably increase to the same level as sentence repetition. By this account, the pattern of repetition and comprehension performance for these types of sentences captures a dissociation between the relative syntactic and phonological storage skills of 5-year old children which is highly specific to this point in the development of skills in the two domains.

A significant advantage to comprehension over repetition performance was obtained in Experiment 1 for sentences containing relative clauses, and the absence of corresponding differences in Experiment 2 is due in part to alpha adjustments necessitated by the large number of post hoc comparisons. It is notable that the relative clause sentences contained more words on average than all other sentence types in Experiment 1. We suggest that such a comprehension advantage will arise in situations when sentences are sufficiently lengthy to tax the limited capacity of phonological short-term memory, but contain syntactic structures that the children are able to analyse accurately. The memory constraint will impair sentence repetition accuracy, whereas comprehension performance will be relatively good as the sentence structures fall within the children's syntactic competence. This possibility could be tested more directly in future research by comparing the repetition and comprehension profiles for short and longer sentences with common syntactic structures.

The significant influences of the phonological memory manipulations in Experiments 1 and 2 on sentence repetition provide little support for the claims of Potter and Lombardi (1990) that temporary phonological representations do not play a role in sentence repetition. The present data are, however, consistent with the view that phonological memory represents only one source of support for sentence repetition. In both experiments a close correspondence was obtained between the accuracy of repetition and comprehension for many of the sentence types, which is entirely consistent with the view that sentences are reconstructed from access to a variety of representations including propositional knowledge generated during the process of comprehension, and lexical and syntactic knowledge (Lee & Williams, 1997; Lombardi & Potter, 1992; Potter & Lombardi, 1990, 1998).

In summary, the present findings suggest that although there is some degree of overlap between the cognitive processes contributing to young children's repetition and understanding spoken sentences, there are also important differences, too. Repetition is strongly supported by access to temporary representations of the phonological form of the sentence held in short-term memory, and to a lesser extent to the stored products of syntactic and conceptual analysis of the sentence structure. These different representations need to be integrated prior to output, possibly in the dynamic and integrative memory system identified by McCarthy and Warrington (1987a), or the episodic buffer (Baddeley, 2000). Comprehension, on the other hand, appears to be much more strongly constrained by the child's ability to process the sentence at the syntactic and conceptual levels.

REFERENCES

Adams, A.-M., & Gathercole, S.E. (1995). Phonological working memory and speech production in young children. *Journal of Speech and Hearing Research*, *38*, 493–414.

Adams, A.-M., & Gathercole, S.E. (1996). Phonological working memory and spoken language development in young children. *Quarterly Journal of Experimental Psychology*, *49*A, 216–233.

Baddeley, A.D. (1986). *Working memory*. Oxford: Oxford University Press.

Baddeley, A.D. (2000). The episodic buffer: A new component of working memory? *Trends in Cognitive Science 4*, 417–423.

Baddeley, A.D., Gathercole, S.E., & Papagno, C. (1998). The phonological loop as a language learning device. *Psychological Review*, *105*, 158–173.

Baddeley, A.D., Lewis, V.J., & Vallar, G. (1984). Exploring the articulatory loop. *Quarterly Journal of Experimental Psychology*, *36*, 233–252.

Baddeley, A.D., Thomson, N., & Buchanan, M. (1975). Word length and the structure of short-term memory. *Journal of Verbal Learning and Verbal Behaviour*, *14*, 575–589.

Baddeley, A.D., Vallar, G., & Wilson, B.A. (1987). Sentence comprehension and phonological memory: Some neuropsychological evidence. In M. Coltheart (Ed.), *Attention and performance XII: The Psychology of reading* (pp. 509–529). Hove, UK: Lawrence Erlbaum Associates Ltd.

Bishop, D. (1982). *Test for reception of grammar (T.R.O.G.)*. Printed for the Medical Research Council by Thomas Leach, Abingdon, Oxon, UK.

Butterworth, B., Campbell, R., & Howard, D. (1986). Uses of short-term memory: A case study. *Quarterly Journal of Experimental Psychology*, *38*, 705–737.

Caplan, D., Rochon, E., & Waters, G.S. (1992). Articulatory and phonological determinants of word length effects in span tasks. *Quarterly Journal of Experimental Psychology*, *45*A, 177–192.

Caplan, D., & Waters, G.S. (1990). Short-term memory and language comprehension: A critical review of the psychological literature. In G. Vallar & T. Shallice (Eds.), *Neuropsychological impairments of short-term memory* (pp. 337–389). Cambridge: Cambridge University Press.

Caplan, D., & Waters, G.S. (1994). Articulatory length and phonological similarity in span tasks: A reply to Baddeley and Andrade. *Quarterly Journal of Experimental Psychology*, *47*A, 1055–1062.

Caramazza, A., & Zurif, E.B. (1976). Dissociation of algorithmic and heuristic processes in language comprehension: Evidence from aphasia. *Brain and Language*, *3*, 572–582.

Cowan, N., Day, L., Sault, S., Keller, T., Johnson, T., & Flores, L. (1992). The role of verbal output time in the effects of word length on immediate memory. *Journal of Memory and Language*, *31*, 1–17.

Dosher, B.A., & Ma, J.J. (1998). Output loss or rehearsal loop? Output-time versus pronunciation-time limits in immediate recall for forgetting-matched materials. *Journal of Experimental Psychology: Learning, Memory, and Cognition*, *24*(2), 316–335.

Friedrich, F.J., Martin, R., & Kemper, S.J. (1985). Consequences of a phonological decoding deficit on sentence processing. *Cognitive Neuropsychology, 2*, 385–412.

Gathercole, S.E. (1995). The assessment of phonological memory skills in preschool children. *British Journal of Educational Psychology, 65*, 155–164.

Gathercole, S.E. (1999). Cognitive approaches to the development of short-term memory. *Trends in Cognitive Science, 3*, 410–418.

Gathercole, S.E., & Baddeley, A.D. (1996). *The Children's Test of Nonword Repetition*. London, UK: Psychological Corporation.

Hanten, G., & Martin, R.C. (2000). Contributions of phonological and semantic short-term memory to sentence processing: Evidence from two cases of closed head injury in children. *Journal of Memory and Language, 43*, 335–361.

Jarvella, R.J. (1971). Syntactic processing of connected speech. *Journal of Verbal Learning and Verbal Behavior, 10*, 409–416.

Lee, M.-W., & Williams, J.N. (1997). Why is short-term sentence recall verbatim? An evaluation of the role of lexical priming. *Memory & Cognition, 25*, 156–172.

Lombardi, L., & Potter, M.C. (1992). The regeneration of syntax in short term memory. *Journal of Memory and Language, 31*, 713–733.

Lovatt, P., Avons, S.E., & Masterson, J. (2000). The word length effect and disyllabic words. *Quarterly Journal of Experimental Psychology, 53*A, 1–22.

Mann, V.A., Shankweiler, D., & Smith, S.T. (1984). Children's memory for word lists and sentence strings in relation to reading ability. *Memory and Cognition, 8*, 329–355.

Martin, R.C. (1990). Neuropsychological evidence on the role of short-term memory in sentence processing. In G. Vallar & T. Shallice (Eds.), *Neuropsychological impairments of short-term memory* (pp. 390–427). Cambridge: Cambridge University Press.

Martin, R.C. (1993). Short-term memory and sentence processing: Evidence from neuropsychology. *Memory and Cognition, 21*, 76–183.

Martin, R.C., Lesch, M.F., & Bartha, M.C. (1999). Independence of input and output phonology in word processing and short-term memory. *Journal of Memory and Language, 41*, 3–29.

Martin, R.C., Shelton, J.R., & Yaffee, L.S. (1994). Language processing and working memory: Neuropsychological evidence for separate phonological and semantic capacities. *Journal of Memory and Language, 33*, 83–111.

McCarthy, R.A., & Warrington, E.K. (1987a). The double dissociation of short-term memory for lists and sentences. *Brain, 110*, 1545–1563.

McCarthy, R.A., & Warrington, E.K. (1987b). Understanding: A function of short-term memory? *Brain, 110*, 1565–1578.

Metsala, J.L. (1999). Young children's phonological awareness and nonword repetition as a function of vocabulary development. *Journal of Educational Psychology, 91*, 3–19.

Miller, G., & Selfridge, J. (1950). Verbal context and the recall of meaningful material. *American Journal of Psychology, 63*, 176–187.

Potter, M.C., & Lombardi, L. (1990). Regeneration in the short-term recall of sentences. *Journal of Memory and Language, 29*, 633–654.

Potter, M.C., & Lombardi, L. (1998). Syntactic priming in immediate recall of sentences. *Journal of Memory and Language, 38*, 265–282.

Raven, J. (1978). *Raven's Coloured Progressive Matrices*. London: H.K. Lewis & Co Ltd.

Saffran, E.M., & Martin, O.S.M. (1975). Immediate memory for lists of words and sentences in a patient with deficient auditory short-term memory. *Brain and Language, 2*, 420–433.

Saffran, E.M., & Martin, N. (1990). Short-term memory impairment and sentence processing: A case study. In G. Vallar & T. Shallice (Eds.), *Neuropsychological impairments of short-term memory* (pp. 428–447). Cambridge: Cambridge University Press.

Shankweiler, D., Smith, S.T., & Mann, V.A. (1984). Repetition and comprehension of spoken sentences by reading-disabled children. *Brain and Language, 23*, 241–257.

Vallar, G., & Baddeley, A.D. (1984). Phonological short-term store, phonological processing and sentence comprehension: A neuropsychological case study. *Cognitive Neuropsychology, 1*, 121–141.

Willis, C.S. (1997). [*Unpublished PhD thesis*] Lancaster University, UK.

APPENDIX

Sentences employed in Study 1

Reversible active sentences
Short words
The fox is chased by the horse
The sheep is pushed by the boy
The man is chased by the fox
The cow is pushed by the girl

Longer words
The rabbit is chased by the donkey
The elephant is pushed by the policeman
The butterfly is chased by the chicken
The lady is pushed by the elephant

X-but-not-Y construction
Short words
The box but not the chair is red
The cat is big but not black
The horse but not the boy is standing
The girl is sitting but not eating

Longer words
The butterfly but not the flower is red
The teddy bear is yellow but not big
The rabbit but not the elephant is eating
The policeman is sitting but not eating

Embedded sentence
Short words
The book the pen is on is red
The sheep the cow runs after is black
The shoe the comb is on is blue
The dog the girl runs after is big

Longer words
The pencil the strawberry is on is yellow
The elephant the tiger runs after is little
The button the tomato is on is orange
The chicken the policeman runs after is enormous

Above/below
Short words
The ball is above the cup
The comb is below the spoon
The star is above the book
The cake is below the star

Longer words
The banana is above the flower
The strawberry is below the animal
The flower is above the potato
The banana is below the orange

Relative clause
Short words
The book is on the box that is red
The girl chases the sheep that is big
The square is in the star that is blue
The dog chases the horse that is brown

Longer words
The aeroplane is on the table that is broken
The policeman chases the rabbit that is big
The umbrella is on the bottle that is yellow
The elephant chases the donkey that is little

In/on
Short words
The cup is in the box
The ball is on the blue box
The red book is in the star
The knife is on the boot

Longer words
The water is in the bottle
The banana is on the little basket
The umbrella is in the yellow basket
The triangle is on the circle

MEMORY, 2001, 9 (4/5/6), 365–381

Working memory and inferences: Evidence from eye fixations during reading

Manuel G. Calvo
University of La Laguna, Tenerife, Spain

Eye fixations during reading were monitored to examine the relationship between individual differences in working memory capacity—as assessed by the reading span task—and inferences about predictable events. Context sentences predicting likely events, or non-predicting control sentences, were presented. They were followed by continuation sentences in which a target word represented an event to be inferred (inferential word) or an unlikely event (non-predictable word). A main effect of reading span showed that high working memory capacity was related to shorter gaze durations across sentence regions. More specific findings involved an interaction between context, target, and reading span on late processing measures and regions. Thus, for high- but not for low-span readers, the predicting condition, relative to the control condition, facilitated reanalysis of the continuation sentence that represented the inference concept. This effect was revealed by a reduction in regression-path reading time in the last region of the sentence, involving less time reading that region and fewer regressions from it. These results indicate that working memory facilitates elaborative inferences during reading, but that this occurs at late text-integration processes, rather than at early lexical-access processes.

Using on-line eye-movement monitoring, this study aims to examine elaborative inferences in low and high working memory capacity readers. Elaborative inferences have previously been investigated using the eye-tracking methodology (Garrod, O'Brien, Morris, & Rayner, 1990; O'Brien, Shank, Myers, & Rayner, 1988), although these studies did not consider individual differences in working memory. Kennison and Clifton (1995) assessed eye fixations in low and high working memory span readers, although their measures were concerned with processes of reading explicit text rather than with inferences. A recent study by Estevez and Calvo (2000) has addressed the contribution of working memory to the time course of elaborative inferences using a naming task at different points in time during reading. However, this technique provides only momentary snapshots of activation of inference concepts. The present study represents a step forward, in that continuous monitoring of cognitive activity will be assessed, as reflected in eye fixations. Fixation times have been shown to be a sensitive on-line measure of cognitive processes in reading (see Rayner, 1998), and their use provides a more ecologically valid measure than naming (O'Brien, Raney, Albrecht, & Rayner, 1997).

Working memory is a cognitive mechanism responsible for the transient storage and computation of currently activated mental representations (Baddeley, 1986; Just & Carpenter, 1992; see Miyake & Shah, 1999). Functionally, working memory is resource-limited, as there is a maximum amount of representations that can be simultaneously activated, and there are important individual differences in the amount of resources available for meeting the processing and storage demands. Considerable evidence suggests that

Requests for reprints should be sent to Manuel G. Calvo, Departamento de Psicología Cognitiva, Universidad de La Laguna, 38205 Tenerife, Spain. Email: mgcalvo@ull.es

This research was supported by Grant PB97-1481 from the DGESIC, Spanish Ministry of Education and Science, and Grant COF1999/012 from the DGUI, Canary Islands Government. I am grateful to Enrique Meseguer for his assistance in data collection, and to Keith Rayner for his helpful comments on an earlier version of this paper.

http://www.tandf.co.uk/journals/pp/09658211.html DOI:10.1080/09658210143000083

working memory capacity constrains several aspects of reading comprehension (see Carpenter, Miyake, & Just, 1994; Daneman & Merikle, 1996; Gathercole & Baddeley, 1993).

Nevertheless, most prior studies have been concerned with comprehension of information explicitly signalled by the text. Fewer studies have investigated the role of working memory in constructing inferences (i.e., activation of representations implicitly suggested by the text). Two main groups of inferences in reading have been distinguished—bridging and elaborative inferences (see Singer, 1994). The former make sentences or texts coherent, and are necessary for comprehension. The latter extend and refine explicit information in the message, but they are not necessary. A major finding regarding the role of working memory in bridging inferences is that it facilitates them only when text demands increase (e.g., number of sentences between the two pieces of information that must be linked) (Daneman & Carpenter, 1980; Gutiérrez-Calvo, Castillo, & Espino, 1996; Singer, Andrusiak, Reisdorf, & Black, 1992; Singer & Ritchot, 1996; Yuill, Oakhill, & Parkin, 1989). Regarding elaborative inferences, there is an argument to support the hypothesis that working memory capacity constrains them more than bridging inferences. Whereas bridging inferences can occur automatically during reading, elaborative inferences are assumed to involve strategic post-lexical processes. In fact, bridging inferences are drawn immediately (less than 500 ms after the inducing context; Magliano, Baggett, Johnson, & Graesser, 1993; Millis & Graesser, 1994). In contrast, elaborative inferences take much longer to develop (more than 500 ms; Calvo & Castillo, 1996, 1998; Fincher-Kiefer, 1995, 1996; Till, Mross, & Kintsch, 1988). Several authors have suggested that working memory constraints will only reveal themselves in tasks that force the reader to engage in controlled effortful processing (Conway & Engle, 1996). If so, then elaborative inferences are expected to provide a good way of examining the contribution of working memory capacity.

Dixon, LeFevre, and Twilley (1988) and Whitney, Ritchie and Clark (1991), investigated the contribution of working memory capacity to elaborative inferencing. In Dixon et al.'s study (1988) subjects were required to read narrative passages and answer questions after each one. To answer the questions, subjects had to make plausible inferences about the motivations and actions of characters in the story. Working memory capacity, as assessed by the reading span task (Daneman & Carpenter, 1980), was positively related to inferential comprehension in Dixon et al.'s study. Nevertheless, this relationship disappeared when the working memory score was introduced as a predictor in a regression analysis together with prior vocabulary knowledge, which remained the only significant predictor of inferences. Whitney et al. (1991) asked participants high and low in reading span to "think out loud" while reading passages in which there were ambiguous referents (e.g., *things*) and actions (e.g., *do*). The participants talked about what they thought was happening in the story and what could be expected to occur later, based on a current description. Whitney et al. (1991) found that low-span readers actually produced more elaborations than high-span readers, although the former frequently committed themselves to wrong interpretations early in the passage and forced the remaining text to fit into them. The findings from these two studies are not conclusive about the role of working memory in elaborative inferences. As Dixon et al. (1988) used memory measures after the passages had been presented, they could not determine whether inferences were made on-line during comprehension or whether inferences were reconstructions at the time of test. The on-line measure during comprehension that Whitney et al. (1991) used is susceptible to voluntary control by readers, and therefore can reflect response selection rather than genuine inference processing.

Investigation of one type of elaborative inferences, i.e., those involving predictable events, has provided some advances in the on-line assessment of inference processing. These inferences are anticipations of likely events, i.e., representations of "what will happen next", based on the application of our prior world knowledge to the explicit information in a message (e.g., McKoon & Ratcliff, 1986). For example, (*she*) *wrote* might be a predictive inference drawn when reading that *She owed a letter to her mother, so she picked up some paper and sat down.* Inferences about predictable events have received considerable attention in reading research (e.g., Calvo, 2000; Calvo & Castillo, 1996, 1998; Calvo, Castillo, & Estevez, 1999; Fincher-Kiefer, 1995; Keefe & McDaniel, 1993; Klin, Guzmán, & Levine, 1999a; Millis & Graesser, 1994; Murray, Klin, & Myers, 1993; Trabasso & Magliano, 1996). These inferences are not automatic; they take about one additional second to construct after the inducing context (Calvo &

Castillo, 1998; Calvo et al., 1999; Fincher-Kiefer, 1995).

The fact that predictive inferences occur with some delay suggests that they are dependent on the limited and effortful working memory resources. Accordingly, individual differences in working memory capacity are expected to be strongly related to predictive inferences. The more activation that is available for meeting the computational and storage demands of language processing, the more likely it is that readers will be able to draw inferences on-line during comprehension. Estevez and Calvo (2000) have recently found evidence supporting this hypothesis. These authors varied the interval (50 vs 550 vs 1050 ms) between the end of an inducing context sentence (predictive of a likely event) and the onset of an inferential target word representing the predictable event, which the participants were to name as quickly as possible. Relative to a control condition (in which the prior context did not predict any particular event), in the inducing condition there was facilitation in naming the inferential target word (a) for both low and high working memory participants 1050 ms after the context, (b) only for those high in working memory capacity 550 ms after the context, and (c) for neither group of participants 50 ms after the context. These results suggest that high working memory capacity accelerates the time course of predictive inferences, although it does not make them become automatic.

Nevertheless, this conclusion might have some limitations, due to the relatively artificial procedure that Estevez and Calvo (2000) used for presenting the context sentences (one word at a time, in a fixed-pace mode). Although this procedure was necessary to determine the time course of inferences, it might have truncated normal reading processes. Furthermore, one potential reason why low-capacity participants failed to generate inferences earlier could be that the presentation rate of context sentences was too fast for these subjects to comprehend the explicit information, thus delaying the construction of inferences. Accordingly, in the present study an eye-tracking paradigm was used, which allows more natural reading. High and low reading span participants were presented with inducing and control context sentences, followed by continuation sentences that included a pre-target region, a target word (representing either a predictable event or an unlikely event), a post-target region, and a final region (see Table 1 and the Appendix), while eye movements were monitored.

The questions that the current experiment addresses are whether and when working memory capacity affects inferences predictive of events during reading. The comparison between an inducing context condition and a lexically equivalent, but non-predicting, control condition is crucial to determine *whether* inferences are drawn. Thus, evidence for inferences will involve facilitation in reading the continuation sentence that represents the predicted event following the inducing context, relative to when the sentence follows the control context. The particular region of the continuation sentence, as well as the type of eye-fixation measures in which the inducing vs control condition difference occurs, will reveal *when* the inferences are drawn. Thus, if inferences are drawn at early processing stages, then facilitation will occur on the target word itself and will be detected by initial processing measures, such as first-fixation duration or gaze duration. But if inferences are drawn with delay, involving reanalysis or integration processes, then facilitation will appear in the post-target and/or final regions, or it will be detected only by late processing measures, such as regression-path reading time (see description of measures in the Method section).

Regarding the contribution of working memory capacity, two complementary hypotheses can be stated. First, high-span readers draw predictive inferences and low-span readers do not. If so, only the former participants, but not the latter, will

TABLE 1

Example of passage, including the predicting and the control context, and the continuation sentence with its four regions

(PREDICTING CONTEXT): Three days before the *examination the *pupil went to the *library, looked for a separate *table and opened his *notebook.
(CONTINUATION SENTENCE): (PRE-TARGET) The pupil (TARGET) *studied* [*slept*] (POST-TARGET) for an hour (FINAL) approximately.
(CONTROL CONTEXT): The *pupil, who was a little tired after finishing his *examination, forgot his *notebook and left it on a *table in the *library.
(CONTINUATION SENTENCE): (PRE-TARGET) The pupil (TARGET) *studied* [*slept*] (POST-TARGET) for an hour (FINAL) approximately.

Words in italics represent target words—the inferential word (*studied*) outside the brackets; the non-predictable word (*slept*) inside the brackets. Asterisks indicate content words shared by the predicting and the control contexts to control for word-based priming. The words in parentheses and the asterisks did not appear in the stimuli.

show the aforementioned facilitation effect, i.e., shorter reading times for the inferential version of continuation sentences following the predicting context than following the control context.[1] Second, high-span readers draw predictive inferences faster than low-span readers. If so, even if facilitation is found for low-span scorers, this effect will take place at a later stage (e.g., a farther region following the target word) for them than for their high-span counterparts, thus revealing a different time course of inference processing for each group or readers.[2]

PRE-EXPERIMENTAL PHASE: ASSESSMENT OF WORKING MEMORY CAPACITY AND VOCABULARY KNOWLEDGE

One week before the experiment, there was a selection phase in which the working memory capacity of 81 Spanish psychology undergraduates was assessed, as well as their prior vocabulary knowledge. I was mainly concerned with individual differences in working memory capacity. However, these have proved to correlate with word or vocabulary knowledge, which is also significantly related to inferences (e.g., Dixon et al., 1988; Singer et al., 1992). As a consequence, the potential relationship between working memory span and inference processing could be partly due to vocabulary differences, if high- and low-span participants are not equated in their prior word knowledge.

Vocabulary knowledge test

I developed a computer version of the Spanish multiple-choice vocabulary comprehension subscale of the PMA test (Primary Mental Abilities; Thurstone & Thurstone, 1979). The vocabulary test involves selecting a synonym from four alternatives for each of 50 target words. In the computer version, on each trial a target word appears on a computer screen, with four additional words, for a maximum of 12 seconds. The participant has to press one of four keys on the computer keyboard, which correspond to each of the four alternative words on the screen. When a choice is made (either correct or incorrect), or if there is no response within 12 seconds, the words corresponding to the current trial disappear and the participant is asked to proceed to the following trial when s/he is ready, by pressing the spacebar. The number of correct and incorrect responses, and omissions, as well as their latencies, are collected. The number of correct responses provides a measure of availability of vocabulary, whereas the latencies for these responses are assumed to assess accessibility (or speed of lexical access).

Reading span task

To assess working memory capacity in reading, I used a computer version in Spanish (developed by Gutiérrez-Calvo, Jiménez, & Castillo, 1996) of the reading span task originally devised by Daneman and Carpenter (1980). The task requires the participant to read a set of unrelated sentences, each of which is between 13 and 16 words long, one sentence at a time, at his/her own pace. The number of sentences is progressively increased from two to five sentences across successive set-size levels. There are five different trials at each set-size (number-of-sentences) level. After reading each sentence in a set, the participant decides whether it is true or false (by pressing one of two keys), which requires comprehension of the sen-

[1] Facilitation refers to shorter processing time, rather than lower probability of fixation. One reason for this is that different mechanisms are involved in the two main decisions to be taken in eye-movement control during reading: when and where to move the eyes (see, for example, Rayner, 1998). The *when* decision (which results in fixation time effects; that is, how long a word is fixated and when to move to the next word) is largely governed by cognitive processes associated with comprehension of the fixated word. In contrast, the *where* decision (which results in probability of fixation; that is, whether, where, and how often a word is fixated) is mainly driven by low-level visual features such as word length. Accordingly, in order to detect a high-level process such as inferencing, the most appropriate measure is fixation time, thus involving the cognitive *when* mechanism. Nevertheless, as measures related to the oculomotor *where* mechanism have sometimes been influenced by semantic contextual factors (e.g., Rayner & Well, 1996), I am also including fixation probability in an exploratory approach.

[2] There are two aspects in this second hypothesis, depending on whether we define "faster" processing in terms of time or of space. If the time notion is used, then high-span readers will show facilitation in early eye-movement processing measures (see *Measures*, such as first fixation duration, etc.), whereas low-span readers will show facilitation in late measures (such as regression-path time, etc.), all on the same target word region. However, if the space notion is used, then facilitation in either of these measures will emerge for high-span readers in a region closer to the target word, whereas for low-span readers facilitation will emerge in a more remote region following the target word. As predictive inferences have been shown to develop with delay in prior research, it is likely that the space notion will be more discriminative than the time notion (because no early measure will probably be affected).

tence (thus taxing the processing component of working memory). The sentences are concerned with relatively well-known facts. After having read all the sentences in each set, the participant tries to recall the final word of each sentence (thus taxing the temporary storage component of working memory). The test determines the maximum number of sentences per set for which the participant can recall all the final words, while answering the comprehension questions correctly. The largest set size for which the participant successfully recalls all of the final words for at least three of five trials is defined as his or her reading span.

Participants with the lowest (N = 20; M = 1.95) and with the highest (N = 20; M = 4.32) scores in the reading span task, $t(38)$ = 20.52, $p < .0001$, were selected to take part in the following experiment. The low- and the high-span groups were equivalent in vocabulary availability, M = 37.1 vs 38.5 words out of 50, respectively; $t(38)$ = 1.20, p = .24, *ns*, and accessibility, M = 4364 vs 3882 ms, respectively; $t(38)$ = 1.59, p = .12, *ns*, scores. This rules out the possibility that the expected effects of working memory capacity on inferences could be accounted for by prior vocabulary knowledge.

EXPERIMENT: MONITORING OF EYE MOVEMENTS DURING READING

Method

Participants. The 20 high-span scorers and the 20 low-span scorers that were selected in the pre-experimental phase were assigned to a high and a low working memory capacity group, respectively. They received course credit.

Materials. A total of 40 short Spanish passages were presented (see Table 1 and the Appendix), each of which was composed of (a) one predicting context sentence, (b) one non-predicting, control context sentence, (c) one continuation sentence including a target word that represented the to-be-inferred event (inferential target word), and (d) one continuation sentence including a target word that represented an unlikely event (non-predictable target word). Besides the *target* word, there were three regions in the continuation sentence: *pre-target* (one or two words long), *post-target* (two or three words), and *final* (one or three words), which were identical for both continuation sentences (c, and d; only the target word was different). Four versions of each passage were constructed (see Design and the Appendix). Each participant was presented with one of these versions (a different version for each passage). Thus, on each trial, each participant read either a predicting or a control context of each passage, followed by a continuation sentence including either an inferential or an non-predictable target word.

Norming data. Prior to the experiment, several norming studies and analyses were conducted to validate the materials (see details in Calvo et al., 1999). Essentially, first, word-based priming (Keenan et al., 1990) was controlled by including 42% of the same content words in the predicting and the control contexts. These were words that could be semantically associated with the inferential target words (see words preceded by an asterisk in Table 1 and the Appendix). They were rearranged in the control contexts so that they did not suggest the inference. Second, in a sentence-completion study, we confirmed that the predicting contexts did induce the presumed inferences, and that these could be expressed linguistically. The participants in this study wrote one-word continuations about "what might happen next" following the event that was described in each context sentence. These one-word predictions were subsequently used as target words. The inferential target words were mentioned by 82% of the participants after the predicting contexts, and by 8% after the control contexts; the respective figures for the non-predictable target words were 2% and 3%. Finally, we checked that the predicting and the control contexts were equivalent in number of words (M = 20.6, for both contexts), and that the inferential and the non-predictable target words were equivalent (all ts < 1.0) in number of characters (M = 6.6 vs 6.7, respectively) and lexical frequency (M = 33.4 vs 35.4, respectively; Alameda & Cuetos, 1995).

Design. A 2 (Reading span: high vs low) × 2 (Priming context: predicting vs control) × 2 (Target type: inferential vs non-predictable)[3]

[3]The non-predictable condition was included as an additional control condition: (a) to detect potential interference effects in the predicting + non-predictable version (which was not the case); (b) to minimise conscious and voluntary inferences (in the predicting + inferential versions), as a strategy to meet the demands of the experiment; (c) to rule out the possibility that the effects of the predicting context could be simply due to spillover effects (i.e., the fact that the predicting context were easier to read than the control context, and that this could affect the reading of the continuation sentence).

design was used, with span as a between-subjects factor, and context and target as within-subject factors. I constructed four versions of each passage (see Appendix), and then they were combined in four lists of stimuli to address the design requirements (i.e., orthogonal and counterbalanced combination of the context and target factors). Thus, each list contained four different versions of the materials, with one version for each group of 10 passages: 10 predicting contexts followed by inferential-target continuation sentences (version 1); 10 control contexts followed by inferential-target continuation sentences (version 2); 10 predicting contexts followed by non-predictable-target continuation sentences (version 3); and 10 control contexts followed by non-predictable-target continuation sentences (version 4). The assignment of target words to the predicting or the control context was reversed across the lists so that a given participant saw a particular context and target only once. Each participant received one list, with 40 trials in random order. It should be noted that, for each participant, only 25% of the trials (predicting + inferential) induced inferences, whereas 50% were neutral (control), and 25% (predicting + non-predictable) clearly discouraged such inferential activity.

Apparatus. Eye movements were recorded by a Fourward Optical Technologies Dual Purkinje Image 5.5 Eyetracker, which has a resolution of less than 10 min of arc. The eyetracker was interfaced with an IBM-compatible PC that controlled stimulus display and data storage. The passages were each presented in three lines up to 80 characters per line, in standard upper- and lower-case format. The continuation sentence, with its four regions, was located on the third line. The position of the eye was sampled every millisecond. The computer was also interfaced with a super-VGA visual display unit on which the stimulus passages were presented. The display was 60 cm from the participant's eye, and four characters equalled 1 degree of visual angle. Viewing was binocular, although eye movements were monitored from the participant's right eye. Participants viewed the screen with their heads positioned in a deep chin rest and a forehead rest, with a strip around the head, to minimise movements.

Procedure. Before the experiment started, participants were informed that the study was concerned with reading comprehension of short passages displayed on a screen. They were told to read at their normal rate and to comprehend the sentences as well as they could. They were also informed that they would periodically be asked to answer comprehension questions about the passages. Then the participant sat in front of the eyetracker. Following a calibration period, participants read six practice passages before the 40 experimental passages. When readers finished each passage, they pressed a key and the computer displayed a comprehension question (e.g., *Was the pupil in a bookshop*, for the example presented in Table 1), and then proceeded to the next passage. Half of these questions had "yes" answers, and half "no". Readers responded to the questions by pressing one of two buttons.

Measures. Two groups of eye-movement measures (see Liversedge, Paterson, & Pickering, 1998; Rayner et al., 1989) were examined for each of the four regions of the continuation sentence. First, measures of initial or *early* processing: (a) *probability of fixation*, which is the probability that a region is fixated when it is initially encountered; (b) *first-fixation duration*, which is the duration of the first fixation on the region independent of the number of fixations on it; and (c) *gaze duration* (or first-pass reading time), which is the sum of all fixations on a region prior to moving to another region, either to the right or to the left. Second, measures of reanalysis or *late* processing: (d) *regression-path reading time*, which is the sum of all fixations between the moment when the eyes enter a region from the left and the moment when the eyes fixate any region to the right of that region—this includes the duration of all consecutive fixations *within* a region *plus all* subsequent fixations on prior regions, until the reader leaves the region in a forward direction; (e) *right-bounded time*, which is the sum of all fixations *within* a region before the eyes fixate any region to the right of it; and (f) *probability of regressions* (i.e., backward eye movements from a region) to preceding regions, and *re-reading time* of those regions (i.e., time spent in regressions, which corresponds to regression-path time for a region minus time spent in that particular region). In fact, regression-path time is the sum of right-bounded time and re-reading time. Measures of reanalysis are assumed to indicate processing difficulty at the region from which they originate. Figure 1 shows a hypothetical example of the eye-movement measures.

In addition, I collected three more measures to *control* for possible differences in oculomotor

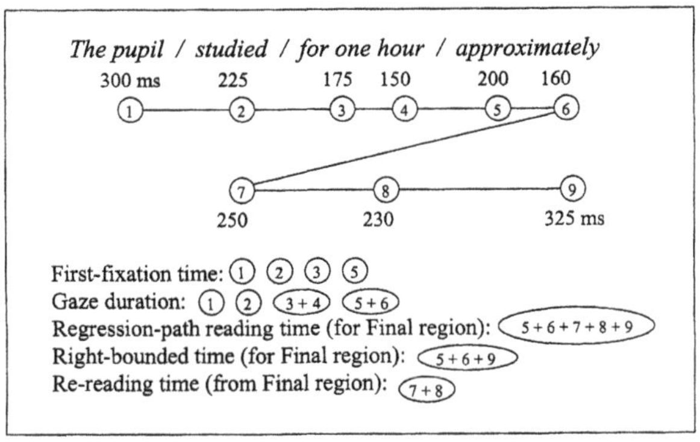

Figure 1. Hypothetical record illustrating eye-movement measures.

factors, or perceptual span, between the low- and the high-reading span groups: (g) *launch site* of the fixation prior to entering the target word, i.e., the last location of the eyes before first landing on the target word (in number of characters backwards from the beginning of the target word), (h) *length* of forward *saccade* from the pre-target region to the target word in the first pass (in number of characters), and (i) *landing position* of first fixation on the target word (in number of characters forward from the beginning of the target word).

Results

Preliminary analyses. No significant differences emerged as a function of reading span (all *t*s < 1) in *comprehension* of explicit information (low span: *M* = 83% of questions correct; high span: *M* = 84%), nor in *total reading time* of the *context* sentences, either predicting (*M* low span = 5916 ms; high span = 5684), or control (*M* low span = 6256 ms; high span = 5874).

Accordingly, I proceeded to analyse the data concerned with the *continuation* sentences. For each dependent measure and region, 2 (Span) × 2 (Context) × 2 (Target) ANOVAs were carried out, using both subjects (F_1) and items (F_2) as random effects.[4] Interactions were analysed by means of planned comparisons between the predicting and the control condition: If an inference is drawn, then facilitation (i.e., shorter reading times) should be found in continuation sentences that include the inferential target word following a predicting context, relative to a control context.

Oculomotor control measures. The ANOVAs yielded no significant effects on any of these measures. Reading span was unrelated to launch site (*M* low span = 4.94 character spaces; high span = 4.93), saccade length (*M* low span = 7.3 chrs; high span = 7.6) and landing position (*M* low span = 3.01 chrs; high span = 3.03).

Initial processing: First-fixation probability and duration, and gaze duration. Mean scores for each of these three measures across regions in the inferential version are shown in Figure 2. There were no significant effects on probability of fixations or on first-fixation duration. Main effects of reading span emerged on gaze duration in the pre-target region, $F_1(1, 38) = 6.40, p < .025$; $F_2\ (1, 78) = 10.33, p < .01$, the target word, $F_1(1, 38) = 2.83, p = .10$; $F_2\ (1, 78) = 6.13,\ p < .025$, the post-target region, $F_1(1, 38) = 13.16, p < .001$; $F_2(1, 78) = 9.94, p < .01$, and the final region $F_1(1, 38) = 4.94, p < .05$; $F_2(1, 78) = 10.13, p < .01$, with the low-span group spending more time reading these regions (*M* pre-target = 365 ms; target = 338; post-target = 478; final = 708) than the high-span group (*M* pre-target = 313 ms; target = 306; post-target = 408; final = 596). There were no context by target interactive effects on any of these measures for either reading span group, thus showing no early inferential activation.[5]

Late processing: Regression-path reading time. No reliable effects appeared in the pre-target and target regions. However, there was a three-way interaction in the *final* region, $F_1(1, 38) = 5.73, p < .025$; $F_2(1, 78) = 3.43, p < .068$. Planned contrasts indicated that, when continuation sentences included an inferential target word, high-span readers spent less regression-path time following a predicting context (*M* = 1417 ms) than

[4] For first-fixation duration, gaze duration, regression-path reading time, right-bounded time, and re-reading time, only trials with first-pass fixations were included in the analyses (that is, zero scores—skipped zones—were not included). Excluding zero scores for these regions is the preferred strategy (Rayner et al., 1989, pp. 29–32; see also Garrod & Terras, 2000, for regression-path reading time). In contrast, zero scores are central to the definition of probability of fixation and probability of regressions, and were therefore included in the analyses as valid cases.

[5] In a further attempt to explore potential early effects, I reanalysed the data using a transformed measure of eye-fixations per character, rather than the whole time per word or region. In addition, the main analyses excluded 0-ms fixations that occurred when readers skipped a region. I subsequently performed a second set of analyses that included 0-ms fixations (see Pickering & Traxler, 1998, p. 945). The results of these analyses match the results of the main analyses, so I do not report them.

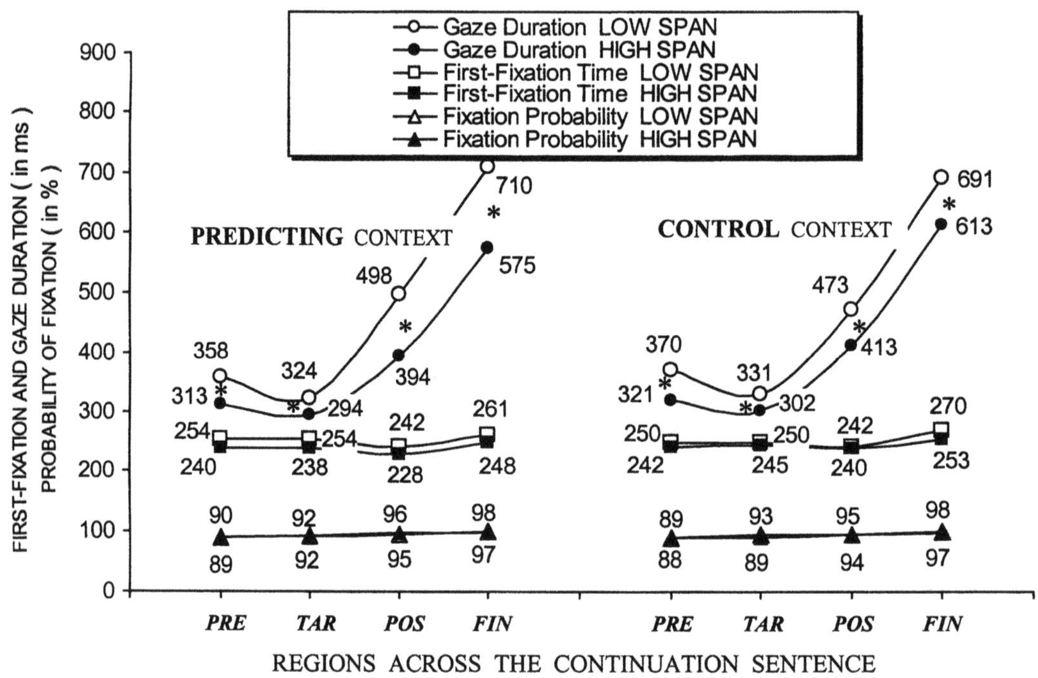

Figure 2. Mean fixation probability in the first pass (in % of participants), first-fixation duration (in ms), and gaze duration (in ms) in reading the pre-target (PRE), target (TAR), post-target (POS), and final (FIN) regions of the inferential version of the continuation sentence, following the predicting context and the control context, as a function of reading span. Asterisks indicate significant differences between the low- and the high-span groups.

following a control context (M = 1816 ms), $F_1(1, 19) = 11.12$, $P < .01$; $F_2(1, 39) = 4.12$, $p < .05$; for low-span readers, there was a non-significant opposite trend (M = 1815 vs 1693 ms). When continuation sentences included a non-predictable target word, planned contrasts revealed no significant effects, either for high-span readers (M predicting = 1671 ms; control = 1741) or for low-span readers (1766 vs 1999 ms). Activation scores (i.e., predicting–control difference) across the four regions are shown in Figure 3.

In addition to this facilitation effect on the final region, there was a similar, though less consistent, effect on the *post-target* region. Thus, a Span × Context interaction appeared only when the inferential version was analysed separately, $F_1(1, 38) = 7.39$, $p < .025$; $F_2(1, 38) = 12.87$, $p < .001$. The high-span group spent less time reading the inferential version following the predicting context (M = 600 ms) than following the control context (M = 967 ms), $F_1(1, 19) = 11.76$, $p < .01$; $F_2(1, 39) = 21.19$, $p < .0001$, whereas the low-span group showed an opposite non-significant trend (M = 834 vs 783 ms). Nevertheless, a three-way interaction did not emerge (both Fs < 1) probably because there was a non-significant trend in the same direction for the non-predictable version ($p_1 = .07$; $p_2 = .10$; M high span + predicting context = 838 ms; high span + control context = 1003; low span + predicting context = 788; low span + control context = 783; see activation scores in Figure 3).

Accordingly, the regression-path time data, particularly those concerned with the final region, show the pattern of facilitation effects predicted by the first hypothesis. As facilitation was found only for the high-span group, there is no specific evidence for the second hypothesis regarding a differential time course of inferential activation for either reading span group.

Late processing: Right-bounded time vs regressions in the post-target/final regions. The total regression-path time that I have just analysed involves the sum of time spent in reading a particular region (i.e., right-bounded time) *and* in possible regressions to prior regions. Each component is separated in the following analyses.

Regarding *right-bounded time* in the *post-target* region, there was no reliable effect, including the three-way interaction (both Fs < 1). In contrast, in the *final* region there was a significant three-way interaction, $F_1(1, 38) = 8.49$, $p < .01$; $F_2(1, 78) = 4.26$, $p < .05$. Planned contrasts indicated that,

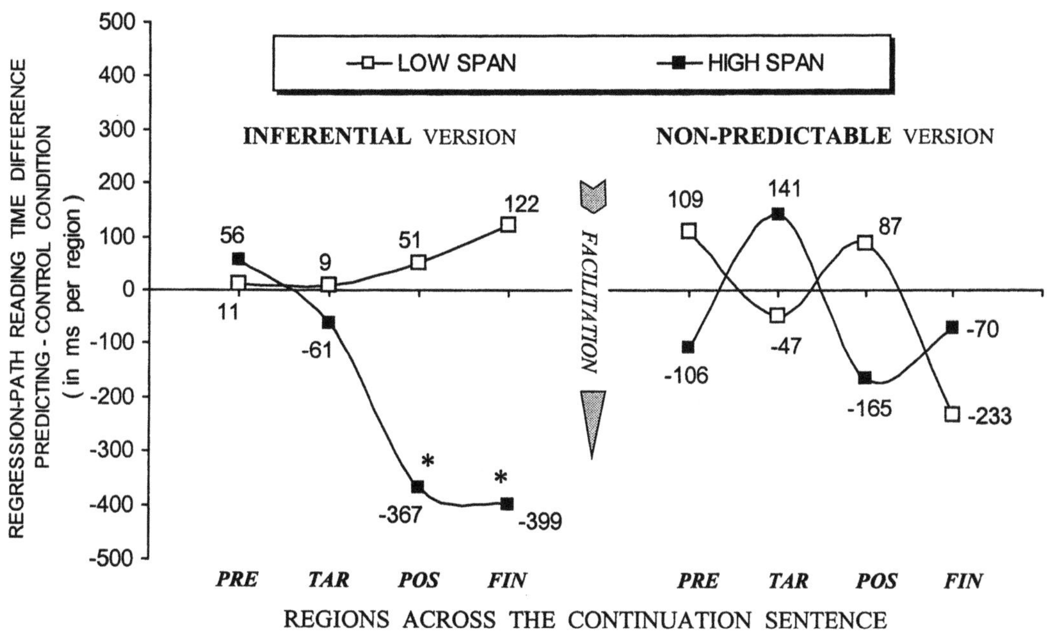

Figure 3. Difference scores (predicting–control context) in *regression-path reading time* (in ms) across the pre-target (PRE), target (TAR), post-target (POS), and final (FIN) regions of the continuation sentence, for the inferential and the non-predictable versions, as a function of reading span. Negative scores indicate facilitation in the predicting condition; positive scores indicate inhibition. Asterisks show significant difference scores.

when continuation sentences included an inferential target word, high-span readers spent less time in the final region following a predicting context (M = 725 ms) than following a control context (M = 824 ms), $F_1(1, 19) = 4.41$, $p = .05$; $F_2(1, 39) = 4.10$, $p = .05$; for low-span readers, there was an opposite trend of borderline significance in the subjects analysis (M = 852 vs 802 ms), $F_1(1, 19) = 3.86$, $p = .07$; $F_2 < 1$. When continuation sentences included a non-predictable target word, planned contrasts revealed no significant effects, either for high-span readers (M predicting context = 832 ms; control context = 796) or low-span readers (877 vs 915 ms). Activation scores (i.e., predicting–control difference) across the four regions are presented in Figure 4.

Regarding *regressions*, I analysed their probability and duration. First, there was no three-way interaction on the *probability* of regressions from the *final* region. A Context × Span interaction appeared only in the inferential version, $F_1(1, 38) = 4.44$, $p < .05$; $F_2(1, 38) = 3.28$, $p = .08$. Thus, there were fewer regressions for the high-span group following a predicting (M = .44) than a control (M = .57) context, $F_1(1, 19) = 6.38$, $p < .025$; $F_2(1, 39) = 3.82$, $p = .06$, whereas there was a non-significant opposite trend for the low-span group (M = .55 vs .50; both Fs < 1). The lack of a three-way interaction was probably due to the existence of a similar interactive trend for the non-predictable version ($p_1 = .12$; $p_2 = .17$; M high span + predicting context = .55; high span + control context = .64; low span + predicting context = .56; low span + control context = .53).[6] Second, for re-reading *time*, the three-way interaction in the *final* region was not significant either ($p_1 = .11$; $p_2 = .21$). A Context × Span interaction for the inferential version only approached significance in the subjects analysis, $F_1(1, 38) = 3.77$, $p = .06$; $p_2 = .25$, with the high-span group spending less time in regressions from the final region following a predicting context (M = 692 ms) than following a control context (M = 992 ms), whereas the low-span group showed the reverse trend (M = 964 vs 890 ms). Accordingly, regressions were affected in the same direction as right-bounded time,

[6] The reported regression scores correspond to the *final* region (54%) of a two-sentence pair on each trial. A main function of regressions is concerned with integration processes (see Vitu, McConkie, & Zola, 1998). As these processes normally occur at the end of sentences, it is understandable that the probability of regressions increases at these zones. Regression scores for the other regions were much smaller (pre-target: 4%; target: 7%; post-target: 11%). Accordingly the average percentage of regressions across the sentence was 19%. This is actually only a little higher than the normal pattern of regressions in reading for adult readers across text (between 10 and 15% of all fixations are regressions, according to Rayner, 1998).

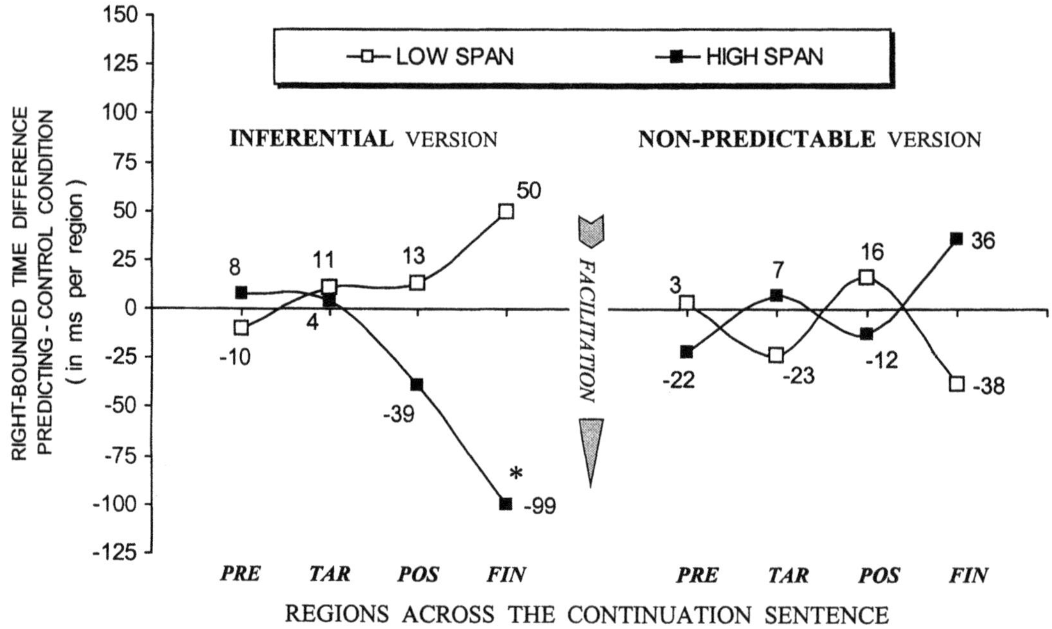

Figure 4. Difference scores (predicting–control context) in *right-bounded time* (in ms) across the pre-target (PRE), target (TAR), post-target (POS), and final (FIN) regions of the continuation sentence, for the inferential and the non-predictable versions, as a function of reading span. Negative scores indicate facilitation in the predicting condition; positive scores indicate inhibition. Asterisks show significant difference scores.

although the effects on regressions were weaker. This suggests that, in the predicting + inferential condition, high memory span facilitates reading of the final region *itself* (i.e., less right-bounded time) more than regressions from the final region.

DISCUSSION

The major findings of this study involved an interaction between reading span, context, and target on late eye-movement processing measures: (a) for readers high in reading span, but not for their low-span counterparts, a predicting context—relative to a control context—facilitated reading of information representing an event to be inferred; however, (b) this facilitatory effect of reading span did not affect early processing of the target word, but rather it took place in the final region of a continuation sentence that was consistent with the suggested event; and, more specifically, (c) facilitation involved spending less time reading the final region itself, rather than less time and fewer regressions to prior regions from the final region. These results support two main conclusions. First, working memory capacity makes a significant contribution to predictive inferences during reading, with high- but not low-span readers drawing inferences on-line. Second, the beneficial influence of high working memory affects late processes involving reanalysis or integration, but it does not extend to early lexical-access processes. In addition to the interactive influence on inferencing, there was a main effect of reading span on gaze duration across the regions of the continuation sentence, with high-span readers having shorter fixation times than low-span readers. This effect reveals a general processing difficulty for readers low in working memory capacity, affecting early processes such as lexical access.

In the present study there were no main effects of the context *per se* on early eye-movement measures, nor was inferential activity detected in these measures. This seems inconsistent with prior studies showing early contextual effects (e.g., Altarriba, Kroll, Sholl, & Rayner, 1996) and early inferential effects (e.g., Myers et al., 2000). One possible reason for this discrepancy is the nature of the contextual source, and the nature of the inference, in the different studies (see Calvo & Meseguer, 2001; Calvo, Meseguer, & Carreiras, in press). Different sources have been shown to affect different processing stages. Thus, Garrod and Terras (2000) found delayed contextual resolution effects (i.e., regression-path time from the post-target region) while lexical effects appeared earlier (i.e., gaze duration during the first pass). In the present study, the lexical source was probably similar in both the predicting and the control context conditions (due to word-based priming control; this is why there were no differences in early measures). In contrast, both conditions differed in the global integration source, with the predicting context inducing an inference representing the whole situation described in the context. (This is why the effects appeared on late measures reflecting post-access integration processes.) Furthermore, the nature of the inference involved, i.e., anticipation of an outcome of the overall situation portrayed in the context involves forward elaboration, which has been shown to take time to develop (e.g., Calvo et al., 1999; Till et al., 1988). In contrast, some studies on backward bridging inferences have detected earlier effects in eye-movement measures (Myers et al., 2000; O'Brien et al., 1997). This is understandable if we take into account that bridging inferences are necessary for comprehension and therefore may occur automatically (e.g., Magliano et al., 1993; Millis & Graesser, 1994). Two studies investigating elaborative inferences (O'Brien et al., 1988; and Garrod et al., 1990) found gaze duration facilitation on the target word, but the effects carried over into the post-target region, thus showing a delay. This suggests that, although the process may begin as soon as the reader views the target word, it is not completed until after the eyes have left this word.

Whether and when working memory contributes to inferences

The fact that readers high in memory span found it easier to read the continuation sentence that represented the to-be-inferred event following an inducing context, in comparison with when the same continuation sentence followed a control context, suggests that the inferential concept was activated some time after having read the inducing context. Presumably, it is the activation of this concept that would have enabled high-span readers to comprehend the corresponding words (i.e., inferential version of the continuation sentence) more readily.

Prior research on predictive inferences has demonstrated that normal readers *can* draw them on-line if the context highly constrains the predictability of a main consequence (Calvo & Castillo, 1996, Calvo et al., 1999; Fincher-Kiefer, 1995, 1996; Keefe & McDaniel, 1993; Klin et al., 1999a; Klin, Murray, Levine, & Guzmán, 1999b; Murray et al., 1993; Whitney, Ritchie, & Crane, 1992). However, no evidence has been found in some studies (Magliano et al., 1993; Millis & Graesser, 1994; Potts, Keenan, & Golding, 1988), or only "minimal" evidence (Duffy, 1986; McKoon & Ratcliff, 1986, 1989). Furthermore, studies using eye-movement measures to investigate a related type of inference (i.e., elaboration of contextually appropriate meanings or instantiation of noun category) found evidence of on-line inferential activity only when the context sentence strongly suggested an implied concept (O'Brien et al., 1988), and when there was an anaphoric relationship between the implying and the implied concepts (Garrod et al., 1990).

In the present study, working memory span has proved important: Whereas readers high in span are able to draw predictive inferences, their low-span counterparts are not. This suggests that not only factors related to the stimulus materials (e.g., context constraints), but also individual differences in working memory capacity, could account for inconsistent findings between different studies. The usual averaging of data across participants can hide relevant individual differences, and give the impression that a particular cognitive process is either generally performed or not performed by most readers. At least, it is very likely that high-level processes, such as elaborative inferences, are performed by some readers but not by others, or with different efficiency.

As high-span readers showed facilitation in late processing measures, such as regression-path reading time at the end of the continuation sentence, it follows that these readers made inferences with some delay (see Garrod & Terras, 2000, for similar effects with normal readers). However, the fact that facilitation occurred in the final region should not be taken as an indication that inferences were made precisely when reading this region. Rather it reveals that, when readers arrived at the final region, the inferential concept had already reached enough activation to make processing of this region easier. So the inference must have been initiated earlier. Actually, if inferences had been delayed to be made at the end of the continuation sentence, interference should have occurred at that time, rather than facilitation. The reason is that the resource demands of these inferences (e.g., Calvo et al., 1999) would have added to the demands of the necessary wrap-up at the end of sentences (Kintsch, 1988). If so, additional reading time should have been observed in the predicting + inferential condition, which is opposite to what happened.

Nevertheless, if inferences had been *completely* generated during reading of the inducing context, then facilitation should have appeared on the target word of the continuation sentence, and/or in early processing measures, such as gaze duration. As there were no such early effects, it is possible that the inferential concepts were only partially or generically activated (e.g., the pupil *read* or *worked*, etc.) by the time the target word was initially encountered. Only after the participant had read the inferential target word would the inference be completed (e.g., *studied*). This interpretation is consistent with the hypothesis that predictive inferences are drawn only minimally (McKoon & Ratcliff, 1986, 1989), or that they do not take a highly specific form (Duffy, 1986). Because of insufficient early activation of the inferential concept, initial access to the target word meaning would not be affected. However, once this concept is completed and refined when the target word is processed, it becomes capable of affecting later text-integration processes, as revealed by the facilitation effects that emerged after the target word was read.

Contrast between continuous reading and discrete naming

These findings and conclusions can be compared with those of a related study (Estevez & Calvo, 2000), in which the same context sentences were presented one word at a time in a fixed-pace mode, followed by a single target word that the participants were to name (with no continuation sentence). In this study, inferences were not generally made within 50 ms of the end of the inducing context; only the high-span participants—not their low-span counterparts—constructed inferences within the first 550 ms after the context; and most participants drew inferences within a 1050-ms interval, regardless of memory span. From Estevez and Calvo's (2000) study, it follows that both high- and low-span readers can make these inferences on-line, although the former can execute the process more efficiently, as they need less processing time than the latter. This is partly consistent with the present study: (a) predictive inferences could be detected only at late processing stages (i.e., 550 or 1050 ms, or last word); and (b) not even the high-span readers were able to draw inferences immediately after the context (i.e., 50 ms, or target word). However, the results of both studies differ in that the low-span readers generated inferences in one study but not in the other. An explanation of this apparent inconsistency and its practical implications for normal reading in naturalistic conditions are considered next.

The reason why low-span readers could generate inferences in the naming study (Estevez & Calvo, 2000) within 1050 ms after the inducing context, but not in the present eye-fixation study, is probably not due to insufficient processing time in the present study, which used self-paced presentation (whereas it was fixed-paced in the naming study). Rather, a relevant factor is concerned with whether there is additional text after the target word. It should be noted that in the naming study each trial ended with the target word to be named, whereas in the eye-movement study two additional regions (post-target and final) had to be read. Accordingly, if low-span individuals need about 1 second to construct inferences (as revealed by the naming study), then in naturalistic reading (and listening) conditions, by the time inferences could be generated, a reader (or listener) would normally be processing the next sentence or region. As a consequence, given the severe constraints on working memory during continuous discourse processing (see Gathercole & Baddeley, 1993), we can expect that low-span readers do not generate inferences. Processing of explicit information in the next sentence would interfere with the construction of inferences from the preceding sentence. In normal conditions, readers would not have that much time (one additional second) to make the inference. If they did, not only would their reading speed be slowed down, but the processes of explicit information comprehension would be impeded.

This could explain why the so-called less-skilled readers perform especially poorly on tasks that involve elaborative inferences (Hannon & Daneman, 1998; Long, Oppy, & Seely, 1994). When reading continuous text, low-span readers probably use a "wait and see" strategy regarding implicit information (which implies "go on reading explicit text"); they would make on-line inferences only when required. In contrast, high-span readers can share resources both for inferences and explicit comprehension, as elaborative inferences are much less time-consuming for these readers (less than 550 ms; Estevez & Calvo, 2000).

How and why working memory favours elaborative inferencing

A plausible explanation for the beneficial, though delayed, effect of high working memory capacity relies on two major premises. First, predictive inferences are elaborations that need time to construct, beyond comprehension of explicit information (i.e., more than 500 additional ms in normal readers: Calvo et al., 1999; Fincher-Kiefer, 1995). This implies that these inferences are probably using the limited and effortful resources of working memory (Conway & Engle, 1996; Estevez & Calvo, 2000). Second, processing of the end of sentences typically requires more time than other parts of the sentence (Haberlandt & Graesser, 1985; Just & Carpenter, 1980). These additional demands presumably involve integrative processes that normally take place at the end of sentences (Kintsch, 1988). Accordingly, it is reasonable that high working memory facilitates predictive inferences: The more capacity a reader has available, the more s/he will be able to draw optional elaborations during reading, concurrently with the obligatory textbase representation (see Just & Carpenter, 1992; Singer & Ritchot, 1996). Furthermore, it is reasonable that the facilitating effect of high working memory appears at the end of continuation sentences. A main function of working memory is to keep a current mental representation temporarily activated while subsequent information is processed, in order to integrate them (Gathercole & Baddeley, 1993; Just & Carpenter, 1992). An elaborative inference following the inducing context will save time in integrating the context with the congruent (i.e., inferential) version of the continuation sentence. It is, therefore, understandable that this advantage reveals itself especially when integrative processes are usually more demanding, i.e., at the end of the continuation sentence.

In an alternative explanation, one could argue that neither high- nor low-span readers draw inferences on-line. If they did, we should have observed predictability effects on the target word, rather than in the final region. The advantage that high-span readers showed at the end of continuation sentences could occur because they are more skilled at integrating new material with previously encountered material. However, if so, a main effect of memory span should have occurred at the end of the continuation sentence regardless of whether the context was predicting or control, and whether the continuation sentence included an inferential or a non-predictable target. Contrary to this explanation is the fact that facilitation was selective, i.e., particularly in the predicting + inferential condition, as revealed by the three-way interactions. This reveals that there is more than a global difference in integrative processing as a function of working memory capacity. Rather, high-span readers were more efficient (i.e., spent less time) than low-span readers specifically in the particular condition where predictive inferences could be generated. This is consistent with the hypothesis that integrative processes are facilitated by high working memory capacity precisely *because* high-span readers generate inferences that help integrate new information with previous information.[7]

Working memory and oculomotor vs cognitive eye-movement control

The present findings are relevant to discussion of the role of working memory in eye-movement control in reading. Readers' eye behaviour has two main components—fixations and saccades—that are assumed to be governed by two relatively independent mechanisms (see Rayner, 1998). An oculomotor control mechanism is influenced by low-level visual factors, such as word length, predetermined scanning routines, and perceptual span. This mechanism is mainly responsible for *where* a saccade is targeted (i.e., fixation location), and impinges on eye-movement variables such as launch site, saccade amplitude, landing position of the eyes, and probability of fixation. A cognitive control mechanism is regulated by on-going comprehension processes, such as lexical access and post-access integration of meanings (see Reichle, Pollatsek, Fisher, & Rayner, 1998), as revealed by its sensitivity to factors such as word lexical frequency and contextual predictability. This mechanism is mainly responsible for *when* to move to another word (i.e., fixation duration),

[7] Alternatively, it might still be argued that the advantage of high-span readers for processing sentences containing predictable events could be that these events are easier to integrate into the discourse representation than less predictable events. This is compatible with previous findings regarding the influence of context on the processing of upcoming words (e.g., Hess, Foss, & Carroll, 1995; Schwanenflugel & White, 1991). But this would lead us to accept the idea that the contribution of high working memory capacity to integrative processes is greater when integration is easier than when it is more difficult. This, however, is the opposite of what we should expect, according to the conceptualisation of working memory.

impinging on variables such as gaze duration, regression-path time, or second-pass time. Other variables such as regressions may be affected by both mechanisms (see Vitu et al., 1998). Accordingly, working memory is unlikely to affect the oculomotor mechanism. In contrast, working memory is likely to influence the cognitive mechanism, in so much as working memory is defined as the number of representations that can be simultaneously activated for integration, and as cognitive processes such as lexical access and integration use working memory resources. The fact that reading span was related to gaze duration and regression-path time, that it affected regressions only relatively, and that it was unrelated to probability of fixations, launch site, saccade length, and landing position, is consistent with this view (see also similar findings in Kennison & Clifton, 1995).

In general, as in Kennison and Clifton's (1995) study (see also Jared, Levy, & Rayner, 1999)[8], in the present experiment eye fixations revealed that low-span readers experienced more difficulty during reading than high-span readers. As suggested by Kennison and Clifton (1995), this difficulty might affect lexical processes. The reason is that, in the current study, memory span affected one early processing measure, such as gaze duration (Kennison & Clifton, 1995, and Jared et al., 1999, also found significant effects on early eye-movement measures). Nevertheless, the difficulty is particularly evident in late measures, such as regression-path time; furthermore, this occurs at the end of the sentence, which suggests that integrative processes are strongly affected. This is consistent with the conceptualisation of working memory as a limited-capacity system that is involved in the transient storage of activated representations, in order to assemble them online. The effect of working memory is stronger at the end of the sentence, when more information needs to be maintained activated for integration.

[8] Jared et al. (1999) found that good readers had significantly shorter gaze durations than poor readers. Skilled reading was determined on the basis of the participants' performance on the Comprehension subtest of the Nelson-Denny Reading Test. As performance on this subtest has proved to correlate with performance on the Reading Span Task (significant positive correlations range from .29 to .46: Baddeley, Logie, Nimmo-Smith, & Brereton, 1985; Dixon et al., 1988; Singer et al., 1992), Jared et al.'s (1999) findings may also be relevant to the effects of reading span in our study.

REFERENCES

Alameda, J.R., & Cuetos, F. (1995). *Diccionario de frecuencia de las unidades lingüísticas del castellano* [Dictionary of lexical frequencies of Spanish linguistic units]. Oviedo, Spain: SEP, Universidad de Oviedo.

Altarriba, J., Kroll, J.F., Sholl, A., & Rayner, K. (1996). The influence of lexical and conceptual constraints on reading mixed-language sentences: Evidence from eye fixations and naming times. *Memory and Cognition*, *24*, 477–492.

Baddeley, A.D. (1986). *Working memory*. Oxford: Oxford University Press.

Baddeley, A., Logie, R., Nimmo-Smith, I., & Brereton, N. (1985). Components of fluent reading. *Journal of Memory and Language*, *24*, 119–131.

Calvo, M.G. (2000). The time course of predictive inferences depends on contextual constraints. *Language and Cognitive Processes*, *15*, 293–319.

Calvo, M.G., & Castillo, M.D. (1996). Predictive inferences occur on-line, but with delay: Convergence of naming and reading times. *Discourse Processes*, *22*, 57–78.

Calvo, M.G., & Castillo, M.D. (1998). Predictive inferences take time to develop. *Psychological Research*, *61*, 249–260.

Calvo, M.G., Castillo, M.D., & Estevez, A. (1999). Online predictive inferences in reading: Processing time *during* vs. *after* the priming context. *Memory and Cognition*, *27*, 834–843.

Calvo, M.G., & Meseguer, E. (2001). Eye movements and processing stages in reading: Relative contribution of visual, lexical, and contextual factors. *Manuscript submitted for publication.*

Calvo, M.G., Meseguer, E., & Carreiras, M. (in press). Inferences about predictable events: Eye movements during reading. *Psychological Research.*

Carpenter, P.A., Miyake, A., & Just, M.A. (1994). Working memory constraints in comprehension: Evidence from individual differences, aphasia, and aging. In M.A. Gernsbacher (Ed.), *Handbook of psycholinguistics* (pp. 1075–1122). San Diego, CA: Academic Press.

Conway, A.R.A., & Engle, R.W. (1996). Individual differences in working memory capacity: More evidence for a general capacity theory. *Memory*, *4*, 577–590.

Daneman, M., & Carpenter, P.A. (1980). Individual differences in working memory and reading. *Journal of Verbal Learning and Verbal Behavior*, *19*, 450–466.

Daneman, M., & Merikle, P.M. (1996). Working memory and language comprehension: A meta-analysis. *Psychonomic Bulletin and Review*, *3*, 422–443.

Dixon, P., LeFevre, J., & Twilley, L.C. (1988). Word knowledge and working memory as predictors of reading skill. *Journal of Educational Psychology*, *80*, 465–472.

Duffy, S.A. (1986). Role of expectations in sentence integration. *Journal of Experimental Psychology: Learning, Memory, and Cognition*, *12*, 208–219.

Estevez, A., & Calvo, M.G. (2000). Working memory capacity and time course of predictive inferences. *Memory*, *8*, 51–61.

Fincher-Kiefer, R. (1995). Relative inhibition following the encoding of bridging and predictive inferences. *Journal of Experimental Psychology: Learning, Memory, and Cognition, 21*, 981–995.

Fincher-Kiefer, R. (1996). Encoding differences between bridging and predictive inferences. *Discourse Processes, 22*, 225–246.

Garrod, S., O'Brien, E.J., Morris, R.K., & Rayner, K. (1990). Elaborative inferencing as an active or passive process. *Journal of Experimental Psychology: Learning, Memory, and Cognition, 16*, 250–257.

Garrod, S., & Terras, M. (2000). The contribution of lexical and situational knowledge to resolving discourse roles: Bonding and resolution. *Journal of Memory and Language, 42*, 526–544.

Gathercole, S.E., & Baddeley, A.D. (1993). *Working memory and language*. Hove, UK: Lawrence Erlbaum Associates Ltd.

Gutiérrez-Calvo, M.G., Castillo, M.D., & Espino, O. (1996). Memoria operativa y procesos de integración en la comprensión de textos [Working memory and integration processes in text comprehension]. *Anuario de Psicología, 70*, 3–18.

Gutiérrez-Calvo, M.G., Jiménez, A., & Castillo, M.D. (1996). Medida de la memoria operativa: Versión informatizada y adaptación al castellano de la tarea de "Reading Span" [Assessment of working memory: Computerized version and Spanish adaptation of the "Reading Span" task]. *Psicologica, 17*, 215–228.

Haberlandt, K., & Graesser, A.C. (1985). Component processes in text comprehension and some of their interactions. *Journal of Experimental Psychology: General, 114*, 357–374.

Hannon, B., & Daneman, M. (1998). Facilitating knowledge-based inferences in less-skilled readers. *Contemporary Educational Psychology, 23*, 149–172.

Hess, D.J., Foss, D.J., & Carroll, P. (1995). Effects of global and local context on lexical processing during language comprehension. *Journal of Experimental Psychology: General, 124*, 62–82.

Jared, D., Levy, B.A., & Rayner, K. (1999). The role of phonology in the activation of word meanings during reading: Evidence from proofreading and eye movements. *Journal of Experimental Psychology: General, 128*, 219–264.

Just, M.A., & Carpenter, P. (1980). A theory of reading: From eye fixations to comprehension. *Psychological Review, 87*, 329–354.

Just, M.A., & Carpenter, P.A. (1992). A capacity theory of comprehension: Individual differences in working memory. *Psychological Review, 99*, 122–149.

Keefe, D.E., & McDaniel, M.A. (1993). The time course and durability of predictive inferences. *Journal of Memory and Language, 32*, 446–463.

Keenan, J.M., Golding, J.M., Potts, G.R., Jennings, T.M., & Aman, C.J. (1990). Methodological issues in evaluating the occurrence of inferences. In A.C. Graesser & G.H. Bower (Eds.), *Inferences and text comprehension* (pp. 295–312). San Diego, CA: Academic Press.

Kennison, S.M., & Clifton, C. (1995). Determinants of parafoveal preview benefit in high and low working memory capacity readers: Implications for eye movement control. *Journal of Experimental Psychology: Learning, Memory, and Cognition, 21*, 68–81.

Kintsch, W. (1988). The role of knowledge in discourse comprehension: A construction-integration model. *Psychological Review, 95*, 163–182.

Klin, C.M., Guzmán, A.E., & Levine, W.H. (1999a). Prevalence and persistence of predictive inferences. *Journal of Memory and Language, 40*, 593–604.

Klin, C.M., Murray, J.D., Levine, W.H., & Guzmán, A.E. (1999b). Forward inferences: From activation to long-term memory. *Discourse Processes, 27*, 241–260.

Liversedge, S.P., Paterson, K.B., & Pickering, M.J. (1998). Eye movements and measures of reading time. In G. Underwood (Ed.), *Eye guidance in reading and scene perception* (pp. 55–75). Oxford: Elsevier.

Long, D.L., Oppy, B.J., & Seely, M.R. (1994). Individual differences in the time course of inferential processing. *Journal of Experimental Psychology: Learning, Memory, and Cognition, 20*, 1456–1470.

Magliano, J.P., Baggett, W.B., Johnson, B.K., & Graesser, A.C. (1993). The time course of generating causal antecedent and causal consequence inferences. *Discourse Processes, 16*, 35–53.

McKoon, G., & Ratcliff, R. (1986). Inferences about predictable events. *Journal of Experimental Psychology: Learning, Memory, and Cognition, 12*, 82–91.

McKoon, G., & Ratcliff, R. (1989). Semantic association and elaborative inference. *Journal of Experimental Psychology: Learning, Memory, and Cognition, 15*, 326–338.

Millis, K.K., & Graesser, A.C. (1994). The time-course of constructing knowledge-based inferences for scientific texts. *Journal of Memory and Language, 33*, 583–599.

Miyake, A., & Shah, P. (Eds.) (1999). *Models of working memory*. New York: Cambridge University Press.

Murray, J.D., Klin, C.M., & Myers, J. (1993). Forward inferences in narrative text. *Journal of Memory and Language, 32*, 464–473.

Myers, J.L., Cook, A.E., Kambe, G., Mason, R.A., & O'Brien, E.J. (2000). Semantic and episodic effects on bridging inferences. *Discourse Processes, 29*, 179–199.

O'Brien, E.J., Raney, G.E., Albrecht, J.E., & Rayner, K. (1997). Processes involved in the resolution of explicit anaphors. *Discourse Processes, 23*, 1–24.

O'Brien, E.J., Shank, D.M., Myers, J.L., & Rayner, K. (1988). Elaborative inferences during reading: Do they occur on-line? *Journal of Experimental Psychology: Learning, Memory, and Cognition, 14*, 410–420.

Pickering, M.J., & Traxler, M.J. (1998). Plausibility and recovery from garden paths: An eye-tracking study. *Journal of Experimental Psychology: Learning, Memory, and Cognition, 24*, 940–961.

Potts, G.R., Keenan, J.M., & Golding, J.M. (1988). Assessing the occurrence of elaborative inference: Lexical decision versus naming. *Journal of Memory and Language, 27*, 399–415.

Rayner, K. (1998). Eye movements in reading and information processing: 20 years of research. *Psychological Bulletin*, *124*, 372–422.

Rayner, K., Sereno, S.C., Morris, R.K., Schmauder, A.R., & Clifton, C. (1989). Eye-movements and on-line comprehension processes. *Language and Cognitive Processes*, *4 (special issue)*, 21–49.

Rayner, K., & Well, A.D. (1996). Effects of contextual constraint on eye movements in reading: A further examination. *Psychonomic Bulletin and Review*, *3*, 504–509.

Reichle, E.D., Pollatsek, A., Fisher, D.L., & Rayner, K. (1998). Toward a model of eye movement control in reading. *Psychological Review*, *105*, 125–157.

Schwanenflugel, P.J., & White, C.R. (1991). The influence of paragraph information on the processing of upcoming words. *Reading Research Quarterly*, *26*, 160–177.

Singer, M. (1994). Discourse inference processes. In M.A. Gernsbacher (Ed.), *Handbook of psycholinguistics* (pp. 479–516). San Diego, CA: Academic Press.

Singer, M., Andrusiak, P., Reisdorf, P., & Black, N.L. (1992). Individual differences in bridging inference processes. *Memory and Cognition*, *20*, 539–548.

Singer, M., & Ritchot, K.F.M. (1996). The role of working memory capacity and knowledge access in text inference processing. *Memory and Cognition*, *24*, 733–743.

Thurstone, L.L., & Thurstone, T.G. (1979). *Primary Mental Abilities Test*. Madrid: TEA Ediciones.

Till, R.E., Mross, E.F., & Kintsch, W. (1988). Time course of priming for associate and inference words in a discourse context. *Memory and Cognition*, *16*, 283–298.

Trabasso, T., & Magliano, J.P. (1996). Conscious understanding during comprehension. *Discourse Processes*, *21*, 255–287.

Vitu, F., McConkie, G.W., & Zola, D. (1998). About regressive saccades in reading and their relation to word identification. In G. Underwood (Ed.), *Eye guidance in reading and scene perception* (pp. 101–124). Oxford: Elsevier.

Whitney, P., Ritchie, B.G., & Clark, M.B. (1991). Working memory capacity and the use of elaborative inferences in text comprehension. *Discourse Processes*, *14*, 133–145.

Whitney, P., Ritchie, B.G., & Crane, R.S. (1992). The effect of foregrounding on readers' use of predictive inferences. *Memory and Cognition*, *20*, 424–432.

Yuill, N., Oakhill, J., & Parkin, A. (1989). Working memory comprehension ability and resolution of text anomaly. *British Journal of Psychology*, *80*, 351–361.

APPENDIX

Example (as translated into English) of the four versions of passages combining a predicting and a control context with an inferential and a non-predictable target word in the continuation sentence. Target words in italics (*inferential* targets outside the brackets; *non-predictable* targets inside the brackets). Asterisks indicate content words shared by the predicting and the control context, to control for word-based priming. Slashes (/) in the continuation sentence indicate region boundaries (i.e., pre-target, target, post-target, and final).

Versions 1 and 3: Predicting Context + Inferential [Non-Predictable] Target Word Three days before the *examination the *pupil went to the *library, looked for a separate *table and opened his *notebook. / The pupil / *studied* [*slept*] / for an hour / approximately.
Versions 2 and 4: Control Context + Inferential [Non-Predictable] Target Word The *pupil, who was a little tired after finishing his *examination, forgot his *notebook and left it on a *table in the *library. / The pupil / *studied* [*slept*] / for an hour / approximately.

Versions 1 and 3: Predicting Context + Inferential [Non-Predictable] Target Word The woman went into the *church, spoke with the *priest for a few minutes and afterwards *knelt down in front of the *altar. / The woman / *prayed* [*wrote*] / silently / with devotion.
Versions 2 and 4: Control Context + Inferential [Non-Predictable] Target Word After having spoken with the *priest for a few minutes, in front of the *church's *altar, the woman *knelt down to do her shoe up. / The woman / *prayed* [*wrote*] / silently / with devotion.

Versions 1 and 3: Predicting Context + Inferential [Non-Predictable] Target Word The *angry *bees *flew out of the *hive and some of them *threw themselves at Julia's arm. / The bees / *stung* [*soiled*] / Julia's / arm.
Versions 2 and 4: Control Context + Inferential [Non-Predictable] Target Word Julia was *angry because someone had *thrown rubbish near the new *hive and the *bees had *flown out. / The bees / *stung* [*soiled*] / Julia's / arm.

Versions 1 and 3: Predicting Context + Inferential [Non-Predictable] Target Word When Eva saw her *father in the *airport, she ran up to him, and he *bent down over his *child. / The father / *embraced* [*frowned at*] / the child / as usual.
Versions 2 and 4: Control Context + Inferential [Non-Predictable] Target Word Before the trip with Eva, the *father *bent down to show a scale model of the *airport to his *child. / The father / *embraced* [*frowned at*] / the child / as usual.

Versions 1 and 3: Predicting Context + Inferential [Non-Predictable] Target Word When the *party was over, there were *bags and *papers all over the *floor, so Susanna picked up the *broom. / Susanna / *swept* [*mopped*] / the floor / thoroughly.
Versions 2 and 4: Control Context + Inferential [Non-Predictable] Target Word In order to decorate the *party, Susanna hung up the coloured *papers with the *broom that was on the *floor. / Susanna / *swept* [*mopped*] / the floor / thoroughly.

Versions 1 and 3: Predicting Context + Inferential [Non-Predictable] Target Word Early in the morning the *gardener took the *hose, connected it to the *water *tap and started his work. / The gardener / *irrigated* [*pruned*] / the plants / of the garden.
Versions 2 and 4: Control Context + Inferential [Non-Predictable] Target Word With *water, the *gardener cleaned the *hose and the *tap that the painters had carelessly soiled the day before. / The gardener / *irrigated* [*pruned*] / the plants / of the garden.

Versions 1 and 3: Predicting Context + Inferential [Non-Predictable] Target Word While Maria *walked *barefoot over the rocks, she *put her foot *down, without realising, on a piece of *glass which had been left on the *floor. / Maria / *cut herself* [*slipped*] / with pain / at that moment.
Versions 2 and 4: Control Context + Inferential [Non-Predictable] Target Word In order to avoid *putting her dirty shoes *down on the *floor, Maria *walked *barefoot up to the *glass display cabinet to place the present in it. / Maria / *cut herself* [*slipped*] / with pain / at that moment.

MEMORY, 2001, *9* (4/5/6), 383–394

Short-term memory and working memory as indices of children's cognitive skills

Una M.Z. Hutton and John N. Towse
Royal Holloway, University of London, UK

In the current literature, empirical and conceptual distinctions have been drawn between a more or less passive short-term memory (STM) system and a more dynamic working memory (WM) system. Distinct tasks have been developed to measure their capacity and research has generally shown that, for adults, WM, and not STM, is a reliable predictor of general cognitive ability. However, the locus of the differences between the tasks has received little attention. We present data from children concerning measures of matrices reasoning ability, reading, and numerical skill along with forward and backward order serial recall of WM, STM, and STM with articulatory suppression tasks. As indices of children's cognitive skills, STM and WM are shown to be rather similar in terms of memory *per se*. Neither the opportunity for rehearsal nor task complexity provides satisfactory explanations for differences between memory tests.

Memory researchers, it seems, like to exploit dichotomies in their field. One long-standing controversy relates to arguments between a unitary view of memory (Laming, 1999; Melton, 1963) and a duplex account that distinguishes short- and long-term stores (Baddeley & Scott, 1971; Shallice & Warrington, 1970). In recalling a sequence of items, a distinction is often made between the advantage for the initial (primacy) and final (recency) list items. Much has also been written of the difference between verbal and visuo-spatial based memories, particularly relevant in a developmental context where children's reliance on these codes appears to vary (e.g., Hitch, Halliday, Schaafstal, & Schraagen, 1988).

Another popular dichotomy distinguishes short-term memory (STM) and working memory (WM). The traditional concept of STM describes a more or less passive temporary memory store, the capacity of which is typically assessed via the immediate serial recall of lists of information (e.g., Atkinson & Shiffrin, 1968). The concept of WM, as well as being chronologically more recent, describes a more dynamic system, concerned with the temporary retention and transformation of information in support of cognitive activity (Baddeley & Hitch, 1974). Although STM and WM clearly share a close relationship, both referring to transient memory, it has been argued on both empirical and conceptual grounds that there are nonetheless important distinctions to be made. After reviewing these, we report a study that evaluates several pertinent issues in a developmental context and makes for a richer appreciation of the two concepts.

STM tasks commonly require just the preservation of sequential order information. For example, the digit span task requires subjects to read or listen to lists of temporally separated digits and then repeat the sequence. In the span format, the number of list items increases until errors exceed threshold. Measuring WM is less straightforward in that there are widely differing views as to what represents the core of WM (Miyake &

Requests for reprints should be sent to Una Hutton, Department of Psychology, Royal Holloway, University of London, Egham, Surrey TW20 0EX, UK.

The data have been collected as part of a postgraduate research programme currently funded by the Economic and Social Research council. We are grateful to Andy Haswell for adapting computer code to produce the software for this study, John Wilding for insightful comments on a previous version of this paper, and anonymous reviewers for their constructive suggestions for improvement.

http://www.tandf.co.uk/journals/pp/09658211.html DOI:10.1080/09658210042000058

Shah, 1999). Nonetheless, the most common way of measuring WM capacity involves *working memory span* tasks, which essentially contain both a memory and a processing element. For example, the reading span task (Daneman & Carpenter, 1980) involves reading and comprehending sentences and remembering the sentence-final words for subsequent recall. Counting span involves counting arrays and remembering the count totals for subsequent recall (Case, Kurland, & Goldberg, 1982). Operation span involves solving arithmetic problems and remembering sums or accompanying words (Turner & Engle, 1989). Therefore, an important commonality of working memory span tasks is that they involve completing an additional processing task before each to-be-remembered item becomes apparent.

There are several differences between data from STM and WM tests among children and adults. WM scores are often lower than their STM counterparts, sometimes half the value. More important, perhaps, WM tasks are often better predictors of complex cognitive skills. Research has consistently demonstrated significant relationships between WM and a range of abilities, including reading comprehension (Daneman & Carpenter, 1980, 1983), language comprehension (King & Just, 1991; MacDonald, Just, & Carpenter, 1992), reasoning (Kyllonen & Christal, 1990), mental arithmetic (Ashcraft, 1995; Logie, Gilhooly, & Wynn, 1994), and general intelligence (Daneman & Tardif, 1987). Among adults, STM is not consistently related to ability (e.g., Perfetti & Lesgold, 1977; but see Turner & Engle, 1989). Developmental studies have also reported STM to be a weaker predictor of cognitive performance than WM (Daneman & Blennerhassett, 1984; Leather & Henry, 1994).

It is therefore important to consider the psychological features responsible for STM and WM performance. According to one theoretical view, tasks like reading span and counting span involve a limited-capacity system in which resources are consumed by either the processing or memory components, leading to a trade-off in resource availability (Case et al., 1982; Daneman & Carpenter, 1980). As complex cognitive tasks likewise comprise elements of both retention and transformation, they too rely on a central limited-capacity system, and so correlate well with working memory span tasks. STM may be less successful at capturing variance in cognitive skills because it assesses only the memory component of the system.

However, this resource-sharing account of WM span performance has been questioned. Towse and Hitch (1995) argued that evidence for a trade-off, with for example impaired memory performance following an increase in processing demand, could be an artefact. High processing demand might not impair retention functions directly, but rather might slow processing down and therefore increase the amount of forgetting that takes place. Towse and Hitch (1995) reported that children's counting span was equivalent across conditions comparable in duration but differing in difficulty. This supports an alternative interpretation of WM, according to which forgetting over time is more important than resource-sharing. Subsequent research also favours this *task-switching* account (Hitch, Towse & Hutton, in press; Towse, Hitch & Hutton, 1998, 2000).

The task-switching model, then, suggests that WM phenomena may be an emergent property of the dynamics of memory degradation. By avoiding the need to invoke some explanatory mechanism such as resource-sharing within a central executive, WM is placed on a more similar footing to STM. For example, to *some* extent at least the processing component of WM tasks could be regarded as a recall delay, emphasising children's ability to engage in rapid processing in order to limit forgetting. Consistent with that view, processing time and working memory span correlate in children (Hitch et al., in press; Towse et al., 1998). In these terms, task configurations may differentiate WM and STM more than fundamentally different underlying memory mechanisms. A major aim of the present study is therefore to compare WM and STM tasks directly among children. By collecting relevant on-line data, it is possible to evaluate whether the superior predictive ability of WM disappears once statistically shorn of its processing time influence, as the task-switching model suggests.

Engle, Tuholski, Laughlin, and Conway (1999b) investigated the relationship between STM and WM in adults. They found that STM and WM latent variables were highly intercorrelated, but that when variance common to both tasks was removed WM was related to fluid intelligence whereas STM was not. Engle, Kane, and Tuholski (1999a) argue that WM and STM tasks are not "pure" measures of underlying abilities, but nonetheless propose that WM capacity can be equated to the capacity for controlled processing, which in turn reflects general fluid intelligence. According to this position, the extent to which

STM or WM tasks correlate with complex cognition will depend on the demand for controlled attention.

We evaluated this controlled attention hypothesis by comparing different forms of memory tasks, as varying their attentional demands should produce corresponding changes in the relationship with standardised ability measures. Achieving this goal is difficult because it requires manipulations of the relevant construct, yet the computations that are constitutive of controlled attention are not well defined. Here, two manipulations are considered. One involves children recalling the presented sequence in reverse order, because a number of authors argue that backward recall increases the task demands, making for a working memory or executive task (see Elliott, Smith & McCulloch, 1997; Gathercole, 1999; Gathercole & Pickering, 2000; Groeger, Field, & Hammond, 1999; Rosen & Engle, 1997). A second manipulation of STM is the inclusion of articulatory suppression requirements. This is likely to make retention more difficult, almost certainly less successful. Furthermore, Cantor, Engle, and Hamilton (1991) suggest that one reason STM may not correlate with cognitive abilities is that individual differences in rehearsal strategies are important for STM but not WM. If this is the case, then curtailing rehearsal in STM will lead to stronger relationships with cognitive abilities and align the task with WM.

The study sampled two groups, at 8 and 11 years of age. Previous studies have investigated the task-switching model in children of this age (e.g., Towse et al., 1998). By the age of 8 years, we can expect that many children will be using articulatory rehearsal to support at least some memory tasks (Henry & Millar, 1993), making it feasible to examine rehearsal in different situations. Furthermore, the ages represent an important period for the development of reading and number skills at the upper end of primary school, allowing us to examine the role of memory in this development.

In summary, the present study compares STM and WM across development in terms of absolute measures and intercorrelations between variables. "General" reasoning and more specific reading and maths performance provided target skills to be explained. Three primary issues were addressed. First, if WM differs from STM among children because the former incorporates a processing element, then controlling for WM processing differences should make the tasks comparable. In contrast, if WM is inherently different, then it should retain its predictive power. Second, if WM is a better predictor of ability because it represents a "purer" measure of temporary memory not confounded by individual differences in rehearsal strategies, then WM and STM performed with articulatory suppression should predict ability better than a standard STM task. Third, if controlled attention mediates the relationship between measures of temporary memory and ability, then backward recall tasks should correlate more highly with ability than forward recall tasks.

METHOD

Design and participants

A mixed design involved age (8 and 11 years) and testing order (using Latin square design) as between-subjects variables, with memory span (STM, WM, and STMAS—STM with articulatory suppression) and recall order (forward and backward) as within-subject variables. Parental consent was obtained for 58 children from two age groups, reflecting class assignment, while full datasets are available for 54. There were 29 "8 years-olds", mean age 7 years 7 months, ranging 7;1 to 8;1. There were 25 "11 year-olds" mean age 10 years 9 months, ranging 10;3 to 11;3.

Apparatus and materials

A single experimenter conducted all trials. A Macintosh Powerbook 5300c computer presented all the memory tasks, which commenced with two items to remember. There were three trials available at each list length and provided two of these were recalled correctly, sequence length increased by one item and testing continued to a maximum length of eight items. Testing stopped when children made errors on more than one trial at a sequence length. The experimenter entered children's recall responses via an external keyboard.

Short-term memory

Stimulus items were single digit numbers, generated by random selection without replacement. They appeared in black type, approximately 2 cm high, within red rectangles, behind which were drawn partially occluded rectangles representing subsequent stimuli. Digits remained on-screen for 1 second with 0.5 second inter-stimulus intervals.

Working memory

Stimulus problems appeared in black type (within red rectangles, behind which outline edges of subsequent problems could be partially seen) approximately 2 cm high in the format $a + b = c$, where c was the to-be-remembered number and a and b were numbers between 0 and 14. Problems were selected at random without replacement for each trial, from a pool of 100 sums with 10 problms for each numerical answer from 1–9 (with a total of 37 addition and 63 subtraction sums).

Recall conditions

The computer cued serial order recall with a screen comprising yellow rectangles (n = list-length for that trial) and a moving blue question mark, as shown in Figure 1. On forward recall trials, the question mark symbol moved successively downwards after each response was entered, whereas on backward recall trials the question mark symbol moved in the opposite direction.

Ability measures

There were three ability measures: Raven's Standard Progressive Matrices ("matrices") (Raven, Court, & Raven, 1990), BAS Single Word Reading Test ("reading"), and BAS Basic Number Skills Test ("number") (Elliott, 1983). Matrices and reading tests required verbal responses (written down by the experimenter) and number tests involved subjects' individually written responses.

Procedure

Each child was initially informed that they would be playing a variety of games over the forthcoming weeks, and then completed four sessions. Two sessions involved a memory task followed by an ability task, one session involved a memory task alone, and one session involved the number test alone. All sessions took place individually in a quiet room except for the number test which children completed in their class. Session order, recall instruction order, and the pairing of ability and memory tasks were counterbalanced as equally as possible.

The experimenter initially explained each game using laminated practice cards to illustrate the computer screens. The experimenter repeated this explanation if subject made any errors on a practice trial. Satisfied that the child understood the task, the experimenter initiated a "Get Ready" instruction in the centre of the screen. Following a manual key press by the experimenter, the first trial commenced.

STM trials required children to read the numbers silently as they appeared on the screen. Children repeated the phrase "la la" throughout the presentation phase of STMAS trials. The experimenter gave an example of the suppression speed required (i.e., normal speech pace) and informally monitored children's repetition speed. On WM tasks, children silently read through each sum as soon as it appeared, and gave their answer out loud so that the experimenter could type this into the computer. Children recalled the items in forward or backward order, with recall order tests blocked together. Children began recall as soon as

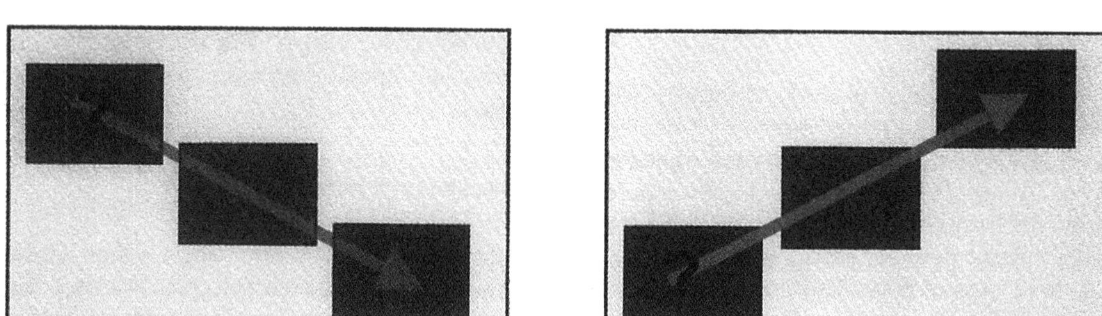

Figure 1. Recall cues for forward and backward order tasks in lists of three items. Arrows indicate direction of cue movement.

they saw the on-screen cue. It was emphasised that it would be easy to forget items and in these cases children should offer a "don't know" response. The experimenter typed children's verbal responses into the computer, which provided visual feedback following each trial. If a child gave more than two incorrect answers to the sums in the WM task, a reminder to solve the sums accurately appeared below the recall feedback.

RESULTS

Visual inspection of the standard deviations, skewness, and kurtosis values for the memory and ability measures indicated satisfactory distribution profiles for most variables. However, reading scores exhibited considerable skew: further inspection identified two extreme values (year 1 case, $z = 3.22$; year 2 case, $z = 3.67$) and as this appeared to be a specific reading problem for these participants, they were excluded from analyses. Re-examination of the descriptive statistics for the remaining participants indicated much improved skewness and kurtosis values. As reported in Table 1, older children obtained significantly higher ability scores than younger children; for matrices, $F(1,51) = 26.50$; $p < .001$, reading, $F(1,51) = 16.26$; $p < .001$, and number, $F(1,51) = 40.01$; $p < .001$.

TABLE 1
Mean ability scores for 8 and 11-year-olds

Age group	*Matrices (total score 60)*	*Reading (total score 90)*	*Number (total score 34)*
8-year-olds	25.4 (8.49)	67.9 (15.0)	16.1 (5.86)
11-year-olds	37.3 (8.08)	80.8 (4.8)	24.3 (2.59)

(n = 52) Standard deviations in parentheses.

Span was estimated following the procedure in Towse et al. (1998). Thus, each score represents the maximum sequence length where recall was correct on 2/3 trials, plus a fraction based on the quality of recall at the next, terminal, level. Overall, as shown in Table 2, older children reached significantly higher span scores, $F(1,46) = 26.08$; $p < .001$[1]. There were also significant differences between memory tasks, $F(2,92) = 50.21$; $p < .001$, and a significant task by year group interaction, $F(2,92) = 3.68$; $p < .05$—older children obtained significantly higher recall on all the memory tasks (all six *ps* < .05 or better[2]) and the age differences were particularly apparent in the WM tasks.

Forward recall yielded higher spans than backward recall, $F(1,46) = 59.79$; $p < .001$, and there was a significant memory task by recall instruction interaction, $F(2,92) = 12.57$; $p < .001$. While forward span was higher than backward span for STM, $t(51) = 7.18$; $p < .05$, and WM, $t(51) = 6.77$; $p < .05$, the difference was not significant for STMAS, $t(51) = 2.06$; ns. There was no significant recall by year interaction, $F(1,46) < 1$. The three-way interaction between recall, task, and year group was also non-significant, $F(2,92) < 1$. Between-task comparisons confirmed that WM scores were significantly lower than STM scores for forward and backward recall, $t(51) = 9.23$; $p < .05$ and $t(51) = 9.59$; $p < .05$ respectively. Articulatory suppression significantly reduced STM scores for forward, $t(51) = 6.37$; $p < .05$, but not backward recall, $t(51) = 2.55$, ns. WM scores were lower than STMAS, a non-significant difference for forward recall, $t(51) = 0.94$, but significant for backward recall, $t(51) = 6.47$; $p < .05$.

TABLE 2
Mean memory span scores for 8- and 11-year-olds

	STM		*STMAS*		*WM*	
Age group	*Forward*	*Backward*	*Forward*	*Backward*	*Forward*	*Backward*
8-year-olds	4.82 (0.88)	3.77 (0.60)	3.68 (0.83)	3.51 (0.77)	3.28 (1.3)	2.42 (0.81)
11-year-olds	5.37 (0.88)	4.60 (0.79)	4.52 (1.00)	4.24 (0.75)	4.6 (1.16)	3.58 (0.97)

(n = 52) Standard deviations in parentheses.

[1] All probability statements incorporate Greenhouse-Geisser corrected values where the Mauchly sphericity test was significant.

[2] Bonferroni corrections were used throughout.

Although the main effect of test-administration order was non-significant, there was a significant interaction between order and task, $F(4, 92) = 3.48$; $p < .05$. WM performance appeared to vary little across test order, whereas STM was lower when it appeared as the first test. All other interactions involving order were non-significant ($ps < .05$).

Analyses of individual differences

Table 3 reports the correlation matrix of the relationship between all variables (three ability measures, six memory tasks, age, and processing time). The lower panel, in italics, displays the partial correlations between the measures when controlling for age[3], where it is apparent that controlling for this variable depressed the associations. STM and WM span measures correlated significantly with all three ability measures. Furthermore, WM scores showed stronger relationships with ability than STM scores, although statistical comparison of correlations (Clark-Carter, 1997) indicated that differences reached significance for number skills only, $t(49) = 1.89$; $p < .05$, 1-tailed test. Articulatory suppression improved the relationship between STM and ability although differences were not significant; for matrices, $t(49) = 0.88$; ns, reading, $t(49) = 0.45$, and number, $t(49) = 1.11$; ns.

The role of processing time

One question motivating the present study was the influence of processing time as a possible explanation for the commonly found predictive advantage of WM tests over STM tests. Thus, the partial correlations between WM and ability, having controlled for age and processing time, were calculated in order to assess the role of processing time as a mediator in the WM–ability relationship. Table 4 reports these statistics (central column). WM for forward recall order still correlated with reading but not with number or matrices. A similar pattern was observed with backward recall. Note than in each case, the relationships are left *weaker* than the corresponding value between STM and ability with age partialled out (right-hand column). The same conclusion is reached when processing time only (i.e., not age) is partialled out of the WM associations $r(49) = .43$, $p < .01$, $r(49) = .25$ respectively, for these values are in the direction of being smaller than those between STM and ability.

To consider the relationship between the various memory tasks and ability measures, a number of hierarchical multiple regressions were conducted. By controlling the entry of variables, it was possible to assess the extent to which memory tasks explain unique variance in an ability measure.

TABLE 3
Bivariate correlations between ability measures and memory tasks for all children

	Matrices	*Reading*	*Number*	*STMF*	*STMB*	*STMASF*	*STMASB*	*WMF*	*WMB*	*TIME*	*AGE*
Matrices		.52**	.62**	.43**	.53**	.55**	.52**	.53**	.55**	−.75**	.63**
Reading	*.30***		.67**	.51**	.46**	.57**	.39**	.59**	.58**	−.56**	.50**
Number	*.33**	*.52***		.44**	.69**	.59**	.55**	.52**	.58**	−.71**	.68**
STMF	*.36**	*.45***	*.38***		.42**	.29*	.34*	.76**	.47**	−.41**	.26*
STMB	*.32**	*.28**	*.55***	*.35**		.44**	.44**	.53**	.56**	−.45**	.50**
STMASF	*.38***	*.44***	*.43***	*.20ns*	*.27**		.65**	.37**	.30*	−.58**	.46**
STMASB	*.34**	*.21ns*	*.38***	*.25ns*	*.28**	*.54***		.43**	.48**	−.58**	.45**
WMF	*.35**	*.48***	*.33**	*.74***	*.40***	*.21ns*	*.28**		.71**	−.51**	.44**
WMB	*.31**	*.43***	*.34**	*.41***	*.40***	*.07ns*	*.31**	*.62***		−.60**	.55**
TIME	*−.57***	*−.36***	*−.49***	*−.33**	*−.20ns*	*−.42***	*−.43***	*−.33**	*−.38***		*−.65***

(n = 52)
** Correlation is significant at the .01 level (2-tailed).
* Correlation is significant at the .05 level (2-tailed).
Type in italics represents correlation coefficients with age partialled.

[3] Statistical significance involves 2-tailed tests unless otherwise stated.

TABLE 4
The role of processing time in the memory–ability relationships

Ability task	*WM–ability relationships*		*STM–ability relationships*
	Age partialled	*Age and time partialled*	*Age partialled*
MATRICES	**0.35**	0.14	**0.36**
READING	**0.48**	**0.41**	**0.45**
NUMBER	**0.33**	0.20	**0.38**

Bold type indicates significant correlation coefficients.

For matrices, with age on the first step and the memory tasks blocked by recall order on steps 2 and 3, neither forward recall tasks together, Change $R^2 = 0.05$; $F(3, 44) = 1.61$; ns, nor backward recall tasks together, Change $R^2 = 0.02$; $F(3, 44) = 1.68$; ns, contributed any additional variance to matrices when entered last. With separate treatment of recall order conditions, only the STMASf measure contributed unique variance to matrices when entered after other variables, Change $R^2 = 0.06$; $F(1, 47) = 5.78$; $p < .05$.

Analyses of reading showed significant effects of entering both forward recall tasks last, Change $R^2 = 0.14$; $F(3, 44) = 4.82$; $p < .001$, and both backward recall tasks last, Change $R^2 = 0.08$; $F(3, 44) = 2.91$; $p < .05$. With separate treatment of recall order tasks, STMASf, Change $R^2 = 0.09$; $F(1, 47) = 8.40$; $p < .01$, and WMb, Change $R^2 = 0.08$; $F(1, 47) = 6.03$; $p < .05$, added variance when entered last. Analysis of number indicated backward recall but not forward recall tasks contributed unique variance to number when entered last, Change $R^2 = 0.09$; $F(3, 44) = 4.11$; $p < .05$, Change $R^2 = 0.04$; $F(3, 44) = 1.88$; ns, respectively. Separate recall order analyses showed STMASf, Change $R^2 = 0.07$; $F(1, 47) = 8.36$; $p < .01$, and STMb, Change $R^2 = 0.09$; $F(1, 47) = 11.91$; $p < .005$, contributed unique variance to number skill.

TABLE 5
The role of rehearsal in the memory–ability relationship

	STM Forward	*STM Backward*
Matrices	**Change $R^2 = 0.06$; $F(1, 48) = 6.27$; $p < .05$**	Change $R^2 = 0.04$; $F(1, 48) = 4.06$; $p = .05$
Reading	**Change $R^2 = 0.10$; $F(1, 48) = 9.11$; $p < .05$**	Change $R^2 = 0.02$; $F(1, 48) = 1.06$; ns
Number	**Change $R^2 = 0.07$; $F(1, 48) = 8.78$; $p < .01$**	**Change $R^2 = 0.03$; $F(1, 48) = 4.22$; $p < .05$**

Summary of multiple regression statistics.
Bold type indicates STMAS contributed significant variance to ability measures.

The role of rehearsal

The contrast between the predictive success of STMS and STMAS illuminated the role of rehearsal in the memory–ability relationships. Table 5 displays the relevant statistical effects. After age on the first step and STM on the second step, STMAS on the third step did contribute significant variance in matrices scores under forward recall, whereas for backward recall the effect was marginal. In similar regression models, STMAS also explained unique variance in reading for the forward but not backward recall tasks, as well as unique variance in number skills for both recall orders.

The role of attention

The importance of recall order instructions on the predictive power of the memory tests is illustrated in Table 6. In the case of STM, with age entered on the first step and forward recall on the second

TABLE 6
The role of attentional demands in the memory–ability relationship

	STM	*STMAS*	*WM*
Matrices	Change $R^2 = 0.03$; $F(1, 48) = 2.45$; ns	Change $R^2 = 0.01$; $F(1, 48) = 1.37$; ns	Change $R^2 = 0.01$; $F(1, 48) = 0.76$; ns
Reading	Change $R^2 = 0.01$; $F(1, 48) = 1.00$; ns	Change $R^2 = 0.00$; $F(1, 48) = 0.10$; ns	Change $R^2 = 0.02$; $F(1, 48) = 1.73$; ns
Number	**Change $R^2 = 0.11$; $F(1, 48) = 14.42$; $p < .001$**	Change $R^2 = 0.02$; $F(1, 48) = 1.67$; ns	Change $R^2 = 0.02$; $F(1, 48) = 1.76$; ns

Summary of multiple regression statistics.
Bold type indicates that backward recalled tasks contributed significant variance.

step, backward recall then contributed significant additional variance to number skills but not matrices or reading. In the case of WM and STMAS, backward recall did not contribute significant additional variance after forward recall on any of the three ability measures. Furthermore, entering instead forward recall after backward recall, there were significant effects with STM, STMAS, and WM in the prediction of reading, Change $R^2 = 0.11$; $F(1, 48) = 8.72$; $p < .05$, Change $R^2 = 0.11$; $F(1, 48) = 8.91$; $p < .05$, and Change $R^2 = 0.06$; $F(1, 48) = 4.89$; $p < .05$ respectively. Forward recall STMAS also contributed significant variance over backward recall in predicting number, Change $R^2 = 0.04$; $F(1, 48) = 4.27$; $p < .05$.

Developmental change and individual differences

Within the experimental design, it was possible to examine separately younger and older children's individual differences in the prediction of target skills, as well as assess the role of age as a mediating variable in the regression analyses. In most cases results were consistent in both age groups, although there were some age-related changes too, and intimations that STM tasks showed more developmental sensitivity than the WM tasks (which might reflect differing reliance on rehearsal across the age groups). At the same time, inconsistencies and lack of significance in some of the findings, attributable in part to the loss of experimental power, make strong interpretation problematic (a full set of age-specific analyses can be obtained from the first author).

Overview

The preceding analyses describe a data set in which many of the variables interrelate, and yet the measures are clearly not interchangeable. To provide an additional perspective on memory performance, principal components and factor analyses were conducted. The Kaiser-Meyer-Olkin measure of sampling adequacy was 0.734, suggesting that such analyses are appropriate (Field, 2000) even though based on a small dataset. Principal components analysis extracted two components on the basis of substantial eigenvalues, which together explained 74.1% of variance. This two-factor solution structure kept forward and backward tasks together, but distinguished STMAS (comprising one component) from STM and WM (both comprising another component); loadings afer varimax rotation are presented in the Appendix. It is worth noting that unweighted and generalised least squares, maximum likelihood, principal axis factoring, alpha factoring, and image factoring extraction techniques all produced essentially comparable two-factor patterns, emphasising the stability of the solution. In summary, the analyses converge with preceding results to indicate articulatory suppression makes short-term memory more, not less, distinct from WM.

DISCUSSION

To summarise, analysis showed substantial developmental improvement across a range of memory tasks. Standard STM tasks yielded the highest span while WM tasks yielded the lowest in both age groups. With conventional recall instructions articulatory suppression reduced STM performance to that of WM. Many of the variables intercorrelated. The zero-order correlations confirmed previous reports that WM tends to correlate more highly with ability measures than does STM. However, controlling for individual differences in the arithmetic processing task eliminated this advantage to WM tasks. Some analyses also showed that backward recall and articulatory suppression requirements made a difference to the characteristics of STM tasks.

It is important to acknowledge that the present analyses assume the various measures of memory have been estimated reliably, and to an equivalent extent. If one memory task measurement was less reliable than another, then clearly this could attenuate the relationship with ability scores. The present study, in common with many involving working memory span, did not collect test–retest reliability, so this issue cannot be addressed precisely (for exceptions with adults, see Klein & Fiss, 1999; Waters & Caplan, 1996. Hitch et al., in press, report data among children using multiple measures and a test–retest interval of 12 months). However, inspection of the correlations to identify the strongest association establishes a rough lower bound of reliability. Among forward order recall, WM and STM correlate .76 while STMAS in forward and backward recall order correlate .65. Clearly, therefore, all the tasks manifest the statistical potential for healthy correlations with ability.

The overlap between STM and WM and the mediating influence of processing time

WM correlated with all three ability measures. STM, in the form of a visually presented digit span task, also correlated with ability. Indeed, although the correlations involving STM were rather modest, they were robust and withstood partialling out of several other variables[4] (see also Towse & Houston-Price, in press, who report significant correlations between children's digit span and BAS achievement scores).

The present experiment allows a more detailed analysis of STM and WM, comparing these tasks after statistical control of individual differences in the processing component of working memory. Although it is often ignored, the present results confirm that among children, working memory processing time can act as an important mediator of ability (see also Hitch et al., in press). The results indirectly support the task-switching model of working memory span by showing how the temporal duration of the processing operation can influence span performance. The present analyses demonstrated that, having controlled for processing time and age, the relationships between STM and abilities were quantitatively *superior* to the WM scores (the direction of effect means this cannot be simply an issue of poor experimental power). Furthermore, WM measures no longer correlated with matrices or number after controlling for processing time.

Thus, the results illustrate the potential danger in ignoring the influence of processing time, as it may confound the relationships between children's memory *per se* and cognitive skill. At the same time, it is important to reiterate that these conclusions apply to children; among adults processing rate does not appear to account—at least directly—for span differences (Conway & Engle, 1996; Engle, Cantor, & Carullo, 1992; Towse et al., 2000). In the same vein, we note that the oft-reported superior predictive performance of WM tasks is most frequently based on a consideration of the adult, rather than developmental, literature and without controlling for differences in the processing task (e.g., Daneman & Carpenter, 1980; Daneman & Blennerhassett, 1984).

Articulatory rehearsal as a critical difference between STM and WM

One previous account of the differential relationships between WM and STM tasks and abilities proposes that conventional STM measures are confounded by a variety of strategies including rehearsal (Cantor et al., 1991; Cohen & Sandberg, 1980). It is possible that STM tasks afford greater opportunity for rehearsal during the inter-stimulus intervals and/or at the recall stage, as only one operation is required compared with two operations in WM tasks—processing *in addition* to retention. However, we believe it is also possible to argue the reverse case, the WM tasks may actually offer more opportunity for rehearsal. The scheduling of various aspects of the task is under the control of the subject and thus the opportunity exists to rehearse memoranda before beginning any subsequent processing operation.

Imposing articulatory suppression requirements during stimulus presentation largely blocked the opportunity for rehearsal on a STM task. If rehearsal normally masks the relationship between STM and ability, then not only would absolute span scores for STMAS be low, but also there would be a stronger relationship between STMAS and WM than between STM and WM. However, with age or with age and processing time partialled out, although there *were* significant correlations between the STM and WM tasks, there was no correlation between forward recall STMAS and either forward or backward recall WM tasks. Neither did STM correlate with forward or backward STMAS. Furthermore, of the forward recall tasks, only STMAS accounted for unique variance in all three ability measures. Thus, while they are related, preventing rehearsal on STM renders performance more different from rather than more similar to WM, a conclusion reinforced by the principal components analysis. That is, the STMAS tasks appear to be qualitatively different from both the WM and the STM tasks and also more predictive of children's ability.

One possible explanation for the pattern of findings is that articulatory suppression makes the STM task sensitive to how children manage the complex task requirements of interleaving encoding and maintenance operations with con-

[4] Although some children received a variant of STM—with articulatory suppression—prior to their STM test, analysis of just those children who performed STM first also demonstrated strong correlations between STM and abilities. It is therefore unlikely that the administration of two STM tasks is responsible for the present findings.

current articulation. At any rate, as WM and STM are more similar than WM and STMAS, and as STMAS is predictive of ability measures in instances where WM is not, we conclude that STM and WM cannot be distinguished merely by the presence of rehearsal in the former task. Instead, we suggest it is more plausible to assume that both STM and WM tasks involve rehearsal, and thus account for why STM with suppression behaved differently from both STM and WM. In summary, while support is obtained for the conclusion that rehearsal strategies may negatively impact on the relationship between short-term memory span and ability (Cantor et al., 1991), this does not fully describe the differences between memory tasks.

The controlled attention hypothesis of working memory

Engle et al. (1999a) argue that WM tasks involve controlled attentional processing. The present study manipulated this factor by requiring children to recall to-be-remembered items in forward or backward order. Backward recall has been demonstrated to be a more effortful task, possibly involving controlled attention. Engle et al. (1999b) have suggested that, although backward recall may involve increased attentional demands, it is not a good measure of adults' working memory because the procedures would be highly automatised. However, this argument does not necessarily hold true for children because sequencing the order of items might well involve greater attentional demands, being less proceduralised. Backward recall tasks produced lower span scores than their forward recall analogues (although not significant for the more poorly recalled STMAS), confirming the additional task difficulty. Yet the backward recall tasks were *not* universally more highly correlated with abilities. Neither forward nor backward recalled tasks together uniquely contributed significant variance to the explanation of matrices. Backward and not forward recall tasks uniquely predicted number skills, but both backward and forward recall tasks contributed significantly to reading skill. Furthermore, only backward recall STM contributed unique variance to any ability measure—for number—when entered after the forward recall analogue, whereas forward recall STMAS predicted number over the backward recall version. Thus, in certain cases forward recall tasks, with lower attentional demands, were more strongly related to ability measures than backward recall tasks.

The preceding conclusions again emphasise differences between memory tasks as well as specificity to skill and achievement domains, and suggest further that increasing "attentional demands" need not enhance the relationship between memory task and ability for children. In general, the supposedly most attention-demanding tasks, those with the greatest subjectively rated difficulty, were less strongly correlated with abilities. As alluded to in the introduction, it is always possible to respond that controlled attention was not appropriately manipulated. However, this rather begs the question of the value of the controlled attention construct and certainly emphasises the necessity to define the concept in a precise and non-circular way.

Overall, the present study stresses a number of important points in the conceptualisation of STM and WM. It appears that what holds for WM in adults may not be equally true for children, and vice versa. The study highlights the value of taking account of children's on-line processing during WM tasks, and in doing so suggests that among children WM and STM may, at least in some circumstances, be rather equivalent. Data suggest the locus of differences between STM and WM does not lie just in differential opportunity for rehearsal, because curtailing rehearsal in STM makes the task more different from, not more similar to, WM. It seems that a more complete description of the range of retention strategies and task characteristics is required to understand the relationship between memory tasks. A straightforward dichotomy between STM and WM represents a considerable oversimplification.

REFERENCES

Ashcraft, M.H. (1995). Cognitive psychology and simple arithmetic: A review and summary of new directions. *Mathematical Cognition*, *1*(1), 3–34.

Atkinson, R.C., & Shiffrin, R.M. (1968). Human memory: A proposed system and its control processes. In K.W. Spence & J.T. Spence (Eds.), *The psychology of learning and motivation: Advances in research and theory* (Vol 2, pp. 89–195). London: Academic Press.

Baddeley, A.D., & Hitch, G.J. (1974). Working memory. In G.H. Bower (Ed.), the psychology of learning and motivation. *Advances in research and theory* (Vol 8, pp. 47–89). London: Academic Press.

Baddeley, A.D., & Scott, D. (1971). Short-term forgetting in the absence of proactive inhibition. *Quarterly Journal of Experimental Psychology*, *23*, 275–283.

Cantor, J., Engle, R.W., & Hamilton, G. (1991). Short-term memory, working memory and verbal abilities: How do they relate? *Intelligence*, *15*, 229–246.

Case, R., Kurland, M.D., & Goldberg, J. (1982). Operational efficiency and the growth of short-term memory span. *Journal of Experimental Child Psychology*, *33*, 386–404.

Clark-Carter, D. (1997). *Doing quantitative psychological research: From design to report*. Hove, UK: Psychology Press.

Cohen, R.L., & Sandberg, T. (1980). Intelligence and short-term memory: A clandestine relationship. *Intelligence*, *4*, 319–331.

Conway, A.R.A., & Engle, R.W. (1996). Individual differences in working memory capacity: More evidence for a general capacity theory. *Memory*, *4*, 577–590.

Daneman, M., & Blennerhassett, A. (1984). How to assess the listening comprehension skills of pre-readers. *Journal of Educational Psychology*, *76*(6), 1372–1381.

Daneman, M., & Carpenter, P.A. (1980). Individual differences in working memory and reading. *Journal of Verbal Learning and Verbal Behavior*, *19*, 450–466.

Daneman, M., & Carpenter, P.A. (1983). Individual differences in integrating information between and within sentences. *Journal of Experimental Psychology: Learning, Memory and Cognition*, *9*, 561–584.

Daneman, M., & Tardif, T. (1987). Working memory and reading skill reexamined. In M. Coltheart (Ed.), *Attention and performance XII: The psychology of reading* (pp 491–508). Hove, UK: Lawrence Erlbaum Associates Ltd.

Elliot, C.D. (1983). *British Abilities Scale, Technical manual*. Windsor, UK: NFER-Nelson.

Elliott, C.D., Smith, P., & McCulloch, K. (1997). *British Ability Scales II. Technical manual*. Windsor, UK: NFER-Nelson.

Engle, R.W., Cantor, J., & Carullo, J.J. (1992). Individual differences in working memory and comprehension: A test of four hypotheses. *Journal of Experimental Psychology: Learning, Memory and Cognition*, *18*, 972–992.

Engle, R.W., Kane, M.J., & Tuholski, S.W. (1999a). Individual differences in working memory capacity and what they tell us about controlled attention, general fluid intelligence, and functions of the pre-frontal cortex. In A. Miyake & P. Shah (Eds.), *Models of working memory: Mechanisms of active maintenance and active control* (pp. 102–134). Cambridge: Cambridge University Press.

Engle, R.W., Tuholski, S.W., Laughlin, J.E., & Conway, A.R.A. (1999b). Working memory, short-term memory and general fluid intelligence: A latent variable approach. *Journal of Experimental Psychology: General*, *128*, 309–331.

Field, A. (2000). *Discovering statistics using SPSS for Windows*. London: Sage.

Gathercole, S. (1999). Cognitive approaches to the development of short-term memory. *Trends in Cognitive Science*, *3*(11), 410–418.

Gathercole, S.E., & Pickering, S.J. (2000). Working memory deficits in children with low achievements in the national curriculum at 7 years of age. *British Journal of Educational Psychology*, *70*, 177–194.

Groeger, J.A., Field, D., & Hammond, S.M. (1999). Measuring memory span. *International Journal of Psychology*, *34*(5/6), 359–363.

Henry, L.A., & Millar, S. (1993). Why does memory span improve with age? A review of the evidence for two current hypotheses. *European Journal of Cognitive Psychology*, *5*(3), 241–287.

Hitch, G.J., Halliday, M.S., Schaafstal, A.M., & Schraagen, J.M.C. (1988). Visual working memory in young children. Memory and Cognition, *16*, 120–132.

Hitch, G.J., Towse, J.N., & Hutton, U. (in press). What limits working memory span? Theoretical accounts and applications for scholastic development. *Journal of Experimental Psychology: General*.

King, J., & Just, M.A. (1991). Individual differences in syntactic processing: The role of working memory. *Journal of Memory and Language*, *30*, 580–602.

Klein, K., & Fiss, W.H. (1999). The reliability and stability of the Turner and Engle working memory task. *Behavior, Research Methods, Instruments, & Computers*, *31*(3), 429–432.

Kyllonen, P.C., & Christal, R.E. (1990). Reasoning ability is (little more than) working-memory capacity?! *Intelligence*, *14*, 389–433.

Laming, D. (1999). Testing the idea of distinct storage mechanisms in memory. *International Journal of Psychology*, *34*(5/6), 419–426.

Leather, C.V., & Henry, L.A. (1994). Working memory span and phonological awareness tasks as predictors of early reading ability. *Journal of Experimental Child Psychology*, *58*, (1), 88–111.

Logie, R.H., Gilhooly, K.J., & Wynn, V. (1994). Counting on working memory in mental arithmetic. *Memory and Cognition*, *22*, 395–410.

MacDonald, J.M.A., Just, M.A., & Carpenter, P.A. (1992). Working memory constraints on the processing of syntactic ambiguity. *Cognitive Psychology*, *24*, 56–98.

Melton, A.W. (1963). Implications of short-term memory for a general theory of memory. *Journal of Verbal Learning and Verbal Behavior*, *2*, 1–21.

Miyake, A., & Shah, P. (1999). Toward unified theories of working memory: Emerging general consensus, unresolved theoretical issues and future directions. In A. Miyake & P. Shah (Eds.), *Models of working memory: Mechanisms of active maintenance and executive control* (pp. 442–481). Cambridge: Cambridge University Press.

Perfetti, C.A., & Lesgold, A.M. (1977). Discourse comprehension and sources of individual differences. In M.A. Just & P.A. Carpenter (Eds.), *Cognitive processes in comprehension*. Hillsdale, NJ: Lawrence Erlbaum Associates Inc.

Raven, J.C., Court, J.F., & Raven, J. (1990). *Standard progressive matrices*. Oxford: Oxford Psychologists Press.

Rosen, V.M., & Engle, R.W. (1997). The role of working memory capacity in retrieval. *Journal of Experimental Psychology: General*, *126*, 211–227.

Towse, J.N., & Hitch, G.J. (1995). Is there a relationship between task demand and storage space in tests of working memory? *Quarterly Journal of Experimental Psychology*, *48*A(1), 108–124.

Towse, J.N., Hitch, G.J., & Hutton, U. (1998). A reevaluation of working memory capacity in children. *Journal of Memory and Language*, *39*, 195–217.

Towse, J.N., Hitch, G.J., & Hutton, U. (2000). On the interpretation of working memory span in adults. *Memory and Cognition*, *28*, 341–348.

Towse, J.N., & Houston-Price, C.M.T. (in press). Combining representations in working memory: A brief report. *British Journal of Developmental Psychology*.

Turner, M.L., & Engle, R.W. (1989). Is working memory capacity task dependent? *Journal of Memory and Language*, *28*, 127–154.

Shallice, T., & Warrington, E.K. (1970). Independent functioning of verbal memory stores: A neuropsychological study. *Quarterly Journal of Experimental Psychology*, *22*, 261–273.

Waters, G.S., & Caplan, D. (1996). The measurement of verbal working memory capacity and its relation to reading comprehension. *Quarterly Journal of Experimental Psychology*, *49*A(1), 51–70.

APPENDIX

Component loadings from Principal Components Analysis of memory scores, with varimax rotation.

Component	*1*	2
STM (forward)	.844	.097
STM (backward)	.586	.471
WM (forward)	.905	.219
WM (backward)	.771	.296
STMAS (forward)	.144	.896
STMAS (backward)	.268	.846

MEMORY, 2001, 9 (4/5/6), 395–421

Working memory in spelling: Evidence from backward typing

Elisabet Service and Raija Turpeinen
University of Helsinki, Finland

Theories of spelling (Margolin, 1984; Nolan & Caramazza, 1983) propose a working memory system for storing order and identity information of letters during the spelling process. Capacity limitations related to the use of such a graphemic buffer were explored. Participants had to type words backwards. Longer pauses between key presses were assumed to signal points at which graphemic buffer contents were refreshed. Five- and six-letter words were divided by a major pause into chunks of two and three letters, partly coinciding with syllables. Articulatory suppression had no effect on performance. Increasing the length of the stimuli to seven to eight letters resulted in major pauses occurring at syllable boundaries, and performance becoming vulnerable to articulatory suppression but not foot tapping. Forward typing resulted in a similar pause pattern. The results suggest that chunks of approximately three letters can be handled at any one time. For short words the task seems to rely on non-phonological modes of coding, whereas longer words appear to require the use of a phonological code, possibly for keeping track of progress through the word.

This study attempts to look at online spelling in terms of processes in working memory (WM) that activate relevant knowledge in long-term memory (LTM), i.e. orthographic knowledge, and control spelling output (in this case typing). In terms of the WM framework put forward by Baddeley and Hitch (Baddeley, 1992, 1986; Baddeley & Hitch, 1974), we conclude that all three WM components: the phonological loop, concerned with phonologically coded information, the visuo-spatial sketchpad, concerned with spatial information, and the central executive, concerned with WM process management, have a role to play.

The empirical evidence derives from a task of backward spelling. This task should activate orthographical word representations in LTM in a similar way as forward spelling. However, read-out from these representations for output production could be different, as no familiar chunks are available for either processing letter sequence knowledge or producing chunked motor output. If chunking is not needed, and the word representations can be handled as orthographic wholes, spelling should proceed at an even pace with more or less invariable pause-length between produced letters. If chunking is normally employed in the spelling process then backward spelling should be slowed down, as either backward chunks have to be formed on the fly, or the letter order in forward chunks has to be reversed. In both cases, boundaries of chunks should be revealed by pauses in output. We analysed pauses between letters to find out WM capacity limitations in spelling (i.e., the need for chunks). In addition, we used secondary tasks to explore the involvement of different WM components in spelling.

Neuropsychological theories of spelling propose that a working memory system for storing order and identity information of letters is used during spelling (Caramazza, Miceli, Villa, &

Requests for reprints should be sent to Elisabet Service, Department of Psychology, P.O. Box 13 (Meritullinkatu 1), FIN-00014 Helsinki, Finland. Email: elisabet.service@helsinki.fi

This study was supported by the Academy of Finland (grants 39253 and 74080 to the first author). We wish to thank Jussi Piitulainen at the Department of Linguistics, University of Helsinki, for help with sampling stimulus words from a large magazine corpus.

http://www.tandf.co.uk/journals/pp/09658211.html DOI:10.1080/09658210143000137

Romani, 1987; Margolin, 1984; Miceli, Silveri, & Caramazza, 1985; Nolan & Caramazza, 1983). In the writing process this graphemic (or orthographic) buffer is assumed to receive information from more central components of the writing system. These central components produce spellings along two or three routes: a phonological sublexical route, depending on phoneme–grapheme conversion from phonological representations, and possibly two lexical routes relying on LTM orthographic whole-word representations: one directly connected to output representations and one reaching output via semantic representations (Margolin, 1984). The graphemic buffer receives output from the central spelling processes, and is in turn thought to feed information about letter ordering to more peripheral processing stages, determining physical output, like letter shapes, typing responses, oral letter names, or other spelling responses. Lately, the graphemic buffer has also been related to reading performance (Caramazza, Capasso, & Miceli, 1996). The quality and modality of graphemic buffer representations remains an empirical question. Patients thought to suffer from a defective graphemic buffer typically show error patterns sensitive to letter position in strings, as well as to string length, but not to lexical factors like word frequency or imageability (e.g., Hillis & Caramazza, 1989; Posteraro, Zinelli, & Mazzucchi, 1988). Longer strings give rise to more errors for these patients. The positioning of the errors depends on the type of graphemic buffer dysfunction the patient has. Two patients, described as suffering from, in one case a left-lateralised and in the other a right-lateralised, disruption of attention affecting the reading from an "inner screen" created by the graphemic buffer, selectively made errors at the beginnings or the ends of words, respectively (Caramazza & Hillis, 1990; Hillis & Caramazza, 1989). Other patients thought to suffer from graphemic buffer dysfunction have typically produced errors predominantly occurring in the middle region of words (Caramazza et al., 1987; Posteraro et al., 1988). Letters in middle positions also seem to be most vulnerable to slips of the pen in normal participants (Wing & Baddeley, 1980). However, as the capacity of the graphemic buffer in normal participants is not known it is unclear whether words of different lengths can justifiably be included in the same analysis of error positions, as they were in the Wing and Baddeley study.

Information on the capacity limitations under which spelling proceeds after a graphemic buffer representation has been created is presently not available. Such information is in fact not available for any part of the spelling process, as limits on amount of information flow or decay functions are not known for the different storage and processing components believed to contribute to performance. Attempts to assess the kind of capacity that might be involved when the contents of the graphemic buffer are being processed have, however, been made outside writing research. Zhang and Simon (1985) explored STM capacity for different kinds of Chinese writing symbols. In Chinese logographic script most words are presented by composite signs consisting of two graphic characters, each pronounced as one syllable. Graphically, characters consist of so-called radicals and some additional parts. There are slightly more than 200 different radicals. Readers of Chinese are familiar with all the radicals. However, most radicals have no pronounceable names. This makes it possible to use semantic radicals as material in testing Chinese speakers' memory for familiar visual symbols that are not pronounceable. In Zhang and Simon's experiments mean span for unrelated semantic radicals was 2.7, while mean span for the visually more complicated but pronounceable characters was 6.4, and that for whole words 3.8. Thus span for pronounceable material seemed to depend on spoken length, as has been found for phonologically coded material in many experiments (Baddeley, Thomson, & Buchanan, 1975). Span for the unpronounceable radicals was considerably lower, suggesting a capacity limit of 2–3 familiar items, possibly stored in the visuo-spatial sketchpad. If the graphemic buffer relies on representations similar to those used in the span task with radicals, we have to assume that the graphemic representations for most alphabetic words exceed either its capacity for storage or for the read-out processes necessary for further preparation of the spelling response. If that is the case the spelling process must require that longer letter strings be broken up into smaller chunks for the reproduction of letter order.

Another experiment relevant to capacity limitations for producing ordered letter strings investigated copy-typing. Inhoff and Wang (1992) studied eye movements during copy-typing under various conditions. They concluded that the so-called keystroke span, consisting of three characters to the right of fixation, reflects the number of identified letters in the process of being translated into manual movements. A smaller window than three letters slows typing down. Possibly, the keystroke span depends on a representational format used in the graphemic buffer. The capacity of this type of letter-order information comes very close to the short-term memory span for unpronounceable, but familiar, Chinese characters, reported by Zhang and Simon. The question for spelling is, thus, to what extent does performance depend on graphemic buffer capacity limitations and are these limitations the same as those affecting the remembering of unpronounceable graphic symbols and the translating of visual symbols into manual movements in typing?

The work presented here attempts to explore graphemic buffer capacity using a backward spelling task. Backward spelling of familiar words is assumed to first proceed like forward spelling to create a letter order representation in the graphemic buffer. If the buffer is limited in capacity only part of the word may be represented at any one point in time. A graphemic buffer capacity limitation would probably be reflected in LTM orthographic representations so that these would consist of letter chunks of an optimal size for the buffer. Such chunks could then be loaded into the buffer at the same time as letter sequences already fully programmed were being written. This would make it difficult to use pauses in production to detect spelling chunk boundaries. In backward spelling any stored letter chunks within words could not be used without reversing the letter order in them. This reversal process can be expected to create a detectable pause in writing. Such pauses could thus mark the chunks that are represented in the graphemic buffer. It is also possible that the graphemic buffer has the capacity to represent whole words, but that the read-out process from this buffer to motor programming is of limited capacity and that WM has to alternate between "looking" at the graphemic representation and programming output. This would again result in pauses marking letter groupings programmed in one go. In forward writing such alternation would deal with familiar chunks and could be fast enough to overlap with motor production, so no pauses could be detected. In backward spelling new "backward chunks" would have to be created, which would presumably be time-consuming enough to cause pauses in motor output.

The backward spelling task has previously been used for the study of visual imagery (Hampson & Morris, 1978; Wippich, Mecklenbräuker, & Halfter, 1989). Based on a series of oral forward and backward spelling experiments Hampson and Morris argued that backward spelling consists of a process of image generation and directed scanning. For long words the process of image generation is assumed to be repeated during the spelling process so that a refreshed image of the word is achieved.

The WM model by Baddeley and Hitch proposes three components: a visuo-spatial sketchpad to store visual and spatial information, a phonological loop for maintaining phonologically coded verbal information, and a capacity-limited central executive for managing processing and information maintenance in the two modality-specific components. Lately, a modality-neutral episodic buffer component has been added to deal with temporarily activated material from LTM (Baddeley, 2000). Although backward spelling has previously been used to tap visuo-spatial processing, it is quite possible that the spelling process recruits other WM systems as well. In a review of typing research, Viviani and Terzuolo (1983) conclude that pronounceability rather than familiarity (lexical status) of material affects patterns in typing. In our study, we used articulatory suppression (repetition of a meaningless syllable) as a secondary task to probe phonological-loop involvement in the backward spelling task.

We studied a variant of the backward spelling task that involved typing. We assumed that longer pauses between key presses while typing words backwards indicated when the graphemic buffer was loaded or refreshed by image generation or some other process. Whether consistent pauses do occur in such a task was explored by subjecting the times between key presses to a cluster analysis and to a subsequent analysis of variance. Even-length pauses between letters would be indicative of a smoothly proceeding read-out from a stable representation in the buffer, whereas consistent grouping of letters between longer pauses could be thought to reflect a buffer-reloading process, and to give us an estimate of the number of letters that could be handled without refreshing the graphemic buffer contents. Alternatively, letter grouping could reflect the size of the chunks that can be read out from the graphemic buffer in one go. We will return to this alternative interpretation for letter grouping in backward typing in the general discussion. For now all hypotheses will be formulated in terms of storage rather than processing capacity.

In a pilot experiment we explored 10-letter words, which were expected to almost certainly exceed buffer or read-out capacity. Hampson and Morris (1978) found that backward spelling times per letter were longer for eight-letter words than four-letter words. They interpreted this as a sign of the longer words exceeding buffer capacity and therefore requiring refreshing of the letter-order images during the spelling process. Also the results concerning memory for unpronounceable graphic symbols (Zhang & Simon, 1985) and the keystroke span in typing (Inhoff & Wang, 1992) suggest that 10-letter words exceed graphemic buffer capacity. We therefore thought that if a regular pattern of longer pauses in spelling words backwards was to be found, 10-letter words should show it. The results of an initial analysis of letter grouping did not look very encouraging from the point of view of finding chunks in the letter string. Clusters appeared tight only for the two letters typed first and the three letters typed last. However, when we analysed the three most frequently occurring syllable structures in our stimuli, we found letter groupings, mostly coinciding with syllables consisting of two or three letters. The attempt to use articulatory suppression as a secondary task had to be abandoned because of unacceptably high error rates.

Our first experiment focused on the working memory codes used in backward typing. If the task depends on phonological coding, performance should be impaired when a phonological secondary task has to be carried out concurrently with the typing. Based on our results in the pilot experiment we also wanted to find out if there was an effect of the syllabic structure of the words to be spelled. Hampson and Morris (1978) had found that their participants spelled six-letter words backwards faster if these consisted of two syllables than if they only had one. This was thought to be the result of two-syllable words more readily lending themselves to being split into two strings of letters that could be separately generated if the whole word exceeded buffer capacity. We assumed that major pauses at syllable boundaries would signal stopping points for buffer reloading. Syllables would be natural sublexical units to be used in parsing the letter string, especially if phonological processing were involved in the task. The stimulus words in the first experiment were relatively short, five or six letters, to enable us to use articulatory suppression as a secondary task. The second experiment looked at words of intermediate length, i.e. seven to eight letters. The third experiment compared the effect of a foot-tapping task to that of articulatory suppression in the previous experiment in order to establish to what extent secondary-task interference is modality-independent. Finally, a fourth experiment explored pauses in forward typing of single items.

EXPERIMENT 1: FINNISH 5–6-LETTER WORDS

The results of the pilot experiment suggested that if graphemic representations were broken down during spelling the resulting units might be syllables, thus coinciding with familiar sublexical units from speech. We originally thought, as Hampson and Morris (1978), that backward spelling was a task mainly involving visual or spatial representations. However, our preliminary finding of letter grouping into syllables suggested that the phonological loop might, indeed, be involved as well. Phonological syllable boundaries are very salient to Finnish speakers. A rule that states that a consonant followed by a vowel starts a new syllable covers 90.8% of cases. The majority of the remaining cases are covered by five other rules, leaving only a few lexical exceptions (Karlsson, 1982). The Finnish orthography is almost fully transparent, with the consequence that phonological syllables have their orthographic parallels.

The effect of syllabic structure on backward typing was studied by using three kinds of Finnish two-syllable words. The words could consist of syllable structures with (i) 2 + 3 letters (ri + kos), (ii) 3 + 2 letters (kir + ja), and (iii) 4 + 2 letters (haus + ka). The effect of phonological coding was investigated by including a condition with articulatory suppression as a secondary task. In this the participants repeatedly pronounced the syllable "palah" (a Finnish equivalent to "blah"). Although the experiment is exploratory in nature, we started out with a number of tentative hypotheses. First, based on the pilot experiment and the literature reviewed earlier, we expected to find one relatively longer pause between typed letters, at least for the six-letter words, showing where participants stopped to refresh the graphemic buffer. If five-letter words were also longer than the buffer could handle, without its contents being refreshed while typing, they too should have at least one longer pause. An even distribution of the length of pauses between typed letters would be a sign of a smooth read-out from a buffer with no need for reloading during the task. Second, we thought that syllable boundaries would be likely to determine the positions of the generated pauses. This might be connected to the use of phonological coding, as syllables are primarily phonotactic units of word structure. However, in addition, the existence of special graphotactic syllables specific to writing (dealing with, for example, letters corresponding to silent sounds), and represented in the orthographic lexicon, has been argued by Caramazza and Miceli (1990). Third, we hypothesised that the representations used in the task would be either visual or abstract spatial because some patients' spatial attention disorders also affect their writing (Caramazza & Hillis, 1990; Hillis & Caramazza, 1989). In addition, if phonological coding were not needed, the articulatory suppression task should not interfere with backward spelling accuracy or time. Interference effects would point to phonological processes being involved.

Method

Participants. A total of 10 university students who reported being used to typing and being familiar with the 10-finger system were tested in the condition with two-syllable words without suppression, and 10 different participants in the condition with articulatory suppression. One participant in the no-suppression condition was subsequently dropped because of typing times twice as long as the mean.

Stimuli. The stimulus words to be spelled were common Finnish two-syllable content words with frequencies varying between 8 and 2303 in the Finnish frequency dictionary, which is based on a corpus of 480,301 word tokens (Saukkonen, Haipus, Niemikorpi, & Sulkala, 1979). There were 50 words of the 2 + 3-letter type, 50 words of the 3 + 2-letter type, and 50 words of the 4 + 2-letter type. Of the six-letter words 26 had a double consonant in letter positions 4 and 5. In addition, a 15-word practice list with two-syllable words was used.

Procedure. The participants sat in front of a PC screen. They were told that they would first see a fixation point in the middle of the screen. Shortly afterwards a word written in block capitals would replace the fixation point for a short time. As soon as they saw the word they should say it aloud and start typing it backwards. The words appeared in block capitals over a visual angle of 1.8 degrees for the five-letter words and 2.2 degrees for the six-letter words. The display times used were 2000 ms for the fixation point, 500 ms for the two-syllable words, and 500 ms for a mask consisting of Xs covering the words. This allowed comfortable word recognition with the pronunciation of the word preventing the participants from reading it backwards. The last letter that they had typed was always visible in a position below the midpoint of the row of Xs on the screen for a short while. When participants had finished typing a word they pressed the RETURN-key and a new fixation point appeared. In the condition with articulatory suppression the participants repeated "palah" starting as soon as they had pronounced the word and continuing till the word was typed. Performance was supervised by an experimenter who made sure that there were no pauses in the repeated articulation.

Scoring. Strings containing errors were removed from the analysis of writing times and their number divided by the number of words in the stimulus list was recorded as a *proportion of errors* for each participant and word type. A computer program recorded the times between the onset of the stimulus and the first key press, and subsequently the intervals between each key press. The time before the first key press will be referred to as the *latency* of the response. The sum of the intervals between key presses was divided by the number of letters in the word to yield *time per letter*. For the cluster analysis the interval times were transformed into temporal distances from the first key press. For instance, the distance for the third keystroke was a sum of the interval between the first keystroke and the second keystroke and the interval between the second keystroke and the third keystroke. The distances were then entered as co-ordinates into a single-linkage cluster analysis. This type of cluster analysis always looks for the nearest neighbour, i.e., the shortest distance between two co-ordinates (here the shortest time between two key presses), a co-ordinate and the outermost co-ordinate of a cluster (here the shortest time between a single key press for a letter and an adjacent letter already included in a cluster), or between the outermost co-ordinates of two clusters (here the time between two adjacent letters both already included in clusters), in order to join them into a new cluster. The result is a tree structure with each node joining two points or clusters.

Results

Letter grouping. The results of the cluster analyses for the five-letter words are presented in Figure 1 and for the six-letter words in Figure 2. The three word types all show a consistent pattern of pauses over conditions and participants. The overall structure for both types of five-letter words is the same, with a major pause between the first two letters typed (the last two letters of the word) and the three remaining letters. Within the cluster of three letters, the last two to be typed form a nested cluster. However, the major pause looks relatively longer when it coincides with a syllable boundary as in the case of 3 + 2-type words. We wondered whether the syllable structure created from reading the words backwards might play a role. Most of the 2 + 3-type words

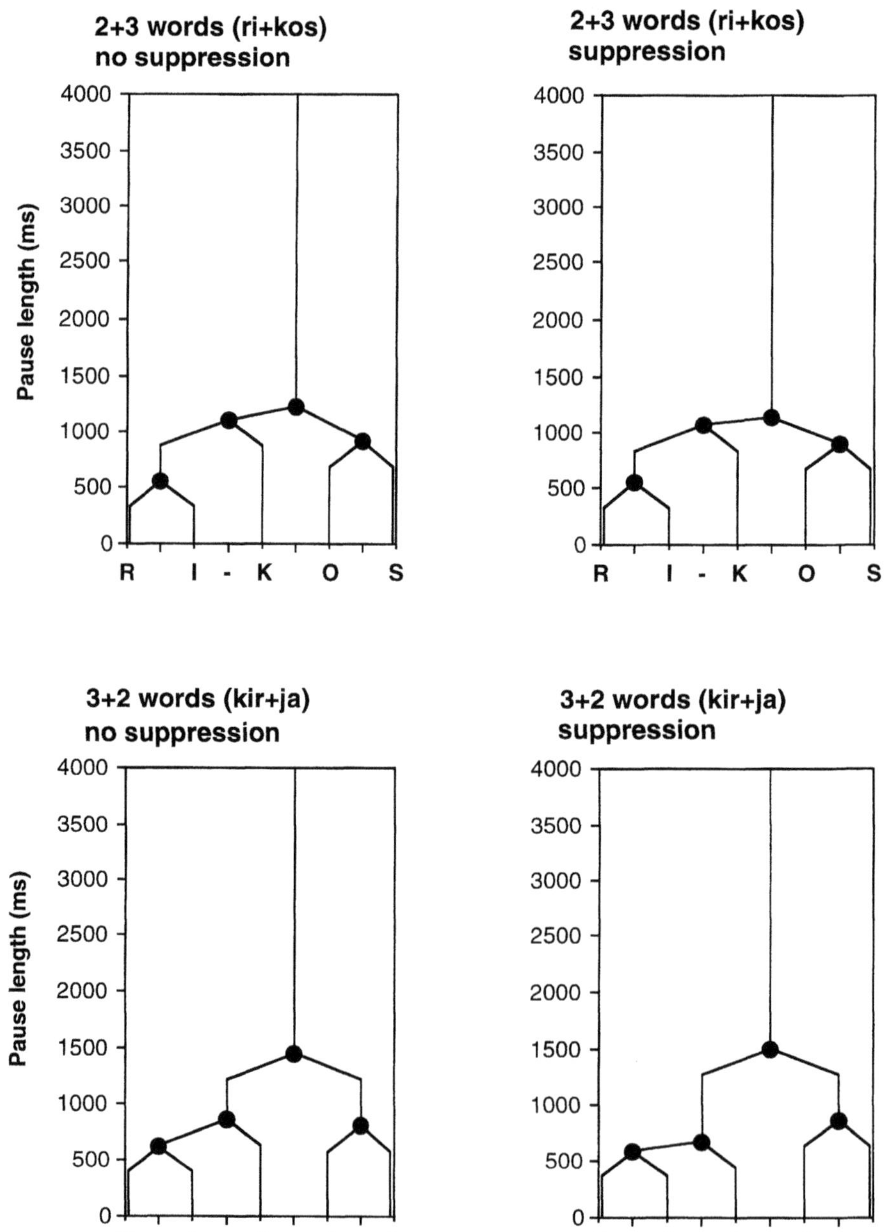

Figure 1. Letter clusters for five-letter words of two types written in conditions with or without articulatory suppression. The letters shown were typed from right to left.

resulted in a 2 + 3 syllable structure when read backwards (e.g. RI + KOS → SO + KIR). As this structure coincides with the result of the cluster analysis we analysed the remaining 16 words with a different structure (e.g. AS + KEL → LEK + SA) separately. However, the tree produced for these items looks identical to that for the rest of the items.

The cluster analysis was backed up by separate analyses of variance for the two word types with five letters. The 2 × 4 repeated-measures ANOVAs had condition (no suppression vs suppression) as a between-subjects factor and interval number (1–4 in the order of typing) as a within-subject factor. The individual intervals were then compared by pairwise contrasts. A significance level of $p < .05$ was adopted for these comparisons. All reported p-values were corrected using the Greenhouse-Geisser epsilon.

The analysis for 2 + 3-type words showed no trace of effect of condition ($p = .99$), i.e. writing time was not affected by articulatory suppression. Interval number, however, had a highly significant effect, $F(3, 51) = 30.58$, $p = .0001$, showing that all pauses were not of equal length. The pause between syllables (no. 3) was significantly longer than two of the three syllable-internal pauses (nos. 1 and 4) but not significantly different from the long syllable-internal interval (no. 2). The analysis thus pointed to a grouping structure with two long pauses (nos. 2 and 3) one of which coincided with a syllable boundary whereas the other did not. No significant interaction was found between condition and interval number, suggesting that articulatory suppression did not affect the pattern of pause lengths as seen in the cluster trees.

A similar ANOVA was run on the interval lengths in 3 + 2-type words. Again there was no detectable effect of condition on the mean length of the intervals. The main effect of interval number was again highly significant, $F(3, 51) = 45.98$, $p = .0001$. Pairwise contrasts between different intervals showed that the pause at the syllable boundary (no. 2) was significantly longer than any other pause in the words. There was again no interaction between the effect of condition and that of interval number. Clearly articulatory suppression did not affect letter grouping for these words. The results for all the five-letter words can be summarised by saying that there was one long pause after two letters had been written. This coincided with the syllable boundary for the 3 + 2-type words. The 2 + 3-type words had an additional long pause at their syllable boundary.

In making up the stimuli with six letters we found that a large number of words with the 4 + 2 structure that we wished to use had double consonants (geminates). We decided to include such words but to analyse them separately, as patient data in the literature suggested that geminates had a special status in graphemic representations (Caramazza & Miceli, 1990; Jónsdóttir, Shallice, & Wise, 1996). We therefore analysed the 26 words with double consonants in these positions and the 24 words without geminates separately (see Figure 2). When no double consonants were involved the major pause occurred again at the syllable boundary, after the first two letters had been typed. The pause between the third letter and the remaining three letters clustered together is nearly as long as the main pause, suggesting that this letter is typed on its own and is not grouped together with letters on either side. For the six-letter words with a double consonant the pattern is different. They form two clear clusters of three letters with a major pause between them. Both identical letters making up the double consonant are included in the cluster with the letters typed first.

The cluster analysis was again complemented with 2 × 5 analyses of variance similar to the ones reported earlier. Words with or without geminates were investigated separately. Mean interval length between letters in words without double consonants was not affected by articulatory suppression but the effect of interval number was once again highly significant, $F(4, 68) = 33.34$, $p = .0001$, indicating that some pauses were longer than others. Pairwise contrasts showed that interval no. 2, which coincided with the syllable boundary, was significantly longer than three of the syllable-internal pauses but did not differ from the fourth, interval no. 3. This result can be summarised by saying that there were two long pauses. One of them coincided with the syllable boundary (no. 2), whereas the other followed it (no. 3), so that together they left the third letter typed more or less on its own. There was again no sign of interaction between condition and interval number ($p = .92$), showing that articulatory suppression did not affect letter grouping in these words.

The results of the analysis of variance were somewhat different for the words with double consonants in letter positions 4 and 5. There was no effect of condition but again a substantial main effect of interval number, $F(4, 68) = 45.96$, $p = .0001$. This time the pause between syllables (no. 2)

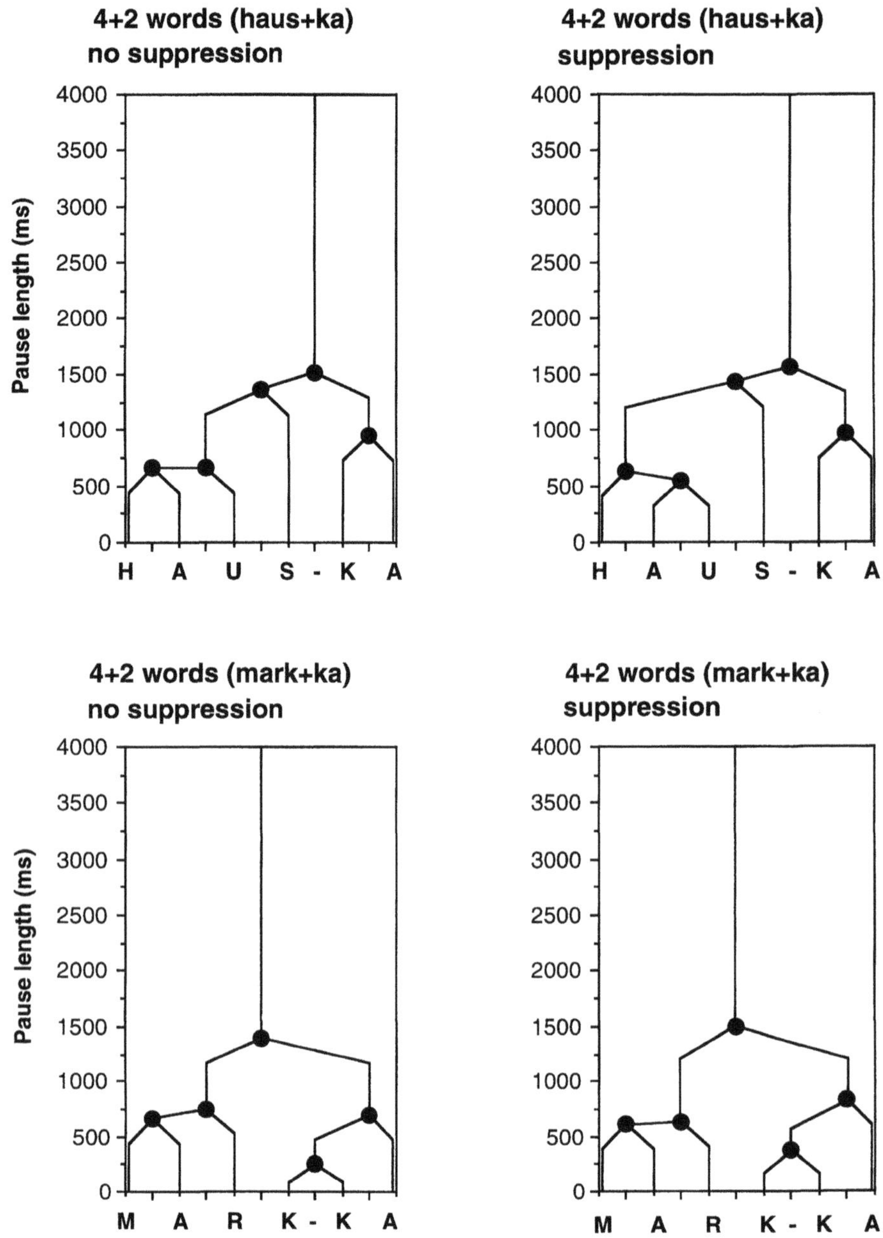

Figure 2. Letter clusters in six-letter words with or without a consonant geminates in letter positions 4 and 5. The letters shown were typed from right to left.

was significantly shorter than any other pause in the word. This was also the pause between the two identical consonants. The syllable-internal pause no. 3 was longer than any other pause while the three remaining pauses did not differ from each other. These results can be summarised by saying that there was one long pause (no. 3) and short pauses with one very short pause (no. 2 between the identical consonants). As with the word types reported earlier, there was again no interaction between condition and interval number, supporting the earlier findings of articulatory suppression not affecting letter grouping when two-syllable words are typed backwards.

Performance over participants was very consistent, with some variation occurring only for the 2 + 3-type words. Individual cluster structures, or trees, differed from the mean over participants for one participant in the case of 2 + 3-type words in the no-suppression condition. This participant had a major pause separating the first typed letter from the rest of the word rather than the two first typed letters and the remainder. In the suppression condition one participant produced a similar tree and four participants produced trees in which the longest pause coincided with the syllable boundary.

The overall pattern for typing backwards five- to six-letter words thus seems to be that first two letters are typed, then there is a pause, then three more letters are typed, if that is all that remains. If there are four left, one is typed, there is a pause again, and the word is finished off by typing the last three. If a consonant is repeated in the letter positions 4 and 5 of a six-letter word it is included in the cluster typed first. This pattern seems to compete with a tendency to use syllable boundaries for grouping letters, as can be seen in the 2 + 3-letter words. In these words the two strategies are in conflict and in the mean data there are long pauses both after two letters and at the syllable border, after three letters. Individual preferences are visible in the data of single participants.

We looked at the effects of condition and word length by comparing five-letter words and six-letter words (see Table 1 for means) in three ANOVAs with condition (no suppression/suppression) as a between-subjects variable and word length as a within-subjects variable, and with latency of first keystroke, time per letter, and number of errors as dependent variables.

Latency. An analysis including only those six-letter stimuli that did not have geminates showed no significant effects or interactions, suggesting that neither the difference in length between five-letter words and six-letter words nor articulatory suppression affected the time of preparation for the first keystroke.

Time per letter. An ANOVA excluding the six-letter words with consonant geminates showed a significant main effect of word length, $F(1,17) = 13.9$, $p < .005$, with letters in six-letter words taking longer to spell. There was no effect of articulatory suppression ($p = .98$) and no significant interaction between the two variables.

Proportion of errors. The number of errors as a proportion of presented words of different lengths showed a significant effect of word length, $F(1,17) = 8.42$, $p < .01$, when stimuli did not include words with double consonants. The error percentage for six-letter words was about twice that for five-letter words. Neither the effect of articulatory suppression nor the interaction between the two variables was significant.

Bigram frequencies. It could be argued that the syllable boundary effects that we found were artifacts based on low probabilities for bigrams straddling syllable boundaries. Such low bigram probabilities at syllable boundaries have been found in English (Seidenberg, 1987). We explored this by using a bigram frequency table for Finnish based on three 8000-character samples of Finnish text (Mikkonen, 1972). For the stimulus words of the four types we studied, in no case were the bigram frequencies across syllable boundaries significantly lower than average bigram frequencies. This was true for both the bigrams in a forward and a backward order. Thus, the detected longer pauses at syllable boundaries do not seem to have resulted from rare bigrams in those positions.

Discussion

Our first hypothesis was that participants would produce a consistent pattern of short and long pauses between typed letters within words,

TABLE 1
Mean latencies, times per letter, and error percentages for different word types with or without articulatory suppression in Experiment 1

	Latency (ms)		*Time per letter (ms)*		*Errors %*	
Word type	*No sup.*	*Art. sup.*	*No sup.*	*Art. sup.*	*No sup.*	*Art. sup.*
5 letters	2039 (444)	2264 (733)	693 (282)	692 (197)	7.6 (7.1)	9.9 (8.8)
6 letters, no geminate	2259 (849)	2234 (775)	799 (293)	794 (267)	12.5 (11.4)	25.4 (23.9)
6 letters, geminate	1997 (559)	2136 (645)	567 (196)	588 (159)	3.4 (4.1)	13.1 (12.5)

Standard deviations in parentheses.

reflecting graphemic buffer refreshment. The results of the experiment show that when two-syllable Finnish words of five to six letters are typed backwards the letters tend to be produced in clusters of two or three between longer pauses. Groups exceeding three letters were avoided. This finding points to a capacity limitation affecting the storage in or read-out from the graphemic buffer in the backward typing task.

Our second hypothesis was that longer pauses would occur at syllable boundaries. This hypothesis received support, but the picture turned out to be more complicated. When a syllable boundary separated the two letters typed first from the rest of the word, it was always marked by a long pause, except in the case of the boundary separating two identical consonants. If the remaining part of the word was three letters, these were all typed closely together. If it was four letters, one middle letter was typed on its own. Finally, if the syllable boundary was after three letters, participants showed a competing strategy of pausing already after two letters. Taken together, the results suggest that syllable boundaries are important in dividing up the word into smaller units. However, it appears that there is a tendency to minimise memory load at the beginning of the task, resulting in a strategy of trying to make the first letter grouping consist of two letters only. That the task gets easier towards the end is suggested by the fact that the intervals separating the last letters tend to be shorter than the first interval at the beginning of the task. Interval no. 1 was significantly longer than interval no. 4 in 2 + 3-type words and 3 + 2-type words. It was also longer than both intervals no. 4 and no. 5 in 4 + 2-type words without consonant geminates.

Our third hypothesis concerned the use of phonological coding in the task. We hypothesised that backward typing is a task based on graphemic representations with no need for phonological recoding. Our results show that articulatory suppression did not interact with interval number in determining the length of pauses between letters in any of the word types we explored. Neither did it have an effect on the latency of the first keystroke, the typing time per letter, or the proportion of errors. Phonological recoding based on an articulatory process did not appear to affect the organisation of typing output for five-letter words or six-letter words without geminates.

The six-letter words were written more slowly and had more errors than the five-letter words, at least when words with geminates were excluded. We therefore thought that growing word length may increase the difficulty of the backward spelling task so that phonological coding becomes necessary to provide additional memory support. This could have been the reason why articulatory suppression had such a detrimental effect in our pilot studies with 10-letter words. We now decided to explore words of intermediate length. They could be used together with articulatory suppression and did not create great problems, like 10-letter words did, for finding a sufficient number of stimulus items with a controlled syllable structure. Our main question was whether phonological codes were used in typing seven- to eight-letter words backwards.

EXPERIMENT 2: FINNISH 7–8-LETTER WORDS

Experiment 2 explored the effect of articulatory suppression on seven-letter words of two different syllabic structures and eight-letter words with a third syllabic structure. The participants took part in two experimental conditions: one with, and one without, articulatory suppression. On the basis of our results with 10-letter words we expected syllable structure to be the major strategy for chunking words of this length. We reasoned that five-letter words may have shown alternative chunking principles because they could be chunked in one go and only one major division border had to be kept in working memory. With longer words, remembering how much progress through the word one had made might become an increasingly capacity-demanding task. One way of reducing processing cost would be to use already familiar chunks, like syllables or morphemes, to divide up the word. Another way of coping with the task of keeping track of one's place in the word might be to use a phonological code for place marking. Our words now approached the length of the 10-letter words that had proved to be difficult to write backwards under articulatory suppression in pilot experiments. We thought that the reason may have been overloading of more central working memory (central executive) resources if a phonologically coded slave system (the phonological loop) was made unavailable. We therefore now expected articulatory suppression to impair performance by increasing the number of errors as well as typing time per letter as signs of increased demands on executive and monitoring processes in working memory. However, we did not think that it would have any effect on the way letter groups were made up. They should depend on graphemic buffer capacity and therefore not be affected by the availability of a phonological code. Only if performance fell apart altogether would we expect participants to abandon chunking into two-letter and three-letter groups. Our hypothesis for seven- to eight-letter words was thus that they should show chunking into syllables. Articulatory suppression should impair performance by decreasing accuracy and writing speed but should not affect the grouping of letters.

Method

Participants. There were 12 participants who all took part in both a condition without articulatory suppression and a condition with articulatory suppression. All participants reported doing typing regularly. However, 3 participants of the original 15 were excluded because of unsatisfactory typing skills (one for using one hand only, two for making an excessive number of errors, 56/90 and 72/90 errors respectively).

Stimuli. The stimulus words were 30 Finnish three-syllable, seven-letter words of the 2 + 3 + 2 type (va + hin + ko), 30 Finnish three-syllable, seven-letter words of the 3 + 2 + 2 type (han + ka + la), and 30 Finnish eight-letter words of the 3 + 3 + 2 (mai + non + ta) type. The words had text frequencies of 5–551 per 600,000 words in the text base based on magazine text of the Department of Linguistics at the University of Helsinki. A 10-word list with five-letter and six-letter words was used in a practice condition preceding the experimental conditions. The stimulus words were randomly mixed into one 90-word list, which was then split into two lists of 45 words each to allow the participants to take a rest and change condition in the middle of the experiment.

Procedure. The experimental procedure was the same as in Experiment 1. This time the experiment was run on a Macintosh II cx microcomputer and the words appeared in black Helvetica 24 pt bold print on a light screen. The seven-letter words stretched over a width of 35 mm and the eight-letter words over 40 mm, the respective visual angles from a viewing distance of 45 cm being 4.4° and 5° respectively. The presentation times used were 2000 ms for the fixation point and 500 ms for the words, which were then replaced by a mask consisting of Xs that remained on the screen till the first letter was typed. Half of the participants were in the articulatory suppression condition during the first half of the experiment, and half in the no-suppression condition. For the other half of participants the order of conditions was reversed.

Results

Letter grouping. The results of the cluster analyses for the three word types can be seen in Figures 3 and 4. As can be seen in the graphs, the general shapes of the trees are rather similar in the two experimental conditions. For the 3 + 2 + 2 words the cluster structures are exactly the same, perfectly reflecting the syllabic structure of the words, although showing longer pauses in the middle of the word. For the 2 + 3 + 2 words the condition without suppression also results in a syllable tree. The structure is slightly different in the suppression condition with the first letter typed in the middle syllable seemingly more on its own. However, the change in grouping depends on very small absolute differences. Lastly, the cluster structures for the two conditions with eight-letter words both follow the words' syllable structures but the long pause after the chunk of two letters written first seems to be lengthened in the suppression condition.

In order to see which differences between pauses were statistically reliable, the intervals between letters for the seven-letter words of the 2 + 3 + 2 type and 3 + 2 + 2 type as well as the eight-letter words were separately subjected to 2 × 6 or 2 × 7 repeated measures analyses of variance with experimental condition (no suppression or suppression) and interval number (1–6 or 1–7) as the repeated measures. The interval means were then compared in pairs using contrasts. All reported significance levels have again been adjusted using the Greenhouse-Geisser (G-G) epsilon. Significant effects are ones with the adjusted $p < .05$.

Results of these analyses (see Table 2) indicate that for the 2 + 3 + 2 words the effect of condition was not significant whereas the main effect of interval number was significant, $F(5, 55) = 8.76$, $p < .005$. Neither was there a significant interaction between interval number and condition and thus no evidence for articulatory suppression influencing letter grouping. Pairwise contrasts revealed that the longest interval was the one

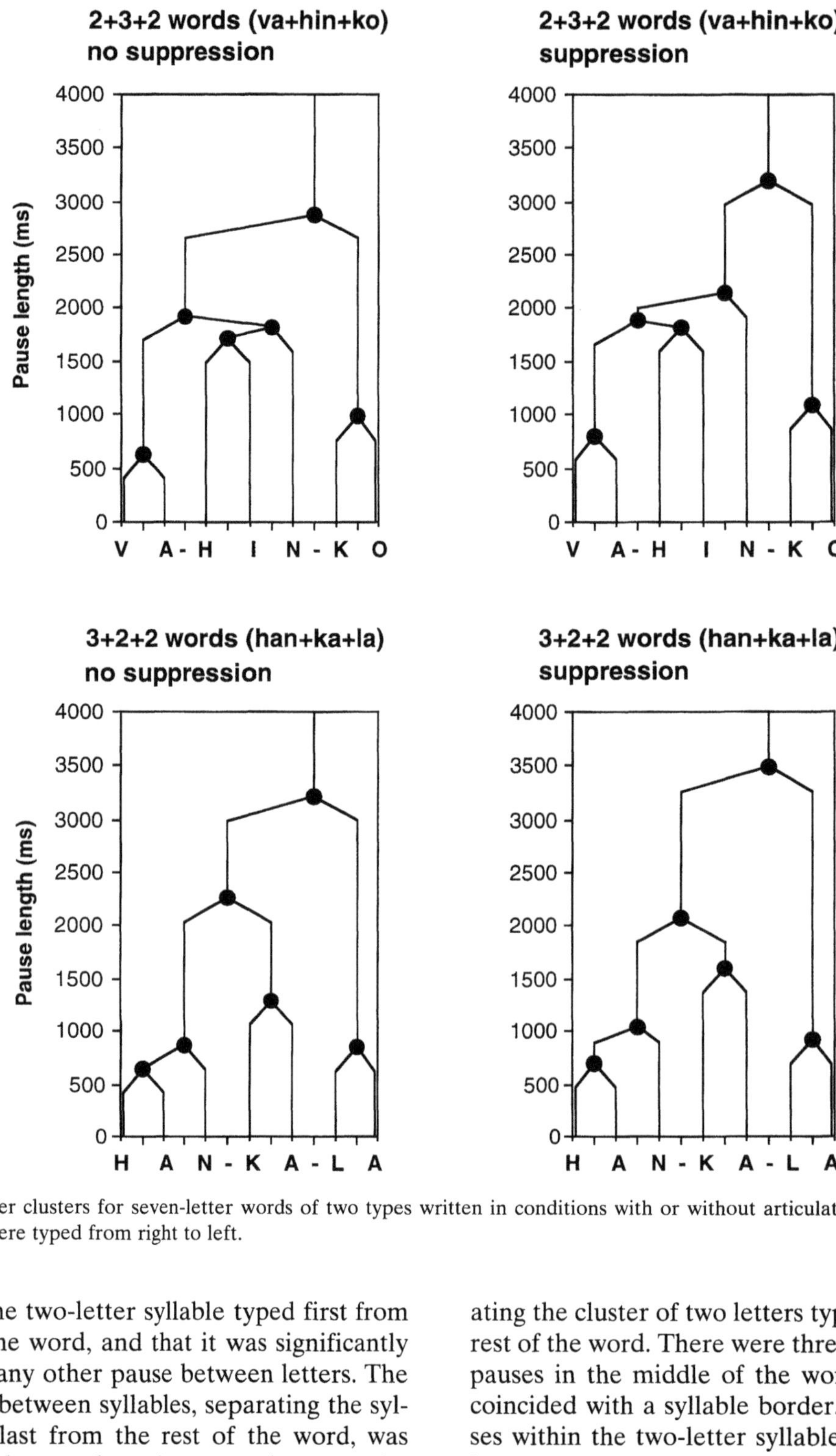

Figure 3. Letter clusters for seven-letter words of two types written in conditions with or without articulatory suppression. The letters shown were typed from right to left.

separating the two-letter syllable typed first from the rest of the word, and that it was significantly longer than any other pause between letters. The other pause between syllables, separating the syllable typed last from the rest of the word, was significantly longer than the pause between the two letters within that syllable and nearly significantly longer than the pause between the two letters in the syllable typed first ($p = .058$) but did not significantly differ from pauses within the middle syllable of the word. In summary, there was one major pause at a syllable border separating the cluster of two letters typed first from the rest of the word. There were three medium-length pauses in the middle of the word, one of which coincided with a syllable border. Lastly, the pauses within the two-letter syllables typed first and last were short.

For the 3 + 2 + 2 words, both the main effects of condition, $F(1, 11) = 5.69$, $p < .05$, and interval number, $F(5, 55) = 30.12$, $p = .0001$, were significant. However, their interaction was not, once again revealing no effect of concurrent articulation on letter grouping. The effect of suppression

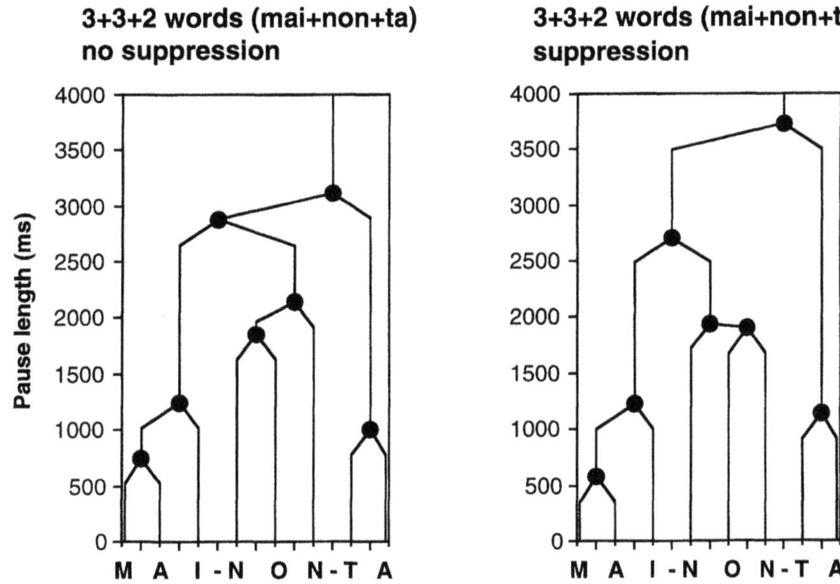

Figure 4. Letter clusters for eight-letter words written in conditions with or without articulatory suppression. The letters shown were typed from right to left.

TABLE 2
Pairwise contrasts between inter-letter pauses between and within syllables in seven- and eight-letter words in Experiment 2

Type of word								
2 + 3 + 2 (va-hin-ko)			*3 + 2 + 2 (han-ka-la)*			*3 + 3 + 2 (mai-non-ta)*		
Between vs within	*Within vs within*	*Between vs between*	*Between vs within*	*Within vs within*	*Between vs between*	*Between vs within*	*Within vs within*	*Between vs between*
2 > 1	1 ≈ 3	*2 > 5*	*2 > 1*	1 ≈ 3	*2 > 4*	*2 > 1*	1 ≈ 3	2 ≈ 5
2 > 3	1 ≈ 4		*2 > 3*	1 ≈ 5		*2 > 3*	1 ≈ 4	
2 > 4	1 ≈ 6		*2 > 5*	1 ≈ 6		*2 > 4*	1 ≈ 6	
2 > 6	3 ≈ 4		*2 > 6*	3 ≈ 5		*2 > 6*	1 ≈ 7	
5 ≈ 1	*3 > 6*		*4 > 1*	3 ≈ 6		*2 > 7*	3 ≈ 4	
5 ≈ 3	*4 > 6*		*4 > 3*	5 ≈ 6		*5 > 1*	3 ≈ 6	
5 ≈ 4			*4 > 5*			*5 > 3*	3 ≈ 7	
5 > 6			*4 > 6*			*5 > 4*	4 ≈ 6	
						5 > 6	*4 > 7*	
						5 > 7	6 ≈ 7	

Pauses are numbered in the order of typing, i.e., from the end of the word. Significant differences are in italics and marked with the direction of the difference, non-significant ones are marked with ≈.

was to make the intervals longer. One-degree-of-freedom contrasts (Table 2) showed that the pause between the syllable typed first and the rest of the word was significantly longer than any other pause between letters. The other pause between syllables, between the letter typed fourth and the letter typed fifth (no. 4), was significantly longer than the remaining pauses between letters. In summary, these words gave rise to two long pauses, both coinciding with syllable boundaries. Of these, the pause after the first two letters was longer. All pauses within syllables were relatively short.

For the eight-letter words of the 3 + 3 + 2 type, both main effects turned out to be significant. Suppression made intervals between letters longer, $F(1, 11) = 5.67$, $p < .05$, and different intervals differed in length, $F(6, 66) = 14.02$, $p < .0005$. The interaction between condition and interval number was again not significant but did approach significance ($p = .0698$), pointing to a possible effect of concurrent articulation on letter grouping in longer words. Pairwise comparisons of pause lengths (see Table 2) can be briefly described by saying that there were two long pauses, coinciding with the syllable boundaries, and shorter pauses within syllables. There also seemed to be a tendency for the first long pause, after two letters had been typed, to be even longer in the suppression condition.

To summarise the analysis of interval lengths, for none of the three word types was there a significant interaction between experimental condition (no suppression or suppression) and interval number. Thus suppression did not seem to affect the length of different intervals differently, although it did significantly lengthen all intervals for the 3 + 2 + 2 words and the longer 3 + 3 + 2 words. A very strong conclusion here is prevented by the fact that the interaction did approach significance for the longest, eight-letter, words. The pause separating the two-letter syllable typed first was significantly longer than all pauses within syllables for all three word types. The pause separating the two syllables typed later was always longer than syllable-internal pauses for the 3 + 2 + 2-type and the 3 + 3 + 2-type words. However, for words of the 2 + 3 + 2 type it was not significantly different from the pauses within the middle syllable, and even the difference between it and the pause within the cluster typed first only approached significance.

Repeated-measures ANOVAs with latency of the first keystroke, time per letter, and proportion of errors as the dependent variables and experimental condition (no suppression vs suppression) and word length (7 vs 8) as within-subject independent variables were run to find out whether articulatory suppression had any overall harmful effects on the backward spelling task with medium-length words. The mean data for the measures can be found in Table 3.

Latency. The analysis showed that concurrent articulation resulted in a significantly longer initial latency than in the condition without a secondary task, $F(1,11) = 30.14$, $p < .0005$, but the difference in word length between seven-letter and eight-letter words had no effect ($p = .81$) on the delay. Neither was there a significant interaction between condition and word length.

Time per letter. The results for typing time per letter showed that significantly more time was required under articulatory suppression, $F(1,11) = 5.81$, $p < .05$, and in the eight-letter words compared with the seven-letter words, $F(1,11) = 5.72$, $p < .05$. The interaction between condition and word length was not significant.

Proportion of errors. The third ANOVA, with the proportion of errors as the dependent variable, also showed a significant effect of condition, $F(1,11) = 7.62$, $p < .05$, with more errors being produced in the suppression condition. The effect of word length was not significant. Neither was the interaction between condition and word length.

Bigram frequencies. We again checked whether the syllable boundaries in our stimuli were characterised by bigram troughs either in the backward or the forward typing direction. In no case was there a significantly lower probability than mean bigram probability for the bigrams at syllable boundaries in our stimuli.

Discussion

Experiment 2 attempted to explore the possible disruptiveness of articulatory suppression and its possible effects on letter clustering when words of medium length were typed backwards. A second

TABLE 3
Mean latencies, times per letter, and error percentages for words of different length with or without articulatory suppression in Experiment 2

	Latency (ms)		*Time per letter (ms)*		*Error %*	
Word type	*No sup.*	*Art. sup.*	*No sup.*	*Art. sup.*	*No sup.*	*Art. sup.*
7 letters	1767 (361)	2170 (412)	1058 (317)	1152 (414)	16.3 (6.9)	30.8 (19.8)
8 letters	1836 (371)	2074 (394)	1113 (354)	1280 (484)	19.3 (10.4)	36.7 (24.5)

Standard deviations in parentheses.

question concerned the influence of syllable structure on the chunking of letters in words during backward typing. It should first be pointed out that for none of the three word types was the interaction between experimental condition and interval number significant. This supports a conclusion that articulatory suppression did not change the way letters were chunked together in the backward typing process. However, an interaction approaching significance for the eight-letter words leaves open the question of whether letter grouping might not be affected by concurrent articulation in longer words than those studied here.

The lack of a significant interaction justifies comparison of different intervals within words with a fixed syllable structure. Such comparisons revealed overall a strong effect of syllable boundary giving rise to longer pauses. There was one exception to this pattern. In the seven-letter words of the 2 + 3 + 2-type only the pause occurring at the syllable boundary separating the two letters typed first from the rest of the word is consistently longer than syllable internal intervals. This pattern is accompanied by a loosely structured middle syllable, suggesting that the three letters belonging to it were typed more or less separately. Possibly, a middle syllable consisting of three letters is rather straining for the system. All three significant comparisons between syllable internal pauses involved longer intervals between letters in a three-letter middle syllable. Two occurred in the 2 + 3 + 2-type words and the third in the 3 + 3 + 2-type words. The syllables typed first and last again show very short pauses between letters, suggesting that grouping there is consistent and tight.

Although articulatory suppression did not have an effect on the way letters were grouped, it did significantly lengthen the latency before the first stroke and typing time per letter. It also increased the number of errors. Assuming that articulatory suppression disrupts the use of phonological codes, these results suggest that the backward typing of seven- to eight-letter words does involve phonological coding. However, the effects found are in line with our hypothesis that a phonological code is used to monitor progress through longer words that need to be divided into more than two chunks of two or three letters. When the possibility of using phonological memory as an additional resource in monitoring progress is removed by forcing the participants to repeat a meaningless syllable, more strain is put on executive processes and an increase in errors and time can be seen. An inspection by eye of the length of the pauses between letter groups in the five- to six-letter words in Experiment 1 and the longer words used here reveals that pauses in the middle of the longer words tend to be substantially longer than in short words. This is another sign suggesting that long words are processed differently from short words. Possibly the longer pauses reflect refreshing time for a phonological as well as a graphemic buffer.

The time increase with articulatory suppression occurred both before the first keystroke and in intervals between keystrokes, suggesting that planning time, as well as possibly execution time, was involved. One could argue, however, that the effect would be the same for any secondary task taxing central resources and that phonological codes therefore need not be assumed to play a role in the task. The third experiment was carried out to investigate this possibility by replacing the articulatory task in Experiment 2 with a foot-tapping task. If foot tapping interferes with performance in a similar way as articulatory suppression, we cannot say anything definite about the modality of the representations used and have to conclude that backward typing of longer words is sensitive to any simple secondary task.

EXPERIMENT 3: FINNISH 7–8-LETTER WORDS WITH FOOT TAPPING

Experiment 3 is an almost exact replication of Experiment 2 with the difference that the articulatory suppression condition was replaced by a condition in which the participants had to tap continuously with their dominant foot.

Method

Participants. Originally 14 participants were tested. Of these two were excluded because of very high error rates (44/90 and 67/90 errors). The remaining participants were students, who were paid a small reward, and staff at the Psychology Department at the University of Helsinki. All participants were used to typing.

Stimuli and procedure. The same stimuli were used as in Experiment 2 and the procedure was identical to Experiment 2 in the condition without secondary task. In the secondary task condition participants were asked to start tapping at a comfortable rate with their dominant foot as soon as they had pronounced the word shown to them on the screen. Tapping was continued throughout the response till the appearance of the next fixation point. The experimenter was present throughout the experiment to make sure that participants actually kept tapping without pausing.

Results

Letter grouping. The tree structures resulting from cluster analyses run on the intervals between typed letters for the 3 + 2 + 2-type words (Figure 5) were very similar to those in Experiment 2. Also the clustering of letters in 2 + 3 + 2-type words (Figure 5) was similar to that in Experiment 2 although the middle syllable was broken up even more clearly than in the earlier experiment. The

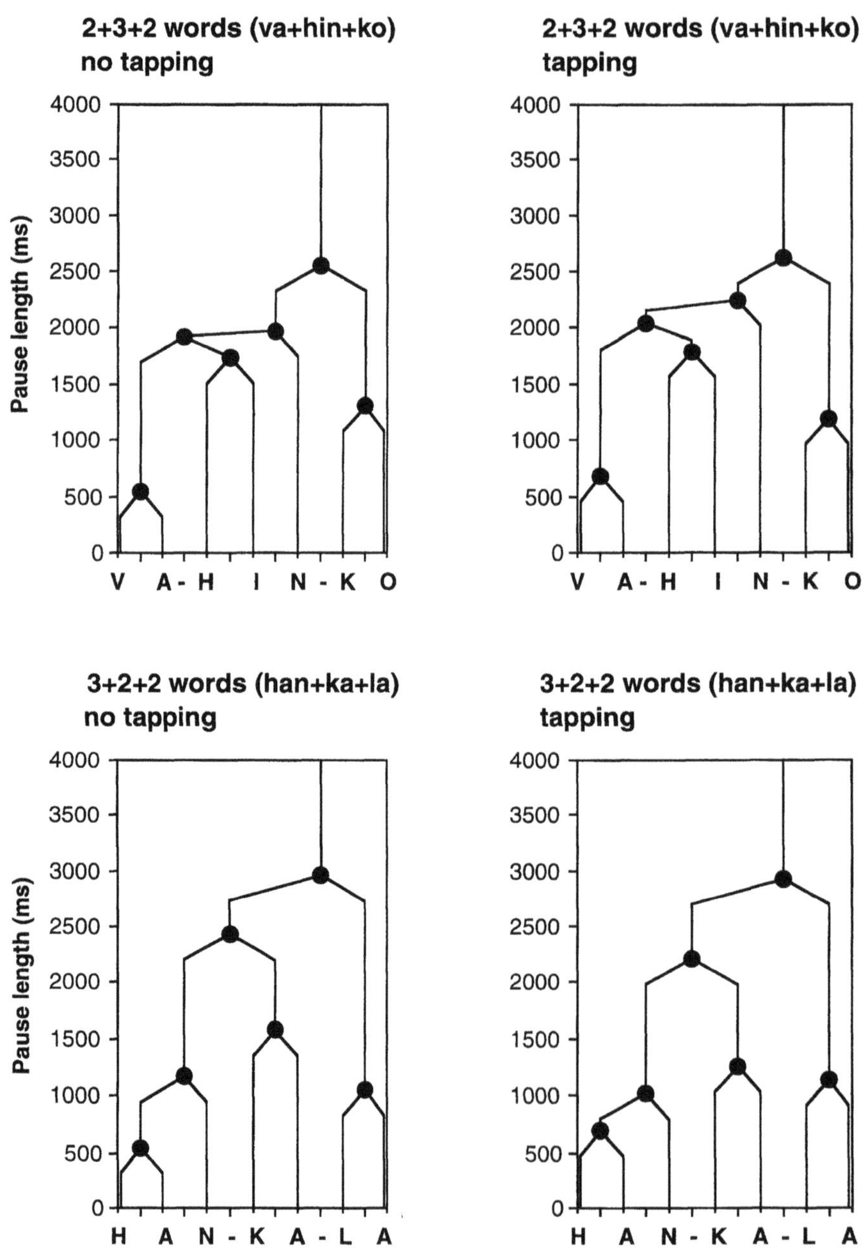

Figure 5. Letter clusters for seven-letter words of two types written in conditions with or without foot tapping. The letters shown were typed from right to left.

trees for the 3 + 3 + 2-type words (Figure 6) closely resembled those produced in Experiment 2 in the no suppression condition.

Repeated measures analyses of variance with condition (no tapping vs tapping) as a within-subject variable and interval number (1–6 or 1–7) as a within-subject variable were again carried out on the interval lengths in the three word types. For the words of the 2 + 3 + 2-type the analysis did not show an effect of condition but a highly significant main effect of interval number, $F(5, 55) = 7.38$, $p < .005$. The interaction between condition and interval number was non-significant ($p = .99$). A summary of pairwise comparisons is presented in Table 4.

Pairwise comparisons of the intervals in words of the 2 + 3 + 2-type replicated the major findings for this type of words in Experiment 2. The overall pattern strengthened the impression from the previous experiment of there being two tight letter groupings coinciding with syllables: one at the beginning and the other one at the end of typing.

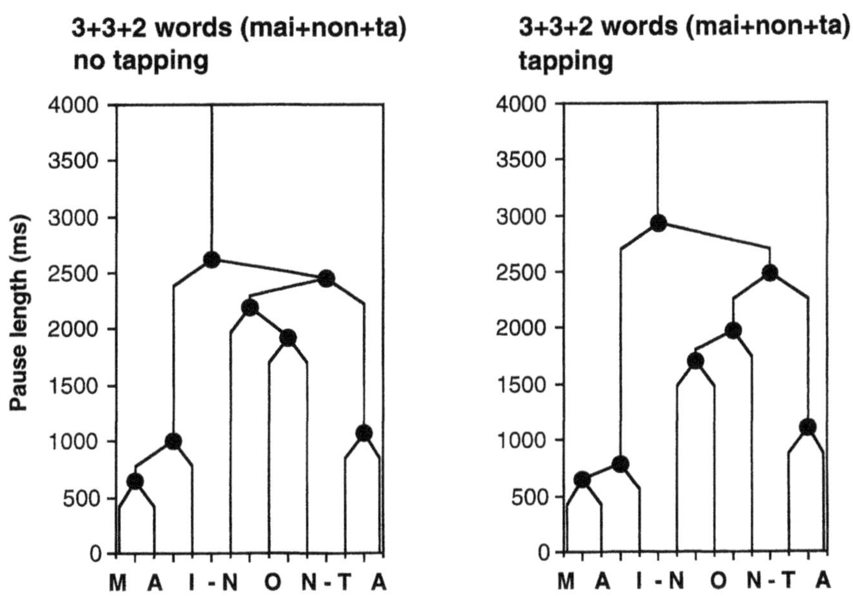

Figure 6. Letter clusters for eight-letter words written in conditions with or without foot tapping. The letters shown were typed from right to left.

TABLE 4
Pairwise contrasts between inter-letter pauses between and within syllables in seven- and eight-letter words in Experiment 3

Type of word								
2 + 3 + 2 (va-hin-ko)			*3 + 2 + 2 (han-ka-la)*			*3 + 3 + 2 (mai-non-ta)*		
Between vs within	*Within vs within*	*Between vs between*	*Between vs within*	*Within vs within*	*Between vs between*	*Between vs within*	*Within vs within*	*Between vs between*
2 > 1	1 ≈ 3	2 ≈ 5	*2 > 1*	1 ≈ 3	*2 > 4*	*2 > 1*	1 ≈ 3	2 ≈ 5
2 ≈ 3	1 ≈ 4		*2 > 3*	1 ≈ 5		2 ≈ 3	1 ≈ 4	
2 > 4	1 ≈ 6		*2 > 5*	1 ≈ 6		*2 > 4*	1 ≈ 6	
2 > 6	3 ≈ 4		*2 > 6*	3 ≈ 5		*2 > 6*	1 ≈ 7	
5 > 1	*3 > 6*		*4 > 1*	*3 > 6*		*2 > 7*	3 ≈ 4	
5 ≈ 3	*4 > 6*		*4 > 3*	5 ≈ 6		*5 > 1*	*3 > 6*	
5 ≈ 4			*4 > 5*			*5 > 3*	*3 > 7*	
5 > 6			*4 > 6*			*5 > 4*	4 ≈ 6	
						5 > 6	*4 > 7*	
						5 > 7	6 ≈ 7	

Pauses are numbered in the order of typing, i.e. from the end of the word. Significant differences are in italics and marked with the direction of the difference, non-significant ones with ≈.

The letters of the longer middle syllable appeared to be typed more individually.

The ANOVA for words of the 3+2+2-type also revealed a significant effect of interval number, $F(5,55)=34.00$, $p<.0001$, but no effect of tapping ($p=.82$). Pairwise comparisons confirmed the division of the word into syllabic letter clusters as in Experiment 2.

The ANOVA results for the 3+3+2-type words resemble those for the two other types of words, with a highly significant effect of interval number, $F(6,66)=13.70$, $p<.0001$, and a non-significant effect of condition ($p=.71$). Although the cluster trees look slightly different from those in Experiment 2, there were again few differences between the pairwise comparisons between intervals in the two experiments. Again the overall impression is of tight syllable grouping at the beginning and the end of the word but of a more loosely grouped three-letter middle syllable.

So far the results look very much like the ones in Experiment 2, with the exception that tapping does not seem to affect interval length in any of the word types whereas articulatory suppression lengthened intervals for two of the three word types. The most interesting part of the analysis concerns the effects of tapping on latency, time per letter, and proportion of errors, as these measures all showed detrimental effects of suppression in Experiment 2. Similar analyses of variance as in Experiment 2 looking at the effects of experimental condition and word length on the three variables were therefore carried out. The means of these variables can be seen in Table 5.

Latency. The results showed neither an effect of condition nor of word length on the latency of the first keystroke. The interaction between the two variables did not approach significance either. Thus the results replicated those for word length in Experiment 2 but differed from those for the secondary task. It should be pointed out, however, that there was a non-significant tendency for the initial pause to be longer in the tapping condition ($p=.0962$).

Time per letter. The effect of condition on time per letter was non-significant ($p=.748$) as well, whereas the effect of word length approached, but did not reach, significance ($p=.0754$). There was again no significant interaction between the two variables. Thus neither the significant effect of secondary task nor of word length in Experiment 2 was replicated. However, there was a tendency for long words to take longer per letter.

Proportion of errors. Our final analysis investigating effects on typing accuracy failed to show any effect of condition ($p=.848$) or of word length or the interaction between the two variables. It thus replicated the lack of word length effect in Experiment 2, but the significant effect of articulatory suppression in that experiment was not replicated for the foot-tapping secondary task.

Discussion

Experiment 3 was designed to explore the possibility that the effects of articulatory suppression on the latency of the initial keystroke, typing time per letter, and proportion of errors, all present in Experiment 2, may be general consequences of pairing backward typing with any secondary task. The fact that foot tapping was not accompanied by significant changes in any of these measures lends support to our original conclusion that articulatory suppression harms task performance because it specifically interferes with phonological

TABLE 5
Mean latencies, times per letter, and error percentages for words of different length with or without foot tapping in Experiment 3

	Latency (ms)		*Time per letter (ms)*		*Errors (%)*	
Word type	*No tapping*	*Tapping*	*No tapping*	*Tapping*	*No tapping*	*Tapping*
7 letters	1861 (1018)	2105 (952)	1052 (434)	1059 (401)	20.5 (13.5)	20.5 (9.1)
8 letters	1898 (969)	2108 (868)	1106 (468)	1121 (451)	21.7 (15.8)	20.4 (14.7)

Standard deviations in parentheses.

codes. A counter argument to this interpretation would be that foot tapping was somehow an easier task than continuous repetition of a meaningless syllable. None of the participants complained about articulatory suppression being difficult *per se*, although some of them felt that foot tapping got to be tiring towards the end of the experiment.

Although there were no significant interference effects of foot tapping on any of the performance measures we looked at, there was a tendency for the latency from stimulus onset to beginning of typing to be longer in the tapping condition. This could be a sign of interference in the first planning stage before a word was tackled. The load on working memory is presumably highest at this point when the graphemic buffer representation for the word has to be set up and a strategic plan made for how to proceed. This is possibly also the stage when the word gets parsed into syllabic units, a process that can depend on either phonological or orthographic coding. It could therefore be assumed that this stage in the task would be highly vulnerable to any secondary task taxing central working memory resources. As latency was not affected by articulatory suppression for the five- to six-letter words, this possible vulnerability does not seem to extend to short words.

Although Experiment 3 was not designed to be a replication of the results obtained in Experiment 2, it is worth emphasising the high degree of similarity in letter grouping between the data from the two experiments. When a great number of pairwise comparisons are made, the probability of some of them being significant as a result of chance factors increases. There was, however, a remarkable stability over the mean comparisons made on the data from Experiments 2 and 3, supporting our previous conclusions that participants behave in systematic ways when they group letters between pauses in typing backwards.

EXPERIMENT 4: FORWARD TYPING OF 7–8-LETTER ITEMS

The last experiment was designed to study pause structure in a forward typing task. In this case there is no need for reading out the letters in reversed order from an orthographic lexical representation, and major pauses may not occur if graphemic buffer processes are fast and can run in parallel with motor execution. We ran the experiment with the same seven- to eight-letter word stimuli as in Experiments 2 and 3 and additional pseudowords with the same syllable structures. Pseudowords were included to find out the importance of lexical representations. As Finnish orthography is almost 100% transparent, written pseudowords are easy to code phonologically for WM maintenance. It is also easy to parse these phonological representations into syllables. There were two conditions: one with articulatory suppression and one without. In standard formulations of the working memory framework by Baddeley and Hitch (Baddeley, 1986, 1997) written pseudowords should not be phonologically coded under articulatory suppression. Syllabic effects should then depend on orthographic rather than phonological representations. Our main question in Experiment 4 was whether the results from Experiments 2 and 3 could be replicated using a forward typing task. In addition we were interested to see whether there would be a three-way interaction between lexical status, condition, and interval number, suggesting that letters in pseudowords are differently grouped when phonological coding is blocked.

Method

Participants. There were 20 student participants, who volunteered for course credit or out of interest. All were used to typing but none was an exceptionally fast typist.

Stimuli. We used the 90 stimuli from Experiments 2 and 3. In addition 30 "pseudowords" of the 2+3+2 type, 30 "pseudowords" of the 3+2+2 type, and 30 "pseudowords" of the 3+3+2 type were selected from an old Finnish-Swedish dictionary (Lönnrot, 1958/1880) among entries that are not in use in modern Finnish.

Design and procedure. Condition (no suppression/suppression), syllabic structure, and lexicality (word/pseudoword) were varied within-subject. For maximal comparability between experiments, all participants typed words before they were presented with pseudowords. Half of the participants received the first half of the words while they were constantly repeating "palah" and the second half of words with no secondary task. For the other half of the participants this order was reversed. The order of articulatory suppression/no suppression was similarly varied between participants when they typed pseudowords. The procedure was in other respects the same as in Experiment 2.

Results and discussion

For space purposes, only the letter grouping analysis is reported for the forward typing task. The results of the cluster analyses for the six item types can be seen in Figures 7, 8, and 9. The first thing to notice is that all pauses are much shorter than in the backward typing experiments, of the order of a sixth of those pauses. It should be kept in mind that typing order for the letters is now reversed. The longest pause in all cases again occurs after the first typed syllable (creating a mirror image shape for the forward trees compared to the backward trees), and the only deviation from syllable grouping is the second letter of the middle syllable in 2 + 3 + 2-type pseudowords, which is

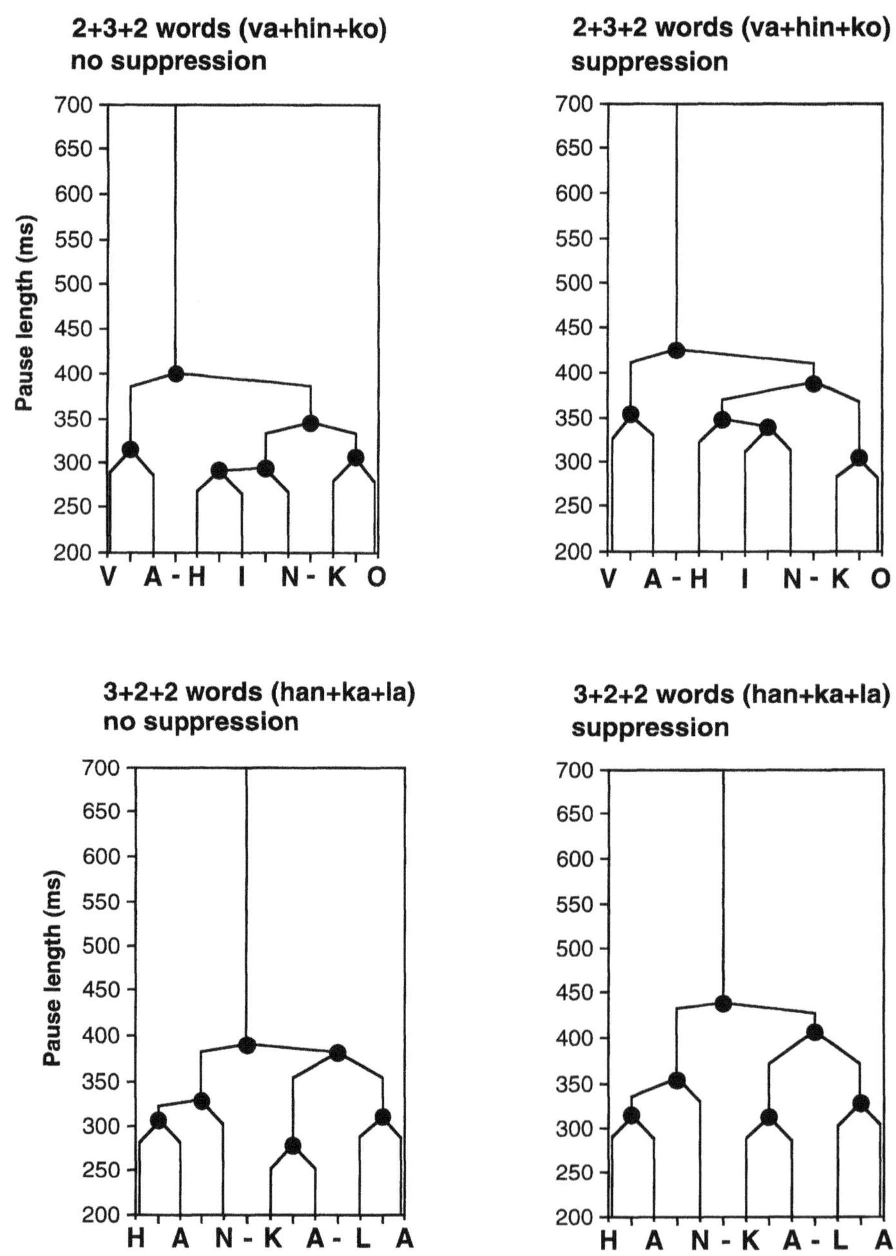

Figure 7. Letter clusters for seven-letter words of two types written in conditions with or without articulatory suppression. The letters shown were typed from left to right.

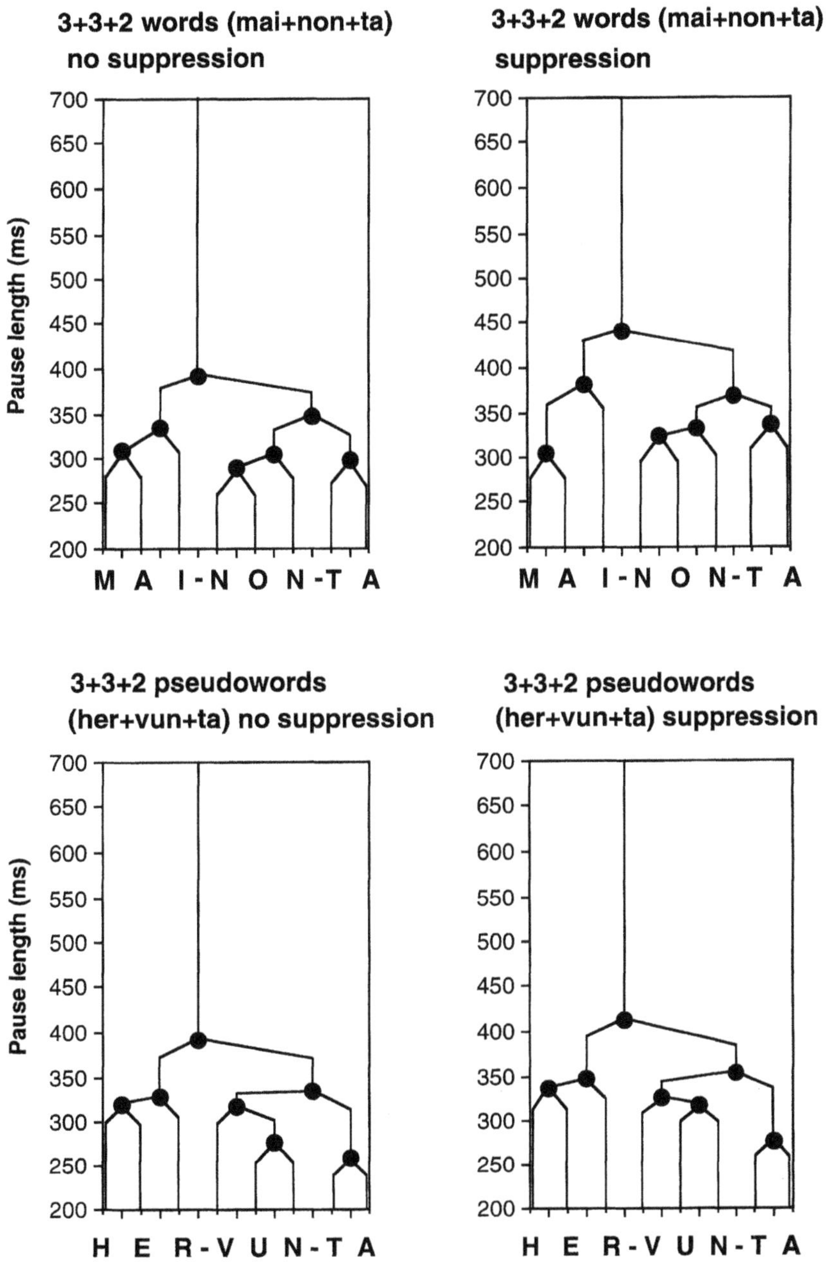

Figure 8. Letter clusters for eight-letter words and pseudowords written in conditions with or without articulatory suppression. The letters shown were typed from left to right.

typed more or less on its own under articulatory suppression. Similar long pauses in three-letter middle syllables were also seen in the backward typing experiments.

The intervals between letters for the two types of seven-letter words and pseudowords as well as eight-letter words and pseudowords were subjected to three separate ANOVAs with lexical status (word vs pseudoword), experimental condition, and interval number as independent variables. The only significant main effect was that of interval number: for 2+3+2 items, $F(5, 95) = 18.44$, $p < .0001$; for 3+2+2 items, $F(5, 95 = 18.91$, $p < .0001$; and for 3+3+2 items, $F(6, 114) = 18.62$, $p < .0001$. The pairwise contrasts can be seen in Tables 6 and 7. The main story is that the first syllable in all cases is separated from the rest of the word by the longest pause in the word, and pauses within syllables generally become shorter towards the end of the word. The middle syllable is also reliably separated from the last syllable. In all three analyses,

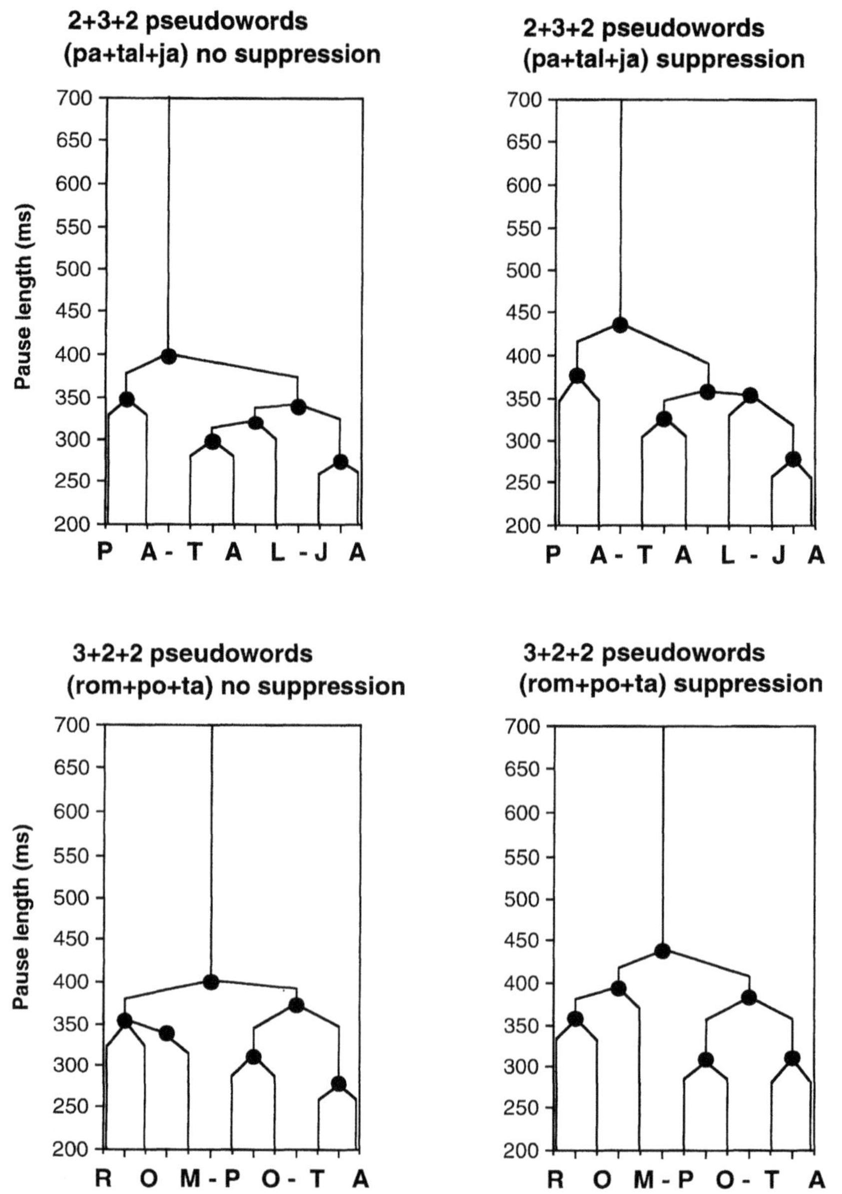

Figure 9. Letter clusters for seven-letter pseudowords of two types written in conditions with or without articulatory suppression. The letters shown were typed from left to right.

the interaction between lexical status and interval number was significant: for 2 + 3 + 2 items, $F(5, 95) = 3.85$, $p < .05$; for 3 + 2 + 2 items, $F(5, 95) = 6.16$, $p < .001$; and for 3 + 3 + 2 items, $F(6, 114) = 3.47$, $p < .01$. This interaction appears to stem from generally longer pauses between syllables, and shorter pauses within the first and the middle syllables, in words that in pseudowords (see Tables 6 and 7 and Figures 7–9), thus accentuating the syllabic organisation in words compared to pseudowords.

The results show that although pauses in forward typing were considerably shorter than in backward typing, the pattern of pauses was similar with respect to a clearly separated syllable typed first and the letters forming the last typed syllable grouped together. The similarity of pausing patterns in forward and backward typing is clearest in the case of 2 + 3 + 2 type words, which are symmetrical with respect to syllable-length in the two typing directions. A long (three-letter) middle syllable was even less clearly separated from the last typed syllable in forward typing than in backward typing. Both typing directions showed tighter clustering for two-letter syllables than three-letter syllables.

TABLE 6
Pairwise contrasts between inter-letter pauses between and within syllables in seven- and eight-letter words in Experiment 4

Type of word								
2+3+2 (va-hin-ko)			*3+2+2 (han-ka-la)*			*3+3+2 (mai-non-ta)*		
Between vs within	*Within vs within*	*Between vs between*	*Between vs within*	*Within vs within*	*Between vs between*	*Between vs within*	*Within vs within*	*Between vs between*
2 > 1	1 ≈ 3	*2 > 5*	*3 > 1*	1 ≈ 2	3 ≈ 5	*3 > 1*	*1 < 2*	*3 > 6*
2 > 3	1 ≈ 4		*3 > 2*	1 ≈ 4		*3 > 2*	1 ≈ 4	
2 > 4	1 ≈ 6		*3 > 4*	1 ≈ 6		*3 > 4*	1 ≈ 5	
2 > 6	3 ≈ 4		*3 > 6*	*2 > 4*		*3 > 5*	1 ≈ 7	
5 ≈ 1	3 ≈ 6		*5 > 1*	2 ≈ 6		*3 > 7*	*2 > 4*	
5 > 3	4 ≈ 6		*5 > 2*	4 ≈ 6		*6 > 1*	*2 > 5*	
5 > 4			*5 > 4*			6 ≈ 2	*2 > 7*	
5 > 6			*5 > 6*			*6 > 4*	4 ≈ 5	
						6 > 5	4 ≈ 7	
						6 > 7	5 ≈ 7	

Pauses are numbered in the order of typing, i.e. from the beginning of the word. Significant differences are in italics and marked with the direction of the difference, non-significant ones are marked with ≈.

TABLE 7
Pairwise contrasts between inter-letter pauses between and within syllables in seven- and eight-letter pseudowords in Experiment 4

Type of word								
2+3+2 (pa-tal-ja)			*3+2+2 (rom-po-ta)*			*3+3+2 (her-vun-ta)*		
Between vs within	*Within vs within*	*Between vs between*	*Between vs within*	*Within vs within*	*Between vs between*	*Between vs within*	*Within vs within*	*Between vs between*
2 > 1	*1 > 3*	*2 > 5*	*3 > 1*	1 ≈ 2	*3 > 5*	*3 > 1*	1 ≈ 2	*3 > 6*
2 > 3	1 ≈ 4		*3 > 2*	*1 > 4*		*3 > 2*	1 ≈ 4	
2 > 4	*1 > 6*		*3 > 4*	*1 > 6*		*3 > 4*	*1 > 5*	
2 > 6	3 ≈ 4		*3 > 6*	*2 > 4*		*3 > 5*	*1 > 7*	
5 ≈ 1	*3 > 6*		5 ≈ 1	*2 > 6*		*3 > 7*	2 ≈ 4	
5 > 3	*4 > 6*		5 ≈ 2	4 ≈ 6		6 ≈ 1	*2 > 5*	
5 ≈ 4			*5 > 4*			6 ≈ 2	*2 > 7*	
5 > 6			*5 > 6*			6 ≈ 4	4 ≈ 5	
						6 > 5	*4 > 7*	
						6 > 7	5 ≈ 7	

Pauses are numbered in the order of typing, i.e. from the beginning of the word. Significant differences are in italics and marked with the direction of the difference, non-significant ones are marked with ≈.

In no case were there significant interactions between suppression condition and interval number. It therefore seems that the syllables used in typing are not products of phonological processing during the spelling task. Moreover, as they were more salient in words than pseudowords and there was no three-way interaction between lexical status, condition, and interval number, they appear to reflect the structure of orthographic representations that is well established in the case of familiar words.

GENERAL DISCUSSION

Chunk size and codes in the graphemic buffer

The experiments reported here set out to explore the characteristics of the graphemic buffer as revealed in a backward typing task. Because backward typing had not been used for this purpose before, the results necessarily consist of both findings concerning the characteristics of this task and findings about the hypothesised graphemic buffer and its use.

We first asked whether backward typing could be used for studying the capacity of the graphemic buffer. We hypothesised that this buffer might use a visuo-spatial representational format. On the basis of research into memory for unpronounceable visual symbols (Zhang & Simon, 1985) and the size of text window used in copy-typing (Inhoff & Wang, 1992) we hypothesised that the graphemic buffer might be used to process two to three letters at any one point in time. If this were the case we might expect participants to stop after every two or three letters to refresh the graphemic buffer in a backward typing task, which forced them to produce the letters of a familiar letter sequence in an unfamiliar order. Our findings from all three backward typing experiments show that no more than three letters are normally produced close together. They also show that participants behave in systematic and consistent ways when they divide up words of different lengths in order to reproduce the reversed letter orderings. The answer to our general question therefore seems to be that there may indeed be a WM process with a capacity of two to three letters that is used in backward typing. Such an estimate is also consistent with the chunking of the two to three letters forming the first syllable in words in our forward typing task. Later syllables were sometimes less salient in this task, possibly due to overlapping graphemic buffer and motor production processes.

We also asked how chunks of two to three letters are created. The pilot experiment with 10-letter words suggested syllables were important. Experiment 1 looked at shorter words of five to six letters. A somewhat more complicated picture emerged. Syllable structure did seem to play a decisive role, but there were other factors present as well. Thus, when syllables of four letters made up the first syllable (i.e., the one to be typed last) one letter tended to be typed separately from the cluster of three that followed. On the other hand, if the four-letter syllable ended in a consonant that was repeated at the beginning of the next syllable, the two identical consonants were grouped together and the syllable boundary ignored. This result echoed patient data in which the error probabilities for consonant clusters in writing were totally different depending on whether the clusters consisted of two identical consonants or two different consonants (Caramazza & Miceli, 1990; Tainturier & Caramazza, 1996). A third complication concerned a strategy seemingly competing with syllable parsing that tried to keep the first typed cluster down to two letters, and resulted in two long pauses in words in which the second syllable (to be typed first) consisted of three letters. Experiments 2, 3, and 4 with seven- to eight-letter words suggested that grouping was tight for the first two-letter syllable chunk to be typed as well as the last two- to three-letter group, but that a middle syllable exceeding two letters caused performance to suffer so that relatively long pauses were also produced inside this syllable. Clearly more experiments should be carried out with different kinds of syllable structures to explore short and long syllables in the middle of the word and grouping in languages with typically longer syllables than in Finnish.

One of our worries was that backward typing might be accomplished using phonological representations and might not therefore be the ideal task to study the graphemic buffer after all. We explored this in Experiments 1 and 2 with short and medium-length words. When five- to six-letter words were spelled backwards we found no sign of articulatory suppression influencing either letter grouping, typing time, or errors. The picture was different for seven- to eight-letter words. Here concurrent articulation seemed to harm initial planning, reflected in the latency before the first keystroke, as well as typing time per letter, and spelling accuracy. It did not, however, interact with letter grouping. Neither was there an interaction between articulatory suppression and letter grouping in the forward typing task in Experiment 4. It therefore appears that the limits to letter grouping are determined by a non-phonological low-capacity mechanism, and that phonological coding may be used to cope with the organisational and monitoring aspects of the task. Possibly, keeping track of progress within a word is accomplished differently for short and long words. In short words it seems possible to do this without resorting to phonological representations. It could be done, for instance, by including the last letter in one letter group as the first letter in another letter group or by somehow marking the letters at group borders. In long words, single letters do not provide unambiguous position cues and therefore other units, like phonotactic or graphotactic syllables, may have to be used. These are well suited to parallel phonological representation.

How does backward spelling relate to forward spelling?

When we decided to use backward spelling to explore the characteristics of the graphemic buffer we had grounds for not using normal forward spelling. We reasoned that if there are graphemic buffer capacity limitations at work in writing, these would be very hard to detect in normal forward typing. First, the processes involving the chunks used would be highly automatised, making all operations fast and difficult to observe. Second, the familiar phonological form of the word could at all times support the correct chaining of chunks. Also, other chaining cues, for instance visual or manual, may be present at all times, making it possible for participants to plan ahead so that no detectable pauses in output occur. However, a crucial question is whether the kind of possibly visuo-spatial representations thought to be used in backward spelling are needed at all in forward spelling. Perhaps the graphemic buffer is a modality-free ordering device for letters to be typed (Greenwald & Berndt, 1999). Evidence from patients suggests that spatial representations are needed in spelling. Some patients, for instance NG (Caramazza & Hillis, 1990), HD, and ML (Hillis & Caramazza, 1989), show signs of impaired attention on either side in space, producing at least subclinical signs of neglect. They also show writing deficits affecting selectively either the beginnings or ends of words. The spatial problems of these patients suggest that during writing there is, at some level in the system, an active spatial representation of the orthographic structure of the whole word, or at least whole morphemes, and that some patients with hemi-attentional problems are not aware of one side of this representation.

It could also be argued that the graphemic buffer is not identical with whatever buffer it is that causes grouping into two- to three-letter chunks in backward typing. It is possible—and this is how it has been described in theories of writing (Caramazza & Miceli, 1990; Caramazza et al., 1987; Margolin, 1984)—that the graphemic buffer contains an abstract representation of the orthographic structure of a whole word. This then gets chunked into two- to three-letter groups for projection onto a limited-capacity "inner screen" for odd tasks like backward spelling, but is available in its entirety for reproduction of letters in their familiar order. We would like to propose that a whole-word representation with marked syllable boundaries is indeed activated in the graphemic buffer. However, read-out from this representation uses the visuo-spatial sketchpad to "look at" two- to three-letter chunks at a time for motor planning. This can be seen in forward typing as well as in backward typing, although only at the very beginnings and ends of words. Support for the interpretation that the visuo-spatial sketchpad is involved comes from further work in our laboratory, showing that secondary tasks involving either mental imagery or spatio-motor programming interfere with backward typing and change letter grouping in five-letter words. Another piece of indirect evidence is that in a case study of a person with congenital visuo-spatial difficulties we found that the subject was practically unable to spell words backwards.

Capacity for storage and processes in backward typing

Three kinds of problems need to be handled in spelling after an orthographic representation has been activated in long-term memory. Keeping this representation active throughout spelling should be the task of the graphemic buffer. As longer words take longer to write, they put higher demands on the maintenance of this representation. A second problem to be solved involves what Wing and Baddeley (1980) described as a serial retrieval process from this representation. Although we set out to explore the capacity of the graphemic buffer, it now seems to us that what we found are the capacity limits of this read-out process, which possibly relies on visuo-spatial representations of chunks of two or three letters. It is possible that three units is also more generally a maximum size of grouped material being serially processed in working memory (Broadbent, 1975). Three or four has also been put forward as the capacity limit for visual attention (Bundesen, 1990; Duncan & Humphreys, 1989) and subitisation—the non-serial process of rapid numerosity processing (see e.g., Watson & Humpreys, 1999).

To cope with the capacity limitations of the read-out process the representation of the whole word needs to be chunked into groups of two to three letters. Syllables seem to provide a good starting point for this process. Jónsdóttir et al. (1996) have suggested that syllables need not be present in orthographic representations in LTM. Effects of syllable structure on the performance of some graphemic buffer patients could be based on their reliance on phonological mediation in spelling. It is possible that there are differences between languages in this respect. In Finnish, syllable boundaries are nearly always unambiguous in speech. A transparent orthography makes it easy also to represent syllables graphemically. The consistent grouping of the letters in the first syllable in the words typed forwards suggest that syllables do, indeed, play a role in typing Finnish words forwards as well as backwards. Moreover, the organisation of pauses to reflect syllable structure was not affected by articulatory suppression. This makes it unlikely that syllables are computed online from phonological representations. A more credible assumption is that graphotactic syllables are represented in the orthographic LTM of a Finnish speaker. This conclusion is supported by the finding of longer inter-syllabic pauses in forward typing of real words than of pseudowords.

To accomplish successful spelling, a number of organising and other processes, typically attributed to the central executive, are also needed. One such process is active monitoring of progress through the word. Because landmarks in grapheme sequences may not always be very salient, this process might be aided by using phonological representations and/or morpheme boundaries. This is assumed to be the reason why articulatory suppression has such a detrimental effect on the backward typing of long words but little effect on short words. Our participants seemed to get into trouble because of the added strain of keeping the orthographic word-level representation alive by some sort of forward-scanning process (Hampson & Morris, 1978) while read-out was done chunk by chunk in the opposite direction. The task got very hard with longer words: error rates were 7.6%, 12.5%, 16.3%, 19.3%, and 36.5% for word lengths 5, 6 (without consonant geminates), 7, 8, and 10. It was also hard under suppression: error rates 9.9%, 25.4%, 30.8%, and 36.7% for word lengths 5, 6 (without consonant geminates), 7, and 8. What makes forward writing hard for some patients could be a fast decay rate of whole-word orthographic representations or an impaired process that refreshes these representations. This could make refreshment cycles short and result in frequent switching between refreshment processes and executive processes connected with read-out and output planning. The task demands would then resemble those posed by backward typing on normal participants. The aforementioned hypothetical components affecting spelling at the graphemic buffer level need to be explored with more varied materials and writing tasks to further clarify what we now know to be a much more complex stage in the writing process than the mere serial conversion of mental letters to written output.

REFERENCES

Baddeley, A. (1992). Working memory. *Science*, *255*, 556–559.

Baddeley, A. (2000). The episodic buffer: A new component of working memory? *Trends in Cognitive Sciences*, *4*, 1364–1366.

Baddeley, A.D. (1986). *Working memory*. Oxford: Clarendon Press.

Baddeley, A.D. (1997). *Human memory: Theory and practice* (2nd Edn.). Hove, UK: Psychology Press.

Baddeley, A.D., & Hitch, G. (1974). Working memory. In G. Bower (Ed.), *The psychology of learning and motivation* (Vol. 8). New York: Academic Press.

Baddeley, A.D., Thomson, N., & Buchanan, M. (1975). Word length and the structure of short-term memory. *Journal of Verbal Learning and Verbal Behavior*, *14*, 575–589.

Broadbent, D.E. (1975). The magic number seven after fifteen years. In K.A. & A. Wilkes (Eds.), *Studies in long-term memory*. London: Wiley.

Bundesen, C. (1990). A theory of visual attention. *Psychological Review*, *97*, 523–547.

Caramazza, A., Capasso, R., & Miceli, G. (1996). The role of the graphemic buffer in reading. *Cognitive Neuropsychology*, 13, 673–698.

Caramazza, A., & Hillis, A. (1990). Spatial presentation of words in the brain implied in the studies of a unilateral neglect patient. *Nature*, *346*, 267–269.

Caramazza, A., & Miceli, G. (1990). The structure of graphemic representations. *Cognition*, *37*, 243–297.

Caramazza, A., Miceli, G., Villa, G., & Romani, C. (1987). The role of the graphemic buffer in spelling: Evidence from a case of acquired dysgraphia. *Cognition*, *26*, 59–85.

Duncan, J., & Humphreys, G.W. (1989). Visual search and stimulus similarity. *Psychological Review*, *96*, 433–458.

Greenwald, M.L., & Berndt, R.S. (1999). Impaired encoding of abstract letter order: Severe alexia in a mildly aphasic patient. *Cognitive Neuropsychology*, *16*, 513–556.

Hampson, P.J., & Morris, P.E. (1978). Some properties of the visual imagery system investigated through backward spelling. *Quarterly Journal of Experimental Psychology*, *30A*, 655–664.

Hillis, A.E., & Caramazza, A. (1989). The graphemic buffer and attentional mechanisms. *Brain and Language*, *36*, 208–235.

Inhoff, A.W., & Wang, J. (1992). Encoding of text, manual movement planning, and eye–hand coordination during copytyping. *Journal of Experimental Psychology: Human Perception and Performance*, *18*(2), 437–448.

Jónsdóttir, M.K., Shallice, T., & Wise, R. (1996). Phonological mediation and the graphemic buffer disorder in spelling: Cross-language differences? *Cognition*, *59*, 169–197.

Karlsson, F. (1982). *Suomen kielen äänne-ja muotorakenne [Finnish phonology and morphology].* Helsinki: Werner Söderström Osakeyhtiö.

Lönnrot, E. (1958/1880). *Suomalais-ruotsalainen sanakirja [Finnish-Swedish dictionary].* Helsinki: Werner Söderström Osakeyhtiö.

Margolin, D.I. (1984). The neuropsychology of writing and spelling: Semantic, phonological, motor and perceptual processes. *Quarterly Journal of Experimental Psychology*, *36A*, 49–489.

Miceli, G., Silveri, C.M., & Caramazza, A. (1985). Cognitive analysis of a case of pure dysgraphia. *Brain and Language*, *25*, 187–212.

Mikkonen, V. (1972). Suomen kielen kirjainten frekvenssi-ja informaatio-ominaisuuksia. [Frequency and information characteristics of letters in the Finnish language]. In O. Järvikoski (Ed.), *Acta Botnica.* Turku: The Ostrobotnian Nation of Turku University.

Nolan, K., & Caramazza, A. (1983). An analysis of writing in a case of deep dyslexia. *Brain and Language*, *20*, 305–328.

Posteraro, L., Zinelli, P., & Mazzucchi, A. (1988). Selective impairment of the graphemic buffer in acquired dysgraphia: A case study. *Brain and Language*, *35*, 274–286.

Saukkonen, P., Haipus, M., Niemikorpi, A., & Sulkala, H. (1979). *Suomen kielen taajuussanasto [Finnish-language Frequency Dictionary].* Porvoo: Werner Söderström Osakeyhtiö.

Seidenberg, M.S. (1987). Sublexical structures in visual word recognition: Access units or orthographic redundancy? In M. Coltheart (Ed.), *Attention and Performance XII. The psychology of reading* (pp. 245–263). Hove, UK: Lawrence Erlbaum Associates Ltd.

Tainturier, M.-J., & Caramazza, A. (1996). The status of double letters in graphemic representations. *Journal of Memory and Language*, *35*, 53–73.

Viviani, P., & Terzuolo, C. (1983). The organization of movement in handwriting and typing. In B. Butterworth (Ed.), *Language production, Vol. 2. Development, writing and other language processes* (pp. 103–146). London: Academic Press.

Watson, D.G., & Humpreys, G.W. (1999). The magic number four and temporo-parietal damage: Neurological impairments in counting targets among distractors. *Cognitive Neuropsychology*, *16*, 609–629.

Wing, A.M., & Baddeley, A.D. (1980). Spelling errors in handwriting: A corpus and a distributional analysis. In U. Frith (Ed.), *Cognitive processes in spelling* (pp. 251–285). London: Academic Press.

Wippich, W., Mecklenbräuker, S., & Halfter, M. (1989). Implicit memory in spelling from word images. *Psychological Research*, *51*, 208–216.

Zhang, G., & Simon, H. (1985). STM capacity for Chinese words and idioms: Chunking and the acoustical loop hypothesis. *Memory & Cognition*, *13*(3), 193–201.

MEMORY, 2001, 9 (4/5/6), 423–432

The development of visuo-spatial working memory

Susan J. Pickering
University of Bristol, UK

Children's performance on tests of visuo-spatial working memory improves with age, although relatively little is known about why this happens. One explanation concerns the development of the ability to recode visually presented information into phonological form. This process appears to be used from around 8 years of age and is a major contributor to tasks in which stimuli can be verbally labelled. However, evidence suggests that phonological recoding cannot account for all of the age-related change in performance on visuo-spatial working memory tasks. In this review, four other mechanisms (knowledge, processing strategies, processing speed, and attentional capacity) are considered in terms of their contribution to children's visuo-spatial working memory development.

Working memory can be thought of as the "moment-to-moment monitoring, processing, and maintenance of information" (Baddeley & Logie, 1999, p.28). To date, the most influential account of working memory has been provided by the multi-component model, originally proposed by Baddeley and Hitch in 1974, and later modified by Baddeley (1986). A key feature of this model is the existence of specialised components for dealing with different aspects of working memory activity. At least three major components are thought to contribute to the functioning of working memory. These include a central executive, which is involved in the control and regulation of the working memory system, and two domain-specific "slave systems" responsible for dealing with information that is in either phonological or visuo-spatial form.

The model of working memory just described is based on empirical evidence from a range of sources, including healthy and brain-damaged adults, and children (see Baddeley & Logie, 1999, for a review). However, in its current state, the model is most suited to a description of working memory function that is in both a mature and an unimpaired form. While the specification of a fully functioning working memory system is the first important step to understanding how this aspect of human cognition is organised, it is also critical to understand how this pattern of mature functioning is reached. The study of working memory in children of different ages can provide important evidence regarding the nature of the immature memory system, and the changes that must occur for mature working memory function to be achieved. The focus of this paper is the development of working memory in the visuo-spatial domain.

The multi-component model has been the subject of a great deal of investigation over the last 25 years, and a range of evidence has been found both to support the model, and to further specify its structure and function. However, much of this research has tended to be concerned with just one of the three components, namely, the phonological loop. Comparatively little is known about the visuo-spatial sketchpad, although in recent years there has been an increase in the research activity devoted to understanding this component of working memory.

Isolating the visuo-spatial sketchpad component using experimental tasks has proved parti-

Requests for reprints should be sent to Susan J. Pickering, University of Bristol, Department of Experimental Psychology, Bristol, BS8 1TN, UK. Email: s.pickering@bris.ac.uk

The author is supported by a grant from the Medical Research Council of Great Britain, awarded to Professors Alan Baddeley and Sue Gathercole (M36006). Grateful thanks are given to Drs Annabel Thorn and Chris Jarrold, and two anonymous reviewers, for their comments on this manuscript.

http://www.tandf.co.uk/journals/pp/09658211.html DOI:10.1080/09658210143000182

cularly difficult, largely because of the requirement to present material that can only be coded in visuo-spatial form. Many types of visuo-spatial image, such as pictures of familiar objects, can be coded in working memory using phonological or semantic representations. "Pure" measures of visuo-spatial working memory are, therefore, more difficult to develop. Two tasks that meet the criteria for use as measures of the visuo-spatial sketchpad are the Corsi blocks (e.g., Milner, 1971) and the visual patterns test (e.g., Della Sala et al., 1999). Each involves the presentation of abstract visuo-spatial information for immediate recall or recognition.

The Corsi blocks task is typically administered using a three-dimensional apparatus involving nine blocks attached to a board in a non-symmetrical arrangement (see Figure 1a for an illustration). The experimenter taps a selection of the blocks in a pre-specified sequence (usually at the rate of one block per second) and the participant is asked to repeat the sequence. Difficulty level is manipulated by altering the number of blocks included in the sequence and a Corsi blocks span score can be calculated on the basis of the longest sequence that can be recalled correctly. The visual patterns task is administered using two-dimensional matrices, like that shown in Figure 1b. Half of the cells in each matrix are filled, and these filled cells form the memory items. The patterns created by the filled and unfilled cells are designed to be relatively abstract, consequently minimising the potential for using anything other than visuo-spatial coding. Scores on this task can be expressed in terms of a pattern span, based on the maximum number of filled squares in the matrix that can be remembered.

Children's performance on the Corsi blocks and visual patterns test increases with age. This is clearly illustrated in a study by Logie and Pearson (1997) in which recall and recognition versions of both tasks were administered to children of 5/6, 8/9 and 11/12 years of age. Performance on all tasks was found to improve significantly with age, as shown in the graph in Figure 2. Similar increases in performance are demonstrated by studies in which each test has been administered separately. For example, in a study of Corsi block recall with 288 children between the ages of 7 and 15 years, Issacs and Vargha-Khadem (1989) found that span increased from an average of 4.1 to 5.6 blocks. Comparable results were obtained in two

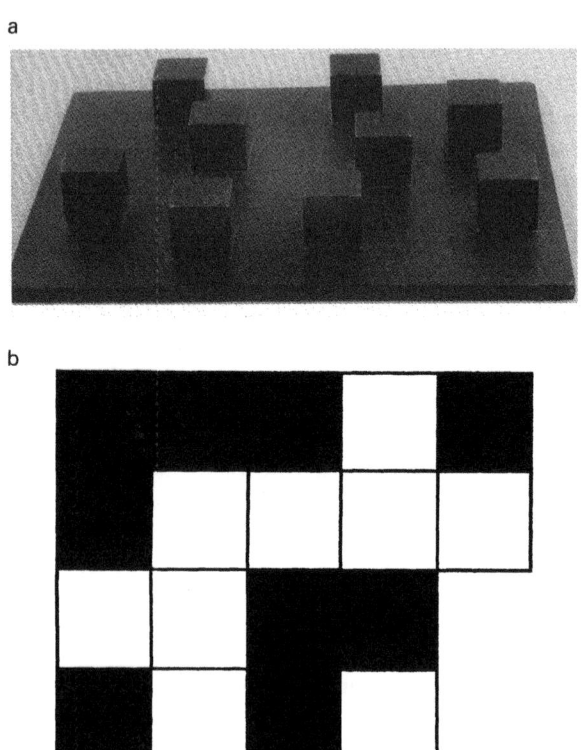

Figure 1. Tests of visuo-spatial working memory: (a) The Corsi blocks task; (b) Stimulus pattern from the visual patterns task.

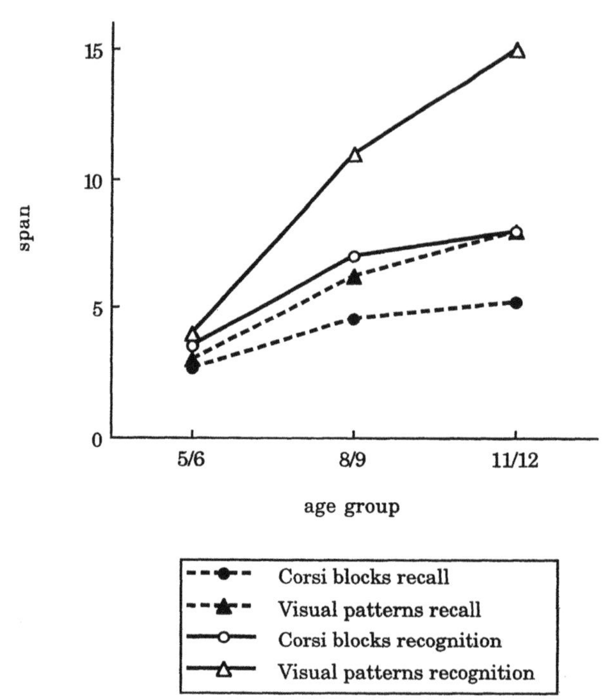

Figure 2. Children's performance on the Corsi blocks task and visual patterns task as a function of age and output mode (based on data from Logie & Pearson, 1997).

studies by Orsini (1994; Orsini et al., 1987). Age-related increases in performance on the visual patterns task are demonstrated by two studies involving children of 5, 7, and 10 years of age, and adults (Miles, Morgan, Milne, & Morris, 1996; Wilson, Scott, & Power, 1987).

What is not clear from these studies is the cause of these improvements in performance. Is there an increase in the capacity of the visuo-spatial sketchpad during childhood, or do changes in strategic activity affect the amount of information that can be retained?

One important line of evidence on children's memory for visually presented information comes from studies involving the recall of pictured objects (e.g., Hitch, Halliday, Dodd, & Littler, 1989; Hitch, Halliday, Schaafstal, & Heffernan, 1991; Hitch, Halliday, Schaafstal, & Schraagen, 1988; Longoni & Scalisi, 1994; Palmer, 2000; Walker, Hitch, Doyle, & Porter, 1994). Although not strictly a "pure" test of visuo-spatial working memory, performance on these tests provides us with some important indications as to the developmental changes that may occur in children's use of the visuo-spatial sketchpad. Across a range of studies, it has been found that very young children appear to encode pictures of objects in visual form. However, after the age of 8 years, children tend to use a more phonological approach to remembering the same pictures.

This developmental change in the coding of nameable pictures is clearly illustrated in an experiment by Hitch and colleagues (1988) involving visual similarity effects and word length effects in 5- and 10-year-old children. These effects are known to be good indices of the use of the visuo-spatial sketchpad and the phonological loop of working memory, respectively, and as such provide evidence of how children of different ages encode memory items. Participants carried out an object recall task with three conditions, in which visual similarity and word length were systematically manipulated. An additional manipulation was included for the 5-year-old group in which half of the participants were instructed to say the names of the objects during presentation. Three important findings emerged from this study. First, young children who labelled the objects performed better than those who did not, suggesting that a process of labelling improves recall. Second, only the 5-year-old children were affected by the visual similarity of the items, suggesting that a visual code was used to maintain information in memory only for these children. Finally, the older group were significantly affected by the name length of the objects, suggesting that they were using a phonological code in working memory.

The presence of a visual similarity effect for the younger group indicates that this group use visuo-spatial working memory to store visually presented information. Hitch et al. (1988) suggest that young children store this type of information in terms of features such as shape, orientation, and detailed appearance. When different objects share visual features, problems can occur during the reconstruction of partially decayed items in memory. However, this reliance on visual working memory in object recall tasks appears to decline during childhood, being replaced by a method of encoding that involves the verbal labels of objects rather than their appearance, and allowing maintenance of information via phonological rehearsal.

There is evidence to suggest that visuo-spatial tasks other than those involving nameable pictures might also be subject to a process of phonological recoding. For example, Fenner, Heathcote, and Jerrams-Smith (2000) found that children's performance on a wayfinding task showed a different pattern of relationships with phonological and visuo-spatial working memory at different ages. Wayfinding is described as "the ability to learn, recall and follow a route through the environment" (p.167) and in this study it was measured in terms of children's ability to accurately walk around a route demonstrated by the experimenter. In children of 5/6 years, wayfinding ability was found to be strongly related to visuo-spatial ability. However this was not the case for the 9/10-year-old children. The authors suggest that whereas young children lack the capacity to form mental models of their environment in a propositional (verbal) format, the use of this type of coding increases with age.

Miles et al. (1996) investigated the extent to which developmental increases in visual patterns task performance could be explained in terms of phonological coding of pattern stimuli. In this study, participants engaged in concurrent articulatory suppression during presentation, maintenance, and output of the matrix patterns. Continuously repeating an utterance (such as "the") interferes with the activity of the phonological loop, and consequently prevents the phonological recoding of visuo-spatial information. It was found that whereas the performance of 10-year-olds and adults was detrimentally affected by the secondary task, the performance of 5- and 7-year-olds was not. It should be noted, however, that the effects of articulatory suppression were moderate and were not found consistently across the study. Nonetheless, the results do indicate that given the opportunity to do so, older children and adults can use phonological processes in order to carry out even a relatively "pure" visuo-spatial working memory task.

Why is it that, in tasks involving visually presented information, young children use a visuo-spatial code and older children use a phonological code? Hitch et al. (1988) have suggested that young children may not have sufficient information-processing capacity to carry out the phonological recoding operations used by older children. They may also be unaware that labelling stimuli would be advantageous. Longoni and Scalisi (1994) proposed that young children use a visual code because they are modality-dependent. Moreover, memory codes are activated automatically, rather than consciously, at this age. Consequently, if information in a memory task is presented in spoken format, it will be encoded phonologically. If it is presented visually, it will be encoded visually. Older children, in contrast, are able to use both phonological and visual codes when dealing with visually presented information.

A series of experiments examining the development of phonological recoding ability in children between 3 and 8 years of age are reported by Palmer (2000). Her findings suggest a relatively complex pattern of developmental change in the coding of pictured objects in working memory. Like Longoni and Scalisi (1994), Palmer suggests that early use of visual coding of objects is explained by the fact that very young children are bound to the perceptual characteristics of the stimuli. Moreover, if verbal labels are made available, they will not be used during encoding unless the relevant phonological representations are activated in long-term memory to a level that can compete with visual coding. In other words, unless the label is specifically drawn to the child's attention, it will not be utilised in the memory task.

Palmer suggests that children go on to use a process of dual coding, prior to the development of the ability to switch attention between different types of active representations in long-term memory and inhibit information of a less relevant nature. Dual coding is an intermediate strategy, in which having multiple representations of the memory items provides a better basis for recall than visual representations alone (e.g., Paivio, 1971). However, the most sophisticated form of memory activity is considered to be automatic phonological coding. Palmer argues that older children are able to use this strategy when recalling nameable objects because they have developed the ability to switch attention from an automatic response based on the presentation modality (visual) to a controlled response based on the (spoken) output requirements of the task.

What factors are responsible for bringing about this change in coding behaviour? Two particular explanations have emerged. First, it has been suggested that the ability to translate information from a visual to a phonological form in a memory task is closely related to the acquisition of literacy (e.g., Fastenau, Conant, & Lauer, 1998; Hitch et al., 1988; Logie, Della Sala, Wynn, & Baddeley, 2000). Fastenau and colleagues suggest that reading instruction is an important factor in the increasing use of phonological processes in visuo-spatial tasks. Evidence to support this view comes from studies in Zaire (Conant et al., 1997b) and Laos (Conant et al., 1997a) in which it has been found that literate and non-literate children show different patterns of performance on phonological and visuo-spatial memory tasks.

A second factor thought to play a role in developmental changes in phonological recoding is the maturation of functions associated with the central executive component of working memory. The central executive is hypothesised to be involved in a range of cognitive processes such as attention, inhibition, switching, planning, and the simultaneous storage and processing of information (see Baddeley, 1996, for a review). Palmer has suggested that age-related changes in memory for visually presented information may be dependent on activities such as these. In other words, for older children and adults, the operation of working memory is contingent on the efficient allocation of (phonological and visuo-spatial) slave system resources by the central executive. Luciana and Nelson (1998) also relate the maturation of higher-order cognitive functions such as those just outlined to changes in working memory performance. They suggest that whereas the early stages of development of working memory involve refinement of basic perceptual and sensorimotor functions, subsequent developmental changes are based on the maturation of neurological networks that serve to integrate complex processes associated with working memory function.

Children's visuo-spatial working memory development therefore appears to be significantly related to the use of phonological recoding strategies. However, visual codes do not appear to be abandoned completely during development. Evidence suggests that this form of coding continues to play a role in immediate memory for visually presented information, even after a phonological recoding strategy has been acquired (Brandimonte, Hitch, & Bishop, 1992; Della Sala, Logie, Marchetti, & Wynn, 1991; Hitch, Woodin, & Baker, 1989; Logie et al., 2000). For example, in a study by Logie and colleagues (2000), visual similarity effects were found across a series of experiments in which word and letter stimuli were presented to adult participants. One possible explanation for this finding is that the development of working memory involves an increase in the number of codes available in a memory task, rather than the substitution of one code for another (Hitch et al., 1988, 1989). This is consistent with the idea of the mature working memory system being capable of a process of dual coding (Paivio, 1971; Palmer, 2000). Palmer suggests that in the fully developed working memory system, visual and phonological coding actually exist together on a continuum, under the control of attentional and inhibitory mechanisms.

However there are a number of problems with the view that the development of visuo-spatial working memory is attributable purely to changes in the use of phonological recoding. First, while it is clear that children's performance on the Corsi blocks task increases with age, it is not clear how the memory stimuli in this task could be encoded verbally. During task presentation children are required to encode a series of vectors of movement between a limited number of spatial targets. Names, directions, and other methods of verbally marking visuo-spatial items are much less applicable here than in tasks involving patterns or line drawings of objects. Indeed, adults' performance on the Corsi blocks task has been found to be unaffected by the inclusion of concurrent articulatory suppression (e.g., Farmer, Berman, & Fletcher, 1986), suggesting that verbal coding is not used in this task.

Second, work in our own laboratory suggests that although verbal recoding may be a useful strategy for carrying out the visual patterns task, it is not the only mechanism responsible for children's improvement in performance with age. Pickering, Gathercole, Hall, and Lloyd (2001) presented a computerised version of the visual pattern task to children of 6 and 10 years of age and adults. During presentation and maintenance of stimuli participants also engaged in one of two secondary tasks selected to interfere with either phonological loop or visuo-spatial sketchpad functioning (articulatory suppression or spatial tapping). It was found that whereas spatial tapping did significantly impair performance, articulatory suppression did not, indicating that visuo-spatial rather than phonological processes were being used in the memory task.

If developmental changes in children's visuo-spatial working memory performance cannot entirely be explained by the use of phonological recoding of memory items, what other mechanisms might be responsible for observed increases in Corsi blocks and visual patterns span? Two recent reviews of children's working memory provide us with some important ideas on this issue. Although not directly addressing development in the visuo-spatial domain, Cowan (1997) and Gathercole (1999) have outlined a number of cognitive capacities that appear to change with age, consequently affecting performance on tasks of working memory. Cowan suggests that changes in knowledge, processing strategies, processing speed, attentional and processing capacity, and passive memory loss and storage capacity, are likely to influence performance on working memory tasks. Focusing more specifically on the phonological loop, Gathercole (1999) reports a range of mechanisms that have been linked to developmental increases on tasks designed to measure this aspect of working memory. These include the perceptual analysis of incoming information, the nature of sensory memory and short-term storage, memory for order, and subvocal rehearsal. Retrieval processes, and in particular, the use of long-term memory to reconstruct partial memory traces (redintegration) (Roodenrys, Hulme, & Brown, 1993), are also considered.

Little is known about whether mechanisms like these play a role in the development of visuo-spatial working memory. However, by relating these mechanisms to the visuo-spatial domain it might be possible to provide some testable ideas about the factors responsible for visuo-spatial working memory development. Four mechanisms in particular—changes in the contents of long-term memory, changes in processing strategies, increases in processing speed, and changes in attentional capacity—seem particularly relevant to the processes involved in carrying out tasks such as the Corsi blocks and visual patterns tasks. In the remainder of this review, each of these four mechanisms is discussed in the context of existing evidence on the development of children's visuo-spatial working memory.

KNOWLEDGE

As children get older the content of their long-term memory increases and becomes more refined. Increases in knowledge provide a greater opportunity for grouping information in a working memory task in meaningful ways, often referred to as "chunking". It has been known for some time that chunking can increase performance in phonological working memory tasks (e.g., Miller, 1956), and it is suggested that the process of grouping memory items on the basis of information held in long-term memory leads to a reduction in the quantity of information that needs to be held in working memory (Cowan, 1997).

The role of children's knowledge in working memory tasks was demonstrated in a study by Chi (1978). In this study, participants' ability to recall chessboard configurations was investigated in relation to their knowledge of chess. It was found that children who were experienced chess players were better at recalling the location of pieces on the board, although only when pieces were arranged in legitimate configurations. It is particularly interesting to note that children who were experienced players performed better on the memory task than adults who were novice players, reinforcing the importance of domain-specific knowledge over general experience.

It seems very likely that children's knowledge about the visuo-spatial features of their world increases with age and through schooling. Such changes in visuo-spatial knowledge could conceivably affect performance on tasks of visuo-spatial working memory by changing the way that information is encoded. That is, information contained in long-term memory might provide a basis for meaningfully grouping memory items in order to decrease working memory load. For example, it might be possible to use a process of chunking in the Corsi blocks task to encode a six-item sequence as two three-block sequences. In doing this, the nature of the representation held in working memory is altered.

Similar processes may also be brought to bear in the visual patterns task. Avons and Phillips (1986) suggest that two different levels of processing may occur during the encoding of abstract visual patterns. One is a low-level description in which the spatial relationships between basic elements of the pattern are specified. The other is a higher-order description based on pre-existing knowledge. Although visual pattern stimuli are designed to be abstract in nature, it is often possible to identify more familiar sub-patterns within the matrix, the recall of which can be supported by information held in long-term memory. Consistent with this suggestion, a study by Avons (1980, cited in Wilson et al., 1987) found that adults' memory for patterns was much better if the patterns contained letter-like shapes.

Wilson and colleagues (1987) have suggested that developmental changes in performance on the visual patterns task may be the result of "an increase in the lexicon of shapes which can be immediately recognised" (p.253). Pickering and Jarrold (2001) investigated the role of knowledge of shapes and patterns on visuo-spatial working memory performance in a recent study. In this study, adult participants were presented with visual pattern stimuli for immediate recall. All stimuli had previously been rated by a separate group of adult participants as to how "pattern-like" they considered them to be (on a scale of 1–5). Performance in the recall test was found to be much higher when participants were presented with stimuli given high "pattern-likeness" ratings compared with those given low ratings. This study provides preliminary evidence that recognition of familiar structures within abstract patterns is an important factor in performance on visuo-spatial working memory tasks. Indeed, in one account of visuo-spatial working memory (Logie, 1995), it is suggested that information actually gains access to the working memory system via long-term memory. According to this view, by the time information enters working memory it is already in the form of an "interpreted package", rather than a set of meaningless items (Ellis, Della Sala, & Logie, 1996).

The notion of familiarity and processes of chunking in visuo-spatial working memory is, however, less well developed than in the phonological domain. It is not clear exactly what constitutes a "visual chunk" (Vecchi, Montecellai, & Cornoldi, 1995), or what kind of long-term knowledge would benefit performance on visuo-spatial working memory tasks. In phonological loop tasks, the notion of a chunk is more readily identifiable as a meaningful set of phonological items. In addition, it has been demonstrated that developmental increases in children's knowledge of their language contribute to performance on phonological working memory tasks. For example, Gathercole, Frankish, Pickering, and Peaker (1999) found that by 6 years of age, children are capable of using both lexical and phonotactic knowledge in order to reconstruct partial phonological memory traces. If long-term knowledge does play an important role in the development of children's visuo-spatial working memory, it is necessary to ask whether there is a visuo-spatial equivalent to lexical and phonotactic knowledge, and if so, what form it takes. Does it, for example, depend on the principles of geometry and the acquisition of a knowledge base of shapes?

PROCESSING STRATEGIES

The second mechanism considered with respect to children's visuo-spatial working memory development is processing strategies, "the potentially conscious, deliberate, and controllable cognitive plans adopted to enhance performance in a memory task" (Schneider & Sodian, 1997, p.443). Studies of the development of strategy use in children reveal some general principles. For example, Cowan (1997) notes improvements across childhood in children's knowledge and understanding of strategies and their use in particular situations, the ability to implement strategies without undue effort, and the ability to use more efficient versions of a strategy. Schneider and Sodian (1997) provide an account of how strategy use develops in four different phases across childhood. In the first phase children show a "mediation deficiency", in that even when instructed in a particular strategy, performance is not improved by its use. In the next phase (production deficiency) children do not use a strategy spontaneously, but will do so if prompted. This is followed by a period of "utilisation deficiency" (Miller, 1990), usually in the early phases of strategy acquisition, when strategic activity is carried out, but does not benefit recall. In the final phase there is mature and sophisticated strategy use. Consequently, it can be seen that although children do develop strategic approaches to carrying out memory tasks, strategy use is far from being an all-or-nothing phenomenon during childhood.

Two major forms of processing strategy have been identified: organisation and rehearsal (Goswami, 1998). This review will concentrate on rehearsal, as the ability to organise memory items is closely linked to the use of existing knowledge in working memory tasks, discussed earlier. Rehearsal is generally viewed as a process of refreshing items in memory to prevent decay (Gathercole, 1999). In phonological working memory tasks this process can be covert or overt, and usually consists of the repetition of a memory list until output is required. With respect to the development of strategies in phonological working memory, it has been suggested that children do not rehearse auditory speech material until around the age of 7 years (Gathercole, Adams, & Hitch, 1994; Gathercole & Hitch, 1993). However, the use of this strategy increases over childhood (Flavell, Beach, & Chinsky, 1966). Moreover, children can be trained to rehearse, with subsequent improvements in memory performance (Naus, Ornstein, & Aivano, 1977). Quality of rehearsal appears to change over childhood too (Cowan, 1997). For example, it appears that older children are more likely to use a cumulative rehearsal strategy in which a greater number of memory items are linked together in a sequence during each repetition of the list.

Although there appears to be a general view that visuo-spatial information can be rehearsed in memory, the processes involved are not as well understood as for rehearsal in the phonological domain. One suggestion is that visuo-spatial rehearsal involves an internal allocation of attention to different locations in space (Baddeley, 1986). Logie (1995) compares the functions of a modified visuo-spatial sketchpad to Kosslyn's (1980) view of visual imagery. Kosslyn proposed the existence of a visual buffer, linked to an area of attentional focus, and on whose contents a number of operations (such as panning, zooming, scanning, generating, and regenerating) could operate. In Logie's model, two subcomponents known as the "visual cache" and the "inner scribe" provide the basis for a rehearsal mechanism. Information stored in the visual cache can be refreshed by the inner scribe using a process related to movement planning. Logie's description of the functions of the visual cache and inner scribe has much in common with the phonological store and articulatory rehearsal mechanism of phonological working memory. However, it is unclear how far analogies between the two slave systems can be taken. If the developmental changes in the use of phonological rehearsal are mirrored in visuo-spatial working memory, this may go some way to explaining age-related increases in visuo-spatial memory task performance. The nature of visuo-spatial rehearsal and its contribution to increased performance on visuo-spatial working memory tasks is an important topic for future studies.

PROCESSING SPEED

A third factor thought to contribute to increases in children's working memory is processing speed (Cowan, 1997). Changes in speed of processing are believed to be dependent on neurological maturation (Kail & Salthouse, 1994) and it has been suggested that faster rates of processing can reduce the effects of decay and interference in working memory in at least two ways (Cowan, 1997). The first is in terms of faster rates of rehearsal, which, in the phonological domain, has been linked to faster rates of articulation (Cowan et al., 1998). The second is in terms of an increase in the speed of memory search (Cowan, 1992; Cowan, Wood, & Borne, 1994). Although there is no direct evidence to link faster rates of processing to increases in visuo-spatial working memory, it seems plausible that this mechanism could influence performance across childhood. It might be the case, for example, that processing speed is linked to speed and efficiency of visuo-spatial rehearsal. It is also likely that retrieval speed is an important factor. Anecdotal observations of children's performance on the Corsi blocks and visual patterns tasks suggest that those who respond quickly are more likely to recall correctly. Evidence from adults provides support for a contribution of general, rather than domain-specific, processing speed to visuo-spatial working memory tasks. Smyth and Scholey (1996) found that articulation rate was related to performance on both a visual pattern recall and a Corsi blocks task.

ATTENTIONAL CAPACITY

The final factor to be considered in terms of its contribution to children's visuo-spatial memory development is changes in attentional capacity. In particular, it seems plausible that changes in the amount of information that can be subsumed within the focus of attention at one time (Cowan, 1997) will affect performance on visuo-spatial working memory tasks. Inhibition of irrelevant information during a task is also likely to be important. Attention and inhibition are thought to be dependent on the activity of the frontal lobes, which do not reach full maturity until adolescence (Yakovelev & Lecours, 1967). Consequently, the contribution of attentional processes to visuo-spatial working memory tasks is unlikely to be at its most powerful until this stage of development. Attention and inhibition are also viewed as processes carried out by the central executive of working memory (Baddeley, 1986). Relatively little is known about the development of the central executive over childhood, however some have suggested that this component of working memory is particularly important to visuo-spatial memory tasks, largely because of the significant attentional requirements of many visuo-spatial tasks (Baddeley, personal communication). Developmental studies of the role of attention and inhibition in children's visuo-spatial working memory could provide important evidence of how central executive processes are linked to visuo-spatial task performance.

CONCLUSIONS

What, then, is the cause of increases in visuo-spatial working memory performance during childhood? In many cases it seems likely that children get better at remembering visuo-spatial information because they convert the information into a phonological code. The availability of both a phonological and a visual representation in working memory serves two purposes. First, it provides a more robust means of maintaining information, and second it provides a choice of representational forms upon which attention can be focused, depending on the requirements of the task. Development of phonological recoding processes may be linked to learning to read, itself a process of phonological recoding. However, the most efficient use of this strategy may also require the contribution of the central executive component of working memory.

Other processes may also influence visuo-spatial working development. Task performance is likely to benefit from a permanent base of relevant knowledge, within which novel memory items can be interpreted. Processing strategies such as visuo-spatial rehearsal may also be important. Finally, the maturation of the neurological system, and corresponding changes in attentional capacity and processing speed, could also play an important role in the development of visuo-spatial working memory.

REFERENCES

Avons, S.E., & Phillips, W.A. (1986). Representation of matrix patterns in long- and short-term memory. *Acta Psychologica, 65*, 227–246.

Baddeley, A., & Logie, R. (1999). Working memory: The multiple component model. In A. Miyake & P. Shah (Eds.), *Models of working memory* (pp.28–61). New York: Cambridge University Press.

Baddeley, A.D. (1986). *Working memory*. Oxford: Oxford University Press.

Baddeley, A.D. (1996). Exploring the central executive. *Quarterly Journal of Experimental Psychology, 49*A, 5–28.

Baddeley, A.D., & Hitch, G. (1974). Working memory. In G.A. Bower (Ed.), *Recent advances in learning and motivation*, Vol. 8 (pp.47–90). New York: Academic Press.

Brandimonte, M.A., Hitch, G.J., & Bishop, D.V.M. (1992). Influence of short-term memory codes on visual image processing: Evidence from image transformation tasks. *Journal of Experimental Psychology: Learning, Memory and Cognition, 18*, 157–165.

Chi, M.T.H. (1978). Knowledge structures and memory development. In R.S. Siegler (Ed.), *Children's thinking: What develops?* Hillsdale, NJ: Lawrence Erlbaum Associates Inc.

Conant, L.L., Fastenau, P.S., Giordani, B., Boivin, M.J., Chounramany, C., Xaisida, S., Choulamountary, L., Pholsena, P., & Olness, K. (1997a). Relationships among memory span tasks: A cross-cultural developmental perspective [Abstract]. *The Clinical Neuropsychologist, 11*, 304.

Cowan, N. (1992). Verbal memory span and the timing of spoken recall. *Journal of Memory and Language, 31*, 668–684.

Cowan, N. (1997). The development of working memory. In N. Cowan (Ed.), *The development of memory in childhood* (pp.163–199). Hove, UK: Psychology Press.

Cowan, N., Wood, N.L., & Borne, D.N. (1994). Reconfirmation of the short-term storage concept. *Psychological Science, 5*, 103–106.

Cowan, N., Wood, N.L., Wood, P.K., Keller, T.A., Nugent, L.D., & Keller, C.V. (1998). Two separate verbal processing rates contributing to short-term memory span. *Journal of Experimental Psychology: General, 127*, 141–160.

Della Sala, S., Gray, C., Baddeley, A., Allamano, N., & Wilson, L. (1999). Pattern span: A tool for unwelding visuo-spatial memory. *Neuropsychologia, 37*, 1189–1199.

Della Sala, S., Gray, C., Baddeley, A., & Wilson, L. (1997). *Visual Patterns Test*. Bury St Edmunds, UK: Thames Valley Test Company.

Della Sala, S., Logie, R., Marchetti, C., & Wynn, V. (1991). Case studies in working memory: A case for single cases? *Cortex, 27*, 169–191.

Ellis, A.X., Della Sala, S., & Logie, R.H. (1996). The bailiwick of visuo-spatial working memory: Evidence from unilateral spatial neglect. *Cognitive Brain Research, 3*, 71–78.

Farmer, E.W., Berman, J.V.F., & Fletcher, Y.L. (1986). Evidence for a visuo-spatial sketchpad in working memory. *Quarterly Journal of Experimental Psychology, 38*A, 675–688.

Fastenau, P.S., Conant, L.L., & Lauer, R.E. (1998). Working memory in young children: Evidence for modality-specificity and implications for cerebral reorganisation in early childhood. *Neuropsychologia, 36*, 643–652.

Fenner, J., Heathcote, D., & Jerrams-Smith, J. (2000). The development of wayfinding competency: Asymmetrical effects of visuo-spatial and verbal ability. *Journal of Environmental Psychology, 20*, 165–175.

Flavell, J.H., Beach, D.H., & Chinsky, J.M. (1966). Spontaneous verbal rehearsal in a memory task as a function of age. *Child Development, 37*, 283–299.

Gathercole, S.E. (1999). Cognitive approaches to the development of short-term memory. *Trends in Cognitive Sciences, 3*, 410–419.

Gathercole, S.E., Adams, A-M., & Hitch, G.J. (1994). Do young children rehearse? An individual differences analysis. *Memory and Cognition, 22*, 201–207.

Gathercole, S.E., Frankish, C.R., Pickering, S.J., & Peaker, S. (1999). Phonotactic influences on short-term memory. *Journal of Experimental Psychology: Learning, Memory and Cognition, 25*, 84–95.

Gathercole, S.E., & Hitch, G.J. (1993). Developmental changes in short-term memory: A revised working memory perspective. In A. Collins, S.E. Gathercole, M.A. Conway, & P.E. Morris (Eds.), *Theories of memory* (pp.189–210). Hove, UK: Lawrence Erlbaum Associates Ltd.

Goswami, U. (1998). *Cognition in children*. Hove, UK: Psychology Press.

Hitch, G.J., Halliday, M.S., Dodd, A., & Littler, J.E. (1989). Development of rehearsal in short-term memory: Differences between pictorial and spoken stimuli. *British Journal of Developmental Psychology, 7*, 347–362.

Hitch, G.J., Halliday, M.S., Schaafstal, A.M., & Heffernan, T.M. (1991). Speech, "inner speech", and the development of short-term memory: Effects of picture labelling on recall. *Journal of Experimental Child Psychology, 51*, 220–234.

Hitch, G.J., Halliday, M.S., Schaafstal, A.M., & Schraagen, J.M.C. (1988). Visual working memory in children. *Memory and Cognition, 16*, 120–132.

Hitch, G.J., Woodin, M.E., & Baker, S. (1989). Visual and phonological components of working memory in children. *Memory and Cognition, 17*, 175–185.

Issacs, E.B., & Vargha-Khadem, F. (1989). Differential course of development of spatial and verbal memory span: A normative study. *British Journal of Developmental Psychology, 7*, 377–380.

Kail, R., & Salthouse, T.A. (1994). Processing speed as a mental capacity. *Acta Psychologica, 86*, 199–255.

Kosslyn, S.M. (1980). *Image and mind*. Cambridge, MA: Harvard University Press.

Logie, R.H. (1995). *Visuo-spatial working memory*. Hove, UK: Lawrence Erlbaum Associates Ltd.

Logie, R.H., Della Sala, S., Wynn, V., & Baddeley, A.D. (2000). Visual similarity effects in immediate verbal serial recall. *Quarterly Journal of Experimental Psychology, 53*A, 626–646.

Logie, R.H., & Pearson, D.G. (1997). The inner eye and the inner scribe of visuo-spatial working memory:

Evidence from developmental fractionation. *European Journal of Cognitive Psychology*, *9*, 241–257.
Longoni, A.M., & Scalisi, T.G. (1994). Developmental aspects of phonemic and visual similarity effects: Further evidence in Italian children. *International Journal of Behavioural Development*, *17*, 57–71.
Luciana, M., & Nelson, C.A. (1998). The functional emergence of pre-frontally-guided working memory systems in four- to eight-year-old children. *Neuropsychologia*, *36*, 273–293.
Miles, C., Morgan, M.J., Milne, A.B., & Morris, E.D.M. (1996). Developmental and individual differences in visual memory span. *Current Psychology*, *15*, 53–67.
Miller, G.A. (1956). The magical number seven, plus or minus two: Some limits on our capacity for processing information. *Psychological Review*, *63*, 81–97.
Miller, P.H. (1990). The development of strategies of selective attention. In D.F. Bjorklund (Ed.), *Children's strategies: Contemporary views of cognitive development* (pp.157–184). Hillsdale, NJ: Lawrence Erlbaum Associates Inc.
Milner, B. (1971). Interhemispheric differences in the localisation of psychological processes in man. *British Medical Bulletin*, *27*, 272–277.
Naus, M.J., Ornstein, P.A., & Aivano, S. (1977). Developmental changes in memory: The effects of processing time and rehearsal instructions. *Journal of Experimental Child Psychology*, *23*, 237–251.
Orsini, A. (1994). Corsi's block-tapping test: Standardisation and concurrent validity with WISC-R for children aged 11 to 16. *Perceptual and Motor Skills*, *79*, 1547–1554.
Orsini, A., Grossi, D., Capitani, E., Laicona, M., & Vallar, G. (1987). Verbal and spatial immediate memory span: Normative data from 1355 adults and 1112 children. *Italian Journal of Neurological Sciences*, *8*, 539–548
Paivio, A. (1971). *Imagery and verbal processes*. New York: Holt, Rinehart & Winston.
Palmer, S. (2000). Working memory: A developmental study of phonological recoding. *Memory*, *8*, 179–193.
Pickering, S.J., Gathercole, S.E., Hall, M., & Lloyd, S. (2001). Development of memory for pattern and path: Further evidence for the fractionation of visuo-spatial memory. *Quarterly Journal of Experimental Psychology*, *54A*, 397–420.
Pickering, S.J., & Jarrold, C.R. (2001). Long-term memory and short-term visuo-spatial recall—the role of "pattern-likeness". *Manuscript in preparation.*
Roodenrys, S., Hulme, C., & Brown, G. (1993). The development of short-term memory span: Separable effects of speech rate and long-term memory. *Journal of Experimental Child Psychology*, *56*, 431–442.
Schneider, W., & Sodian, B. (1997). Memory strategy development: Lessons from longitudinal research. *Developmental Review*, *17*, 442–461.
Smyth, M.M., & Scholey, K.A. (1996). The relationship between articulation time and memory performance in verbal and visuo-spatial tasks. *British Journal of Psychology*, *87*, 179–191.
Vecchi, T., Montecellai, M.L., & Cornoldi, C. (1995). Visuo-spatial working memory: Structures and variables affecting a capacity measure. *Neuropsychologia*, *33*, 1549–1564.
Walker, P., Hitch, G.J., Doyle, A., & Porter, T. (1994). The development of short-term visual memory in young children. *International Journal of Behavioural Development*, *17*, 73–89.
Wilson, J.T.L., Scott, J.H., & Power, K.G. (1987). Developmental differences in the span of visual memory for pattern. *British Journal of Developmental Psychology*, *5*, 249–255.
Yakovelev, P.I., & Lecours, A.R. (1967). The myelinogenetic cycles of regional maturation of the brain. In A. Minkowski (Ed.), *Regional development of the brain in early life*. Oxford: Blackwell.

MEMORY, 2001, 9 (4/5/6), 433–444

The effects of eye and limb movements on working memory

Bonnie M. Lawrence, Joel Myerson, Heather M. Oonk, and Richard A. Abrams
Washington University, USA

Three experiments examined the role of eye and limb movements in the maintenance of information in spatial working memory. In Experiment 1, reflexive saccades interfered with memory span for spatial locations but did not interfere with memory span for letters. In Experiment 2, three different types of eye movements (reflexive saccades, pro-saccades, and anti-saccades) interfered with working memory to the same extent. In all three cases, spatial working memory was much more affected than verbal working memory. The results of these two experiments suggest that eye movements interfere with spatial working memory primarily by disrupting processes localised in the visuospatial sketchpad. In Experiment 3, limb movements performed while maintaining fixation produced as much interference with spatial working memory as reflexive saccades. These results suggest that the interference produced by eye movements is not the result of their visual consequences. Rather, all spatially directed movements appear to have similar effects on visuospatial working memory.

Working memory is a cognitive system involved in the temporary maintenance and manipulation of information (Baddeley, 1986; Baddeley & Logie, 1999). According to Baddeley (1986), the cognitive architecture of working memory consists of a central executive, an articulatory loop, and a visuospatial sketchpad. The central executive is an attentional control mechanism that is responsible for selecting information for temporary maintenance and for delegating resources within the working memory system. The articulatory loop and the visuospatial sketchpad subsystems are responsible for the temporary maintenance of verbal and visuospatial information, respectively. Both subsystems are commonly thought to include a passive perceptual store and an active rehearsal mechanism for maintaining the contents of the store, and researchers have been interested in determining the processes underlying the maintenance of information in the two subsystems. In the verbal working memory subsystem, a subvocal rehearsal process is thought to underlie the maintenance of information in the passive store (i.e., Awh et al., 1996; Baddeley, Lewis, & Vallar, 1984; Salame & Baddeley, 1982). In the spatial working memory subsystem, a rehearsal process involving eye movements or the covert analogue of eye movements has been proposed (Baddeley, 1986), but the effects of such movements have not been systematically examined.

The results of an unpublished experiment by Idzihowski, Baddeley, Dimbleby, and Park (cited in Baddeley, 1986) support an eye-movement-based rehearsal process. In this experiment, subjects were required to detect changes in the form of a visual stimulus while simultaneously maintaining the locations of digits in working memory. The stimulus was either stationary (requiring no eye movements) or moving (requiring pursuit eye movements), and results revealed that pursuit eye

Requests for reprints should be sent to Bonnie M. Lawrence, Department of Anatomy and Neurobiology, Washington University School of Medicine, Box 8108, 660 South Euclid Avenue, St. Louis, Missouri 63110, USA. Email: bonnie@eye-hand.wustl.edu

This research was supported by a Grants-in-Aid of Research Award from Sigma Xi, awarded to Bonnie M. Lawrence, and grant R01-MH45145 from the National Institutes of Health to Richard A. Abrams. We thank Sandra Hale for her comments and assistance throughout this project.

http://www.tandf.co.uk/journals/pp/09658211.html DOI:10.1080/09658210143000047

movements interfered with the maintenance of spatial locations. Related findings were reported by Hale et al. (1996, Experiment 3). In their experiment, subjects were required to remember a series of visually cued locations. Following presentation of each cued location, subjects were required to execute an eye movement to a visual target, and these eye movements interfered with the maintenance of spatial information in working memory.

Although the results of the Idzihowski et al. and Hale et al. (1996) experiments are consistent with an eye-movement-based rehearsal process, important limitations characterise these experiments, and an understanding of the relationship between eye movements and spatial working memory has yet to emerge. Specifically, because neither of the experiments examined the effect of eye movements on verbal working memory, it is possible that eye movements interfere with working memory in general (i.e., the central executive) and not spatial working memory (i.e., the visuospatial sketchpad) in particular. In addition, because Idzihowski et al. required smooth pursuit eye movements and because Hale et al. did not precisely measure eye movements, it is unclear whether *saccadic* eye movements interfere with the maintenance of information in spatial working memory.

Furthermore, if saccadic eye movements interfere with spatial working memory, it is unclear whether or not this interference effect is dependent on the type of saccadic eye movement executed, or even whether interference will result from any type of spatially directed movement, regardless of whether it is an eye movement or a limb movement. This is an important issue because a comparison of the effects of different types of eye and limb movements might help to localise the source of the interference produced by eye movements. One possibility is that all types of eye movements interfere equally, perhaps because of the resulting shift in spatial coordinates or because of accompanying shifts of attention (e.g., Shepherd, Findlay, & Hockey, 1986). Another possibility is that certain types of eye movements interfere more than others. For example, if anti-saccades (i.e., eye movements executed away from a spatial cue) interfere to a greater degree than other types of eye movements, it would suggest that central executive processes play an important role in eye-movement interference. This is because anti-saccades involve not only programming a movement away from the cue, but also inhibition (presumably an executive function) of a reflexive saccade in the direction of the cue. A final possibility is that *any* type of spatially directed movement will interfere. Although simultaneous eye and limb movements have been shown to interfere with spatial working memory (Hale et al., 1996; Smyth & Scholey, 1994), the effects of limb movements executed in the absence of eye movements have not been studied.

Accordingly, the present study compared the effects of different types of spatially directed movements (i.e., reflexive saccades, symbolically cued pro-saccades, anti-saccades, and limb movements) on working memory. First, however, we sought to establish whether eye movements had differential effects on spatial and verbal working memory. Interference common to both types of working memory would suggest that eye movements interfere with central executive processes, whereas interference specific to one domain would suggest that processes associated with that particular subsystem were being affected. In addition, the effects of peripheral flashes while subjects were required to maintain fixation, which presumably required inhibition of reflexive saccades, were also assessed.

EXPERIMENT 1

The purpose of this experiment was to determine if eye movements selectively interfere with the maintenance of information in spatial working memory. The working memory tasks required subjects to remember either a series of letters or a series of spatial locations. In between presentation of the memory items, subjects performed one of three secondary tasks. In the baseline condition, the secondary task was simply to maintain fixation. The present experiment also included two other secondary task conditions in which subjects saw a peripheral flash. In one of these conditions, subjects were required to maintain fixation, whereas in the other condition, subjects executed an eye movement to the location where the flash occurred. The latter two secondary tasks both presumably elicited a shift of attention (e.g., Muller & Rabbitt, 1989; Theeuwes, 1992; Yantis, 1993, but see Yantis & Jonides, 1990), but only one of them required the execution of an eye movement whereas the other required the inhibition of an eye movement. If either of the latter two conditions affected memory for both digits and locations, they would presumably do so by affecting executive processes that were not specific to one domain, whereas domain-specific effects would provide evidence of selective disruption of either the verbal or visuospatial subsystems (Baddeley, 1986).

Method

Subjects. A total of 24 undergraduate students from Washington University completed the experiment in a 2-hour session for course credit.

Apparatus and procedure. Subjects were seated in a dimly lit room with their chins supported by a chin rest in order to maintain stable head position and keep their eyes a constant distance (55 cm) from the video monitor. Subjects performed verbal and spatial working memory tasks similar to those used in Hale et al. (1996, Experiment 1). These primary tasks were accompanied by a secondary task requiring fixation, a secondary task requiring a shift of attention but no eye movement, or a secondary task involving a reflexive saccade. The corresponding three secondary task conditions were termed fixate, fixate plus, and reflexive. The timing and sequences of events are presented in Figure 1.

The spatial working memory task consisted of a series of yellow Xs (1.5° × 1.5°) each presented for 1250 ms in one of 16 cells of a 4 × 4 grid (6.2° × 6.2°) located in the centre of the screen. The locations of the Xs were selected randomly without replacement for each series such that no location occurred more than once in a series. Two rectangles (0.5° × 0.6°) were presented concurrently with the grid, one located 6.5° to the left of screen centre and one located 6.5° to the right of screen centre. Subjects were instructed to remember the locations of the Xs because they would be asked to indicate the locations of the Xs on the monitor with an erasable pen. At the end of each series, an empty grid signalled subjects to recall the locations of the memory items.

The verbal working memory task consisted of a series of yellow letters (0.5° × 0.6°), each presented for 1250 ms in a box located in the centre of the display. The letters were selected from the following set (B, D, F, G, H, K, L, M, N, Q, R, S, T, W, and X) randomly without replacement for each series such that no letter occurred more than once in a series. Two rectangles (0.5° × 0.6°) were presented simultaneously with the letter, one located 6.5° to the left of screen centre and one

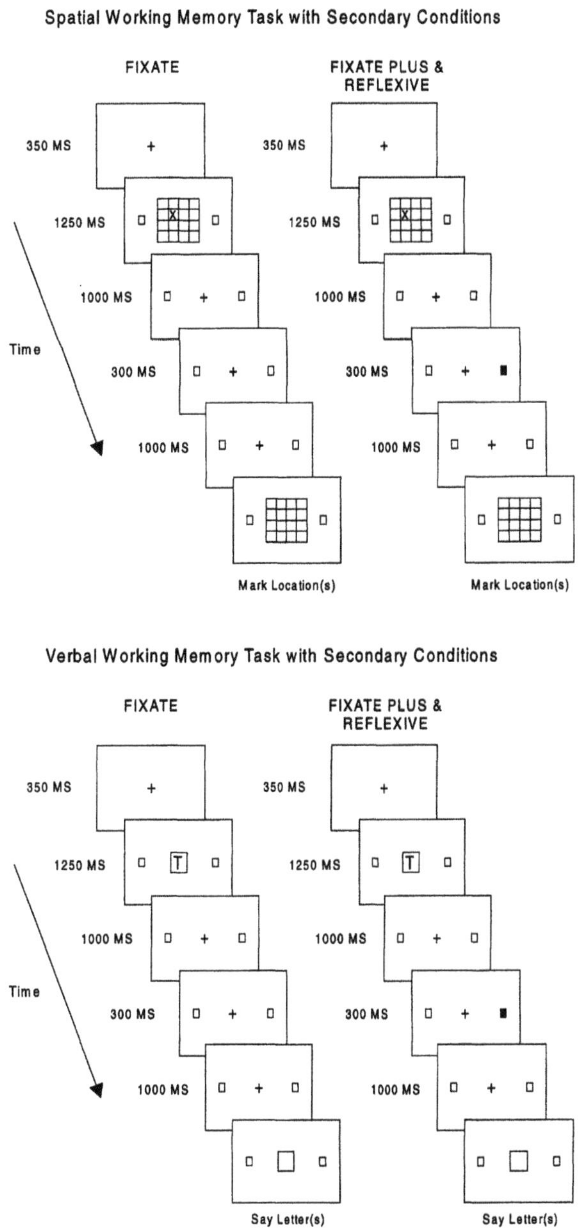

Figure 1. Procedure and sample stimuli (for a series length of one item) for the spatial and verbal secondary task conditions of Experiment 1. When the series length was more than one item, the same procedure (with a different location or letter) was repeated (without the final recall stimulus) for each item. The recall stimulus (the cue for the participant to either mark the spatial locations that appeared previously or recite the letters that appeared previously) was presented once per trial after all of the items had been presented. The fixate plus and reflexive saccade conditions differed only in instruction to the subject (see Method section).

located 6.5° to the right of screen centre. Subjects were instructed to remember the identity and temporal order of the letters because they would be asked to recall the letters at the end of a series. At the end of each series, an empty purple box appeared to signal subjects to recall the memory items in the correct order.

The secondary tasks were interleaved between the presentation of the primary (working memory) task items (Xs or letters) so that completion of the secondary task would not interfere with encoding of the primary task items. In all conditions, the secondary task stimulus consisted of a white central crosshair (0.3° × 0.3°) which appeared simultaneously along with rectangles presented 6.5° to the left and to the right of the centre of the screen. In the fixate condition, the stimulus events consisted of a crosshair and rectangles presented for 2300 ms, and subjects were required to maintain fixation on the crosshair. In the fixate plus condition, the stimulus events consisted of a crosshair and rectangles presented for 1000 ms after which one of the rectangles was cued by filling it in completely with white for 300 ms. This was followed by a crosshair and rectangles presented for 1000 ms. Subjects were required to maintain fixation on the crosshair throughout. Each rectangle had a 0.5 probability of being the one that was filled. In the reflexive condition, the stimulus events were the same as in the fixate plus condition, but subjects were required to execute an eye movement to the filled box. In all conditions, the background colour was dark grey, and the borders of the rectangles and of the box surrounding the letters were white, as were the lines of the grid.

The number of memory items (i.e., series length) was determined by a psychophysical staircase procedure (Levitt, 1970). Each condition began with a series of three letters or Xs. Initially, if the response to the series was correct (i.e., all items were correctly recalled), the number of items in the next series was increased by two. This procedure was followed until the first incorrect response (i.e., one or more items incorrectly recalled), after which the number of items in the next series was decreased by one. Subsequently, the number of items in a series was increased or decreased by one depending on whether the response to the previous series had been correct or incorrect, respectively. Each condition was terminated after the third reversal (i.e., a series with an incorrect response followed immediately by a series with a correct response). Subjects received three practice series prior to each condition.

Eye movement monitoring. Stimulus presentation was computer-controlled as was the acquisition of eye movement data. Eye position was monitored using an ISCAN (Cambridge, MA) RK426pc video-based eye movement monitor. The eye movement monitor was calibrated at the beginning of each experimental condition by presenting five evenly spaced points across the display which subjects were required to fixate.

Eye position was recorded at a rate of 60 Hz for 2000 milliseconds beginning after the offset of each memory item. In order to identify saccades, the eye position signal was filtered and differentiated so that a smooth velocity record was obtained. The beginning of an eye movement was defined as the first moment in time when the velocity exceeded 10°/s for at least 32 ms with the constraint that velocity subsequently exceeded 30°/s. In the fixate and fixate plus conditions, an error message was presented if an eye movement was made between memory items when subjects were supposed to be fixating the crosshair. In the reflexive condition, an error message was presented if the eye movement was too fast (latency less than 80 ms), too slow (latency greater than 2000 ms), or in the wrong direction from that cued by the filled rectangle. If an eye movement error occurred, the series was aborted and immediately rerun at the same series length but with different memory items.

Design. The two primary working memory tasks (verbal and spatial) were crossed with the three secondary task conditions (fixate, fixate plus, reflexive) to produce a total of six experimental conditions. All subjects participated in all six conditions. Half of the subjects performed the spatial working memory task conditions first, and half performed the verbal working memory task conditions first. The order of secondary task conditions was completely counterbalanced across subjects.

Results

Analysis of the eye movement latencies revealed that there was no significant difference between the latencies from the reflexive conditions of the spatial ($M = 233.0$ ms) and verbal ($M = 231.8$ ms) working memory tasks, $t(23) < 1$. For these conditions, only data from those series in which saccades towards the appropriate target occurred were included in the analyses of the memory data. For the fixate and fixate plus conditions, only data from series in which no eye movements occurred were included in the analyses.

Verbal and spatial memory spans were determined for each subject in each of the secondary task conditions. As in experiments previously conducted in our laboratory (Jenkins, Myerson, Joerding, & Hale, 2000), span was defined as the amount of information (i.e., the number of items) for which the probability of all items being maintained accurately in memory is 0.5 (i.e., the series length that could be correctly recalled 50% of the time). The method by which spans were determined is analogous to a procedure used to estimate psychometric functions. More specifically, the probability of recalling an entire series was determined for each series length that a subject encountered within a particular condition, and then these probabilities were plotted as a function of series length. Linear interpolation was performed on the data from all series lengths ranging from the longest series for which a subject had 100% accuracy to the longest series encountered by that subject. For example, if a subject had 100% correct at series lengths 3, 4, and 5, and the longest series presented according to the staircase procedure was 8, the probabilities for series lengths 5 to 8 were used in the regression analysis. The series length at which the regression equation predicted a probability of .5 was used as an index of the individual's memory span.

Mean verbal and spatial spans in each secondary task condition are presented in Figure 2. As may be seen, eye movements and peripheral flashes produced large decreases in spatial but not verbal spans. A 2 (primary task: spatial and verbal) × 3 (secondary task: fixate, fixate plus, reflexive) repeated measures analysis of variance (ANOVA) on memory spans revealed a significant main effect of secondary task, $F(2, 46) = 20.37$, $p < .001$, and a significant primary task × secondary task interaction, $F(2, 46) = 12.98$, $p < .001$. Although verbal spans tended to be larger than spatial spans, the difference did not reach statistical significance, $F(1, 23) = 3.93$, $p = .06$. Planned comparisons in the verbal domain revealed no significant differences between the fixate and the fixate plus conditions, $F(1, 23) = 2.85$, $p > .10$, or between the fixate and reflexive conditions, $F(1, 23) = 1.62$, $p > .20$. Planned comparisons in the spatial domain revealed no significant difference between the fixate and the fixate plus conditions, $F(1, 23) < 1$. However, memory spans were significantly smaller in the reflexive condition than in the fixate condition, $F(1, 23) = 40.90$, $p < .001$.

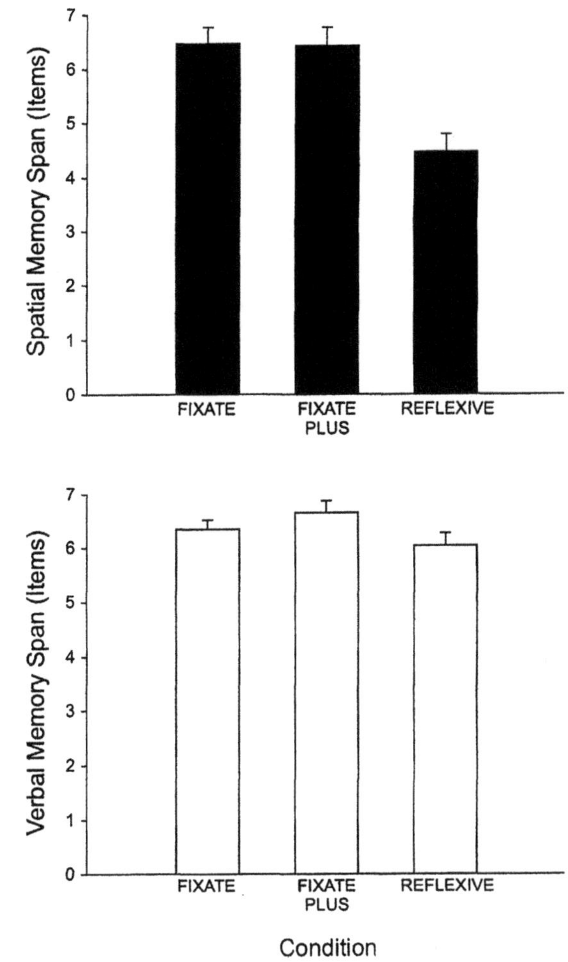

Figure 2. The mean verbal and spatial spans for each secondary task condition of Experiment 1, with standard error bars.

Discussion

In the current experiment, reflexive eye movements significantly interfered with spatial, but not verbal, working memory. In contrast, peripheral flashes in the absence of eye movements did not interfere with the maintenance of either spatial or verbal information in working memory, suggesting that the inhibition of a saccade does not interfere with the maintenance of information in working memory.

The present finding that saccadic eye movements selectively interfere with spatial working memory is consistent with the findings of Hale et al. (1996). Hale et al. found that eye movements alone were sufficient to interfere with spatial working memory, although they did not monitor eye movements precisely or examine the effects of eye movements on verbal working memory. Notably, the results of the present experiment demonstrate that saccadic eye movements selectively interfere with the maintenance of information in spatial working memory.

EXPERIMENT 2

The results of Experiment 1 suggest that eye movements selectively interfere with spatial, but not verbal, working memory. It is possible, however, that this interference may be dependent on the type of eye movement executed in that experiment. In Experiment 1, eye movements were summoned by peripheral cues. Eye movements can also be voluntarily generated in response to a central, symbolic cue in the absence of any peripheral stimulus events. Furthermore, eye movements can be executed in a direction away from a peripheral event. Such eye movements are known as anti-saccades and involve the inhibition of a reflexive saccade and the execution of a pro-saccade (Guitton, Buchtel, & Douglas, 1985).

Moreover, reflexive saccades, pro-saccades, and anti-saccades are thought to be mediated by neurobiologically distinct networks (Pierrot-Deseilligny et al., 1995). For example, the parietal eye fields are believed to be responsible for the triggering of reflexive saccades, whereas the frontal eye fields are thought to be responsible for the production of pro-saccades. Furthermore, the prefrontal cortex is thought to be responsible for the inhibition of reflexive saccades in the anti-saccade paradigm. The involvement of prefrontal cortex is especially relevant because it is frequently associated with executive processes as well as with working memory (e.g., Goldman-Rakic, 1996; Roberts, Hager, & Heron, 1994). Because of the various differences in the mechanisms involved in the different types of eye movements, it is possible that the pattern of interference effects in spatial working memory may be dependent on the type of eye movement executed. The purpose of Experiment 2 was to address this possibility. The procedure used in Experiment 2 was similar to that used in Experiment 1 with the addition of secondary tasks requiring pro-saccades and anti-saccades.

Method

Subjects. A total of 20 undergraduate students were obtained from a subject pool maintained by the Department of Psychology at Washington University. Subjects were paid $15 upon completion of two $1\frac{1}{2}$ hour sessions.

Apparatus and procedure. The equipment was the same as that used in Experiment 1. The procedure was similar to that in Experiment 1 except that two secondary tasks were added, one involving a pro-saccade and one involving an anti-saccade. In the pro-saccade condition, the central fixation cross was replaced by an arrow that pointed to either the right or left rectangle, to which subjects executed a saccade. The stimulus events in the anti-saccade condition were the same as in the reflexive saccade and fixate plus conditions. That is, either the right or left rectangle was randomly filled. In the anti-saccade condition, subjects then executed a saccade to the rectangle that was *not* filled, whereas in the reflexive saccade condition, subjects executed a saccade towards the filled rectangle.

The timing for the fixate plus and reflexive saccade conditions was the same as in Experiment 1. For the pro-saccade condition, the fixation cross appeared for 500 ms, and then was replaced by either a left- or right-pointing arrow which was present for 800 ms. The duration of the fixation cross in the fixate condition was 800 ms, similar to the amount of time that subjects fixated prior to executing a pro-saccade (duration of the fixation cross plus saccade latency). The experiment consisted of two separate sessions conducted on separate days. Half of the subjects completed the spatial working memory conditions in the first session, and half of the subjects completed the verbal working memory conditions in the first session.

Design. The two primary working memory tasks (verbal and spatial) were crossed with the five secondary task conditions (fixate, fixate plus, reflexive saccade, pro-saccade, and anti-saccade) to produce a total of ten experimental conditions. All subjects participated in all conditions. Half of the subjects performed the spatial working memory task conditions first and half performed the verbal working memory task conditions first. The order of secondary task conditions was completely counterbalanced across subjects.

Results

The mean eye movement latencies for each secondary task condition are shown in Table 1. A 2 (primary task: spatial and verbal) × 3 (secondary task: reflexive-saccade, pro-saccade, and anti-saccade) repeated measures ANOVA on the eye movement latencies revealed no main effect of primary task, $F(1,19) < 1$. However, there was a main effect of secondary task, $F(2,38) = 15.46$, $p < .001$, reflecting the fact that the latencies of pro-saccades and anti-saccades were slower than those of reflexive saccades. There was no primary task × secondary task interaction, $F(2,38) = 1.42$, $p > .20$.

Verbal and spatial memory spans were determined for each subject in each condition in the same manner as in Experiment 1. For the fixate and fixate plus conditions, only data from series in which no eye movements occurred were included in the analyses. For the reflexive, pro-saccade, and anti-saccade conditions, only data from series in which saccades towards the appropriate target occurred were included in the analyses.

Mean verbal and spatial spans in each secondary task condition are represented in Figure 3. As may be seen, eye movements and peripheral flashes produced larger decreases in spatial spans than in verbal spans, and the three different types of eye movements all had very similar effects. A 2 (primary task: spatial and verbal) × 5 (secondary task: fixate, fixate plus, reflexive saccade, pro-saccade, and anti-saccade) repeated measures ANOVA revealed a main effect of secondary task, $F(4,76)$, $p < .001$, and a primary task × secondary task interaction, $F(4,76) = 4.41$, $p < .01$. There was no main effect of primary task on memory span, $F(1,19) < 1$.

TABLE 1
Eye movement (EM) mean latencies and standard errors from Experiment 2

EM	*Spatial*	*Verbal*
Reflexive	297.6 (19.6)	280.8 (15.2)
Pro-saccade	364.8 (14.7)	355.3 (11.9)
Anti-saccade	342.1 (22.5)	346.4 (19.1)

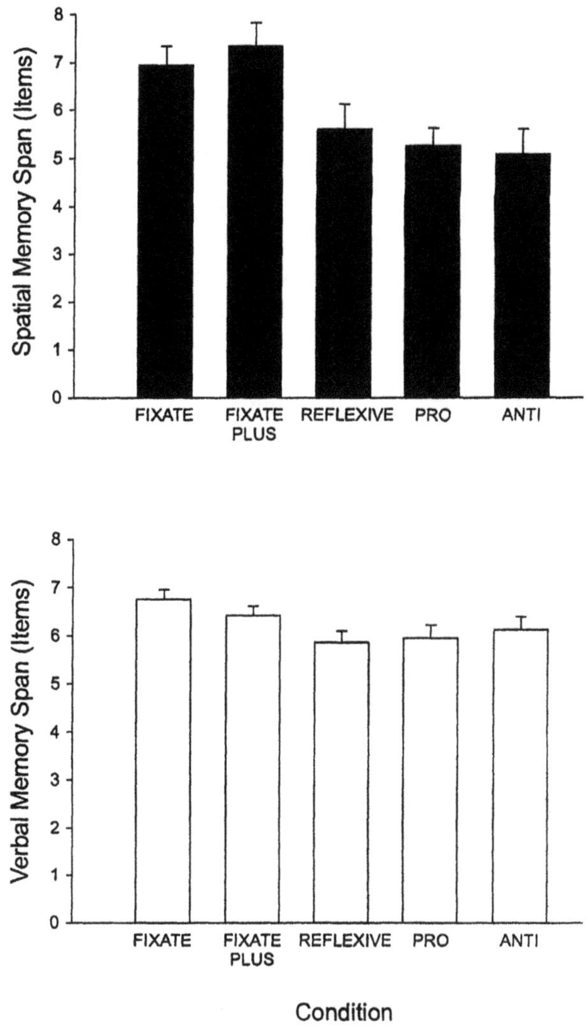

Figure 3. The mean verbal and spatial spans for each secondary task condition of Experiment 2, with standard error bars.

Planned comparisons of the fixate and fixate plus conditions revealed no significant differences in either domain [for spatial working memory, $F(1,19) = 1.19$, ns; for verbal working memory, $F(1,19) = 3.11$, ns]. Planned comparisons of the three eye movement conditions within each domain also revealed no significant differences in either domain (all Fs < 1). Accordingly, for each domain, the data from the fixate and fixate plus conditions (i.e., no eye movement) were collapsed as were the data from the three eye movement conditions (i.e., eye movement). Comparisons of the no-eye-movement and eye-movement condititions within each domain revealed that eye movements significantly interfered with both verbal and spatial working memory; $t(19) = 4.40$, $p < .001$, and $t(19) = 6.25$, $p < .001$, respectively.

As a result, the collapsed data were then subjected to a 2 (primary task: spatial and verbal) × 2 (secondary task: eye movement and no eye movement) repeated measures ANOVA in order to compare the magnitude of interference effects in the two domains. Analysis revealed no main effect of primary task, $F(1,19) < 1$, a main effect of secondary task, $F(1,19) = 45.84$, $p < .001$, and a significant interaction between primary and secondary task, $F(1,19) = 18.36$, $p < .001$, reflecting the fact that the magnitude of the interference effect for spatial working memory was greater than that for verbal working memory. As can be seen in Figure 4, the decrease in memory span due to eye movements was actually three times as large for spatial working memory ($M = 1.8$ items lost) as for verbal working memory ($M = 0.6$ items lost).

Discussion

The results of Experiment 2 indicated that all three types of eye movements (reflexive saccades, pro-saccades, and anti-saccades) significantly interfered with the maintenance of information in spatial working memory and that the magnitude of the interference effect was independent of the type of eye movement executed. In contrast, peripheral flashes did not interfere with memory for spatial locations. A similar pattern was observed with respect to verbal working memory, but the amount of interference produced by eye movements was much smaller. These findings (i.e., the differential sensitivity of spatial working memory and the similar effects of different types of eye movements) suggest that the observed interference primarily reflects a general characteristic of the way in which the eye movement system interacts with the system responsible for spatial working memory. The results of the analysis of eye movement latencies are consistent with this suggestion. This analysis revealed no significant differences between latencies in the spatial and verbal domains, implying that the greater effect of eye movements on memory for locations was due to the greater sensitivity of spatial working memory rather than to any difference between the eye movements executed in the verbal and spatial working memory conditions.

In Experiment 2, eye movements had a significantly greater effect on spatial working memory than on verbal working memory, whereas in Experiment 1, eye movements affected spatial working memory but did not significantly affect verbal working memory. It is possible that this difference between the results of the present two experiments reflects sample differences or that the addition of more secondary task conditions, with a resultant increase in the number of times the primary task had to be performed, increased subjects' sensitivity to inteference. The important point, however, is that the results of both of the present experiments are in agreement with respect to the fact that eye movements produce much more interference with spatial than with verbal working memory. Even in Experiment 2, where some effect on verbal working memory was observed, the effect on spatial working memory was approximately three times as large. These results suggest that eye movement interference with spatial working memory is primarily at the level of the visuospatial sketchpad.

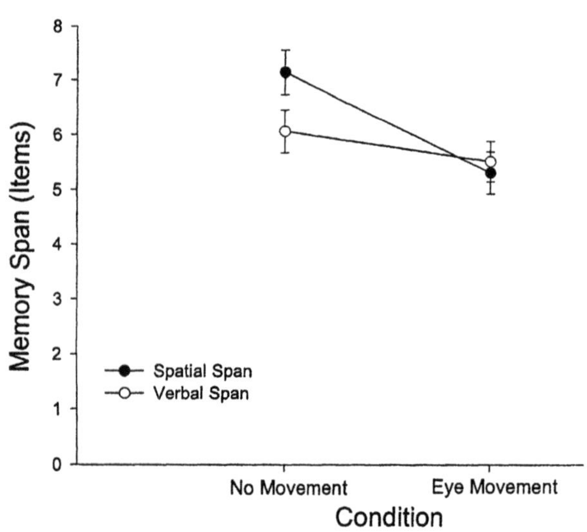

Figure 4. The mean verbal and spatial memory spans for secondary conditions without an eye movement requirement (fixate and fixate plus) and those secondary conditions with an eye movement requirement (reflexive, pro- and anti-saccade) from Experiment 2, with standard error bars.

EXPERIMENT 3

Although the previous two experiments demonstrate that eye movements interfere with spatial working memory, it is possible that eye movements interfere because of their visual consequences (i.e., because they produce visual transients, saccadic suppression, and changes in retinal coordinates) or because they are spatially planned and executed movements. That is, it is possible that *any* spatially directed movement would interfere with the maintenance of information in spatial working memory. Hale et al. (1996, Experiment 3) demonstrated that the concurrent execution of eye and limb movements interferes with spatial working memory to a significantly greater extent than the execution of eye movements alone. Although these results suggest that limb movements interfere with spatial working memory, it is possible that the interference in the Hale et al. experiment did not result from the execution of the limb movements *per se*, but from an interaction between the eye and limb movement systems (e.g., Bekkering et al., 1994; Bekkering et al., 1995). Therefore, the purpose of the present experiment was to determine if limb movements executed in the absence of eye movements interfere with spatial working memory.

Method

Subjects. A total of 18 undergraduate students from Washington University completed the experiment in a 1-hour session for course credit.

Apparatus and procedure. The apparatus for Experiment 3 was the same as that used in the previous experiments except for the addition of a button panel (47 cm in length) containing three equally spaced (12.5 cm between each button) buttons (6 cm in diameter), which rested on the subject's lap. The button panel was not visible to the subject while they were performing the experiment. Eye movement monitoring was also the same as in the previous experiments except for slight changes in the time requirements that were modified to be the same as those for limb movement monitoring (described later).

The presentation of stimuli for the primary spatial working memory task interleaved with either a secondary task requiring fixation (*fixate*), a secondary task requiring a limb movement (*limb*), or a secondary task requiring a reflexive eye movement (*reflexive*). For both working memory and secondary task stimuli, the background colour was dark grey.

The stimuli for the working memory task consisted of a series of blue circles (1.25° in diameter), each presented for 2000 ms in one of 20 cells of a white cross-shaped grid (4.7° × 4.7°) located in the centre of the screen. The locations of the circles were selected randomly without replacement for each series such that no location could be cued more than once in a series. The centrally located cell was filled white and could not contain a memory item (i.e., a circle). This was because a discrimination stimulus would appear in that same location during the secondary task. Subjects were instructed to remember the locations of the circles as accurately as possible. At the end of each series, the appearance of an empty grid signalled subjects to recall the memory items by moving a mouse cursor to each of the previously cued locations, clicking the left mouse button once in each location. Subjects signalled the completion of the recall period by clicking once in the space outside the grid. A 200 Hz tone was sounded if the subjects did not correctly recall the memory items.

The number of memory items (i.e., the series length) was determined by a modified version of the WAIS–III memory span procedure (Wechsler, 1997) rather than by the staircase procedure used previously. Like the WAIS-III procedure, subjects were given two trials at each series length until they missed two trials at any one series length. Unlike the WAIS-III procedure, when subjects missed two trials at any one series length, they were given one last trial at a series length of one item less. If the subject was correct on this trial, their span was determined to be the length of the series in this trial. If, however, the subject was incorrect on this trial, their span was determined to be this series length minus half an item. Each condition began with a series of two memory items.

The secondary tasks were interleaved between the presentation of each of the working memory items (i.e., circles), as opposed to simultaneously with the primary memory items, so that completion of the secondary task would not interfere with encoding of the primary task items. In all conditions, the secondary task discrimination stimulus consisted of either a white "x" (0.6°) or a white "+" (0.6°) which appeared for 2500 ms in all conditions. Each discrimination stimulus had a 50% probability of appearing.

In the fixate condition, subjects were required to maintain fixation on the centre of the screen where the stimulus appeared. In addition, subjects were required to maintain hand position on the centre button of the button pad. In both the reflexive and limb conditions, the stimulus appeared in the periphery (i.e., 6.5° to the left or the right of fixation) signalling the direction of the to-be-executed movement. In the reflexive condition, subjects were required to execute an eye movement in the direction of the peripheral stimulus and then execute an eye movement back to the centre of the screen. In this condition, subjects were required to maintain hand position on the centre button. In the limb condition, subjects were to execute a limb movement to the button in the corresponding direction of the peripheral item (i.e., left or right) and then execute a limb movement back to the centre button.

Limb movement monitoring. In all conditions, an error message was presented if the subject's hand was not on the centre button prior to the presentation of each working memory item. After the onset of the secondary task stimulus, an error message was presented in the fixate and reflexive conditions if the subject's hand was not on the centre button throughout the presentation of the secondary task stimuli. In the limb condition, error messages were also presented under the following circumstances: if the subject's hand was not on the centre button by 100 ms after the onset of the secondary task stimulus; if the subject's hand was not removed from the centre button until 700 ms after the onset of the secondary task stimulus; if the subject's hand was not removed from the centre button and 2333 ms had passed, or if 2333 ms had passed and the subject's hand was not back to the centre button. If one of the preceding errors occurred, the memory trial was aborted and immediately rerun at the same series length.

Design. Subjects participated in all three separately blocked conditions (fixate, reflexive, limb). The order of conditions was completely counterbalanced across subjects. Subjects received six practice trials prior to each condition. Practice consisted of two trials each at series lengths one, two, and three.

Results

The mean saccade latency in the reflexive condition was 278.2 ms (SD = 60.0). The mean limb movement latency in the limb condition was 419.7 ms (SD = 43.8). The mean memory spans and standard errors for each task condition are presented in Figure 5. A one-way repeated measures ANOVA conducted on memory spans indicated a significant main effect of condition, $F(2,34) = 8.02$, $p < .005$, reflecting the fact that memory spans in the reflexive and limb conditions were smaller than the memory spans in the fixate condition. Planned comparisons revealed a significant difference in memory spans between the fixate and the limb conditions, $t(17) = 3.06$, $p < .01$. There was also a significant difference in memory spans between the fixate and reflexive conditions $t(17) = 3.42$, $p < .005$, but no significant difference between the limb and reflexive conditions $t(17) < 1.0$.

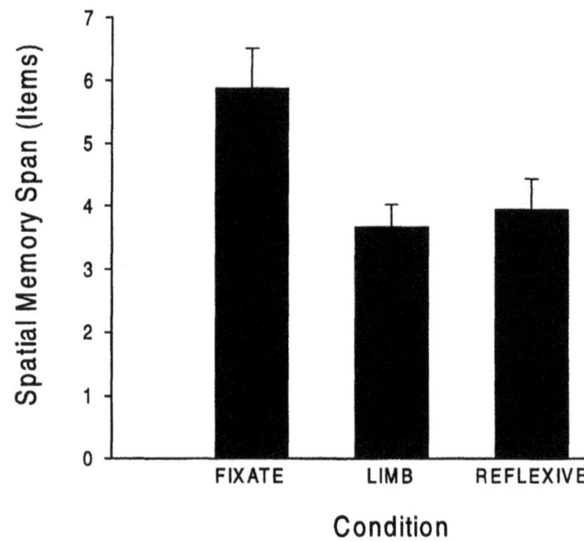

Figure 5. The mean spatial spans for each secondary task condition of Experiment 3, with standard error bars.

Discussion

The results of Experiment 3 indicate that both eye movements (executed in the absence of limb movements) and limb movements (executed in the absence of eye movements and without visual guidance) interfere with spatial working memory. These results suggest that a common aspect of spatially directed movements (e.g., movement planning or shifts of spatial attention), rather than some property specific to a particular type of movement (e.g., the visual consequences of eye movements or the visual and kinesthetic consequences of limb movements), underlies the interference with spatial working memory observed in all three of the present experiments.

GENERAL DISCUSSION

The results of Experiment 1 revealed that reflexive eye movements selectively interfered with the maintenance of location information in working memory. This finding was replicated in Experiment 2, which yielded the additional finding that other types of eye movements, specifically anti-saccades and pro-saccades, also significantly interfere with spatial working memory. Moreover, the magnitude of the interference effects in the spatial working memory domain was independent of the type of eye movement executed, and was much greater than the interference effects in the verbal domain. The results of Experiment 3 indicated that limb movements also interfere with spatial working memory. Taken together, the present findings suggest that interference results from a common property of spatially directed movements, and that the effects of this common property are primarily localised within the visuospatial sketchpad.

In addition, the results of the first two experiments suggest that the inhibition of a saccade does not interfere with the maintenance of information in spatial or verbal working memory. In both experiments, the fixate plus condition, in which subjects were required to inhibit a saccade to a peripheral flash, failed to produce interference with spatial working memory. Moreover, there were no significant differences among the different types of eye movements in the amount of interference they produced, even though one of them (anti-saccades) required inhibition of reflexive saccades. Both the lack of effect of inhibition on memory for locations and the relative insensitivity of verbal working memory to eye movements suggest that such movements exert their effects more on the visuospatial sketchpad and less on the central executive component of working memory which is often assumed to be responsible for inhibitory control (e.g., Engle, Tuholski, Laughlin, & Conway, 1999).

The finding that eye movements of various kinds interfere with the maintenance of information in spatial working memory would be consistent with Baddley's (1986) suggestion that eye-movement-based rehearsal subserves the maintenance of spatial information. That is, it could be that secondary tasks requiring eye movements interrupt rehearsal, resulting in the loss of spatial information. However, the present finding that a secondary task requiring limb movements also interferes with working memory for locations (Experiment 3) is not readily explainable in terms of an eye-movement-based rehearsal process. Moreover, the eye movement rehearsal interpretation assumes that rehearsal is necessary to maintain information in working memory, whereas the results of recent studies both by psychologists, (e.g., Washburn & Astur, 1998) and cognitive neuroscientists (e.g., Fuster, 1995) raise the possibility that visuospatial information does not have to be rehearsed in order to be maintained.

What mechanism or mechanisms might be responsible for interference by eye and limb movements? If one assumes that a single common mechanism is involved, then the mechanism would appear to involve some property common to spatially directed movements in general, rather than a mechanism that relies on properties specific to one particular type of movement (e.g., the visual consequences of saccades). For example, both eye and limb movements, rather than interrupting a rehearsal sequence, may interrupt activity in the positive feedback loop between prefrontal and posterior cortices that, it has been hypothesised, serves to maintain visuospatial information (Chafee & Goldman-Rakic, 2000; Fuster, 1995; Hale et al., 1996).

Other possible mechanisms for interference with memory for locations involve the effects of shifting spatial attention and planning spatially directed movements. More specifically, shifts in spatial attention may interfere because they interrupt an attention-based rehearsal process or simply because attention is required to maintain spatial information (Awh, Jonides, & Reuter-Lorenz, 1998; Smyth & Scholey, 1994). Alternatively, movement planning might interfere either directly by interrupting rehearsal, or indirectly because such planning itself involves shifts of spatial attention (Rizzolatti, Riggio, & Sheliga, 1994). Finally, it is possible that different mechanisms are involved in the interference produced by different types of movement. Obviously, further research will be needed to discriminate between these possibilities, but the present results suggest that, whatever the mechanism or mechanisms involved, spatially directed movements interfere with working memory primarily by disrupting processes localised in the visuospatial sketchpad.

REFERENCES

Awh, E., Jonides, J., & Reuter-Lorenz, P.A. (1998). Rehearsal in spatial working memory. *Journal of Experimental Psychology: Human Perception and Performance*, *24*, 780–790.

Awh, E., Jonides, J., Smith, E.E., Schumacher, E.H., Koeppe, R.A., & Katz, S. (1996). Dissociation of storage and rehearsal in verbal working memory: Evidence from PET. *Psychological Science*, *7*, 25–31.

Baddeley, A.D. (1986). *Working memory*. Oxford: Oxford University Press.

Baddely, A., Lewis, V., & Vallar, G. (1984). Exploring the articulatory loop. *The Quarterly Journal of Experimental Psychology*, *36*, 233–252.

Baddeley, A.D., & Logie, R.H. (1999). Working memory: The multiple-component model. In A. Miyake & P. Shah (Eds.), *Models of working memory: Mechanisms of active maintenance and executive control* (pp. 28–61). New York: Cambridge University Press.

Bekkering, H., Adam, J.J., Kingma, L., Huson, A., & Whiting, H.T.A. (1994). Reaction time latencies of eye and hand movements in single and dual-task conditions. *Experimental Brain Research*, *97*, 471–476.

Bekkering, H., Adam, J.J., van den Aarssen, A., Kingma, H., & Whiting, H.T.A. (1995). Interference between saccadic eye and goal-directed hand movements. *Experimental Brain Research*, *106*, 475–484.

Chafee, M.V., & Goldman-Rakic, P.S. (2000). Inactivation of parietal and prefrontal cortex reveals interdependence of neural activity during memory-guided saccades. *Journal of Neurophysiology*, *83*, 1550–1566.

Engle, R.W., Tuholski, S.W., Laughlin, J.E., & Conway, A.R.A. (1999). Working memory, short-term memory, and general fluid intelligence: A latent-variable approach. *Journal of Experimental Psychology: General*, *128*, 309–331.

Fuster, J.M. (1995). *Memory in the cerebral cortex: An empirical approach to neural networks in the human and nonhuman primate*. Cambridge, MA: MIT Press.

Goldman-Rakic, P.S. (1996). The prefrontal landscape: Implications of functional architecture for understanding human mentation and the central executive. *Philosophical Transactions of the Royal Society of London, Biological Sciences*, *351*, 1445–1453.

Guitton, D., Buchtel, H.A., & Douglas, R.M. (1985). Frontal lobe lesions in man cause difficulties in suppression of reflexive glances and in generating goal-directed saccades. *Experimental Brain Research*, *58*, 455–472.

Hale, S., Myerson, J., Rhee, S.H., Weiss, C.S., & Abrams, R.A. (1996). Selective interference with the maintenance of location information in working memory. *Neuropsychology*, *10*, 228–240.

Jenkins, L., Myerson, J., Joerding, J., & Hale, S. (2000). Converging evidence that visuospatial cognition is more age-sensitive than verbal cognition. *Psychology and Aging*, *15*, 157–175.

Levitt, H. (1970). Transformed up–down methods in psychoacoustics. *The Journal of the Acoustical Society of America*, *49*, 467–477.

Muller, H., & Rabbitt, P. (1989). Reflexive and voluntary orienting of attention: Time course of activation and resistance to disruption. *Journal of Experimental Psychology: Human Perception and Performance*, *15*, 315–330.

Pierrot-Deseilligny, C., Rivaud, S., Gaymard, B., Muri, R., & Vermersch, A. (1995). Cortical control of saccades. *Annals of Neurology*, *37*, 557–567.

Rizzolatti, G., Riggio, L., & Sheliga, B.M. (1994). Space and selective attention. In C. Umilta & M. Moscovitch (Eds.), *Attention and performance 15: Conscious and nonconscious information processing* (pp. 232–265). Cambridge, MA: MIT Press.

Roberts, R.J., Hager, L.D., & Heron, C. (1994). Prefrontal cognitive processes: Working memory and inhibition in the antisaccade task. *Journal of Experimental Psychology: General*, *123*, 374–393.

Salame, P., & Baddeley, A.D. (1982). Disruption of short-term memory by unattended speech: Implications for the structure of working memory. *Journal of Verbal Learning and Verbal Behavior*, *21*, 150–164.

Shepherd, M., Findlay, J., & Hockey, R. (1986). The relationship between eye movements and spatial attention. *Quarterly Journal of Experimental Psychology*, *38*A, 475–491.

Smyth, M.M., & Scholey, K.A. (1994). Interference in immediate spatial memory. *Memory and Cognition*, *22*, 1–13.

Theeuwes, J. (1992). Perceptual selectivity for color and form. *Perception & Psychophysics*, *51*, 599–606.

Washburn, D.A., & Astur, R.S. (1998). Nonverbal working memory of humans and monkeys: Rehearsal in the sketchpad? *Memory & Cognition*, *26*, 277–286.

Wechsler, D. (1997). *Wechsler Adult Intelligence Scale – III: Administration and scoring manual*. San Antonio, CA: Psychological Corporation.

Yantis, S. (1993). Stimulus-driven attentional capture. *Current Directions in Psychological Science*, *2*, 156–161.

Yantis, S., & Jonides, J. (1990). Abrupt visual onsets and selective attention: Voluntary versus automatic allocation. *Journal of Experiment Psychology: Human Perception and Performance*, *16*, 121–134.

MEMORY, 2001, 9 (4/5/6), 445–457

Field dependence–independence from a working memory perspective: A dual-task investigation of the Hidden Figures Test

Akira Miyake, Alexander H. Witzki, and Michael J. Emerson
University of Colorado at Boulder, USA

Field dependence–independence (FDI) is a construct intensively investigated within cognitive style research, but its cognitive underpinnings are not clearly specified. We propose that performance on FDI tasks primarily reflects the operations of the visuospatial and executive components of working memory. We tested this hypothesis in a dual-task experiment with a commonly used measure of FDI, the Hidden Figures Test. The results showed that performance on this test was impaired by concurrent performance of secondary tasks that primarily tap the visuospatial component (spatial tapping) and the executive component (2-back and random number generation), but was almost unaffected by other secondary tasks (simple tapping and articulatory suppression). Moreover, an analysis of secondary task performance ruled out the possibility of strategic trade-offs and revealed an intriguing dissociation for two different sets of "randomness" indices for the random number generation task. These results support the hypothesised mapping between FDI and working memory components and suggest that the dual-task paradigm can provide a useful way to bring underspecified constructs like FDI into closer alignment with theoretical ideas developed within cognitive psychology.

The view that individuals differ systematically in how they prefer to approach tasks or solve problems has provided a central basis for research on cognitive styles. Perhaps the most intensively studied cognitive style is field dependence–independence (FDI), originally proposed by Witkin (Witkin et al., 1962). FDI is a dimension that reflects the tendency of an individual to perceive entire fields as a whole (field-dependent) or focus on isolable components of a field (field-independent). More specifically, field-dependent individuals show a high degree of "dependence on the structure of the prevailing visual field," whereas field-independent individuals "deal with the presented field analytically" and mentally "separate an item from the configuration in which it occurs" (Witkin, 1964, p. 176).

The notion of FDI can be illustrated more concretely by describing some tasks commonly used to measure this dimension. Two traditional measures of FDI are the Rod-and-Frame Test and the Embedded Figures Test. In the Rod-and-Frame Test, a participant sits in a dark room in which only an illuminated rod and frame are visible. The frame is tilted off angle, and the participant's task is to align the rod to the true vertical, without being influenced by the orientation of the frame. In the Embedded Figures Test, the task is to find a simple figure hidden inside a more complex pattern. Illustrated in Figure 1 is a widely used variant of this test, the Hidden Figures Test, which we will focus on in this article. This test requires participants to identify which one of the five simple figures is embedded inside the

Requests for reprints should be sent to Dr Akira Miyake, Department of Psychology, University of Colorado at Boulder, 345 UCB, Boulder, CO 80309-0345 USA. Email: miyake@psych.colorado.edu

This work was supported in part by a National Science Foundation grant (IBN-9873492).

We thank Amy Howerter for her help in running the experiment and Naomi P. Friedman, Hirohito Kondo, and Priti Shah for providing comments on an earlier version of this article.

http://www.tandf.co.uk/journals/pp/09658211.html DOI:10.1080/09658210143000029

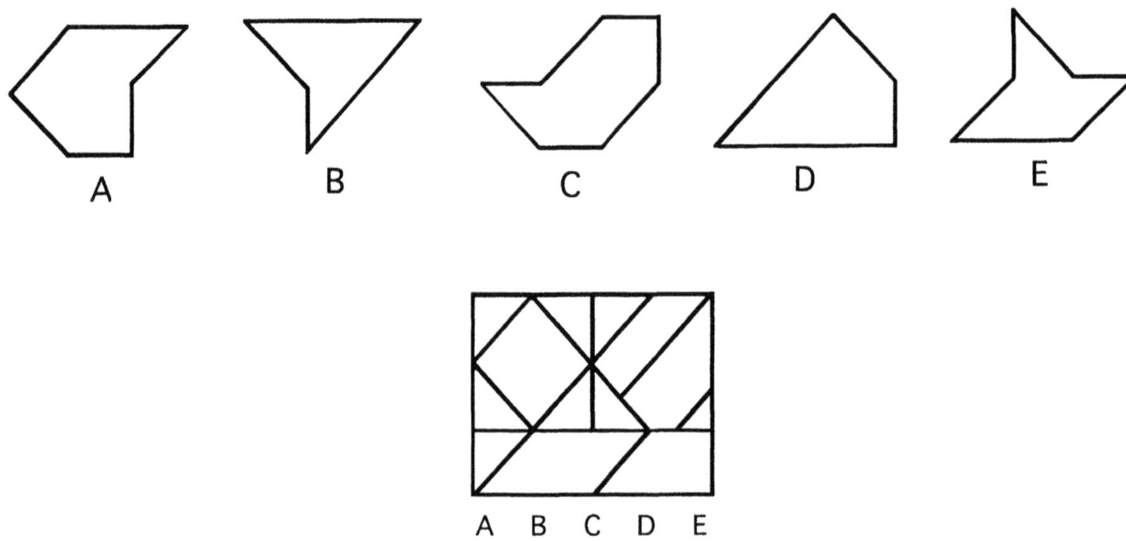

Figure 1. A sample item representative of the problems in the Hidden Figures Test. The task is to determine which one of the five simpler figures is hidden in the more complex figure. The correct answer for this problem is "A".

complex figure. Thus, these FDI measures all assess the degree to which the participant can make judgements independently of distracting contextual information (i.e., the tilted frame and the extra lines in complex drawings).[1] Cognitive style research has relied on these measures to examine the role of FDI in a variety of situations, such as school achievement (Tinajero & Paramo, 1998), second language learning (Bialystok & Hakuta, 1994), sports performance (McMorris, 1992), and social-cultural functioning (Berry, 1991).

Despite its apparent popularity, however, the notion of FDI is problem-laden from a cognitive standpoint. One major problem concerns the key assumption that FDI is a dimension of cognitive style, rather than cognitive ability. In other words, most cognitive style research implicitly or explicitly assumes that there is no inherent reason to consider one end of the FDI dimension more preferable than the other, because field dependence and independence are just two different ways of perceiving and processing cognitive information.

Although this "FDI is a style" assumption is still prevalent, existing evidence seriously challenges that assumption. Arguably the most serious challenge comes from McKenna's (1984) extensive review of correlational studies involving the Embedded Figures Test. His review compellingly demonstrated that there is a close relationship between FDI and various ability-related constructs, such as spatial ability (especially spatial visualisation ability) and general fluid intelligence. For example, MacLeod et al. (1986) showed in a confirmatory factor analysis study that the construct of FDI (as measured by both the Rod-and-Frame Test and the Embedded Figures Test) was essentially indistinguishable from the construct of spatial ability (as measured by the Space Relations Test and the Block Design Test). Similarly, in a developmental study, Case and Globerson (1974) showed that both the Rod-and-Frame Test and the Embedded Figures Test were moderately correlated with the Raven Progressive Matrices Test ($r=.64$ and .40, respectively), a hallmark test of general fluid intelligence. These results not only suggest that FDI reflects a dimension of cognitive ability, but also reveal that the notion of FDI remains vague and that its cognitive underpinnings are not clearly understood.

In this article, we attempt to specify the cognitive underpinnings of FDI from a working memory perspective. Working memory refers to a

[1] Although some doubts concerning whether these measures of FDI tap the same underlying construct have been raised, the Rod-and-Frame Test and the Embedded Figures Test have consistently demonstrated moderate correlations (usually, $r=.30$–.55) with each other (Case & Globerson, 1974; MacLeod, Jackson, & Palmer, 1986; Witkin et al., 1962). In addition, various factor-analytic studies have shown that several paper-and-pencil tasks commonly used as FDI measures (including the Hidden Figures Test) often, if not always, load on the same factor, usually referred to as the "closure flexibility" factor (Carroll, 1993; Lohman, 1988).

system or a set of processes that underlie active maintenance of task-relevant information during the performance of complex cognitive tasks, such as spatial thinking, problem solving, and language comprehension. Although a number of influential models and theories of working memory exist (Miyake & Shah, 1999), perhaps the most influential framework has been Baddeley's (1986) multicomponent model (Baddeley & Logie, 1999). This model postulates two distinct domain-specific subsystems, the *visuospatial sketchpad* and the *phonological loop*, which are responsible for maintaining and processing visuospatial and verbal–phonological information, respectively. The third subsystem in the model is a central, general-purpose control structure called the *central executive*, which regulates the operation of the other two domain-specific subsystems and performs a host of so-called executive functions (Baddeley, 1996).

Within this framework, we propose that FDI can be conceptualised in terms of the efficiency of the functioning of two of its components, the visuospatial sketchpad and the central executive. The involvement of the visuospatial sketchpad appears essential because FDI tasks all require temporary maintenance of some visuospatial information. For example, to perform the Hidden Figures Test, participants must temporarily maintain the shape of each simple figure while simultaneously scanning and analysing the more complex figure. Although the specific role of the central executive in the performance of the Hidden Figure Test is less clear, it is likely to play a crucial role in developing and implementing efficient strategies, keeping track of various possible solutions, and deliberately ignoring distracting information present in the complex figure. Interestingly, this working memory interpretation of FDI nicely corresponds to Witkin and Goodenough's (1981, p. 47) two-component view of FDI, which consisted of "reliance on vestibular or visual-field reference" (corresponding to the visuospatial component) and "cognitive restructuring" (corresponding to the executive component).

Existing data provide tantalising evidence for this proposed mapping between FDI and the working memory components, although no direct evidence currently exists. Recall that previous correlational studies suggested that FDI is closely associated with spatial ability as well as general fluid intelligence (McKenna, 1984). Importantly, both of these mental abilities have recently been linked to working memory, especially its visuospatial and executive components, respectively. Shah and Miyake (1996), for example, demonstrated that spatial ability (specifically spatial visualisation ability) is strongly related to individual differences in spatial, but not necessarily verbal, working memory capacity (see also Miyake et al., in press). Evidence also points to a link between working memory (particularly its executive aspects) and general fluid intelligence (Engle, Kane, & Tuholski, 1999; Kyllonen, 1996). Recent correlational analyses, for example, demonstrated that performance on fluid intelligence tasks such as the Raven Progressive Matrices Test or Cattell's Culture Fair Test depends crucially on the effective execution and coordination of various executive processes (Carpenter, Just, & Shell, 1990; Duncan et al., 1996; Engle, Tuholski, Laughlin, & Conway, 1999). Moreover, Robinson and Bennink (1978) showed that field-independent individuals, as measured by the Embedded Figures Test, were better than field-dependent individuals at performing a complex cognitive task while concurrently maintaining a heavy memory load. Given that dual tasking is considered one of the major functions of the central executive (Baddeley, 1996), this result further points to the hypothesised link between FDI and executive functioning. Thus, even though the currently available evidence is indirect, the proposed two-component mapping between FDI and working memory is a plausible one.

The main purpose of the present study was to provide more direct experimental evidence for the proposed relationship between FDI and working memory components. Specifically, we used the dual-task interference paradigm to assess which of the working memory components are implicated in the performance of the Hidden Figures Test. In this paradigm, a cognitive task of interest is performed by itself and also with a secondary task considered to tap mainly one of the subcomponents of working memory. If the secondary task disrupts the performance of the primary cognitive task when compared to the control single-task condition, then it is usually inferred that the subcomponent tapped by the secondary task is involved in the performance of the primary task. This dual-task paradigm has been used effectively to elucidate various working memory demands implicated in the performance of complex cognitive tasks, including reasoning (Gilhooly, Logie, & Wynn, 1999), problem solving (Phillips et al.,

1999), chess playing (Robbins et al., 1996), and mental arithmetic (Logie, Gilhooly, & Wynn, 1994).

In this study, we used five secondary tasks to tap different subcomponents of working memory. *Simple tapping*, which requires tapping one's index finger continuously at one location, was used as a secondary task that may impose some small amount of general attentional demand but does not selectively tax any particular working memory component. We used *articulatory suppression* and *spatial tapping* as secondary tasks that specifically tap each of the two domain-specific subsystems. Articulatory suppression, which requires participants to repeatedly say a familiar word or phrase aloud, primarily interferes with the operation of the phonological loop, whereas spatial tapping, which requires participants to tap a spatial pattern repeatedly with their index fingers, primarily interferes with the operation of the visuospatial sketchpad.

In addition, we used the *2-back* task and the *random number generation (RNG)* task as two secondary tasks that heavily tax the operations of the executive component. The 2-back task is used frequently in working memory research, particularly in the context of neuroimaging studies, and requires participants to decide whether each letter matches the one presented two items earlier. This task has been considered to implicate a variety of executive functions, such as temporally tagging incoming letters, updating and monitoring actively maintained information, and inhibiting incorrect responses (Cohen et al., 1997; Jonides & Smith, 1997). RNG is another frequently used task, particularly in the context of dual-task studies. Although attempts to specify the cognitive processes underlying RNG performance have begun only recently, this task is considered to heavily implicate the operations of the central executive, because it requires actively monitoring candidate responses and suppressing responses that would lead to well-learned or stereotyped sequences, particularly counting responses (Baddeley, Emslie, Kolodny, & Duncan, 1998; Towse, 1998).

Although the primary reason for choosing the 2-back and RNG tasks was their prevalent use in working memory research, there was an additional novel reason for including RNG as a secondary executive task. Recent studies of RNG have indicated that different indices of "randomness" may capture different facets of executive functioning. For example, two recent principal components analyses of common randomness indices demonstrated that the indices load on multiple, largely uncorrelated components (Miyake et al., 2000; Towse & Neil, 1998). One subset of indices, thought to assess the degree to which each number is produced equally frequently, loaded highly on one of the components (which Towse and Neil interpreted as the "equality of response usage" component), whereas a second subset of indices, thought to be sensitive to the degree to which well-learned counting sequences—both counting up (e.g., 4–5) and counting down (e.g., 7–6)—are produced, loaded highly on another component (interpreted as the "prepotent associates" component). Interestingly, these two components were subsequently found to correlate differentially with different executive functions; specifically, the "equality of response usage" component was primarily associated with one's ability to update and monitor working memory representations, and the "prepotent associates" component was primarily associated with one's ability to deliberately inhibit dominant or prepotent responses (Miyake et al., 2000). Thus we reasoned that, to the extent that these randomness indices tap different executive functions, the patterns of dual-task interference produced by the two sets of indices might illuminate the nature of executive processes implicated in the performance of the Hidden Figures Test.

On the basis of the proposal that performance on FDI tasks strongly implicates the operations of the visuospatial and executive components of working memory, our prediction was that concurrent performance of the spatial tapping, 2-back, and RNG tasks should significantly disrupt performance on the Hidden Figures Test, whereas concurrent performance of the articulatory suppression and simple tapping tasks should not. Moreover, these effects should be observed in the absence of a strategic trade-off between the primary and secondary tasks.

METHOD

Participants

A total of 75 undergraduate students at the University of Colorado participated in this experiment for partial course credit. The participants were randomly assigned to one of the five experimental groups ($N = 15$ each) that differed in the secondary task they performed.

Materials

The Hidden Figures Test. The Hidden Figures Test (Ekstrom, French, Harman, & Dermen, 1976), illustrated in Figure 1, is a close variant of Witkin's Embedded Figures Test and is widely used as a measure of FDI (e.g., Noppe, 1985; Rickards, Fajen, Sullivan, & Gillespie, 1997; Schmidt & Stephans, 1991). In this test, each participant is presented with five simple figures (available for inspection at all times throughout the test) and then must decide which one of the five is embedded in each of the complex figures. There are two parallel sections of this test, each of which consists of 16 problems that are approximately equivalent in terms of difficulty (i.e., the problems do not become progressively more difficult within each section). The presentation of the two sections under the single-task and dual-task conditions was counterbalanced. The dependent measure for this task was the number of correctly answered items.

Secondary tasks. Three of the secondary tasks (articulatory suppression, simple tapping, and spatial tapping) had a similar structure. For these three tasks, a metronome was used to pace the responses (750 ms per response).

The *articulatory suppression* task required participants to repeat aloud the phrase "one, two, three" once per beat (i.e., say "one, two, three" every 750 ms). Note that this rate of articulatory suppression is much faster and is physically more demanding than the typical rate (i.e., 1 s) used in other dual-task studies (for example, the Gilhooly et al., 1999, study required participants to repeat the word "go" at the rate of one per second). This was done to maximise the demand on the phonological loop and thereby increase the likelihood of this secondary task impairing the primary task performance. Given that we predict a null effect for this secondary task (i.e., no significant interference effect on the Hidden Figure Test), we reasoned that it would be important to make the articulatory suppression task as demanding of the phonological loop resources as possible.

The two tapping tasks both required participants to make key-press responses once per 750 ms. In the case of the *simple tapping* task, participants pressed the "2" key on a numerical keypad, whereas in the *spatial tapping* task, participants tapped a square spatial pattern around a numerical keypad by pressing the numbers 1, 4, 7, 8, 9, 6, 3, and 2 in order. In both simple and spatial tapping tasks, participants used one finger of their preferred hand for tapping. To avoid the possibility that dual-task performance decrement was caused by input-level interference (i.e., the inability to look at the Hidden Figures Test booklet and the keypad at the same time), we instructed participants to perform the assigned task without looking down at the keypad. To encourage participants to keep looking at the test booklet, we covered each participant's hand with a box and thereby prevented visual feedback.

The *2-back* task required participants to listen to a series of consonant letters presented at the rate of one letter every 2 s. Their task was to say "Yes" aloud whenever a consonant was identical to the one presented two items before. For example, if the last two letters presented were *P* and *K* and the next presented letter was *P*, participants should answer "Yes". The *RNG* task required participants to say aloud a random number from 1 to 9 in time with a metronome (one number per second), and the participants were instructed to make the series of numbers as random as possible. To illustrate the concept of randomness (with replacement), participants were given the analogy of picking a number out of a hat, reading it aloud, putting it back in the hat, and picking the next number. The importance of maintaining a consistent response rhythm was also emphasised.

To rule out the possibility of strategic trade-offs between the primary and secondary tasks, we analysed participants' secondary task performance data under both single-task (baseline assessment) and dual-task conditions. For the articulatory suppression task, the dependent measure we used was the number of times the phrase "one, two, three" was articulated. For both the simple tapping and spatial tapping tasks, it was the number of appropriate key presses made. Note that these dependent measures are essentially indices of how well participants were able to keep up with the pace of the metronome (i.e., how well they were able to avoid skipping responses) under single-task and dual-task situations. For the 2-back task, the dependent measure was the number of correct responses (maximum of 10 correct in the single-task condition and 40 correct in the dual-task condition). Finally, for the RNG task, we analysed the responses using Towse and Neil's (1998) RgCalc program. This program produces many commonly used randomness indices, from which we chose a set of six as the main dependent measures for this study. These six randomness indices were selected because, in two previous principal components analyses (Miyake et al., 2000; Towse & Neil, 1998), three of them (i.e., redundancy, coupon, and mean repetition gap) loaded consistently highly on the "equality of response usage" component, whereas the other three (i.e., adjacency, the turning point index, and runs) loaded consistently highly on the "prepotent associates" component (see Towse & Neil, 1998, for more detailed descriptions of these measures).

When these secondary task measures were analysed, some adjustments had to be made because of the difference in the length of time each secondary task was performed under single-task (1.5 min) and dual-task (6 min) conditions. For the articulatory suppression, simple tapping, spatial tapping, and 2-back tasks, we adjusted the score of each participant's baseline performance by multiplying it by four. For the RNG task, we compared the response sequence produced by each individual during the single-task condition (baseline assessment) to the same number of responses that he or she produced during the initial period of the dual-task condition (i.e., approximately the first 1.5 min of dual-task performance). This method of adjustment was adopted for the RNG task because the results of a Monte Carlo simulation study we conducted prior to the data analysis showed that many of the randomness indices are highly sensitive to the length of the response sequence being analysed (i.e., more responses tend to produce better randomness scores).[2]

[2]We used Towse and Neil's (1998) RgCalc program to perform the Monte Carlo simulation study. In this analysis, we first used the program's random generator to generate 100 sequences each of 90 random numbers and 360 random numbers (corresponding to the longest sequence lengths that could be produced in the single-task and dual-task conditions, respectively, in the current study) and then evaluated the extent to which the difference in sequence lengths produced a systematic bias in each randomness index. The results of the analysis indicated that many of the indices were highly sensitive to sequence length and that only three indices were relatively unaffected by sequence length (adjacency, coupon, and the turning point index). For these three measures, the pattern of secondary task decrement reported in the Results section remained essentially identical even when the baseline sequence (i.e., the sequence of numbers produced in 1.5 min) was compared to the entire dual-task sequence (i.e., the sequence of numbers produced during the entire 6 min of dual-task performance).

Procedure

Participants performed the experimental tasks in the following order: baseline assessment for the secondary task, the Hidden Figures Test in the single-task condition, and then in the dual-task condition. They were first given instructions for the secondary task and practised that task for 30 s so that they were able to perform it smoothly (in the case of the simple and spatial tapping tasks, without having to look down at the keypad). Participants then performed the secondary task for 1.5 min for baseline assessment. Next, the participants read the instructions of the Hidden Figures Test. After receiving two practice items, they were given 6 min to answer as many items correctly as possible. During this single-task condition, the metronome was turned on (one beat every 750 ms in the articulatory suppression, simple tapping, and spatial tapping conditions, one beat every 2 s in the 2-back condition, and one beat per s in the RNG condition) to ensure that experimental effects could not be explained by the sound of the metronome in the dual-task condition. Participants in the articulatory suppression, 2-back, and RNG conditions marked their answers on the Hidden Figures Test booklet, whereas participants in the two tapping conditions orally reported their answers to the experimenter. Finally, participants were given 6 min to answer as many items correctly as possible of the second part of the Hidden Figures Test while simultaneously performing the secondary task.

RESULTS

Primary task performance

We first conducted a series of planned comparisons to examine the effect of each secondary task on the participants' performance of the Hidden Figures Test. Specifically, we used a paired t test (one-tailed) to compare the baseline and dual-task performances on this test for each of the five groups. Figure 2 presents the mean performance on the Hidden Figures Test in the single-task and dual-task conditions for each of the five dual-task groups. Figure 3A summarises the impact of the secondary tasks on the Hidden Figures Test in terms of percentage decrement.

As predicted, concurrent performance of the secondary task significantly disrupted performance on the Hidden Figures Test when the

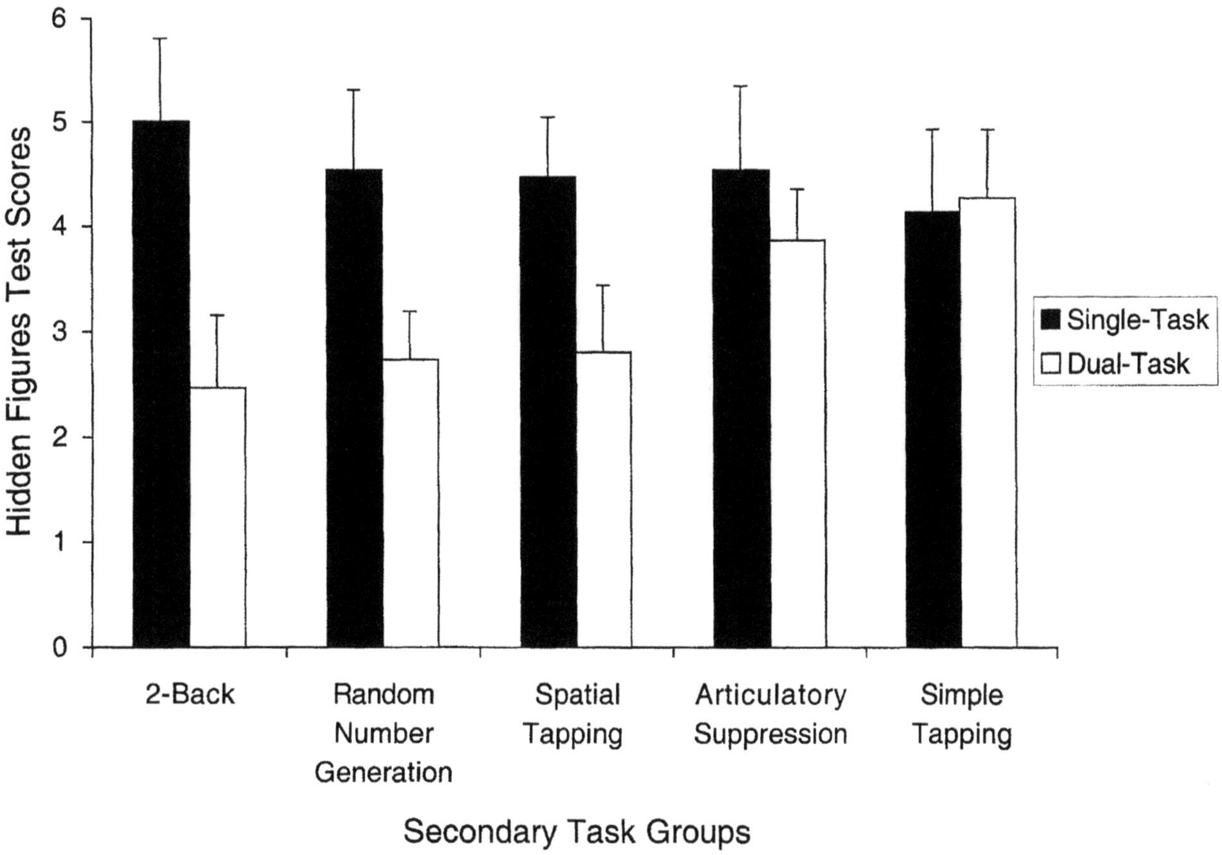

Figure 2. The mean performance on the Hidden Figures Test in the single-task and dual-task conditions for each of the five dual-task groups (the error bars represent standard error). Concurrent performance of secondary tasks impaired participants' Hidden Figures Test performance in the 2-back, random number generation (RNG), and spatial tapping groups, but not in the articulatory suppression and simple tapping groups.

concurrent task was primarily executive or spatial in nature. Concurrent performance of the executive tasks led to a considerable drop in the Hidden Figure Test performance, a 51% decrement in the 2-back condition, $t(14) = 2.92$, $p < .01$, and a 40% decrement in the RNG condition, $t(14) = 2.00$, $p < .05$. Performance decrement was also considerable in the spatial tapping condition (a 37% decrement), $t(14) = 2.99$, $p < .01$.

In contrast, dual-task requirements did not significantly impair performance on the Hidden Figures Test in the articulatory suppression condition (a 15% decrement), $t(14) = 1.09$, $p > .10$, despite our attempts to make this task more demanding on the phonological loop resources than is usually the case. Also, there was virtually no dual-task interference effect in the simple tapping condition (a 3% increase), $t(14) = -.20$, $p > .10$.

In summary, the primary task data clearly showed that only the secondary tasks that are considered to tap the executive and spatial components significantly disrupted performance on the Hidden Figures Test. This pattern of results is highly consistent with the predictions based on the proposed mapping between FDI and working memory.

Secondary task performance

When the secondary tasks are complex, participants sometimes strategically trade off their performance between the primary and the secondary tasks (e.g., Bourke, Duncan, & Nimmo-Smith, 1996; Hegarty, Shah, & Miyake, 2000). To rule out the possibility that the results reflected such a strategic trade-off, we also examined the participants' performance on the secondary task by performing a series of planned comparisons (one-tailed). Table 1 summarises the results, and Figure 3B illustrates the impact of the Hidden Figures Test on the secondary task performance in terms of percentage decrement.

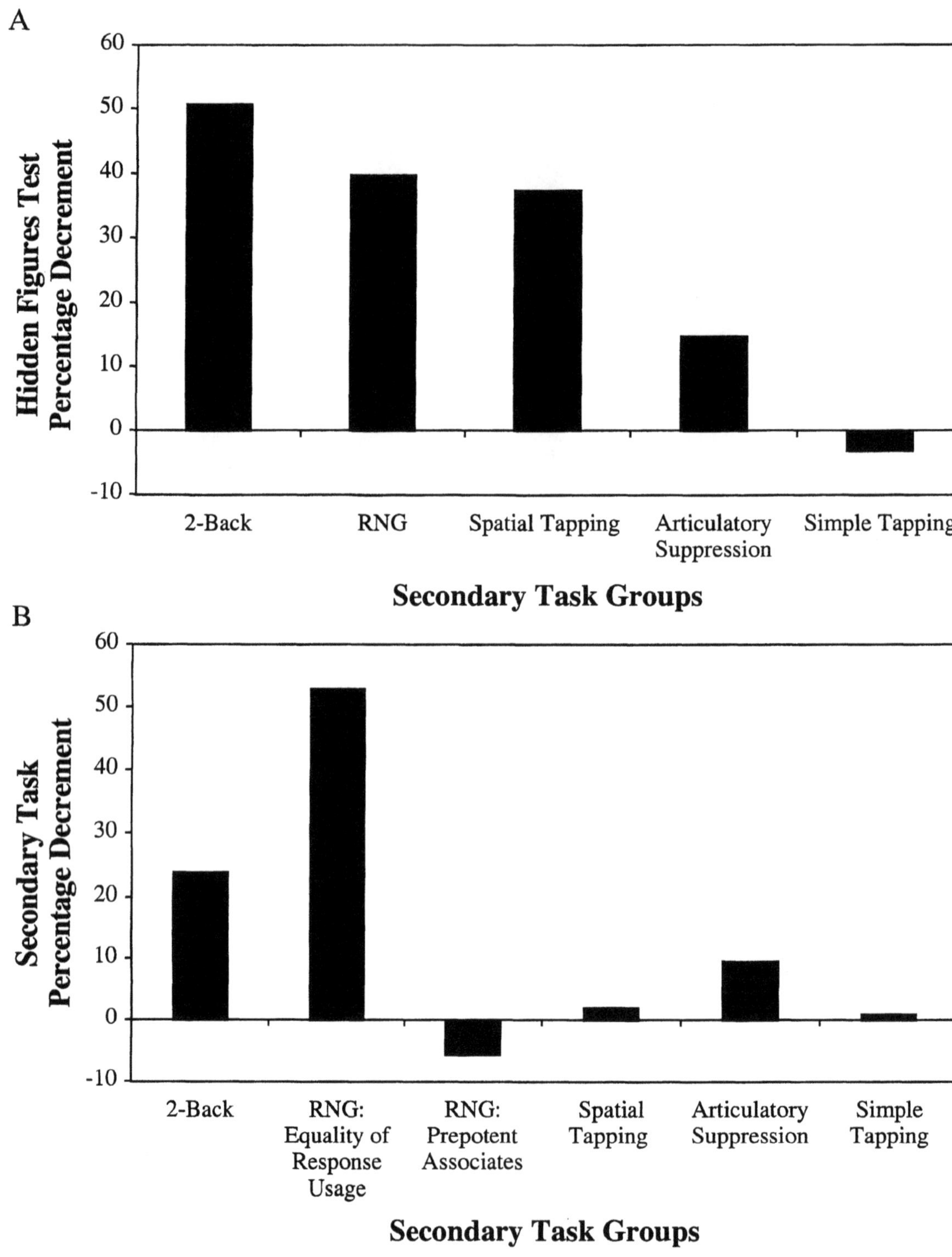

Figure 3. The percentage decrement for the Hidden Figures Test (Figure 3A) and for secondary task performance (Figure 3B) in each of the dual-task conditions. The pattern of interference was similar for the primary and secondary tasks, indicating that the results cannot be accounted for in terms of a strategic trade-off between them.

Performance on the 2-back task was significantly worse in the dual-task condition than in the single-task condition, $t(14) = 8.79$, $p < .01$, with the magnitude of the performance decrement a substantial 24%. The corresponding analysis of performance on the RNG task (the directionality of all measures was adjusted so that bigger scores reflect better performance) showed an interesting dissociation. The three indices associated with the "equality of response usage" component each

TABLE 1
Mean secondary task performance under single-task and dual-task conditions (standard deviations in parentheses)

Secondary Task	*Condition* *Single-Task*	*Dual-Task*
2-Back[a]	37.60 (3.31)	28.60 (4.26)
Random Number Generation		
"Equality of Response Usage" Indices		
Redundancy	1.16 (.70)	2.66 (2.27)
Coupon	17.20 (3.76)	21.49 (8.26)
Mean Repetition Gap	8.65 (.17)	8.32 (.38)
"Prepotent Associates" Indices		
Adjacency	40.23 (8.17)	37.67 (8.23)
Turning Point Index	79.26 (11.22)	80.30 (11.03)
Runs	1.44 (.71)	1.31 (.69)
Spatial Tapping[b]	475.20 (4.06)	465.27 (9.44)
Articulatory Suppression[c]	461.07 (23.54)	417.27 (22.99)
Simple Tapping[b]	472.53 (3.34)	468.40 (3.87)

Because the baseline assessment of secondary task performance in the single-task condition lasted for only 1.5 min (as opposed to 6 min in the dual-task condition), the entries for the means of the single-task condition in this table, except the randomness indices, are multiplied by four to facilitate the comparison.

[a] The total number of correct responses. [b] The total number of key presses. [c] The total number of times that the phrase "one, two, three" was articulated.

demonstrated a significant decrement from baseline performance to dual-task performance, $t(14) = 3.08$, $p < .01$, for redundancy, $t(14) = 2.06$, $p < .05$, for coupon, and $t(14) = 2.92$, $p < .01$, for mean repetition gap. In contrast, none of the three indices associated with the "prepotent associates" component showed significant differences between the baseline and dual-task conditions, $t(14) = -1.28$, $p > .10$, for adjacency, $t(14) = -.39$, $p > .10$, for the turning point index, and $t(14) = -.72$, $p > .10$, for runs. As illustrated in Figure 3B, the performance change was sizeable for the three "equality of response usage" indices (an average of 53% decrement), but was virtually absent for the three "prepotent associates" indices (an average of 6% increase).[3] Possible interpretations of this dissociation will be considered later in the Discussion section.

The dual-task decrements for the other, simpler secondary tasks were also statistically significant, $t(14) = 3.64$, $p < .01$, for spatial tapping, $t(14) = 8.33$, $p < .01$, for articulatory suppression, and $t(14) = 2.87$, $p < .01$, for simple tapping, indicating that there was some general attentional cost associated with performing these tasks simultaneously with the Hidden Figures Test. As indicated in Figure 3B, however, the magnitude of the decrement was relatively small for these three tasks: the decrement was restricted to 2% for the spatial tapping condition, 10% for the articulatory suppression, and 1% for the simple tapping condition.

Although the magnitude of the decrement of secondary task performance in the articulatory suppression condition (10%) was somewhat larger than that in the two tapping conditions, it simply reflected the fact that repeatedly saying the phrase "one, two, three" at the rate of 750 ms per phrase over a 6 min period without a break was a physically demanding task. Most participants needed to take an increasing number of short pauses over the course of 6 min to continue the dual-task performance. Indeed, if only the first 1.5 min of articulatory suppression was considered (the baseline assessment for the secondary task lasted 1.5 min), the magnitude of decrement was only 4%, no longer significantly different from the

[3] We also conducted these analyses using Evans's (1978) RNG measure. Although this measure is arguably the most prevalently used index of randomness, we did not include it in the main analysis because it loaded highly on more than one component in Towse and Neil's (1998) principal components analysis. Perhaps reflecting this ambiguity, Evans's RNG score showed a marginally significant change from the single-task to the dual-task condition (an 8% decrement), despite the fact that it tends to correlate more strongly with the "prepotent responses" indices than with the "equality of response usage" indices.

single-task condition, $t(13) = 1.55$, $p < .10$.[4] Given that the speed of key presses required for the two tapping conditions was not as demanding (i.e., one key press every 750 ms), there was no such effect of fatigue.

A more surprising result may be the significant yet small (2%) dual-task interference effect found for the spatial tapping condition. Given that the spatial tapping task had a major detrimental effect on the Hidden Figure Test performance (a 37% decrement; see Figure 3A), why was the effect so small for the secondary task performance? As it happens, for this secondary task, the dual-task decrement seems to have taken the form of increased variability in performance, rather than decreased mean scores. As shown in Table 1, the standard deviation (SD) for the spatial tapping condition increased substantially from 4.06 (single-task) to 9.44 (dual-task), suggesting that some individuals in the spatial tapping condition experienced considerable difficulty keeping up with the pace of the metronome while performing the Hidden Figures Test. In contrast, the degree of change in SDs for the articulatory suppression and simple tapping conditions was much smaller.

Taken together, then, the pattern of interference observed for the secondary task performance generally mirrored the pattern observed for the primary task performance (i.e., clear evidence of performance decrement for the executive tasks and for spatial tapping, but not for articulatory suppression and simple tapping). Thus, there was no evidence for the hypothesis that the pattern of interference found for the primary task was due to a strategic trade-off with secondary task performance.

DISCUSSION

The results of the current dual-task study were highly consistent with our predictions. Performance on the Hidden Figures Test was significantly disrupted by concurrent performance of a secondary spatial task (spatial tapping) and two secondary executive tasks (2-back and RNG), but not by concurrent performance of a secondary verbal task (articulatory suppression) or a control task (simple tapping). The data from the secondary task performance also ruled out the possibility of strategic trade-offs between the primary and secondary tasks. These results, then, support the hypothesis that performance on the Hidden Figures Test depends on the efficient operations of the visuospatial and executive components of working memory.

One alternative explanation that needs to be considered is that the overall patterns of interference outlined earlier may have simply reflected the differences in the difficulty level of the secondary tasks. Although this interpretation cannot be completely ruled out, none of the secondary tasks was particularly difficult when performed by itself. In the RNG task, for example, the average number of digits produced during baseline assessment was 95% of maximum, indicating that participants were generally able to produce responses in time with the metronome. Even for the 2-back task, the mean accuracy in the single-task condition was 94%, almost at the ceiling level. Moreover, although articulatory suppression did not show a strong impact on the Hidden Figures Test performance in this study (despite our attempts to make it relatively demanding), it has been shown to severely disrupt the performance of various cognitive tasks, including immediate serial recall (Baddeley, Lewis, & Vallar, 1984) and mental arithmetic (Logie et al., 1994). Thus, the pattern of interference reported in this paper is unlikely to have arisen as a result of task difficulty alone.

It is also important to acknowledge that the current study demonstrated the involvement of the visuospatial and executive components of working memory within the context of only one prevalent measure of FDI, the Hidden Figures Test. Thus, the extent to which the proposed mapping between FDI and working memory is generalisable to other well-accepted FDI measures (such as the Rod-and-Frame Test) remains to be seen. Nevertheless, we believe that the current results more likely reflect the aspects of the Hidden Figures Test requirements that are common to other FDI measures, because, as we reviewed earlier, a host of FDI measures (i.e., not just the Hidden or Embedded Figures Test but also the Rod-and-Frame Test) show significant correlations with both spatial ability (MacLeod et al., 1986) and general fluid intelligence measures like the Raven Progressive Matrices Test (Case & Globerson, 1974; McKenna, 1984). Such evidence seems to go against the view that the results reported in this study are specific only to the Hidden Figures Test and instead suggests that the proposed mapping between FDI and working

[4] The data from one participant were lost for this analysis due to equipment malfunction.

memory may be extended to other measures of FDI as well.

One interesting finding from the current dual-task study was that, in our analysis of secondary task performance, there was a strikingly clear dissociation between the two sets of randomness indices (i.e., those associated with "equality of response usage" and those associated with "prepotent associates"). More specifically, the "equality of response usage" indices showed a large dual-task decrement (51%), whereas the "prepotent associates" indices did not (a 6% increase). What does this dissociation mean?

One possibility is that the dissociation between the two sets of indices may be due to a relative insensitivity of the "prepotent associates" indices (i.e., adjacency, turning point index, and runs) to detect dual-task decrements. However, this explanation seems unlikely because at least one of the "prepotent associates" indices, adjacency, has been shown to be sensitive to experimental demands (Towse, 1998; Towse & Valentine, 1997). One study (Towse, 1998), for example, independently manipulated production speed and set size (the number of response alternatives) for the RNG task. The adjacency index was significantly affected by production speed, but not by set size, whereas the redundancy index (associated with "equality of response usage") showed the opposite pattern. In another study (Towse & Valentine, 1997), adjacency, but not redundancy, was found to be sensitive to the concurrent requirement of suppressing two preselected responses (e.g., avoiding the responses of 3 and 7) during the generation of numbers. These previously reported dissociations make it highly unlikely that the "prepotent associates" indices were simply insensitive to dual-task demands.

A more plausible—and theoretically more interesting—possibility is that the interference patterns produced by the two sets of randomness indices are telling us something about the underlying processes or abilities involved in FDI tasks. Given the previously suggested link between the "equality of response usage" indices and one's ability to update and monitor working memory representations (Miyake et al., 2000), the virtually identical pattern of interference shown by all three of the "equality of response usage" indices suggests that the major role of the central executive in the performance of the Hidden Figure Test may be to keep track of all possible solutions and the answer figures that have been tried for each complex figure in the Hidden Figures Test. Moreover, given the suggested link between the "prepotent associates" indices and one's ability to inhibit prepotent responses (Miyake et al., 2000), the null results shown by all three of the "prepotent associates" indices might mean that inhibition, at least the type of inhibition involved in deliberately suppressing prepotent or automatic responses, is not playing a major role in performance on the Hidden Figures Test.

Although these interpretations are speculative and require further empirical validation, the different interference patterns demonstrated by the two sets of randomness indices are interesting from a methodological point of view. So far, most dual-task studies that used RNG as a secondary task have relied on only one or two "favourite" randomness indices to assess changes in secondary task performance. Even when multiple indices are used, they are sometimes of the same type. Our results suggest that it is far more preferable to use multiple randomness indices that have been shown to tap different aspects of executive functioning and examine whether these indices show systematic patterns of differential decrement under dual-task situations. To the extent that different indices are sensitive to different underlying executive processes, the RNG task may serve as a useful tool to specify the nature of executive processes involved in the primary task.

In conclusion, the results from our dual-task study suggest that the notion of FDI can be reinterpreted from the perspective of working memory. Specifically, performance on FDI tasks reflects the efficiency of the operations of the visuospatial and executive components of working memory. The visuospatial component (the visuospatial sketchpad) appears to help the individual actively maintain relevant visuospatial information, whereas the executive component (the central executive) may play a role in keeping track of and monitoring the solutions and previous attempts. According to this mapping, individual variation in FDI is likely to arise because individuals differ in the capacity of the visuospatial sketchpad as well as in the efficiency of central executive functioning (or the efficiency of various subfunctions performed by the executive, particularly the updating and monitoring operations). Such a view is in contrast with the common "FDI is a style" notion and, together with the correlational findings reviewed earlier, strongly suggests that FDI should be construed as a cognitive ability, rather than a cognitive style.

REFERENCES

Baddeley, A.D. (1986). *Working memory*. New York: Oxford University Press.

Baddeley, A.D. (1996). Exploring the central executive. *Quarterly Journal of Experimental Psychology, 49*A, 5–28.

Baddeley, A.D., Emslie, H., Kolodny, J., & Duncan, J. (1998). Random generation and the executive control of working memory. *Quarterly Journal of Experimental Psychology, 51*A, 819–852.

Baddeley, A.D., Lewis, V.J., & Vallar, G. (1984). Exploring the articulatory loop. *Quarterly Journal of Experimental Psychology, 36A*, 233–252.

Baddeley, A.D., & Logie, R.H. (1999). Working memory: The multiple-component model. In A. Miyake & P. Shah (Eds.), *Models of working memory: Mechanisms of active maintenance and executive control* (pp. 28–61). New York: Cambridge University Press.

Berry, J.W. (1991). Cultural variations in field dependence–independence. In S. Wapner & J. Demick (Eds.), *Field dependence–independence: Cognitive style across the life span* (pp. 289–308). Hillsdale, NJ: Lawrence Erlbaum Associates Inc.

Bialystok, E., & Hakuta, K. (1994). *In other words: The science and psychology of second-language acquisition*. New York: Basic Books.

Bourke, P.A., Duncan, J., & Nimmo-Smith, I. (1996). A general factor involved in dual-task performance decrement. *Quarterly Journal of Experimental Psychology, 49*A, 525–545.

Carpenter, P.A., Just, M.A., & Shell, P. (1990). What one intelligence test measures: A theoretical account of the processing in the Raven Progressive Matrices Test. *Psychological Review, 97*, 404–431.

Carroll, J.B. (1993). *Human cognitive abilities: A survey of factor-analytic studies*. New York: Cambridge University Press.

Case, R., & Globerson, T. (1974). Field independence and central computing space. *Child Development, 45*, 772–778.

Cohen, J.D., Perlstein, W.M., Braver, T.S., Nystrom, L.E., Noll, D.C., Jonides, J., & Smith, E.E. (1997). Temporal dynamics of brain activation during a working memory task. *Nature, 386*, 604–608.

Duncan, J., Emslie, H., Williams, P., Johnson, R., & Freer, C. (1996). Intelligence and the frontal lobe: The organization of goal-directed behavior. *Cognitive Psychology, 30*, 257–303.

Ekstrom, R.B., French, J.W., Harman, H.H., & Dermen, D. (1976). *Kit of factor-referenced cognitive tests*. Princeton, NJ: Educational Testing Service.

Engle, R.W., Kane, M.J., & Tuholski, S.W. (1999). Individual differences in working memory capacity and what they tell us about controlled attention, general fluid intelligence, and functions of the prefrontal cortex. In A. Miyake & P. Shah (Eds.), *Models of working memory: Mechanisms of active maintenance and executive control* (pp. 102–134). New York: Cambridge University Press.

Engle, R.W., Tuholski, S.W., Laughlin, J.E., & Conway, A.R.A. (1999). Working memory, short-term memory, and general fluid intelligence: A latent variable approach. *Journal of Experimental Psychology: General, 128*, 309–331.

Evans, F.J. (1978). Monitoring attention deployment by random number generation: An index to measure subjective randomness. *Bulletin of the Psychonomic Society, 12*, 35–38.

Gilhooly, K.J., Logie, R.H., & Wynn, V. (1999). Syllogistic reasoning tasks, working memory, and skill. *European Journal of Cognitive Psychology, 11*, 473–498.

Hegarty, M., Shah, P., & Miyake, A. (2000). Constraints on using the dual-task methodology to specify the degree of central executive involvement in cognitive tasks. *Memory & Cognition, 28*, 376–385.

Jonides, J., & Smith, E.E. (1997). The architecture of working memory. In M.D. Rugg (Ed.), *Cognitive neuroscience* (pp. 243–276). Cambridge, MA: MIT Press.

Kyllonen, P.C. (1996). Is working memory capacity Spearman's *g*? In I. Dennis & P. Tapsfield (Eds.), *Human abilities: Their nature and measurement* (pp. 49–75). Mawhah, NJ: Lawrence Erlbaum Associates Inc.

Logie, R.H., Gilhooly, K.J., & Wynn, V. (1994). Counting on working memory in arithmetic problem solving. *Memory & Cognition, 22*, 395–410.

Lohman, D.F. (1988). Spatial abilities as traits, processes, and knowledge. In R.J. Sternberg (Ed.), *Advances in the psychology of human intelligence* (Vol. 4, pp. 181–248). Hillsdale, NJ: Lawrence Erlbaum Associates Inc.

MacLeod, C.M., Jackson, R.A., & Palmer, J. (1986). On the relation between spatial ability and field dependence. *Intelligence, 10*, 141–151.

McKenna, F.P. (1984). Measures of field dependence: Cognitive style or cognitive ability? *Journal of Personality and Social Psychology, 47*, 593–603.

McMorris, T. (1992). Field independence and performance in sport. *International Journal of Sport Psychology, 23*, 14–27.

Miyake, A., Friedman, N.P., Emerson, M.J., Witzki, A.H., Howerter, A., & Wager, T.D. (2000). The unity and diversity of executive functions and their contributions to complex "frontal lobe" tasks: A latent variable analysis. *Cognitive Psychology, 41*, 49–100.

Miyake, A., Friedman, N.P., Rettinger, D.A., Shah, P., & Hegarty, M. (in press). How are visuospatial working memory, executive functioning, and spatial abilities related? A latent variable analysis. *Journal of Experimental Psychology: General.*

Miyake, A., & Shah, P. (Eds.). (1999). *Models of working memory: Mechanisms of active maintenance and executive control.* New York: Cambridge University Press.

Noppe, L.D. (1985). The relationship of formal thought and cognitive styles to creativity. *Journal of Creative Behavior, 19*, 88–96.

Phillips, L.H., Wynn, V., Gilhooly, K.J., Della Sala, S.,

& Logie, R.H. (1999). The role of memory in the Tower of London task. *Memory*, *7*, 209–231.

Rickards, J.P., Fajen, B.R., Sullivan, J.F., & Gillespie, G. (1997). Signaling, notetaking, and field independence–dependence in text comprehension and recall. *Journal of Educational Psychology*, *89*, 508–517.

Robbins, T.W., Anderson, E.J., Barker, D.R., Bradley, A.C., Fearnyhough, C., Henson, R., Hudson, S.R., & Baddeley, A.D. (1996). Working memory in chess. *Memory & Cognition*, *24*, 83–93.

Robinson, J.A., & Bennink, C.D. (1978). Field articulation and working memory. *Journal of Research in Personality*, *12*, 439–449.

Schmidt, C.P., & Stephans, R. (1991). Locus of control and field dependence as factors in students' evaluations of applied music instruction. *Perceptual and Motor Skills*, *73*, 131–136.

Shah, P., & Miyake, A. (1996). The separability of working memory resources for spatial thinking and language processing: An individual differences approach. *Journal of Experimental Psychology: General*, *125*, 4–27.

Tinajero, C., & Paramo, M.F. (1998). Field dependence–independence cognitive style and academic achievement: A review of research and theory. *European Journal of Psychology of Education*, *13*, 227–251.

Towse, J.N. (1998). On random generation and the central executive of working memory. *British Journal of Psychology*, *89*, 77–101.

Towse, J.N., & Neil, D. (1998). Analyzing human random generation behavior: A review of methods used and a computer program for describing performance. *Behavior Research Methods, Instruments, & Computers*, *30*, 583–591.

Towse, J.N., & Valentine, J.D. (1997). Random generation of numbers: A search for underlying processes. *European Journal of Cognitive Psychology*, *9*, 381–400.

Witkin, H.A. (1964). Origins of cognitive style. In C. Sheerer (Ed.), *Cognition: Theory, research, and promise* (pp. 172–205). New York: Harper & Row.

Witkin, H.A., Dyk, R.B., Faterson, H.F., Goodenough, D.R., & Karp, S.A. (1962). *Psychological differentiation*. New York: Wiley.

Witkin, H.A., & Goodenough, D.R. (1981). *Cognitive styles: Essence and origins*. New York: International Universities Press.

Subject Index

For Product Safety Concerns and Information please contact our EU
representative GPSR@taylorandfrancis.com
Taylor & Francis Verlag GmbH, Kaufingerstraße 24, 80331 München, Germany

www.ingramcontent.com/pod-product-compliance
Ingram Content Group UK Ltd.
Pitfield, Milton Keynes, MK11 3LW, UK
UKHW051358190926
475701UK00013B/1005

* 9 7 8 1 1 3 8 8 7 7 8 6 3 *